Tenth Workshop on Innovative Use of NLP for Building Educational Applications 2015

Held at NAACL HLT 2015

Denver, Colorado, USA
4 June 2015

ISBN: 978-1-5108-0440-1

Printed from e-media with permission by:

Curran Associates, Inc.
57 Morehouse Lane
Red Hook, NY 12571

Some format issues inherent in the e-media version may also appear in this print version.

Printed by Curran Associates, Inc. (2015)

For permission requests, please contact the Association for Computational Linguistics at the address below.

Association for Computational Linguistics
209 N. Eighth Street
Stroudsburg, Pennsylvania 18360

Phone: 1-570-476-8006
Fax: 1-570-476-0860

acl@aclweb.org

Additional copies of this publication are available from:

Curran Associates, Inc.
57 Morehouse Lane
Red Hook, NY 12571 USA
Phone: 845-758-0400
Fax: 845-758-2634
Email: curran@proceedings.com
Web: www.proceedings.com

Table of Contents

Introduction

We are excited to be holding the 10th anniversary the BEA workshop. Since starting in 1997, the BEA workshop, now one of the largest workshops at NAACL/ACL, has become one of the leading venues for publishing innovative work that uses NLP to develop educational applications. The consistent interest in and growth of the workshop has clear ties to societal need and related advances in the technology, and the maturity of the NLP/education field. NLP capabilities now support an array of learning domains, including writing, speaking, reading, and mathematics. Within these domains, the community continues to develop and deploy innovative NLP approaches for use in educational settings. In the writing and speech domains, automated writing evaluation (AWE) and speech scoring applications, respectively, are commercially deployed in high-stakes assessment and instructional settings, including Massive Open Online Courses (MOOCs). We also see widely-used commercial applications for plagiarism detection and peer review. Major advances in speech technology, have made it possible to include speech in both assessment and Intelligent Tutoring Systems. There has been a renewed interest in spoken dialog and multi-modal systems for instruction and assessment as well as feedback. We are also seeing explosive growth of mobile applications for game-based applications for instruction and assessment. The current educational and assessment landscape, continues to foster a strong interest and high demand that pushes the state-of-the-art in AWE capabilities to expand the analysis of written responses to writing genres other than those traditionally found in standardized assessments, especially writing tasks requiring use of sources and argumentative discourse.

The use of NLP in educational applications has gained visibility outside of the NLP community. First, the Hewlett Foundation reached out to public and private sectors and sponsored two competitions: one for automated essay scoring, and the other for scoring of short answer, fact-based response items. The motivation driving these competitions was to engage the larger scientific community in this enterprise. MOOCs are now beginning to incorporate AWE systems to manage the thousands of constructed-response assignments collected during a single MOOC course. Learning@Scale is a recent venue for discussing NLP research in education. The NLP-TEA workshop, now in its second year (NLP-TEA2), gives special attention to papers working on Asian languages. The Speech and Language Technology in Education (SLaTE), now in its sixth year, promotes the use of speech and language technology for educational purposes. Another breakthrough for educational applications within the CL community is the presence of a number of shared-task competitions over the last three years. There have been three shared tasks on grammatical error correction with the most recent edition hosted at CoNLL 2014. In 2014 alone, there were four shared tasks for NLP and Education-related areas.

As a community, we continue to improve existing capabilities and to identify and generate innovative ways to use NLP in applications for writing, reading, speaking, critical thinking, curriculum development, and assessment. Steady growth in the development of NLP-based applications for education has prompted an increased number of workshops, typically focusing on one specific subfield. In this volume, we present papers from these subfields: tools for automated scoring of text and speech, automated test-item generation, dialogue and intelligent tutoring, evaluation of genres beyond essays, feedback studies, grammatical error detection, native language identification, and use of corpora. One of the oral presentations proposes a Shared Task that addresses the task of automated evaluation of scientific writing. This presentation will also be presented as a poster to allow greater opportunity for discussion beyond the main conference day.

We received 44 submissions and accepted 10 papers as oral presentations and 19 as poster presentation and/or demos. Each paper was reviewed by three members of the Program Committee who were believed to be most appropriate for each paper. We continue to have a very strong policy to deal with conflicts of interest. First, we made a concerted effort to not assign papers to reviewers if the paper had an author from their institution. Second, with respect to the organizing committee, authors of papers for which there was a conflict of interest recused themselves from the discussion and decision making.

This workshop offers an opportunity to present and publish work that is highly relevant to ACL, but is also highly specialized, and so this workshop is often a more appropriate venue for such work. The Poster session offers more breadth in terms of topics related to NLP and education, and maintains the original concept of a workshop. We continue to believe that the workshop framework designed to introduce work in progress and new ideas needs to be revived, and we hope that we have achieved this with the breadth and variety of research accepted for this workshop. The total number of acceptances represents a 66% acceptance rate across oral (23%) and poster presentations (43%).

While the field is growing, we do recognize that there is a core group of institutions and researchers who work in this area. With a higher acceptance rate, we were able to include papers from a wider variety of topics and institutions. The papers accepted to this workshop were selected on the basis of several factors, including the relevance to a core educational problem space, the novelty of the approach or domain, and the strength of the research.

The accepted papers were highly diverse, falling into the following themes:

Speech-based and dialogue applications: Loukina et al. compare several methods of feature selection for speech scoring systems and show that the use of shrinkage methods such as Lasso regression makes it possible to rapidly build models that both satisfy the requirements of validity and intepretability; Volodina and Pijetlovic present the development and the initial evaluation of a dictation and spelling prototype exercise for second language learners of Swedish based on text-to-speech technology in a CALL context.; Somasundaran et al. investigate linguistically-motivated features for automatically scoring a spoken picture-based narration task by building scoring models with features for story development, language use and task relevance of the response; Jaffe et al. present a log-linear ranking model for interpreting questions in a virtual patient dialogue system.

Automated writing evaluation: Rahimi et al. present an investigation of score prediction for the "organization" dimension of an assessment of analytical writing for writers in the lower grades; Napoles and Callison-Burch explore applications of automatic essay scoring applied to a corpus of essays written by college freshmen and discuss the challenges related to evaluation of essays that do not have a highly-constrained structure; Zesch et al. analyze the potential of recently proposed methods for semi-supervised learning based on clustering for short-answer scoring; Ramachandran et al. present a new approach that uses word-order graphs to identify important patterns from scoring rubrics and top-scoring student answers; Farra and Somasundaran investigate whether the analysis of opinion expressions can help in scoring persuasive essays, and predict holistic essay scores using features extracted from opinion expressions and topical elements; Zesch et al. investigate task-independent features for automated essay scoring and evaluate their transferability on English and German datasets; Ramachandran et al. use an extractive summarization tool called MEAD to extract a set of responses that may be used as alternative reference texts to score responses; Mathew et al. identified computational challenges in restructuring encyclopedic resources (like Wikipedia or thesauri) to reorder concepts with the goal of helping learners navigate through a concept network; Goutte et al. extract, from the text of the test items, keywords that are most relevant knowledge components, and using a small dataset from the PSLC datashop, they show that this is surprisingly effective; Yannakoudakis and Cummins perform a systematic study to compare the efficacy of different automated text scoring metrics under different experimental conditions; Chen et al. introduce a novel framework based on a probabilistic model for emotion wording assistance; Madnani et al. conduct a crowd-sourced study on Amazon Mechanical Turk to answer questions concerning the effects of type and amount of writing feedback; Wilson and Martin conduct a quasi-experimental study comparing the effects of a feedback condition on eighth-grade students' writing motivation and writing achievement.

Test-item generation: Beinborn et al. describe a generalized framework for test difficulty prediction that is applicable to several languages and test types., and develop two ranking strategies for candidate evaluation inspired by automatic solving methods based on language model probability and semantic relatedness; Niraula and Rus discuss a study that uses active learning for training classifiers to judge the quality of gap-fill questions; Kumar et al. describe RevUP , a system that deals with automatically generating gap-fill questions.

Error detection: Ledbetter and Dickinson describe a morphological analyzer for learner Hungarian, built upon limited grammatical knowledge of Hungarian requiring very few resources and flexible enough to do both morphological analysis and error detection, in addition to some unknown word handling; Kochmar and Briscoe present a novel approach to error correction in content words in learner writing focusing on adjective–noun (AN) combinations.

Use of corpora and annotation: Willis discusses the Amati system which aims to help human markers improve the speed and accuracy of their marking for short-answer question types; Wang et al. present the Jinan Chinese Learner Corpus, a large collection of L2 Chinese texts produced by learners that can be used for educational tasks, such as automated essay scoring.

Native language identification: Malmasi and Cahill propose a function to measure feature independence for an NLI system, and analyze its effectiveness on a standard NLI corpus; Malmasi et al. examine different ensemble methods, including an oracle, to estimate the upper limit of classification accuracy for NLI, and show that the oracle outperforms state-of-the-art systems, and present a pilot study of human performance for NLI, the first such experiment.

A shared task proposal (Daudaravicius) discusses a shared task for evaluating scientific writing, and describes the corpus and evaluation metrics associated with this task.

We wish to thank everyone who submitted a paper, all of the authors for their contributions, the members of the Program Committee for their thoughtful reviews, and everyone who attended this workshop. We would especially like to thank our sponsors: American Institutes for Research, Appen, Educational Testing Service, Grammarly, McGraw-Hill Education/CTB, Pacific Metrics, Pearson and Turnitin LightSide, whose contributions allowed us to subsidize students at the workshop dinner, and make workshop T-shirts! In addition, we thank Joya Tetreault for creating the T-shirt design.

Joel Tetreault, Yahoo Labs
Jill Burstein, Educational Testing Service
Claudia Leacock, McGraw-Hill Education/CTB

Organizers:

Joel Tetreault, Yahoo Labs
Jill Burstein, Educational Testing Service
Claudia Leacock, McGraw-Hill Education/CTB

Program Committee:

Lars Ahrenberg, Linköping University, Sweden
Laura Allen, Arizona State University, USA
Timo Baumann, Universität Hamburg, Germany
Lee Becker, Hapara, USA
Beata Beigman Klebanov, Educational Testing Service, USA
Delphine Bernhard, LiLPa, Université de Strasbourg, France
Suma Bhat, University of Illinois, USA
Kristy Boyer, North Carolina State University, USA
Chris Brew, Thomson-Reuters Research, UK
Ted Briscoe, University of Cambridge, UK
Chris Brockett, Microsoft Research, USA
Julian Brooke, University of Toronto, Canada
Aoife Cahill, Educational Testing Service, USA
Min Chi, North Carolina State University, USA
Martin Chodorow, Hunter College and the Graduate Center, CUNY, USA
Mark Core, University of Southern California, USA
Markus Dickinson, Indiana University, USA
Myroslava Dzikovska, University of Edinburgh, UK
Keelan Evanini, Educational Testing Service, USA
Mariano Felice, University of Cambridge, UK
Michael Flor, Educational Testing Service, USA
Jennifer Foster, Dublin City University, Ireland
Thomas François, Université Catholique de Louvain, Belgium
Anette Frank, Heidelberg University, Germany
Michael Gamon, Microsoft Research, USA
Binyam Gebrekidan Gebre, Max Planck Institute for Psycholinguistics, Netherlands
Kallirroi Georgila, University of Southern California, USA
Dan Goldwasser, Purdue University, USA
Cyril Goutte, National Research Council, Canada
Iryna Gurevych, University of Darmstadt, Germany
Trude Heift, Simon Fraser University, Canada
Michael Heilman, Civis Analytics, USA
Derrick Higgins, Civis Analytics, USA
Andrea Horbach, Saarland University, Germany
Chung-Chi Huang, National Institutes of Health, USA

Radu Ionescu, University of Bucharest, Romania
Ross Israel, Factual, USA
Levi King, Indiana University, USA
Ola Knutsson, Stockholm University, Sweden
Ekaterina Kochmar, University of Cambridge, UK
Mamoru Komachi, Tokyo Metropolitan University, Japan
Lun-Wei Ku, Academia Sinica, Taiwan
John Lee, City University of Hong Kong, Hong Kong
Sungjin Lee, Yahoo Labs, USA
Samuel Leeman-Munk, North Carolina State University, USA
Chee Wee (Ben) Leong, Educational Testing Service, USA
James Lester, North Carolina State University, USA
Annie Louis, University of Edinburgh, UK
Anastassia Loukina, Educational Testing Service, USA
Xiaofei Lu, Penn State University, USA
Wencan Luo, University of Pittsburgh, USA
Nitin Madnani, Educational Testing Service, USA
Shervin Malmasi, Macquarie University, Australia
Montse Maritxalar, University of the Basque Country, Spain
Mourad Mars, Umm Al-Qura University, KSA
Aurélien Max, LIMSI-CNRS and Univ. Paris Sud, France
Julie Medero, Harvey Mudd College, USA
Detmar Meurers, Universität Tübingen, Germany
Lisa Michaud, Merrimack College, USA
Rada Mihalcea, University of Michigan, USA
Michael Mohler, Language Computer Corporation, USA
Jack Mostow, Carnegie Mellon University, USA
Smaranda Muresan, Columbia University, USA
Ani Nenkova, University of Pennsylvania, USA
Hwee Tou Ng, National University of Singapore, Singapore
Rodney Nielsen, University of North Texas, USA
Alexis Palmer, Saarland University, Germany
Aasish Pappu, Yahoo Labs, USA
Ted Pedersen, University of Minnesota, Duluth, USA
Ildiko Pilan, University of Gothenburg, Sweden
Heather Pon-Barry, Mount Holyoke College, USA
Patti Price, PPRICE Speech and Language Technology, USA
Martí Quixal, Universität Tübingen, Germany
Lakshmi Ramachandran, Pearson, USA
Vikram Ramanarayanan, Educational Testing Service, USA
Arti Ramesh, University of Maryland, College Park, USA
Andrew Rosenberg, CUNY Queens College, USA
Mihai Rotaru, Textkernel, Netherlands
Alla Rozovskaya, Columbia University, USA
C. Anton Rytting, University of Maryland, USA
Keisuke Sakaguchi, Johns Hopkins University, USA

Conference Program

Thursday, June 4, 2015

8:45–9:00 ***Load Presentations***

9:00–9:15 ***Opening Remarks***

9:15–9:40 *Candidate evaluation strategies for improved difficulty prediction of language tests*
Lisa Beinborn, Torsten Zesch and Iryna Gurevych

9:40–10:05 *Feature selection for automated speech scoring*
Anastassia Loukina, Klaus Zechner, Lei Chen and Michael Heilman

10:05–10:30 *Incorporating Coherence of Topics as a Criterion in Automatic Response-to-Text Assessment of the Organization of Writing*
Zahra Rahimi, Diane Litman, Elaine Wang and Richard Correnti

10:30–11:00 ***Break***

11:00–11:25 *Automatic morphological analysis of learner Hungarian*
Scott Ledbetter and Markus Dickinson

11:25–11:45 *Automated Scoring of Picture-based Story Narration*
Swapna Somasundaran, Chong Min Lee, Martin Chodorow and Xinhao Wang

11:45–12:05 *Measuring Feature Diversity in Native Language Identification*
Shervin Malmasi and Aoife Cahill

12:05–12:25 *Automated Evaluation of Scientific Writing: AESW Shared Task Proposal*
Vidas Daudaravicius

12:30–2:00 ***Lunch***

2:00–3:30 ***Poster Sessions***

2:00–2:45 ***Poster Session A***

Scoring Persuasive Essays Using Opinions and their Targets
Noura Farra, Swapna Somasundaran and Jill Burstein

Towards Automatic Description of Knowledge Components
Cyril Goutte, Guillaume Durand and Serge Leger

The Impact of Training Data on Automated Short Answer Scoring Performance
Michael Heilman and Nitin Madnani

Interpreting Questions with a Log-Linear Ranking Model in a Virtual Patient Dialogue System
Evan Jaffe, Michael White, William Schuler, Eric Fosler-Lussier, Alex Rosenfeld and Douglas Danforth

Identifying Patterns For Short Answer Scoring Using Graph-based Lexico-Semantic Text Matching
Lakshmi Ramachandran, Jian Cheng and Peter Foltz

Lark Trills for Language Drills: Text-to-speech technology for language learners
Elena Volodina and Dijana Pijetlovic

The Jinan Chinese Learner Corpus
Maolin Wang, Shervin Malmasi and Mingxuan Huang

Reducing Annotation Efforts in Supervised Short Answer Scoring
Torsten Zesch, Michael Heilman and Aoife Cahill

Annotation and Classification of Argumentative Writing Revisions
Fan Zhang and Diane Litman

2:45–3:30 ***Poster Session B***

Embarrassed or Awkward? Ranking Emotion Synonyms for ESL Learners' Appropriate Wording
Wei-Fan Chen, MeiHua Chen and Lun-Wei Ku

RevUP: Automatic Gap-Fill Question Generation from Educational Texts
Girish Kumar, Rafael Banchs and Luis Fernando D'Haro

Preliminary Experiments on Crowdsourced Evaluation of Feedback Granularity
Nitin Madnani, Martin Chodorow, Aoife Cahill, Melissa Lopez, Yoko Futagi and Yigal Attali

Thursday, June 4, 2015 (continued)

Oracle and Human Baselines for Native Language Identification
Shervin Malmasi, Joel Tetreault and Mark Dras

Using PEGWriting® to Support the Writing Motivation and Writing Quality of Eighth-Grade Students: A Quasi-Experimental Study
Joshua Wilson and Trish Martin

Towards Creating Pedagogic Views from Encyclopedic Resources
Ditty Mathew, Dhivya Eswaran and Sutanu Chakraborti

Judging the Quality of Automatically Generated Gap-fill Question using Active Learning
Nobal Bikram Niraula and Vasile Rus

Generating Reference Texts for Short Answer Scoring Using Graph-based Summarization
Lakshmi Ramachandran and Peter Foltz

Evaluating the performance of Automated Text Scoring systems
Helen Yannakoudakis and Ronan Cummins

Task-Independent Features for Automated Essay Grading
Torsten Zesch, Michael Wojatzki and Dirk Scholten-Akoun

3:30–4:00 ***Break***

4:00–4:25 *Using Learner Data to Improve Error Correction in Adjective–Noun Combinations*
Ekaterina Kochmar and Ted Briscoe

4:25–4:50 *Using NLP to Support Scalable Assessment of Short Free Text Responses*
Alistair Willis

4:50–5:15 *Automatically Scoring Freshman Writing: A Preliminary Investigation*
Courtney Napoles and Chris Callison-Burch

5:15–5:30 ***Closing Remarks***

Gold Sponsors

Silver Sponsor

Candidate Evaluation Strategies for Improved Difficulty Prediction of Language Tests

Lisa Beinborn[◇], **Torsten Zesch**[‡], **Iryna Gurevych**[◇§]

◇ UKP Lab, Technische Universität Darmstadt
‡ Language Technology Lab, University of Duisburg-Essen
§ UKP Lab, German Institute for Educational Research
`http://www.ukp.tu-darmstadt.de`

Abstract

Language proficiency tests are a useful tool for evaluating learner progress, if the test difficulty fits the level of the learner. In this work, we describe a generalized framework for test difficulty prediction that is applicable to several languages and test types. In addition, we develop two ranking strategies for candidate evaluation inspired by automatic solving methods based on language model probability and semantic relatedness. These ranking strategies lead to significant improvements for the difficulty prediction of cloze tests.

1 Introduction

In learning scenarios, evaluating the learner's proficiency is crucial to assess differences in learner groups and also individual learner progress. This kind of evaluation is usually performed over the learner's results on certain tasks or tests. For informative results, it is important that the test difficulty is suitable for the learner. It needs to be challenging enough to avoid boredom and stagnation, but the learner should still be able to solve the task at least partially. In this work, we focus on language proficiency tests and aim at predicting the difficulty for five different test datasets.

Understanding the challenging elements of a task is an essential prerequisite for learner support. In natural language processing, human performance is usually considered as the gold standard for automatic approaches. The models are tuned and adjusted to reach human-like results. In learning settings, the human performance is flawed because of limited knowledge and lack of experience. In this work, we thus apply a reverse approach: we exploit strategies from automatic solving to model human difficulties.

To enable the experiments, we retrieved datasets from various testing institutions and conducted a learner study to obtain error rates for an additional test type.[1] For a better understanding of the differences between test types, we first calculate the candidate space of potential answers and compare it to learner answers. We assume that higher answer ambiguity leads to higher difficulty. As all datasets allow binary scoring (correct/wrong), the difficulty of an item is interpreted as the proportion of wrong answers, also referred to as the error rate. We then build a generalized difficulty prediction framework based on an earlier approach we presented in Beinborn et al. (2014a) which was limited to English and to one specific test type. We evaluate the prediction for different test types and languages and obtain remarkable results for French and German.

Many language tests are designed as multiple choice questions. The generalized prediction approach lacks predictive power for this format because the evaluation strategy for the answer candidates is solely based on word frequency. We develop two strategies for more sophisticated candidate ranking that are inspired by automatic solving methods based on language models and semantic relatedness. We show that the candidate ranking can successfully model human evaluation strategies and leads to improved difficulty prediction for cloze tests.

[1] The dataset is available at: https://www.ukp.tu-darmstadt.de/data/c-tests

Proceedings of the Tenth Workshop on Innovative Use of NLP for Building Educational Applications, 2015, pages 1–11, Denver, Colorado, June 4, 2015.

In order to establish common ground, we first introduce the concept of reduced redundancy testing and the most popular test types.

2 Reduced Redundancy Tests

In language learning, most proficiency tests rely on the principle of reduced redundancy testing as introduced by Spolsky (1969). He formalized the idea that "natural language is redundant" and that the proficiency level of language learners can be estimated by their ability to deal with reduced redundancy. For testing, redundancy can be reduced by eliminating (partial) words from a text to create a gap. The learner is then asked to fill in the gaps i.e. to complete the missing words.

Reduced redundancy tests can be distinguished into *open* and *closed* answer formats. In open formats, the learner has to actually produce the solution, while it can be selected from a small fixed set of multiple choice options in closed formats. This technique provides full control over the candidate space, but the selection of good answer options (distractors), that are not a proper solution, is a difficult task. Most previous works in the field of educational natural language processing focus on the generation of distractors to manipulate the difficulty, i.e. for cloze tests (Zesch and Melamud, 2014; Mostow and Jang, 2012; Agarwal and Mannem, 2011; Mitkov et al., 2006), vocabulary exercises (Skory and Eskenazi, 2010; Heilman et al., 2007; Brown et al., 2005) and grammar exercises (Perez-Beltrachini et al., 2012).

In addition to the answer format, the test types can be distinguished by the gap type and the deletion rate. On the local level, the gap type determines which portion of the word is deleted. On the global test level, the deletion rate determines the distribution of gaps in the text. A higher number of gaps per sentence results in a higher redundancy reduction. This increases the dependency between gaps as the mutilated context of a single gap can only be recreated by solving the surrounding gaps.

2.1 Cloze test

Cloze tests have been introduced by Taylor (1953) and have become the most popular form of reduced redundancy testing. In cloze tests, full words are deleted from a text. This strategy requires comprehensive context, so the deletion rate is usually every 7th word or higher (Brown, 1989). The main problem with cloze tests is that the gaps are usually highly ambiguous and the set of potential solutions cannot be exactly anticipated (Horsmann and Zesch, 2014). Therefore, most cloze tests are designed as closed formats, so that the correct solution can be selected from a set of distractors (see Figure 1 for an example).

13. His characteristic talk , with its keen ____ of detail and subtle power of inference held me amused and enthralled.

- instincts
- presumption
- observance
- expiation
- implements

Figure 1: Example for a cloze question, the solution is *observance*.

2.2 C-test

Although the cloze test is widely used, the setup contains several weaknesses such as the small number of gaps and the ambiguity of the solution. The C-test is an alternative of the cloze test that has been developed by Klein-Braley and Raatz (1982). The C-test construction principle enables a higher number of gaps on less text, every second word of a short paragraph is transformed into a gap. As this high deletion rate would lead to an unfeasible degree of redundancy reduction, only the second "half" of the word is deleted to narrow down the candidate space, see the example below.

Vacc___ like penic___ and ot___ antibiotics th___ were disco___ as a dir___ result are lik___ the grea___ inventions o___ medical sci___.[2]

2.3 Prefix deletion test

The prefix deletion test is a more difficult variant of the C-test that can be used to assess more advanced students up to native speakers (Sigott and Köberl, 1996). In this case, the first "half" of the word (the prefix) is deleted. As word endings vary less than word onsets (at least for the languages under study), the candidate space is increased and allows alternative solutions that are equally valid. See the previous

[2]Solutions: *Vaccines, penicillin, other, that, discovered, direct, likely, greatest, of, science*

example as a prefix deletion test below.

___ines like ___illin and ___er antibiotics ___at were ___vered as a ___ect result are ___ely the ___test inventions ___f medical ___nce.

In standard C-tests, a big challenge is to select the correct inflection of the solution, especially for languages with a rich morphology. In prefix deletion tests, the inflected ending of the word is already provided and thus the focus is shifted towards semantic challenges. Psycholinguistic experiments have shown that the information value of the initial part of a word is higher than the final part (Broerse and Zwaan, 1966; Kinoshita, 2000). This supports the assumption that prefix deletion tests are more difficult.

In general, the following hypothesis is supposed: A higher degree of redundancy reduction for the gap results in a bigger candidate space and leads to increased difficulty (compare the results by Sigott and Köberl (1996)). In the following section, we provide an approximation of the candidate space for each test variant.

3 Candidate Space

The main difference between the different test types is the number of competing candidates. In this section, we analyze the candidate space for the three languages English, French and German and for the test types cloze, C-test and prefix deletion. We calculate the candidates for each word in the vocabulary and then average the results for words with the same length to approximate the candidate space.

Language	Words	Mean word length
English (American)	99,171	8.5 ±2.6
French	139,719	9.6 ±2.6
German	332,263	12.0 ±3.5

Table 1: Vocabulary size and mean word length for different languages

Candidate space for different languages We focus on English, French and German because they are used in our datasets. The word list package provided by Ubuntu for spell-checking serves as vocabulary.[3]

The size of the lists vary depending on the morphological richness of the language; the German list is more than three times bigger than the English one (see Table 1). It should also be noted that the average word length is much higher for German. This is mainly due to the existence of noun compounds that concatenate two or more words into one.

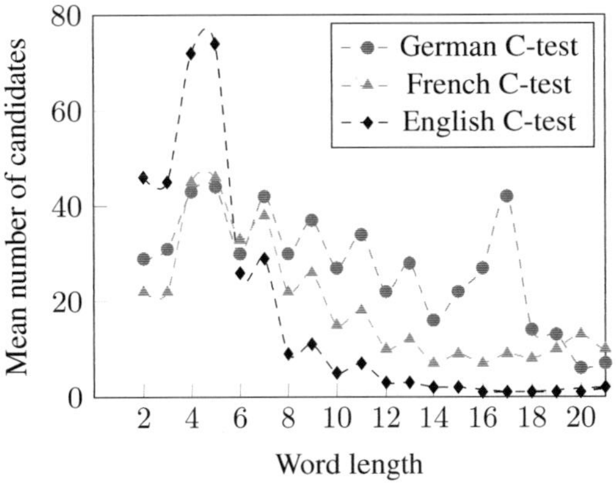

Figure 2: Mean number of candidates for different test types with respect to word length

Figure 2 illustrates how the candidate space varies for the languages under study. It can be seen that for English the candidate space is maximized for extremely short words and decreases rapidly with increased word length. In comparison, the French and in particular the German candidate space is more leveled: it is smaller for short words, but bigger and more constant for longer words.

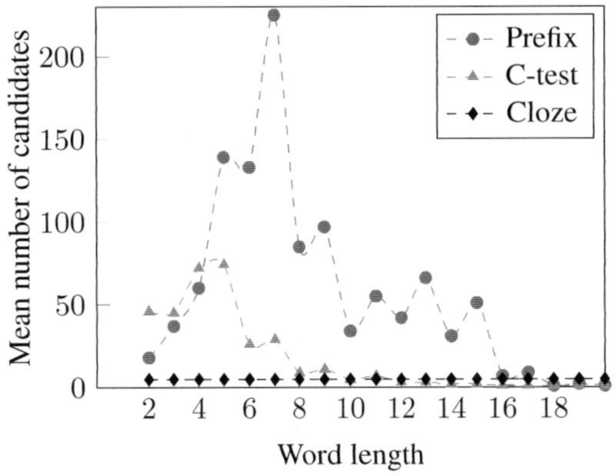

Figure 3: Mean number of English candidates for different test types with respect to word length

Candidate space for different test types Figure 3 shows the English candidate space for the test types.

[3]http://packages.ubuntu.com/de/lucid/wordlist, 15.12.2014

The number of candidates for the cloze test with five distractors is of course always five. Compared to the C-test, the candidate space for the prefix deletion test is extremely large, in particular for words with medium length (five to nine characters). This could be an explanation why this test type is considered to be more difficult than the standard C-test. However, following this hypothesis, the cloze tests should be fairly easy given the consistently small candidate space. The obtained error rates and the feedback of our test participants do not support this assumption. This gives rise to the idea that the candidate space considered by the learner differs from the computational one.

Candidate evaluation by learners When solving open formats, the learners cannot consider the full candidate space; only the words that are in the active vocabulary of the learner are accessible. In addition, the context can lead to priming effects and the test situation might alter the stress level of the participant and apply further restrictions.

From the above arguments, one would expect that the learner's candidate space is smaller than the objective candidate space. However, we need to take into account that learners also consider wrong options, see the different learner answers for the gap *appro*___ in Figure 4, for example. The computational candidate space on the left consists of only 9 candidates, but the participants provided 68 different answers along with the solution *appropriate* (and only four of them intersect with the candidate space). This example highlights the importance of modelling productive difficulties for test types with open answer format.

For the closed cloze test, the candidate space is constant. The learners seem to consider even fewer options, on average only three of the five provided answers are actually selected. For closed formats, it is thus more relevant to model candidate ambiguity. In the following section, we analyze if the difficulty prediction can be performed for all test types despite the varying candidate space.

4 Difficulty prediction

Teachers are often not able to correctly anticipate the difficulties a learner might face. For the example in Section 2, one would probably expect high error rates for *vaccines* and *penicillin*, while the problems with *likely* and *that* might come as a surprise (see Figure 5). For optimal learner support, it is important to predict these difficulties.

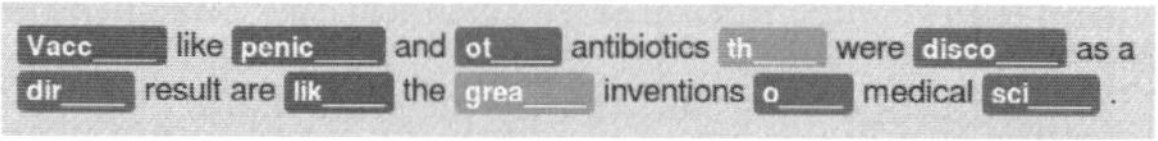

Figure 5: Visualization of gap difficulty. Easy gaps are marked green, intermediate gaps yellow and difficult gaps red.

4.1 Previous work

The earliest analyses of test difficulty operate on the level of the full text instead of individual gaps. Klein-Braley (1984) performs a linear regression analysis with only two difficulty indicators – average sentence length and type-token ratio – and obtained useful predictions of the mean test difficulty for her target group. Eckes (2011) also focuses on the mean test difficulty and aims at calibrating C-tests using a Rasch model to build a test pool.

Kamimoto (1993) performs classical item analysis on the gap level and creates a tailored C-test that only contains selected gaps which better discriminate between students. However, the gap selection is based on previous test results instead of gap features and cannot be applied on new tests.

In previous work (Beinborn et al., 2014a), we reported the first results for automatic difficulty prediction on the gap level. We introduced a model for the difficulty prediction of English C-test gaps that combines aspects of text and word difficulty with properties of the candidate space and gap dependencies. As the current work builds on this model, we summarize the feature space below.

Text difficulty For all test types, the difficulty of the test text determines the available context for the participant. A more challenging text increases the difficulty of all gaps as the participant's orientation in the text becomes more complicated (compare Brown (1989)). The difficulty of the underlying text can be determined by readability features. Our approach combines traditional features as the average sentence and word length with more advanced features from all linguistic levels (e.g. lexical, syntactic, semantic, discourse) including features specific to readability for language learning as for example

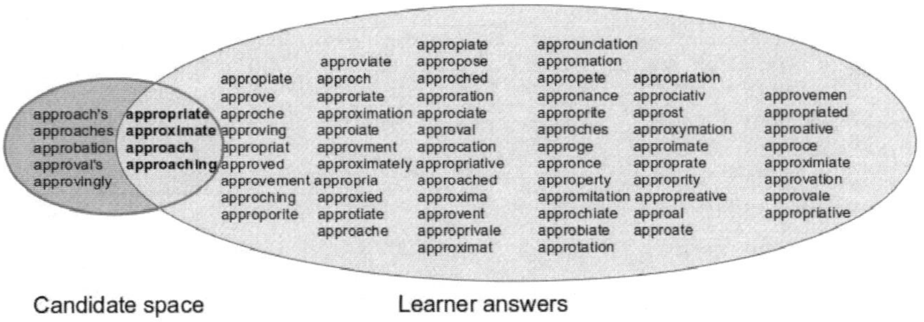

Figure 4: The candidates for the gap *appro*___: The computational candidate space is on the left, the answers provided by the students are on the right.

the "cognateness of words" (Beinborn et al., 2014b).

Word difficulty On a more local level, the difficulty of the particular solution word determines whether the participant is even capable of knowing the solution. Previous work by Brown (1989) and Sigott (1995) shows that the word class and the word frequency correlate with the gap difficulty. In addition, Klein-Braley (1996) analyzed error patterns in C-tests that are related to production problems (correct word stem in wrong form) and early closure (the participant selects a solution that works locally, but not in the larger context). In previous work, we operationalized and extended these findings by implementing many word difficulty features targeted at morphology, word frequency, cognateness and spelling (Beinborn et al., 2014a).

Test parameters In our previous work, we focused on English C-Tests, so the test parameters were fixed to a deletion rate of two, the C-test gap type and an open answer format. In order to evaluate the candidate space, we calculated the number of candidates and ranked them based on their frequency in the context. Due to the high deletion rate, the context is limited to the direct left and right neighbor. In addition, we evaluated the position of the gap and the solution frequency of the previous gap to assess dependencies between items.

4.2 Our generalized approach

Our approach for automatic difficulty prediction builds on the model introduced earlier for English C-tests as summarized above (Beinborn et al., 2014a). We reduce the feature set (from 87 to 70) and only include those features that can be adapted to all our target languages and test types. This comprises features estimating the difficulty of the solution and its direct context (cognateness, frequency, word class, inflection, compound structure, spelling difficulty, etc.)[4], the readability of the text (type-token-ratio, number of clauses, average word and sentence length, etc.) and the test parameters (number of candidates, position of gap, etc). We also adapt the pipelines to include proper German and French pre-processing using DkPro (de Castilho and Gurevych, 2014) and adapt the candidate calculation to the different test types.

In order to assure comparability to previous work, we also use support vector machines for regression in Weka (Hall et al., 2009) through the DKPro TC framework (Daxenberger et al., 2014).

4.3 Data

Table 2 provides an overview of the test datasets used in this paper. It consists of four open formats and one closed format with multiple choice options. The number of participants is averaged over the texts because each participant worked with 5 texts in the open formats.[5] The error rates should not be compared across test types because the participants had different levels of language proficiency. The high standard deviations indicate that each test contains gaps that are rather easy and others that are extremely difficult. In Beinborn et al. (2014a) we have shown that the error rate for a single item remains

[4]For the English C-test, we consider the cognateness to German because it is the L1 of the majority of the participants. For the French and German tests, we do not have information about the L1. We therefore consider the cognateness with English because we assume that most participants have at least rudimentary knowledge of English.

[5]The total number of participants is thus much higher, but this is not relevant for the error rate calculation

Format	Test type	Texts	Gaps	Particip.	Avg. error rate
Open	C-test en	39	775	210	.35±.25
	C-test fr	40	799	24	.52±.28
	C-test de	82	1,640	251	.55±.26
	Prefix de	14	348	225	.36±.23
Closed	Cloze en	100	100	22	.27±.22

Table 2: Overview of test data

quite stable for varying sample sizes.

C-test We use the same English C-test data as in our previous work (Beinborn et al., 2014a) and additionally obtained French tests. In both cases, the tests served as a placement test at the language centre of the TU Darmstadt in order to assign students to language levels. The participants had heterogeneous backgrounds regarding their language proficiency and mother tongue, but the majority was German. Furthermore, we received German C-tests from the TestDaf institute that have been administered to foreign students who apply for studying in Germany. It is a subset of the data described in Eckes (2011).

Prefix deletion For the prefix deletion test, we received German tests from the University of Duisburg-Essen that test the proficiency of prospective teachers.[6] The participants are a mix of native German speakers and students with migratory background (26%). Their language proficiency is much higher than that of the participants in the other tests.

Cloze tests For cloze tests, we could not find any test data with error rates. We thus conducted a study to collect error rates ourselves using the Microsoft sentence completion dataset.[7] For this dataset, Zweig and Burges (2012) transformed 1400 sentences from 5 Sherlock Holmes novels (written by Arthur Conan Doyle) into cloze tests. In each selected sentence, they replace a low-frequency content word with a gap and provide the solution along with 4 distractors (so-called closed cloze). The distractors were generated automatically based on n-gram frequencies and then handpicked by human judges. It should be noted that all distractors form grammatically correct sentences and that the n-gram probabilities for the answer options are comparable.

[6]http://zlb.uni-due.de/sprachkompetenz

[7]http://research.microsoft.com/en-us/projects/scc/, 15.12.2014

Dataset	LOO Gaps	LOO Texts
C-test en	.55	.47
C-test fr	.70	.67
C-test de	.63	.61
Prefix de	.54	.27
Cloze en	.20	.20

Table 3: Pearson correlation for difficulty prediction results in an leave-one-out cross-validation setting on the gap and on the text level

We tested a subset of the cloze questions with an eloquent native speaker of English and he answered 100% correctly. In order to determine the difficulty for language learners, we set up 10 web surveys with 10 questions each (as in Figure 1) and asked advanced learners of English to answer them.

4.4 Prediction Results

Table 3 shows the correlation between the measured human error rates and the predictions of our generalized prediction approach. It should be noted that we used the same features for each dataset. In practical applications, it would of course be possible to tune the feature selection for each task separately. For research purposes, however, we are interested in creating uniform conditions to allow a more meaningful comparison.

In our previous approach, we performed leave-one-out testing on all gaps to account for the small amount of training data. As each text of the open format test types contains 20 gaps, leave-one-out testing on all gaps increases the risk of over-fitting the model to specific text properties. For a more realistic prediction setting, we additionally perform leave-one-out testing on the texts, i.e. we always test on 20 gaps from one coherent text. We will focus on the results reported for this scenario, although they are slightly worse. The baseline, that always predicts the mean error rate, yields a correlation of 0 for all test types.

Languages The results show that the difficulty prediction can be successfully adapted to other languages. The correlation for the English C-tests is a bit lower than in previous work (0.60) because we reduced the set of features as described above. This allowed us to obtain results for German and French that are even better than the ones previously reported for English.

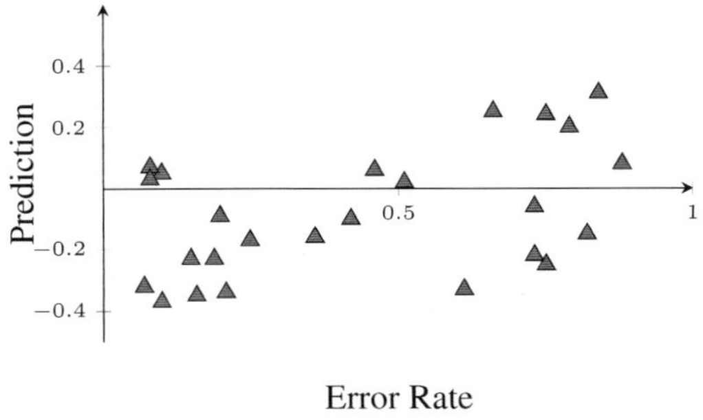

Figure 6: Biased prediction for the outlier text in the prefix deletion dataset

Test Types The results for the test types show that the prediction framework struggles with the prefix deletion and the cloze tests. One obvious reason could be the size of the training data which is significantly smaller for these tasks.

We first have a closer look at the prefix deletion test to explain the strong decline for leave-one-out cross-validation on texts. We find that the most significant prediction errors can be found for one particular text. This text exhibits a very high readability (e.g. low type-token and pronoun ratio, few adjectives and adverbs), but contains many difficult gaps. This combination has not been observed in the training data which explains that the difficulty of all gaps is strongly underestimated (resulting in negative values for the predicted error rates).

Figure 6 shows that the differences between gaps are actually predicted quite well, one could simply add a constant factor (of about 0.4) to receive an acceptable prediction. For the purpose of the error analysis, we remove that particular text from the evaluation and re-calculate the results. This yields a more reasonable Pearson correlation of 0.43 and shows that the difference between LOO on gaps and on text is due to over-fitting to text properties of the training data. This effect would surely decrease with more training data as can be seen for the bigger French and German datasets.

For the cloze test on the other hand, something more essential is going wrong. In Section 3, we have seen that the main difference for this test type is the closed candidate space. The features modelling production problems are thus not relevant here. While the number of the candidates is fixed, the set is still very variable because the distractors can be freely selected from the whole vocabulary. The better the

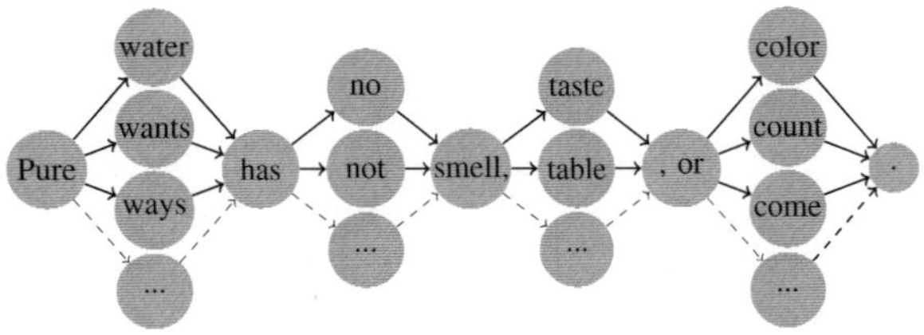

Figure 7: The search space for the sentence *Pure wa___ has n___ smell, ta___, or co___.* In this graph, the solution is always the topmost candidate, the candidate space is simplified.

distractors fit the gap, the more difficult it gets for the learner to select the solution, as in the following example:

When his body had been carried from the cellar we found ourselves still confronted with a problem which was almost as ____ as that with which we had started.

[tall, loud, invisible, quick, formidable]

Only very few learners managed to identify the solution *formidable* in this case, while the example in Figure 1 was quite easy for them. For difficulty prediction, it is therefore important to estimate the ambiguity of the answer options. In the remainder of the paper, we examine whether strategies that have been successfully applied for automatic solving of language tests can also provide insights into human difficulties with candidate ambiguity.

5 Candidate evaluation strategies

The main challenge for solving a reduced redundancy test consists in identifying the most suitable candidate in the candidate space. The context fitness of a candidate can be evaluated based on language model probabilities and on semantic relatedness between the candidate and the context.

LM-based approach A probabilistic language model (LM) calculates the probability of a phrase based on the frequencies of lower order n-grams extracted from training data (Stolcke, 1994). This can be used to predict the fitness of a word for the sentential context. Bickel et al. (2005), for example, evaluate the use of probabilistic language models to support auto-completion of sentences in writing editors. In the completion scenario, only the left context is available, while the learner can also consider the right context in language tests. Zweig et al. (2012)

thus model the problem of solving cloze tests by applying methods from lexical substitution to evaluate and rank the candidates. The part to be substituted is a gap and the set of "substitution candidates" is already provided by the answer options.

Unfortunately, we cannot rely on static sentences for the open test formats as the context needs to be determined by solving the surrounding gaps. For each gap, we take all candidates into account and generate all possible sentences resulting from the combinations with the candidates of subsequent gaps. This can lead to strong dependencies between items, i.e. solving a subsequent item is facilitated, if the previous one has been solved correctly. As a consequence, we need to evaluate a combinatorial search space that grows exponentially with the number of gaps in the sentence (see Figure 7). We thus use a pruning step after each gap that scores the generated sub-sentences using a language model and only keeps the n best. For the closed cloze test, the number of generated sentences is of course limited to the number of candidates (5) because each sentence contains only one gap.

We use 5-gram language models that are trained on monolingual news corpora using berkeleylm with Kneser-Ney smoothing.[8] Zweig et al. (2012) trained their models explicitly on training data only from Sherlock Holmes novels. In order to better simulate learner knowledge, we use rather small and controlled training data from the Leipzig collection (Quasthoff et al., 2006) consisting of one million sentences for each language.

For solving the test, we then select the generated sentence with the highest log-probability in the language model and count how many gaps are solved correctly. If several sentences obtain the same probability, we pick one at random. We run this strategy ten times and average the results. For comparison, we implement a baseline that always selects the most frequent candidate without considering the context.

Semantic relatedness approach Language models cannot capture relations between distant words in the sentence. To account for this constraint, Zweig et al. (2012) include information from latent semantic analysis (Deerwester et al., 1990). For this method, every word is represented by a vector of related words that is calculated on the basis of training data. The semantic relatedness between two words can then be expressed by the cosine similarity of the two vectors. Similar to Zweig et al. (2012), we sum over the cosine similarity between the candidate and every content word in the sentence to calculate the candidate fitness. While they calculate relatedness based on a latent semantic analysis index of the domain-specific Holmes corpus, we use explicit semantic analysis (Gabrilovich and Markovitch, 2007) calculated on Wikipedia to better model the learner's general domain knowledge.[9] The semantic approach cannot be applied on open formats because semantic relatedness is not informative for function words and inflections.

	Human	Baseline	LM-Based	Semantic
C-test en	.68	.11	.76	-
C-test fr	.48	.10	.79	-
C-test de	.45	.09	.76	-
Prefix de	.64	.09	.73	-
Cloze en	.70	.21	.26	.32

Table 4: Solving accuracy for the different candidate evaluation strategies

Results The accuracy of the automatic solving strategies and the average human performance in Table 4 shows that the LM-based solving strategy strongly outperforms the baseline and can also beat the average human solver for the open test formats.[10] Even the large candidate space of the prefix deletion test can be disambiguated quite well. For the cloze tests, the candidate ambiguity seems to be more challenging. The LM-based candidate evaluation only performs slightly better than the baseline due to the fact that the distractor generation approach assured comparable context frequency of all candidates. The semantic relatedness approach works slightly better, but also fails to select the correct candidate in most cases.

Not surprisingly, our results for the cloze tests are worse than those obtained with domain-specific corpora in previous work. However, we are not interested in developing a perfect solving method, but aim at modelling the difficulty for the learner. A

[8] http://code.google.com/p/berkeleylm, 15.12.2014

[9] Index retrieved from https://public.ukp.informatik.tu-darmstadt.de/baer/wp_eng_lem_nc_c.zip, 30.03.2015

[10] The human results should not be compared across test types as the participant groups had different backgrounds and different language proficiency.

question is less likely to be solved if the context fitness of a distractor is rated higher than that of the solution. The failures of the automatic solving might hence be indicative for the difficulty prediction for cloze tests.

6 Improved difficulty prediction

The solving approaches described above provide a ranking of the candidates that can be instrumental for difficulty prediction. We develop two new features that evaluate the context fitness of the candidates based on the measures described above and return the rank of the solution. We assume that a gap is more difficult if the solution is not the top-ranked candidate.

We have seen that many of the difficulty features that have been developed for the C-test are not applicable for the cloze data. The C-test difficulty has been modelled by estimating the size of the candidate space (which is constant in this case), production difficulties (which are not relevant in closed formats), and a frequency-based ranking of the candidates (which has been controlled by the test designers). The remaining features measure the readability of the text, the frequency of the direct context, and the word class of the gap and provide important information about the general difficulty of the gap independent of the answer options. We analyze if the ranking features can then capture the important aspect of candidate ambiguity to improve difficulty prediction for cloze tests.

Results The results in Table 5 show that reducing the feature set to those that are actually relevant for closed formats already has a small effect, but it is not significant. Adding the ranking features then leads to a strong improvement in difficulty prediction. The best result is obtained with the semantic relatedness ranking.

We explained above that the LM-based approach is not suitable for solving this cloze dataset because the answer options have been controlled with respect to frequency. However, the participants are not aware of this constraint, and frequency effects actually do play a role in learner processing. This explains that LM-based ranking can also be beneficial for difficulty prediction.

Our results show that modelling the context fitness of the candidates is essential for predicting the difficulty of closed cloze tests.[11]

	# Features	Pearson's r
Standard features	70	.20
Reduced features	33	.24
Reduced + LM ranker	34	.38*
Reduced + Semantic ranker	34	**.42***
Reduced + LM + Semantic ranker	35	.39*

Table 5: Improved prediction results for cloze tests. Significant differences to the result with the standard features are indicated with * ($p<0.01$).

7 Conclusions

In this work, we have performed difficulty prediction for different types of reduced redundancy testing for several languages. To our knowledge, this is the first approach to predict the difficulty of prefix deletion tests, cloze tests and French and German C-tests. We obtained remarkably good results for French and German that were even better than the ones previously reported for English. In practical teaching scenarios, the feature selection could be further tuned to the respective test type and learner group.

In order to improve difficulty prediction for closed test formats, we developed two ranking strategies for candidate evaluation inspired by automatic solving methods. The approaches evaluate the fitness of a candidate in the sentential context based on language model probability and semantic relatedness. We have reached significant improvements of the difficulty prediction for closed cloze tests by including these ranking features. Especially the semantic approach seems to be a good model for human evaluation strategies.

For future work, we will extend our analysis to a bigger set of closed test formats and work towards better models of learner knowledge.

Acknowledgments

This work has been supported by the Volkswagen Foundation as part of the Lichtenberg-Professorship Program under grant No. I/82806, and by the Klaus Tschira Foundation under project No. 00.133.2008.

[11] For the open test formats, the additional features had almost no effect.

References

Manish Agarwal and Prashanth Mannem. 2011. Automatic Gap-fill Question Generation from Text Books. pages 56–64. Association for Computational Linguistics.

Lisa Beinborn, Torsten Zesch, and Iryna Gurevych. 2014a. Predicting the difficulty of language proficiency tests. *Transactions of the Association for Computational Linguistics*, 2:517–529.

Lisa Beinborn, Torsten Zesch, and Iryna Gurevych. 2014b. Readability for foreign language learning: The importance of cognates. *International Journal of Applied Linguistics*.

Steffen Bickel, Peter Haider, and Tobias Scheffer. 2005. Predicting sentences using N-gram language models. In *Proceedings of the conference on Human Language Technology and Empirical Methods in Natural Language Processing - HLT '05*, pages 193–200, Morristown, NJ, USA, October. Association for Computational Linguistics.

Aleid C Broerse and EJ Zwaan. 1966. The information value of initial letters in the identification of words. *Journal of Verbal Learning and Verbal Behavior*, 5(5):441–446.

Jonathan C Brown, Gwen A Frishkoff, and Maxine Eskenazi. 2005. Automatic Question Generation for Vocabulary Assessment. In *HLT '05: Proceedings of the conference on Human Language Technology and Empirical Methods in Natural Language Processing*, pages 819–826, Morristown, NJ, USA. Association for Computational Linguistics.

James Dean Brown. 1989. Cloze item difficulty. *JALT journal*, 11:46–67.

Johannes Daxenberger, Oliver Ferschke, Iryna Gurevych, and Torsten Zesch. 2014. DKPro TC: A Java-based Framework for Supervised Learning Experiments on Textual Data. In *Proceedings of 52nd Annual Meeting of the Association for Computational Linguistics: System Demonstrations*, pages 61–66, Baltimore, Maryland, June. Association for Computational Linguistics.

Richard Eckart de Castilho and Iryna Gurevych. 2014. A broad-coverage collection of portable NLP components for building shareable analysis pipelines. *Proceedings of the Workshop on Open Infrastructures and Analysis Frameworks for HLT*, pages 1–11.

Scott C. Deerwester, Susan T Dumais, Thomas K. Landauer, George W. Furnas, and Richard A. Harshman. 1990. Indexing by latent semantic analysis. *Journal of the American Society for Information Science*, 41(6):391–407.

Thomas Eckes. 2011. Item banking for C-tests: A polytomous Rasch modeling approach. *Psychological Test and Assessment Modeling*, 53(4):414–439.

Evgeniy Gabrilovich and Shaul Markovitch. 2007. Computing Semantic Relatedness using Wikipedia-based Explicit Semantic Analysis. In *Proceedings of the 20th International Joint Conference on Artificial Intelligence*, pages 1606–1611.

Mark Hall, Eibe Frank, Geoffrey Holmes, Bernhard Pfahringer, Peter Reutemann, and Ian H. Witten. 2009. The WEKA data mining software: an update. 11(1).

Michael J Heilman, Kevyn Collins-Thompson, Jamie Callan, and Maxine Eskenazi. 2007. Combining lexical and grammatical features to improve readability measures for first and second language texts. In *Proceedings of NAACL-HLT*, pages 460–467.

Tobias Horsmann and Torsten Zesch. 2014. Towards automatic scoring of cloze items by selecting low-ambiguity contexts. *NEALT Proceedings Series Vol. 22*, pages 33–42.

Tadamitsu Kamimoto. 1993. Tailoring the Test to Fit the Students: Improvement of the C-Test through Classical Item Analysis. *Language Laboratory*, 30:47–61, November.

Sachiko Kinoshita. 2000. The left-to-right nature of the masked onset priming effect in naming. *Psychonomic Bulletin & Review*, 7(1):133–141, March.

Christine Klein-Braley and Ulrich Raatz. 1982. Der C-Test: ein neuer Ansatz zur Messung allgemeiner Sprachbeherrschung. *AKS-Rundbrief*, 4:23 – 37.

Christine Klein-Braley. 1984. Advance Prediction of Difficulty with C-Tests. In Terry Culhane, Christine Klein-Braley, and Douglas K. Stevenson, editors, *Practice and problems in language testing*, volume 7.

Christine Klein-Braley. 1996. Towards a theory of C-Test processing. In Rüdiger Grotjahn, editor, *Der C-Test. Theoretische Grundlagen und praktische Anwendungen 3*, pages 23–94. Brockmeyer, Bochum.

Ruslan Mitkov, Le An Ha, and Nikiforos Karamanis. 2006. A computer-aided environment for generating multiple-choice test items. *Natural Language Engineering*, 12(2):177–194, May.

Jack Mostow and Hyeju Jang. 2012. Generating Diagnostic Multiple Choice Comprehension Cloze Questions. pages 136–146.

Laura Perez-Beltrachini, Claire Gardent, and German Kruszewski. 2012. Generating Grammar Exercises. In *Proceedings of the Seventh Workshop on Building Educational Applications Using NLP*, pages 147–156.

Uwe Quasthoff, Matthias Richter, and Christian Biemann. 2006. Corpus portal for search in monolingual corpora. In *Proceedings of the fifth international conference on language resources and evaluation*, volume 17991802.

Günther Sigott and Johann Köberl. 1996. Deletion patterns and C-test difficulty across languages. In Rüdiger Grotjahn, editor, *Der C-Test. Theoretische Grundlagen und praktische Anwendungen 3*, pages 159–172. Brockmeyer, Bochum.

Günther Sigott. 1995. The C-test: some factors of difficulty. *AAA. Arbeiten aus Anglistik und Amerikanistik*, 20(1):43–54.

Adam Skory and Maxine Eskenazi. 2010. Predicting Cloze Task Quality for Vocabulary Training. In *The 5th Workshop on Innovative Use of NLP for Building Educational Applications (NAACL-HLT)*. Association for Computational Linguistics.

Bernard Spolsky. 1969. Reduced Redundancy as a Language Testing Tool. In G.E. Perren and J.L.M. Trim, editors, *Applications of linguistics*, pages 383–390. Cambridge University Press, Cambridge, August.

Andreas Stolcke. 1994. *Bayesian learning of probabilistic language models*. Ph.D. thesis, University of California, Berkeley.

Wilson L. Taylor. 1953. "Cloze procedure": a new tool for measuring readability. *Journalism Quarterly*, 30:415–433.

Torsten Zesch and Oren Melamud. 2014. Automatic Generation of Challenging Distractors Using Context-Sensitive Inference Rules. In *Proceedings of the Ninth Workshop on Innovative Use of NLP for Building Educational Applications*, pages 143–148. Association for Computational Linguistics.

Geoffrey Zweig and Chris JC Burges. 2012. A challenge set for advancing language modeling. In *Proceedings of the NAACL-HLT 2012 Workshop: Will We Ever Really Replace the N-gram Model? On the Future of Language Modeling for HLT*, pages 29–36. Association for Computational Linguistics.

Geoffrey Zweig, John C Platt, Christopher Meek, Christopher JC Burges, Ainur Yessenalina, and Qiang Liu. 2012. Computational approaches to sentence completion. In *Proceedings of the 50th Annual Meeting of the Association for Computational Linguistics: Long Papers-Volume 1*, pages 601–610. Association for Computational Linguistics.

Feature selection for automated speech scoring

Anastassia Loukina, Klaus Zechner, Lei Chen, Michael Heilman*
Educational Testing Service
660 Rosedale Rd
Princeton, NJ, USA
{aloukina, kzechner, lchen}@ets.org, mheilman@civisanalytics.com

Abstract

Automated scoring systems used for the evaluation of spoken or written responses in language assessments need to balance good empirical performance with the interpretability of the scoring models. We compare several methods of feature selection for such scoring systems and show that the use of shrinkage methods such as Lasso regression makes it possible to rapidly build models that both satisfy the requirements of validity and intepretability, crucial in assessment contexts as well as achieve good empirical performance.

1 Introduction

In this paper we compare different methods of selecting the best feature subset for scoring models used in the context of large-scale language assessments, with a particular look at the assessment of spoken responses produced by test-takers.

The basic approach to automatically scoring written or spoken responses is to collect a training corpus of responses that are scored by human raters, use machine learning to estimate a model that maps response features to scores from this corpus , and then use this model to predict scores for unseen responses (Page, 1966; Burstein et al., 1998; Landauer et al., 2003; Eskenazi, 2009; Zechner et al., 2009; Bernstein et al., 2010). While this method is often quite effective in terms of producing scoring models that exhibit good agreement with human raters, it can lend itself to criticism from the educational measurement community if it fails to address certain basic considerations for assessment design and scoring that are common practice in that field.

For instance, Ramineni and Williamson (2013) argue that automated scoring not only has to be reliable (i.e., exhibiting a good empirical performance as demonstrated, for example, by correlations between predicted and human scores), but also valid. One very important aspect of validity is to what extent the automated scoring model reflects important dimensions of the construct measured by the test (a construct is the set of knowledge, skills, and abilities measured by a test). For example, a speaking proficiency test for non-native speakers may claim that it assesses aspects such as fluency, pronunciation, and content accuracy in a test-taker's spoken response(s). If the features that contribute to the scoring models can be seen as measuring all of these aspects of spoken language well, the model would be considered valid from a construct point of view. However, if certain dimensions of the construct are not represented (well) by the feature set used in the scoring model, and/or features contained in the model address aspects not considered to be relevant for measuring the test construct, the construct validity of the scoring model would not be considered ideal (cf. also Bernstein et al. (2010) and Williamson et al. (2012) who make similar argument).

Furthermore, relative contributions by features to each construct dimension should be easily obtainable from the scoring model. To satisfy this requirement, machine-learning approaches such as support vector machines (SVMs) with non-linear kernels

*Currently at Civis Analytics

Proceedings of the Tenth Workshop on Innovative Use of NLP for Building Educational Applications, 2015, pages 12–19,
Denver, Colorado, June 4, 2015.

may be less ideal than a simple straightforward linear regression model, where the contribution of each feature in the model is immediately obvious.

Finally, the contribution of each feature to the final score should be consistent with the relevant constructs: if all of the features in the model are designed to be positively correlated with human scores, the coefficients of all such features in the final model should be positive as well.

Fulfilling all of these requirements when building automated scoring models is not trivial and has, in the past, typically involved the participation and advice of human content and measurement experts whose role it is to optimize the feature set so that it adheres to the aforementioned criteria as much as possible, while still allowing for good empirical performance of the resulting automated scoring model (Zechner et al., 2009; Cheng et al., 2014). However, there are certain limitations to this manual process of scoring- model building, not the least of which is the aspect of time it takes to build models with iterative evaluations and changes in the feature set composition.

Alternatively, one can compute a large number of potential features and then use automatic feature selection to identify the most suitable subset. This second approach is commonly used in studies that aim to maximize the performance of machine-learning systems (cf. for example, Hönig et al. (2010) among many others), but to our knowledge, it has not yet been applied in the assessment context where model performance needs to be balanced with model validity in terms of construct coverage and other constraints such as feature polarity.

We consider several methods of automatic feature selection commonly applied to linear models (Hastie et al., 2013). These include subset selection methods such as step-wise feature selection as well as shrinkage methods such as Lasso regression (Tibshirani, 1996). We focus on feature selection methods that can be scaled to a large number of features which exclude, for example, the best-subset approach, which becomes unfeasible for more than 30–40 features. We also exclude methods that use derived input such as principal component regression or partial least squares because the contribution of each feature in the final model would be more difficult to interpret. Finally, we consider feature selection methods which make it possible to restrict the coefficients to positive values. Such restriction is not specific to automated scoring and therefore various algorithms have been developed to address this requirement (see, for example, Lipovetsky (2009) for further discussion). We consider several of such methods including non-negative least squares regression Lawson and Hanson (1981) and a constrained version of Lasso regression (Goeman, 2010).

In this paper we address the following questions: (a) What methods of automatic feature selection can address all or most of the requirements of automated scoring and therefore are most suitable for this purpose? (b) Does more constrained selection affect the performance of such scoring models? (c) How do models based on automated feature selection compare to models based on human expert feature selection in terms of empirical performance and construct coverage?

The paper is organized as follows: Section 2 provides a description of the data used in this study, further details about the feature-selection methods, and the parameter setting for these methods. Section 3 presents the comparison between different feature-selection methods in terms of performance, coefficient polarity, and construct coverage of the selected feature subset. Finally, Section 4 summarizes the results of our experiments.

2 Data and Methodology

2.1 Data

The study is based on spoken responses to an English language proficiency test. During the original test administration, each speaker provided up to six responses. Two of the items required test takers to listen to an audio file and respond to a prompt about the conversation or lecture they heard. For the other two items, the test takers were required to read a short passage and listen to an audio file, and then integrate information from both sources in their responses to that prompt. The remaining two items asked the speakers to discuss a particular topic. All responses consisted of unscripted speech and were no longer than 1 minute each.

Both the training and evaluation sets included responses from about 10,000 speakers. With few exceptions, the training set included one response from each speaker, for a total of 9,956 responses and 9,312 speakers. The evaluation set included a similar number of speakers (8,101), but we used all available responses for each speaker, for a total of 47,642 responses[1]. There was no overlap of speakers or prompts between the two sets.

All responses were assigned a holistic proficiency score by expert raters. The scores ranged from 1 (low proficiency) to 4 (high proficiency). The raters evaluated the overall intelligibility of responses, grammar, the use of vocabulary, and topic development. About 10% of the responses in the evaluation set and all responses of the training set were scored by two raters. The agreement between the two raters was Pearson's r = 0.63 for the training set and r = 0.62 for the evaluation set.

2.2 Features

For each response, we extracted 75 different features which covered five aspects of language proficiency: fluency, pronunciation accuracy, prosody, grammar, and vocabulary. Some examples of such features include speech rate (fluency), normalized acoustic model score (pronunciation accuracy), language model score (grammar), and average lexical frequency of words used in the response(vocabulary). Several features were closely related: for example, the speech rate was measured in both words per second and syllables per second.

All features are designed to be positively correlated with human proficiency scores. For features that have a negative correlation with a proficiency score (such as the number of disfluencies), the values are multiplied by -1 so that the final correlation is always positive.

The features for the baseline EXPERT model were manually selected by an expert in English language learning to fulfill the criteria described in 1. The expert only had access to the training set while doing the feature selection. The model included 12 features which represented the five dimensions of language proficiency described above. The features were then used as independent variables in an ordinary least squares (OLS) linear regression using the proficiency score assigned by the first rater as the dependent variable.

We also built scoring models using all 75 features and several methods of automatic feature selection, following (Hastie et al., 2013). These are listed in Table 1.

Table 1: The methods used for automatic feature selection in this study

Name	Description
ALL	No feature selection. This model uses OLS regression and all 75 available features.
STEP	Features were identified by hybrid stepwise selection with search in both directions
NNLS	Features were identified by fitting the non-negative least squares regression model. (Lawson and Hanson (1981) as implemented by Mullen and Van Stokkum (2012))
LASSO	Used features that were assigned non-zero coefficients after fitting a Lasso regression (Tibshirani, 1996). All estimated coefficients were restricted to be non-negative (Goeman, 2010; Goeman et al., 2012). See 2.3 for details about parameter tuning.

We used 10-fold cross-validation on the training set to estimate model performance and tune the parameters for the Lasso regression. The allocation of responses between the folds was the same for all models. In all cases, the feature selection was applied separately to each fold.

The models were evaluated by the correlation between predicted and observed scores, the number of features in the final model, the percentage of features with positive coefficients, and by the number of constructs that were represented in the automatically selected subset model.

2.3 Setting parameters for LASSO model

We trained two versions of the LASSO models: LASSO where λ parameter for $L1$-regularization was tuned empirically to achieve the best model fit and LASSO* where λ was set to obtain the smallest pos-

[1]A small number of responses originally collected from these speakers were not included in the evaluation set due to their low audio quality or other problems.

sible set of features without a substantial loss in performance.

To set λ for LASSO*, we used the algorithm described in Park and Hastie (2007) to identify the values of λ that corresponded approximately to changes in feature sets. This was done separately for each fold.

We then computed the model performance for each feature set and identified the best performing set of each size (in many cases different values of λ produced several different feature sets with the same number of features). Figure 1 shows the performance obtained for models with different numbers of features selected by LASSO across the ten folds.

The figure shows that the number of features (12) in the EXPERT model may be insufficient to include all information covered by the features.[2] The average correlation for models with this number of features was $r = 0.63$. The optimal number of features for this dataset appeared to be around 21–25 features. We therefore set λ to $\sqrt{n * lg(p)}$, where n is the number of cases and p is the total number of features. For this dataset, this rule-of-thumb value forced a more aggressive feature selection and produced a model with approximately 25 features.

3 Results

3.1 Model performance

Figure 2 and Table 2 show that the models with automatic feature selection consistently outperformed the baseline EXPERT model (paired t-test with Holm's adjustment for multiple comparisons: $p < 0.00001$ for all models). Note that all of these models also used a higher number of features than what was included in the EXPERT model.

The models that did not have restrictions on positive coefficients achieved the highest performance. However, half of the coefficients in both STEP and ALL were negative. This is partially due to the fact that many features were highly correlated which resulted in what is known as "multicollinearity distortion of regression coefficients" (cf. also Lipovetsky (2009) for further discussion). Therefore the models created using these feature-selection methods violated the criterion that the coefficient assigned to each feature must have the same sign as the marginal correlation between that feature and human score.

[2]The figure shows the performance of the best performing set consisting of 12 features as identified by LASSO. These were not the same features as selected by the expert

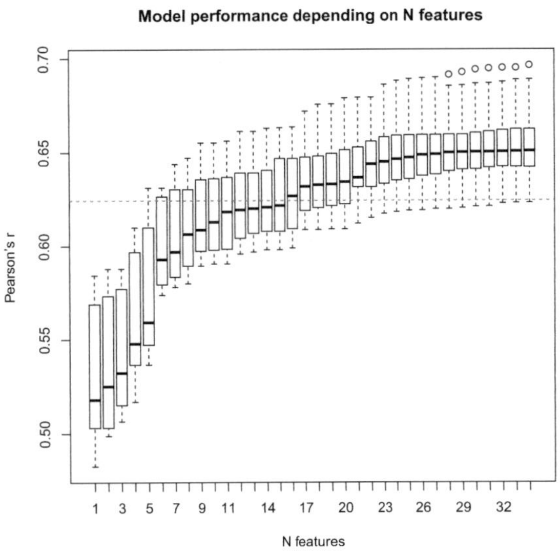

Figure 1: The performance of models based on LASSO feature selection by the number of features. The boxplots show the results across 10 folds of the training set. The horizontal line shows the performance at $N_{feat} = 12$ ($r = 0.63$), the size of the subset in the EXPERT model.

The methods which restricted feature selection to positive coefficients (NNLS, LASSO and LASSO*) addressed this problem, but the performance of these models was somewhat lower ($r = 0.65$ vs. $r = 0.67$, $p < 0.001$) which suggests that there is further interaction between different features that are not currently captured by a model restricted to positive coefficients.

There was no significant difference in performance between NNLS, LASSO and LASSO* but the NNLS and LASSO models included more features than LASSO* model, making them more difficult to interpret. LASSO* appeared to reach the best compromise between model complexity and model performance.

Finally, we evaluated the extent to which the performance of LASSO models was due to the different methods of coefficient estimation. We used the feature set selected by LASSO* to fit an OLS regression and compared the performance of the two models. There was no difference in performance between the models with coefficients estimated by OLS or penalized coefficients, but the two-step approach resulted in models with small negative coefficients in four out of ten folds. Therefore we used the original LASSO* with penalized coefficients for final evaluation.

Table 2: Maximum and minimum number of features selected by each model (N_{min} and N_{max}), average ratio of features assigned positive coefficients to the total N features (P/N) and average Pearson's r between predicted and observed scores r_{resp} across 10 folds

	N_{min}	N_{max}	P/N	r_{resp}
EXPERT	12	12	1	0.606
ALL	75	75	0.55	0.667
STEP	37	43	0.62	0.667
NNLS	32	37	1.00	0.655
LASSO	32	36	1.00	0.655
LASSO*	22	27	1.00	0.649

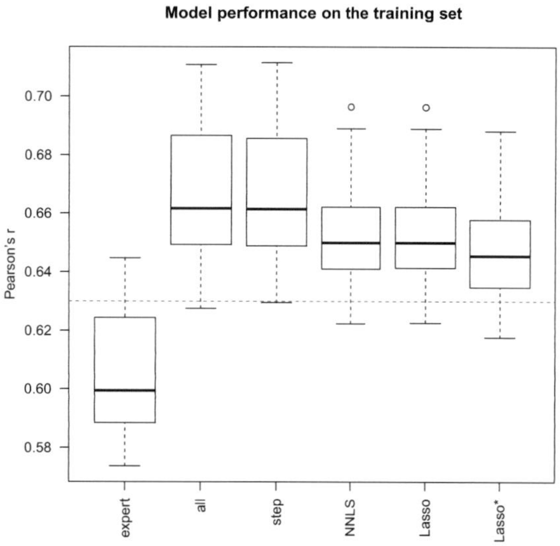

Figure 2: Model performance (Pearson's r) across 10 folds. Feature selection was performed separately at each fold. The horizontal line indicates the agreement between two human raters.

3.2 Model performance on unseen data

We then applied these feature selection methods to the whole training set and evaluated their performance on the unseen evaluation set. The results were consistent with the results of the cross-validation and are shown in Table 3.

The LASSO* model trained on the entire training set included 25 features, all of which had positive coefficients. The correlation between the predicted and observed scores was r_{resp} = 0.653, which was above the EXPERT baseline (r_{resp} = 0.607).

In addition to response-level agreement, we also computed the agreement for scores aggregated by speaker. During the test administration, the scores for all six responses given by each speaker are summed to compute an overall speaking proficiency score. Therefore, speaker-level agreement r_{sp} was calculated as the correlation coefficient (Pearson's r) between the summed observed scores and the summed predicted scores for each speaker. Following operational practice, this was only done for 7,390 speakers, where scores were available for 5 or more responses.[3]. We found that the model created using the LASSO* feature selection also outperformed the EXPERT model for speaker-level agreement with r_{sp} increasing from 0.78 to 0.84.

Table 3: Model performance on the unseen evaluation set using different feature- selection methods. The agreement between two human raters for this data is r_{resp}=0.62 for single responses. The human-human agreement for the aggregated speaker-level score, r_{sp}, was not available for this particular data since only a small subset of responses were scored by two human raters. Based on other data from the same test, r_{sp} between two human raters is expected to be around 0.9

	N_{feat}	P/N	r_{resp}	r_{sp}
EXPERT	12	1	0.61	0.78
ALL	75	0.55	0.67	0.86
STEP	40	0.65	0.67	0.86
NNLS	37	1	0.66	0.85
LASSO	36	1	0.66	0.85
LASSO*	25	1	0.65	0.84

3.3 Construct coverage

All methods of automatic feature selection produced feature subsets that represented the five subconstructs covered by the expert model: fluency, pronunciation accuracy, prosody, grammar, and vocabulary sophistication. In the rest of this section we

[3]If only 5 responses were available for a given speaker, the mean of these scores was added to their sum in order to estimate the overall speaker score.

Table 4: Relative weights of features representing different constructs covered by the scoring models.

Construct	EXPERT	LASSO*
Delivery		
Fluency	0.580	0.527
Pronunciation accuracy	0.098	0.151
Prosody	0.080	0.035
Total for delivery:	0.759	0.712
Language use		
Grammar	0.155	0.103
Vocabulary	0.086	0.183
Total for Language Use:	0.241	0.286

only consider in detail the features included in the LASSO* model which was selected in 3.1 as the best compromise between model complexity and model performance.

The selected model included 25 features covering all of the constructs currently represented by the expert model. To evaluate the construct coverage of each model we first computed standardized weights for each features. We then scaled the standardized weights for each model so that their sum equaled 1 and refer to them as "relative weights." Finally, we computed the sum of relative weights of all features representing a given construct or sub-construct. The results are shown in Table 4.

The two models, EXPERT and LASSO* closely matched in terms of construct coverage: delivery features in both models accounted for about 70-75% of the final score, with most weight given to fluency features, followed by pronunciation accuracy and rhythm. Language-use features accounted for 25% of the final score, but the relative weights of sub-constructs differed between the two models: while the EXPERT model assigned more weight to grammar features, the LASSO* model assigned more weight to vocabulary features.

4 Discussion

Building automated scoring models for constructed responses, such as spoken or written responses in language assessments, is a complex endeavor. Aside from the obvious desire for high empirical performance, as measured in terms of agreement between predicted and human scores, a number of important considerations from educational measurement should be taken into account as well. They include, foremost, the validity of the scoring model and, in particular, to what extent features that measure certain aspects of the construct are represented in the model, and features that are not related to the construct are not. Additionally, the relative contribution of each feature to the score based on the model should be transparent to the test taker and score user. Finally, each feature's contribution to the score must be in the same polarity as its marginal correlation with the criterion score (human score or dependent variable).

Because of this complexity, scoring models for constructed responses were typically built in the past using human experts who selected features based on these criteria in an iterative fashion, training and evaluating scoring models after each feature set was chosen.

In this paper, we applied different methods of feature selection in order to select the best feature set for the automated scoring of spoken responses to an English language proficiency test. We aimed to simultaneously achieve optimal construct coverage, maximal interpretability of the resulting scoring model, and good empirical performance.

For research question (a), what methods of feature selection are most suitable for the automated scoring of spoken responses, we found that a model based on Lasso regression fine-tuned to enforce more aggressive feature selection reaches a good compromise between relatively small number of features and good agreement with human scores. In addition, this model could also satisfy the requirement that all coefficients are positive. Finally, the LASSO* model represented all constructs included into the EXPERT model.

Our results showed that some of the constraints imposed by the requirements to model interpretability decrease model performance in comparison to unconstrained models (research question b). Thus, the requirement to keep all coefficients positive in line with feature interpretation reduced response-level performance of the model from 0.667 to 0.65. While the difference is relatively small, it is statistically significant. More research is needed to explore whether the information lost due to this constraint may be relevant to the constructs covered by the model and can be incorporated into a future model by developing new combined features.

Finally, for research question (c), how automatic and expert feature selection compare in terms of empirical performance and construct coverage, we found that in comparison to expert feature selection, computing a large number of features with subsequent automatic selection leads to higher performance (for LASSO*: $r = 0.84$ vs. $r = 0.78$ on the evaluation set for aggregated scores for each test taker) while maintaining construct validity and interpretability of the resulting models. Furthermore, the feature subset produced by LASSO* closely matched the EXPERT model in terms of the relative contribution of each construct.

To summarize, the application of Lasso regression to feature selection for automated speech scoring made it possible to rapidly build models which both achieved higher performance than the expert baseline and also satisfied the requirements of construct coverage and interpretability of the model posed by the assessment context. In this respect, Lasso regression was superior to other common methods of feature selection such as step-wise selection, which could not satisfy all of these requirements.

In this study, the features selected by LASSO* showed consistently good construct coverage across 10 folds of the training set. Yet it is possible that for a different dataset the LASSO* method may lead to a feature subset which is considered sub-optimal by an expert. In this case, the automatically selected feature set can be adjusted by the expert to ensure appropriate construct coverage by adding additional features to the model or removing unwanted features from the original feature set and re-running the model to estimate the coefficients. Of course, such adjustments may lead to a loss in performance, in which case the optimal balance between construct validity and model performance will be determined by other considerations such as the nature of the assessment or the role of the automated scoring system in determining the final score.

5 Conclusion

In this paper we compared a range of different methods for the purpose of feature selection for the automated scoring models of spoken language in the context of language assessment and educational measurement.

Based on a number of criteria as to what constitutes scoring models that have not only high empirical performance, are valid from a construct point of view, and interpretable for the test taker or score user, we demonstrated that in using the LASSO* method all criteria can be satisfied: the resulting scoring model has construct coverage commensurate to that built by a human expert and its empirical performance is, at the same time, superior.

In future work, we plan to refine the automated feature selection process by using construct constraints directly in the feature selection procedure.

Acknowledgments

We would like to thank Lawrence Davis and Florian Lorenz for their feedback and discussion; Keelan Evanini, Jidong Tao and Su-Youn Yoon for their comments on the final draft and René Lawless for editorial help.

References

Jared Bernstein, Alistaire Van Moere, and Jian Cheng. 2010. Validating automated speaking tests. *Language Testing*, 27(3):355–377.

Jill Burstein, Karen Kukich, Susanne Wolff, Chi Lu, Martin Chodorow, Lisa Braden-Harder, and Mary Dee Harris. 1998. Automated scoring using a hybrid feature identification technique. In *Proceedings of the 36th annual meeting on Association for Computational Linguistics - and 17th International Conference on Computational Linguistics*, volume 1, pages 206–210, Morristown, NJ, USA. Association for Computational Linguistics.

Jian Cheng, Yuan Zhao D'Antilio, Xin Chen, and Jared Bernstein. 2014. Automatic Assessment of the Speech of Young English Learners. *Proceedings of the 9th Workshop on Innovative Use of NLP for Building Educational Applications*, pages 12–21.

Maxine Eskenazi. 2009. An overview of spoken language technology for education. *Speech Communication*, 51(10):832–844.

Jelle J. Goeman, Rosa Meijer, and Nimisha Chaturverdi. 2012. Penalized L1 (lasso and fused lasso) and L2 (ridge) penalized estimation in GLMs and in the Cox model. R package version 0.9-42.

Jelle J. Goeman. 2010. L1 penalized estimation in the Cox proportional hazards model. *Biometrical journal*, 52(1):70–84.

Trevor Hastie, Robert Tibshirani, and Jerome Friedman. 2013. *The Elements of Statistical Learning: Data Mining, Inference, and Prediction, Second Edition (Springer Series in Statistics)*. Springer, 2nd edition.

Florian Hönig, Anton Batliner, Karl Weilhammer, and Elmar Nöth. 2010. Automatic assessment of non-native prosody for english as L2. *Speech Prosody 2010*, 100973(1):1–4.

Thomas K. Landauer, D. Laham, and Peter W. Foltz. 2003. Automated scoring and annotation of essays with the Intelligent Essay Assessor. In Mark D. Shermis and Jill C. Burstein, editors, *Automated essay scoring: A cross-disciplinary perspective*, pages 87–112. Erlbaum, Hillsdale, NJ.

Charles L. Lawson and Richard J. Hanson. 1981. *Solving Least Squares Problems*. Prentice-Hall, Englewood Cliffs, NJ, January.

Stan Lipovetsky. 2009. Linear regression with special coefficient features attained via parameterization in exponential, logistic, and multinomiallogit forms. *Mathematical and Computer Modelling*, 49(7-8):1427–1435.

Katharine M. Mullen and Ivo H.M. Van Stokkum. 2012. nnls: The Lawson-Hanson algorithm for non-negative least squares (NNLS). R package version 1.4.

Ellis B. Page. 1966. The imminence of... grading essays by computer. *The Phi Delta Kappan*, 47(5):238–243.

Mee Young Park and Trevor Hastie. 2007. L1-regularization path algorithm for generalized linear models. *Journal of the Royal Statistical Society: Series B (Statistical Methodology)*, 69(4):659–677.

Chaitanya Ramineni and David M. Williamson. 2013. Automated essay scoring: Psychometric guidelines and practices. *Assessing Writing*, 18(1):25–39, January.

Robert Tibshirani. 1996. Regression shrinkages and selection via the Lasso. *Journal of the Royal Statistical Society: Series B (Statistical Methodology)*, 58(1):267–288.

David M. Williamson, Xiaoming Xi, and F. Jay Breyer. 2012. A framework for evaluation and use of automated scoring. *Educational measurement: issues and practice*, 31(1):2–13.

Klaus Zechner, Derrick Higgins, Xiaoming Xi, and David M. Williamson. 2009. Automatic scoring of non-native spontaneous speech in tests of spoken English. *Speech Communication*, 51(10):883–895.

Incorporating Coherence of Topics as a Criterion in Automatic Response-to-Text Assessment of the Organization of Writing

Zahra Rahimi[1], **Diane Litman**[1,2,3], **Elaine Wang**[3], **Richard Correnti**[3]
[1]Intelligent Systems Program, [2]Department of Computer Science
[3]Learning Research and Development Center
University of Pittsburgh
Pittsburgh, PA 15260
{zar10,dlitman,elw51,rcorrent}@pitt.edu

Abstract

This paper presents an investigation of score prediction for the Organization dimension of an assessment of analytical writing in response to text. With the long-term goal of producing feedback for students and teachers, we designed a task-dependent model that aligns with the scoring rubric and makes use of the source material. Our experimental results show that our rubric-based model performs as well as baselines on datasets from grades 6-8. On shorter and noisier essays from grades 5-6, the rubric-based model performs better than the baselines. Further, we show that the baseline model (lexical chaining) can be improved if we extend it with information from the source text for shorter and noisier data.

1 Introduction

As a construct, 'Organization' has figured in systems for scoring student writing for decades. On the NAEP (National Assessment of Educational Progress), the organization of the text, coherence, and focus are judged in relation to the writer's purpose and audience (National Assessment Governing Board, 2010) to determine a single holistic score. Alternatively, when organization is considered as a separate dimension, some surface features of organization are considered. Such surface features include: effective sequencing; strong inviting beginning; strong satisfying conclusion; and smooth transitions[1]. Assessments aligned to the Common Core State Standards (CCSS), the academic standards adopted widely in 2011 that guide K-12 education, reflect a shift in thinking about the scoring of organization in writing to consider the coherence of ideas in the text[2]. The consideration of coherence as a critical aspect of organization of writing is relatively new.

Notably, prior studies in natural language processing have examined the concept of discourse coherence, which is highly related to the coherence of topics in an essay, as a measure of the organization of analytic writing. For example, in Somasundaran et al. (2014) the coherence elements are adherence to the essay topic, elaboration, usage of varied vocabulary, and sound organization of thoughts and ideas. In Crossley and McNamara (2011) the elements are effective lead, clear purpose, clear plan, topic sentences, paragraph transitions, organization, unity, perspective, conviction, grammar, syntax, and mechanics.

Many computational methods are used to measure such elements of discourse coherence. Vector-based similarity methods measure lexical relatedness between text segments (Foltz et al., 1998) or between discourse segments (Higgins et al., 2004). Centering theory (Grosz et al., 1995) addresses local coherence (Miltsakaki and Kukich, 2000). Entity-based essay representation along with type/token ratios for each syntactic role is another method to evaluate coher-

[1]Retrieved from http://www.rubrics4teachers.com/pdf/6TRAITSWRITING.pdf, February 25, 2015

[2]See, e.g., Grades 4 and 5 Expanded rubric for analytic and narrative writing retrieved from http://www.parcconline.org/sites/parcc/files/Grade 4-5 ELA Expanded Rubric FOR ANALYTIC AND NARRATIVE WRITING_0.pdf

Proceedings of the Tenth Workshop on Innovative Use of NLP for Building Educational Applications, 2015, pages 20–30,
Denver, Colorado, June 4, 2015.

ence (Burstein et al., 2010) that is shown in Burstein et al. (2013) to be a predictive model on a corpus of essays from grades 6-12. Lexical chaining addresses multiple aspects of coherence such as elaboration, usage of varied vocabulary, and sound organization of thoughts and ideas (Somasundaran et al., 2014). Discourse structure is used to measure the organization of argumentative writing (Cohen, 1987; Burstein et al., 1998; Burstein et al., 2003b).

In previous studies, assessments of text coherence have been task-independent, which means that these models are designed to be able to evaluate the coherence of the response to any writing task. Task-independence is often the goal for automated scoring systems, but it is also important to measure the quality of students' organization skills when they are responding to a task-dependent prompt. One advantage of task-dependent scores is the ability to provide feedback that is better aligned with the task.

One of the types of writing emphasized in the CCSS is writing in response to text (Correnti et al., 2013). In as early as the fourth and fifth grades, students are expected to write analytical responses to text, which involves making claims and marshalling evidence from a source text to support a viewpoint.

The Response-to-Text Assessment (RTA) (Correnti et al., 2013; Correnti et al., 2012) was developed for research purposes to study upper-elementary students' text-based writing skills. The RTA is evaluated with a five-trait rubric. Efforts to automate the assessment of student responses have been underway to support scaling up the use of the RTA in research and also to explore the potential of providing feedback on student writing to teachers. Specifically, evaluation of the Evidence dimension is investigated in Rahimi et al. (2014). In the present study, we aim to design a model to evaluate the Organization dimension of the RTA.

Our study differs in three noteworthy ways from previous studies aiming to evaluate organization. Insofar as the Organization dimension of the RTA concerns the coherence of the essay, this is similar to previous investigations that operationalize this trait as adherence to the essay topic, sentence-to-sentence flow, and logical paragraph transitions. Specifically, however, Organization as conceived by the RTA also concerns how well the pieces of evidence provided from the text are organized to make a strong argument. In this sense, what matters is coherence around the ordering of pieces of evidence.

This additional aspect of Organization is important to the evaluation of the RTA and to text-based writing in general; yet, available models for assessing coherence do not capture this aspect, primarily because Organization has been treated largely as task-independent. As such, these models are insufficient for our purposes, even if they might perform well on score prediction. For our study, then, we set out to design a model that draws upon information from the source text as well as the scoring rubric to assess Organization in RTA.

Second, while past studies have focused on the writing of advanced students (i.e., in high school and beyond), we evaluate the writing of students in grades 5 through 8. An implication of this is that the pieces are typically very short, full of grammatical and spelling errors, and not very sophisticated in terms of organization. This difference in the population under study renders our task more complex than in previous studies.

Third, we sought to develop a model that is consistent with the rubric criteria and easily explainable. Such a model has greater potential to generate useful feedback to students and teachers.

In this paper, we first introduce the data (a set of responses written by 5th and 6th graders, and a set by students in grades 6-8). Next, we explain the two different structures we designed from which we extracted features. Then we explain the features, experiments, and results. We show that in general, our rubric-based task-dependent model performs as well as (if not better than) the rigorous baselines we used. Moreover, we show that different approaches to evaluating organization in student writing work differently on different populations. On shorter and noisier essays from grades 5-6, the rubric-based model performs better than the baselines. Meanwhile, for essays from grades 6-8, our rubric-based model does not perform significantly differently from the baselines; however, the combination of our new features with the baselines performs the best. Finally, we show that even a lexical chaining baseline can be improved with the use of topic information from the source text.

Excerpt from the article: The people of Sauri have made amazing progress in just four years. The Yala Sub-District Hospital has medicine, free of charge, for all of the most common diseases. Water is connected to the hospital, which also has a generator for electricity.
Prompt: The author provided one specific example of how the quality of life can be improved by the Millennium Villages Project in Sauri, Kenya. Based on the article, did the author provide a convincing argument that winning the fight against poverty is achievable in our lifetime? Explain why or why not with 3-4 examples from the text to support your answer.
Essay with score of 1 on Organization dimension: Yes because Poverty should be beaten. Their are solutions to the Promblem that keep people impoverished. In 2004 two adults and three children was rushed to the hospital because of a disease. The disease was called Malaria. Mosquitoes carry Malaria. They pass it to people by bitting them. 20,000 kids die from malaria each day. A brighter future is a better life and better health. Poverty means to be Poor or have no money. People can end poverty. Ending poverty is easy. In 2004 Hannah Sachs visited the Millenium Villages Project in Kenya, a country in Africa. While they was there they saw people that were bare footed and had tattered clothing. The country that they went to had Poverty. She felt bad for the people. The Millennium Villages Project was created to help reach the Millennium Development Goals.
Essay with score of 4 on Organization dimension: This story convinced me that "winning the fight against poverty is achievable because they showed many example in the beginning and showed how it changed at the end. One example they sued show a great amount oF change when they stated at first most people thall were ill just stayed in the hospital Not even getting treated either because of the cost or the hospital didnt have it, **but at the end it stated they now give free medicine to most common deseases**. Anotehr amazing change is in the beginning majority of the childrenw erent going to school because the parents couldn't affford the school fee, and the kdis didnt like school because tehre was No midday meal, and Not a lot of book, pencils, and paper. Then in 2008 the perceNtage of kids going to school increased a lot because they Now have food to be served aNd they Now have more supplies. So Now theres a better chance of the childreN getting a better life The last example is Now they dont have to worry about their families starving because Now they have more water and fertalizer. They have made some excellent changes in sauri. Those chaNges have saved many lives and I think it will continue to change of course in positive ways

Table 1: A small excerpt from the *Time for Kids* article, the prompt, and sample low and high-scoring essays from grades 5–6.

2 Data

Our dataset consists of student writing from the RTA introduced in Correnti et al. (2013). Specifically, we have two datasets from two different age groups (grades 5-6 and grades 6-8), which represent different levels of writing proficiency.

The administration of the RTA involves having the classroom teacher read aloud a text while students followed along with their own copy. The text is an article from *Time for Kids* about a United Nations effort (the Millennium Villages Project) to eradicate poverty in a rural village in Kenya. After a guided discussion of the article as part of the read-aloud, students wrote an essay in response to a prompt that requires them to make a claim and support it using details from the text. A small excerpt from the article, the prompt, and two student essays from grades 5-6 are shown in Table 1.

Our datasets (particularly responses by students in grades 5-6) have a number of properties that may increase the difficulty of the automatic essay assessment task. The essays in our datasets are short, have many spelling and grammatical errors, and the modal essays score at a basic level on Organization. Some statistics about the datasets are in Table 2.

The student responses have been assessed on five dimensions, each on a scale of 1-4 (Correnti et al., 2013). Half of the assessments are scored by an expert. The rest are scored by undergraduate students trained to evaluate the essays based on the criteria. The corpus from grades 5-6 consists of 1580 essays, with 602 of them double-scored for inter-rater reliability. The other corpus includes 812 essays, with almost all of them (802) double-scored. Inter-rater agreement (Quadratic Weighted Kappa) for Organization on the double-scored portion of the grades 5-6 and 6-8 corpora respectively are 0.68 and 0.69.

Dataset		Mean	SD
5–6 grades	# words	161.25	92.24
	# unique words	93.27	40.57
	# sentences	9.01	6.39
	# paragraphs	2.04	1.83
6–8 grades	# words	207.99	104.98
	# unique words	113.14	44.14
	# sentences	12.51	7.53
	# paragraphs	2.71	1.74

Table 2: The two dataset's statistics

In this paper we focus only on predicting the score of the Organization dimension. The distribution of Organization scores is 398 (25%) ones, 714 (46%) twos, 353 (22%) threes, and 115 (7%) fours on the grades 5-6 dataset, and 128 (16%) ones, 316 (39%) twos, 246 (30%) threes, and 122 (15%) fours on the grades 6-8 dataset. Higher scores on the 6–8 corpus indicate that the essays in this dataset have better organization than the student essays in the 5–6 dataset. The rubric for this dimension is shown in Table 3.

1	2	3	4
Strays frequently or significantly from main idea*	Attempts to adhere to the main idea*	Adheres to the main idea* (i.e., The main idea is evident throughout the response)	Focuses clearly on the main idea throughout piece* and within paragraph
Has little or no sense of beginning, middle, and end(2) (i.e., Lacks topic and concluding sentence, or has no identifiable middle)	Has a limited sense of beginning, middle, and end(2) (i.e., Lacks a topic or concluding sentence, or has short development in middle)	Has an adequate sense of beginning, middle, and end(2) (topic and concluding sentences may not quite match up. Or, may be missing a beginning or ending, but organization is very clear and strong	Has a strong sense of beginning, middle, and end (2) (i.e., Must have topic sentence and concluding sentence that match up and relate closely to the same key idea, and well-developed middle)
Has little or no order; May feature a rambling collection of thoughts or list-like ideas with little or no flow(4)(5)	Attempts to address different ideas in turn+, in different parts of the response(3) (i.e., Some ideas may be repeated in different places)	Addresses different ideas in turn+, in different parts of the response(3), although multiple paragraphs may not be used(1)	Features multiple appropriate paragraphs (1), each addressing a different idea+
Consists mostly of a summary or copy of the whole text or large sections of the text (The organization of the response is necessarily the organization of the original text)	Has some uneven or illogical flow from sentence to sentence or idea to idea (3)	Demonstrates logical flow from sentence to sentence and idea to idea(3)	Demonstrates logical and seamless flow from sentence to sentence and idea to idea(3)
*In implementation, when scoring the rubric experts and trained coders considered the coherence of the evidence in support of the author's main claim for the text. Thus, in implementation coders placed pre-eminence on whether the evidence contributing support to the original claim formed a coherent body of evidence.			
+When scoring the rubric, experts and trained coders considered whether the different ideas were presented in a logical order to evaluate how well they worked together to form coherent evidence for the main claim. The sequence of the evidence as well as how well the author elaborated different pieces of evidence, in turn, were both considered when coding. (4)(5)			

Table 3: Rubric for the Organization dimension of RTA. The numbers in the parentheses identify the corresponding feature group in section 4 that is aligned with that specific criteria.

3 Topic-Grid and Topic Chains

Lexical chains (Somasundaran et al., 2014) and entity grids (Burstein et al., 2010) have been used to measure lexical cohesion. In other words, these models measure the continuity of lexical meaning. Lexical chains are sequences of related words characterized by the relation between the words, as well as by their distance and density within a given span. Entity grids capture how the same word appears in a syntactic role (Subject, Object, Other) across adjacent sentences.

Intuitively, we hypothesize that these models will not perform as well on short, noisy, and low quality essays as on longer, better written essays. When the essays are short, noisy, and of low quality (i.e., limited writing proficiency), the syntactic information may not be reliable. Moreover, even when there is elaboration on a single topic (continuation of meaning), there may not be repetition of identical or similar words. This is because words that relate to a given topic in the context of the article may not be deemed similar according to external similarity sources such as WordNet. Take, for example, the following two sentences:

"The hospitals were in bad situation. There was no electricity or water."

In the entity grid model, there would be no transition between these two sentences because there are no identical words. The semantic similarity of the nouns "hospitals" and "water" is very low and there would not be any chain including a relation between the words "hospitals", "water", and "electricity". But if we look at the source document and the topics within it, these two sentences are actually addressing a very specific sub-topic. Therefore, we think there should be a chain containing both of these words and a relation between them.

More importantly, what we are really interested in evaluating in this study is the organization and cohesion of pieces of evidence, not the lexical cohesion.

These reasons, altogether, motivated us to design new topic-grid and topic chain models (inspired by entity-grids and lexical chains), which are more related to our rubric and may be able to overcome the issues we mentioned above.

A topic-grid is a grid that shows the presence or absence of each topic addressed in the source text (i.e., the article about poverty) in each text unit of a written response. The rows are analogous to the words in an entity-grid, except here they represent topics instead of individual words. The columns are text units. We consider the unit as a sentence or a sub-sentence (since long sentences can include more than one topic and we don't want to lose the ordering and transition information from one topic to the next). We explain how we extract the units later in this section.

To build the grids, we use the information in the source text. That is, we had experts of the RTA manually extract the exhaustive list of topics discussed in the article. Similarly, in other studies on evaluation of content (typically in short answer scoring), the identification of concepts and topics is manual (Liu et al., 2014). Since the source text explicitly addresses the conditions in a Kenyan village before and after the United Nations-intervention, and since the prompt leads students to discuss the contrasting conditions at these different time points, we extract topics that provided evidence for the "before" and "after" states, respectively. That is, except for some general topics which are related to the conclusion of the text, for each major topic *t* the experts define two sub-topics t_{before} and t_{after} by listing specific examples related to each sub-topic .

The resulting list of topics was used to generate the rows of the topic-grid. The experts defined 7 different topics; 4 of them have before and after states, resulting in 11 sub-topics in total. Each sub-topic is defined by an exhaustive list of related examples from the text. For instance, the topic "Hospitals_after" (extracted from part of the article mentioned in Table 1) includes 5 examples that are shown here by their domain words (we use the stemmed version of the words): "*1. Yala sub-district hospital medicine 2. medicine free charge 3. water connected hospital 4. hospital generator electricity 5. medicine common diseases*".

Following this, each text unit of the essay is automatically labeled with topics using a simple window-based algorithm (with a fixed window size = 10), which relies on the presence and absence of topic-words in a sliding window and chooses the most similar topic to the window. (Several equally similar topics might be chosen). If there are fewer than two words in common with the most similar topic, the window is annotated with no topic. We did not use spelling correction to handle topic words with spelling errors, although it is in our future plan.

	1	2	3	4	5	6	7	8	9	10
Hospitals.b	-	x	-	-	-	-	-	-	-	-
Hospitals.a	-	-	x	-	-	-	-	-	-	-
Education.b	-	-	-	x	-	-	-	-	-	-
Education.a	-	-	-	-	x	x	-	-	-	-
Farming.b	-	-	-	-	-	-	x	-	-	-
Farming.a	-	-	-	-	-	-	-	x	-	-
General	x	-	-	-	-	-	-	-	x	x

Topic	Chain
Hospitals	(b,2),(a,3)
Education	(b,4),(a,5),(a,6)
Farming	(b,7),(a,8)

Table 4: The topic-grid (on the top) and topic-chains (on the bottom) for the example essay with score=4 in Table 1. *a* and *b* indicate *after* and *before* respectively.

The rule is that each column in the grid represents a text unit. A text unit is a sentence if it has no disjoint windows annotated with different topics. Otherwise, we break the sentence into multiple text units where each of them covers a different topic (the exact boundaries of the units are not important). Finally, if the labeling process annotates a single window with multiple topics, we add a column to the grid with multiple topics present in it.

See Table 4 for an example of a topic-grid for the essay with the score of four in Table 1. Consider the third column in the grid. It represents the bold text unit (the second part of the second sentence) in Table 1. The corresponding sentence has two text units since it covers two different topics "Hospitals_before" and "Hospitals_after". The "x" in the third column indicates the presence of the topic "Hospital_after" which is mentioned above. The topics that are not mentioned in the essay are not included in the grid.

Then, chains are extracted from the grid. We have one chain for each topic *t* including both t_{before} and t_{after}. Each node in a chain carries two pieces of information: the index of the text unit it appears in and whether it is a *before* or *after* state. We do not consider chains related to general topics that do not have a *before* or *after* state. Examples of topic-chains are presented in Table 4. Finally, we extract several features, explained in section 4, from the grid and the chains to represent some criteria from the rubric.

4 Features

As indicated above, one goal of this research in predicting Organization scores is to design a small set of rubric-based features that performs acceptably and also models what is actually important in the rubric. To this end, we designed 5 groups of features, each addressing one criterion in the rubric. Some of these features are not new and have been used before to evaluate the organization and coherence of the essay; however, the features based on the topic-grid and topic-chains (inspired by entity-grids and lexical chains) are new and designed for this study. The use of *before* and *after* information to extract features is based on the rubric and the nature of the prompt, and it can be generalized to other contrasting prompts. Below, we explain each of the features and its relation to the rubric. Each group of features is indicated with a number that relates it to the corresponding criteria in the rubric in Table 3.

(1) Surface: Captures the surface aspect of organization; it includes two features: *number of paragraphs* and *average sentence length*. Multiple paragraphs and medium-length sentences help readers follow the essays more easily.

(2) Discourse structure: Investigates the discourse elements in the essays. We cannot expect the essays written by students in grades 5-8 to have all the discourse elements mentioned in Burstein et al. (2003a), as might be expected of more sophisticated writers. Indeed, most of the essays in our corpora are short and single-paragraph (the median of # paragraphs is one). In terms of the structure, then, taking cues from the rubric, we are interested in the extent to which it has a clear beginning idea, concluding sentence, and well-developed middle.

We define two binary features, *beginning* and *ending*. In the Topic-list, there is a general topic that represents general statements from the text and the prompt. If this topic is present at the beginning or at the end of the grid, the corresponding feature gets a value of 1. A third feature measures if the beginning and the ending match. We measure LSA-similarity (Landauer et al., 1998) of 1 to 3 sentences from the beginning and ending of the essay with respect to the length of the essay. The LSA is trained by the source document and the essays in the training corpus. The number of sentences are chosen based on the average essay length.

(3) Local coherence and paragraph transitions: Local coherence addresses the rubric criterion related to logical sentence-to-sentence flow. It is measured by the average LSA (Foltz et al., 1998) similarity of adjacent sentences. Paragraph transitions capture the rubric criterion of discussing different topics in different paragraphs. It is measured by the average LSA similarity of all paragraphs (Foltz et al., 1998). For an essay where each paragraph addresses a different topic, the LSA similarity of paragraphs should be less than for an essay in which the same topic appears in different paragraphs. For one paragraph essays, we divide the essays into 3 equal parts and calculate the similarity of 3 parts.

(4) Topic development: Good essays should have a developed middle relevant to the assigned prompt. The following features are designed to capture how well-developed an essay is:

Topic-Density: Number of topics covered in the essay divided by the length of the essay. Higher Density means less development on each topic.

Before-only, After-only (i.e., Before and after the UN-led intervention referenced in the source text): These are two binary features. It measures if all the sentences in the essay are labeled only with "before" or only with "after" topics. A weak essay might, for example, discuss at length the condition of Kenya before the intervention (i.e., address several "before" topics) without referencing the result of the intervention (i.e., "after" topics).

Discourse markers: Four features that count the discourse markers from each of the four groups: contingency, expansion, comparison, and temporal, extracted by "AddDiscourse" connective tagger (Pitler and Nenkova, 2009). Eight additional features represent count and percentage of discourse markers from each of the four groups that appear in sentences that are labeled with a topic.

Average Chain Size: Average number of nodes in chains. Longer chains indicate more development on each topic.

Number and percentage of chains with variety: A chain on a topic has variety if it discusses both aspects ('before' and 'after') of that topic.

(5) Topic ordering and patterns: It is not just the number of topics and the amount of development on each topic that is important. More important is how students organized these topics in their essays. Logical and strategic organization of topics helps to strengthen arguments. Meanwhile, as reflected in the rubric in Table 3, little or no order in the discussion of topics in the essay means poor organization. In this section we present the features we designed to assess the quality of the essays in terms of organization of topics.

Levenshtein edit-distance of the topic vector representations for "befores" and "afters", normalized by the number of topics in the essay. If the essay has a good organization of topics, it should cover both the *before* and the *after* examples on each discussed topic. It is also important that they come in a similar order. For example, suppose the following two vectors represent the order of topics in an essay: befores=[3,4,4,5] , afters=[3,6,5]. First we compress the vectors by combining the adjacent similar topics. In this example topic number 4 will be compressed. So the final vectors are: befores=[3,4,5] , afters=[3,6,5]. The normalized Levensthein between these two vectors is 1/4, which shows the number of edits required to change one number string into the other normalized by total number of topics in the two vectors. The greater the value, the worse the pattern of discussed topics.

Max distance between chain's nodes: Large distance can be a sign of repetition. The distance between two nodes is the number of text units between those nodes in the grid.

Number of chains starting and ending inside another chain: There should be fewer in well-organized essays.

Average chain length (Normalized): The length of the chain is the sum of the distances between each pair of adjacent nodes. The normalized feature is divided by the length of the essay.

Average chain density: Equal to average chain size divided by average chain length.

5 Experiments and Results

5.1 Experimental Setup

We configure a series of experiments to test the validity of three hypotheses: H1) the new features perform better than the baselines; H2) the topic-grid model performs better on shorter and noisier essays than longer and well-written essays; H3) the lexical chaining baseline can be improved with the use of topic information from the source document.

For all experiments we use 10 runs of 10 fold cross validation using Random Forest as a classifier (max-depth=5). We also tried some other classification and regression methods, such as logistic regression and gradient boosting regression, and all the conclusions remained the same. Since our dataset is imbalanced, we use SMOTE (Chawla et al., 2002) oversampling method. This method involves creating synthetic minority class examples. We only oversampled the training data, not the testing data.

All performance measures are calculated by comparing the classifier results with the first human rater's scores. We chose the first human rater because we do not have the scores of the second rater for the entire dataset. We report the performance as Quadratic Weighted Kappa, which is a standard evaluation measure for essay assessment systems. We use corrected paired t-test (Bouckaert and Frank, 2004) to measure the significance of any difference in performance.

We use two well-performing baselines from recent methods to evaluate organization and coherence of the essays. The first baseline (EntityGridTT) is based on the entity-grid coherence model introduced by Barzilay and Lapata (2005). This method has been used to measure the coherence of student essays (Burstein et al., 2010). It includes transition probabilities and type/token ratios for each syntactic role as features. We perform a set of experiments using different configurations for the entity-grid baseline, and we find that the best model is an entity-grid model with history=2, salience=1, syntax=on and type/token ratios. We therefore use this best configuration in all experiments. It should be noted that this works to the advantage of the entity-grid baseline since we do not have parameter tuning for the other models.

The second baseline (LEX1) is a set of features extracted from Lexical Chaining (Morris and Hirst, 1991). We use Galley and McKeown (2003) lexical chaining and extract the first set of features (LEX1) introduced in Somasundaran et al. (2014). We do not implement the second set because we do not have the annotation or the tagger to tag discourse cues.

	Model	(5–6)	(6–8)
1	EntityGridTT	0.42	0.49
2	LEX1	0.45	0.53 (1)
3	EntityGridTT+LEX1	0.46 (1)	0.54 (1)
4	Rubric-based	**0.51** (1,2,3)	0.51
5	EntityGridTT+Rubric-based	0.49 (1,2,3)	0.53 (1)
6	LEX1+Rubric-based	**0.51** (1,2,3)	0.55 (1)
7	EntityGridTT+LEX1 +Rubric-based	0.50 (1,2,3)	**0.56** (1)

Table 5: Performance of our rubric-based model compared to the baselines on both datasets. The numbers in parenthesis show the model numbers which the current model performs significantly better than.

	Model	Train(5–6) Test(6–8)	Train(6–8) Test(5–6)
1	EntityGridTT	0.51 (2)	0.43
2	LEX1	0.43	0.41
3	EntityGridTT+LEX1	0.52 (2)	0.42
4	Rubric-based	0.56 (2)	**0.47** (1,2,3)
5	EntityGridTT+LEX1 +Rubric-based	**0.58** (2,3,1)	0.45

Table 6: Performance of our rubric-based model compared to the baselines. Each time, we train the models on one dataset and test on the other. The numbers in parenthesis show the model numbers which the current model performs significantly better than.

5.2 Results and Discussion

We first examine the hypothesis that the new features perform better than the baselines (H1). The results on the corpus of grades 5-6 (see Table 5) show that the new features (Model 4) yield significantly higher performance than either baseline (Models 1 and 2) or the combination of the baselines (Model 3). The results of Models 5, 6, and 7 show that our new features capture information that is not in the baseline models since each of these three models is significantly better than models 1, 2, and 3 respectively. The best result in all experiments is bolded.

We repeated the experiments on the corpus of grades 6-8. The results in Table 5 show that there is no significant difference between the rubric-based model and the baselines, except that in general, models that include lexical chaining features perform better than those with entity-grid features.

We configured another experiment to examine the generalizability of the models across different grades. In this experiment, we used one dataset for model training and the other for testing. We divided the test data into 10 disjoint sets to be able to perform significance tests on the performance measure. The results in Table 6 show that for both experiments, the rubric-based model performs at least as well as the baselines. Where the training is on grades 6-8 and we test the model on the shorter and noisier set of 5-6, the rubric-based model performs significantly better than the baselines. Where we test on the 6-8 corpus, the rubric-based model performs better than the baselines (although not always significantly), and adding it to the baselines (Model 5) adds value to them significantly.

Altogether, our first and second hypotheses seem to hold. On the grade 5-6 data, the rubric-based model performs better than the baselines; for grades 6-8, the rubric-based features add value to the baselines. That is, with shorter and noisier essays, models based on coarse-grained topic information outperform state-of-the-art models based on syntactic and lexical information. Moreover, while the state of the art models perform better on better-written essays, to get an even better performing model for essays written by younger children, we need a model that examines more and different aspects of organization. Additionally, we believe that the rubric-based, task-dependent model yields more information about students' writing skills that could be fed back to teachers (and students) than the baselines.

Next, we repeated all of the experiments using each of the isolated groups of features. The results in Table 7 show that Topic-Development and Topic-Ordering are the most predictive set of features. While the topic-based features may not be better than the baselines, they can be improved. One potential improvement is to enhance the alignment of the sentences with their corresponding topics (since we currently use a very simple model for alignment). Moreover, we believe that the topic ordering features are more substantive and potentially provide more useful information for students and teachers.

We also conducted an ablation test to investigate how important each group of features is in the new model. In the first phase, we remove each group of features and select the one that decreases the performance most significantly. This group of features has the greatest influence after accounting for all other

	Model	(5–6) Cross-val	(6–8) Cross-val	Train(5–6) Test(6–8)	Train(6–8) Test(5–6)
1	TopicDevelopment	0.40	0.42	0.43	0.36
2	TopicOrdering	0.40	0.43	0.44	0.43
3	TopicDevelopment+TopicOrdering	0.42	0.45	0.46	0.40
4	Surface	0.32	0.40	0.42	0.35
5	LocalCoherence+ParagraphTransition	0.20	0.21	0.23	0.18
6	DiscourseStrucutre	0.25	0.19	0.26	0.22

Table 7: Performance of each group of features in isolation. The first two columns are for cross validation experiments. The last two column are the results for training on one corpus and testing on the other one.

features. In the second phase, we repeat the experiment, having already removed the most influential feature. We continue the experiment until we have reached a single group of features. The results show that the features in order of their importance are: $Surface > TopicOrdering > LocalCoherence + ParagraphTransitions > DiscourseStructure > TopicDevelopment$. In this test, surface features were more influential than topic ordering, despite the fact that topic-ordering in isolation is more predictive than surface features. One potential reason might be that the surface features may not be correlated with other task-dependent features such as topic-ordering and topic development. Examining the correlation between some of the features across feature groups is an area for future investigation.

As for Hypothesis 3, as we suggested in section 3, to measure the coherence in our text-based essays, we need to use the information from the source text. To reprise the example in section 3, we think there should be a chain containing both of the words "hospital" and "water", and a relation between them. To examine this claim, we modified the lexical chaining algorithm in such a way that it uses both external sources to measure semantic similarity and also our list of topics extracted from the source text. If we are adding a word w_1 from subtopic t_1 and there is a chain containing a word w_2 on the same subtopic t_1, there should be a relation in the chain between w_1 and w_2. If there is no Strong or Extra-Strong semantic relation between w_1 and w_2, we consider the relation as Medium-Strong. The relations are defined per Hirst and St-Onge (1998).

Table 8 presents the effect of this modification on the performance. As hypothesized, the modified version performs significantly better than the base lexical chains on essays from grades 5-6.

	Model	(5-6)	(6-8)
1	LEX1	0.45	0.53
2	LEX1+Topic	**0.48** (1)	**0.54**

Table 8: Performance of the baseline and the topic-extended lexical chaining model on the two datasets.

6 Conclusion and Future Work

We present the results for predicting the score of the Organization dimension of a response-to-text assessment in a way that aligns with the scoring rubric. We used two datasets of essays written by students in grades 5-8. We designed a set of features aligned with the rubric that we believe will be meaningful and easy to interpret given the writing task. Our experimental results show that our task-dependent model (consistent with the rubric) performs as well as either baseline on both datasets. On the shorter and noisier essays from grades 5-6, the rubric-based model performs better than the baselines. On the better-written essays from grades 6-8, the rubric-based features can add value to the baselines. We also show that the lexical chaining baseline can be improved on shorter and noisier data if we extend it using task-dependent information from the text.

There are several ways to improve our work. First, we plan to use a more sophisticated method to annotate text units, such as information retrieval based approaches.We need to tune all our parameters that were chosen intuitively or were set to the default value. We will test the generalizability of our model by using other texts and prompts from other response-to-text writing tasks. We would also like to extract topics and words automatically, as our current approach requires these to be manually defined by experts (although this task needs to be only done once for each new text and prompt).

Acknowledgments

This work was supported by the Learning Research and Development Center at the University of Pittsburgh. We thank the ITSPOKE group for their helpful feedback and suggestions.

References

Regina Barzilay and Mirella Lapata. 2005. Modeling local coherence: An entity-based approach. In *Proceedings of the 43rd Annual Meeting on Association for Computational Linguistics*, ACL '05, pages 141–148.

Remco R Bouckaert and Eibe Frank. 2004. Evaluating the replicability of significance tests for comparing learning algorithms. In *Advances in knowledge discovery and data mining*, pages 3–12.

Jill Burstein, Karen Kukich, Susanne Wolff, Chi Lu, and Martin Chodorow. 1998. Enriching automated essay scoring using discourse marking. In *Proceedings of the Workshop on Discourse Relations and Discourse Marking, Annual Meeting of the Association of Computational Linguistics*.

Jill Burstein, Martin Chodorow, and Claudia Leacock. 2003a. Criterion sm : Online essay evaluation: An application for automated evaluation of student essays. In *Proceedings of the Fifteenth Annual Conference on Innovative Applications of Artificial Intelligence*.

Jill Burstein, Daniel Marcu, and Kevin Knight. 2003b. Finding the write stuff: Automatic identification of discourse structure in student essays. *IEEE Intelligent Systems*, 18(1):32–39, January.

Jill Burstein, Joel Tetreault, and Slava Andreyev. 2010. Using entity-based features to model coherence in student essays. In *Human Language Technologies: The 2010 Annual Conference of the North American Chapter of the Association for Computational Linguistics*, HLT '10, pages 681–684.

Jill Burstein, Joel Tetreault, and Martin Chodorow. 2013. Holistic discourse coherence annotation for noisy essay writing. *Dialogue & Discourse*, 4(2):34–52.

Nitesh V. Chawla, Kevin W. Bowyer, Lawrence O. Hall, and W. Philip Kegelmeyer. 2002. Smote: Synthetic minority over-sampling technique. *Journal of Artificial Intelligence Research*, 16:321–357.

Robin Cohen. 1987. Analyzing the structure of argumentative discourse. *Comput. Linguist.*, 13(1-2):11–24, January.

Richard Correnti, Lindsay Clare Matsumura, Laura S Hamilton, and Elaine Wang. 2012. Combining multiple measures of students' opportunities to develop analytic, text-based writing skills. *Educational Assessment*, 17(2-3):132–161.

Richard Correnti, Lindsay Clare Matsumura, Laura S Hamilton, and Elaine Wang. 2013. Assessing students' skills at writing in response to texts. *Elementary School Journal*, 114(2):142–177.

Scott A Crossley and Danielle S McNamara. 2011. Text coherence and judgments of essay quality: Models of quality and coherence. In *Proceedings of the 29th Annual Conference of the Cognitive Science Society*, pages 1236–1241.

Peter W Foltz, Walter Kintsch, and Thomas K Landauer. 1998. The measurement of textual coherence with latent semantic analysis. *Discourse processes*, 25(2-3):285–307.

Michel Galley and Kathleen Mckeown. 2003. Improving word sense disambiguation in lexical chaining. In *In Proceedings of IJCAI*, pages 1486–1488.

Barbara J Grosz, Scott Weinstein, and Aravind K Joshi. 1995. Centering: A framework for modeling the local coherence of discourse. *Computational linguistics*, 21(2):203–225.

Derrick Higgins, Jill Burstein, Daniel Marcu, and Claudia Gentile. 2004. Evaluating multiple aspects of coherence in student essays. In *HLT-NAACL*, pages 185–192.

Graeme Hirst and David St-Onge. 1998. Lexical chains as representations of context for the detection and correction of malapropisms. *WordNet: An electronic lexical database*, 305:305–332.

T.K. Landauer, P.W. Foltz, and D. Laham. 1998. An introduction to latent semantic analysis. *Discourse processes*, 25:259–284.

Ou Lydia Liu, Chris Brew, John Blackmore, Libby Gerard, Jacquie Madhok, and Marcia C Linn. 2014. Automated scoring of constructed-response science items: Prospects and obstacles. *Educational Measurement: Issues and Practice*, 33(2):19–28.

Eleni Miltsakaki and Karen Kukich. 2000. Automated evaluation of coherence in student essays. In *Proceedings of LREC 2000*.

Jane Morris and Graeme Hirst. 1991. Lexical cohesion computed by thesaural relations as an indicator of the structure of text. *Comput. Linguist.*, 17(1):21–48.

Emily Pitler and Ani Nenkova. 2009. Using syntax to disambiguate explicit discourse connectives in text. In *Proceedings of the ACL-IJCNLP 2009 Conference Short Papers*, pages 13–16.

Zahra Rahimi, Diane J Litman, Richard Correnti, Lindsay Clare Matsumura, Elaine Wang, and Zahid Kisa.

2014. Automatic scoring of an analytical response-to-text assessment. In *Intelligent Tutoring Systems*, pages 601–610. Springer.

Swapna Somasundaran, Jill Burstein, and Martin Chodorow. 2014. Lexical chaining for measuring discourse coherence quality in test-taker essays. In *Proceedings of COLING 2014, the 25th International Conference on Computational Linguistics: Technical Papers*, pages 950–961. Dublin City University and Association for Computational Linguistics.

Automatic morphological analysis of learner Hungarian

Scott Ledbetter
Indiana University
Bloomington, IN, USA
saledbet@indiana.edu

Markus Dickinson
Indiana University
Bloomington, IN, USA
md7@indiana.edu

Abstract

In this paper, we describe a morphological analyzer for learner Hungarian, built upon limited grammatical knowledge of Hungarian. The rule-based analyzer requires very few resources and is flexible enough to do both morphological analysis and error detection, in addition to some unknown word handling. As this is work-in-progress, we demonstrate its current capabilities, some areas where analysis needs to be improved, and an initial foray into how the system output can support the analysis of interlanguage grammars.

1 Introduction and Motivation

While much recent research has gone into grammatical error detection and correction (Leacock et al., 2014), this work has a few (admitted) limitations: 1) it has largely focused on a few error types (e.g., prepositions, articles, collocations); 2) it has largely been for English, with only a few explorations into other languages (e.g., Basque (de Ilarraza et al., 2008), Korean (Israel et al., 2013)); and 3) it has often focused on errors to the exclusion of broader patterns of learner productions—a crucial link if one wants to develop intelligent computer-assisted language learning (ICALL) (Heift and Schulze, 2007) or proficiency classification (Vajjala and Loo, 2013; Hawkins and Buttery, 2010) applications or connect to second language acquisition (SLA) research (Ragheb, 2014). We focus on Hungarian morphological analysis for learner language, attempting to build a system that: 1) works for a variety of morphological errors, providing detailed information for each; 2) is feasible for low-resource languages; and 3) provides analyses for correct and incorrect forms, i.e., is both a morphological analyzer and an error detector. Perhaps unsurprisingly, we find that the best way to accomplish these goals is to hearken back to the *parsing ill-formed input* literature (see Heift and Schulze, 2007, ch. 2) and develop a rule-based system, underscoring the point that different kinds of linguistic properties require different kinds of systems (see Leacock et al., 2014, ch. 7).

We hope to make the analysis of Hungarian morphology maximally useful. Consider ICALL system development, for example: successful systems not only provide meaningful feedback for learners but also model learner behavior (e.g., Amaral and Meurers, 2008). To do this requires tracking correct and incorrect use of different linguistic phenomena (e.g., case). Furthermore, one likely wants to keep track of individual differences between learners as well as to track general developmental trends—a point relevant to SLA research more generally (Dörnyei, 2010; Gass and Selinker, 2008).

In addition to providing a platform for ICALL development and SLA research, another long-term goal of our project is to develop an annotated corpus of learner Hungarian, including both linguistic and error annotation. The exact delineation between the two kinds of annotation is an open question (Ragheb and Dickinson, 2014), and building an analyzer which does both can show the link for at least certain types of errors. Additionally, the link between corpus data and automatic analysis is part

Proceedings of the Tenth Workshop on Innovative Use of NLP for Building Educational Applications, 2015, pages 31–41,
Denver, Colorado, June 4, 2015.

of an important feedback loop: if one views error detection as the relaxation of grammatical constraints (Reuer, 2003; Schwind, 1995), it is important to determine which constraints may be relaxed—given the huge space of possible variation (e.g., reordering affixes)—and this work is a step in that direction.

One further point is worth mentioning: the analyzer we describe makes use of a limited amount of grammatical knowledge in a rule-based system, allowing for potential application to other languages with minimal effort and resources. Our hope is that this can provide a basis for research into other lesser-resourced languages and some less-investigated error types. The system is also flexible and adaptable, designed to allow for the variation and inconsistencies expected of early learner language.

The paper is organized as follows. In Section 2 we discuss facts about Hungarian relevant for building an analyzer, as well as previous research in relevant areas, and in Section 3 we describe the data used for analysis. We turn to the actual analyzer in Section 4, employing a simple chart-parsing strategy that allows for feature clashes and crucially relies on a handful of handwritten affixes, which essentially encode the "rules" of the grammar (i.e., the approach is fairly lexicalized). The evaluation in Section 5 is tripartite, reflecting our different goals: evaluating the quality of assigned morphological tags (Section 5.1), the error detection capabilities (Section 5.2), and the ability to extract information for learner modeling (Section 5.3). The work is still in progress, and thus the evaluation also points to ways in which the system can be improved.

2 Background and Previous Work

2.1 Hungarian

Hungarian is an agglutinative language belonging to the Finno-Ugric family. It has a rich inflectional and derivational morphological system, as illustrated in (1). Verbs take suffixes to indicate number, person, tense, and definiteness, as in (1a), in addition to suffixes which alter aspectual quality or modality. Nouns, meanwhile, take suffixes for number, internal and external possession, and case (1b), of which there are 20 (e.g. inessive in (1b)), many of which roughly correspond to adpositions in other languages. Allomorphs of most suffixes are selected based on vowel harmony, for which features (e.g. +BK) must match, as with the inessive case in (1b) and (1c). For both verbs and nouns, the ordering of grammatical suffixes is fixed (Törkenczy, 2008).

(1) a. fut -ott -ál
run -PST -2SG.INDEF
'you [2sg.] ran'

b. könyv -eim -ben
book[-BK] -1SG.PL[-BK] -INESSIVE[-BK]
'in my books'

c. ház -ban
house[+BK] -INESSIVE[+BK]
'in (a) house'

The rich morphology of Hungarian necessitates taking the morpheme as the basic unit of analysis. A single morpheme can convey a wealth of information (e.g. person, number, definiteness on verb suffixes), and a sufficiently extensive set of phonological and morphological features must be used, particularly if one is to capture individual variation.

2.2 Morphological analysis for Hungarian

Morphological analysis for agglutinative languages tends to be based on finite-state transducers (Koskenniemi, 1983; Oflazer, 1994; Özlem Çetinoğlu and Kuhn, 2013; Aduriz et al., 2000). These are robust, but the process is not quickly adaptable to other languages, as every rule is language-specific, and there is no clear way to handle learner innovations.

For Hungarian, HuMor (High-speed Unification Morphology) (Prószéky and Kis, 1999) uses a bank of pre-encoded knowledge in the form of a dictionary and feature-based rules. Megyesi (1999) extends the Brill tagger (Brill, 1992), a rule-based tagger, with simple lexical templates. Tron et al. (2005) derive a morphological analyzer, Hunmorph, from a language-independent spelling corrector, using a recursive affix-stripping algorithm that relies on a dictionary to remove affixes one by one until a root morpheme is found. The dictionary is customizable to other languages, and the idea of using affix-removal to identify stems is similar to our technique

(Section 4). Morphdb (Trón et al., 2006), a lexical database for Hungarian, encodes only irregularities and uses features on the appropriate lexical items to apply the proper phonological and morphological processes during analysis. These various tools have been incorporated into a variety of other Hungarian systems (Halácsy et al., 2006; Bohnet et al., 2013; Farkas et al., 2012; Zsibrita et al., 2013). For approaches like Hunmorph and Morphdb that rely on a dictionary, unknown words are the main problem—also a crucial issue for innovative learner forms.

2.3 Grammatical error detection

There is some work exploring morphological derivations in learner language. Dickinson (2011) looks for stem-suffix mismatches to identify potential errors (for Russian) and uses heuristics to sort through multiple analyses. There is, however, no evaluation on learner data. We focus on building a small grammar to explicitly license combinations and provide a variety of evaluations on real learner data. Prior work in L2 Hungarian uses the HunLearner corpus (Durst et al., 2014; Vincze et al., 2014) to develop systems to automatically identify errors. Our work explores similar directions, focusing not only on the identification of non-target forms but also systematically describing them and making that information available in the form of morphological annotation.

The work presented here is related to the idea of constraint relaxation and constraint ranking (e.g., Menzel, 2006; Schwind, 1995), wherein grammatical constraints are defeasible (see Leacock et al., 2014, ch. 2). In the case of morphology, the primary process of relaxing constraints is in allowing stems and affixes to combine which are generally not allowed to do so (see also Section 4).

There is a wealth of research on statistical error detection and correction of grammatical errors for language learners (Leacock et al., 2014), including for Hungarian (Durst et al., 2014; Vincze et al., 2014). As has been argued before (e.g., Chodorow et al., 2007; Tetreault and Chodorow, 2008), statistical methods are ideal for parts of the linguistic system difficult to encode via rules. Since Hungarian morphology is a highly rule-governed domain of the language and since we want detailed linguistic information for feedback, we do not focus on statistical methods here. We hope, however, to eventually obtain an appropriate distribution of errors in order to incorporate probabilities into the analysis.

The emphasis on rule-based error detection allows one to connect the work to broader techniques for modeling learner behavior, in the context of ICALL exercises (Thouësny and Blin, 2011; Heift, 2007) or in mapping and understanding development (cf. Vajjala and Loo, 2013; Vyatkina, 2013; Yannakoudakis et al., 2012). Our evaluation thus focuses on multiple facets of the output and its use (Section 5).

3 Data and Annotation

3.1 Corpus

The corpus was collected from L1 English students of Hungarian at Indiana University and is divided into three levels of proficiency (Beginner, Intermediate, Advanced) as determined by course placement in one of three two-semester sequences. The corpus consists of journal entries, each a minimum ten sentences in length on a topic selected by the student.

The corpus at present contains data for 14 learners (9 Beginner, 1 Intermediate, 4 Advanced), 9391 sentences total, with 10 annotated journals. The corpus represents both cross-sectional and longitudinal data. Productions from multiple learners can be compared across or (for beginners) within proficiency levels, and a single learner's data over time can also be analyzed. Additionally, passages are often longer and feature more descriptive language than those produced for grammatical exercises.

3.2 Annotation

Each journal has been transcribed manually and annotated for errors with EXMARaLDA (Schmidt, 2010).[1] The text is segmented on morpheme boundaries, and errors are identified in four different tiers, matched to a target form. The annotation scheme is specifically for Hungarian, but the principles behind it can be extended to other morphologically rich languages (Dickinson and Ledbetter, 2012).

The annotation marks different types of errors re-

[1] `http://www.exmaralda.org/en_index.html`

flecting different levels of linguistic analysis. For instance, for (2), the annotation shows a CL (vowel length) error on the verb stem and an MAD (definiteness) error on the verb suffix—i.e. the definite suffix does not agree with the indefinite noun complements—as shown in Figure 1.

(2) **Ajanl** **-om** bor -t , nem sör -t
recommend 1SG.DF wine ACC , not beer ACC
'I recommend wine, not beer.'

TXT	Ajanlom		bort		,	nem	sört		.
SEG	Ajanl	om	bor	t	,	nem	sör	t	.
CHA	CL								
MOR		MAD							
TGT	Ajánl	ok	bor	t	,	nem	sör	t	.

Figure 1: Error annotation for (2)

There are four basic error annotation categories, reflecting *character* (CHA, e.g., vowel harmony, phonological confusion), *morphological* (MOR, e.g., agreement in person, case), *grammatical relation* (REL, e.g., case, root selection), and *sentence* (SNT, e.g., insertion, ordering) errors. A full list of categories can be found in Dickinson and Ledbetter (2012). Different categories of errors can be annotated for the same word, and error spans can overlap if necessary. A target (TGT) sentence is also provided. The morphological analyzer discussed in section 4 is designed to recognize errors within the morphological (MOR) and character (CHA) tiers.

4 Morphological Analysis

Our goal for analyzing a word is to provide its derivation, in order to support morphological analysis, error detection, and learner modeling. A derivation here refers to a breakdown of a word's internal structure into individual morphemes, i.e., a root morpheme plus affixes, and we want to provide as much of a derivation as we can even when: a) the root is unknown, or b) the learner has misapplied an affix (e.g., it is inappropriate for the rest of the word). We discuss the knowledge base (Section 4.1), the basic algorithm (Section 4.2), and our first pass at making the analyzer more robust (Section 4.3).

4.1 Knowledge base

There are two parts to the knowledge base, a handcrafted suffix base and a dictionary obtained from another project. The dictionary is obtained from *A Magyar Elektronikus Könyvtár*.[2] To model lesser-resourced situations, one can experiment with differing sizes of this lexicon; in general, this type of resource does not have to contain much information.

The suffix base, on the other hand, is where we encode the rules for morphological combination, and it thus must be developed with more care. We use 205 affixes, including those for noun case, plurals, verb conjugation, and possession. An affix corresponds to a set of possible categories, the encoding inspired by the Combinatory Categorial Grammar (CCG) framework (Steedman and Baldridge, 2011). For example, the accusative case marker *-t* has one possible category KN\N, indicating that it would create a new category KN (cased noun phrase) if it was combined with a noun (N) on the left.

Each affix category contains features describing relevant linguistic properties. For example, features for the entry for the affix *-ot* indicates that: a) it contains back vowels and b) it is accusative case when combined with a noun stem. As another example, the plural noun suffix *-ok* also contains back vowels, but its features furthermore indicate a stem-lowering effect—i.e. successive affixes must adhere to a restricted subset of allomorphs based on vowel harmony. The suffix base represents our grammar engineering, but, as noted, it is quite small.

4.2 Building an analysis

To efficiently determine the correct combinations of root and affixes, we use a basic CYK chart parsing algorithm (Cocke and Schwartz, 1970), treating each letter as a unit of analysis; as suffixes drive the analysis, we process from right to left. At each possible interval of starting and ending sequences within a word, the system verifies if the sequence is either attested in the affix base or in the dictionary of attested language forms. If the sequence is found, a corresponding category is placed into

[2] `http://www.mek.iif.hu/porta/szint/egyeb/szotar/ssa-dic/`

the chart. While finite-state techniques are the standard for morphological analyzers (section 2.2), chart parsing is easy to implement and makes the processing architecture extendible to syntactic phenomena.

Consider *házot* ('house+ACC'), indexed in (3) and with a corresponding chart in Figure 2. Here, both *-t* and *-ot* can be suffixes, but as only *ház*—and not *házo*—is a verified noun (the N in cell 2–5), the segmentation *ház+ot* provides the correct analysis.

(3) $*_5\,h_4\,á_3\,z_2\,o_1\,t_0$

					4
					3
N					2
N_{hyp}					1
KN			KN\N	KN\N	0
5	4	3	2	1	

Figure 2: Chart for (3)

As the system is affix-driven, if no root is found matching an item in the dictionary, the system can posit a possible stem for the word based on the affixes that *were* found. This possible stem is then added to the chart like an attested root, with the information noted that it is hypothesized, indicated here as N_{hyp} in cell 1–5. This ability to hypothesize is an important feature of the analyzer, as it allows for "erroneous" or "nonstandard" root morphemes, crucial to analyzing learner language.

4.3 Constraint relaxation

When general categories are combined in the chart (Section 4.2), features of affixes and stems are also compared. Any inconsistencies violating the grammar of Hungarian are marked. A sample derivation obtained from the chart in Figure 2 is given in Figure 3, here with one feature shown. The stem requires a lowered allomorph (*-at*) of the accusative suffix, but the unlowered allomorph is provided.

h á z   o t
N[+LOW]   KN\N[-LOW]
KN[!LOW]

Figure 3: Feature clash during derivation

The feature clash here indicates a learner innovation, providing some analysis of the their current understanding of the language. Importantly for processing, we currently require: a) equivalence of main categories (e.g., KN\N must combine with N), and b) proper ordering of affixes. Neither of these relaxations seemed to be required for our data, though future analysis may prove otherwise. In that light, we can note the importance of the grammar-writer to put relaxable constraints (e.g., sub-category information) into features and non-relaxable constraints into the main categories.

5 Evaluation

As mentioned earlier, we evaluate the system in three different ways. First, we treat the system as a straight morphological analyzer and evaluate the quality of assigned morphological tags (Section 5.1). Secondly, employing some constraint relaxation abilities, we evaluate the system's capabilities in performing error detection (Section 5.2). Finally, we illustrate the ability of the system to provide information on interlanguage grammars, namely the ability to help distinguish between individual learners and levels of learners (Section 5.3).

5.1 Morphological analysis

The system is first evaluated in terms of accuracy of morphological analysis, both on native (L1) and learner (L2) data. For every word, the system returns one or more derivations, representing the internal structure of the word, and the associated morphological features, here represented as a morphological code. Take, for example, the verb in (4a).

(4) a. lát -t -ál
see -PST -2SG.INDEF
'you saw'

b. V m i s 3 s - - - n
0 1 2 3 4 5 6 7 8 9

The morphological code in (4b) for the verb follows the scheme used to annotate the Szeged Corpus (Csendes et al., 2004), applicable to multiple languages. Each numbered field corresponds to a feature, and different letters or numbers give the values.

After the initial verb indicator (V), the code in (4b) indicates: main verb (m), indicative mood (i), past tense (s), third person (3), singular (s), indefinite (n). Three fields are unused (e.g., one for grammatical gender, not found in Hungarian).

As the system is fairly resource-light (Section 4.1), we do not expect state-of-the-art accuracy, but we do need to gauge whether it is effective enough for our purposes and to know how to improve for the future. We start by investigating its general accuracy on L1 data, presenting the analyzer with a selection of native Hungarian data from the Szeged Corpus (Csendes et al., 2004), taking the first 1000 tokens from a section of compositions (in order to verify results by hand and to compare to the 1021 tokens of learner data discussed below). The results are in the *Total* column of Table 1.

	Total	POS	+N	POS+N
Precision	0.308	—	0.307	—
Recall	0.262	—	0.315	—
Accuracy	0.467	0.568	0.505	0.592
Unk. POS	0.425	0.425	0.425	0.425
Unk. Word	0.067	0.067	0.067	0.067

Table 1: Morphological analysis on L1 Hungarian data

The corpus provides both a single, context-specific tag and a list of all appropriate tags, and we use a set of measures to reflect this situation. **Precision** is calculated as the number of codes produced by the analyzer that appear in the gold standard *list* divided by the total number of codes produced, and **recall** is the number of codes produced by the analyzer that appear in the gold standard *list* divided by the total number of codes in the gold standard. **Accuracy** is the percentage of cases where the analyzer produces, among its output, the correct *context-specific* gold tag. As the analyzer doesn't have access to part of speech data in its dictionary, it may recognize a word but have no tag for it, in which case it produces an **unknown POS** tag. Finally, when the analyzer cannot produce a derivation, it returns an **unknown word** tag.

We can see in Table 1 that the analyzer provides the correct tag in only 47% of the 1000 test cases. Yet the frequency of the *unknown POS* tag indicates that nearly half of the time, the analyzer recognizes the word but cannot determine its internal structure—i.e., we are not positing incorrect codes so much as positing nothing. The majority of these words are monomorphemic nouns, pronouns, adjectives, or adverbs: without the overt morphology indicated by the affixes in the knowledge base, the analyzer relies only on the dictionary, which contains no information about part of speech. Precision and Recall seem fairly low, but a closer inspection of the data reveals that a number of codes are mostly correct, differing from the gold standard by only one or two fields. Taking into account only part of speech (*POS*), accuracy increases to nearly 57%.

Because nouns were one of the most common parts of speech for which the analyzer could determine no structure, a second evaluation was performed, positing an additional noun tag in each case where the *unknown POS* tag was returned (*+N*). Precision fell by a slim margin (due to the increase in proposed tags), while Recall rose by about 5% and Accuracy by 4%. Taking into account only part of speech (*POS+N*, Accuracy reaches 59%.

Our second analysis targets learner data. In this analysis, the corrected forms for 1021 words produced by L2 Hungarian learners were manually annotated with morphological codes from the Szeged Corpus scheme. These gold standard codes were compared to those returned by the analyzer, as above with the native data. The design of the analyzer emphasizes flexibility, and we compare stricter and more permissive derivations, ignoring feature clashes that would otherwise result in an incomplete parse of a given word (Section 4.3). Results are in Table 2, where $Total_{Strict}$ reflects the performance of the analyzer when run with strict settings, i.e., no feature clashes allowed, and $Total_{Free}$ reflects performance when feature clashes are allowed (and recorded) during derivation. The same tokens were also analyzed by the *magyarlanc* tool (Zsibrita et al., 2013), developed for analyzing the standard language, as a benchmark (*ML*). *Magyarlanc* returns only one analysis per word, and thus accuracy was the principal measure for comparison.

Accuracy is on a par with the native L1 data when the system is used with strict settings, and approxi-

	Total_{Strict}	Total_{Free}	ML
Accuracy	0.499	0.509	0.846
Unk. POS	0.499	0.499	—
Unk. Word	0.109	0.097	0.027

Table 2: Morph. analysis on corrected L2 Hungarian data

mately half of the test cases were recognized by the analyzer. With flexibility, accuracy increases by 1% and the unknown word rate decreases by about the same margin. *Magyarlanc* outperforms the system, but even on corrected learner data, accuracy is 85%.

The final analysis is on raw learner data (the same 1021 words with no corrections) to test the analyzer's flexibility with the idiosyncracies in authentic learner language. Results are in Table 3.

	Total_{Strict}	Total_{Free}	ML
Accuracy	0.464	0.478	0.753
Unk. POS	0.456	0.456	—
Unk. Word	0.137	0.119	0.074

Table 3: Morph. analysis on raw L2 Hungarian data

Accuracy is still fairly low, with a slim increase in performance with the more permissive settings. With *magyarlanc*, accuracy falls by about 10%. For both, the unknown word rate is higher than with corrected data. Again, a large proportion of the test cases involve monomorphemic words for which the analyzer recognizes no internal structure. Access to POS data, as with *magyarlanc*, would greatly improve performance. In general, however, an emphasis on flexibility and adaptability seems to have benefits for describing learner language, decreasing unknown word rate and maintaining accuracy.

5.2 Error detection

The next evaluation assesses the system's ability to automatically detect errors in learner data. As discussed in Section 4.3, an error occurs when features clash (cf. Figure 3). Feature clashes also arise from unknown words, as the category of a word not in the dictionary is unspecified. Evaluation of the system as a whole is given in the *Total* column of Table 4.

Precision is the number of correctly identified errors divided by the number of errors suggested by the analyzer. **Recall** is the number of correctly identified errors divided by the number of errors in the gold annotation. The **F_1 score** is the harmonic mean of precision and recall; because precision is critical when providing feedback to learners, **$F_{0.5}$** is also given, weighing precision more heavily. Precision in Table 4 is very low, below 40%; i.e., 60% of the "errors" identified by the morphological analyzer are false positives. Recall is better, at over 60%.

	Total	Morph	Char
Precision	0.380	0.380	0.380
Recall	0.625	0.789	0.938
F_1	0.472	0.513	0.541
$F_{0.5}$	0.412	0.424	0.431

Table 4: Error detection using only dictionary stems

The morphological analyzer is not currently designed to handle syntax errors or many agreement errors, as it considers only one word at a time. Thus, additional scores are calculated for errors below the tier of syntax (see Section 3.2). In the *Morph* column, only those errors from the morphological tier and below are considered (i.e., *Morph* and *Char*). For *Char*, only those errors from the character tier are considered. Recall improves considerably by this restricted focus, up to nearly 94% for *Char*.

Considering the importance of precision, the analyzer needs much improvement. A closer analysis illustrates some of the problems with the algorithm and with the test data. The vast majority of false positives (˜40%) are for proper names. Most named entities are obviously not in the dictionary (excepting, e.g., *Magyarország* 'Hungary'), and the system cannot recognize them. As described in Section 4, the analyzer can posit hypothetical stems to complete a derivation, estimating words as they exist in the learner's vocabulary. A second evaluation was performed, allowing the system to hypothesize that any unknown word may be a valid item in the learner's vocabulary. Results are in Table 5.

Precision sees a modest increase to 40%, while recall falls to less than 10%. Limiting the scope of analysis once more increases recall (to nearly 7%), but the F-scores remain less than half of those in the

	Total	Morph.	Char.
Precision	0.400	0.400	0.400
Recall	0.038	0.043	0.067
F_1	0.070	0.078	0.114
$F_{0.5}$	0.139	0.152	0.200

Table 5: Error detection including hypothesized stems

previous evaluation. Investigating the system's performance more closely once again reveals a problem with unknown words and proper names. While the analyzer is able to posit hypothetical lexical entries, including nouns, it is impractical to allow any unknown word to be a potential noun. One of the most frequent errors, especially for beginners, is vowel length. Allowing any word to be hypothesized allows any number of these errors to go unnoticed. A possible solution for vowel length errors is to run a spelling corrector as part of the pipeline (Durst et al., 2014), and more generally a short list of common Hungarian names could improve performance.

Another problem for the analyzer is the appearance of irregular stems in the derivation. For example, the analyzer correctly produces a derivation for *megyek* ('I go', dictionary form *megy*) but not for *mennek* ('they go'). The derived base form *men* must be deemed a new word and potential error. One way to combat this problem is to encode irregular lexical items into the knowledge base of the system.

One final issue is the limited scope of the system. The most frequent source of errors is due to Hungarian's extensive case system. The analyzer can identify accusative or nominative case on nouns, for example, but because it considers each word individually, it cannot determine whether there is an error. Performance improves when excluding such types, but adding context-sensitivity is a crucial future step.

5.3 Grammar extraction

The final evaluation is the most exploratory, involving the extraction of properties which might be useful for comparing different learners. The space of possibly relevant metrics is quite large (Lu, 2010, 2012; Vajjala and Loo, 2013; Vyatkina, 2013; Yannakoudakis et al., 2012), and in this exploratory study we focus on a small number of metrics surrounding: a) complexity, and b) paradigm coverage. An overall goal is to sort out features which are good at distinguishing learner level from those which characterize individual learner differences.

Complexity Complexity is often used to describe the syntax of learners and the structure of their sentences. We consider the average number of **morphemes per word (MPW)** and of **words per sentence (WPS)**. Tokenization and segmentation are performed by the analyzer (and checked for accuracy). The last five journal entries for each learner are analyzed, to avoid masking change over time, as interlanguage is always changing.

	MPW	WPS
Beg01	1.38	5.79
Beg02	1.40	4.37
Beg03	1.52	3.84
Beg04	1.31	5.43
Beg06	1.52	5.75
Beg08	1.44	2.81
Beg09	1.58	3.28
Int01	1.51	6.40
Adv01	1.60	15.73
Adv02	1.66	10.90

Table 6: Complexity measures for learners of Hungarian

The beginning learners produce a range of morphemes per word, with some even approaching the production of the advanced learners. Even the least morphologically productive learner (Beg04) attains 1.31 morphemes per word. This particular aspect of morphological complexity, while it increases with greater proficiency, seems to be a largely individual feature of learner language, making it a potential candidate for classification tasks to identify specific learners or to characterize individual differences. Sentence length, while it has individual variation, seems to increase over the course of acquisition and thus may be an indicator of proficiency.

Coverage Taking Hungarian's morphological richness into account, we propose **paradigm coverage** to represent the frequency of different verb forms within the same tense and mood (here, present indicative), thus showcasing how much of the paradigm space a learner is using. Any occurrence of the appropriate verbal affix on any verb is counted, and the sum of the affix frequencies is normalized by dividing by the number of journal entries. Given space constraints, only one beginning and one advanced learner are presented in Figures 4 and 5. Average frequencies for the indefinite form are in light gray and for the definite in dark gray.[3]

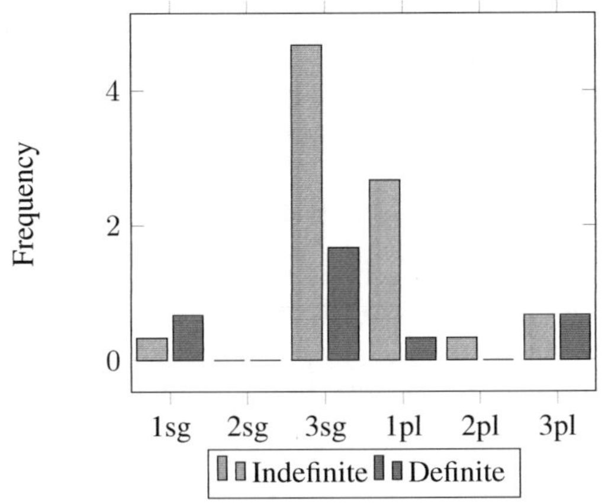

Figure 4: Affix coverage for learner Beg01

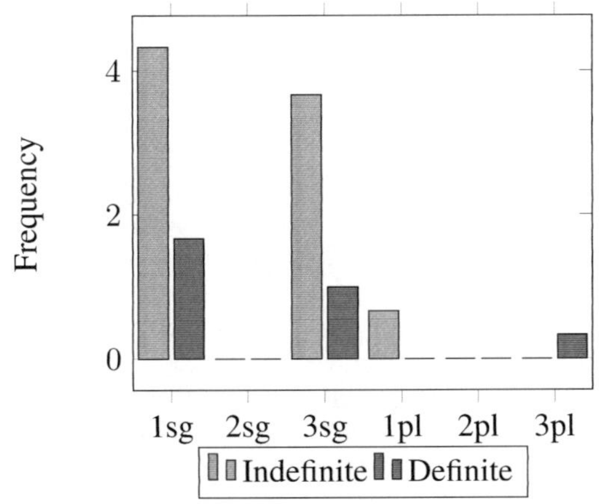

Figure 5: Affix coverage for learner Adv02

While there are definitely genre effects (e.g., lack of second person), the individual differences here may help form a more complete picture of a learner's interlanguage. Learner Beg01 appears to have some of the most complete knowledge of the present indicative paradigm among beginners, with representation in the first and third person singular and plural, definite and indefinite. Learner Adv02 exhibits many instances of the first person, characteristic of narrative description. This metric seems to be unique to individual learners (and their choice of topic), as some beginning learners exhibit more complete paradigms than the advanced learners.

To return to the theme of the whole paper: regardless of the conclusions drawn exactly from such paradigms, it is only by automatic morphological analysis that one is able to investigate differences in morphological complexity and paradigm coverage.

6 Summary and Outlook

We have presented a rule-based morphological analysis system for learner Hungarian, employing constraint relaxation, and have performed three different evaluations to illustrate its utility for linguistic analysis, error analysis, or downstream applications. We have used very little in the way of hand-built resources, and, while the system still needs improvement, the information captured by the analyzer already shows promise for describing the interlanguage of learners of Hungarian.

There are a number of ways to improve the system. Named entities in particular have been a problem for other approaches (Durst et al., 2014), and we intend to use similar methods to increase accuracy, including lists of common names. While syntactic context is presently unavailable to the analyzer for disambiguation, we hope to extend the methodology to syntax in the future. We also intend to explore how a record of language use may aid in disambiguation: if an ambiguous stem has only ever occurred previously with verbal morphology, for example, there is a good chance that its current use is as a verb. Finally, given a desire to be resource-light and applicable to other languages, one may investigate iterative bootstrapping methods to allow for the reduction of the initial size of the knowledge base, instead building a gradual inventory through analyzing a set of learner data itself.

[3]Definiteness is decided by the object of the verb, i.e., *a cat* (indefinite) or *the cat* (definite).

Acknowledgments

We would like to thank the participants of the IU CL discussion group, as well as the three anonymous reviewers, for their many helpful comments.

References

Itziar Aduriz, Eneko Agirre, Izaskun Aldezabal, Iñaki Alegria, Xabier Arregi, Jose Maria Arriola, Xabier Artola, Koldo Gojenola, Aitor Maritxalar, Kepa Sarasola, and Miriam Urkia. 2000. A word-grammar based morphological analyzer for agglutinative languages. In *Proceedings of the 18th conference on Computational linguistics (COLING 2000), vol. 1*, pages 1–7.

Luiz Amaral and Detmar Meurers. 2008. From recording linguistic competence to supporting inferences about language acquisition in context: Extending the conceptualization of student models for intelligent computer-assisted language learning. *Computer-Assisted Language Learning*, 21(4):323–338.

Bernd Bohnet, Joakim Nivre, Igor Boguslavsky, Richárd Farkas, Filip Ginter, and Jan Hajic. 2013. Joint morphological and syntactic analysis for richly inflected languages. *Transactions of the Association for Computational Linguistics*, 1(1):415–428.

Eric Brill. 1992. A simple rule-based part of speech tagger. In *Proceedings of the DARPA Speech and Natural Language Workshop*, pages 112–116.

Martin Chodorow, Joel Tetreault, and Na-Rae Han. 2007. Detection of grammatical errors involving prepositions. In *Proceedings of the 4th ACL-SIGSEM Workshop on Prepositions*, pages 25–30.

John Cocke and Jacob T. Schwartz. 1970. *Programming languages and their compilers: Preliminary notes*. CIMS, NYU, second edition.

Dóra Csendes, János Csirik, and Tibor Gyimóthy. 2004. The szeged corpus: A pos tagged and syntactically annotated hungarian natural language corpus. In *Text, Speech and Dialogue: 7th International Conference, TSD*, pages 41–47.

Arantza Díaz de Ilarraza, Koldo Gojenola, and Maite Oronoz. 2008. Detecting erroneous uses of complex postpositions in an agglutinative language. In *Proceedings of COLING-08*. Manchester.

Markus Dickinson. 2011. On morphological analysis for learner language, focusing on russian. *Research on Language and Computation*, 8(4):273–298.

Markus Dickinson and Scott Ledbetter. 2012. Annotating errors in a hungarian learner corpus. In *Proceedings of the 8th Language Resources and Evaluation Conference (LREC 2012)*.

Zoltán Dörnyei. 2010. *The Psychology of the Language Learner: Individual Differences in Second Language Acquisition*. Routledge.

Péter Durst, Martina Katalin Szabó, Veronika Vincze, and János Zsibrita. 2014. Using automatic morphological tools to process data from a learner corpus of hungarian. *Apples Journal of Applied Language Studies*, 8(3):39–54.

Richárd Farkas, Veronika Vincze, and Helmut Schmid. 2012. Dependency parsing of hungarian: Baseline results and challenges. In *Proceedings of the 13th Conference of the European Chapter of the Association for Computational Linguistics*, pages 55–65.

Susan M. Gass and Larry Selinker. 2008. *Second Language Acquisition: An Introductory Course*. Routledge, third edition.

Péter Halácsy, András Kornai, Csaba Oravecz, Viktor Trón, and Dániel Varga. 2006. Using a morphological analyzer in high precision POS tagging of Hungarian. In *Proceedings of LREC*, pages 2245–2248.

John A. Hawkins and Paula Buttery. 2010. Criterial features in learner corpora: Theory and illustrations. *English Profile Journal*, 1(1):1–23.

Trude Heift. 2007. Learner personas in call. *CALICO Journal*, 25(1):1–10.

Trude Heift and Mathias Schulze. 2007. *Errors and Intelligence in Computer-Assisted Language Learning: Parsers and Pedagogues*. Routledge.

Ross Israel, Markus Dickinson, and Sun-Hee Lee. 2013. Detecting and correcting learner korean particle omission errors. In *Proceedings of the 6th International Joint Conference on Natural Language Processing (IJCNLP 2013)*, pages 1419–1427. Nagoya, Japan.

Kimmo Koskenniemi. 1983. *Two-level morphology: A general computational model for word-form recognition and production*. Ph.D. thesis, University of Helsinki, Helsinki.

Claudia Leacock, Martin Chodorow, Michael Gamon, and Joel Tetreault. 2014. *Automated Grammatical Error Detection for Language Learners*. Synthesis Lectures on Human Language Technologies. Morgan & Claypool Publishers, second edition.

Xiaofei Lu. 2010. Automatic analysis of syntactic complexity in second language writing. *International Journal of Corpus Linguistics*, 15(4):474–496.

Xiaofei Lu. 2012. The relationship of lexical richness to the quality of esl learners' oral narratives. *The Modern Language Journal*, 96(2):190–208.

Beáta Megyesi. 1999. Improving Brill's POS tagger for an agglutinative language. In *Proceedings of the Joint SIGDAT Conference on Empirical Methods in Natural Language Processing and Very Large Corpora*, pages 275–284.

Wolfgang Menzel. 2006. Detecting mistakes or finding

misconceptions? diagnosing morpho-syntactic errors in language learning. In Galia Angelova, Kiril Simov, and Milena Slavcheva, editors, *Readings in Multilinguality*, pages 71–77. Incoma Ltd., Shoumen, Bulgaria.

Kemal Oflazer. 1994. Two-level description of turkish morphology. *Literary and Linguistic Computing*, 9(2):137–148.

Özlem Çetinoğlu and Jonas Kuhn. 2013. Towards joint morphological analysis and dependency parsing of turkish. In *Proceedings of the 2nd International Conference on Dependency Linguistics (DepLing 2013)*, pages 23–32.

Gabor Prószéky and Balazs Kis. 1999. A unification-based approach to morpho-syntactic parsing agglutinative and other (highly) inflectional languages. In *Proceedings of the 37th annual meeting of the Association for Computational Linguistics on Computational Linguistics*, pages 261–268.

Marwa Ragheb. 2014. *Building a Syntactically-Annotated Corpus of Learner English*. Ph.D. thesis, Indiana University, Bloomington, IN.

Marwa Ragheb and Markus Dickinson. 2014. Developing a corpus of syntactically-annotated learner language for English. In *Proceedings of the 13th International Workshop on Treebanks and Linguistic Theories (TLT13), Poster Session*. Tübingen, Germany.

Veit Reuer. 2003. Error recognition and feedback with lexical functional grammar. *CALICO Journal*, 20(3):497–512.

Thomas Schmidt. 2010. Linguistic tool development between community practices and technology standards. In *Proceedings of the Workshop on Language Resource and Language Technology Standards*. Malta.

Camilla B. Schwind. 1995. Error analysis and explanation in knowledge based language tutoring. *Computer Assisted Language Learning*, 8(4):295–324.

Mark Steedman and Jason Baldridge. 2011. Combinatory categorial grammar. In Robert Borsley and Kersti Börjars, editors, *Non-Transformational Syntax: Formal and Explicit Models of Grammar*. Wiley-Blackwell.

Joel Tetreault and Martin Chodorow. 2008. The ups and downs of prepositions error detection in ESL writing. In *Proceedings of the 22nd International Conference on Computational Linguistics (Coling 2008)*, pages 865–872.

Sylvie Thouësny and Françoise Blin. 2011. Modeling language learners' knowledge: What information can be inferred from learners' free written texts? In M. Levy, F. Blin, C. Bradin Siskin, and O. Takeuchi, editors, *WorldCALL: International Perspectives on Computer-Assisted Language Learning*, pages 114–127. Routledge, New York.

Miklós Törkenczy. 2008. *Hungarian Verbs and Essentials of Grammar, 2nd ed.* McGraw-Hill, New York.

Viktor Tron, Gyögy Gyepesi, Péter Halácsky, András Kornai, László Németh, and Dániel Varga. 2005. Hunmorph: Open source word analysis. In *Proceedings of the Workshop on Software*, pages 77–85. Association for Computational Linguistics.

Viktor Trón, Péter Halácsy, Péter Rebrus, András Rung, Péter Vajda, and Eszter Simon. 2006. Morphdb.hu: Hungarian lexical database and morphological grammar. In *Proceedings of 5th International Conference on Language Resources and Evaluation (LREC)*, pages 1670–1673.

Sowmya Vajjala and Kaidi Loo. 2013. Role of morpho-syntactic features in estonian proficiency classification. In *Proceedings of the Eighth Workshop on Innovative Use of NLP for Building Educational Applications*, pages 63–72.

Veronika Vincze, János Zsibrita, Péter Durst, and Martina Katalin Szabó. 2014. Automatic error detection concerning the definite and indefinite conjugation in the hunlearner corpus. In *Proceedings of the 9th Language Resources and Evaluation Conference (LREC 2014)*.

Nina Vyatkina. 2013. Specific syntactic complexity: Developmental profiling of individuals based on an annotated learner corpus. *The Modern Language Journal*, 97:11–30.

Helen Yannakoudakis, Ted Briscoe, and Theodora Alexopoulou. 2012. Automating second language acquisition research: Integrating information visualisation and machine learning. In *Proceedings of the EACL 2012 Joint Workshop of LINGVIS & UNCLH*, pages 35–43.

János Zsibrita, Veronika Vincze, and Richárd Farkas. 2013. Magyarlanc: A toolkit for morphological and dependency parsing of hungarian. In *Proceedings of RANLP*, pages 763–771.

Automated Scoring of Picture-based Story Narration

Swapna Somasundaran[1], **Chong Min Lee**[1], **Martin Chodorow**[2] **and Xinhao Wang**[1]
[1]Educational Testing Service, 660 Rosedale Road, Princeton, NJ 08541, USA
[2]Hunter College and the Graduate Center, CUNY, New York, NY 10065, USA
{ssomasundaran,clee001,xwang002}@ets.org
martin.chodorow@hunter.cuny.edu

Abstract

This work investigates linguistically motivated features for automatically scoring a spoken picture-based narration task. Specifically, we build scoring models with features for story development, language use and task relevance of the response. Results show that combinations of these features outperform a baseline system that uses state of the art speech-based features, and that best results are obtained by combining the linguistic and speech features.

1 Introduction

Story-telling has been used in evaluating the development of language skills (Sun and Nippold, 2012; McKeough and Malcolm, 2011; Botvin and Sutton-Smith, 1977). It has also been incorporated into assessment of English language proficiency in tests such as ETS's TOEFL Junior Comprehensive Test[1], where English language skills of non-native middle-school students are tested on a task designed to elicit stories based on pictures. The Six-Picture Narration task presents a series of six pictures (similar to a comic strip) to the test taker, who must orally produce a story which incorporates the events depicted in the pictures. As the scoring guide[2] for this task indicates, in addition to fluidity of speech and few pronunciation errors, high scoring responses must also show good command of language conventions, including grammar and word usage, and must also be relevant to the task.

Previous work (Evanini and Wang, 2013) explored automated assessment of the speech component of the spoken responses to the picture narration task, but the linguistic and narrative aspects of the response have not received much attention. In this work, we investigate linguistic and construct-relevant aspects of the test such as (1) relevance and completeness of the content of the responses with respect to the prompt pictures, (2) proper word usage (3) use of narrative techniques such as detailing to enhance the story, and (4) sequencing strategies to build a coherent story.

The contribution of this work is three-fold. First, we improve the construct coverage of the automated scoring models by incorporating evaluation of elements prescribed in the scoring rubric. Second, our linguistically motivated features allow for clear interpretation and explanation of scores, which is especially important if the automated scoring is to be employed for educational purposes. Finally, our results are promising – we show that the combination of linguistic and construct-relevant features which we explore in this work outperforms the state of the art baseline system, and that the best performance is obtained when the linguistic and construct-relevant features are combined with the speech features.

2 Related Work

Evanini et al. (2013; 2014) use features extracted mainly from speech for scoring the picture narration task. They employ measures capturing fluency,

[1]Details of the task and sample can be found at https://toefljr.caltesting.org/sampleQuestions/TOEFLJr/s-movietheater.html

[2]https://www.ets.org/s/toefl_junior/pdf/toefl_junior_comprehensive_speaking_scoring_guides.pdf

Proceedings of the Tenth Workshop on Innovative Use of NLP for Building Educational Applications, 2015, pages 42–48,
Denver, Colorado, June 4, 2015.

prosody and pronunciation. Our work explores the other (complementary) dimensions of the test such as language use, content relevance and story development.

Somasundaran and Chodorow (2014) construct features for awkward word usage and content relevance for a written vocabulary test which we adapt for our task. Discourse organization features have been employed for essay scoring of written essays in the expository and argumentative genre (Attali and Burstein, 2006). Our discourse features are focused on the structure of spoken narratives. Our relevance measure is intended to capture topicality while providing leeway for creative story telling, which is different from scoring summaries (Loukina et al., 2014). King and Dickinson (2013) use dependency parses of written picture descriptions. Given that our data is automatically recognized speech, parse features are not likely to be reliable. We use measures of n-gram association, such as pointwise mutual information (PMI), that have a long history of use for detecting collocations and measuring their quality (see Manning and Schütze (1999) and Leacock et al. (2014) for reviews). Our application of a large n-gram database and PMI is to encode language proficiency in sentence construction without using a parser.

Picture description tasks have been employed in a number of areas of study ranging from second language acquisition to Alzheimer's disease (Ellis, 2000; Forbes-McKay and Venneri, 2005). Picture-based story narration has also been used to study referring expressions (Lee et al., 2012) and to analyze child narratives (Hassanali et al., 2013).

3 Data

The TOEFL Junior Comprehensive assessment is a computer-based test intended for middle school students around the ages of 11 - 15, and is designed to assess a student's English communication skills. As mentioned above, we focus on the Six-Picture Narration task. Human expert raters listen to the recorded responses, which are about 60 seconds in duration, and assign a score to each on a scale of 1 - 4, with score point 4 indicating an excellent response. In this work, we use the automatic speech recognition (ASR) output transcription of the responses (see (Evanini and Wang, 2013) for details).

	Total	—Score Distribution—			
		1	2	3	4
Train	877	142	401	252	82
Eval	674	132	304	177	61

Table 1: Number of responses and score distributions for training and evaluation datasets.

The data consists of 3440 responses to 6 prompts, all of which were scored by human raters. Table 1 shows the data size and partitions for the experiments as well as the score distributions. An ASR partition (with 1538 responses) was created and used for training the speech recognition models and was used also for our linguistic feature development. *Train* was used for cross validation experiments as well as for training a final model that was evaluated on *Eval* evaluation dataset. Quadratic Weighted Kappa (QWK) between human raters for Train is 0.69 and for Eval is 0.70. Responses containing anomalous test taker behavior (such as non-English responses or non-responses) and responses with severe technical difficulties (such as static or background noise) receive separate ratings and are excluded from this study. This filtering resulted in a total of 874 responses in Train and 672 responses in Eval data sets.

4 Features

We explore five different feature sets to help us answer the following questions about the response: Did the test taker construct a story about the pictures in the prompt (or did he/she produce an irrelevant response instead?) (*Relevance*); Did the test taker use words appropriately in the response? Proper usage of words and phrases is characterized by the probabilities of the contexts in which they are used (*Collocation*); Did the test taker adequately organize the narrative? (*Discourse*); Did the test taker enhance the narrative by including details (*Detailing*); and Did the test taker develop the story through expression of emotion and character development? (*Sentiment*)

4.1 Relevance

In order to test if a given response tells a story that is relevant to the pictures in the prompt, we calculate the overlap of the content of the response and the content of the pictures similar to (Somasundaran and Chodorow, 2014). To facilitate this, each prompt is associated with a reference corpus containing a detailed description of each picture, and also an overall narrative that ties together the events in the pictures. Each reference corpus was created by merging the picture descriptions and narratives that were generated independently by 10 annotators.[3] To calculate overlap, stop words were first removed from lemmatized versions of the response and the reference corpus.

Because test-takers often use synonyms and other words related to the prompt, we expanded the content words in the reference corpus by adding their synonyms, as provided in Lin's thesaurus (Lin, 1998) and in WordNet, and also included their WordNet hypernyms and hyponyms. This gave us the following 6 features which measure the overlap, or coverage, between the lemmatized response and the lemmatized (i) reference corpus (*lemmas*), (ii) reference corpus expanded using Lin's thesaurus (*cov-lin*), (iii) reference corpus expanded using WordNet Synonyms (*cov-wn-syns*), (iv) reference corpus expanded using WordNet Hypernyms (*cov-wn-hyper*), (v) reference corpus expanded using WordNet Hyponyms (*cov-wn-hypo*), and (vi) reference corpus expanded using all of the above methods (*cov-all*).

4.2 Collocation

Inexperienced use of language is often characterized by inappropriate combinations of words, indicating the writer's lack of knowledge of collocations. In order to detect this, we calculate the Pointwise Mutual Information (PMI) of all adjacent word pairs (bigrams), as well as all adjacent word triples (trigrams) in the Google 1T web corpus (Brants and Franz, 2006). The higher the value of the PMI, the more common is the collocation for the word pair/triple in well formed texts. On the other hand, negative values of PMI indicate that the given word pair or triple is less likely than chance to occur together. We hypothesized that this would be a good indicator of awkward usage, as suggested in Chodorow and Leacock (2000).

The PMI values for adjacent words obtained over the entire response are then assigned to bins, with 8 bins for word pairs and another 8 for word triples following the procedure from (Somasundaran and Chodorow, 2014). Each of the 8 bins represents a range of PMI : $p > 20, 10 < p \leq 20, 1 < p \leq 10, 0 < p \leq 1, -1 < p \leq 0, -10 < p \leq -1, -20 < p \leq -10, p \leq -20$.

We generate two sets of features based on the proportions of bigrams/trigrams falling into each bin, resulting in a total of 16 features. In addition to binning, we also encode as features the maximum, minimum and median PMI value obtained over all bigrams and trigrams. These encode the best and the worst word collocations in a response as well as the overall general quality of the response.

4.3 Discourse

Stories are characterized by events that are related (and ordered) temporally or causally. In order to form a coherent narrative, it is often necessary to use proper transition cues to organize the story. Intuitively, coherent responses are more likely to have these cues than less coherent responses.

In order to detect discourse organization cues, we use two lexicons. The first was obtained from the Penn Discourse Treebank (PDTB) annotation manual (Prasad et al., 2008). The second was developed by manually mining websites giving advice on good narrative writing. The two lexicons gave us a total of over 550 cues. From the PDTB and our lexicon, we extracted the number of times each connective was encountered in a particular sense (sense information such as "Temporal" or "Cause" is directly provided in the PDTB manual, and we added similar information to our manually collected lexicon) and used the frequencies to construct a probability distribution over the senses for that cue. Then, for each response, we produced the following features: the number of cues found in the response (*totalCuesCount*), the number of cues found in the response divided by the number of words in the response (*normalizedCuesCount*), the number of cues belonging to the temporal category (*temporalCuesCount*), the number of cues belonging to the causal category (*causalCuesCount*), the sum of the probabilities of belonging to the temporal category for each cue found in

[3] We do not calculate agreement as producing different descriptions and having variety was the goal of the task of reference corpus creation.

the response (*temporalCuesScore*), the sum of the probabilities of belonging to the causal category for each cue found in the response (*causalCuesScore*).

4.4 Detailing

We hypothesized that better responses would show evidence of effective narrative techniques, such as providing vivid descriptions of the events and providing depth to the story. For example, one could say *"In the afternoon a boy and a man went to the library."*, or make the story more interesting by assigning names to the characters and places as *"One day John went to the Central Public Library because he wanted to do some research for his science project. An old man was walking behind him; his name was Peter. "*

We observed that certain syntactic categories, such as adjectives and adverbs, come into play in the process of detailing. Also, detailing by providing names to the characters and places results in a higher number of proper nouns (NNPs). Thus our detailing feature set consists of the following features: a binary value indicating whether the response contains any proper nouns (*presenceNames*), the number of proper nouns in the response (*countNames*), a binary value indicating whether the response contains any adjectives (*presenceAdj*), the number of adjectives in the response (*countAdj*), a binary value indicating whether the response contains any adverbs (*presenceAdv*), the number of adverbs in the response (*countAdv*). We use separate features for counts and presence of the syntactic category in order to balance the trade-off between sparsity and informativeness. The count features are more informative, but they can be sparse (especially for higher counts).

4.5 Sentiment

One common technique used in developing a story is to reveal the character's private states, emotions and feelings. This requires the use of subjectivity and sentiment terms.

We use lexicons for annotating sentiment and subjective words in the response. Specifically, we use a sentiment lexicon (*ASSESS*) developed in previous work in assessments (Beigman Klebanov et al., 2013) and the MPQA subjectivity lexicon (Wilson et al., 2005). ASSESS lexicon assigns a positive/negative/neutral polarity probability profile to its entries, and MPQA lexicon associates a positive, negative or neutral polarity category to its entries. We consider a word from the ASSESS lexicon to be polar if the sum of positive and negative probabilities is greater than 0.65 (we arrived at this number after manual inspection of the lexicon). This gives us the subjectivity feature set comprised of the following features: A binary value indicating whether the response contains any polar words from the ASSESS lexicon (*presencePolarProfile*), the number of polar words from the ASSESS lexicon found in the response (*cntPolarProfile*), a binary value indicating whether the response contains any polar words from the MPQA lexicon (*presenceMpqaPolar*), the number of polar words from the MPQA lexicon found in the response (*cntMpqaPolar*), a binary value indicating whether the response contains any neutral words from the MPQA lexicon (*presenceMpqaNeut*), the number of neutral words from the MPQA lexicon found in the response (*cntMpqaNeut*).

We construct separate features from the ASSESS lexicon and the MPQA lexicon because we found that the neutral category had different meanings in the two lexicons – even the neutral entries in the MPQA lexicon are valuable as they may indicate speech events and private states (e.g. view, assess, believe, cogitate, contemplate, feel, glean, think etc.). On the other hand, words with a high probability of being neutral in the ASSESS lexicon are non-subjective words (e.g. woman, undergo, entire, technologies).

5 Experiments

For our experiments, we used a supervised learning framework, with the data described above, to build scoring models based on our feature sets. We evaluated several different learning algorithms and found that a Random Forest Classifier consistently produced the best results in cross-validation experiments on the training data when we used our features as well as when we used the baseline set of features. Hence, all of our results in this section are reported using this Random Forest learner. Performance was calculated using Quadratic Weighted Kappa (QWK) (Cohen, 1968), which is the standard evaluation metric used in automated scoring. QWK measures the agreement between the system score and the

Feature set	CV	Eval
Relevance	0.43	0.46
Collocation	0.48	0.40
Discourse	0.25	0.27
Details	0.18	0.21
Subjectivity	0.17	0.16
EW13 baseline	0.48	0.52
All Feats	0.52	0.55
All Feats + EW13	0.58	0.58

Table 2: Performance of different feature sets.

Feature set	Performance
EW13 baseline	0.48
EW13 + Relevance	0.54
EW13 + Collocation	0.57
EW13 + Discourse	0.49
EW13 + Details	0.50
EW13 + Subjectivity	0.50

Table 3: Performance of the Baseline when each individual feature set is added to it.

human-annotated score, correcting for chance agreement and penalizing large disagreements more than small ones.

5.1 Baseline

We use the previous state-of-the-art features from Evanini and Wang (2013) as our baseline *(EW13)*. They are comprised of the following subsets: fluency (rate of speech, number of words per chunk, average number of pauses, average number of long pauses), pronunciation (normalized Acoustic Model score, average word confidence, average difference in phone duration from native speaker norms), prosody (mean duration between stressed syllables), and lexical choice (normalized Language Model score).

5.2 Results and Analysis

We performed cross validation on our training data (Train) and also performed training on the full training dataset with evaluation on the Eval data. Table 2 reports our results on 10-fold cross validation experiments on the training data (CV), as well results when training on the full training dataset and testing on the evaluation dataset (Eval). The first 5 rows report the performance of the individual feature sets described in Section 4. Not surprisingly, each individual feature set is not able to perform as well as the EW13 baseline, which is comprised of an array of many features that measures various speech characteristics. One exception to this is the collocation feature set that performs as well as the EW13 baseline in the cross validation experiments. Notably, the combination of all five feature sets proposed in this work (*All Feats*), performs better than the EW13 baseline, indicating that our relevance and linguistic features are important for scoring for this spoken response item type. Finally the best performance is obtained when we combine our features with the speech-based features. This improvement of All Feats + EW13 over the baseline is statistically significant at $p < 0.01$, based on 10K bootstrap samples (Zhang et al., 2004). Somewhat surprisingly, the testing on the evaluation dataset showed slightly better performance for most types of features than the cross validation testing. We believe that this might be due to the fact that, for the Eval results, all the training data were available to train the scoring models.

We also performed analysis on the Train set to see if the baseline's performance is impacted when each of our individual feature sets is added to it. As shown in Table 3, each of the feature sets is able to improve the baseline's performance (of 0.48 QWK). Specifically, Discourse and Subjectivity produce a slight improvement while Relevance produces modest improvement. However, only the improvement produced by the Collocation features was statistically significant ($p < 0.01$)

6 Conclusions

In this work, we explored five different types of linguistic features for scoring spoken responses in a picture narration task. The features were designed to capture language proficiency, story development and task relevance. Our results are promising: we found that each feature is able to combine well with a state of the art speech feature system to improve results. The combination of the linguistic features achieved better overall performance than the speech features alone. Finally the best performance was achieved when linguistic and speech features were combined.

References

Yigal Attali and Jill Burstein. 2006. Automated essay scoring with e-rater v. 2.0. *Journal of Technology, Learning, and Assessment*, 4:3.

Beata Beigman Klebanov, Jill Burstein, and Nitin Madnani. 2013. Sentiment profiles of multi-word expressions in test-taker essays: The case of noun-noun compounds. In *ACM Transactions on Speech and Language Processing*, volume 10(3).

Gilbert J. Botvin and Brian Sutton-Smith. 1977. The development of structural complexity in children's fantasy narratives. *Developmental Psychology*, 13(4):377 – 388.

Thorsten Brants and Alex Franz. 2006. Web 1T 5-gram Version 1. In *Linguistic Data Consortium, Philadelphia.*

Martin Chodorow and Claudia Leacock. 2000. An unsupervised method for detecting grammatical errors. In *Proceedings of the Conference of the North American Chapter of the Association of Computational Linguistics (NAACL)*, pages 140–147.

Jacob Cohen. 1968. Weighted kappa: Nominal scale agreement provision for scaled disagreement or partial credit. *Psychological Bulletin*, 70(4).

Rod Ellis. 2000. Task-based research and language pedagogy. *Language teaching research*, 4(3):193–220.

Keelan Evanini and Xinhao Wang. 2013. Automated speech scoring for non-native middle school students with multiple task types. In *Proceedings of Interspeech*, pages 2435–2439.

Keelan Evanini, Michael Heilman, Xinhao Wang, and Daniel Blanchard. 2014. Automated scoring for TOEFL Junior comprehensive writing and speaking. Technical report, ETS, Princeton, NJ.

KE Forbes-McKay and Annalena Venneri. 2005. Detecting subtle spontaneous language decline in early Alzheimers disease with a picture description task. *Neurological sciences*, 26(4):243–254.

Khairun-nisa Hassanali, Yang Liu, and Thamar Solorio. 2013. Using Latent Dirichlet Allocation for child narrative analysis. In *Proceedings of the 2013 Workshop on Biomedical Natural Language Processing*. Association for Computational Linguistics.

Levi King and Markus Dickinson. 2013. Shallow semantic analysis of interactive learner sentences. In *Proceedings of the Eighth Workshop on Innovative Use of NLP for Building Educational Applications*, pages 11–21, Atlanta, Georgia, June. Association for Computational Linguistics.

Claudia Leacock, Martin Chodorow, Michael Gamon, and Joel Tetreault. 2014. *Automated Grammatical Error Detection for Language Learners*. Synthesis Lectures on Human Language Technologies. Morgan & Claypool.

Choonkyu Lee, Smaranda Muresan, and Karin Stromswold. 2012. Computational analysis of referring expressions in narratives of picture books. In *Proceedings of the NAACL-HLT 2012 Workshop on Computational Linguistics for Literature*, pages 1–7, Montréal, Canada, June. Association for Computational Linguistics.

Dekang Lin. 1998. Automatic retrieval and clustering of similar words. In *Proceedings of the 17th international conference on Computational linguistics-Volume 2*, pages 768–774. ACL.

Anastassia Loukina, Klaus Zechner, and Lei Chen. 2014. Automatic evaluation of spoken summaries: the case of language assessment. In *Proceedings of the Ninth Workshop on Innovative Use of NLP for Building Educational Applications*, pages 68–78, Baltimore, Maryland, June. Association for Computational Linguistics.

Christopher Manning and Hinrich Schütze. 1999. *Foundations of Statistical Natural Language Processing*. MIT Press.

Anne McKeough and Jennifer Malcolm. 2011. Stories of family, stories of self: Developmental pathways to interpretive thought during adolescence. *New Directions for Child & Adolescent Development*, 2011(131):59 – 71.

Rashmi Prasad, Nikhil Dinesh, Alan Lee, Eleni Miltsakaki, Livio Robaldo, Aravind Joshi, and Bonnie Webber. 2008. The Penn Discourse Treebank 2.0. In *Proceedings of the Sixth International Conference on Language Resources and Evaluation (LREC'08)*, Marrakech, Morocco, May. European Language Resources Association (ELRA).

Swapna Somasundaran and Martin Chodorow. 2014. Automated measures of specific vocabulary knowledge from constructed responses (use these words to write a sentence based on this picture). In *Proceedings of the Ninth Workshop on Innovative Use of NLP for Building Educational Applications*, pages 1–11. Association for Computational Linguistics.

Lei Sun and Marilyn A Nippold. 2012. Narrative writing in children and adolescents: Examining the literate lexicon. *Language, speech, and hearing services in schools*, 43(1):2–13.

Theresa Wilson, Janyce Wiebe, and Paul Hoffmann. 2005. Recognizing contextual polarity in phrase-level sentiment analysis. In *Proceedings of the conference on Human Language Technology and Empirical Methods in Natural Language Processing (HLT-EMNLP)*, pages 347–354. Association for Computational Linguistics.

Ying Zhang, Stephan Vogel, and Alex Waibel. 2004. Interpreting bleu/nist scores: How much improvement do we need to have a better system? In *Proceedings of the International Conference on Language Re-*

sources and Evaluation (LREC). European Language Resources Association (ELRA).

Measuring Feature Diversity in Native Language Identification

Shervin Malmasi
Centre for Language Technology
Macquarie University
Sydney, NSW, Australia
shervin.malmasi@mq.edu.au

Aoife Cahill
Educational Testing Service
660 Rosedale Rd
Princeton, NJ 08541, USA
acahill@ets.org

Abstract

The task of Native Language Identification (NLI) is typically solved with machine learning methods, and systems make use of a wide variety of features. Some preliminary studies have been conducted to examine the effectiveness of individual features, however, no systematic study of feature interaction has been carried out. We propose a function to measure feature independence and analyze its effectiveness on a standard NLI corpus.

1 Introduction

Researchers in Second Language Acquisition (SLA) investigate the multiplex of factors that influence our ability to acquire new languages and chief among these is the role of the learner's mother tongue. This core factor has recently been studied in the task of Native Language Identification (NLI), which aims to infer the native language (L1) of an author based on texts written in a second language (L2). Machine Learning methods are usually used to identify language use patterns common to speakers of the same L1 (Tetreault et al., 2012). While NLI has applications in security, most research has a strong linguistic motivation relating to language teaching and learning. In this context, by identifying L1-specific language usage and error patterns, NLI can be used to better understand SLA and develop teaching methods, instructions and learner feedback that is tailored to their mother tongue (Malmasi and Dras, 2014b).

Although researchers have employed tens of feature types, no effort has been made to measure the overlap of information they capture. Results from previous studies show that while some feature types yield similar accuracies independently, combining them can improve performance (Brooke and Hirst, 2012). This indicates that the information they capture is diverse, but how diverse are they and how can we measure the level of independence between the feature types?

This is a question that has not been tackled in NLI, despite researchers having examined numerous feature types to date. We examine one approach to measuring the degree of diversity between features and perform several analyses based on the results.

2 Data and Methodology

We use the TOEFL11 corpus (Blanchard et al., 2013) released with the 2013 NLI shared task (Tetreault et al., 2013). It includes 12,100 learner texts from 11 L1 groups, divided into train, dev. and test sets.

We use a linear Support Vector Machine[1] to perform multi-class classification in our experiments.

We experiment with a wide range of previously used syntactic and lexical features: Adaptor Grammars (AG) (Wong et al., 2012), character n-grams (Tsur and Rappoport, 2007),[2] Function word unigrams and bigrams (Malmasi et al., 2013), Lemma and Word n-grams, CFG Production Rules (Wong and Dras, 2011), Penn Treebank (PTB) part-of-speech n-grams, RASP part-of-speech n-grams (Malmasi et al., 2013), Stanford Dependencies with POS transformations (Tetreault et al., 2012), and Tree Substitution Grammar (TSG) fragments (Swanson and Charniak, 2012). The individual feature accuracies[3] are shown in Figure 1.[4]

[1] We use LIBLINEAR. Additional preliminary experiments with alternative learners yielded similar results.

[2] We treat character n-grams as lexical features in this work but restrict our investigation to 1–3-grams. Recent work has also shown improvements from longer sequences (Jarvis et al., 2013; Ionescu et al., 2014).

[3] Obtained by training on the TOEFL11 train and development sets and evaluating on the test set.

[4] Listed in alphabetical order.

Proceedings of the Tenth Workshop on Innovative Use of NLP for Building Educational Applications, 2015, pages 49–55,
Denver, Colorado, June 4, 2015.

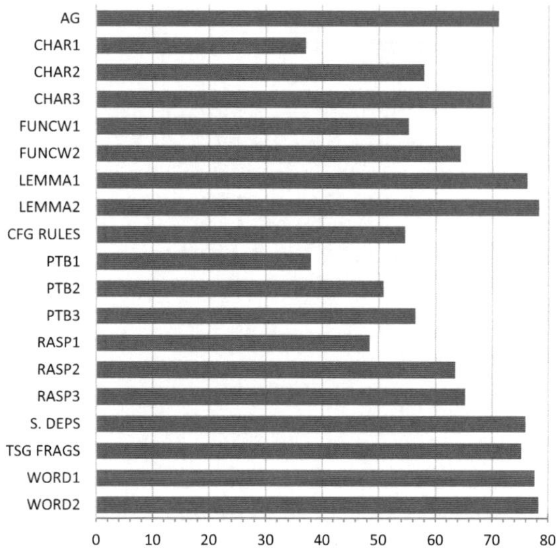

Figure 1: Individual classification accuracy for each one of our features on the TOEFL11 test set.

3 Measuring Feature Diversity

An ablation study is a common approach in machine learning that aims to measure the contribution of each feature in a multi-component system. This ablative analysis is usually carried out by measuring the performance of the entire system with all components (*i.e.* features) and then progressively removing the components one at a time to measure how the performance degrades.[5]

While useful for estimating the potential contribution of a component, this type of analysis does not directly inform us about the pairwise relation between any two given components. This shortcoming has been noted by other researchers, *e.g.* Wellner et al. (2009, p. 122), and highlights the need to quantify the overlap between any two given components in a system. Our approach to quantifying the diversity between two feature types is based on measuring the level of agreement between the two for predicting labels on the same set of documents. Here, we aim to examine feature differences by holding the classifier parameters and data constant.

Past research suggests that Yule's Q-coefficient statistic (Yule, 1912) is a useful measure of pairwise dependence between two classifiers (Kuncheva et al., 2003). This notion of dependence relates to complementarity and orthogonality, and is an important factor in combining classifiers (Lam, 2000).

Yule's Q statistic is a correlation coefficient for binary measurements and can be applied to classifier outputs for each data point where the output values represent correct (1) or incorrect (0) predictions made by that learner. Each classifier C_i produces a result vector $y_i = [y_{i,1}, \ldots, y_{i,N}]$ for a set of N documents where $y_{i,j} = 1$ if C_i correctly classifies the jth document, otherwise it is 0. Given these output vectors from two classifiers C_i and C_k, a 2×2 contingency table can be derived, as shown in Table 1.

	C_k **Correct**	C_k **Wrong**
C_i **Correct**	N^{11}	N^{10}
C_i **Wrong**	N^{01}	N^{00}

Table 1: Contingency table for two classifiers.

Here N^{11} is the frequency of items that both classifiers predicted correctly, N^{00} where they were both wrong, and so on. The Q-coefficient for the two classifiers can then be calculated as:

$$Q_{i,k} = \frac{N^{11}N^{00} - N^{01}N^{10}}{N^{11}N^{00} + N^{01}N^{10}}.$$

This distribution-free association measure[6] is based on taking the products of the diagonal cell frequencies and calculating the ratio of their difference and sum. Q ranges between -1 to $+1$, where -1 signifies negative association, 0 indicates no association (independence) and $+1$ means perfect positive correlation (dependence).

Here our classifiers are always of the same type, a linear SVM, but they are trained with different features on the same data, allowing us to measure the dependence between feature types themselves.

4 Results

The matrix of the Q-coefficients for all features is shown graphically in Figure 2. The most discernible feature is the red cluster in the bottom left of the matrix. This region covers the correlations between syntactic and lexical features, showing that they differ the most.

Another interesting aspect is the strong correlations between the lexical features, shown by the clustering of high values in the bottom right corner. It also shows that character n-grams capture similar information to word unigrams and bigrams. Even character unigrams – the lowest performing lexical feature – show much stronger dependence with word unigrams than other syntactic features. Additionally, the high values in the bottom middle section

[5]Other variations exist, *e.g.* compare Richardson et al. (2006) and Wellner et al. (2009)

[6]This is equivalent to the 2×2 version of Goodman and Kruskal's gamma measure for ordinal variables.

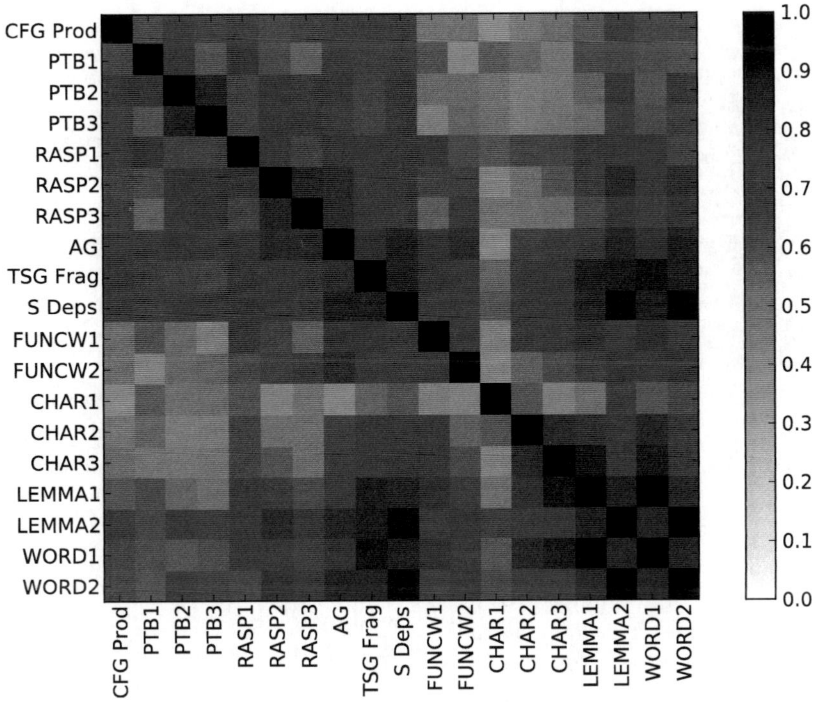

Figure 2: The Q-coefficient matrices of our feature set. The matrices are displayed as heat maps.

of the matrix show that Stanford Dependencies and TSG fragments largely capture the same information as Word and Lemma bigrams. These issues are explored further in §5.

In contrast to the lexical features, the syntactic ones show much lower inter-correlation levels, evidenced by lower values in the top left corner and absence of a visible cluster. This seems to indicate that there is greater diversity among these features.

Such analyses can help us better understand the linguistic properties of features and guide interpretation of the results. This knowledge can also be useful in creating classifier ensembles. One goal in creating such committee-based classifiers is the identification of the most diverse independent learners and this method can be applied to that end. To assess this, we also measure the accuracy for all 171 possible feature pair combinations f_i and f_j in our feature set. Each pair is combined in a weighted sum ensemble classifier (Malmasi et al., 2013) and run against the TOEFL11 test set. For each pair we also calculate the relative increase over only using the more accurate feature of the two;[7] this measures

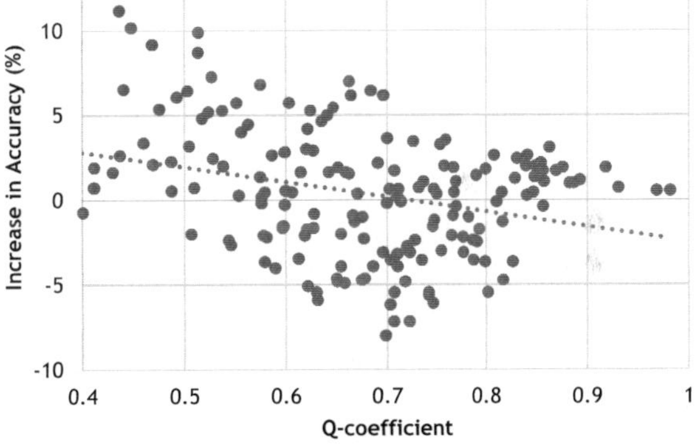

Figure 3: Scatterplot of the Q-coefficient vs relative increase in accuracy for all 171 feature pairs.

the net effect of combining the two: positive for improvements and negative for degradation.

The increase for each pair is compared against the Q-coefficient, and Pearson's correlation for the two variables shows a medium, statistically significant negative correlation ($r = -.303$, $p = .000$). A scatterplot is shown in Figure 3, where we observe that almost all feature pairs with $Q < 0.5$ yielded a net increase while many pairs with $Q > 0.6$ resulted in performance degradation.

The measure is particularly useful when comparing features with similar individual accuracy to identify sets with the highest diversity. This is because

[7]The relative increase is defined as:
$Accuracy_{f_i+f_j} - max(Accuracy_{f_i}, Accuracy_{f_j})$
An alternative metric here for this could be the "Oracle" baseline used by Malmasi et al. (2015).

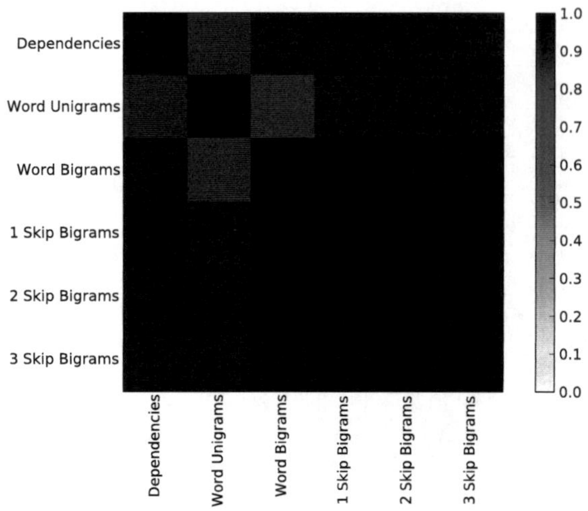

Figure 4: The Q-coefficient matrix for dependencies, word n-grams and skip-grams.

diversity itself cannot be the sole criterion for feature selection; a weak feature such as character unigrams will be very diverse to a strong one like POS n-grams but this does not *ipso facto* make it a good feature and we must also consider accuracy.

5 Analyzing Words and Dependencies

Grammatical dependencies have been found to be a very useful NLI feature and thought to capture a "more abstract representation of syntactic structures" (Tetreault et al., 2012; Bykh and Meurers, 2014). Accordingly, we were initially surprised to find the high correlation between dependencies and word bigrams ($Q = 0.93$). However, this relation may not be unexpected after all.

One source of supporting evidence comes from examining dependency distances. Using English data,[8] Liu (2008) reports a Mean Dependency Distance (MDD) of 2.54 with 51% of the dependencies being adjacent and thus also captured by word bigrams. This also suggests that we can capture more of this information by considering non-adjacent tokens. We test this hypothesis by using k-skip word bigrams (Guthrie et al., 2006) as classification features, with $k = 1$–3.

The 1-skip bigrams yield an accuracy of 79.3% on the TOEFL11 test set, higher than either word bigrams or Stanford Dependencies. The 2- and 3-skip grams achieve 78.4% and 77.9%. The matrix of Q-coefficients for these features is shown in Figure 4, showing that the 1-skip word bigrams feature is the closest to the dependencies feature with a Q-coefficient of 0.96. It is also the closest to standard word unigrams and bigrams with Q-coefficients of 0.91 and 0.97, respectively.

These results suggest that skip-grams are a very useful feature for NLI.[9] They could also be used as a substitute for dependencies in scenarios where running a full parser may not be feasible, *e.g.* real-time data processing. Moreover, with NLI being investigated with other languages (Malmasi and Dras, 2014a), this feature can be a good approximation of the dependencies feature for low-resourced languages without an accurate parser. However, results may vary by language and possibly genre (Liu, 2008). We also note that the skip-gram feature space grows prodigiously as k increases.

Another related issue is whether sub-lexical character n-grams are independent of word features. Previously, Tsur and Rappoport (2007) hypothesized that these n-grams are discriminative due to writer choices "strongly influenced by the phonology of their native language". Nicolai and Kondrak (2014) also investigate the source of L1 differences in the relative frequencies of character bigrams. They propose an algorithm to identify the most discriminative words and subsequently, the bigrams corresponding to these words. They found that removing a small set of highly discriminative words greatly degrades the accuracy of a bigram-based classifier. Based on this they conclude that bigrams capture differences in word usage and lexical transfer rather than L1 phonology. Evidence from our analysis also points to a similar pattern with the predictions of character bigrams and trigrams being strongly correlated with word and lemma unigrams.

Such lexical transfer effects have been previously noted by others (Odlin, 1989). The effects are mediated not only by cognates and word form similarities, but also semantics and meanings. We also examine the link between L1 and word usage.

Using the Etymological WordNet[10] database (de Melo, 2014), we extracted two lists of English words with either Old English (508 words) or Latin origins (1,310 words). These words were used as unigram features to train two classifiers. The F1-scores for classification on TOEFL11 are shown in Figure 5. The Old English words, with their West Germanic roots, yield the best results for classifying German data. Conversely, the Latinate features achieve the

[8] 120k sentences averaging 21 tokens each.

[9] Hladka et al. (2013) and Henderson et al. (2013) previously used a skip-gram variant that did not include 0 skips as per (Guthrie et al., 2006) and did not improve accuracy.

[10] http://www1.icsi.berkeley.edu/%7edemelo/etymwn/

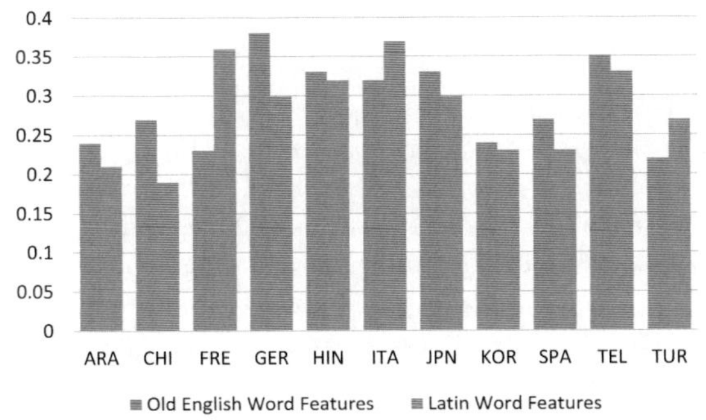

Figure 5: F1-scores for classifying L1 using English words with Old English or Latin origins.

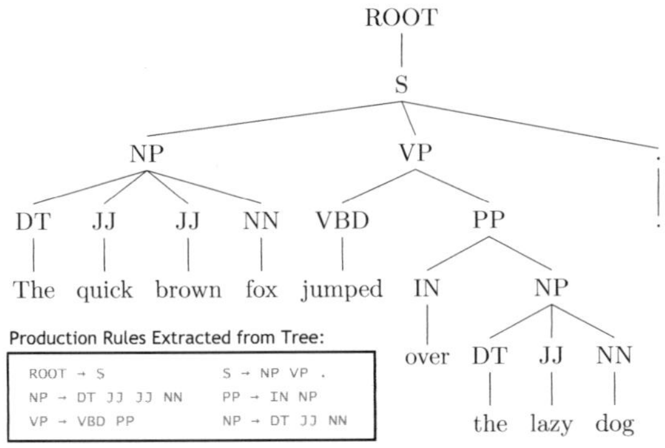

Figure 6: A constituent parse tree for an example sentence along with the context-free grammar production rules which can be extracted from it.

best results for Italian followed by French, both languages descended from Latin.

This experiment, albeit limited in scope, provides some empirical evidence suggesting that small sets of words can capture lexical transfer effects potentially mediated by L1 similarity and cognates.

6 Parent-Annotated CFG Rules

As demonstrated by our results, CFG production rules are a diverse syntactic feature with good accuracy. This feature type is processed by first generating constituent parses for each sentence and then extracting its production rules,[11] excluding lexicalizations. Each rule is then used as a feature. Figure 6 illustrates this with an example tree and its rules. They have been successfully used in NLI (Wong and Dras, 2011) and in this section we experiment with a new extension of this feature type previously not applied to NLI.

Parent-annotated PCFG models have previously been applied in parsing and shown to yield improved results over other models (Johnson, 1998). In this experiment we apply this feature to NLI and evaluate whether it can provide any improvement over standard production rule models.

[11]These are the phrase structure rules used to generate constituent parts of sentences, such as noun phrases.

```
ROOT       → S^<ROOT>              VP^<S>   → VBD PP^<VP>
S^<ROOT> → NP^<S> VP^<S> .   PP^<VP>  → IN NP^<PP>
NP^<S>     → DT JJ JJ NN           NP^<PP>  → DT JJ NN
```

Figure 7: Parent-annotated CFG rules from Fig. 4.

This feature involves a modification of the linguistic tree representation, appending the category of each node's parent as additional contextual information (Johnson, 1998, p. 623). This transformation can be described as adding "pseudo context-sensitivity" (Charniak and Carroll, 1994). Figure 7 shows the parent-annotated CFG rule features extracted from the tree shown in Figure 6.

Testing this feature on the TOEFL11 test set, we achieve an accuracy of 55.6%, a $+1.3\%$ increase over the standard CFG rules feature. Analyzing feature diversity, we observe a Q-coefficient of 0.92 between the two CFG rule based features. These results show that parent annotation leads to a sizeable increase in accuracy and also a notable change in diversity levels.

Although these initial results suggest that this is a useful feature, more testing with other data can help determine if these patterns hold across corpora (Malmasi and Dras, 2015). This additional information could also help in other tasks such as language transfer hypothesis formulation (Malmasi and Dras, 2014b) through the examination of more specific environmental contexts for features.

We leave to future work the investigation of improved ensemble classifiers that would be informed by the results of this study. The exploration of other linguistic tree representations and transformations, including Chomsky Normal Form, is another avenue for future work.

7 Conclusion

In this work we examined a method for measuring feature diversity in NLI and highlighted several interesting trends. We demonstrated how this analysis can be used to better understand the information captured by features and used it to examine the relationship between lexical features. We show that a variant of 1-skip bigrams can in fact be a useful feature and also proposed a new NLI feature, parent-annotated CFG rules, showing how feature diversity can guide feature engineering.

Acknowledgments

We would like to thank the anonymous reviewers for their helpful comments. We would also like to thank Keelan Evanini, Yoko Futagi and Jidong Tao for their thoughtful suggestions for improving this work.

References

Daniel Blanchard, Joel Tetreault, Derrick Higgins, Aoife Cahill, and Martin Chodorow. 2013. TOEFL11: A Corpus of Non-Native English. Technical report, Educational Testing Service.

Julian Brooke and Graeme Hirst. 2012. Robust, Lexicalized Native Language Identification. In *Proceedings of COLING 2012*, pages 391–408, Mumbai, India, December. The COLING 2012 Organizing Committee.

Serhiy Bykh and Detmar Meurers. 2014. Exploring Syntactic Features for Native Language Identification: A Variationist Perspective on Feature Encoding and Ensemble Optimization. In *Proceedings of COLING 2014, the 25th International Conference on Computational Linguistics: Technical Papers*, pages 1962–1973, Dublin, Ireland, August. Dublin City University and Association for Computational Linguistics.

Eugene Charniak and Glenn Carroll. 1994. Context-sensitive statistics for improved grammatical language models. In *AAAI*, pages 728–733.

Gerard de Melo. 2014. Etymological wordnet: Tracing the history of words. In *Proceedings of the Ninth International Conference on Language Resources and Evaluation (LREC-2014)*. European Language Resources Association (ELRA).

David Guthrie, Ben Allison, Wei Liu, Louise Guthrie, and Yorick Wilks. 2006. A Closer Look at Skip-gram Modelling. In *Proceedings of the Fifth International Conference on Language Resources and Evaluation (LREC 2006)*, pages 1222–1225, Genoa, Italy.

John Henderson, Guido Zarrella, Craig Pfeifer, and John D. Burger. 2013. Discriminating Non-Native English with 350 Words. In *Proceedings of the Eighth Workshop on Innovative Use of NLP for Building Educational Applications*, pages 101–110, Atlanta, Georgia, June. Association for Computational Linguistics.

Barbora Hladka, Martin Holub, and Vincent Kriz. 2013. Feature Engineering in the NLI Shared Task 2013: Charles University Submission Report. In *Proceedings of the Eighth Workshop on Innovative Use of NLP for Building Educational Applications*, pages 232–241, Atlanta, Georgia, June. Association for Computational Linguistics.

Radu Tudor Ionescu, Marius Popescu, and Aoife Cahill. 2014. Can characters reveal your native language? A language-independent approach to native language identification. In *Proceedings of the 2014 Conference on Empirical Methods in Natural Language Processing (EMNLP)*, pages 1363–1373, Doha, Qatar, October. Association for Computational Linguistics.

Scott Jarvis, Yves Bestgen, and Steve Pepper. 2013. Maximizing Classification Accuracy in Native Language Identification. In *Proceedings of the Eighth Workshop on Innovative Use of NLP for Building Educational Applications*, pages 111–118, Atlanta, Georgia, June. Association for Computational Linguistics.

Mark Johnson. 1998. PCFG models of linguistic tree representations. *Computational Linguistics*, 24(4):613–632.

Ludmila I Kuncheva, Christopher J Whitaker, Catherine A Shipp, and Robert PW Duin. 2003. Limits on the majority vote accuracy in classifier fusion. *Pattern Analysis & Applications*, 6(1):22–31.

Louisa Lam. 2000. Classifier combinations: implementations and theoretical issues. In *Multiple classifier systems*, pages 77–86. Springer.

Haitao Liu. 2008. Dependency distance as a metric of language comprehension difficulty. *Journal of Cognitive Science*, 9(2):159–191.

Shervin Malmasi and Mark Dras. 2014a. Chinese Native Language Identification. *Proceedings of the 14th Conference of the European Chapter of the Association for Computational Linguistics*.

Shervin Malmasi and Mark Dras. 2014b. Language Transfer Hypotheses with Linear SVM Weights. In *Proceedings of the 2014 Conference on Empirical Methods in Natural Language Processing (EMNLP)*, Doha, Qatar, October. Association for Computational Linguistics.

Shervin Malmasi and Mark Dras. 2015. Large-scale Native Language Identification with Cross-Corpus Evaluation. In *Proceedings of NAACL-HLT 2015*, Denver, Colorado, June. Association for Computational Linguistics.

Shervin Malmasi, Sze-Meng Jojo Wong, and Mark Dras. 2013. NLI Shared Task 2013: MQ Submission. In *Proceedings of the Eighth Workshop on Innovative Use of NLP for Building Educational Applications*, pages 124–133, Atlanta, Georgia, June. Association for Computational Linguistics.

Shervin Malmasi, Joel Tetreault, and Mark Dras. 2015. Oracle and Human Baselines for Native Language Identification. In *Proceedings of the Tenth Workshop on Innovative Use of NLP for Building Educational Applications*, Denver, Colorado, June. Association for Computational Linguistics.

Garrett Nicolai and Grzegorz Kondrak. 2014. Does the phonology of L1 show up in L2 texts? In *Proceedings of The 52nd Annual Meeting of the Association for Computational Linguistics (ACL)*, pages 854–859.

Terence Odlin. 1989. *Language Transfer: Cross-linguistic Influence in Language Learning*. Cambridge University Press, Cambridge, UK.

Matthew Richardson, Amit Prakash, and Eric Brill. 2006. Beyond PageRank: machine learning for static ranking. In *Proceedings of the 15th international conference on World Wide Web*, pages 707–715. ACM.

Benjamin Swanson and Eugene Charniak. 2012. Native Language Detection with Tree Substitution Grammars. In *Proceedings of the 50th Annual Meeting of the Association for Computational Linguistics (Volume 2: Short Papers)*, pages 193–197, Jeju Island, Korea, July. Association for Computational Linguistics.

Joel Tetreault, Daniel Blanchard, Aoife Cahill, and Martin Chodorow. 2012. Native Tongues, Lost and Found: Resources and Empirical Evaluations in Native Language Identification. In *Proceedings of COLING 2012*, pages 2585–2602, Mumbai, India, December. The COLING 2012 Organizing Committee.

Joel Tetreault, Daniel Blanchard, and Aoife Cahill. 2013. A Report on the First Native Language Identification Shared Task. In *Proceedings of the Eighth Workshop on Innovative Use of NLP for Building Educational Applications*, pages 48–57, Atlanta, Georgia, June. Association for Computational Linguistics.

Oren Tsur and Ari Rappoport. 2007. Using Classifier Features for Studying the Effect of Native Language on the Choice of Written Second Language Words. In *Proceedings of the Workshop on Cognitive Aspects of Computational Language Acquisition*, pages 9–16, Prague, Czech Republic, June. Association for Computational Linguistics.

Ben Wellner, James Pustejovsky, Catherine Havasi, Anna Rumshisky, and Roser Sauri. 2009. Classification of discourse coherence relations: An exploratory study using multiple knowledge sources. In *Proceedings of the 7th SIGdial Workshop on Discourse and Dialogue*, pages 117–125. Association for Computational Linguistics.

Sze-Meng Jojo Wong and Mark Dras. 2011. Exploiting Parse Structures for Native Language Identification. In *Proceedings of the 2011 Conference on Empirical Methods in Natural Language Processing*, pages 1600–1610, Edinburgh, Scotland, UK., July. Association for Computational Linguistics.

Sze-Meng Jojo Wong, Mark Dras, and Mark Johnson. 2012. Exploring Adaptor Grammars for Native Language Identification. In *Proc. Conf. Empirical Methods in Natural Language Processing (EMNLP)*, pages 699–709.

George Udny Yule. 1912. On the methods of measuring association between two attributes. *Journal of the Royal Statistical Society*, pages 579–652.

Automated Evaluation of Scientific Writing: AESW Shared Task Proposal

Vidas Daudaravičius
VTeX
Mokslininku st. 2a
Vilnius, Lithuania
vidas.daudaravicius@vtex.lt

Abstract

The goal of the Automated Evaluation of Scientific Writing (AESW) Shared Task is to analyze the linguistic characteristics of scientific writing to promote the development of automated writing evaluation tools that can assist authors in writing scientific papers. The proposed task is to predict whether a given sentence requires editing to ensure its "fit" with the scientific writing genre. We describe the proposed task, training, development, and test data sets, and evaluation metrics.

Quality means doing it right when no one is looking.
– Henry Ford

1 Introduction

De facto, English is the main language for writing and publishing scientific papers. In reality, the mother-tongue of many scientists is not English. Writing a scientific paper is likely to require more effort for researchers who are nonnative English speakers compared to native speakers. The lack of authoring support tools available to nonnative speakers for writing scientific papers in English is a formidable barrier nonnative English-speaking authors who are trying to publish, and this is becoming visible in academic community. Many papers, after acceptance to journals, require improvement in overall writing quality which may be addressed by publishers. However, this is not the case with most conference proceedings.

The vast number of scientific papers being authored by nonnative English speakers creates a large demand for effective computer-based writing tools to help writers compose scientific articles. Several shared tasks have been organized (Dale and Kilgarriff, 2011; Dale et al., 2012; Ng et al., 2013; Ng et al., 2014) which constituted a major step toward evaluating the feasibility of building novel grammar error correction technologies. English language learner (ELL) corpora were made available for research purposes (Dahlmeier et al., 2013; Yannakoudakis et al., 2011). An extensive overview of the feasibility of automated grammatical error detection for language learners was conducted by Leacock et al. (2010). While these achievements are critical for language learners, we also need to develop tools that support genre-specific writing features. The shared task proposed here focuses on the genre of scientific writing.

Above and beyond correct use of English conventions, the genre of scientific writing is characterized by features, including, but not limited to declarative voice, and appropriate academic and discipline-specific terminology. There are many issues for writers that are not necessarily related to grammar issues such as, vocabulary usage, and correct word and phrase order among other issues. In addition, many ELL writers have a different way of thinking and reasoning in their native language which may be reflected in their writing. For instance, it is likely that ELLs and native English (EN) writers would write the same text in different ways:

1. ELL *"Completely different role of elastic interaction occurs due to local variations in the strain field..."*

   EN *"Elastic interaction takes on a completely*

Proceedings of the Tenth Workshop on Innovative Use of NLP for Building Educational Applications, 2015, pages 56–63,
Denver, Colorado, June 4, 2015.

different role with local variations in the strain field..."

2. ELL *"The method is straightforward and concise, and its applications is promising."*

   EN *"The method is straightforward and concise, and it holds promise for many applications."*

The difference in the readability and the fluency of texts due to grammatical errors is apparent.

The task of automated writing evaluation applied to scientific writing is critical, but it is not well studied because no data for research have been available until recently when the dataset of language edits of scientific texts was published (Daudaravicius, 2014).

On the other hand, some scientists propose to use Scientific Globish versus scientific English (Tychinin and Kamnev, 2013). The term 'Globish' denotes the international auxiliary language proposed by Jean-Paul Nerrière, which relies on a vocabulary of 1500 English words and a subset of standard English grammar[1]. The proposed adoption of '*scientific Globish*' as a simplified language standard may appeal to authors who have difficulty with English proficiency. However, *Globish* might lead to further deterioration of the quality of English-language scientific writing, and, in general, it cannot be a reasonable direction. Therefore, we propose the *automated evaluation of scientific writing* shared task.

2 Language Quality in Scientific Discourse

In this section, we define the concept of *language quality* and provide examples of previous work that has evaluated scientific writing.

2.1 Definition

While writers may have proficiency in English, they may still struggle to be effective writers in the genre of scientific writing. The concept of '*quality*' in scientific discourse is ill-defined. For instance, a student in a seventh-grade science classroom asked a question '*Maestro, what is quality?*' during an experiment engaging students to address two questions: "*What is the quality of air in my community?*" and "*What is the quality of water in our river?*" (Moje et al., 2001). The student was asking, "*What do you mean when you talk about quality?*" As a result of this question, Maestro Tomas spent a class period working on what it meant to refer to quality, especially in science, and how scientists determined *quality*. In the most explicit discussion, Maestro Tomas told the students that *quality* differs depending on one's purpose, one's background, and one's position (e.g., as a scientist, an activist, an industrialist, a community member).

We find that the concept of *academic language* and the concept of *the language of academic writing* are different at a conceptual level. Krashen and Brown (2007) discuss the concept of academic language proficiency. They argue that academic language proficiency consists of the knowledge of academic language and specialized subject matter. The *academic language* concept can be described as a proper use of discipline-specific and academic vocabulary to express topic and discourse structure.

2.2 Previous work: Scientific Writing Evaluation

Natural language software requirements are the communication medium between users and software developers. Ormandjieva et al. (2007) addressed a problem of writing evaluation of natural language software requirements, and applied a text classification technique for automatic detection of ambiguities in natural language requirements. Sentences were classified as "ambiguous" or "unambiguous", in terms of surface understanding. Fabbrini et al. (2001) present a tool called QuARS (Quality Analyzer of Requirements Specification) for the analysis of textual software requirements. The Quality Model aims at providing a quantitative, corrective and repeatable evaluation of software requirement documents. Berrocal Rojas and Sliesarieva (2010) examine the automated detection of language issues affecting accuracy, ambiguity and verifiability in natural language software requirements. Lexical analysis, syntactic analysis, WordNet (Miller et al., 1993) and VerbNet (Schuler, 2005) were used for the automated quality evaluation. Burchardt et al. (2015) provided practical guidelines for the use of the Multidimensional Quality Metrics (MQM) framework for assessing translation quality in scientific research projects. MQM provide detailed

[1]See: http://en.wikipedia.org/wiki/Globish_(Nerriere)

The boundary problem for $V(t,x)$ is of the form

$$(\partial_t + L - r)V(t,x) = 0, \quad x > h, t < T; \tag{1}$$

$$V(t,x) = 0, \quad x \le h, t \le T; \tag{2}$$

$$V(T,x) = G(x), \quad x > h. \tag{3}$$

Boyarchenko and Levendorskiĭ (BLbook; BLAAP02) derived the generalization of the Black–Scholes equation 1 under a weak regularity condition: the process (t, X_t) in 2D satisfies the (ACP) condition (for the definition, see e.g. (Sa)). Note that the (ACP) condition is satisfied if the process X has a transition density. Equation 1 is understood in the sense of the theory of generalized functions: for any infinitely smooth function u with compact support $\operatorname{supp} u \subset (-\infty, T) \times (h, +\infty)$,

$$(V, (-\partial_t + \tilde{L} - r)u)_{L_2} = 0, \tag{4}$$

where $\tilde{L}$ is the infinitesimal generator of the dual process.

Figure 1: A short example of common academic text writing (from (Kudryavtsev and Levendorskiĭ, 2009)).

The boundary problem for _MATH_ is of the form _MATHDISP_. Boyarchenko and Levendorskii _CITE_ derived the generalization of the Black–Scholes equation (_REF_) under a weak regularity condition: the process _MATH_ in 2D satisfies the (ACP) condition (for the definition, see e.g. _CITE_). Note that the (ACP) condition is satisfied if the process _MATH_ has a transition density. Equation (_REF_) is understood in the sense of the theory of generalized functions: for any infinitely smooth function _MATH_ with compact support _MATH_, _MATHDISP_, where _MATH_ is the infinitesimal generator of the dual process.

Figure 2: The transformation of the text in Fig 1 using named entities.

insights about translation issues/errors on different levels of granularity up to the word or phrase level as input for systematic approaches to overcome translation quality barriers. MQM framework does not provide a translation quality metric, but rather provides a framework for defining task-specific translation metrics. MQM describes three typical layers of annotation in MT development:

- the phenomenological level (target errors/issues);
- the linguistic level (source or target POS, phrases, etc.);
- the explanatory level (source/system-related causes for certain errors).

A wide range of translation quality evaluation aspects show that the field is growing, and more efforts needed to solve many issues of translation quality evaluation.

3 The Language of Scientific Texts

Some elements of scientific writing that are distinct from other genres of writing, include, but are not limited to the following:

- Formal notations, e.g. $f(x) = \cos(x)$.
- Extensive mathematical expressions which can be independent sentences or a continuation of a preceding sentence, see example in Fig 1.
- Discipline-specific terminology.
- Citations.
- Section headers.
- References to other elements of a paper, which are of logical relation only. The scientific writing is highly multidimensional compared to linear daily language.
- Lists and enumerations.
- Bibliography elements.

Domain	The Number of Paragraphs	The Number of Edits
Physics	41,188	164,813
Mathematics	32,981	79,019
Engineering	14,968	43,551
Statistics	12,115	35,988
Computer Science	7,028	16,013
Astrophysics	4,278	15,594
Business and Management	3,454	8,262
Psychology	2,604	6,189
Finance	2,241	6,016
Economics	185	314
Total	**121,042**	**375,759**

Table 1: Main characteristics of the training dataset.

- Figures are also used as the continuation of sentences, though not so frequently.
- Hypertext references.

4 The Task Objectives and Definition

The objectives of the AESW Shared Task are to promote the use of NLP tools to help ELL writers the quality of their scientific writing.

In the scope of the task, the main goals are:

- to identify sentence-level features that are unique to scientific writing;
- to provide a common ground for development and comparison of sentence-level automated writing evaluation systems for scientific writing;
- to establish the state-of-the-art performance in the field.

Some interesting uses of sentence-level quality evaluations are the following:

- automated writing evaluation of submitted scientific articles;
- authoring tools in writing English scientific texts;
- filtering out sentences that need quality improvement.

The task will examine automated evaluation of scientific writing at the sentence-level by using the output of the professionally edited scientific texts, which are text extracts before and after editing (by native English speakers).

The goal of the task is to predict whether a given sentence needs for any kind of editing to improve it. The task is a binary classification task. Two cases of decisions are examined: binary decision (False or True) and probabilistic estimation (between 0 and 1).

5 Data

5.1 The Editing Process

This section describes the role of the professional language editors who completed the data editing described in Section 5.3. *Language editors* are defined as individuals who perform *proofreading* (see Smith (2003)). There are no standards that define language quality. The language editors use best practices, for instance (see Society for Editors and Proofreaders (2015)).

Language editors edited selected papers as part of publishing service. Each edited paper has two versions: text *before* and *after* editing. Language editors do their best to improve writing quality within the limited time span. In this data set, however, there was no double-annotation for quality control. We estimate that approximately 20% of the data may still contain errors, and also that there may be errors in the editors edits.

5.2 Tex2TXT

We use the open-source tool `tex2txt`[2] for the conversion from LaTeX to text, which was developed

[2]See: http://textmining.lt:8080/tex2txt.htm

```
<par pid="9" domain="Physics">
    <edits>
        <edit originalParOffset="7" editedParOffset="7" type="replaced">
            <original>ultimately</original>
            <edited>finally</edited>
        </edit>
    </edits>
    <sentence type="original" sid="9.0">Let us ultimately insist on the fact that the expression in the right hand side _MATH_
                                        is a function of _MATH_ due to the action of the shift and is therefore a different
                                        function than _MATH_. </sentence>
    <sentence type="edited" sid="9.1">Let us finally insist on the fact that the expression in the right hand side _MATH_
                                        is a function of _MATH_ due to the action of the shift and is therefore a different
                                        function than _MATH_. </sentence>
    <sentence type="nonedited" sid="9.2">Only the expectations of both expressions of Eq. (_REF_) are equal.</sentence>
</par>
```

Figure 3: Training data example of the paragraph annotation with data before language editing, after language editing, and the difference.

```
<par pid="9" domain="Physics">
    <sentence sid="9.0">Let us ultimately insist on the fact that the expression in the right hand side _MATH_ is a func-
                        tion of _MATH_ due to the action of the shift and is therefore a different function than _MATH_.
                        </sentence>
    <sentence sid="9.1">Only the expectations of both expressions of Eq. (_REF_) are equal.</sentence>
</par>
```

Figure 4: A sample from the test data.

specifically for this task. The tool is stand-alone and does not require any other LaTeX processing tools or packages. The primary goal was to extract the correct textual information.

5.3 The Data Set

The data set is the collection of text extracts from more than 4,000 published journal articles (mainly from physics and mathematics) *before* and *after* language editing. The data were edited by professional editors (per above) who were native English speakers[3]. Editing includes grammar error corrections, text cleaning, rephrasing, spelling correction, stylistics, and sentence structure corrections. Each extract is a paragraph which contains at least one edit done by language editor. All paragraphs in the dataset were randomly ordered for the source text anonymization purpose. The distribution of paragraphs and edits are presented in Table 1.

Sentences were tokenized automatically, and then both versions – texts *before* and *after* editing – automatically aligned with a modified `diff` algorithm. Each sentence is annotated as either '*original*', or '*edited*', or '*nonedited*'. *Non-edited* sentences contained no errors. The *original text* – the text before language editing – can be restored simply by deleting sentences that are annotated as 'edited'. Also, the *edited text* can be restored simply by deleting sentences that are annotated as 'original'.

The training data: The training data will be at least 121,000 paragraphs with 375,000 edits. The number of edited sentences will be at least 235,000, and the number of original sentences will be at least 234,000. There will be 335,000 sentences that were non-edited. These numbers show that 41% of all sentences were edited. See

[3] VTeX provides LaTeX-based publishing solutions and data services to the scientific community and science publishers. Publishers often request language editing services for papers accepted for publication. The data of our proposed shared task are based on selected papers published in 2006–2009 by Springer publishing company and edited at VTeX by professional language editors.

Figure 3 for an example of annotated training data.

The training data will include annotations to show differences between the 'original' and 'edited' texts. The 'edits' data are used for a quick reference to what the changes are.

The development data: An additional 5,000 paragraphs similar to test data will be provided. The development data set will be comprised of a set of articles that are independent from articles used for compiling the training and test sets. The development data will be distributionally similar to training data and test data with regard to edited and non-edited sentences, and domain.

The test data: An additional 5,000 paragraphs will be provided for testing the registered systems of the AESW Shared Task. The test data set will be comprised of a set of articles that are independent from articles used for compiling the training and development sets. Test paragraphs will retain 'original' and 'nonedited' versions only. The 'edited' sentence version will be removed. The test data anotation will be similar to training and development data. However, no data about edits and sentence class will be provided until submission of system results. See an example in Figure 4.

Shared Task participating teams will be allowed to use external data that are publicly available. Teams will not be able to use proprietary data. Use of external data should be specified in the final system report.

6 The Task and Evaluation

The task is to predict the class of a test sentence: 'original' or 'edited'. In Section 2, we saw that both Boolean and probabilistic prediction are used for various tasks. Therefore, there will be **two tracks of the task**:

Boolean Decision: The prediction of whether a test sentence is edited (TRUE), or before editing and corrections are needed (FALSE).

Probabilistic Estimation: The probability estimation of whether a test sentence is edited ($P = 0$), or before editing and corrections are needed ($P = 1$).

Participating teams will be allowed to submit up to two system results for each track. In total, a maximum of four system results will be accepted. All participating teams are encouraged to participate in both tracks.

The primary goal of the task is to predict 'original' sentences with poor writing quality. Each registered system will be evaluated with a *Detection score*, which is described below.

6.1 Detection score

The score will be an F-score of 'original' class prediction. The score will be computed for both tracks individually. For the Boolean decision track, a gold standard sentence G_i is considered detected if there is an alignment in the set that contains G_i. We calculate *Precision* (*P*) as the proportion of the sentences that were 'original' in the gold standard:

$$P_{bool} = \frac{\#\, Sentence_{detected}}{\#\, Sentence_{spurious} + \#\, Sentence_{detected}}.$$

Similarly, *Recall* (*R*) will be calculated as:

$$R_{bool} = \frac{\#\, Sentence_{detected}}{\#\, Sentence_{gold}}.$$

The *detection score* is the harmonic mean (F-score):

$$DetectionScore_{bool} = 2 \cdot \frac{P_{bool} \cdot R_{bool}}{P_{bool} + R_{bool}}.$$

For the probabilistic estimation track, the Mean squared error (MSE) will be used. A gold standard sentence G_i is assigned to 1 if it is 'original', and to 0 if it is 'nonedited'. A gold standard sentence G_i is considered detected if there is correlation in the set that contains G_i. We calculate *Precision* as the MSE of the sentences E_i that were estimated as 'original', i.e., their estimated probability is above 0.5:

$$P_{prob} = 1 - \frac{1}{n}\sum_{i=1}^{n}(E_{i,\,>0.5} - G_i)^2.$$

The higher the P_{prob} the better the system is. Similarly, we calculate *Recall* as the MSE of the sentences G_i that were 'original' in the gold standard:

$$R_{prob} = 1 - \frac{1}{n}\sum_{i=1}^{n}(E_i - G_{i,original})^2.$$

ID	Type	G_{bool}	G_{prob}	**Boolean Decision Track**			**Probabilistic Estimation Track**		
				TEAM1	**TEAM2**	**TEAM3**	**TEAM1**	**TEAM2**	**TEAM3**
1	original	F	1	F	T	F	0.7	0	1
2	original	F	1	F	T	F	0.8	0	1
3	nonedited	T	0	T	T	F	0.1	0	1
4	nonedited	T	0	F	T	F	0.6	0	1
5	nonedited	T	0	T	T	F	0.2	0	1
6	nonedited	T	0	T	T	F	0.4	0	1
7	original	F	1	F	T	F	0.9	0	1
8	nonedited	T	0	T	T	F	0.1	0	1
9	nonedited	T	0	T	T	F	0.4	0	1
P				**0.75**	**0**	**0.33**	**0.875**	**0**	**0.33**
R				**0.67**	**0**	**1**	**0.953**	**0**	**1**
DetectionScore				**0.71**	**0**	**0.5**	**0.912**	**0**	**0.5**

Table 2: $DetectionScore$ calculation example.

The harmonic mean $DetectionScore_{prob}$ is calculated similarly as $DetectionScore_{bool}$. The higher the $DetectionScore_{prob}$ the better the system is. An example of score calculation is shown in Table 2.

7 Report submission

The authors of participant systems are expected to submit a shared task paper describing their system. The task papers should be 4-8 pages long and contain a detailed description of the system and any further insights.

Acknowledgments

We would like to thank the Springer publishing company for permission to publish a large number of text extracts from published scientific papers. We appreciate the support and help in improving writing quality and organization of this paper from Building Educational Applications (BEA) workshop organisers. And special thanks to Joel Tetreault for the discussions and valuable suggestions. This work has been partially supported by EU Structural Funds administrated by the Lithuanian Business Support Agency (Project No. VP2-1.3-UM-02-K-04-019).

References

Allan Berrocal Rojas and Gabriela Barrantes Sliesarieva. 2010. Automated detection of language issues affecting accuracy, ambiguity and verifiability in software requirements written in natural language. In *Proceedings of the NAACL HLT 2010 Young Investigators Workshop on Computational Approaches to Languages of the Americas*, pages 100–108, Los Angeles, CA.

Aljoscha Burchardt, Kim Harris, Alan K. Melby, and Hans Uszkoreit, 2015. *Multidimensional Quality Metrics (MQM) Definition*. Version 0.3.0 (2015-01-20), http://www.qt21.eu/mqm-definition/definition-2015-01-20.html.

Daniel Dahlmeier, Hwee Tou Ng, and Siew Mei Wu. 2013. Building a large annotated corpus of learner English: The NUS Corpus of Learner English. In *Proceedings of the Eighth Workshop on Innovative Use of NLP for Building Educational Applications*, pages 22–31, Atlanta, GA, June.

Robert Dale and Adam Kilgarriff. 2011. Helping Our Own: The HOO 2011 Pilot Shared Task. In *Proceedings of the Generation Challenges Session at the 13th European Workshop on Natural Language Generation*, pages 242–249, Nancy, France.

Robert Dale, Ilya Anisimoff, and George Narroway. 2012. HOO 2012: A report on the Preposition and Determiner Error Correction Shared Task. In *Proceedings of the Seventh Workshop on Building Educational Applications Using NLP*, pages 54–62, Montréal, Canada.

Vidas Daudaravicius. 2014. Language editing dataset of academic texts. In *Proceedings of the Ninth International Conference on Language Resources and Evaluation (LREC'14)*, Reykjavik, Iceland. European Language Resources Association (ELRA).

F. Fabbrini, M. Fusani, S. Gnesi, and G. Lami. 2001. An automatic quality evaluation for natural language requirements. In *Proceedings of the Seventh International Workshop on RE: Foundation for Software Quality (REFSQ2001)*, pages 4–5.

Stephen Krashen and Clara Lee Brown. 2007. What is academic language proficiency? *STETS Language & Communication Review*, 6(1):252–262.

Oleg Kudryavtsev and Sergei Levendorskiĭ. 2009. Fast and accurate pricing of barrier options under Lévy processes. *Finance and Stochastics*, 13(4):531–562.

Claudia Leacock, Martin Chodorow, Michael Gamon, and Joel Tetreault. 2010. *Automated Grammatical Error Detection for Language Learners*. Morgan and Claypool.

G. Miller, R. Beckwith, C. Fellbaum, D. Gross, and K. Miller. 1993. Introduction to WordNet: An online lexical database. Technical report.

Elizabeth B. Moje, Tehani Collazo, Rosario Carrillo, and Ronald W. Marx. 2001. "Maestro, what is 'quality'?": Language, literacy, and discourse in project-based science. *Journal of Research in Science Teaching*, 38(4):469–498.

Hwee Tou Ng, Siew Mei Wu, Yuanbin Wu, Christian Hadiwinoto, and Joel Tetreault. 2013. The CoNLL-2013 Shared Task on Grammatical Error Correction. In *Proceedings of the Seventeenth Conference on Computational Natural Language Learning: Shared Task*, pages 1–12, Sofia, Bulgaria.

Hwee Tou Ng, Siew Mei Wu, Ted Briscoe, Christian Hadiwinoto, Raymond Hendy Susanto, and Christopher Bryant. 2014. The CoNLL-2014 Shared Task on Grammatical Error Correction. In *Proceedings of the Eighteenth Conference on Computational Natural Language Learning: Shared Task*, pages 1–14, Baltimore, MD, USA.

Olga Ormandjieva, Ishrar Hussain, and Leila Kosseim. 2007. Toward a text classification system for the quality assessment of software requirements written in natural language. In *Fourth International Workshop on Software Quality Assurance: In Conjunction with the 6th ESEC/FSE Joint Meeting*, SOQUA '07, pages 39–45, New York, NY, USA. ACM.

Karin Kipper Schuler. 2005. *Verbnet: A Broad-coverage, Comprehensive Verb Lexicon*. Ph.D. thesis, Philadelphia, PA, USA.

B. Smith. 2003. *Proofreading, Revising & Editing Skills Success in 20 Minutes a Day*. Learning Express Library. Learning Express.

Society for Editors and Proofreaders, 2015. *Ensuring editorial excellence: The SfEP code of practice*. http://www.sfep.org.uk/pub/bestprac/cop5.asp.

Dmitry N. Tychinin and Alexander A. Kamnev. 2013. Scientific Globish versus scientific English. *Trends in Microbiology*, 21(10):504–505.

Helen Yannakoudakis, Ted Briscoe, and Ben Medlock. 2011. A new dataset and method for automatically grading ESOL texts. In *Proceedings of the 49th Annual Meeting of the Association for Computational Linguistics: Human Language Technologies*, pages 180–189, Portland, OR, USA.

Scoring Persuasive Essays Using Opinions and their Targets

Noura Farra
Columbia University
New York, NY 10027
noura@cs.columbia.edu

Swapna Somasundaran
Educational Testing Service
660 Rosedale Road
Princeton, NJ 08540
ssomasundaran@ets.org

Jill Burstein
Educational Testing Service
660 Rosedale Road
Princeton, NJ 08540
jburstein@ets.org

Abstract

In this work, we investigate whether the analysis of opinion expressions can help in scoring persuasive essays. For this, we develop systems that predict holistic essay scores based on features extracted from opinion expressions, topical elements, and their combinations. Experiments on test taker essays show that essay scores produced using opinion features are indeed correlated with human scores. Moreover, we find that combining opinions with their targets (what the opinions are about) produces the best result when compared to using only opinions or only topics.

1 Introduction

In a persuasive essay, test takers are asked to take a stance on a given topic and to write an essay supporting their stance. Consider for example the following essay question, also known as the prompt:

"A teacher's ability to relate well with students is more important than excellent knowledge of the subject being taught."

Test takers have to write an essay describing whether they agree or disagree with the given prompt, using language expressing clear opinions. The scores for these essays are typically influenced by many factors, such as grammar, spelling errors, style and word usage, as well as the persuasiveness component: how well does the writer argue in favor of that writer's position on the subject? In this work, we try to tackle this last aspect, by studying how the expression of opinions influences the scores of expert human graders.

A number of essay scoring systems which rely on Natural Language Processing methods have been developed for automatically scoring persuasive essays, most notably (Page, 1966; Foltz et al., 1999; Burstein, 2003; Rudner and Liang, 2002; Attali and Burstein, 2006). The principal features for automatic essay-scoring have traditionally been based on grammar, usage, mechanics, and style, and have additionally included content-based features such as discourse and topic, as in Attali and Burstein (2006). These kind of features have been shown to have very strong performance in scoring holistic essay scores, and are very highly correlated with expert human scores (Bridgeman et al., 2012). However, in spite of their powerful predictive capability, these automated scoring systems have been criticized for limited coverage of the construct (Deane, 2013; Ben-Simon and Bennett, 2007; Williamson et al., 2012).

Our work addresses this concern by developing features specific to the persuasive construct. Incorporating knowledge of the persuasiveness factor into essay-scoring models can allow us to add features directly related to the scoring construct and to the writing task, which typically asks test takers to state and defend their opinion. Additionally, our linguistically motivated features encode intuitions which could allow for interpretable, useful and explicit feedback to students, test takers and educators regarding the persuasive aspect of the essays.

We build simple essay scoring systems which incorporate persuasiveness by engineering features based on the analysis of opinions expressed in the

Proceedings of the Tenth Workshop on Innovative Use of NLP for Building Educational Applications, 2015, pages 64–74,
Denver, Colorado, June 4, 2015.

essay and whether these opinions are being expressed about relevant topics. Specifically, the developed systems are based on simple features capturing (1) Opinion expressions, (2) Topics, and (3) Opinion-Target pairs which combine opinions with what they are about. We consider different methods for finding opinion-target pairs, and extract features which assess if the opinions in the essay are indeed relevant to the persuasion, and if the stance taken in the essay is consistently maintained. We find that our system predictions are indeed correlated with human scores, and the system using opinion-target information is the best.

The rest of the paper is organized as follows. Section 2 describes related work. In Section 3 we describe how we find opinions, topics and opinion-targets in essays, and Section 4 describes the features used accordingly to build the persuasive essay scoring systems. Section 5 describes our experiments, Section 6 presents analysis, and we conclude in Section 7.

2 Related Work

Automated essay scorers rely on a number of features based on grammar, usage, and content. Notable systems are Project Essay Grader (Page, 1966) which grades essays based on fluency and grammar; IEA (Foltz et al., 1999) which uses both content and mechanics-based features and relies on LSA word vector representations; e-rater (Burstein, 2003; Attali and Burstein, 2006) which combines syntactic, discourse, and topical components; and the Bayesian Essay Test Scoring System (Rudner and Liang, 2002). For a comprehensive description of these automatic essay scoring systems, the reader is referred to Dikli's survey (Dikli, 2006). Recently, there have been attempts to incorporate more non-traditional features for essay scoring; such as Beigman Klebanov and Flor (2013) who examined the relationship between the quality of essay writing and the use of word associations, and accordingly built a system to improve the prediction of holistic essay scores; and Somasundaran et al. (2014) who predicted discourse coherence quality of persuasive essays using lexical chaining techniques.

There has also been work on the study of argumentation in essays. Stab and Gurevych (2014a) propose an annotation scheme and a corpus for annotating different components of arguments and argumentative relations in persuasive essays. In addition, Stab and Gurevych (2014b) propose models for automatically recognizing arguing components in persuasive essays, and identifying whether the arguing components reflect support or non-support. Madnani et al. (2012) proposed a system for distinguishing the "shell" organizational elements of arguing expressions from actual argumentative content. Beigman Klebanov et al. (2013a) identify sentence-level sentiment in persuasive essays by considering the sentiment of multi-word expressions. In our work, we have used lexicons for identifying opinion expressions; however, our methods can be augmented by using such systems.

Opinion analysis has been applied to a number of natural language processing tasks and domains, such as sentiment in movie reviews (Turney, 2002; Pang and Lee, 2004), product reviews (Hu and Liu, 2004; Liu et al., 2005), social media (Go et al., 2009; Agarwal et al., 2011; Bollen et al., 2011), news, blogs, and political and online debates (Mullen and Malouf, 2006; Godbole et al., 2007; Somasundaran and Wiebe, 2009). The use of opinion and sentiment information to predict holistic essay scores, however, has remained unstudied.

Targets of sentiment have been studied in the form of finding features in product reviews (Qiu et al., 2011; Liu et al., 2014) and for classifying online debates (Somasundaran and Wiebe, 2010). The recent 2014 SemEval Task on aspect-based sentiment analysis (Pontiki et al., 2014) was concerned with identifying targets of sentiment in reviews of restaurants and laptops. Jiang et al. (2011) and (Dong et al., 2014) have explored target-dependent classification of sentiment in Twitter. In our work, we take a simple approach to finding targets of opinion expressions, since our focus is on determining whether opinion analysis is useful for persuasive essay scoring, even when using approximate opinion-targets.

3 Opinions and Topics in Persuasive Essays

Intuitively, well-written persuasive essays will clearly state the opinion of the writer and build support for their stance by evoking ideas and concepts that are relevant for the argument. Thus, we investigate the role of opinions, topics, and their interactions in determining overall persuasive essay scores.

3.1 Opinion Expressions

We consider two distinct types of opinions important for persuasion: Sentiment and Arguing. Much work has been done on defining these two types of opinions (Wilson, 2008; Ruppenhofer et al., 2008). We focus on sentiment and arguing because we expect these types of expressions to be common in essays which require persuasion.

Sentiment Expressions Sentiment expressions reveal a writer's judgments, evaluations and feelings, and are likely to be employed to express a preference for a particular position, or to point out the shortcomings of an alternative position. In the following sentence, we see the sentiment expression in bold, and the target in brackets. The writer has a positive evaluation ("learning the most") of teachers' encouragement.

Example 1
At school, I always ***learned the most*** *from [teachers who encouraged me].*

Arguing Expressions Arguing expressions reveal the writer's beliefs and strong convictions, and is seen in the form of reasoning, justification, strong assertions, emphasis, and use of imperatives, necessities and conditionals (Wilson, 2008; Ruppenhofer et al., 2008). In the following sentence, we see the arguing expression in bold, and the target in brackets. Here, the writer clearly emphasizes the position taken with respect to the topic.

Example 2
For these reasons, I claim with confidence *that [excellent knowledge of the subject being taught is secondary to the teacher's ability to relate well with their students].*

We expect that persuasive essays where test takers clearly state their opinions will get better scores than the ones that do not.

3.2 Topical Elements

We define topical elements as words or concepts that are relevant to the topic of the essay, and which usually get invoked in the process of stance-taking. They essentially correspond to "common topics" that test takers are expected to write about when presented with a prompt. For example, given the prompt in Section 1, while words which appear in the prompt (*prompt words*), such as 'teacher', 'student', 'subject', and 'knowledge' are naturally expected, we also expect general topical words such as 'class' and 'school' to occur in response essays. Intuitively, we would expect essays containing sufficient topical elements to get higher scores.

3.3 Opinion Relevancy and Consistency

We expect that well-written persuasive essays will not only express opinions and evoke common topics, but in fact *express opinions about relevant topical elements*. Specifically, we hypothesize that the opinions should be about artifacts relevant to the theme of the essay, and not about irrelevant topics. For example, for the prompt described in Section 1, it is important that there be opinions expressed about topics such as teachers, school, learning, and so on. In addition, the essay also has to reflect a clear attempt at persuasion and stance-taking in relevance to the prompt statement and the underlying theme. We call this *opinion relevancy*.

We also expect that once a stance is taken, there should be sufficient elaboration and development such that the stance is consistently maintained. We hypothesize that essays where test takers support their stance will achieve higher scores than essays where they vacillate between options (for instance, in the example prompt in Section 1, the test taker is unable to decide whether the teachers' ability to relate well is more important or not). We call this *opinion consistency*.

These expectations are more stringent than those discussed in Sections 3.1 and 3.2, and we expect that a scoring system which captures these requirements will likely perform better.

4 Essay Scoring Systems

In order to test the intuitions described in Section 3, we build essay scoring systems based on features extracted from opinions, topics, and opinion-target pairs. We construct three separate systems:

1. **Opinion** This system uses features based on

opinion expressions only, and tests whether expressing opinions influences the essay score.

2. **Topic** This system uses features based on topical expressions alone, and tests whether evoking relevant topics associated with the prompt influences the essay score.

3. **Opinion-Target** This system uses features based on the combination of opinions and their targets, with the goal of measuring opinion relevancy and consistency. This system tests how well the essay score can be predicted based on the interactions of opinions with their targets.

4.1 Opinion System

4.1.1 Finding sentiment and arguing expressions

In order to find sentiment expressions in the essays, we used a combination of two lexicons: the MPQA subjectivity lexicon (Wilson et al., 2005) (Lexicon 1), and the sentiment lexicon developed by Beigman Klebanov et al. (2013b) (Lexicon 2). Each of these lexicons provides for each word, a sentiment polarity (positive, negative, or neutral), along with an indicator of sentiment intensity: strongly or weakly subjective (Lexicon 1) or a probability distribution over the polarity (Lexicon 2). For Lexicon 2, the sentiment polarity for a word is obtained by choosing the polarity corresponding to the highest probability score.

For identifying arguing expressions in the essays, we used an Arguing lexicon developed as part of a discourse lexicon (Burstein et al., 1998). The original lexicon has annotations for different types of expressions, including claim initializations and development, structure, rhetoric, among others. For this work, since we are concerned with arguing expressions that specifically reveal support for or against an idea, we used only lexicon entries which label an expression as *arguing-for* or *arguing-against*. For instance, in Example 2, the writer argues *for* teachers' ability to relate well with their students.

4.1.2 Features

We extract three (global) features based on opinion expressions:

1. The total count of sentiment words in the essay that are found in Lexicon 1 and Lexicon 2 respectively. These counts also include words with subjective neutral polarity.

2. The total count of words in the essay found in the arguing lexicon.

4.2 Topic System

4.2.1 Finding topical elements

In order to determine topical elements, we compute topic signatures (Lin and Hovy, 2000) over each prompt. Topic Signatures are defined as

$$TS = \{topic, signature\}$$

$$= \{prompt, < (t_1, w_1), (t_2, w_2) ... (t_n, w_n) >\}$$

where topic in our case is the prompt. The signature comprises a vector of related terms, where each term t_i is highly correlated with the prompt with an association weight w_i.

For each prompt, we use a corpus of high-scoring essays (that was separate from our training and testing data) to find its topic signature[1]. The top 500 words with the highest signature scores are considered as topical elements for that prompt.

For a given essay, we annotate all prompt words and topic signature words. Note that our topical elements consist entirely of unigrams, but this need not necessarily be the general case (as seen in examples 1 and 2); extending the scope of topical elements to multi-word concepts is a direction for future work.

4.2.2 Features

Based on the prompt words and topical words we extract the following features:

1. The total count of topical words in the essay

2. The total count of actual prompt words

We distinguished between prompt words and topical words as the former measures whether the essay is clearly responding to the prompt, while the latter measures if thematic elements are indeed present in the essay and its arguments.

[1] We used the topic signatures code provided at http://homepages.inf.ed.ac.uk/alouis/topicS.html

4.3 Opinion-Target System

The opinion-target system relies on the extraction of features based on the opinion-target pairs found in the essay. The first step towards building this system is the identification of opinion-target pairs, after which we construct features which measure opinion relevancy and consistency. We investigated simple heuristic-based approaches for finding targets of opinions, described below.

4.3.1 Finding sentiment-target pairs

We explored three methods for finding targets of sentiment expressions. Our simplest approach, ***all-sentence***, finds all sentiment expressions in the sentence and assumes that all words are targets of each expression. This method introduces some noise as it results in some words becoming targets of multiple opinions with possibly conflicting polarities.

Our second approach, ***resolve-sentence***, resolves the sentiment at the sentence-level to a single polarity, as in (Somasundaran and Wiebe, 2010), and then assumes that all nouns, verbs, and adjectives in the sentence are targets. If we consider Example 1, suppose the sentiment of the sentence is resolved to positive, (due to the positive opinion words **learned**, **most**, and **encouraged**) then the words *school*, *teachers*, *learned* and *encouraged* would be considered as the targets. Ideally, we would like only the words *teachers* and *encouraged* to be targets. We note here that in our task a target can actually be a sentiment-containing word such as *encouraged*, which is why we don't disregard sentiment words when finding targets.

Our third method, ***resolve-constituent***, resolves sentiment at the syntactic constituent level instead of the sentence level, and assumes that all nouns, verbs and adjectives in the constituent phrase are targets. For obtaining the phrases, we used the regular expression parser from the Python NLTK toolkit (Bird, 2006) to define a custom grammar that describes noun, verb, and prepositional phrases. The parser uses regular expression rules for grouping words together based on their part of speech tags. Considering our example with this scenario, the phrases *"at school"*, *"I always"*, and *"learned the most from..."* will be considered separately in our grammar, so the word *school* will likely not end up as a target.

To resolve sentence-level or constituent-level polarity, we use a heuristic that aggregates polarity scores from both sentiment lexicons, and chooses the final polarity corresponding to the word with the maximum sentiment intensity.

While these methods are not exact and may lead to over-generating targets, for the purposes of this work (which is to determine whether a basic opinion system is effective in predicting essay scores), we are more interested in high recall of targets then high precision because they will be aggregated at the essay level.

4.3.2 Finding arguing-target pairs

For resolving arguing-target pairs, we use the ***all-sentence*** method. Resolving the dominant arguing polarity at the sentence level would be less straightforward than for sentiment, given that the argument lexicon does not provide us with scores for arguing intensity. Moreover, arguing targets are generally longer (Ruppenhofer et al., 2008); we would expect their spans to extend beyond constituent phrases. Finally, we observed that sentences generally do not contain multiple arguing expressions, thus alleviating the problem of spurious combinations.

4.3.3 Features

The features for the opinion-target system are based on measuring relevancy and consistency of opinions.

Relevancy Relevancy is measured by taking into account how many opinions (or proportion of opinions) are about prompt or topical elements. These include global engineered features as follows:

1. The number of times that topical elements (topic and prompt words) appear as a target in the essay's opinion-target pairs.

2. The ratio of topic targets (opinion-topic pairs) to all opinion-target pairs.

We distinguished between topic targets and prompt targets and also between sentiments which included subjective neutral versus only positive or negative sentiments. We had separate features for sentiment-target pairs and arguing-target pairs, resulting in 13 relevancy features.

Consistency Consistency is measured by determining how often the writer switches opinion polarity when referring to the same target. The consistency features included the following:

1. A binary feature indicating the presence of a reversal ('flip') of opinion towards any target.

2. The number of unique targets which get flipped.

3. The proportion of all flips where the target is a topical element.

4. The proportion of all topical elements which get flipped.

5. Statistics including max, mean, and median number of flips over all targets.

We also separated sentiment-target and arguing-target features, as well as prompt word targets and topic word targets, resulting in a total of 17 consistency features. We note that these features can only capture an approximate picture of consistency, because it is well-known (Aull and Lancaster, 2014) that mature writers tend to state and describe opposing arguments as well as their own.

5 Experiments

5.1 Data

The data used for this study consists of 58K essays, covering 19 different prompts, obtained from the TOEFL® (Test of English as a Foreign Language) persuasive writing task which pertains to essays written by undergraduate and graduate school applicants who are non-native English speakers. All essays are *holistically* scored by experts on an integer scale 0-5, with score point 5 assigned to excellent essays. Detailed studies of human-human agreement for this dataset can be found in Bridgeman et al. (2012). The holistic scores are assigned to essays based on English proficiency, and account for the quality of (and errors in) grammar, language use, mechanics, style, in addition to quality of the persuasive task. The scores for these essays are thus influenced by a number of factors other than the quality of persuasion (essays can get a low score if they use incorrect grammar, even if they make good persuasive arguments). However, we would like to test the extent to which our hypothesis holds when predicting such holistically graded essays.

We split this dataset randomly into a training and test set with proportions of 80% (46,404 essays) and 20% (11,603 essays) respectively. Table 1 shows the score distribution of essays for different score points, in the training and test set respectively. We note that the distribution of scores is unbalanced, with essays having scores 3, 4, and 2 occupying the majority in that order.

5.2 Setup

We modeled the system with a number of different regression learners, which have generally been shown to do well on the essay scoring task. We used a number of learners available from the Python Scikit-learn toolkit (Pedregosa et al., 2011) and the Scikit-learn-Laboratory (Blanchard et al., 2013): the Logistic Regression classifier (**LO**), which uses 6-way classification to predict integer essay scores in the range 0-5, the Linear Regression learner (**LR**), which predicts real-valued scores that are rounded to integers, and the Rescaled Linear Regression learner (**RR**), which rescales the predicted scores based on the training data distribution. Given an input essay, the learners predict essay scores in the range 0-5, based on the features described in Section 4.

We considered a number of evaluation metrics to test for the predictive ability of opinion, topic, and opinion-target information in scoring the essays. We tested if our proposed systems' score predictions are correlated with human scores, by computing the human score correlation *(HSC)* using Pearson's coefficient. As essay length is highly correlated with the human score (Attali and Burstein, 2006; Chodorow and Burstein, 2004), and as many of our features are based on counts, they can be influenced by essay length; so we also compute the partial correlations *(HSC-Part)* accounting for length, by partialing out the length of the essay in words. For measuring the performance of the system, we report Accuracy, F-measure – where we computed the weighted f-score (*F-w*) over the six score points – and Quadratic Weighted Kappa (QWK) (Cohen, 1968), which is the standard metric for essay scoring. Accuracy and F-measure are standard NLP metrics and provide a direct, interpretable measure of system performance which reflects the precision and recall of different

	Train		Test	
Score	**# Essays**	**Distribution(%)**	**# Essays**	**Distribution(%)**
0	278	0.6	65	0.6
1	1,177	2.5	304	2.6
2	6,812	14.7	1,668	14.4
3	27,073	58.3	6,714	57.9
4	8,902	19.2	2,305	19.9
5	2,162	4.7	546	4.7
Total	46,404	100	11,602	100

Table 1: Score distribution of essays in our dataset

score points. QWK corrects for chance agreement between the system prediction and the human prediction, and it also takes into account the extent of the disagreement between labels.

We compared all systems to a baseline *Length*, that predicts an essay score based solely on the length of the essay in words. Due to the strong correlation between length and essay scores, we consider this to be a strong (albeit simple) baseline. Another simple baseline was *Majority*, which always predicts the majority class (score point 3).

5.3 Results

We evaluate each of the Opinion, Topic, and Opinion-Target systems separately, to determine the effect of each and to test the hypotheses described in Section 3.

For the Opinion-Target system, we found that both the *resolve-sentence* and *resolve-constituent* methods (Section 4.3.1) consistently and significantly outperformed the *all-sentence* approach. The difference between *resolve-sentence* and *resolve-constituent* was not statistically significant. Thus we report results for the *resolve-sentence* approach, which had the best performance.

Table 2 shows the results of the correlation experiments for each system and for each of the three learners. We find that predictions based on opinions and topics are positively correlated with human scores. Furthermore, combining opinions with their targets produced the best correlation for all learners, with the Linear Regression predictor achieving the best result (0.53). This result supports our hypothesis that the relevancy and consistency of opinions is more informative than simply measuring whether opinions are expressed or topics are invoked. Our results are particularly promising when considering the fact that the features only capture the persuasivenes component of the holistic score. As noted previously, the holistic score of this English proficiency test depends on a number of factors such as grammar, language usage, mechanics and style: effective persuasion is but one aspect of the score.

When partialing out the effect of length, we find that the partial correlation scores drop, but it is still strong for the Opinion-Target system (0.21 for LR). This drop is unsurprising, as human scores are influenced by the length of the essay, and so are the count-based features. We also note that the correlation results differ between the linear regression predictors (LR and RR) and the LO classifier. This is also expected because LR and RR report the correlation of real numbers while LO reports the correlation of an integer classification.

Next, Table 3 reports the performance for all systems in terms of Accuracy, F-measure, and QWK. For each system and for each metric, we present the results from all learners. For each learner, the results comparing the opinion-target system with the baselines are all statistically significant ($p < 0.0001$); we computed significance for each of the three metrics using the bootstrap sampling method described in (Berg-Kirkpatrick et al., 2012) with a subset size of $n = 11,000$ and $b = 10^4$ subset samples.

When considering the Linear Regression and Logistic Regression classifiers, we observe that the Opinion-Target system significantly outperforms the majority baseline and our other systems across all metrics. On the other hand, when using the Rescaled Regression predictor, the Opinion-Target system is

	LR		RR		LO	
System	**HSC**	**HSC-*Part***	**HSC**	**HSC-*Part***	**HSC**	**HSC-*Part***
Opinion	0.29	0.10	0.28	0.10	0.33	0.07
Topic	0.29	0.081	0.30	0.086	0.33	0.15
Opinion-Target	**0.53**	**0.21**	**0.53**	**0.21**	**0.39**	**0.16**

Table 2: Correlation of System Predictions with Human Scores. The best system correlation is shown in **bold**.

outperformed by the majority baseline (for Accuracy) and the length baseline (for F-measure and QWK). The best QWK score of 0.553 is obtained by the length predictor using the Rescaled Linear Regression predictor, followed by the Opinion-Target system which gets a QWK score of 0.496. We suspect that the rescaling of the training data by the RR learner significantly alters the scores. We note for example that when using the LR predictor, all the predictions of the Length system fall in the range (3,3.5), and hence get rounded to score 3; thus it always predicts the majority class (3) and essentially functions as a majority predictor. This explains why it has a QWK of 0 and an F-measure equal to the majority baseline. On the other hand, when the data is rescaled to match the training data, the Length system predictions are stretched to match the distribution of scores observed in the training data, and the percentage of score 3 predictions drops to 56% of predictions, while the percentage of score 4 predictions jumps to 20%, and the recall of all other score points increases. This makes sense when considering that length predictions are highly correlated with human scores, and thus its linear regression predictions will be correlated with the human score irrespective of the training data distribution. On the other hand, the Opinion-Target system is able to produce more predictions across different score labels even when the test data is not rescaled.

6 Feature Analysis

To explore the impact of the different opinion-target features on essay scores, we tested the performance of individual features in predicting scores for our test set. We evaluated the features based on both accuracy and QWK. Table 4 shows the results, where we show the top 15 features ranked in order of QWK.

We observe that the best feature is the frequency of topic-relevant sentiment-target pairs, counting only positive and negative words (as opposed to neutral lexicon words). This indicates that expressing sentiment clearly in favor of or against the topical words is important for persuasion in this data.

We notice that most of the top-scoring features are sentiment rather than arguing features. This may be because our sentiment-target pairing system was more concise and precise than the arguing-target system. Additionally, our arguing features include strong modal words such as 'must', 'clearly' and 'obviously'. Previous research has shown that while writers with intermediate proficiency use such terms, they are used less often by the most proficient writers (Vázquez Orta and Giner, 2009; Aull and Lancaster, 2014). Thus it is possible that these features would not be found in essays with very high scores, whose writers would likely employ more subtle and sophisticated forms of argumentation.

We also observed that count-based features tend to perform better than their ratio-based counterparts, except in the case of the prompt word adherence feature (10), where the ratio feature actually outperforms the frequency feature (12). It is likely that the length effect is at play here. However, the fact that significant correlations exist, even after accounting for length (as seen in Table 2), indicates that these features are capturing meaningful information.

7 Conclusions

In this work, we investigated features for improving the persuasive construct coverage of automated scoring systems. Specifically, we explored the impact of using opinion and topic information for scoring persuasive essays. We hypothesized that essays with high scores will show evidence of clear and consistent stance-taking towards relevant topics. We built systems using features based on opinions, topics, and opinion-target pairs, and performed experiments with holistically scored data using different learners.

Our results are encouraging. We found that, in spite of the fact that the persuasive component is

	LR			RR			LO		
System	**Acc%**	**F-*w*%**	**QWK**	**Acc%**	**F-*w*%**	**QWK**	**Acc%**	**F-*w*%**	**QWK**
Majority	57.87	42.43	---	**57.87**	42.43	---	57.87	42.43	---
Length	57.87	42.43	0	53.88	**54.11**	**[0.553]**	58.39	44.53	0.141
Opinion	57.85	43.84	0.032	41.33	42.47	0.275	58.38	44.71	0.169
Topic	58.39	43.83	0.0013	40.75	42.00	0.284	58.39	43.83	0.168
Opinion-Target	**59.44**	**[54.20]**	**0.38**	50.31	50.87	0.496	**[59.58]**	**47.35**	**0.249**

Table 3: Performance of different systems measured by accuracy, weighted F-score, and QWK. The best system for each learner is in **bold**. The best overall system for each metric is bracketed. For each learner, the results comparing the different systems are statistically significant ($p < 0.0001$).

Feature Name	**Desc**	**QWK**	**Acc %**
(1) Freq of pos and neg sentiment-topic pairs	Rel	**0.418**	33.3
(2) Freq of all sentiment-topic pairs	Rel	0.411	32.1
(3) Freq of arguing-topic pairs	Rel	0.273	25.7
(4) Mean # of sentiment flips	Con	0.205	**37.3**
(5) Unique # of sentiment flips	Con	0.204	19.2
(6) Ratio of sentiment-topic flips to all topic words	Con	0.202	19.7
(7) Ratio of pos and neg sentiment-topic pairs to all sentiment-target pairs	Rel	0.197	22.9
(8) Freq of all sentiment-prompt pairs	Rel	0.185	21.8
(9) Median # of sentiment flips	Con	0.178	21.6
(10) Ratio of pos and neg sentiment-prompt pairs to all sentiment-target pairs	Rel	0.165	23.5
(11) Max # of sentiment flips	Con	0.162	19.8
(12) Freq of pos and neg sentiment-prompt pairs	Rel	0.160	24.4
(13) Freq of arguing-prompt pairs	Rel	0.159	20.9
(14) Flip presence	Con	0.155	21.2
(15) Ratio of sentiment-topic flips to all sentiment-target flips	Con	0.150	20.7

Table 4: Feature Analysis. A feature is described as 'Rel' if it assesses relevancy and 'Con' if it assesses consistency. Sentiment-topic, Arguing-topic, Sentiment-prompt, and Arguing-prompt refer to the opinion-target pairs where the target is a topic word or prompt word respectively. Ratios are all measured with respect to total number of sentiment-target pairs or arguing-target pairs, except for feature (6) where the ratio is measured against all topic words. This experiment was performed using the Logistic Regression (LO) classifier.

one of many factors influencing the holistic score, our system's predictions were positively correlated with the essay scores. Moreover, combining opinions with their targets, and assessing their relevancy and consistency, resulted in a higher correlation than using only topics or only opinions. We also found that, for most learners, the opinion-target predictor performs better than a system which predicts essay scores based on the length of the essay.

Our initial feature analysis shows that opinion-target features seem to reasonably reflect the importance of persuasion information found in the essays, and that the co-occurrence of polar sentiment words with topic targets is particularly important.

Having demonstrated the viability of the approach using simple methods, our next step is to explore more precise ways of finding opinion-target pairs and topical elements, including resolving negations and co-references, exploring syntactic dependencies, as well as targets spanning multiple words. We also plan to validate our experiments with data from different writing exams. Future work will also involve exploring ways to combine our features with those of other automated scoring systems – such as grammar, usage and mechanics – in order to obtain more robust holistic scoring.

Acknowledgments

We would like to thank all the reviewers for their valuable feedback and comments.

References

Apoorv Agarwal, Boyi Xie, Ilia Vovsha, Owen Rambow, and Rebecca Passonneau. 2011. Sentiment analysis of twitter data. In *Proceedings of the Workshop on Languages in Social Media*, pages 30–38. Association for Computational Linguistics.

Yigal Attali and Jill Burstein. 2006. Automated essay scoring with e-rater® v. 2. *The Journal of Technology, Learning and Assessment*, 4(3).

Laura L Aull and Zak Lancaster. 2014. Linguistic markers of stance in early and advanced academic writing a corpus-based comparison. *Written Communication*, 31(2):151–183.

Beata Beigman Klebanov and Michael Flor. 2013. Word association profiles and their use for automated scoring of essays. In *ACL (1)*, pages 1148–1158.

Beata Beigman Klebanov, Jill Burstein, and Nitin Madnani. 2013a. Sentiment profiles of multiword expressions in test-taker essays: The case of noun-noun compounds. *ACM Transactions on Speech and Language Processing (TSLP)*, 10(3):12.

Beata Beigman Klebanov, Nitin Madnani, and Jill Burstein. 2013b. Using pivot-based paraphrasing and sentiment profiles to improve a subjectivity lexicon for essay data. *TACL*, 1:99–110.

Anat Ben-Simon and Randy Elliot Bennett. 2007. Toward more substantively meaningful automated essay scoring. *The Journal of Technology, Learning and Assessment*, 6(1).

Taylor Berg-Kirkpatrick, David Burkett, and Dan Klein. 2012. An empirical investigation of statistical significance in nlp. In *Proceedings of the 2012 Joint Conference on Empirical Methods in Natural Language Processing and Computational Natural Language Learning*, pages 995–1005. Association for Computational Linguistics.

Steven Bird. 2006. Nltk: the natural language toolkit. In *Proceedings of the COLING/ACL on Interactive presentation sessions*, pages 69–72. Association for Computational Linguistics.

Daniel Blanchard, Michael Heilman, and Nitin Madnani. 2013. Scikit-learn laboratory.

Johan Bollen, Huina Mao, and Alberto Pepe. 2011. Modeling public mood and emotion: Twitter sentiment and socio-economic phenomena. In *ICWSM*.

Brent Bridgeman, Catherine Trapani, and Yigal Attali. 2012. Comparison of human and machine scoring of essays: Differences by gender, ethnicity, and country. *Applied Measurement in Education*, 25(1):27–40.

Jill Burstein, Karen Kukich, Susanne Wolff, Ji Lu, and Martin Chodorow. 1998. Enriching automated essay scoring using discourse marking. In *Workshop on Discourse Relations and Discourse Marking*. ERIC Clearinghouse.

Jill Burstein. 2003. The e-rater® scoring engine: Automated essay scoring with natural language processing.

Martin Chodorow and Jill Burstein. 2004. Beyond essay length: Evaluating e-rater®'s performance on toefl® essays. *ETS Research Report Series*, 2004(1):i–38.

Jacob Cohen. 1968. Weighted kappa: Nominal scale agreement provision for scaled disagreement or partial credit. *Psychological bulletin*, 70(4):213.

Paul Deane. 2013. On the relation between automated essay scoring and modern views of the writing construct. *Assessing Writing*, 18(1):7–24.

Semire Dikli. 2006. An overview of automated scoring of essays. *The Journal of Technology, Learning and Assessment*, 5(1).

Li Dong, Furu Wei, Chuanqi Tan, Duyu Tang, Ming Zhou, and Ke Xu. 2014. Adaptive recursive neural network for target-dependent twitter sentiment classification. In *Proceedings of the 52nd Annual Meeting of the Association for Computational Linguistics*, pages 49–54.

Peter W Foltz, Darrell Laham, and Thomas K Landauer. 1999. The intelligent essay assessor: Applications to educational technology. *Interactive Multimedia Electronic Journal of Computer-Enhanced Learning*, 1(2).

Alec Go, Richa Bhayani, and Lei Huang. 2009. Twitter sentiment classification using distant supervision. *CS224N Project Report, Stanford*, pages 1–12.

Namrata Godbole, Manja Srinivasaiah, and Steven Skiena. 2007. Large-scale sentiment analysis for news and blogs. *ICWSM*, 7.

Minqing Hu and Bing Liu. 2004. Mining and summarizing customer reviews. In *Proceedings of the tenth ACM SIGKDD international conference on Knowledge discovery and data mining*, pages 168–177. ACM.

Long Jiang, Mo Yu, Ming Zhou, Xiaohua Liu, and Tiejun Zhao. 2011. Target-dependent twitter sentiment classification. In *Proceedings of the 49th Annual Meeting of the Association for Computational Linguistics: Human Language Technologies-Volume 1*, pages 151–160. Association for Computational Linguistics.

Chin-Yew Lin and Eduard Hovy. 2000. The automated acquisition of topic signatures for text summarization. In *Proceedings of the 18th conference on Computational linguistics-Volume 1*, pages 495–501. Association for Computational Linguistics.

Bing Liu, Minqing Hu, and Junsheng Cheng. 2005. Opinion observer: analyzing and comparing opinions on the web. In *Proceedings of the 14th international conference on World Wide Web*, pages 342–351. ACM.

Kang Liu, Liheng Xu, and Jun Zhao. 2014. Extracting opinion targets and opinion words from online reviews with graph co-ranking.

Nitin Madnani, Michael Heilman, Joel Tetreault, and Martin Chodorow. 2012. Identifying high-level organizational elements in argumentative discourse. In *Proceedings of the 2012 Conference of the North American Chapter of the Association for Computational Linguistics: Human Language Technologies*, pages 20–28. Association for Computational Linguistics.

Tony Mullen and Robert Malouf. 2006. A preliminary investigation into sentiment analysis of informal political discourse. In *AAAI Spring Symposium: Computational Approaches to Analyzing Weblogs*, pages 159–162.

Ellis B Page. 1966. The imminence of... grading essays by computer. *Phi Delta Kappan*, pages 238–243.

Bo Pang and Lillian Lee. 2004. A sentimental education: Sentiment analysis using subjectivity summarization based on minimum cuts. In *Proceedings of the 42nd annual meeting on Association for Computational Linguistics*, page 271. Association for Computational Linguistics.

Fabian Pedregosa, Gaël Varoquaux, Alexandre Gramfort, Vincent Michel, Bertrand Thirion, Olivier Grisel, Mathieu Blondel, Peter Prettenhofer, Ron Weiss, Vincent Dubourg, et al. 2011. Scikit-learn: Machine learning in python. *The Journal of Machine Learning Research*, 12:2825–2830.

Maria Pontiki, Haris Papageorgiou, Dimitrios Galanis, Ion Androutsopoulos, John Pavlopoulos, and Suresh Manandhar. 2014. Semeval-2014 task 4: Aspect based sentiment analysis. In *Proceedings of the 8th International Workshop on Semantic Evaluation (SemEval 2014)*, pages 27–35.

Guang Qiu, Bing Liu, Jiajun Bu, and Chun Chen. 2011. Opinion word expansion and target extraction through double propagation. *Computational linguistics*, 37(1):9–27.

Lawrence M Rudner and Tahung Liang. 2002. Automated essay scoring using bayes' theorem. *The Journal of Technology, Learning and Assessment*, 1(2).

Josef Ruppenhofer, Swapna Somasundaran, and Janyce Wiebe. 2008. Finding the sources and targets of subjective expressions. In *LREC*.

Swapna Somasundaran and Janyce Wiebe. 2009. Recognizing stances in online debates. In *Proceedings of the Joint Conference of the 47th Annual Meeting of the ACL and the 4th International Joint Conference on Natural Language Processing of the AFNLP: Volume 1-Volume 1*, pages 226–234. Association for Computational Linguistics.

Swapna Somasundaran and Janyce Wiebe. 2010. Recognizing stances in ideological on-line debates. In *Proceedings of the NAACL HLT 2010 Workshop on Computational Approaches to Analysis and Generation of Emotion in Text*, pages 116–124. Association for Computational Linguistics.

Swapna Somasundaran, Jill Burstein, and Martin Chodorow. 2014. Lexical chaining for measuring discourse coherence quality in test-taker essays.

Christian Stab and Iryna Gurevych. 2014a. Annotating argument components and relations in persuasive essays. In *Proceedings of the 25th International Conference on Computational Linguistics (COLING 2014)*, pages 1501–1510.

Christian Stab and Iryna Gurevych. 2014b. Identifying argumentative discourse structures in persuasive essays.

Peter D Turney. 2002. Thumbs up or thumbs down?: semantic orientation applied to unsupervised classification of reviews. In *Proceedings of the 40th annual meeting on association for computational linguistics*, pages 417–424. Association for Computational Linguistics.

Ignacio Vázquez Orta and Diana Giner. 2009. Writing with conviction: The use of boosters in modelling persuasion in academic discourses.

David M Williamson, Xiaoming Xi, and F Jay Breyer. 2012. A framework for evaluation and use of automated scoring. *Educational Measurement: Issues and Practice*, 31(1):2–13.

Theresa Wilson, Janyce Wiebe, and Paul Hoffmann. 2005. Recognizing contextual polarity in phrase-level sentiment analysis. In *Proceedings of the conference on human language technology and empirical methods in natural language processing*, pages 347–354. Association for Computational Linguistics.

Theresa Ann Wilson. 2008. *Fine-grained subjectivity and sentiment analysis: recognizing the intensity, polarity, and attitudes of private states*. ProQuest.

Towards Automatic Description of Knowledge Components

Cyril Goutte
National Research Council
1200 Montreal Rd.
Ottawa, ON K1A0R6
Cyril.Goutte@nrc.ca

Guillaume Durand
National Research Council
100 des Aboiteaux St.
Moncton, NB E1A7R1
Guillaume.Durand@nrc.ca

Serge Léger
National Research Council
100 des Aboiteaux St.
Moncton, NB E1A7R1
Serge.Leger@nrc.ca

Abstract

A key aspect of cognitive diagnostic models is the specification of the Q-matrix associating the items and some underlying student attributes. In many data-driven approaches, test items are mapped to the underlying, latent knowledge components (KC) based on observed student performance, and with little or no input from human experts. As a result, these latent skills typically focus on modeling the data accurately, but may be hard to describe and interpret. In this paper, we focus on the problem of describing these knowledge components. Using a simple probabilistic model, we extract, from the text of the test items, some keywords that are most relevant to each KC. On a small dataset from the PSLC datashop, we show that this is surprisingly effective, retrieving unknown skill labels in close to 50% of cases. We also show that our method clearly outperforms typical baselines in specificity and diversity.

1 Introduction

Recent years have seen significant advances in automatically identifying latent attributes useful for cognitive diagnostic assessment. For example, the Q-matrix (Tatsuoka, 1983) associates test items with skills of students taking the test. Data-driven methods were introduced to automatically identify latent *knowledge components* (KCs) and map them to test items, based on observed student performance, cf. Barnes (2005) and Section 2 below.

A crucial issue with these automatic methods is that latent skills optimize some well defined objective function, but may be hard to describe and interpret. Even for manually-designed Q-matrices, knowledge components may not be described in detail by the designer. In that situation, a data-generated description can provide useful information. In this short paper, we show how to extract keywords relevant to each KC, from the textual content corresponding to each item. We build a simple probabilistic model, with which we score possible keywords. This proves surprisingly effective on a small dataset obtained from the PSLC datashop.

After a quick overview of the automatic extraction of latent attributes in Section 2, we describe our keyword extraction procedure in Section 3. The data is introduced in Section 4, and we present our experimental results and analysis in Section 5.

2 Extraction of Knowledge Component Models

The Rule Space model (Tatsuoka, 1983; Tatsuoka, 1995) was introduced to statistically classify student's item responses into a set of ideal response patterns associated with different cognitive skills. A major assumption of Rule Space is that students only need to master specific skills in order to successfully complete items. Using the Rule Space model for cognitive diagnostics assessment requires experts to build and reduce an incidence or Q matrix encoding the combination of skills, a.k.a. attributes, needed for completing items (Birenbaum et al., 1992) and generating ideal item responses based on the reduced Q matrix (Gierl et al., 2000). The ideal response patterns can then be used to analyze student response patterns.

Proceedings of the Tenth Workshop on Innovative Use of NLP for Building Educational Applications, 2015, pages 75–80,
Denver, Colorado, June 4, 2015.

The requirement for extensive expert effort in the traditional Q matrix design has motivated attempts to discover the Q matrix from observed response patterns, in effect reverse engineering the design process. Barnes (2005) proposed a multi-start hill-climbing method to create the Q-matrix, but experimented only on limited number of skills. Desmarais et al. (2011; 2014) refined expert Q matrices using matrix factorization, Although this proved useful to automatically improve expert designed Q-matrices, non-negative matrix factorization is sensitive to initialization and prone to local minima. Sun et al. (2014) generated binary Q-matrices using an alternate recursive method that automatically estimates the number of latent attributes, yielding high matrix coverage rates. Others (Liu et al., 2012; Chen et al., 2014) estimate the Q-matrix under the setting of well known psychometric models that integrate guess and slip parameters to model the variation between ideal and observed response patterns. They formulate Q-matrix extraction as a latent variable selection problem solved by regularized maximum likelihood, but require to know the number of latent attributes. Finally, Sparse Factor Analysis (Lan et al., 2014) was recently introduced to address data sparsity in a flexible probabilistic model. They require setting the number of attributes and rely on user-generated tags to facilitate the interpretability of estimated factors.

These approaches to the automatic extraction of a Q-matrix address the problem from various angles and an extensive comparison of their respective performance is still required. However, none of these techniques address the problem of providing a textual description of the discovered attributes. This makes them hard to interpret and understand, and may limit their practical usability.

3 Probabilistic Keyword Extraction

We focus on the textual content associated with each item in order to identify the salient terms as keywords. Textual content associated with an item may be for example the body of the question, optional hints or the text contained in the answers (Figure 1).

For each item i, we denote by d_i its textual content (e.g. body text in Figure 1). We also assume a binary mapping of items to K skills c_k, $k = 1 \dots K$. Skills are typically latent skills obtained automatically (unsupervised) from data. They may also be defined by a manually designed Q-matrix for which skill descriptions are unknown. In analogy with text categorization, textual content is a document d_i and each skill is a class (or cluster) c_k. Our goal is to identify keywords from the documents that describe the classes.

For each KC c_k, we estimate a unigram language model based on all text d_i associated with that KC. This is essentially building a Naive Bayes classifier (McCallum and Nigam, 1998), estimating relative word frequencies in each KC:

$$P(w|c_k) = \frac{\sum_{i,d_i \in c_k} n_{wi}}{\sum_{i,d_i \in c_k} |d_i|}, \ \forall k \in \{1 \dots K\}, \quad (1)$$

where n_{wi} is the number of occurrences of word w in document d_i, and $|d_i|$ is the length (in words) of document $|d_i|$. In some models such as Naive Bayes, it is essential to smooth the probability estimates (1) appropriately. However more advanced multinomial mixture models (Gaussier et al., 2002), or for the purpose of this paper, smoothing has little impact. Conditional probability estimates (1) may be seen as the profile of c_k. Important words to describe a KC $c \in \{c_1, \dots c_K\}$ have significantly higher probability in c than in other KCs. One metric to evaluate how two distributions differ is the (symmetrized) Kullback-Leibler divergence:

$$KL(c, \not{c}) = \sum_w \underbrace{(P(w|c) - P(w|\not{c})) \log \frac{P(w|c)}{P(w|\not{c})}}_{k(w)}, \quad (2)$$

where $\not{c}$ means all KCs except c, and $P(w|\not{c})$ is estimated similarly to Eq. 1, $P(w|\not{c}) \propto \sum_{i,d_i \notin c} n_{wi}$.

Note that Eq. (2) is an additive sum of positive, word-specific contributions $k(w)$. Large contributions come from significant differences *either way* between the profile of a KC, $P(w|c)$, and the average profile of all other KCs, $P(w|\not{c})$. As we want to focus on keywords that have significantly *higher* probability for that KC, and diregard words that have higher probability *outside*, we will use a signed score:

$$s_c(w) = |P(w|c) - P(w|\not{c})| \log \frac{P(w|c)}{P(w|\not{c})}, \quad (3)$$

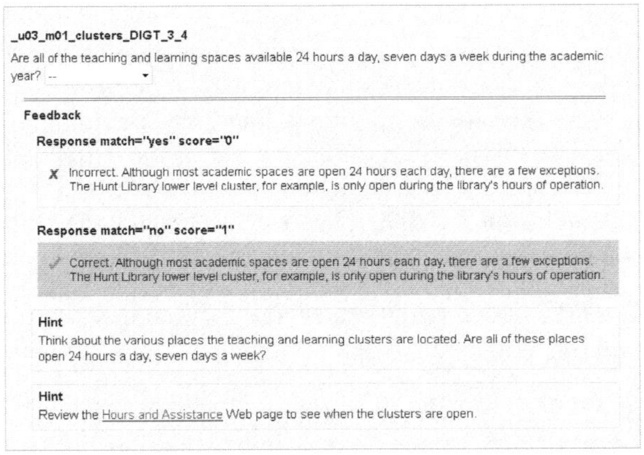

Figure 1: Test item body text, hints and responses.

	body	hint	response	Total
# tokens	31,132	11,505	41,207	83,844

Table 1: Dataset statistics, (# tokens).

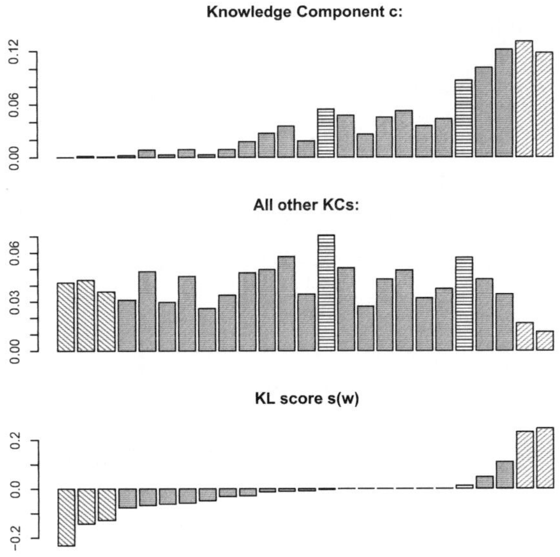

Figure 2: KL score illustration: KC profile (top), profile for all other KCs (middle) and scores (bottom).

where the log ensures that the score is positive if and only if $P(w|c) > P(w|\not{c})$.

Figure 2 illustrates this graphically. Some words (blue horizontal shading) have high probability in c (top) but also outside (middle), hence $s(w)$ close to zero (bottom): they are not specific enough. The most important keywords (green upward shading, right) are more frequent in c than outside, hence a large score. Some words (red downward shading, left) are less frequent in c than outside: they do contribute to the KL divergence, but are atypical in c. They receive a negative score.

4 Data

In order to test and illustrate our method, we focus on a dataset from the PSLC datashop (Koedinger et al., 2010). We used the *OLI C@CM v2.5 - Fall 2013, Mini 1*.[1] This OLI dataset tests proficiency with the CMU computing infrastructure. It is especially well suited for our study because the full text of the items (cf. Fig. 1) is available in HTML format and can be easily extracted. Other datasets only include screenshots of the item, making text extraction more challenging.

There are 912 unique steps in that dataset, and less than 84K tokens of text (Table 1), making it very small by NLP standards. We picked two KC models included in PSLC for that dataset. The **noSA** model has 108 distinct KCs with minimally descriptive labels (e.g. "vpn"), assigning between 1 and 52 items to each KC. The **C75** model is fully unsupervised and has the best BIC reported in PSLC. It contains 44 unique KCs simply labelled *Cxx*, with *xx* between -1 and 91. It assigns 5 to 78 items per KC. In both models there are 823 items with at least 1 KC assigned.

We use a standard text preprocessing chain. All text (body, hint and responses) in the dataset is tokenized and lowercased, and we remove all tokens appearing in an in-house stoplist, as well as tokens not containing at least one alphabetical character.

5 Experimental Results

From the preprocessed data, we estimate all KC profiles using Eq. (1), on different data sources:

1. Only the body of the question ("body"),
2. Body plus hints ("b+h"),
3. Body, hints and responses ("all").

For each KC, we extract the top 10 keywords according to $s_c(w)$ (Eq. 3).

[1] https://pslcdatashop.web.cmu.edu/DatasetInfo?datasetId=827

KC label	#items	Top 10 keywords
_identify-sr	52	phishing email scam social learned indicate legitimate engineering anti-phishing
_p2p	27	risks mitigate applications p2p protected law file-sharing copyright illegal
_print_quota03	12	quota printing andrew print semester consumed printouts longer unused cost
_vpn	11	vpn connect restricted libraries circumstances accessing need using university
_dmca	9	copyright dmca party notice student digital played regard brad policies
_penalties_dmca	2	penalties illegal possible file-sharing fines 80,000 $ imprisonment high years
_penalties_bandwidth	1	maximum limitations exceed times long bandwidth suspended network access

Table 2: Top 10 keywords extracted from the body only of a sample of knowledge components of various sizes.

We first illustrate this on the **noSA** KC model, for which we can use the minimally descriptive KC labels as partial reference. Table 2 shows the top keywords extracted from the body text for a sample of knowledge components. Even for knowledge components with very few items, the extracted keywords are clearly related to the topic suggested by the label.

Although the label itself is not available when estimating the model, words from the label often appear in the keywords (sometimes with slight morphological differences). Our first metric evaluates the quality of the extraction by the number of times words from the (unknown) label appear in the keywords. For the model in Table 2, this occurs in 44 KCs out of the 108 in the model (41%). These KCs are associated with 280 items (34%), suggesting that labels are more commonly found within keywords for small KCs. This may also be due to vague labels for large KCs (e.g. *identify*, *sr* in Table 2), although the overall keyword description is quite clear (*phishing*, *email*, *scam*).

We now focus on two ways to evaluate keyword quality: *diversity* (number of distinct keywords) and *specificity* (how many KC a keyword describes). Desirable keywords are specific to one or few KCs. A side effect is that there should be many different keywords. We therefore compute 1) how many distinct keywords there are overall, 2) how many keywords appear in a single KC, and 3) the maximum number of KCs sharing the same keyword. As a baseline, we compare against the simple strategy that consists in simply picking as keywords the tokens with maximum probability in the KC profile (1). This baseline is common practice when describing probabilistic topic models (Blei et al., 2003).

Table 3 compares KL score ("KL-*" rows) and maximum probability baseline ("MP-*" rows) for the two KC models. The total number of keywords is fairly stable as we extract up to 10 keywords per KC in all cases (some KCs have a single item and not enough text). The KL rows clearly show that our KL-based method generates many more *different* keywords than MP, implying that MP extracts the same keywords for many more KCs.

- With KL, we have up to 727 distinct keywords (out of 995) for **noSA** and 372 out of 440 for **C75**, i.e. an average 1.18 to 1.37 (median 1) KC per keyword. With MP the keywords describe on average 3.1 KC of **noSA**, and 2.97 of **C75**.
- With KL, as many as 577 (i.e. more than half) keywords appear in a single **noSA** KC. By contrast, only as few as 221 MP keywords have a unique KC. For **C75**, the numbers are 316 (72%) vs, 88 to 131.
- With KL, no keyword is used to describe more than 9 to 19 **noSA** KCs and 6 to 12 **C75** KCs. With MP, some keywords appear in as many as 87 **noSA** KCs and all 44 **C75** KCs. This shows that they are much less specific at describing the content of a KC.

These results all point to the fact that the KL-based method provides better *diversity* as well as *specificity* in naming the different KCs.

Source of textual content: Somewhat surprisingly, using less textual content, i.e. body only, consistently produces better diversity (more distinct keywords) and better specificity (fewer KC per keyword). The hint text yields little change and the response text seriously degrades both diversity and specificity, despite nearly doubling the amount of textual data available. This is because responses are

model		total	diff.	uniq.	max
noSA	KL-body	995	**727**	**577**	**9**
	KL-b+h	1005	722	558	10
	KL-all	1080	639	480	19
	MP-body	995	534	365	42
	MP-b+h	1005	521	340	34
	MP-all	1080	352	221	87
C75	KL-body	440	**372**	**316**	**6**
	KL-all	440	328	254	12
	MP-body	440	203	131	33
	MP-all	440	148	88	44
C75 (+sw)	KL-body	440	**377**	**325**	**4**
	KL-all	440	332	261	11
	MP-body	440	76	43	43
	MP-all	440	68	32	44

Table 3: Statistics on various keyword extraction methods. KL (Kullback-Leibler score) and MP (maximum probability) are tested on body only, body+hints (b+h) or all text. We report the total number of keywords extracted (Total), the number of different keywords (diff.), keywords with unique KC (unique) and maximum number of KC per keyword (max). "+sw" indicates stopwords are included (not filtered).

very similar across items. They add textual information but tend to smooth out profiles. This is shown in the comparison between "KL-body" and "MP-all" in Table 4. The latter extracts "correct" and "incorrect" as keywords for most KCs in both models, because these words frequently appear in the response feedback (Fig. 1). KL-based naming discards these words because they are almost equally frequent in all KCs and are not specific enough. Table 4 also shows that MP selects the same frequent words for both KC models. By contrast, the most used KL keywords for **noSA** are not so frequently used to describe **C75** KCs, suggeting that the descriptions are more specific to the models.

Impact of stopwords: The bottom panel of table 3 (indicated by "(+sw)") shows the impact of *not filtering* stopword on the keyword extraction metrics (i.e. keeping stopwords). For KL the impact is small: filtering out stopwords actually degrades performance slightly. The impact on MP is massive: there are up to three times less different keyword (76 vs. 203), and most are high-frequency function words ("to", "of", etc.). The extreme case is "the",

KL-body		
Keyword	#no	#C
use	9	1
following	8	1
access	7	-
andrew	7	2
account	7	-
search	7	2

MP-all		
Keyword	#no	#C
incorrect	87	44
correct	67	41
review	49	22
information	30	20
module	29	9
course	26	9

Table 4: Keywords associated with most KCs in **noSA**, with number of associated KC in **noSA** (#no) and **C75** (#C). Left: KL score on item body; Right: max. probability on all text.

extracted for *all* 44 KCs. Results on **noSA** are similar and not included for brievity.

6 Discussion

We described a simple probabilistic method for knowledge component naming using keywords. This simple method is effective at generating descriptive keywords that are both diverse and specific. We show that our method clearly outperforms the simple baseline that focuses on most probable words, with no impact on computational cost.

Although we only extract key *words* from the textual data, one straightforward improvement would be to identify and extract either multiword terms, which may be more explanatory, or relevant snippets from the data. A related perspective would be to combine our relevance scores with, for example, the output of a parser in order to extract more complicated linguistic structure such as subject-verb-object triples (Atapattu et al., 2014).

Our data-generated descriptions could also be useful in the generation or the refinement of Q-Matrices. In addition to describing knowledge components, naming KCs could offer significant information on the consistency of the KC mapping. This may offer a new and complementary approach to the existing refinement methods based on functional models optimization (Desmarais et al., 2014). It could also complement or replace human input in student model discovery and improvement (Stamper and Koedinger, 2011).

Acknowledgement

We used the 'OLI C@CM v2.5 - Fall 2013, Mini 1 (100 students)' dataset accessed via DataShop (Koedinger et al., 2010). We thank Alida Skogsholm from CMU for her help in choosing this dataset.

References

T. Atapattu, K. Falkner, and N. Falkner. 2014. Acquisition of triples of knowledge from lecture notes: A natural language processing approach. In *7th Intl. Conf. on Educational Data Mining*, pages 193–196.

T. Barnes. 2005. The Q-matrix method: Mining student response data for knowledge. In *AAAI Educational Data Mining workshop*, page 39.

M. Birenbaum, A. E. Kelly, and K. K. Tatsuoka. 1992. *Diagnosing Knowledge States in Algebra Using the Rule Space Model.* Educational Testing Service Princeton, NJ: ETS research report. Educational Testing Service.

David M. Blei, Andrew Y. Ng, and Michael I. Jordan. 2003. Latent dirichlet allocation. *Journal of Machine Learning Research*, 3(Jan):993–1022.

Y. Chen, J. Liu, G. Xu, and Z. Ying. 2014. Statistical analysis of Q-matrix based diagnostic classification models. *Journal of the American Statistical Association.*

M. Desmarais, B. Beheshti, and P. Xu. 2014. The refinement of a Q-matrix: Assessing methods to validate tasks to skills mapping. In *7th Intl. Conf. on Educational Data Mining*, pages 308–311.

M. Desmarais. 2011. Mapping questions items to skills with non-negative matrix factorization. *ACM-KDD-Explorations*, 13(2):30–36.

E. Gaussier, C. Goutte, K. Popat, and F. Chen. 2002. A hierarchical model for clustering and categorising documents. In *Advances in Information Retrieval*, pages 229–247. Springer Berlin Heidelberg.

M.J. Gierl, J. P. Leighton, and S. M. Hunka. 2000. Exploring the logic of Tatsuoka's rule-space model for test development and analysis. *Educational Measurement: Issues and Practice*, 19(3):34–44.

K.R. Koedinger, R.S.J.d. Baker, K. Cunningham, A. Skogsholm, B. Leber, and J. Stamper. 2010. A data repository for the EDM community: The pslc datashop. In C. Romero, S. Ventura, M. Pechenizkiy, and R.S.J.d. Baker, editors, *Handbook of Educational Data Mining*. CRC Press.

A.S. Lan, A.E. waters, C. Studer, and R.G. Baraniuk. 2014. Sparse factor analysis for learning and content analytics. *Journal of Machine Learning Research*, 15:1959–2008, June.

J. Liu, G. Xu, and Z. Ying. 2012. Data-driven learning of Q-matrix. *Applied Psychological Measurement*, 36(7):548–564.

A. McCallum and K. Nigam. 1998. A comparison of event models for naive Bayes text classification. In *AAAI-98 workshop on learning for text categorization*, pages 41–48.

J.C. Stamper and K.R. Koedinger. 2011. Human-machine student model discovery and improvement using DataShop. In *Artificial Intelligence in Education*, pages 353–360. Springer Berlin Heidelberg.

Y. Sun, S. Ye, S. Inoue, and Yi Sun. 2014. Alternating recursive method for Q-matrix learning. In *7th Intl. Conf. on Educational Data Mining*, pages 14–20.

K.K. Tatsuoka. 1983. Rule space: an approach for dealing with misconceptions based on item response theory. *Journal of Educational Measurement*, 20(4):345–354.

K.K. Tatsuoka. 1995. Architecture of knowledge structures and cognitive diagnosis: A statistical pattern recognition and classification approach. In P. D. Nichols, S. F. Chipman, and R. Brennan, editors, *Cognitively Diagnostic Assessment*, pages 327–359. Hillsdale, NJ: Lawrence Erlbaum Associates.

The Impact of Training Data on Automated Short Answer Scoring Performance*

Michael Heilman and **Nitin Madnani**
Educational Testing Service
Princeton, NJ, USA

Abstract

Automatic evaluation of written responses to content-focused assessment items (automated short answer scoring) is a challenging educational application of natural language processing. It is often addressed using supervised machine learning by estimating models to predict human scores from detailed linguistic features such as word n-grams. However, training data (i.e., human-scored responses) can be difficult to acquire. In this paper, we conduct experiments using scored responses to 44 prompts from 5 diverse datasets in order to better understand how training set size and other factors relate to system performance. We believe this will help future researchers and practitioners working on short answer scoring to answer practically important questions such as, "How much training data do I need?"

1 Introduction

Automated short answer scoring is a challenging educational application of natural language processing that has received considerable attention in recent years, including a SemEval shared task (Dzikovska et al., 2013), a public competition on the Kaggle data science website (`https://www.kaggle.com/c/asap-sas`), and various other research papers (Leacock and Chodorow, 2003; Nielsen et al., 2008; Mohler et al., 2011).

The goal of short answer scoring is to create a predictive model that can take as input a text response to a given prompt (e.g., a question about a reading passage) and produce a score representing the accuracy or correctness of that response. One well-known approach is to learn a prompt-specific model using detailed linguistic features such as word n-grams from a large training set of responses that have been previously scored by humans.[1]

This approach works very well when large sets of training data are available, such as in the ASAP 2 competition, where there were thousands of labeled responses per prompt. However, little work has been done to investigate the extent to which short answer scoring performance depends on the availability of large amounts of training data. This is important because short answer scoring is different from tasks where one dataset can be used to train models for a wide variety of inputs, such as syntactic parsing.[2] Current short answer scoring approaches depend on having training data for each new prompt.

Here, we investigate the effects on performance of training sample size and a few other factors, in order to help answer extremely practical questions like, "How much data should I gather and label before deploying automated scoring for a new prompt?" Specifically, we explore the following research questions:

- How strong is the association between training sample size and automated scoring performance?

*Michael Heilman is now a data scientist at Civis Analytics.

[1] Information from the scoring guidelines, such as exemplars for different score levels, can also be used in the scoring model, though in practice we have observed that this does not add much predictive power to a model that uses student responses (Sakaguchi et al., 2015).

[2] Syntactic parsing performance varies considerably depending on the domain, but most applications use parsing models that depend almost exclusively on the Penn Treebank.

Proceedings of the Tenth Workshop on Innovative Use of NLP for Building Educational Applications, 2015, pages 81–85,
Denver, Colorado, June 4, 2015.

- If the training set size is doubled, how much improvement in performance should we expect?
- Are there other factors such as the number of score levels that are strongly associated with performance?
- Can we create a model to predict scoring model performance from training sample size and other factors (and how confident would we be of its estimates)?

2 Short Answer Scoring System

In this section, we describe the basic short answer scoring system that we will use for our experiment. We believe that this system is broadly representative of the current state of the art in short answer scoring. Its performance is probably slightly lower than what one would find for a system highly tailored to a specific dataset. Although features derived from automatic syntactic or semantic parses might also result in small improvements, we did not include such features for simplicity.

The system uses support vector regression (Smola and Schölkopf, 2004) to estimate a model that predicts human scores from vectors of binary indicators for linguistic features. We use the implementation from the scikit-learn package (Pedregosa et al., 2011), with default parameters except for the complexity parameter, which is tuned using cross-validation on the data provided for training. For features, we include indicator features for the following:

- lowercased word unigrams
- lowercased word bigrams
- length bins (specifically, whether the log of 1 plus the number of characters in the response, rounded down to the nearest integer, equals x, for all possible x from the training set)

Note that word unigrams and bigrams include punctuation.

3 Datasets

We conducted experiments using responses to 44 prompts from five different datasets. The data for each of the 44 prompts was split into a training set and a testing set. Table 1 provides an overview of the datasets.

The **ASAP 2** dataset is from the 2012 public competition hosted on Kaggle (`https://www.kaggle.com/c/asap-sas`) and is publicly available.[3] The **Math** and **Reading 1** datasets were developed as part of the Educational Testing Service's "Cognitively Based Assessment of, for, and as Learning" research initiative (Bennett, 2010).[4] The **Reading 2** dataset was developed as part of the "Reading for Understanding" framework (Sabatini and O'Reilly, 2013). The **Science** dataset was developed and scored as part of the Knowledge Integration framework (Linn, 2006). Note that only the ASAP 2 dataset is publicly available.

For all prompts, there are at least 359 training examples (at most 2,633).

4 Experiments

For each prompt, we trained a model on the full training set for that prompt and evaluated on the testing set. In addition, we trained models from randomly selected subsamples of the training set and evaluated on the full testing set. Specifically, we created 20 replications of samples (without replacement) of sizes $2^n * 100$ (i.e., 100, 200, 400, ...) up to the full training sample size. We trained models on these subsamples and evaluated each on the full testing set.

Following the ASAP 2 competition (`https://www.kaggle.com/c/asap-sas/details/evaluation`), we evaluated models using quadratically weighted κ (Cohen, 1968).

For subsamples of the training data, we averaged the results across the 20 replications before further analyses. We used the Fisher Transformation $z(\kappa)$ when averaging because of its variance-stabilization properties. The same transformation was also used

[3] For the ASAP 2 dataset, we used the "public leaderboard" for the testing sets.

[4] The math data came from the 2012 multi-state administration of two multi-prompt tasks: Moving Sidewalks with 1 Rider (prompts 2a, 4a, 4b, 4d, 10b) and Moving Sidewalks with 2 Riders (prompts 3a, 3b, 6a, 6b, 10, 12). The reading data from the 2013 multi-state administration of the following prompts: Ban Ads 1-B, 1-C, 2-C; Cash for Grades 1-B, 1-C, 2; Social Networking 1-B, 1-C, 2; Culture Fair 3-1; Generous Gift 3-1; and Service Learning 3-1. Zhang and Deane (under review) describe the reading data in more detail.

Dataset	No. of Prompts	Score Range	Domain(s)	Task Type	Response Length
ASAP 2	10	0–2 or 0–3	Various (science, language arts, etc.)	Various (description of scientific principles, literary analysis, etc.)	27-66 words
Math	11	0–2	Middle school math	Explanation of how mathematical principles apply to given situations involving linear equations	9-16 words
Reading 1	12	0–3 or 0–4	Middle school reading	Summarization or development of arguments	51-79 words
Reading 2	4	0–3 or 0–4	Middle school reading	Summarization and analysis of reading passages	29-111 words
Science	7	1–5	Middle school science	Explanations and arguments embedded in inquiry science units that call for students to use evidence to link ideas	16-46 words

Table 1: Descriptions of the datasets. The **Response Length** column shows the range of average response lengths (in number of words) across all prompts in a dataset.

N	**mean**	**s.d.**	**med.**	**min.**	**max.**
100	.600	.095	.596	.343	.782
200	.649	.085	.638	.418	.810
400	.688	.085	.692	.473	.828
800	.730	.079	.742	.540	.851
1600	.747	.074	.761	.590	.863

Table 2: Descriptive statistics about performance in terms of averaged quadratically weighted κ for different training sample sizes (N), aggregated across all prompts. "med." = median, "s.d." = standard deviation

by the ASAP 2 competition as part of its official evaluation.

$$z(\kappa) = \frac{1}{2} \ln \frac{1+\kappa}{1-\kappa} \quad (1)$$

$$\kappa_{\text{average}} = z^{-1}\Big(\sum_{\text{prompt}} z(\kappa_{\text{prompt}}) \Big) \quad (2)$$

This gives us a dataset of averaged κ values for different combinations of prompts and sample sizes. Table 2 shows descriptive statistics.

For each data point, in addition to the κ value and prompt, we compute the following:

- `log2SampleSize`: $\log_2$ of the training sample size,

Variable	r
`log2SampleSize`	.550
`log2MinSampleSizePerScore`	.392
`meanLog2NumChar`	-.365
`numLevels`	.033

Table 3: Pearson's r correlations between training set characteristics and human-machine κ.

- `log2MinSampleSizePerScore`:$\log_2$ of the minimum number of examples for a score level (e.g., $\log_2(16)$ if the least frequent score level in the training sample had 16 examples),
- `meanLog2NumChar`: The mean, across training sample responses, of $\log_2$ of the number of characters (a measure of response length),
- `numLevels`: The number of score levels.

For each of these variables, we first compute Pearson's r to measure the association between κ and each variable. The results are shown in Table 3.

Not surprisingly, the variable most strongly associated with performance (i.e., κ) is the $\log_2$ of the number of responses used for training. However, having a large sample does not ensure high human-machine agreement: the correlation between κ and `log2SampleSize` was only $r = .550$. Performance varies considerably across prompts, as illus-

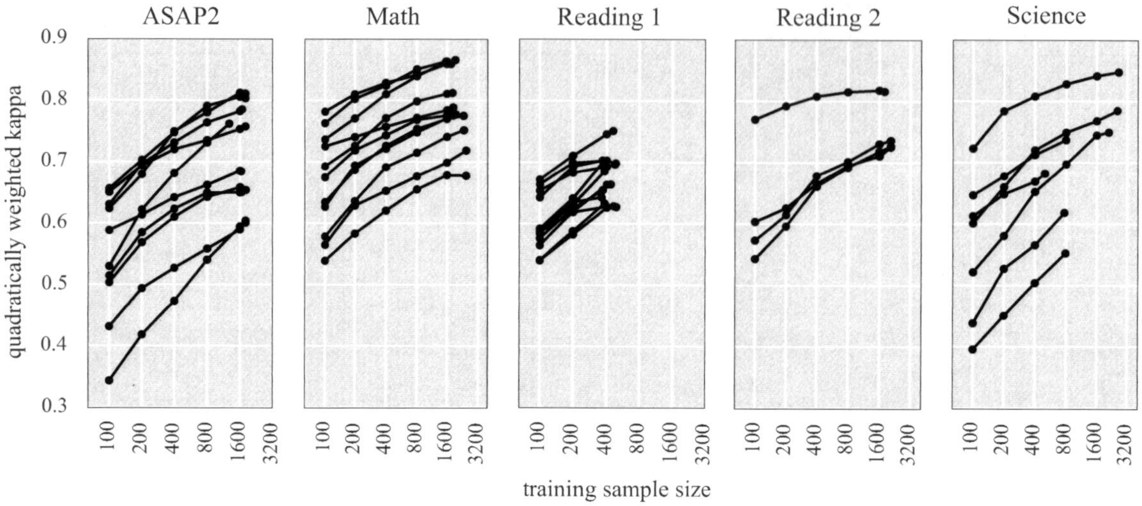

Figure 1: Plots of human-machine agreement versus sample size, for various prompts from different datasets.

trated in Figure 1.

Next, we tested whether we could predict human-machine agreement for different size training sets for new prompts. We used the dataset of κ values for different prompts and training set sizes described above (N = 224). We iteratively held out each dataset and used it as a test set to evaluate performance of a model trained on the remaining datasets. For the model, we used a simple ordinary least squares linear regression model, with the variables from Table 3 as features.[5] For labels, we used $z(\kappa)$ instead of κ, and then converted the models predictions back to κ values using the inverse of the z function (Eq. 1). We report two measures of correlation (Pearson's and Spearman's) and two measures of error (root mean squared error and mean absolute error). The results are shown in Table 4.

Dataset	**pearson**	**spearman**	**RMSE**	**MAE**
ASAP2	.650	.654	.080	.064
Math	.558	.523	.095	.076
Reading 1	.708	.617	.039	.031
Reading 2	.497	.467	.070	.063
Science	.438	.464	.173	.139

Table 4: Results for the predictive model of human-machine κ.

5 Discussion and Conclusion

In response to the research questions we posed earlier, we found that:

- The correlation between training sample size and human-machine agreement is strong, though performance varies considerably by prompt (Table 2 and Figure 1).
- If the training sample is doubled in size, then performance increases .02 to .05 in κ (Table 2). This rate of increase was fairly consistent across prompts. However, as with other supervised learning tasks, there will likely be a point where increasing the sample size does not yield large improvements.
- Variables such as the minimum number of examples per score level and the length of typical responses are also associated with performance (Table 3), though not as much as the overall sample size.
- A model for predicting human-machine agreement from training sample size and other factors could provide useful information to developers of automated scoring, though predictions from our simple model show considerable error (Table 4). More detailed features of prompts,

[5]We prefer to use a simpler linear model instead of a more complex hierarchical model for the sake of interpretability.

scoring rubrics, and student populations might lead to better predictions.

In this paper, we investigated the impact of training sample size on short answer scoring performance. Our results should help researchers and practitioners of automated scoring answer the highly practical question, "How much data do I need to get good performance?", for new short answer prompts. We conducted our experiments using a basic system with only n-gram and length features, though it is likely that the observed trends (e.g., the rate of increase in κ with more data) would be similar for many other systems. Future work could explore issues such as how much performance varies by task type or by the amount of linguistic variation in responses at particular score levels.

Acknowledgements

We would like to thank Randy Bennett, Kietha Biggers, Libby Gerard, Rene Lawless, Marcia Linn, Lydia Liu, and John Sabatini for providing us with the various datasets used in this paper. We would also like to thank Aoife Cahill and Martin Chodorow for their help with the research. Some of the material used here is based upon work supported by the National Science Foundation under Grant No. 1119670 and by the Institute of Education Sciences, U.S. Department of Education, under Grant R305F100005. Any opinions, findings, conclusions, or recommendations expressed in this material are those of the authors and do not necessarily reflect the views of the National Science Foundation, the Institute of Education Sciences, or the U.S. Department of Education.

References

Randy Elliot Bennett. 2010. Cognitively based assessment of, for, and as learning (CBAL): A preliminary theory of action for summative and formative assessment. *Measurement: Interdisciplinary Research and Perspectives*, 8(2–3):70–91.

J. Cohen. 1968. Weighted kappa: Nominal scale agreement with provision for scaled disagreement or partial credit. *Psychological Bulletin*, 70(4).

Myroslava Dzikovska, Rodney Nielsen, Chris Brew, Claudia Leacock, Danilo Giampiccolo, Luisa Bentivogli, Peter Clark, Ido Dagan, and Hoa Trang Dang. 2013. SemEval-2013 Task 7: The Joint Student Response Analysis and 8th Recognizing Textual Entailment Challenge. In *Second Joint Conference on Lexical and Computational Semantics (*SEM), Volume 2: Proceedings of the Seventh International Workshop on Semantic Evaluation (SemEval 2013)*, pages 263–274, Atlanta, Georgia, USA, June.

C. Leacock and M. Chodorow. 2003. c-rater: Scoring of short-answer questions. *Computers and the Humanities*, 37.

Marcia C. Linn. 2006. *The Knowledge Integration Perspective on Learning and Instruction.* Cambridge University Press, Cambridge, MA.

Michael Mohler, Razvan Bunescu, and Rada Mihalcea. 2011. Learning to Grade Short Answer Questions using Semantic Similarity Measures and Dependency Graph Alignments. In *Proceedings of ACL:HLT*, pages 752–762, Portland, Oregon, USA, June.

Rodney D. Nielsen, Wayne Ward, and James H. Martin. 2008. Classification Errors in a Domain-Independent Assessment System. In *Proceedings of the Third Workshop on Innovative Use of NLP for Building Educational Applications*, pages 10–18, Columbus, Ohio, June.

F. Pedregosa, G. Varoquaux, A. Gramfort, V. Michel, B. Thirion, O. Grisel, M. Blondel, P. Prettenhofer, R. Weiss, V. Dubourg, J. Vanderplas, A. Passos, D. Cournapeau, M. Brucher, M. Perrot, and E. Duchesnay. 2011. Scikit-learn: Machine learning in Python. *Journal of Machine Learning Research*, 12:2825–2830.

J. Sabatini and T. O'Reilly. 2013. Rationale for a new generation of reading comprehension assessments. In B. Miller, L. Cutting, and P. McCardle, editors, *Unraveling Reading Comprehension: Behavioral, Neurobiological and Genetic Components*. Paul H. Brooks Publishing Co.

Keisuke Sakaguchi, Michael Heilman, and Nitin Madnani. 2015. Effective Feature Integration for Automated Short Answer Scoring. In *Proceedings of NAACL*, Denver, Colorado, USA.

Alex J. Smola and Bernhard Schölkopf. 2004. A Tutorial on Support Vector Regression. *Statistics and Computing*, 14(3):199–222.

Mo Zhang and Paul Deane. under review. Generalizing automated scoring models in writing assessments. *Submitted to the ETS Research Report Series*.

Interpreting Questions with a Log-Linear Ranking Model in a Virtual Patient Dialogue System

Evan Jaffe and **Michael White** and **William Schuler**
The Ohio State University
Department of Linguistics
jaffe.59@buckeyemail.osu.edu
{mwhite, schuler}@ling.osu.edu

Eric Fosler-Lussier
The Ohio State University
Dept. of Computer Science and Engineering
fosler@cse.ohio-state.edu

Alex Rosenfeld
University of Texas at Austin
Department of Linguistics
alexbrosenfeld@gmail.com

Douglas Danforth
The Ohio State University
Department of Family Medicine
doug.danforth@osumc.edu

Abstract

We present a log-linear ranking model for interpreting questions in a virtual patient dialogue system and demonstrate that it substantially outperforms a more typical multiclass classifier model using the same information. The full model makes use of weighted and concept-based matching features that together yield a 15% error reduction over a strong lexical overlap baseline. The accuracy of the ranking model approaches that of an extensively handcrafted pattern matching system, promising to reduce the authoring burden and make it possible to use confidence estimation in choosing dialogue acts; at the same time, the effectiveness of the concept-based features indicates that manual development resources can be productively employed with the approach in developing concept hierarchies.

1 Introduction

In this paper, we present a log-linear ranking model for interpreting questions in a virtual patient dialogue system, along with initial experiments to determine effective sets of features with this model.

Learning to take a medical history is fundamental to becoming a successful physician. Most methods for assessing history taking skills involve interaction with Standardized Patients (SP) who are actors portraying real patients. SP interviews are effective, but they require significant faculty effort and institutional support. As an alternative, virtual standardized patients (VSPs) can be valuable tools that offer a practical and accessible means of simulating standardized patient encounters. VSP simulations have the potential to allow students to practice their communication and history taking skills before working with Standardized Patients. Students can rehearse interviewing skills in a risk-free environment, providing additional opportunities for practice prior to standardized or real-world patient encounters.

Our VSP system closely models the interaction between doctors and patients. Our virtual patients are avatars representing standardized patients that students can interview and communicate with using natural language. Students take a medical history and develop a differential diagnosis of the virtual standardized patient, much as they would a standardized or actual patient. As shown in Figure 1, the dialogue system is embedded in an immersive learning environment designed to provide student doctors with a sense of presence, allowing them to "suspend disbelief" and behave as if the virtual patient is a real patient. The virtual world platform can be run in a variety of environments; here we focus on text-based interaction for laptops and mobile devices.

The current task is a question matching paradigm where user input is mapped to a set of predefined questions, which have scripted answers created by content authors, as in much previous work on question answering systems (Leuski and Traum, 2011). This approach allows for easier authoring than, for example, systems that use deep natural language understanding (Dzikovska et al., 2012; Dzikovska et al., 2013) or semantic parsing (Artzi and Zettlemoyer, 2013; Berant and Liang, 2014), and yet still achieves the desired learning objectives of the virtual patient system.

To date, the VSP system has been based on the

Proceedings of the Tenth Workshop on Innovative Use of NLP for Building Educational Applications, 2015, pages 86–96,
Denver, Colorado, June 4, 2015.

ChatScript[1] pattern matching engine, which offers a low cost and straightforward approach for initial dialogue system development. In an evaluation where a group of third-year medical students were asked to complete a focused history of present illness of a patient with back pain and develop a differential diagnosis, the VSP system answered 83% of the questions correctly. This level of accuracy sufficed for all students to correctly identify the appropriate differential diagnosis, confirming that the virtual patient can effectively communicate and answer complaint-specific questions in a simulated encounter between a doctor and a patient (Danforth et al., 2009; Danforth et al., 2013).

A limitation of rule-based pattern matching approaches, however, is the need to create all patterns manually and extensively test and refine the system to allow it to answer questions correctly, with no ability to use confidence estimation in making dialogue act decisions. With our log-linear ranking model, we aim to substantially reduce the burden of designing new virtual patients, as well as to make it possible to use confidence estimation to decide when the system should ask the user to clarify or restate his or her question.

To create a corpus for developing our statistical interpretation model, the ChatScript patterns were refined to correct errors found during the evaluation and then run on a set of 32 representative dialogues, with the interpretation of all questions hand-verified for correctness.[2]

The rest of the paper is organized as follows. In Section 2, we discuss related work. In Section 3, we present the log-linear ranking model formally, comparing it to more typical multiclass classification models. In Section 4, we describe the features we investigate in detail, with experimental results and analysis appearing in Section 5. Finally, in Section 6 we conclude with a summary and discussion of avenues for future investigation.

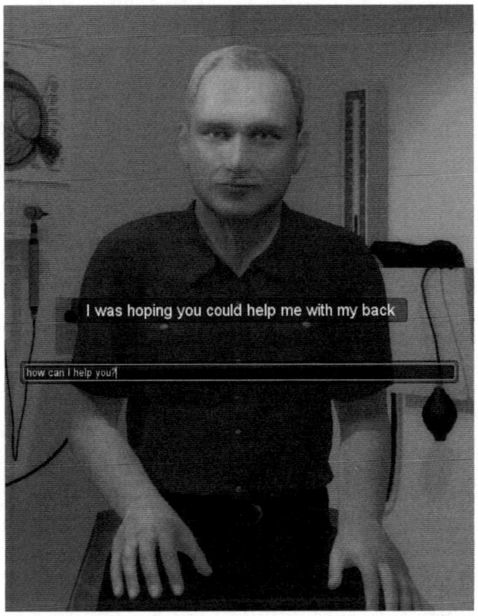

Figure 1: Example exam room and virtual patient avatar. The avatars are programmed to display emotions and movements that are appropriate for the nature of the question, interaction, or condition of the patient.

2 Background and Related Work

In a dialogue system where user utterances are expected to have one of a fixed set of expected interpretations, a straightforward way to implement the natural language understanding component is to map utterances to their interpretations using a multiclass classifier. DeVault et al. (2011) have pursued this approach with an interactive training system designed to enable users to practice multi-party negotiation skills by engaging with virtual humans. They employ a maximum entropy classification model with unigrams, bigrams, skip bigrams and length as features, reporting 87% accuracy in interpretation on transcribed user input (they then go on to show how acceptable accuracy can also be achieved incrementally with noisy ASR output). However, in our domain we find that a similar baseline model—using essentially the same information as the lexical

[1] `http://chatscript.sourceforge.net/`

[2] While the method by which we derived our corpus unfortunately precludes a direct comparison with the ChatScript patterns, since accuracy on the exact set of 32 dialogues in the corpus was not calculated before the patterns were corrected, we note that it is difficult in any case to fairly compare a pattern matching system with a statistical one, as the performance of the former is highly dependent on the time and effort spent refining the patterns. We consider the qualitative differences between the approaches to be of much greater importance, in particular that the machine-learned system can output a useful confidence measure and can be automatically improved with more training data, as discussed below and in Section 5. We are currently gathering a larger corpus of hand-corrected dialogues that will enable a direct comparison of accuracy in future work.

What kind of medicine is that	
u: (what kind of medicine is that)	#must match exactly
u: ([kind type] * ~medicines)	#'kind' or 'type', then any word(s), then a ~medicines concept
u: (what * ~medicines * that)	#'what', then any word(s), then a ~medicines concept, then any word(s), then 'that'

Table 1: Example ChatScript patterns to match the canonical question, *What kind of medicine is that?* Brackets indicate disjunctions of terms, asterisks match zero or more words, and ~prefixes mark concepts, which are themselves disjunctions of terms or other concepts. *u* indicates that the pattern will match a question or statement. See Figure 4 for an example of a ChatScript concept.

overlap baseline discussed below—only achieves a mediocre 67% accuracy; presumably, this discrepancy results from many of the questions the virtual patient is expected to answer being more superficially similar to each other than is the case with DeVault et al.'s training system, thereby making the interpretation task more challenging.

Another way to approach the interpretation task is to view it as one of paraphrase identification, comparing user questions for the virtual patient to a set of expected questions. Since the introduction of the Microsoft Research Paraphrase Corpus (Dolan et al., 2004), or MSRP, there has grown a considerable body of research on paraphrase identification reporting results on this corpus. We draw on this research here, in particular for our baseline feature sets. In adapting these paraphrase identification methods to our setting, however, the question arises as to how to generalize beyond pairwise classification: with the MSRP corpus, the task is to take a pair of superficially similar sentences and classify it as a paraphrase or not a paraphrase, while here the goal is to identify which member of the set of expected questions provides the best match with the user's question. One way to find the best match would be to continue to make use of a binary classifier, selecting the best matching question as the one with the highest probability for the true paraphrase class. Alternatively, one can train a model to rank the competing alternatives, directly selecting the top-ranked option. In the context of question answering, Ravichandran et al. (2003) compared these two methods on the task of answer pinpointing and found that the ranking approach significantly improved upon the pairwise classification approach even using the same features, suggesting that with ranking models the alternatives compete more effectively in training than with binary classifiers, where the pairs are treated in piecemeal fashion. Subsequently, Denis & Baldridge (2007; 2008) also demonstrated a substantial performance improvement using a ranking model for coreference, in comparison to a pairwise classification model. Consequently, in this paper we have adopted the ranking approach.[3]

A perhaps surprising lesson from the paraphrase identification research based on the MSRP corpus is the strong performance of lexical overlap baselines. In particular, Das and Smith (2009) develop a lexical overlap baseline using 1- to 3-gram precision/recall/F-score features over words and stems, reporting 75.4% accuracy on the MSRP corpus. This lexical overlap baseline substantially exceeds many (and perhaps even most) published results on the task, as well as the performance of their own soft alignment model based on quasi-synchronous grammar; moreover, using this much fancier alignment model together with the lexical overlap baseline, they are only able to achieve a 0.7% improvement to 76.1%. Das & Smith's strong results with a lexical overlap baseline echo Wan et al.'s (2006) earlier results using features inspired by the BLEU MT evaluation metric (Papineni et al., 2002). More recently, Madnani et al. (2012) have shown that BLEU can be combined with a variety of newer MT evaluation metrics in classifier obtaining 77.4% accuracy, until recently the best result on the MSRP corpus. In particular, they showed

[3]Note that in general, ranking models allow for a variable number of alternatives, as may be familiar from log-linear parsing models; while allowing for a variable set of prediction options is not necessary in our setting, and thus our ranking model is technically also a multiclass classification model, its feature set is more like those found in typical ranking models than typical classification models, as explained further in Section 3.

that just using BLEU (and two other base metrics using only words, not stems, namely NIST and TER) together with Meteor (Denkowski and Lavie, 2011)—which goes beyond BLEU in employing stems, WordNet synonyms and a database of paraphrases acquired using the pivot method (Bannard and Callison-Burch, 2005)—yields 76.6% accuracy, already one of the best results on this corpus.

Given the strong performance of Das & Smith's lexical overlap baseline, we use these features as a starting point for our log-linear ranking model, and we also combine them with Meteor to yield two competitive baselines. On our corpus, the baselines deliver 75–76% accuracy, much higher than the 67% accuracy of the DeVault et al. multiclass classifier approach. We then add weighted variants of the Das & Smith baseline features, using information content estimated from the Gigaword corpus and a task-specific measure of inverse document frequency, yielding a nearly 3% absolute improvement.

The remaining features we investigate are inspired by our success to date in using handcrafted ChatScript patterns for interpreting user questions. Note that unlike with the MSRP corpus, where the task is to identify unrelated, open domain paraphrases, in our setting the task is to interpret related questions in a constrained domain. As such, it is not overly onerous to arrange relevant words and phrases into a domain-specific concept hierarchy to enhance ChatScript pattern matching. Using the concept hierarchy already developed for use with ChatScript, we are able to achieve a greater than 3% absolute improvement in accuracy over the lexical overlap baseline, indicating that developing such hierarchies may be the most productive way to employ manual development resources. ChatScript additionally makes use of a notion of topic to organize the dialogue, which we incorporate into our model using topic transition features. Finally, to fine tune patterns, ChatScript allows words that should not be matched to be easily specified; as such, we investigate a general method of discovering useful lexically specific features. Unfortunately, however, the topic and lexical features do not yield appreciable gains.

Other approaches to paraphrase identification with the MSRP corpus have been investigated. In particular, vector space models of word meaning have been employed to assess text similarity, representing a rather different angle on the problem in comparison to the methods investigated here, which we plan to explore in future work in combination with our current methods. For example, Rus et al. (2011) make use of Latent Semantic Analysis, a technique they have found effective in their work on interpreting user input in intelligent tutoring systems; however, their results on MSRP corpus lag several percentage points behind the Das & Smith lexical overlap baseline. Socher et al. (2011) present another vector space method making use of recursive autoencoders, enabling vectors for phrases in syntactic trees to be learned. Their method yielded the best published result at the time, though perhaps surprisingly their accuracy is nearly identical to using Meteor together with baseline MT metrics, trailing Madnani et al.'s (2012) best MT metrics combination by half a percentage point. More recently, Ji and Eisenstein (2013) have obtained the best published result on the MSRP corpus by refining earlier distributional methods using supervised information, in particular by discriminatively reweighting individual distributional features and learning the relative importance of the latent dimensions. Xu et al. (2014) have also shown that an approach based on latent alignments can improve upon Ji and Eisenstein's methon on a corpus of Twitter paraphrases.

Finally, Leuski and Traum (2011) present a method inspired by research on cross-language information retrieval that ranks the most appropriate system responses by measuring the similarity between the user's question and the system's potential answers. We have chosen to keep the formulation of the virtual patient's responses separate from question interpretation, though that remains a potential avenue for exploration in future research.

3 Log-Linear Ranking Model

In designing a virtual patient, the content author devises a set of expected questions that the virtual patient can answer. Each expected question has a canonical form, and may additionally have variant forms that have been collected during initial interactions with the virtual patient[4]. Thus, considering the

[4]Variants are identified automatically from training data any time two asked questions are annotated with the same canonical question.

canonical form of the question to be one of its variants, the task of the interpretation model is to predict the correct canonical question for an input question based on one or more known variants of each canonical question.

Formally, we define the likelihood of a canonical question c given an input question x using a log-linear model that marginalizes over the observed variants v of c:

$$P(c|x) = \frac{1}{Z(x)} \sum_{v \in c} \exp\Big(\sum_j w_j f_j(x, v)\Big) \quad (1)$$

Here, the features $f_j(x, v)$ are intended to indicate how well the input question x matches a variant v, and $Z(x)$ normalizes across the variants:

$$Z(x) = \sum_v \exp\Big(\sum_j w_j f_j(x, v)\Big) \quad (2)$$

In training, the objective is to choose weights that maximize the regularized log likelihood of the correct canonical questions c_i for each input x_i:

$$\sum_i \log P(c_i|x_i) - \lambda \sum_j w_j^2 \quad (3)$$

The model is implemented with MegaM,[5] using a default value of $\lambda = 1$ for the Gaussian prior regularization parameter.[6] We also experimented with a linear ranking SVM (Joachims, 2002; Joachims, 2006), but did not observe a performance improvement.

At test time, we approximate[7] the most likely canonical question c^* for input question x as the canonical question $c(v^*)$ for the best matching question variant v^*, i.e. the one with the highest score:

$$\begin{aligned} c^* &= c(v^*), \text{where} \\ v^* &= \text{argmax}_v \textstyle\sum_j w_j f_j(x, v) \end{aligned} \quad (4)$$

In our ranking model, features can be defined that are shared across all question variants. For example, in the next section we make use of an unweighted unigram recall feature, whose value is the percentage of words in v that also appear in x:

$$f_1(x, v) = \text{unigram\_recall}(x, v)$$

In training, a single weight is learned for this feature (rather than one per class), indicating the relative contribution of unigram recall for predicting the correct interpretation. We expect that the trained weights for general features such as this one will carry over reasonably well to new virtual patients, aiding in the process of bootstrapping the collection of training data specific to the new virtual patient.

It is also possible to define lexical- and class-specific features. For example, the following feature indicates a recall miss for a specific word (*ever*) and canonical question (c_{27}):

$$f_2(x, v) = \begin{cases} 1, & \text{if } \textit{ever} \text{ in } v \text{ but not } x \text{ and} \\ & \quad c(v) = c_{27} \\ 0, & \text{otherwise} \end{cases}$$

Sparse features such as this one are intended to fine-tune the predictions that can be made with the more general, dense features like the one above. Note, however, that class-specific features cannot generally be expected to carry over to predictions for new virtual patients (except where the patients are designed to answer some of the same questions).

While our ranking model allows us to make use of features that are defined in terms of the words in both the input question x and a variant question v, it is worth pointing out that most implementations of log-linear classification models require features to be defined only in terms of the input x, with the class implicitly conjoined, and thus with no features shared across classes. For example, Devault et al.'s (2011) maximum entropy classification model—as well as our multiclass baseline model below—makes use of class-specific features indicating n-grams found in the input, such as

$$f_3(x, c) = \begin{cases} 1, & \text{if } \textit{have you} \text{ in } x \text{ and} \\ & \quad c = c_{27} \\ 0, & \text{otherwise} \end{cases}$$

Here, the weight learned in training is indicative of the relative importance of the bigram *have you* for

[5] http://www.umiacs.umd.edu/~hal/megam/

[6] We used MegaM's -explicit format option to implement the ranking model, where each question variant is considered a class, along with the -multilabel option to give a cost of zero to all variants of the correct canonical question and a cost of one to all other variants.

[7] A testing objective that more closely following the training objective was also attempted. This testing method summed over likelihoods of variants for a given canonical question, and then took the argmax over canonical questions. This method did not perform as well as the approximation.

predicting a specific class, i.e. the one for canonical question c_{27}. As noted above, such class-specific features cannot generally be expected to carry over to predictions for new virtual patients, and thus a model consisting of only such features will be of little value for new virtual patients.

4 Features

The features described below are used to create feature subsets evaluated as models. Precision and recall features are defined as being relative to either the asked question or the compared question, respectively. Precision n-gram features, for example, are the ratio of matched n-grams to total n-grams in the asked question. Matching can happen at the exact, stem, concept, or Meteor alignment level.

AlignScore the overall Meteor alignment score

LexOverlap 1- to 3-gram exact/stem unweighted precision/recall/F-score features inspired by Das and Smith

Weighting 1- and 2-gram exact and stem lexical overlap features weighted by IDF and InfoContent

Meteor 1- and 2-gram IDF/InfoContent weighted precision/recall, matched on Meteor alignments

Concept paraphrase-type features based on stem n-gram overlap, but using the concept hierarchy to add further equivalences. Includes 1- and 2-gram precision/recall, weighted and unweighted.

Lex lexical exact match features, as well as precision/recall miss and canonical question-specific precision/recall misses

Topic topic start and transition features

Inverse document frequency weighting is implemented by taking the canonical question and its variants as a document. A gram is weighted based on its frequency in documents, where a gram that only occurs in one or a few documents is more informative than a word that occurs in many documents.

$$\mathrm{IDF}(w) = \log((N+1)/(\mathrm{count}(w)+1))$$

concept: ~medicines [~drugs_legal analgesia **antibiotics** antidote claritin drug drugs hormone hormonal loratidine medication medications medicine meds narcotic 'pain killer' 'pain killers' painkiller pill prescription 'prescription medication' 'prescription medications' remedy steroid tablet tums]

Figure 2: An example ChatScript concept. The *~medicines* concept is defined in the figure, where *antibiotics* is an instance of *medicines*, and *~drugs_legal* is a subconcept of *~medicines*. Each concept is defined as a disjunction of terms, and can include subconcepts.

Asked: what kind of medicine is that
Compared: what type of tablet would that be

↓

Asked: what ~anon of ~medicines is that
Compared: what ~anon of ~medicines would that be

Figure 3: Example sentence pair and derived concept n-gram sequence. The words *kind* and *type* match in an anonymous concept (indicated here as *~anon*) derived from a ChatScript pattern, while the words *medicine* and *tablet* match under the *~medicines* concept.

N is the total number of documents and $\mathrm{count}(w)$ is the number of documents the gram w appears in.

InfoContent weighting uses negative log probabilities of the Gigaword corpus. For bigrams, weighting is calculated as the product of probabilities of a unigram with the conditional probability of the subsequent gram, using Katz backoff.

Concept features are lexical overlap features that use domain-specific knowledge to allow for matching on more words than the exact or stem level. Concept matches occur when a stem matches another stem in a ChatScript concept hierarchy, defined by content authors as labeled classes of equivalent words or phrases.

See Figure 4 for an example. Concepts are used in Chatscript to increase generalizability of the match patterns and reduce authoring burden. To calculate concept features, stems are replaced with the concept name if the stem in the question is listed under a concept in the hierarchy.

Figure 3 shows an example sentence pair and its resulting concept n-gram sequence, given concepts that include *kind* and *type* in an anonymous concept (i.e., an unlabeled disjunction) in one of the ChatScript patterns, along with the words *medicine*

```
Lex:::what
Lex:::of
Lex:::that
LexMissPrec:::kind
LexMissPrec:::medicine
LexMissRec:::type
LexMissRec:::tablet
LexMissRec:::would
LexMissRec:::be
LexMissRecClass:::what_kind_of_tablet_would_that_be:::tablet
LexMissRecClass:::what_kind_of_tablet_would_that_be:::would
LexMissRecClass:::what_kind_of_tablet_would_that_be:::be
```

Figure 4: Example lexical features. These binary features fire in the presence (or absence, in the case of a *Miss*) of a specific word. *Prec* and *Rec* miss features fire when a word appears in one question, but not the other, and is defined in both directions. Here, *LexMissPrec:::kind* fires because *kind* appears in the asked question, but not the compared question. *Class* miss features define lexical misses that are specific to a canonical question, and are similarly defined with *Prec* and *Rec* to refer to the asked and compared question, respectively.

Asked	Correct	Topic
1. hello, mr. covington	hello	~openingdialogue
2. What brings you in today	what brings you in today	~chiefcomplaint
3. Any health problems	what brings you in today	~chiefcomplaint

↓

1. TOPICSTART:::~openingdialogue
2. TOPICTRANS:::~openingdialogue:::~chiefcomplaint
3. SAMETOPIC

Figure 5: Example topic features

and *tablet* being included under the *medicines* topic. Lexical overlap features are then computed on this concept-level n-gram sequence.

Lexical features are binary features that include an exact match or miss. A canonical question-specific miss feature is implemented for precision and recall. See Figure 4 for example lexical features and descriptions, using the running example sentence pair from the concept features.

Topic features keep track of the topic at each point in the dialogue. They include binary transition features that track the current and previous topic, or else the current start topic in the case of the first line of a dialogue. For example, Figure 5 shows the features generated from three example training data. The previous topics are taken from the gold annotation during training and testing. If automatically classified values were used instead of this oracle setting, performance would likely not suffer greatly, given that these features were not found to be very informative and low weights were learned during training.

5 Experiments

The corpus consists of 32 dialogues, which include 918 user turns, with a mean dialogue length of 29 turns. For each turn, the asked question, canonical question, current topic and a question response are annotated. 193 total canonical questions were created by content authors as the fixed set of classes. Correct canonical questions were obtained by running ChatScript, then hand-correcting the output. Any asked questions annotated with the same canonical question are considered variants of that canonical question. There are 787 variants, with a mean of 4.1 variants (standard deviation 4.7) per canonical question. The median number of variants is 2.0, and the maximum number is 34.0.

System accuracy is measured by outputting the correct canonical question, given an input question. Cross-fold validation is run on a per-dialogue basis.Total system accuracy is measured as the mean over all individual cross-fold accuracies.

Results of system accuracy by model are shown in Table 2. The weighted, concept-based, topic-based, and lexical features model (Full-no-meteor) shows a significant improvement over the LexOverlap baseline model, using a McNemar paired chi-square test (chi-square=16.5, p=4.86e-05). At an overall accuracy of 78.6%, this represents an error reduction of 15% over the baseline and approaches the performance of the handcrafted patterns. Of interest, the LexOverlap+concept shows a significant improvement over LexOverlap alone (chi-square=18.3, p=1.95e-05). Meteor features do not show a significant difference when comparing the Full vs. Full-no-meteor model (chi-square=3.2, p=.073), indicating that the concept-based features largely suffice to supply the information provided by WordNet synsets and pivot-method paraphrases in Meteor.

Training with variants as acceptable matches is a useful strategy for this domain, reducing error by 47%, as compared to training without variants. This allows for comparison at test time to not only the

Model Name	Features Included	% Accuracy
Align	Meteor AlignScore feature alone	75.3
LexOverlap	Das and Smith-style lexical overlap baseline	74.9
LexOverlap+lex	adds lexical features	74.1
LexOverlap+topic	adds topic features	75.1
LexOverlap+align	adds Meteor AlignScore	75.8
LexOverlap+weighting	adds weighting features	77.8
LexOverlap+concept	adds concept features	78.1
LexOverlap+concept+weighting	adds weighting and concept features	78.5
Full	all features	77.0
Full-no-meteor	full minus AlignScore and Meteor features	78.6

Table 2: Model results, with a description of their included features

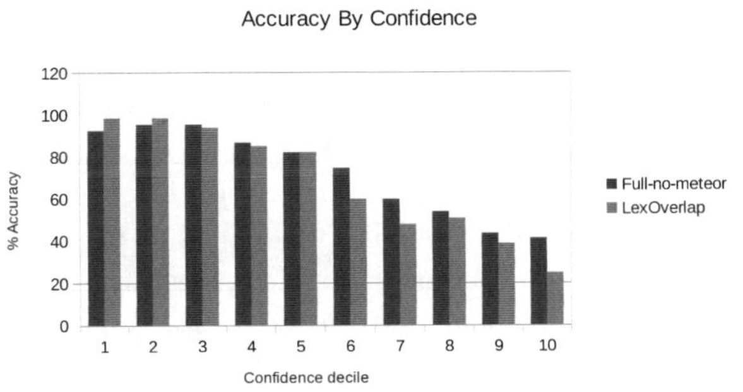

Figure 6: Percent accuracy shown by deciles of decreasing confidence. The most confident deciles have the highest accuracy.

canonical version of a question, but also each correct variant of the canonical version. Matching the correct canonical question or any of its variants results in a correct system response.

In addition, accuracy is higher in cases where the model is most confident, suggesting that confidence can be successfully employed to trigger useful clarification requests, and that training with question variants acquired in previous dialogues yields a large reduction in error. Lastly, an error analysis reveals that many question interpretation errors yield matches that are close enough for the purposes of the dialogue, though some errors remain that reflect misleading lexical overlap, lack of world knowledge or the lack of a dedicated anaphora resolution component.

A measure of system confidence can be obtained from test items' probabilities, and can be compared to accuracy to show that higher confidence system responses are more accurate. Confidence is defined as follows:

$$P(v|x) = \frac{\exp \sum_j w_j f_j(x, v)}{\sum_v \exp \sum_j w_j f_j(x, v)} \quad (5)$$

In Figure 6, test items' answer probability is binned by decile. Mean response accuracy is then calculated for each bin of test items. Future work will use confidence to make discourse management decisions, such as when to answer a question, ask for clarification between close candidates, or give a generic response. Additionally, higher system accuracy is possible if the system is limited to answering higher confidence quantiles.

As an alternative to the log-linear ranking model employed here, a baseline multiclass classifier[8] trained on 1- to 3-gram word and stem indicator features obtains an accuracy of 67%. The ranking system performs better when trained on essentially the same information (LexOverlap), with 75% accuracy.

A ranking model using SVMRank (Joachims, 2002; Joachims, 2006) was also tried, but performance (not shown) was similar to the log-linear model. Future work might explore other machine learning models such as neural networks.

System errors largely fall into a few categories. First, some responses are actually acceptable, but reported as incorrect due to a topic mismatch. For example, the same question *have you ever had this type of pain before* could be labeled as *have you ever had this pain before* or *have you ever had back pain before*, depending on the topic. If the topic was *currentbackpain* or *currentpain*, the gold label could differ. Topics, therefore, exist at varying levels of

[8] `http://scikit-learn.org/`

specificity. Including nearly identical questions in multiple topics promotes question reuse across virtual patients but can be a source of error if the topic is not tracked well.

A second class of errors comes from superficially similar questions, where the most meaningful word or words in the question are not matched. For example *does the pain ever go away* vs. *does rest make the pain go away* would have high lexical overlap, but this does not reflect the fact that the most informative words do not match. Interestingly, we expect that questions that match primarily on common n-grams and not on rarer n-grams have relatively low confidence scores, since the common n-grams would match multiple other questions. Using confidence scoring could help mitigate this error class.

For the previous example, the correct question is actually, *is the pain constant*, which highlights a third kind of error, where some inference or world-knowledge is necessary. Understanding that things that *go away* are not *constant* is an entailment involving negation and is more complicated to capture than using a paraphrase resource.

While room exists for absolute improvement in accuracy, the results are encouraging, given the relatively small dataset and fact that the full model approaches ChatScript pattern-matching system performance (83%). Larger datasets will likely improve accuracy, but given the expense and limited availability of large corpora, we focus on exploring features that maximize limited training data. Annotation is in progress for a larger corpus of 100 dialogues with approximately 5500 user turns.

Qualitatively, the ranking system is less labor-intensive than ChatScript and can use confidence values to drive dialogue act decisions, such as asking the user to rephrase, or to choose between multiple candidate question interpretations. Additionally, the ranking system could potentially be combined with ChatScript to provide ranking when multiple ChatScript patterns match, or to provide a question when no existing ChatScript pattern matches the input.

Better anaphor resolution could help address errors from uninformative pronouns that might not match the canonical question form. Zero-anaphors are missed by the current features and could occur in a dialogue setting such as: *What medications are you taking*, followed by *ok, how often*.

6 Conclusion

In this paper, we have presented a log-linear ranking model for interpreting questions in a virtual patient dialogue system that substantially outperforms a vanilla multiclass classifier model using the same information. In the full model, the most effective features turned out to be the concept-based matching features, which make use of an existing concept hierarchy developed for an extensively handcrafted pattern matching system, and play a similar (but less error-prone) role as WordNet synsets and pivot-based paraphrases in tools such as Meteor. Together with weighted matching features, these features led to a 15% error reduction over a strong lexical overlap baseline, approaching the accuracy of the handcrafted pattern matching system, while promising to reduce the authoring burden and make it possible to use confidence estimation in choosing dialogue acts. At the same time, the effectiveness of the concept-based features indicates that manual development resources can be productively employed in the ranking model by developing domain-specific concept hierarchies.

The student-VSP interaction creates a comprehensive record of questions and the order in which they are asked, which allows for student assessment as well as the opportunity for focused practice and improvement. Indeed, the primary goal of our current research is to leverage the advantages of the VSP system to provide for deliberate practice with immediate feedback.

To better support student practice and assessment, we plan to investigate in future work the impact of more advanced methods for anaphora resolution, as our error analysis suggests that questions containing anaphors are a frequent source of errors. In a dialogue system that uses speech input, we expect automatic speech recognition errors to hurt performance. The exact impact is left as an empirical question for future work. Finally, we also plan to investigate incorporating syntactically-informed vector space models of word meaning into our system, which may help to boost accuracy, especially when acquiring patient-specific training data during the early phase of developing a new virtual patient.

Acknowledgments

We would like to acknowledge Kellen Maicher who created the virtual environment and Bruce Wilcox who authored ChatScript and customized the software for this project. We also acknowledge the expert technical assistance of Laura Zimmerman who managed the laboratory and organized student involvement in this project.

This project was supported by funding from the Department of Health and Human Services Health Resources and Services Administration (HRSA D56HP020687) and the National Board of Medical Examiners Edward J. Stemmler Education Research Fund (NBME 1112-064).

References

Yoav Artzi and Luke Zettlemoyer. 2013. Weakly supervised learning of semantic parsers for mapping instructions to actions. *Transactions of the Association for Computational Linguistics*, 1(1):49–62.

Colin Bannard and Chris Callison-Burch. 2005. Paraphrasing with bilingual parallel corpora. In *Proceedings of ACL*, ACL '05, pages 597–604.

Jonathan Berant and Percy Liang. 2014. Semantic parsing via paraphrasing. In *Proceedings of the 52nd Annual Meeting of the Association for Computational Linguistics (Volume 1: Long Papers)*, pages 1415–1425, Baltimore, Maryland, June. Association for Computational Linguistics.

D. R. Danforth, M. Procter, R. Heller, R. Chen, and M. Johnson. 2009. Development of virtual patient simulations for medical education. *Journal of Virtual Worlds Research*, 2(2):4–11.

D. R. Danforth, A. Price, K. Maicher, D. Post, B. Liston, D. Clinchot, C. Ledford, D. Way, and H. Cronau. 2013. Can virtual standardized patients be used to assess communication skills in medical students? In *Proceedings of the 17th Annual IAMSE Meeting*, St. Andrews, Scotland.

Dipanjan Das and Noah A. Smith. 2009. Paraphrase identification as probabilistic quasi-synchronous recognition. In *Proceedings of the Joint Conference of the 47th Annual Meeting of the ACL and the 4th International Joint Conference on Natural Language Processing of the AFNLP*, pages 468–476, Suntec, Singapore, August. Association for Computational Linguistics.

Pascal Denis and Jason Baldridge. 2007. A ranking approach to pronoun resolution. In *In Proceedings of IJCAI-2007*, Hyderabad, India.

Pascal Denis and Jason Baldridge. 2008. Specialized models and ranking for coreference resolution. In *Proceedings of the 2008 Conference on Empirical Methods in Natural Language Processing*, pages 660–669, Honolulu, Hawaii, October. Association for Computational Linguistics.

Michael Denkowski and Alon Lavie. 2011. Meteor 1.3: Automatic Metric for Reliable Optimization and Evaluation of Machine Translation Systems. In *Proceedings of the EMNLP 2011 Workshop on Statistical Machine Translation*.

David DeVault, Kenji Sagae, and David Traum. 2011. Incremental interpretation and prediction of utterance meaning for interactive dialogue. *Dialogue and Discourse*, 2(1):143–170.

Bill Dolan, Chris Quirk, and Chris Brockett. 2004. Unsupervised construction of large paraphrase corpora: Exploiting massively parallel news sources. In *Proceedings of Coling 2004*, pages 350–356, Geneva, Switzerland, Aug 23–Aug 27. COLING.

Myroslava O. Dzikovska, Peter Bell, Amy Isard, and Johanna D. Moore. 2012. Evaluating language understanding accuracy with respect to objective outcomes in a dialogue system. In *Proceedings of the 13th Conference of the European Chapter of the Association for Computational Linguistics*, pages 471–481, Avignon, France, April. Association for Computational Linguistics.

Myroslava Dzikovska, Elaine Farrow, and Johanna Moore. 2013. Improving interpretation robustness in a tutorial dialogue system. In *Proceedings of the Eighth Workshop on Innovative Use of NLP for Building Educational Applications*, pages 293–299, Atlanta, Georgia, June. Association for Computational Linguistics.

Yangfeng Ji and Jacob Eisenstein. 2013. Discriminative improvements to distributional sentence similarity. In *Proceedings of the 2013 Conference on Empirical Methods in Natural Language Processing*, pages 891–896, Seattle, Washington, USA, October. Association for Computational Linguistics.

Thorsten Joachims. 2002. Optimizing search engines using clickthrough data. In *Proc. KDD*.

Thorsten Joachims. 2006. Training linear svms in linear time. In *Proceedings of the ACM Conference on Knowledge Discovery and Data Mining (KDD)*.

Anton Leuski and David Traum. 2011. Npceditor: Creating virtual human dialogue using information retrieval techniques. *AI Magazine*, 32(2):42–56.

Nitin Madnani, Joel Tetreault, and Martin Chodorow. 2012. Re-examining machine translation metrics for paraphrase identification. In *Proceedings of the 2012 Conference of the North American Chapter of the*

Association for Computational Linguistics: Human Language Technologies, pages 182–190, Montréal, Canada, June. Association for Computational Linguistics.

Kishore Papineni, Salim Roukos, Todd Ward, and Wei-Jing Zhu. 2002. BLEU: a method for automatic evaluation of machine translation. In *Proceedings of the 40th Annual Meeting of the Association for Computational Linguistics (ACL)*, Philadelphia, PA.

Deepak Ravichandran, Eduard Hovy, and Franz Josef Och. 2003. Statistical QA — classifier vs. re-ranker: What's the difference? In *Proceedings of the ACL 2003 Workshop on Multilingual Summarization and Question Answering*, pages 69–75, Sapporo, Japan, July. Association for Computational Linguistics.

Richard Socher and Eric H. Huang and Jeffrey Pennington and Andrew Y. Ng and Christopher D. Manning. 2011. Dynamic Pooling and Unfolding Recursive Autoencoders for Paraphrase Detection. In *Advances in Neural Information Processing Systems 24.*

Vasile Rus, Mihai Lintean, Arthur C. Graesser, and Danielle S. McNamara. 2011. Text-to-text similarity of sentences. In Phillip McCarthy and Chutima Boonthum-Denecke, editors, *Applied Natural Language Processing*. IGI Global.

Stephen Wan, Mark Dras, Robert Dale, and Cecile Paris. 2006. Using dependency-based features to take the 'para-farce' out of paraphrase. In *Proceedings of the Australasian Language Technology Workshop 2006*, pages 131–138, Sydney, Australia, November.

Wei Xu, Alan Ritter, Chris Callison-Burch, William B. Dolan, and Yangfeng Ji. 2014. Extracting lexically divergent paraphrases from Twitter. *Transactions of the Association for Computational Linguistics (TACL)*, 2(1).

Identifying Patterns For Short Answer Scoring Using Graph-based Lexico-Semantic Text Matching

Lakshmi Ramachandran[1], **Jian Cheng**[2] and **Peter Foltz**[1,3]
[1]Pearson, [2]Analytic Measures Inc., [3]University of Colorado
{lakshmi.ramachandran, peter.foltz}@pearson.com
jian.cheng@analyticmeasures.com

Abstract

Short answer scoring systems typically use regular expressions, templates or logic expressions to detect the presence of specific terms or concepts among student responses. Previous work has shown that manually developed regular expressions can provide effective scoring, however manual development can be quite time consuming. In this work we present a new approach that uses word-order graphs to identify important patterns from human-provided rubric texts and top-scoring student answers. The approach also uses semantic metrics to determine groups of related words, which can represent alternative answers. We evaluate our approach on two datasets: (1) the Kaggle Short Answer dataset (ASAP-SAS, 2012), and (2) a short answer dataset provided by Mohler et al. (2011). We show that our automated approach performs better than the best performing Kaggle entry and generalizes as a method to the Mohler dataset.

1 Introduction

In recent years there has been a significant rise in the number of approaches used to automatically score essays. These involve checking grammar, syntax and lexical sophistication of student answers (Landauer et al., 2003; Attali and Burstein, 2006; Foltz et al., 2013). While essays are evaluated for the quality of writing, short answers are brief and evoke very specific responses (often restricted to specific terms or concepts) from students. Hence the use of features that check grammar, structure or organization may not be sufficient to grade short answers.

Regular expressions, text templates or patterns have been used to determine whether a student answer matches a specific word or a phrase present in the rubric text. For example, Moodle (2011) allows for the use of a "Regular Expression Short-Answer question" type which allows instructors or question developers to code correct answers as regular expressions. Consider the question: "What are blue, red and yellow?" This question can evoke a very specific response: "They are colors." However, there are several ways (with the term "color" spelled differently, for instance) to answer this question. E.g. (1) they are colors; (2) they are colours; (3) they're colours; (4) they're colors; (5) colours; or (6) colors. Instead of having to enumerate all the alternatives to this question, the answer can be coded as a regular expression: `(they('|\s(a))re\s)?colo(u)?rs`.

Manually generated regular expressions have been used as features in generating models that score short answers in the Kaggle Short Answer Scoring competition (ASAP-SAS, 2012). Tandalla (2012)'s approach, the best performing one of the competition, achieved a Quadratic Weighted (QW) Kappa of 0.70 using just regular expressions as features. However, regular expression generation can be tedious and time consuming, and the performance of these features is constrained by the ability of humans to generate good regular expressions. Automating this approach would ensure that the process is repeatable, and the results consistent.

We propose an approach to identify patterns to score short answers using the rubric text and top-scoring student responses. The approach involves

Proceedings of the Tenth Workshop on Innovative Use of NLP for Building Educational Applications, 2015, pages 97–106,
Denver, Colorado, June 4, 2015.

(1) identification of classes of semantically related words or phrases that a human evaluator would expect to see among the best answers, and (2) combining these semantic classes in a meaningful way to generate patterns. These patterns help capture the main concepts or terms that are representative of a good student response. We use a word order graph (Ramachandran and Gehringer, 2012) to represent the rubric text. The graph captures order of tokens in the text. We use a lexico-semantic matching technique to identify the degree of relatedness across tokens or phrases. The matching process helps identify alternate ways of expressing the response.

An answer containing the text *diet of koalas* would be coded as follows: `(?=.*(diet|eat(s)?|grub).*) of (?=.*(koala(s)?|koala|opossum).*)`. The patterns generated contain (1) positional constraints (?=, which indicates that the search for the text should start at the beginning, and (2) the choice operator (|), which captures alternate ways of expressing the same term, e.g. `diet` or `eat` or `grub`. We look for match (or non-match) between the set of generated patterns and new short answers.

We evaluate our patterns on short answers from the Kaggle Automated Student Assessment Prize (ASAP) competition, the largest publicly available short answer dataset (Higgins et al., 2014). We compare our results with the those from the competition's best model, which uses manually generated regular expressions. Our aim with this experiment is to demonstrate that automatically generated patterns produce results that are comparable to manually generated patterns. We also tested our approach on a different short answer dataset curated by Mohler et al. (2011).

One of the main contributions of this paper is the use of an automated approach to generate patterns that can be used to grade short answers effectively, while spending less time and effort. The rest of this paper is organized as follows: Section 2 discusses related work that use manually constructed patterns or answer templates to grade student responses. Section 3 contains a description of our approach to automatically generate patterns to grade short answers. Sections 4 and 5 discuss the experiments conducted to evaluate the performance of our patterns in scoring short answers. Section 6 concludes the paper.

2 Related Work

Leacock and Chodorow (2003) developed the use of a short-answer scoring system called C-rater, which focuses on semantic information in the text. They used a paraphrase-recognition based approach to score answers.

Bachman et al. (2002) proposed the use of a short answer assessment system called WebLAS. They extracted regular expressions from a model answer to generate the scoring key. Regular expressions are formed with exact as well as near-matches of words or phrases. Student answers are scored based on the degree of match between the answer and scoring key. Unlike Bachman et al., we do not use patterns to directly match and score student answers. In our approach, text patterns are supplied as features to a learning algorithm such as Random Forest (Breiman, 2001) in order to accurately predict scores.

Mitchell et al. (2003) used templates to identify the presence of sample phrases or keywords among student responses. Marking schemes were developed based on keys specified by human item developers. The templates contained lists of alternative (stemmed) tokens for a word or phrase that could be used by the student. Pulman and Sukkarieh (2005) used hand-coded patterns to capture different ways of expressing the correct answer. They automated the approach of template creation, but the automated ones did not outperform the manually generated templates. Makatchev and VanLehn (2007) used manually encoded first-order predicate representations of answers to score responses.

Brill et al. (2002) reformulated queries as declarative sentence segments to aid query-answer matching. Their approach worked under the condition that the (exact) content words appearing in a query would also appear in the answer. Consider the sample query "When was the paper clip invented?", and the sample answer: "The paper clip is a very useful device. It was patented by Johan Vaaler in 1899." The word *patented* is related in meaning to the term *invented*, but since the exact word is not used in the query, it will not match the answer. We propose a technique that uses related words as part of the patterns in order to avoid overlooking semantically close matches.

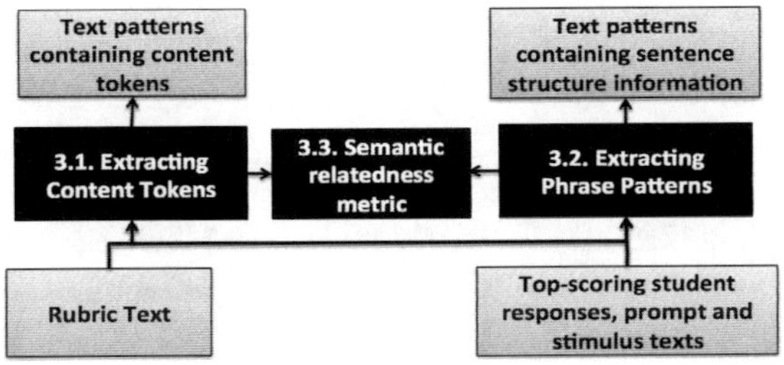

Figure 1: An overview of the approach.

3 Approach

In this section we describe our approach to automatically identify text patterns that are representative of the best answers. We automatically generate two types of patterns containing: (1) content words and (2) sentence structure information. We use the rubric text provided to human graders and a set of top-scored student answers as the input data to generate patterns. Top-scoring responses are those that receive the highest human grades. In our implementation we use the top-scored answers from the training set only. Figure 1 depicts an overview of our approach to automate pattern generation.[1,2]

3.1 Extracting Content Tokens

We rewrite the rubric text in order to generate a string of content words that represent the main points expected to appear in the answer. The aim of our approach is to generate patterns with no manual intervention. The re-writing of the rubric is also done automatically. It involves the removal of stopwords while retaining only content tokens.

We eliminate stopwords and function words in the text and retain only the important prompt-specific content words. Short answer scoring relies on the presence or absence of specific tokens in the student's response. Content tokens are extracted from sample answers, and the tokens are grouped together without taking the order of tokens into consideration.

Students may use words different from those used in the rubric (e.g. synonyms or other semantically related words or phrases). Therefore we have to identify groups of words or phrases that are semantically related. In order to extract semantically similar words specific to the prompt's vocabulary, we look for related tokens in top-scoring answers as well as in the prompt and stimulus texts.

3.1.1 Semantic Relatedness Metric

We use WordNet (Fellbaum, 1998) to determine the degree of semantic match between tokens because it is faster to query than a knowledge resource such as Wikipedia. WordNet has been used successfully to measure relatedness by Agirre et al. (2009).

Match between two tokens could be one of: (1) exact, (2) synonym[3], (3) hypernym or hyponym (more generic or specific), (4) meronym or holonym (sub-part or whole) (5) presence of common parents (excluding generic parents such as *object*, *entity*), (6) overlaps across definitions or examples of tokens i.e., using context to match tokens, or (7) distinct or non-match. Each of these matches expresses different degrees of semantic relatedness across compared tokens. The seven types of matches are weighted on a scale of 0 to 6. An exact match gets the highest weight of 6, a synonym match gets a weight of 5 and so on, and a distinct or non-match gets the least weight of 0.

In the pattern `(?=.*(larg(e)?|size|volum(e)?).*)(?=.*(dry).*)(?=.*(surface).*)`, the set `(?=.*(larg(e)?|size|volum(e)?).*)` contains semantically related alternatives. The pattern looks for the presence of three tokens: any one of the tokens within the first `(?=.*···*)` and tokens `dry` and `surface`. These tokens do not have to appear in any particular order within the student answer. A combination of these tokens should be present in a student answer for it to get a high score. Steps involved in generating content tokens based patterns for the text "size or type of container to use" are described in Algorithm 1.

3.2 Extracting Phrase Patterns

In order to capture word order in the rubric text we extract subject–verb, verb–object, adjective–noun, adverb–verb type structures from the sample answers. The extraction process involves generation of

[1]Prompt: Writing prompt provided to help guide students.

[2]Stimulus: Text presented to students, in addition to the writing prompt, to provide further writing guidance.

[3]We use the part-of-speech of a token to extract the synset from WordNet. This, to an extent, helps disambiguate the sense of a token.

Input: Rubric text, top-scoring answers, and prompt and stimulus texts (if available)
Output: Patterns containing unordered content words.
for *each sentence in the rubric text* **do**
    /* Rubric text: "size or type of container to use" */
    1. Remove stopwords or relatively common words.
    /* Output: size type container use*/
    2. Rank tokens in top-scoring answers, and prompt and stimulus texts based on their frequency, and select the top most frequent tokens.
    /* size container type*/
    3. Identify classes of alternate tokens, for each rubric token, from among most frequent tokens (from Step 2).
    /* {size, large, mass, thing, volume} {container, cup, measure} {type, kind}*/
    4. Stem words and use the suffix as an alternative
    /* container→ (stem: contain, suffix: er) →contain(er)?/
    5. Generate the pattern by AND-ing each of the classes of words.
    /* (?=.*(large|mass|size|thing|volume).*)(?=.*(contain(er)?|cup|measure).*)(?=.*(kind|type).*)
end

Algorithm 1: Generating patterns containing unordered content tokens.

word-order graph representations for the sample answers, and extracting edges representing structural relations listed above.

Generating word-order graphs: We use word-order graphs to represent text because they contain the ordering of words or phrases, which helps capture context information. Context is not available when using just unigrams.

Word graphs have been found to be useful for the task of determining a review's relevance to the submission. Word-order graphs' f-measure on this task is 0.687, while that of dependency graphs is 0.622 (Ramachandran and Gehringer, 2012). No approach is highly accurate, but word graphs work well for this task.

Structure information is crucial in a pattern-

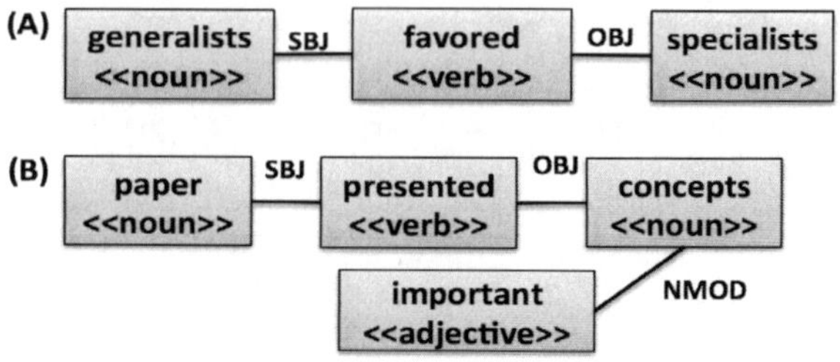

Figure 2: Word-order graphs for texts (A) "Generalists are favored over specialists" and (B) "The paper presented important concepts." Edges in a word-order graph maintain ordering information, e.g. generalists–are favored, paper–presented, important–concepts.

Input: Rubric text, top-scoring answers, and prompt and stimulus texts (if available)
Output: Patterns containing ordered word phrases.
for *each sentence in the rubric text* **do**
    /* Rubric text: "···particles like sodium, potassium ions into membranes···"
    1. Generate word-order graphs from the text, and extract edges from the word-order graph.
    /* The extracted segment: particles like--sodium potassium--ions into membranes. Graph edges are connected with a "--"
    2. Replace stopwords or function words with \w{0,4}.
    /* The segment becomes: particles(\s\w{0,4}\s){0,1} sodium potassium ions(\s\w{0,4}\s){0,1}membranes
    3. Rank tokens in top-scoring answers and prompt and stimulus texts based on their frequency, and select the top most frequent tokens.
    4. Identify class of alternate tokens, for each rubric token, from among most frequent tokens.
    5. Add all synonyms of the rubric token from WordNet to the class of alternatives.
    /* E.g. class of alternate tokens for *sodium*: {potassium, bismuth, zinc, cobalt}, for *potassium*: {tungsten, zinc, calcium, iron, aluminum, tin}, for *membrane*: {film, sheet}
    6. Stem words and generate pattern by AND-ing all classes of words.
end

Algorithm 2: Generating patterns containing sentence structure or phrase pattern information.

generation approach since some short answers may capture relational information. Consider the answer: "Generalists are favored over specialists", to a question on the differences between generalists and specialists. A pattern that does not capture order of terms in the text will not capture the relation that exists between "generalists" and "specialists". Figure 2(A) contains the graph representation for this text.

During graph generation, each sample text is tagged with parts-of-speech (POS) using the Stanford POS tagger (Toutanova et al., 2003), to help identify nouns, verbs, adjectives, adverbs etc. For each sample text consecutive noun components, which include nouns, prepositions, conjunctions and Wh-pronouns are combined to form a noun vertex. Consecutive verbs (or modals) are combined to form a verb vertex; similarly with adjectives and adverbs. When a noun vertex is created the generator looks for the last created verb vertex to form an edge between the two. When a verb vertex is found, the algorithm looks for the latest noun vertex to create a noun–verb edge. Ordering is maintained when an edge is created i.e., if a verb vertex was formed before a noun vertex a verb–noun edge is created, else a noun–verb edge is created. A detailed description of the process of generating word-order graphs is available in Ramachandran and Gehringer (2012).

For this experiment we do not use dense representations of words (e.g. Latent Semantic Analysis (LSA) (Landauer, 2006)) because they are extracted from a large, general corpus and tend to extend the meaning of words to other domains (Foltz et al., 2013). In place of a dense representation we use word-order graphs, since they capture order of phrases in a text.

Substituting stopwords with regular expressions: Stopwords or function words in the extracted word phrases are replaced with the regular expression `(\s\w{0,x}\s){0,n}` where `x` indicates the length of the stopwords or function words, and `n` indicates the number of stopwords that appear contiguously. We use `x=4`, and `n` can be determined while parsing the text. We allow for 0 occurrences of stopwords (`in {0,n}`) between content tokens. Some students may not write grammatically correct or complete answers, but the answer might still contain the right order of the remaining content words, which helps them earn a high score.

Identifying semantic alternatives for content words: Just as in the case of tokens-based patterns (Section 3.1), semantically related words are identified to accommodate alternative responses (relatedness metric described in Section 3.1.1). Tokens in top-scoring answers and prompt texts are ranked based on their frequency, and the most frequent tokens are selected for comparison with words in the rubric text. Apart from that we also add other synonyms of the token to the class of related terms. For instance some synonyms of the token `droplets` are `raindrops, drops`, which are added to its class of semantically related words.

Stemming accommodates typos, the use of wrong tenses as well as the use of morphological variants of the same term (containing singular-plural or nominalized word forms). For instance if "s" is missed in "drops", it is handled by the expression "drop(s)?". These are correctly spelled variants of the same token. We use Porter (1980) stemmer to stem words. The final class of words from the example above looks as follows: `{droplet(s)?, driblet, raindrop(s)?, drop(s)?}`. Humans tend to overlook typos as well as difference in tenses. Therefore the trailing "s" is considered optional.

Algorithm 2 describes steps involved in extracting phrase patterns from a sample answer "···particles like sodium, potassium ions into membranes···". Output of Algorithm 2 is: `particles(\s\w{0,4}\s){0,1}(?=.*(sodium|potassium|bismuth|zinc|cobalt).*)(?=.*(potassium|tungsten|zinc|calcium|iron|aluminum|tin).*)ions(\s\w{0,4}\s){0,1}(?=.*(membrane|film|sheet).*)`. These patterns are also flexible like the token-based ones (with the presence of positional constraints), but it expects content words such as `particles, sodium, potassium, ions` and `membrane` to appear in the text, in that order.

4 Kaggle Short Answer Dataset

The aim of the Kaggle ASAP Short Answer Scoring competition was to identify tools that would help score answers comparable to humans (ASAP-SAS, 2012). Short answers along with prompt texts (and in some cases sample answers) were made available to competitors. The dataset contains 10 different prompts scored on either a scale of 0–2 or 0–3. There were a total of 17207 training and 5224 test answers. Around 153 teams participated in the competition. The metric used for evaluation is QW Kappa. The human benchmark for the dataset was 0.90. The best team achieved a score of 0.77.

4.1 Tandalla's Approach

Tandalla (2012)'s was the best performing model at the ASAP-Short Answer Scoring competition. One of the important aspects of Tandalla's approach was the use of manually coded regular expressions to determine whether a short answer matches (or does not match) a sample pattern. Specific regular expressions were developed for each prompt set, depending on the type of answers each set evoked (e.g. presence of words such as "alligator", "generalist", "specialist" etc. in the text). These patterns were entirely hand-coded, which involved a lot of manual effort. Tandalla built a Random Forest model with the regular expressions as features. This model alone achieved a QW Kappa of 0.70. Tandalla also manually labeled answers to indicate match with the rubric text. A detailed description of the best performing approach is available in Tandalla (2012).

4.2 Experiment

Our aim with this experiment is to compare system-generated patterns with Tandalla's manually generated regular expressions. The goal is to determine the scoring performance of automated patterns, while keeping everything (but the regular expressions) in the best performing approach's code constant.

We substituted the manual regular expressions used by Tandalla in his code with the automated patterns. We then ran Tandalla's code to generate the models and obtain predictions for the test set. We evaluate our approach on each of the 10 prompt sets from the Kaggle short answer dataset.

The final predictions produced by Tandalla's code is the average of four learning models' (two Random Forests and two Gradient Boosting Machines) predictions. The learners were used to build regression (and not discrete) models. We used content tokens and phrase patterns to generate two sets of predictions, one for each run of Tandalla's code. We stacked the output by taking the average of the two sets of predictions.

We compare our model with the following:

1. *Tandalla's model with manually generated regular expressions:* This is the gold standard, since manual regular expressions were a part of the best performing model.

2. *Tandalla's model with no regular expressions:* This model constitutes a lower baseline since the absence of any regular expressions should cause the model to perform worse. Since the code expects Boolean regular expression features as inputs, we generated a single dummy regular expression feature with all values as 0 (no match).

4.3 Results

From Table 1 we see that Tandalla's base code along with our patterns' stacked output performs better than the manual regular expressions. On 8 out of the 10 sets our patterns perform better than the manual regular expressions. Their performance on the remaining 2 sets is better than that of the lower baseline i.e., Tandalla's code with no regular expressions.

The mean QW Kappa achieved by our patterns is 0.78 and that achieved by Tandalla's manual regular expressions is 0.77. Although the QW Kappas are very close (i.e. the difference is not statistically significant), their unrounded difference of 0.00530 is noteworthy as per Kaggle competition's standards. For instance the difference between the first and second place teams (Luis Tandalla and Jure Zbontar) in the competition is 0.00058.[4]

4.4 Analysis of Behavior of Regular Expressions

While the overall performance of the automated regular expressions is better than Tandalla's manual regular expressions, there are some aspects that it may be lacking in when compared with the manual regular expressions.

In the case of Sets 5 and 7, the stacked model performs worse than the model that uses manual regular expressions. This indicates that the manual regular expressions play a very important role for these

[4]Kaggle Public Leaderboard `https://www.kaggle.com/c/asap-sas/leaderboard/public`

Table 1: Comparing performance of models on the test set from the Kaggle ASAP competition. The table contains QW Kappas for each of the ten prompts in the dataset. AutoP: Stacked patterns model. Tandalla's: Tandalla's model with manually generated regular expressions; Baseline: Tandalla's model with no regular expressions.

Approach	Set 1	Set 2	Set 3	Set 4	Set 5	Set 6	Set 7	Set 8	Set 9	Set 10	Mean
AutoP	**0.86**	**0.78**	**0.66**	**0.70**	0.84	**0.88**	0.66	**0.63**	**0.84**	**0.79**	**0.78**
Tandalla's	0.85	0.77	0.64	0.65	**0.85**	0.88	**0.69**	0.62	0.84	0.78	0.77
Baseline	0.82	0.76	0.64	0.66	0.80	0.86	0.63	0.59	0.82	0.76	0.75

prompts. In the case of set 5, the prompt evokes information on the movement of mRNA across the nucleus and ribosomes. We found that:

1. The answers discuss the movement of mRNA in a certain direction, e.g. out of (exit) the nucleus and into the (entry) ribosome. Although students may mention the content terms such as nucleus and ribosome correctly, they tend to miss the directionality (of the mRNA). Since terms such as *into, out of* etc. are prepositions or function words, they get replaced, in our automated approach by `\w{0,x}`. Hence, if the student answer mentions "the mRNA moved *into* the nucleus" as opposed to saying "*out of* the nucleus", our pattern would incorrectly match it.

2. Another reason why automated regular expressions do not perform well is that WordNet treats terms such as *nucleus* and *ribosome* as synonyms. As a result when students interchange the two terms, the regular expression finds incorrect matches. For example an automated pattern for the text "travels from the cytoplasm into the ribosome" is represented as `travels(\s\w{0,4}\s){0,2}(?=.*(cytoplasm|endoplasm(ic)?).*)(\s\w{0,4}\s){0,2}(?=.*(ribosom(e)?|nucleu(s)?).*)`. An incorrect student answer containing "··· mRNA travels from the cytoplasm into the *nucleus* ···" will match this pattern.

As described above we found that retaining stopwords (e.g. prepositions such as "into" or "out of") in the regular expressions may be useful in the case of some prompts. Our approach to regular expression generation may be tweaked to allow the use of stopwords for some prompts. However, our aim is to show that with a generalized approach (in this case one that excludes stopwords) our system performs better than Tandalla's.

In the case of prompt 7, the answers are expected to contain a description of the traits of a character named Rose, as well as an explanation on why students thought that the character was caring. An automated pattern such as: `(?=.*(hard|difficult).*)(?=.*(work(ing)?).*)` captures some of Rose's traits. The answer "Rose was a very hard working girl. She felt really lonely because her dad had just left and her mother worked most of the day." matches the above pattern. However the explanation provided by the student in the second sentence is *not* correct. This answer was awarded a score of 1 by the human grader, but was given a 2 by the system. Although the pattern succeeds in capturing partial information, it does not capture the explanation correctly for this prompt.

5 Mohler et al. (2011)'s Short Answer Dataset

In this section we evaluate our approach on an alternate short answer scoring dataset generated by Mohler et al. (2011). The aim is to show that our method is not specific to a single type of short answer, and could be used successfully on other datasets to build scoring models.

Mohler et al. use a combination of graph-based alignment and lexical similarity measures to grade short answers. They evaluate their model on a dataset containing 10 assignments and 2 examinations. The dataset contains 81 questions with a total of 2273 answers. The dataset was graded by two human judges on a scale of 0–5. Human judges have an agreement of 57.7%.

Mohler et al. apply a 12-fold cross validation over the entire dataset to evaluate their models. On average, the train fold contains 1894 data points

Table 2: Sample questions from a single assignment. Questions in this assignment are about sorting techniques. Since they discuss the same subject a single model can be built for the assignment.

1. In one sentence, what is the main idea implemented by insertion sort?
2. In one sentence, what is the main idea implemented by selection sort?
3. What is the number of operations for insertion sort under a best-case scenario, and what is the best-case scenario?
4. What is the base case for a recursive implementation of merge sort?

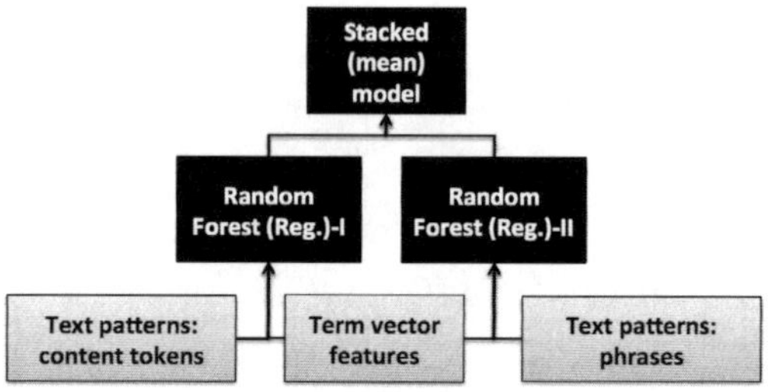

Figure 3: Features used and models built for the experiment on Mohler et al. (2011)'s short answer dataset.

while the test fold contains 379 data points. Models are constructed with data from assignments containing questions on a variety of programming concepts such as the role of a header file, offset notation in arrays and the advantage of linked lists over arrays. Although all the questions are from the same domain (e.g. computer programming) the answers they evoke are very different.

Mohler et al. achieved a correlation of 0.52 with the average human grades, with a hybrid model that used Support Vector Machines as a ranking algorithm. The hybrid model contained a combination of graph-nodes alignment, bag-of-words and lexical similarity features. The best Root Mean Square Error (RMSE) of 0.98 was achieved by the hybrid model, which used Support Vector Regression as the learner. The best median RMSE computed across each individual question was 0.86.

5.1 Experiment and Results

We use the same dataset to extract text patterns. Since patterns are prompt or question specific we cannot create models using the entire dataset like Mohler et al. do. Patterns extracted from across different questions may not be representative of the content of individual questions or assignments. Questions within each assignment are on the same topic. Table 2 contains a list of all questions from Assignment 5, which is about insertion, selection and merge sort algorithms. We therefore extract patterns containing content tokens and phrases for each assignment.

The data for each assignment is divided into train and test sets (80% train and 20% test). The train set contains a total of 1820 data points and the test set contains a total of 453 data points. The train data is used to extract content tokens and phrase patterns from sample answers.

Most short answer grading systems use term vectors as features (Higgins et al., 2014), since they work as a good baseline. Term vectors contain frequency of terms in an answer. We use a combination of term vectors and automatically extracted patterns as features.

We use a Random Forest regressor as the learner to build models. The learner is trained on the average of the human grades. We stack results from models created with each type of pattern to compute final results. Results are listed in Table 3. Our approach's correlation over all the test data is 0.61. The RMSE is 0.86, and the median RMSE computed over questions is 0.77. The improvement in correlation of our stacked model over Mohler et al.'s performance of 0.52 is significant (one tailed test, p-value $= 0.02 < 0.05$, thus the null hypothesis that this difference is a chance occurrence may be rejected). Correlation achieved by using just term vectors is 0.56 (difference from Mohler et al.'s result is not significant). These results indicate that the use of patterns results in an improvement in performance.

The above process was repeated at the granularity level of questions. Data points from each question were divided into train and test sets, and models were built for each training set. There were a total of 1142 training and 1131 test data points. Results from the stacked model are computed over all the test predictions. This model achieved a correlation of 0.61, and an RMSE of 0.88. The median RMSE computed over each of the questions is 0.82.

Table 3: Comparing performance of models on Mohler et al. (2011)'s dataset. Md(RMSE): median RMSE over questions; AutoP (As): Stacked model over assignments; AutoP (Qs): Stacked model over questions; Baseline: Mohler et al.'s best results; Human: Human Average (Mohler et al., 2011). "*" under column Sig. indicates that the difference between our model and the baseline is statistically significant ($p < 0.05$)

Models	R	Sig.	RMSE	Md(RMSE)
AutoP (As)	**0.61**	*	**0.86**	**0.77**
AutoP (Qs)	**0.61**	*	0.88	0.82
Term vectors	0.56		0.92	0.87
Baseline	0.52		0.98	0.86
Human	0.59		0.66	0.61

As can be seen from Table 3 our stacked model performs better in terms of correlation, RMSE and median RMSE over questions than Mohler et al.'s best models. One of the reasons for improved performance could be that models were built over individual assignments or questions rather than over the entire data. Patterns are particularly effective when built over assignments containing the same type of responses. Short answer scoring can be very sensitive to the content of answers. Hence using data from across a variety of assignments could result in a poorly generalized model.

6 Conclusion

Automatically scoring short answers is difficult. For example, none of Kaggle ASAP short answer scoring competitors managed to consistently reach the level of human-human reliability in scoring. The results of the Kaggle competition, however do show that manually generated regular expressions are a promising approach to increase performance. Regular expressions like patterns are easily interpretable features that can be used by learners to boost short answer scoring performance. They capture semantic and contextual information contained within a text. Thus, determining the best ways to incorporate these patterns as well as making it efficient to develop them is critical to improving short answer scoring.

In this paper we introduce an automated approach to generate text patterns with limited human effort, and whose performance is comparable to manually generated patterns. Further we ensure that the method is generalizable across data sets.

We generate patterns from rubrics and sample top-scoring answers. These patterns help capture the desired structure and semantics of answers and act as good features in grading short answers. Our approach achieves a QW Kappa of 0.78 on the Kaggle short answer scoring dataset, which is greater than the QW Kappa achieved by the best performing model that uses manually generated regular expressions. We also show that on Mohler et al. (2011)'s dataset our model achieves a correlation of 0.61 and an RMSE of 0.77. This result is an improvement over Mohler et al. (2011)'s best published correlation of 0.52 and RMSE of 0.86.

References

Eneko Agirre, Enrique Alfonseca, Keith Hall, Jana Kravalova, Marius Paşca, and Aitor Soroa. 2009. A study on similarity and relatedness using distributional and WordNet-based approaches. In *Proceedings of Human Language Technologies: The 2009 Annual Conference of the North American Chapter of the Association for Computational Linguistics*, pages 19–27.

ASAP-SAS. 2012. Scoring short answer essays. ASAP short answer scoring competition system description. `http://www.kaggle.com/c/asap-sas/`.

Yigal Attali and Jill Burstein. 2006. Automated essay scoring with e-rater® v. 2. *The Journal of Technology, Learning and Assessment*, 4(3).

Lyle F Bachman, Nathan Carr, Greg Kamei, Mikyung Kim, Michael J Pan, Chris Salvador, and Yasuyo Sawaki. 2002. A reliable approach to automatic assessment of short answer free responses. In *Proceedings of the 19th international conference on Computational linguistics-Volume 2*, pages 1–4. Association for Computational Linguistics.

Leo Breiman. 2001. Random forests. *Machine learning*, 45(1):5–32.

Eric Brill, Susan Dumais, and Michele Banko. 2002. An analysis of the AskMSR question-answering system. In *Proceedings of the ACL-02 Conference on Empirical Methods in Natural Language Processing - Volume 10*, EMNLP '02, pages 257–264, Stroudsburg, PA, USA.

Susan Dumais, Michele Banko, Eric Brill, Jimmy Lin, and Andrew Ng. 2002. Web question answering: Is more always better? In *Proceedings of the 25th annual international ACM SIGIR conference on*

Research and development in information retrieval, pages 291–298. ACM.

Christiane Fellbaum. 1998. Wordnet: An electronic lexical database. *MIT Press*.

Peter Foltz, Karen Lochbaum, and Mark Rosenstein. 2011. Analysis of student writing for large scale implementation of formative assessment. In *Paper presented at the National Council for Measurement in Education*, New Orleans, LA.

Peter Foltz, Lynn A. Streeter, Karen Lochbaum, and Thomas K. Landauer. 2013. Implementation and applications of the Intelligent Essay Assessor. In *M. Shermis & J. Burstein, (Eds.). Handbook of Automated Essay Evaluation*, pages 68–88, Routledge, NY.

Evgeniy Gabrilovich and Shaul Markovitch. 2007. Computing semantic relatedness using Wikipedia-based explicit semantic analysis. In *Proceedings of the 20th international joint conference on Artifical intelligence*, IJCAI'07, pages 1606–1611.

Derrick Higgins, Chris Brew, Michael Heilman, Ramon Ziai, Lei Chen, Aoife Cahill, Michael Flor, Nitin Madnani, Joel Tetreault, Dan Blanchard, Diane Napolitano, Chong Min Lee, and John Blackmore. 2014. Is getting the right answer just about choosing the right words? The role of syntactically-informed features in short answer scoring. *arXiv*.

Thomas K. Landauer, Darrell Laham, and Peter W. Foltz. 2003. Automated scoring and annotation of essays with the Intelligent Essay Assessor. In *Automated Essay Scoring: A cross-disciplinary perspective*, pages 87–112, Mahwah, NJ: Lawrence Erlbaum Publishers.

Thomas K Landauer. 2006. Latent semantic analysis. *Encyclopedia of Cognitive Science*.

Claudia Leacock and Martin Chodorow. 2003. C-rater: Automated scoring of short-answer questions. In *Computers and the Humanities*, volume 37, pages 389–405. Springer.

Maxim Makatchev and Kurt VanLehn. 2007. Combining bayesian networks and formal reasoning for semantic classification of student utterances. In *Proceedings of the 2007 Conference on Artificial Intelligence in Education: Building Technology Rich Learning Contexts That Work*, pages 307–314, Amsterdam, The Netherlands.

Tom Mitchell, Nicola Aldridge, and Peter Broomhead. 2003. Computerised marking of short-answer free-text responses. In *Manchester IAEA conference*.

Michael Mohler, Razvan Bunescu, and Rada Mihalcea. 2011. Learning to grade short answer questions using semantic similarity measures and dependency graph alignments. *Proceedings of the 49th Annual Meeting of the Association of Computational Linguistics - Human Language Technologies (ACL HLT 2011)*, pages 752–762.

Moodle. 2011. Regular expression short-answer question type. `http://docs.moodle.org/20/en/Regular_Expression_Short-Answer_question_type`.

Martin F Porter. 1980. An algorithm for suffix stripping. In *Program: electronic library and information systems*, volume 14, pages 130–137. MCB UP Ltd.

Stephen G Pulman and Jana Z Sukkarieh. 2005. Automatic short answer marking. In *Proceedings of the second workshop on Building Educational Applications Using NLP*, pages 9–16.

Lakshmi Ramachandran and Edward F. Gehringer. 2012. A word-order based graph representation for relevance identification (poster). *Proceedings of the 21st ACM Conference on Information and Knowledge Management*, pages 2327–2330, October.

Lakshmi Ramachandran and Edward Gehringer. 2013. Graph-structures matching for review relevance identification. In *Proceedings of TextGraphs-8 Graph-based Methods for Natural Language Processing*, pages 53–60, Seattle, Washington, USA, October.

Luis Tandalla. 2012. Scoring short answer essays. ASAP short answer scoring competition–Luis Tandalla's approach. `https://kaggle2.blob.core.windows.net/competitions/kaggle/2959/media/TechnicalMethodsPaper.pdf`.

Kristina Toutanova, Dan Klein, Christopher D. Manning, and Yoram Singer. 2003. Feature-rich part-of-speech tagging with a cyclic dependency network. In *In Proceedings of HLT-NAACL*, pages 252–259.

Yu Wang, Yang Xiang, Wanlei Zhou, and Shunzheng Yu. 2012. Generating regular expression signatures for network traffic classification in trusted network management. In *Journal of Network and Computer Applications*, volume 35, pages 992–1000, London, UK, UK, May. Academic Press Ltd.

Lark Trills for Language Drills: Text-to-speech technology for language learners

Elena Volodina
University of Gothenburg, Dpt of Swedish,
Swedish Language Bank (Språkbanken)
Box 200, 405 30, Gothenburg, Sweden
elena.volodina@svenska.gu.se

Dijana Pijetlovic
Nuance Communications Switzerland AG
Baslerstrasse 30
8048 Zürich, Switzerland
dijana.pijetlovic@nuance.com

Abstract

This paper reports on the development and the initial evaluation of a dictation&spelling prototype exercise for second language (L2) learners of Swedish based on text-to-speech (TTS) technology. Implemented on an already existing Intelligent Computer-Assisted Language Learning (ICALL) platform, the exercise has not only served as a test case for TTS in L2 environment, but has also shown a potential to train listening and orthographic skills, as well as has become a way of collecting learner-specific spelling errors into a database. Exercise generation re-uses well-annotated corpora, lexical resources, and text-to-speech technology with an accompanying talking head.

1 Introduction and background

ICALL – Intelligent Computer-Assisted Language Learning - is an intersection between Computer-Assisted Language Learning (CALL) and Natural Language Processing (NLP) where interests of the one side and technical possibilities of the other meet, e.g. automatic error detection and automatic essay scoring.

Multiple research projects worldwide explore the benefits of NLP in educational applications (Mitkov & Ha 2003; Monaghan & Bridgeman 2005; Heilman & Eskenazi, 2006; Antonsen 2012), some of them being exploited for real-life language teaching (Amaral and Meurers, 2011; Heift, 2003; Nagata, 2009), most of them though staying within academic research not reaching actual users (Nilsson & Borin, 2002; François & Fairon, 2012) or remaining limited by commercial usage (Attali & Burstein, 2006; Burstein et al., 2007).

In the past five decades the area of NLP has witnessed intensive development in Sweden. However, ICALL has remained rather on the periphery of NLP community interests. Among the directions in which ICALL research developed in Sweden, one can name supportive writing systems (Bigert et al., 2005; Östling et al., 2013); exercise generators (Bick 2001, 2005; Borin & Saxena, 2004; Volodina et al., 2014); tutoring systems (Wik 2004, 2011; Wik & Hjalmarsson, 2009).

As can be seen, the number of directions for Swedish ICALL projects is relatively small. Given the potential that NLP holds for CALL community, this fact is rather surprising, if not remarkable.

1.1 Pedagogical Framework

More than a decade ago Council of Europe has adopted a new framework for language learning, teaching and assessment, the *Common European Framework of Reference for Languages* (CEFR; COE, 2001). The CEFR guidelines describe language skills and competences at six proficiency levels (from beginner to proficient): A1, A2, B1, B2, C1, C2. Among those skills, *orthographic skills, listening comprehension, vocabulary range and control,* and *knowledge of lexical elements* are relevant in the context of the exercise described in the paper.

Orthographic control, as defined by the CEFR, is ranging from "*Can copy familiar words and short phrases ... used regularly*" at the beginner level (A1) to "*Writing is orthographically free of error*" at the mastery level (C2) (COE, 2001:118). The same applies to *listening comprehension* which ranges from "*I can recognise fami-*

Proceedings of the Tenth Workshop on Innovative Use of NLP for Building Educational Applications, 2015, pages 107–117,
Denver, Colorado, June 4, 2015. ©2015 Association for Computational Linguistics

liar words and very basic phrases..." at A1 to "*I have no difficulty in understanding any kind of spoken language...*" at C1 (COE 2001:26-27). Criteria for *lexical competence* include *vocabulary range and control* and knowledge of *lexical elements* that stretch over the limits of one single word (2001:110-112).

The proposed *dictation&spelling* exercise is a possible way to improve the above-mentioned competences and skills. Learners first hear the item pronounced by a talking head, and afterwards spell it - item in this context being understood as either a single word, a phrase or a sentence. For teachers, it is rather time-consuming to engage in dictation in an attempt to help students improve their lexical, listening and orthographic skills. In this case, NLP can successfully replace a teacher in this drill-like exercise.

1.2 Use of TTS for L2 learning

TTS is being increasingly used in CALL systems for multiple tasks, such as for listening and dictation practice (Santiago-Oriola, 1999; Huang et al., 2005; Pellegrini et al., 2012; Coniam, 2013), for reading texts aloud (Lopes et al., 2010), and for pronunciation training (Wik, 2011; Wik & Hjalmarsson, 2009).

The Swedish TTS in CALL environment is represented by *Ville* and *Deal* (Wik, 2011; Wik & Hjalmarsson, 2009). *Ville* is a virtual language teacher that assists learners in training vocabulary and pronunciation. The system makes a selection of words that the student has to pronounce. The system analyses students' input and provides feedback on their pronunciation. The freestanding part of *Ville*, called *DEAL*, is a role-playing game for practicing conversational skills. While *Ville* provides exercises in the form of isolated speech segments, *DEAL* offers the possibility to practice them in conversations (Wik & Hjalmarsson, 2009).

Like *Ville*, the dictation&spelling exercise presented here uses TTS technology for training vocabulary. However, unlike *Ville*, the dictation&spelling exercise is (1) focused on spelling rather than pronunciation, and in this respect complements the functionality offered by Ville; (2) is web-based and does not need prior installation; and (3) is designed to address students at different CEFR proficiency levels.

1.3 Research questions

Two important research questions, raised in connection to this project, have influenced the design of the implemented exercise.

(1) Is TTS technology for Swedish mature enough for use in ICALL applications? To answer this question, we included evaluation and a follow-up questionnaire by the end of the project, where users could assess several parameters of the speech synthesizer and express an overall impression of the exercise (Section 3).

(2) What way should feedback on L2 misspellings be delivered? To have a better idea about what typical L2 spelling errors learners of Swedish make, we designed an error database that stores incorrect answers during the exercise. Based on the analysis of the inititally collected errors, we suggest a way to generate meaningful feedback to Swedish L2 learners (Section 4).

The rest of the paper is structured as follows: Section 2 describes the implementation details of the exercise and the database. Section 3 presents the results of the evaluation. Section 4 focuses on the first explorations of the SPEED (SPElling Error Database) and suggests a feedback generation flow. Section 5 concludes the paper and outlines future prospects.

2 Exercise design and implementation

2.1 Resources

A number of computational resources for Swedish have been used in the exercise, namely:

- Corpora available through *Korp*, Språkbanken's infrastrusture for maintaining and searching Swedish corpora (Borin et al., 2012b). All corpora in Korp are accessible via web services and contain linguistic annotation: lemmas, parts-of-speech, morphosyntactic information, dependency relations.
- Lexical resources available through *Karp*, Språkbanken's lexical infrastructure (Borin et al., 2012a*): Kelly word list,* a frequency-based word list of modern Swedish containing 8,500 most important words for language learners with associated CEFR proficiency levels (Volodina & Johansson Kokkinakis, 2012); and *Saldo morphology,* a morphology lexicon of Swedish containing all in-

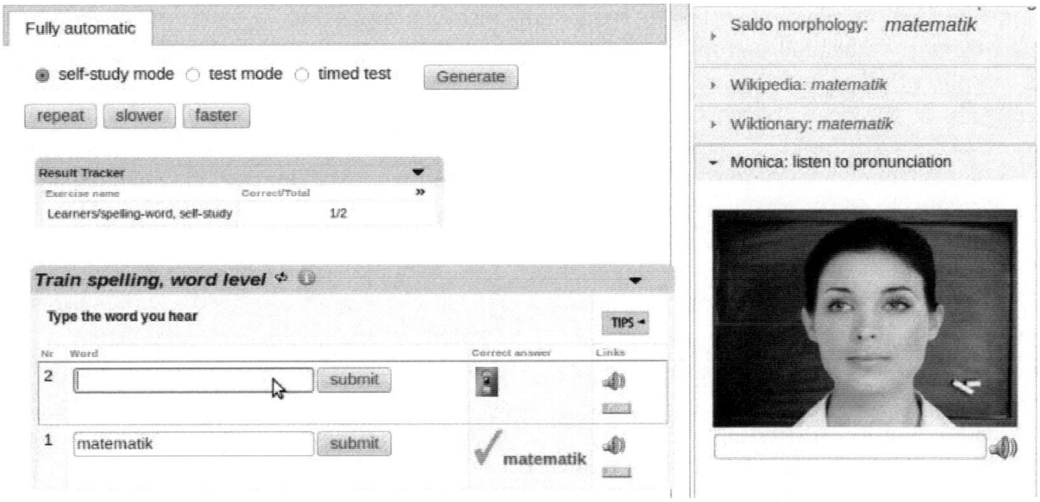

Figure 1. User interface for dictation&spelling exercise, version 2

flected forms for each lemgram (base form + part of speech pair) (Borin, Forsberg & Lönngren, 2013). Karp resources are also accessible through web services.

- *SitePal*'s TTS synthesizer module and a talking head, Monica, who is addressed that way in the paper
- *Lärka*, an ICALL platform for Swedish where the exercise is deployed (Volodina et al., 2014). *Lärka* is an ICALL platform for studying Swedish (in broad sense). It targets two major user groups – students of Linguistics, and L2 learners. The exercise repertoire comprises (1) exercises for training parts-of-speech, syntactic relations and semantic roles for students of Linguistics; and (2) exercises for training word knowledge and inflectional paradigms for L2 learners (Volodina et al., 2014). Features common to all exercises include corpora and lexical resources, training modes, access to reference materials (Figure 1).

2.2 Linguistic levels

According to Nation (2001), aspects of word knowledge include: (1) *Form*: spoken (recognition in speech, pronunciation); written (recognition in texts, spelling); word parts (inflection, derivation, word-building); (2) *Meaning*: form and meaning; concept and references; associations; (3) *Use*: grammatical functions; collocations; constraints on use (register/frequency/etc.)

While the two previously available exercises in Lärka – for training vocabulary knowledge and inflectional paradigms – focus on some aspects of meaning, use and form, the newly added dictation&spelling exercise has extended the spectrum of trained word knowledge aspects to cover other dimensions of form-aspect, namely spoken and written forms, and therefore the exercise has become a natural and welcome addition to the exercise arsenal offered by Lärka.

The exercise is offered at four linguistic levels, each targeting different aspects of word knowledge. The *word level* focuses on pronunciation and spelling of the base form of a word. A target word of an indicated CEFR level is randomly selected from the Kelly list or from a *user-defined list*, an option provided by Lärka where learners can type words they need to train. The target item is then sent to the TTS module to obtain its pronunciation. TTS pronounces the word, while the user needs to spell it (Figure 2).

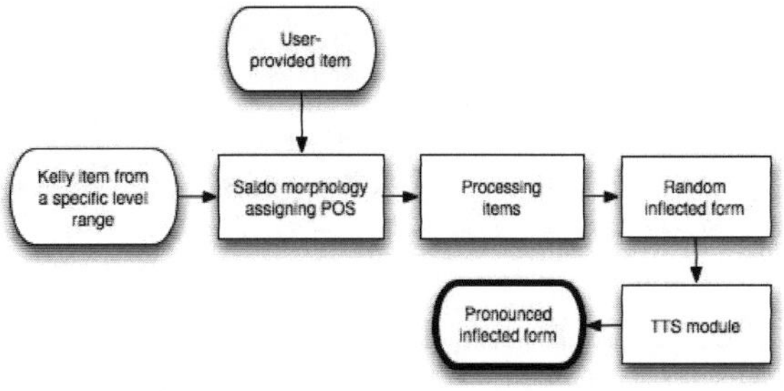

Figure 2. NLP pipeline for word levels. At the non-inflected word level *Saldo morphology* is excluded from the pipeline

The *inflected word level* (Figure 2) also focuses on a single word, however, the learner is made aware of its inflectional patterns, in addition to pronunciation and spelling (learners have to spell the inflected form they hear). Analogous to the word level, the target word is randomly selected from the Kelly list or the user-defined list. Before the item is sent to the TTS module, its different inflected forms are checked in Saldo-morphology, whereas some of the forms, e.g. possessives, are excluded as inappropriate for training through dictation. One random form is used for training.

The *phrase level* offers the target word in some typical context, which alongside demonstrating the item's collocational and distributional patterns, also requires the user to identify (via listening) the number of separate words constituting the phrase. While the implementation for the word and the inflected word levels was straightforward, the implementation for the phrase level needed some workaround to achieve the best phrase accuracy. In this exercise version only noun and verb phrases have been taken into consideration.

For retrieval of the typical phrase patterns, word pictures associated with the target item are retrieved from Korp. A fragment of a word picture for the noun *ord* [word], is shown in Figure 3. The columns on top of Figure 4 provide the most distinguished collocation patterns (prepositions, premodifiers, post-modifiers), underneath followed by the actual lemmas alongside with the number of hits in the corpora. Most typical prepositions used with the noun *ord* are (in translation): *with, without, behind, against, beyond.* Most typical premodifiers are: *free, ugly, beautiful, hard, empty*.

Preposition		Pre-Modifier		ord	Post-Modifier
1. med	9191	1. fri	2353		
2. utan	494	2. ful	314		
3. bakom	235	3. vacker	376		
4. mot	484	4. hård	395		
5. bortom	50	5. tom	208		

Figure 3. Word picture for the noun *ord* [word] in Korp

The number accompanying each of the collocates reflects the number of hits in the corpus. For example, *fri 2353* on top of the second column means that the phrase starting with a pre-modifier *fri* [free] has a pattern *fri + ord* and has been used 2353 times in the corpora where we performed our search. To extract the actual phrase containing *fri ord*, another request is forwarded to Korp where the actual corpus hits are returned (the 2353 of them). Then, any of the sentences can be used for extracting the actual phrase preserving inflections and words that come in-between, e.g. *fria tankar och ord* [free thoughts and words]. After some experiments, we have set the limit at max 6 tokens per phrase.

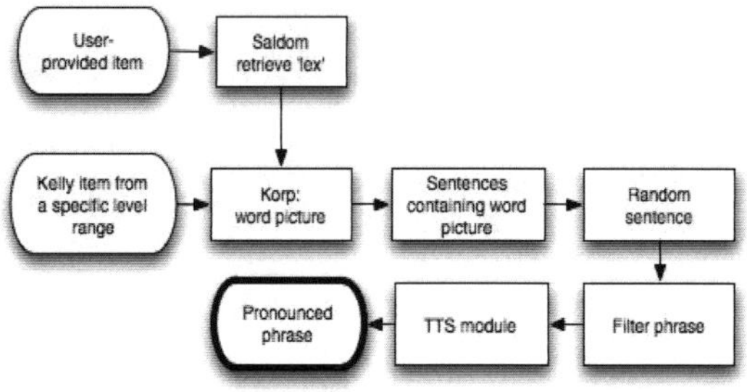

Figure 4. NLP pipeline for the phrase level

The final flow of the exercise generation at the phrase level is shown in Figure 4: A random item from the Kelly list is forwarded to the Korp's word picture web-service, one of the top frequent patterns is selected and the actual KWIC hits are consulted. After the phrase has been selected and adjusted, it is sent to the TTS module for pronunciation. In case of a user-defined word list, the randomly selected item is first sent to Saldo-morphology to check possible word classes associated with the item, one is selected and sent further to Korp for extracting a word picture.

Figure 5. NLP pipeline for the sentence level.

The *sentence level* offers the target item in a sentence context, which sets further demands on listening comprehension and awareness of structures that the target word can be used in. The sentence level is the most challenging for the users, since sentences are usually long and it is difficult to remember all information. Programmatically, though, it is less challenging than the phrase level, unless you want to ensure that learners understand the sentences they get for training. We have used algorithms developed by Pílan et al. (2014) for automatic retrieval of sentences understandable by learners at B1/B2 proficiency levels. Before the sentence is sent to the TTS module, some additional filtering is performed blacklisting sentences of inappropriate length or containing inappropriate tokens (e.g. dates with slashes *30/11/2013*), see Figure 5.

Finally the *performance-based variant* of the exercise offers a path from the word to the sentence level, allowing the user to go over from one level to another according to his/her performance. If 10 items have been spelled correctly, a new level is offered.

2.3 Error database

All user answers are logged in SPEED, the SPElling Error Database, which has been deployed on Karp's backend. SPEED keeps track of:
(1) the session which consists of the date and time when the user has started the exercise. All errors made by that particular user have the same session ID. This way we have a chance to identify some user-specific behaviour and error patterns.
(2) the correct item, its parts-of-speech, the misspelling and the time when the misspelling is added. If an entry for the correct item has already been created, a new misspelling is added to the list of misspellings. Otherwise, a new entry is created.

Since no login information is required to use Lärka (which is a choice made at the departmental level), we cannot log information about learners' first language (L1) background.

3 User evaluation

We have used an off-the-shelf TTS solution offered by SitePal (www.sitepal.com), which offers an optimal combination of voice quality, availability of talking heads, user-friendliness and a reasonable subscription price.

A critical question for this project has been whether the TTS quality of the SitePal's synthesizer is mature enough for use in an ICALL application. A quality of a TTS synthesizer is generally judged by its *naturalness* (i.e. similarity to the human voice), *understandability* (comprehensibility of the message and intelligibility of individual sounds), and *accuracy* (Handley & Hamel, 2005). This is especially significant when applied to L2 context where TTS is used both for setting an example of correct pronunciation and for testing listening comprehension. Besides the three criteria above, the criteria of *language learning potential* and *opportunity to focus on linguistic form* are critical in CALL environment (Chapelle, 2001a, 2001b). If the technology doesn't live up to the demands, this type of exercise should be excluded in want of better technological solutions.

A few studies have evaluated TTS in CALL applications. A study by Pellegrini et al. (2012) compared TTS-produced versus human pre-recorded speech in L2 dictation exercises (sentence level). They found that L2 learners make more mistakes when human voice is heard, thus establishing that (at A2 level) TTS speech is more understandable by L2 learners of Portuguese, most probably due to the speed difference, TTS version being 15% slower. Handley (2009) evaluated TTS modules in four CALL applications using criteria of comprehensibility, acceptability, and appropriateness, and found TTS technology mature enough for use in L2 applications, emphasizing that expressiveness was insufficient. Handley & Hamel (2005) discuss a benchmark for evaluation of speech synthesis for CALL applications. Evaluation focus should differ depending on uses of TTS, since different features play roles for various learning scenarios. They explored appropriateness, acceptability and comprehensibility as potential criteria for the three TTS tasks: reading texts, pronunciation training and dialogue partner, and found that the same TTS module has been evaluated differently depending upon the task it was used for.

3.1 Participants and setting

The evaluation of the exercise was carried out with 10 participants who represented three user groups: beginner levels A1/A2, intermediate levels B1/B2 and advanced levels C1/C2 with 3 participants in each. A native speaker is categorized separately as his/her language knowledge exceeds the CEFR-defined proficiency levels.

The participants have been asked to fill an evaluation form following the experience of working with the exercise. During the exercise, each of the participants spelled at least 40 items: 10 at each of the four linguistic levels. They were also encouraged to test performance-based level. All along the misspellings have been saved to the error database.

3.2 Questionnaire

The purpose of the evaluation has been primarily to evaluate the text-to-speech module and to assess the usefulness of the exercise, based on L2 learner preferences. We have used criteria suggested by Handley and Hamel (2005) and Chapelle (2001a, 2001b) as the basis for our evaluation adding some more questions.

The questionnaire contained 15 questions, of which five were focused on the TTS quality (questions #3-7, Table 1), six - on the exercise and its effectiveness (#8-14), one explicitly asking for the type of feedback learners expect from the program (#15), and the rest were devoted to the user-friendliness of the GUI (#1-2)[1].

All questions (except #15) were evaluated according to a 5-grade scale, where 1 corresponded to *very good* and 5 to *very poor*. Additionally, the evaluators had the possibility to add comments for every question and at the end of the questionnaire.

	A1/A2	B1/B2	C1/C2	Native	all levels
Q1 - Instructions	1	2	2.67	1	**1.8**
Q2 - GUI	1.33	2	2	1	**1.7**
Q3 - Comprehensibility	2	3	2.67	2	**2.5**
Q4 - Intelligibility	2	2.33	3.33	1	**2.4**
Q5 - Avatar	4	3.67	3.67	4	**3.8**
Q6 - Naturalness of speech	1	2.33	2.67	2	**2**
Q7 - Pronunciation	1.67	1.33	2	2	**1.7**
Q8 - Difficulty	2	1.67	3.67	1	**2.3**
Q9 - Word level	1.33	1.67	2	1	**1.8**
Q10 - Phrase level	2.67	2.33	2.67	1	**2.4**
Q11 - Sentence level	3.67	2.67	4	1	**3.2**
Q12 - Sentence length	4	2.33	4	2	**3.3**
Q13 - Speed	2.33	2.33	1.67	2	**2.1**
Q14 - Effectiveness	1.67	2	1.67	2	**1.8**
overall results	2.19	2.26	2.76	1.64	**2.34**

Table 1. Results by question & proficiency level, on the scale 1=very good … 5=very poor

3.3 Evaluation results and discussion

According to the evaluation results (Table 1), the talking head (#5) appears to be the least effective element in the spelling exercises. The unsatisfying results for the speaking head are based hypothetically on the missing facial expression and on its location within the spelling game. Compared to the virtual language teacher Ville, which was developed specifically for educational purposes, the SitePal's talking head seems to have a rather entertaining function. The expressive lip movement that is characteristic of Ville, is clearly missing from Monica.

The *pronunciation* generated by the TTS module (#7), however, is regarded as good despite comments on some smaller pronunciation errors. The user interface (#2) and the quality of pronunciation (#7) are the most satisfactory features. The *naturalness* of speech (#6) is perceived differently among the participants. While the beginner group finds the TTS-produced speech natural and human-like, the advanced group perceives it as least natural. This result is not very surprising as the beginner group is not familiar with the language and therefore is not able to critically judge the naturalness of speech. The native speaker is in general very positive towards the TTS system.

Table 1 shows clearly that the word/inflected word levels (#9) are the most appropriate units for training spelling followed by the phrase level (#10). Phrases need to be adapted to the respective proficiency level in order to achieve the best learning effect. The sentence level (#11) is assessed as the least appropriate one, as the length and the speed rate have been perceived unsuitable for training spelling and listening. The results demonstrate that the *learning potential* at the word and phrase levels is higher than at the sentence level, as perceived by L2 learners.

The results by proficiency level (Table 1) show that there is an obvious tendency to become more critical as the level grows. The proficiency group C1/C2 is the least satisfied one, while the native speaker is the most positive. The reason for that might be that language learners from higher proficiency levels are more critical as their knowledge of the language is better and therefore TTS mistakes are more noticeable, while TTS mistakes might not be that obvious to the learners with lower levels of proficiency. The vocabulary chosen for training spelling and listening at lower levels may also be easier for the TTS system to pronounce. The native speaker shows in general a very positive attitude towards the spelling game as (s)he might be more aware of the difficulty of the language and is therefore more ‘forgiving’. Another reason might be that the native speaker does not assess the spelling exercise from the learner’s point of view and might therefore be less critical.

When it comes to the word level (#9), with the increase of learners' proficiency dissatisfaction also increases (Figure 6). The reason for that might be

[1]Full questionnaire form can be downloaded from http://spraakbanken.gu.se/eng/larka/tts

that the words in the Kelly-list are too advanced for the intermediate level. Some of the advanced participants find the word level not challenging enough as the target words are displayed quickly before they are pronounced. This kind of spelling tip needs to be adapted to the proficiency level.

As for the appropriateness of phrases (#10), the intermediate group is more positive to them than the beginner and advanced groups. The reason for that may lie in the implementation approach. Since words within a phrase do not all belong to the same difficulty level, phrases extracted for the beginner level might be too advanced.

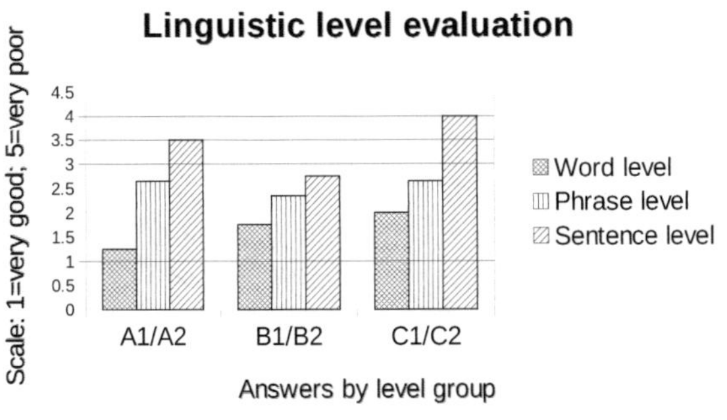

Figure 6. Results by proficiency levels & linguistic levels, on the scale 1=very good … 5=very poor

The sentence level (#11) is in general the most challenging linguistic level for training spelling and listening (Figure 6). The C1/C2 group finds the sentence level in general inappropriate for spelling exercises. The obtained sentences were difficult to follow not only for beginners but even for advanced Swedish L2 learners.

Especially interesting are the comments provided for the question on feedback (#15). The feedback that the participants would like to see in this exercise is grouped into several suggestions:

- A hint on the word form for the inflected forms
- Tips regarding grapheme-phoneme mappings
- English translation of the spelled items
- Possibility to see the correct answer by choice
- Possibility to notify the pronunciation mistakes made by the TTS module
- Detailed feedback on the wrong answers
- Run-time marking of spelling errors

4 Feedback on L2 misspellings

In the pedagogical and psychological studies on feedback one can encounter an extensive amount of different terms, e.g. achievement feedback, assessment feedback (Higgins et al., 2002), formative and summative feedback, feedback on performance (Hyland, 2001), etc. The common ground for all types of feedback is that the student performance (actual level) is compared with the expected performance (reference level) and some information is provided to the learners that should help them develop the target skills further in order to alter the gap between the actual and the reference levels (Ramaprasad, 1983).

Obviously, just stating the presence of the gap ("incorrect") is not sufficient. Feedback becomes useful when ways to improve or change the situation are outlined. To do that, we need to understand the nature of a spelling mistake, and to point learners to the specific aspects of the target language orthography, the phoneme-grapheme mappings in L2; or even to the relation between L1 and the target L2 spelling and pronunciation systems. A lot of studies argue that it is vital to know a learner's L1 for successful error analysis (Tingbjörn & Andersson, 1981; Abrahamsson, 2004; Koppel et al., 2005; Nicolai et al., 2013). Unfortunately, the ICALL platform that is used as a basis for the exercise does not offer any login facility, which makes it impossible to log learners' L1, at least at present. Given that constraint we had to make the best out of the situation. We started looking for a taxonomy of most typical L2 spelling errors which students should be addressed to, independent of their L1.

While there are several available error corpora for other languages (Granger 2003; Tenfjord, Meurer & Hofland 2006), we are aware of only one error database for Swedish, an Error Corpora Database (ECD), which is a collection of different types of errors, among others spelling ones. They have been collected from Swedish newspapers, and analyzed to create an error typology used for developing proof-reading tools for professional writers of Swedish (Wedbjer Rambell, 1999a; Wedbjer Rambell, 1999b). Being a good source for comparison, ECD, however, cannot be applied as it is to the context of Swedish L2 learning. Antonsen (2012) points out that L2 errors differ in nature and type from L1 errors. Rimrott & Heift (2005) found that generic spell-checkers fail to identify L2 errors and therefore special care should be taken to study specific L2 errors. We faced therefore the necessity of collecting a special database of Swedish L2 errors as the first step on the way to useful feedback.

Collecting errors into a database from corpora is a time-consuming process which we could not afford. We have opted for another alternative, inspired by Rodrigues & Rytting (2012), where errors are collected into a database while learners do exercises. Advantages of collecting a corpus by applying this method are numerous: participants are quickly attracted, while cost, time and effort of collecting a corpus are reduced.

While the feedback has not been implemented at this stage, the database has been populated with misspellings and has given us the first insights into the nature of typical L2 errors and prompted some ideas on useful feedback.

4.1 Error log analysis

The initial analysis of the error logs focused on word-level errors, which have been categorized into several error types. The same spelling errors could often be classified into more than one category; e.g. a real word error can be at the same time a performance- or a competence-based error.

There are two major groups of errors, competence-based (55%) and performance-based (17%) ones, that are described here. The rest of the errors (28%) are connected to a group of errors occurring in sentences or phrases where e.g. wrong segmentation or total absence of one or several words are the cause of the error. These errors have been left out of the present analysis.

While performance-based errors are accidental and are easily corrected with a hint to the learner, competence-based errors depend on the lack of or insecure knowledge and need to be explained. Learners need to be made aware of the mappings between orthography and pronunciation in the target language. L1 speakers usually make performance-based errors while in L2 learners' writing competence-based errors dominate (Rimrott & Heift, 2005).

Competence-based errors (55%) occur as a result of not knowing a word's spelling or confusing words. L2 spelling errors are mostly competence-based. This type of errors mainly occurs when the orthographic rules of L2 differ from the ones of L1 or when a language contains special characters or sounds that do not exist in L1. The competence-based errors from the evaluation fall into the four categories described below.

Spelling errors based on *consonant doubling* (28%) belong to one of the most common errors, where either a single consonant is written instead of a double (e.g. *sto**pa*** instead of *sto**pp**a* [thrust]) or a double consonant instead of a single (e.g. *r**imm**ligen* instead of *ri**m**ligen* [reasonably]).

Spelling words that contain *characters with accents/diacritics* (ä, å, ö) present challenge for Swedish L2 learners, due to the difficulty to distinguish between special characters and the orthographically or phonetically similar vowels (23%). For example, the sound of the letter *å* was frequently mistaken for the vowel *o*.

Phonetic errors (25%) appear when parts of words are spelled as they are heard. The most frequent phonetic error in our logs is caused by confusing voiced and voiceless consonants.

Another cause of a typical Swedish L2 misspelling are *consonant clusters* that follow special rules for grapheme-to-phoneme mapping (20%). The letter combination *rl*, for example, is pronounced [l]. The drop of "r"-sound applies also for the combinations *rs*, *rd* and *rt*. Some other problematic clusters are *tj*, *ch*, *hj*, *sk*.

Performance-based errors (17%), the so called 'typos', are caused by addition, deletion, insertion or replacement of one or several letters in a word, often a result of hitting a wrong key or two keys at the same time on the keyboard. Performance-based errors are not always obvious, for example, the misspelling *s**j**ön* (corr. *s**k**ön* [beautiful]) could have been created by confusing the keys *j'* and *k* on the keyboard but could also be categorized as a competence-based phonetic error. The spelling error *förb**'**ttra* (corr. *forb**ä**ttra* [improve]) clearly belongs to the performance-based category.

Spelling mistakes can also result in *real words* (14%) either by chance or because a word is misheard and therefore mistaken for another word. For example, the word *likna**n**de* [similar] could either be mistaken for *liknade* [resembled] or the letter *n* was omitted accidentally, while the word *livs**stil*** [life style] is more likely to be misheard as *livs**tid*** [life time]. Overall, the results show that non-word errors (86%) are significantly more likely to occur than real-word errors (14%).

The first analysis of the error logs inspired us to propose a feedback generation tree (Figure 7). The analysis of a larger database might lead to a more specific decision tree. The tree is build up from the easiest spelling errors to identify to the more difficult ones. All along the error analysis, relevant feedback is provided. If multiple changes are necessary, they are advised step-wise. In case the spelling error cannot be classified, the correct item is shortly exposed.

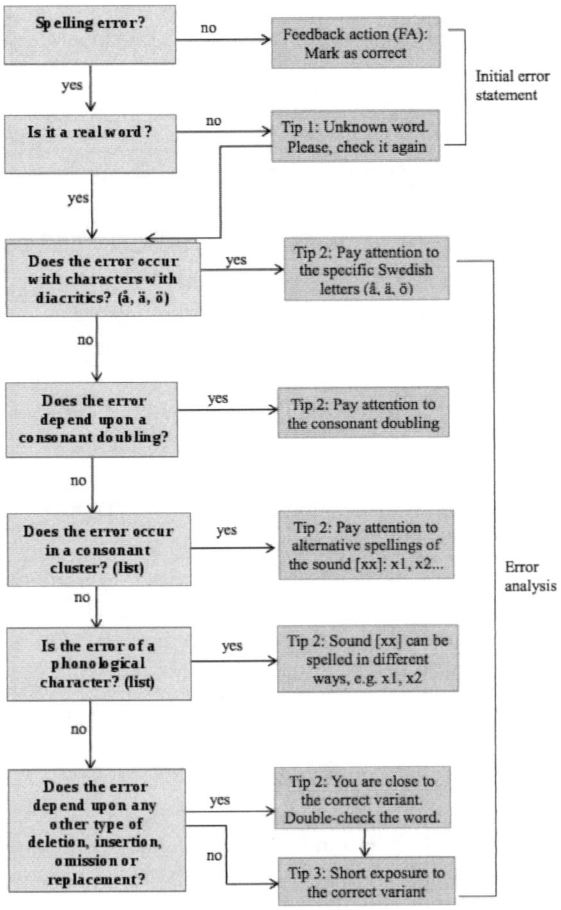

Figure 7. Feedback generation tree

The proposed feedback generation flow would allow to offer the kind of information that can help learners to fill the gap between the reference and the actual level of the assessed spelling error.

5 Concluding remarks

The goals of this project have been, firstly, the implementation of a Swedish dictation&spelling exercise that can provide L2 learners with a tool for training spelling and listening at different linguistic levels; and secondly, the evaluation of the newly implemented module regarding its effectiveness and usefulness. The main focus of the evaluation, in its turn, was to find out whether the TTS technology is mature enough for the use in L2 context and to suggest a way to provide useful feedback on L2 specific misspellings.

The state of TTS development looks very promising for integration of the current TTS synthesizer for Swedish L2 learning. Some improvements might be in place on the Lärka side, especially regarding the placement of the talking head on the screen and adjustment of the pronunciation speed to the level of the learner. However, the naturalness and understandability of the SitePal's TTS module hold a very good level.

The issue of homophones should be solved at word levels, either by counting alternative spellings as correct ones (e.g. flour vs flower) or by offering learners an additional possibility to hear the item in a context of a phrase or a sentence. The latter should help distinguish errors that arise due to learners' inability to recognize the word pronounced out of context versus their not knowing how to spell the word.

Besides, a broader spectrum of lexical resources and detailed feedback are necessary. The taxonomy of spelling errors shows that generating feedback for easily identifiable spelling errors is straightforward while more work is necessary to understand the nature of other types of errors. More detailed evaluations with larger number of participants, and repeated analysis of more extensive error logs are necessary to refine the feedback generation tree. Other suggestions on feedback proposed by evaluation participants will be considered for implementation.

The vocabulary for the word level needs to be expanded with larger lexical resources and domain specific vocabulary lists. The generation pace of phrases has to be accelerated, and the phrase level needs to be adapted to the proficiency level. Since the sentence level is regarded as the least effective one, most improvements are due on this level. The sentence length as well as the speech rate need to be adapted to the proficiency level.

In order to assess the spelling exercises from the pedagogical point of view, an in-class evaluation with teachers needs to be carried out once a new version is in place.

References

Niclas Abrahamsson. 2004. Fonologiska aspekter på andraspråksinlärning och svenska som andraspråk. In: *Hyltenstam Kenneth & Lindberg Inger (eds.) Svenska som andraspråk: i forskning, undervisning och samhälle*. Lund: Studentlitteratur.

Luiz Amaral & Detmar Meurers. 2011. On using intelligent computer-assisted language learning in real-life for-eign language teaching and learning. *ReCALL 23(1)*: 4–24.

Lene Antonsen. 2012. Improving feedback on L2 misspellings – an FST approach. *Proceedings of the SLTC 2012 workshop on NLP for CALL*. Linköping Electronic Conference Proceedings 80: 1–10.

Yigal Attali & Jill Burstein. 2006. Automated essay scoring with e-rater® V.2. *The Journal of Technology, Learning and Assessment 4 (3)*.

Eckhard Bick. 2001. The VISL System: Research and Applicative Aspects of IT-based learning. *Proceedings of NoDaLiDa*. Uppsala, Sweden.

Eckhard Bick. 2005. Grammar for Fun: IT-based Grammar Learning with VISL. In: *Henriksen, Peter Juel (ed.), CALL for the Nordic Languages*. p.49-64. Copenhagen: Samfundslitteratur (Copenhagen Studies in Language).

Johnny Bigert, Viggo Kann, Ola Knutsson & Jonas Sjöbergh. 2005. Grammar Checking for Swedish Second Language Learners. *Chapter in CALL for the Nordic Languages p. 33-47*. Copenhagen Studies in Language 30, Copenhagen Business School. Samfundslitteratur.

Lars Borin, Markus Forsberg & Lennart Lönngren. 2013. SALDO: a touch of yin to WordNet's yang. *Language Resources and Evaluation*, 1-21.

Lars Borin, Markus Forsberg, Leif-Jöran Olsson & Jonatan Uppström. 2012a. The open lexical infrastructure of Språkbanken. *Proceedings of LREC 2012*. Istanbul: ELRA. 3598–3602.

Lars Borin, Markus Forsberg & Johan Roxendal. 2012b. Korp – the corpus infrastructure of Språkbanken. *Proceedings of LREC 2012*. Istanbul: ELRA. 474–478.

Lars Borin & Anju Saxena. 2004. Grammar, Incorporated. In *Peter Juel Henrichsen (ed.), CALL for the Nordic Languages*. Copenhagen Studies in Language 30. p.125-145. Copenhagen: Samfundslitteratur.

Jill Burstein,Jane Shore, John Sabatini, Y Lee, Matthew Ventura. 2007. Developing a reading support tool for English language learners. *Demo Proceedings of NAACL-HLT*.

Carol Chapelle. 2001a. Innovative language learning: Achieving the vision. *ReCALL, 23*(10), 3-14

Carol Chapelle. 2001b. *Computer applications in second language acquisition: Foundations for teaching testing and research*. Cambridge, England: Cambridge University Press.

COE, Council of Europe. 2001. *The Common European Framework of Reference for Languages: Learning, Teaching, Assessment*. Cambridge University Press.

David Coniam. 2013. Computerized dictation for assessing listening proficiency. *CALICO Journal*, Vol.13., Nr 2&3.

Thomas François & Cedrik Fairon. 2012. An "AI readability" formula for French as a foreign language In *Proceedings of the 2012 Conference on Empirical Methods in Natural Language Processing (EMNLP 2012)*, Jeju, 466-477.

Sylviane Granger. 2003. Error-tagged Learner Corpora and CALL: A Promising Synergy. *CALICO Journal*, 20(3), p-p 465-480.

Zöe Handley. 2009. Is text-to-speech synthesis ready for use in computer-assisted language learning? *Speech Communication* , vol. 51, no. 10, pp. 906–919, 2009.

Zöe Handley & Marie-Josée Hamel. 2005. Establishing a methodology for benchmarking speech synthesis for Computer-Assisted Language Learning (CALL). *Language Learning & Technology*, Vol. 9, No. 3, pp. 99-119

Trude Heift. 2003. Multiple learner errors and meaningful feedback: A challenge for ICALL systems. *CALICO Journal*, 20(3), 533–548.

Shang-Ming Huang, Chao-Lin Liu, and Zhao-Ming Gao. 2005. Computer-assisted item generation for listening cloze tests and dictation practice in English. in *Proc. of ICWL*, pp. 197–208.

Michael Heilman, & Maxine Eskenazi. (2006). Language Learning: Challenges for Intelligent Tutoring Systems. *Workshop on Ill-defined Domains in Intelligent Tutoring*, Taiwan

Richard Higgins, Peter Hartley & Alan Skelton. 2002. "The Conscientious Consumer: reconsidering the role of assessment feedback in student learning". *Studies in Higher Education*, Vol.27, No.1, p.53-64

Fiona Hyland. 2001. Providing Effective Support: investigating feedback to distance language learners. *Open Learning*, Vol.16. No.3, p.233-247.

Moshe Koppel, Jonathan Schler, & Kfir Zigdon. 2005. Determining an authors' native language by mining a text for errors. In *Proceedings of the 11th ACM SIGKDD international conference*, 624–628.

José Lopes, Isabel Trancoso, Rui Correia, Thomas Pellegrini, Hugo Meinedo, Nuno Mamede, & Maxine Eskenazi. 2010. Multimedia Learning Materials. In *Proc. IEEE Workshop on Spoken Language Technology SLT, Berkeley*, pp. 109–114.

Ruslan Mitkov & Le An Ha. 2003. Computer-Aided Generation of Multiple-Choice Tests. *Proceedings of the HLT-NAACL 2003* Workshop on Building Educational Applications Using Natural Language Processing, 17-22.

William Monaghan & Brent Bridgeman. 2005. E-Rater as a Quality Control on Human Scores. *ETS R&D Connections*: Princeton, NJ: ETS.

Noriko Nagata. 2009. Robo-Sensei's NLP-based error detec-tion and feed-back generation. *CALICO Journal*, 26(3), 562–579.

Paul Nation. 2001. *Learning Vocabulary in Another Language*, Cambridge University Press, p.477

Garrett Nicolai, Bradley Hauer, Mohammad Salameh, LeiYao, Grzegorz Kondrak. 2013. Cognate and Misspelling Features for Natural Language Identification. In *Proceedings of NAACL-BEA8.*

Kristina Nilsson & Lars Borin. 2002. Living off the Land: The Web as a Source of Practice Texts for Learners of Less Prevalent Languages. *Proceedings of LREC 2002,* Third International Conference on Language Resources and Evaluation p.411-418. Las Palmas: ELRA.

Thomas Pellegrini, Ângela Costa, Isabel Trancoso. 2012. Less errors with TTS? A dictation experiment with foreign language learners. *Thirteenth Annual Conference of the International Speech Communication Association*

Ildikó Pilán, Elena Volodina and Richard Johansson. 2014. Rule-based and machine learning approaches for second language sentence-level readability. *Proceedings of the 9th workshop on Building Educational Applications Using NLP*, ACL 2014.

Arkalgud Ramaprasad. 1983. On the definition of feedback. *Behavioural Science*, Vol.28, p.4-13.

Anne Rimrott & Trude Heift. 2005. Language Learners and Generic Spell Checkers in CALL. *CALICO journal*, Vol.23, No.1.

Paul Rodrigues & C. Anton Rytting. 2012. Typing Race Games as a Method to Create Spelling Error Corpora. *LREC 2012*.

C. Santiago-Oriola. 1999. Vocal synthesis in a computerized dictation exercise. In *Proc. of Eurospeech, 1999*.

Gunnar Tingbjörn, Anders-Börje Andersson. 1981. *Invandrarbarnen och tvåspråkigheten : rapport från ett forskningsprojekt om hur invandrarbarn med olika förstaspråk lär sig svenska.* Liber: Skolöverstyrelsen.

Kari Tenfjord, Paul Meurer & Knut Hofland. 2006. The ASK corpus - A Language Learner Corpus of Norwegian as a Second Language. *Proceedings of LREC 2006.*

Elena Volodina & Sofie Johansson Kokkinakis. 2012. Introducing Swedish Kelly-list, a new lexical e-resource for Swedish. *LREC 2012*, Turkey.

Elena Volodina, Ildikó Pilán, Lars Borin & Therese Lindström Tiedemann. 2014. A flexible language learning platform based on language resources and web services. *LREC 2014*, Iceland.

Olga Wedbjer Rambell. 1999a. Error Typology for Automatic Proof-reading. *Reports from the SCARRIE project*, Ed. Anna Sågvall Hein.

Olga Wedbjer Rambell. 1999b. An Error Database of Swedish. *Reports from the SCARRIE project*, Ed. Anna Sågvall Hein.

Preben Wik. 2004. Designing a Virtual Language Tutor. In *Proc. of The XVIIth Swedish Phonetics Conference, Fonetik 2004*. p. 136-139. Stockholm University, Sweden.

Preben Wik. 2011. *The Virtual Language Teacher: Models and applications for language learning using embodied conversational agents.* PhD Thesis. KTH Royal Institute of Technology

Preben Wik & Anna Hjalmarsson. 2009. Embodied conversational agents in computer assisted language learning. *Speech communication* 51 (10), 1024-1037

Robert Östling, Andre Smolentzov, Björn Tyrefors Hinnerich & Erik Höglin. 2013. Automated Essay Scoring for Swedish. In *Proceedings of the Eighth Workshop on Innovative Use of NLP for Building Educational Applications*, pages 42–47, Atlanta, Georgia, June 13 2013. Association for Computational Linguistics.

The Jinan Chinese Learner Corpus

Maolin Wang[1]**, Shervin Malmasi**[2] **and Mingxuan Huang**[3]

[1]College of Chinese Language and Culture, Jinan University, Guangzhou, China
[2]Centre for Language Technology, Macquarie University, Sydney, NSW, Australia
[3]Guangxi University of Finance and Economics, Nanning, China

[1]`wmljd@126.com`, [2]`shervin.malmasi@mq.edu.au`, [3]`gxmingxh@163.com`

Abstract

We present the Jinan Chinese Learner Corpus, a large collection of L2 Chinese texts produced by learners that can be used for educational tasks. The present work introduces the data and provides a detailed description. Currently, the corpus contains approximately 6 million Chinese characters written by students from over 50 different L1 backgrounds. This is a large-scale corpus of learner Chinese texts which is freely available to researchers either through a web interface or as a set of raw texts. The data can be used in NLP tasks including automatic essay grading, language transfer analysis and error detection and correction. It can also be used in applied and corpus linguistics to support Second Language Acquisition (SLA) research and the development of pedagogical resources. Practical applications of the data and future directions are discussed.

1 Introduction

Despite the rapid growth of learner corpus research in recent years (Díaz-Negrillo et al., 2013), no large-scale corpus of second language (L2) Chinese has been made readily available to the research community.

Learner corpora are often used to investigate learner language production in an exploratory manner in order to generate hypotheses about learner language. Recently, learner corpora have also been utilized in various educational NLP tasks including error detection and correction (Gamon et al., 2013), Native Language Identification (Tetreault et al., 2013) and language transfer hypothesis formulation (Swanson and Charniak, 2014).

While such corpus-based studies have become an accepted standard in SLA research and relevant NLP tasks, there remains a paucity of large-scale L2 corpora. For L2 English, the two main datasets are the ICLE (Granger, 2003) and TOEFL11 (Blanchard et al., 2013) corpora, with the latter being the largest publicly available corpus of non-native English writing.[1] However, this data scarcity is far more acute for L2 other than English and this has not gone unnoticed by the research community (Lozano and Mendikoetxea, 2013; Abuhakema et al., 2008).

The present work attempts to address this gap by making available the Jinan Chinese Learner Corpus (JCLC), an L2 Chinese corpus designed for use in NLP, corpus linguistics and other educational domains. This corpus stands out for its considerable size and breadth of data collection. Furthermore, the corpus – an ongoing project since 2006 – continues to be expanded with new data. In releasing this data we hope to equip researchers with the data to support numerous research directions[2] going forward.

The JCLC is freely available to the research community and accessible via our website.[3] It can be used via a web-based interface for querying the data. Alternatively, the original texts can be downloaded in text format for more advanced tasks.

[1]TOEFL11 contains over 4 million tokens in 12,100 texts.
[2]See section 5 for examples.
[3]`http://hwy.jnu.edu.cn/jclc/`

Proceedings of the Tenth Workshop on Innovative Use of NLP for Building Educational Applications, 2015, pages 118–123,
Denver, Colorado, June 4, 2015.

2 Background

Interest in learning Chinese is rapidly growing, leading to increased research in Teaching Chinese as a Foreign Language (TCFL) and the development of related resources such as learner corpora (Chen et al., 2010).

This booming growth in Chinese language learning (Rose and Carson, 2014; Zhao and Huang, 2010), related to the dramatic globalization of the past few decades and a shift in the global language order (Tsung and Cruickshank, 2011), has brought with it learners from diverse backgrounds. Consequently, a key challenge here is the development of appropriate resources – language learning tools, assessments and pedagogical materials – driven by language technology, applied linguistics and SLA research (Tsung and Cruickshank, 2011). The application of these tools and SLA research can greatly assist researchers in creating effective teaching practices and is an area of active research.

This pattern of growing interest in Chinese is also reflected in the NLP community, evidenced by the continuously increasing research focus on Chinese tools and resources (Wong et al., 2009).

A key application of such corpora is in the field of Second Language Acquisition (SLA) which aims to build models of language acquisition. One aspect of SLA is to formulate and test hypotheses about particularly common patterns of difficulty that impede L2 production among students. This is usually done using the natural language produced by learners to identify deficits in their interlanguage.

A criticism of SLA has been that its empirical foundation is weak (Granger, 2002), casting doubts on the generalizability of results. However, this is beginning to change with the shift towards using large learner corpora. The creation of such corpora has led to an efflorescence of empirical research into language acquisition (Granger, 2002).

The use of NLP and machine learning methods has also extended to SLA, with a new focus on a combined multidisciplinary approach to developing methods for extracting ranked lists of language transfer candidates (Swanson and Charniak, 2014; Malmasi and Dras, 2014c).

3 Data Collection and Design

The JCLC project, started in 2006, aims to create a corpus of non-native Chinese texts, similar to the ICLE. The majority of the data has been collected from foreign students learning Chinese at various universities in China, with some data coming from universities outside China. This data includes both exams and assignments. The texts are manually transcribed with all errors being maintained. Error annotations are not available at this stage.

In order to be representative, the corpus includes student data from a wide range of countries and proficiency levels. 59 different nationalities are represented in the corpus. Proficiency levels are classified according to the length of study and include: beginners (less than 1 year), intermediate (2-3 years) and advanced (3+ years). In selecting texts for inclusion, we strived to maximize representativeness across all proficiencies.

3.1 Data Format

The learner texts are made available as Unicode (UTF-8) text files to ensure maximum compatibility with linguistic and NLP tools.

3.2 Metadata

In order to support different research directions, extensive metadata about each text has been recorded. This metadata is available in text, CSV and Microsoft Excel format. The variables are outlined below.

Writing ID A unique id assigned to each text.

Writing Type Either exam or assignment.

Student ID While student names are redacted, they are each assigned a unique ID which allows for the analysis of longitudinal data in the corpus.

Date The submission date of the writing also enables longitudinal analysis of a student's data.

Gender, Age and Education level This data allows the investigation of other research questions, e.g. the critical age hypothesis (Birdsong, 1999).

Native Language This variable is helpful in studying language transfer effects by taking into account the author's native language.

Other Acquired Languages It should be noted that the currently used learner corpora, including the ICLE and TOEFL11, fail to distinguish whether the learner language is in fact the writer's second language, or if it is possibly a third language (L3). It has been noted in the SLA literature that when acquiring an L3, there may be instances of both L1- and L2-based transfer effects on L3 production (Ringbom, 2001). Studies of such second language transfer effects during third language acquisition have been a recent focus on cross-linguistic influence research (Murphy, 2005). The JCLC is the first large-scale learner corpus to include this information as well.

Proficiency Level Determined by the length of study, as described above, a level of beginner, intermediate or advanced is assigned to each text.

Length of Chinese study The amount of time spent studying Chinese. Study inside and outside China are recorded separately.

Chinese heritage learner This variable indicates if the learner is of Chinese heritage, was exposed to Chinese at home, and if so, which dialect.

4 Corpus Analysis

We now turn to a brief analysis of the corpus. The current version of the JCLC contains 5.91 million Chinese characters across 8,739 texts. The top backgrounds of the learners and their text frequency and mean lengths[4] are shown in Table 1.

We also observe high variability in text lengths across the data.[5] A histogram of the text lengths, shown in Figure 1, confirms this trend. We believe that this is a result of the data being collected from a variety of tasks of different scopes from a range of courses at different institutes. Most texts fall in the 250-700 token range of the distribution.

For text types, 57% of the texts are assignments while the remaining 43% are mostly exams.

We can also look at the distribution of proficiency levels in the data, as shown in Figure 2. The majority of the texts, 65%, fall into the medium category with 21% and 14% in the low and high levels, respectively. Comparing this distribution to that of the data in the TOEFL11, also shown in Figure 2,

[4]As measured by the number of Chinese characters.

[5]The standard deviation in text length is 530 tokens.

Language	Texts	Mean Token Count
Indonesian	3381	663.62
Thai	1307	755.86
Vietnamese	824	721.41
Korean	568	399.45
Burmese	410	776.92
Laotian	398	794.78
Khmer	329	691.62
Filipino	293	1135.90
Japanese	270	446.13
Spanish	198	401.85
Mongolian	119	537.02
Others	642	418.26
Total	**8739**	**675.93**

Table 1: The top native language backgrounds available in the corpus, including document counts and the average number of Chinese tokens per text.

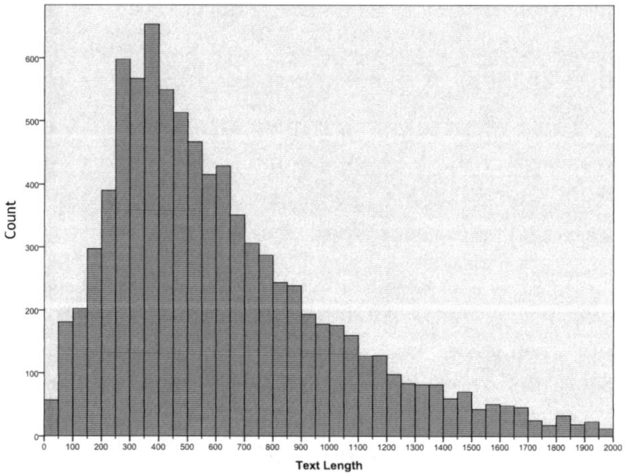

Figure 1: Histogram of text lengths (bin size = 50).

we observe a similar trend with the great majority of the data falling into the medium proficiency bracket. The TOEFL11 has more advanced learners, which is to be expected given that the texts are all collected from a high-stakes exam.

While the data sampling is not equal across all language/proficiency groups we note that this type of imbalance is a perennial problem present in most learner corpora and generally a result of the demographics of the students. Given these constraints, we strived to adhere to key corpus design principles (Wynne, 2005) at all stages.

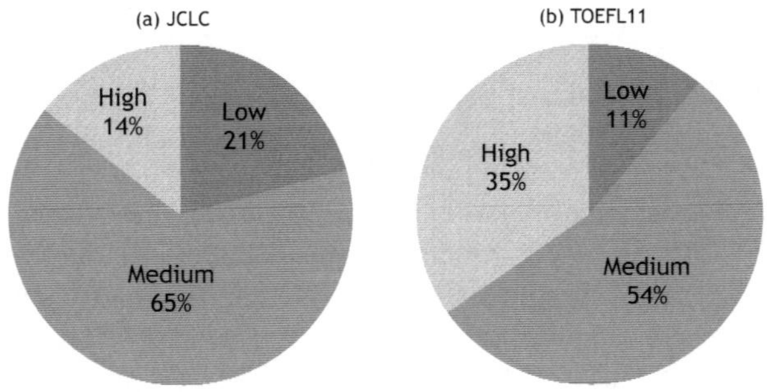

Figure 2: Proficiency distributions in the Jinan Chinese Learner Corpus (left) and the TOEFL11 corpus (right).

In sum, we see that the JCLC is a large corpus and represents various native language and proficiency groups. These characteristics make it suitable for a wide range of research tasks, as described in the next section.

5 Applications

Educational studies in linguistics and NLP have been increasing recently. To this end, this corpus can be used in various areas, as outlined here.

Automatic Essay Scoring is an active area of research that relies on examining the differences between proficiency levels using large learner data and NLP methods (Yannakoudakis et al., 2011). Given the inclusion of proficiency data, the JCLC could also be used to investigate the extension of current automatic grading techniques to Chinese, something which has not been done to date.

Error Detection and Correction There is growing research in building error detection and correction systems trained on learner corpus data (Dahlmeier and Ng, 2011; Han et al., 2010). This was also the focus of a recent shared tasks including Helping Our Own (Dale and Kilgarriff, 2011; Dale et al., 2012) and CoNLL shared tasks (Ng et al., 2013). A recent shared task also focused on Chinese error correction (Yu et al., 2014). This research was also recently extended to Chinese word ordering error detection and correction (Cheng et al., 2014), also using learner texts. The large JCLC can be used in such tasks through the addition of error annotations.

Native Language Identification is the task of inferring an author's native tongue based on their writings in another language (Malmasi and Dras, 2015). This task mainly relies on learner corpora and the JCLC could be directly applied here. A good overview is presented in the review of the recent NLI shared task (Tetreault et al., 2013). NLI methods have already been tested on other languages including Arabic and Finnish (Malmasi and Dras, 2014a; Malmasi and Dras, 2014b).

Transfer Hypothesis Extraction Researchers have recently investigated using data-driven techniques combined with machine learning and NLP to extract language transfer hypotheses from learner corpora (Swanson and Charniak, 2014).

Second Language Acquisition researchers are interested in contrasting the productions of natives and non-natives (Housen, 2002). This is made possible with the JCLC data and the presence of multiple L1s allows for contrastive interlanguage analysis between different native languages as well. The availability of such large-scale data with different L1-L2 combinations can enable broad language acquisition research that can be extrapolated to other learners.

Pedagogical Material Development Learner corpora have been used identify areas of difficulty and enable material designers to create resources that take into account the strengths and weaknesses of students from distinct groups (McEnery and Xiao, 2011). This can also be further expanded to syllabus development where corpus-derived knowledge can be used to guide the design process.

Combined with language transfer analysis, learner data can be used to aid development of pedagogical material within a needs-based and data-driven approach. Once language use patterns are uncovered, they can be assessed for teachability and used to create tailored, native language-specific exercises and teaching material.

Automatic Assessment Generation Combined with the above-mentioned error detection and language transfer extraction methods, this data can be used to automatically generate testing material (e.g. Cloze tests). Following such an approach, recent work by Sakaguchi et al. (2013) made use of large-scale English learner data to generate fill-in-the-blank quiz items for language learners. Previous research in this space had also considered the automatic generation of multiple-choice questions for language testing (Hoshino and Nakagawa, 2005), but without learner data. The use of learner corpora containing naturally produced errors provides a much more promising synergy, enabling the assessment of more complex linguistic errors beyond articles, prepositions and synonyms. With further annotations of the present errors, the JCLC could be used for such tasks.

6 Conclusion and Future Work

The JCLC, a sizeable project that has been ongoing for the last 8 years, has yielded a large-scale language resource for researchers – the first of its kind. As the only such corpus of this size, the JCLC is a valuable resource to support research in various areas, some of which we outlined here.

Research in most of the tasks described in section 5 has focused on English. The availability of the JCLC will enable much of this work to be extended to Chinese, potentially opening new research areas for the community.

The JCLC is an ongoing project and new data continues to be collected and added to the corpus. No fixed target size has been set and it is anticipated that the corpus will grow to be much larger than the current size.

Several directions for future work are under consideration. One avenue is the the creation of further annotation layers over the data to include additional linguistic information such as Chinese word segmentation boundaries, part-of-speech tags, constituency parses and grammatical dependencies. The inclusion of error annotations and manual corrections is another potential avenue for future work.

Another possibility is the addition of a new subcorpus of native texts that can be used as a control group for comparing native and non-native data. This would enable further analysis of learner interlanguage.

Acknowledgments

We would like to thank the three anonymous reviewers for their insightful comments.

References

Ghazi Abuhakema, Reem Faraj, Anna Feldman, and Eileen Fitzpatrick. 2008. Annotating an Arabic Learner Corpus for Error. In *LREC*.

David Birdsong. 1999. *Second Language Acquisition and the Critical Period Hypothesis*. Routledge.

Daniel Blanchard, Joel Tetreault, Derrick Higgins, Aoife Cahill, and Martin Chodorow. 2013. TOEFL11: A Corpus of Non-Native English. Technical report, Educational Testing Service.

Jianguo Chen, Chuang Wang, and Jinfa Cai. 2010. *Teaching and learning Chinese: Issues and perspectives*. IAP.

Shuk-Man Cheng, Chi-Hsin Yu, and Hsin-Hsi Chen. 2014. Chinese Word Ordering Errors Detection and Correction for Non-Native Chinese Language Learners. *Proceedings of COLING 2014*, pages 279–289.

Daniel Dahlmeier and Hwee Tou Ng. 2011. Grammatical error correction with alternating structure optimization. In *Proceedings of the 49th Annual Meeting of the Association for Computational Linguistics: Human Language Technologies-Volume 1*, pages 915–923. Association for Computational Linguistics.

Robert Dale and Adam Kilgarriff. 2011. Helping our own: The HOO 2011 pilot shared task. In *Proceedings of the 13th European Workshop on Natural Language Generation*, pages 242–249. Association for Computational Linguistics.

Robert Dale, Ilya Anisimoff, and George Narroway. 2012. HOO 2012: A report on the preposition and determiner error correction shared task. In *Proceedings of the Seventh Workshop on Building Educational Applications Using NLP*, pages 54–62. Association for Computational Linguistics.

Ana Díaz-Negrillo, Nicolas Ballier, and Paul Thompson. 2013. *Automatic treatment and analysis of learner corpus data*, volume 59. John Benjamins Publishing Company.

Michael Gamon, Martin Chodorow, Claudia Leacock, Joel Tetreault, N Ballier, A Díaz-Negrillo, and P Thompson. 2013. Using learner corpora for automatic error detection and correction. *Automatic treatment and analysis of learner corpus data*, pages 127–150.

Sylviane Granger. 2002. A bird's-eye view of learner corpus research. *Computer learner corpora, second language acquisition and foreign language teaching*, pages 3–33.

Sylviane Granger. 2003. The International Corpus of Learner English: a new resource for foreign language learning and teaching and second language acquisition research. *Tesol Quarterly*, 37(3):538–546.

Na-Rae Han, Joel R Tetreault, Soo-Hwa Lee, and Jin-Young Ha. 2010. Using an error-annotated learner corpus to develop an esl/efl error correction system. In *LREC*.

Ayako Hoshino and Hiroshi Nakagawa. 2005. A real-time multiple-choice question generation for language testing: a preliminary study. In *Proceedings of the second workshop on Building Educational Applications Using NLP*, pages 17–20. Association for Computational Linguistics.

Alex Housen. 2002. A corpus-based study of the L2-acquisition of the English verb system. *Computer learner corpora, second language acquisition and foreign language teaching*, 6:2002–77.

Cristóbal Lozano and Amaya Mendikoetxea. 2013. Learner corpora and second language acquisition. *Automatic Treatment and Analysis of Learner Corpus Data*, 59.

Shervin Malmasi and Mark Dras. 2014a. Arabic Native Language Identification. In *Proceedings of the Arabic Natural Language Processing Workshop (EMNLP 2014)*, pages 180–186, Doha, Qatar, October. Association for Computational Linguistics.

Shervin Malmasi and Mark Dras. 2014b. Finnish Native Language Identification. In *Proceedings of the Australasian Language Technology Workshop (ALTA)*, pages 139–144, Melbourne, Australia.

Shervin Malmasi and Mark Dras. 2014c. Language Transfer Hypotheses with Linear SVM Weights. *Proceedings of the 2014 Conference on Empirical Methods in Natural Language Processing (EMNLP)*.

Shervin Malmasi and Mark Dras. 2015. Large-scale Native Language Identification with Cross-Corpus Evaluation. In *Proceedings of NAACL-HLT 2015*, Denver, Colorado, June. Association for Computational Linguistics.

Tony McEnery and Richard Xiao. 2011. What corpora can offer in language teaching and learning. *Handbook of research in second language teaching and learning. London: Routledge*, pages 364–380.

Shirin Murphy. 2005. Second language transfer during third language acquisition. *Teachers College, Columbia University Working Papers in TESOL & Applied Linguistics*, 3(1).

Hwee Tou Ng, Siew Mei Wu, Yuanbin Wu, Christian Hadiwinoto, and Joel Tetreault. 2013. The CoNLL-2013 Shared Task on Grammatical Error Correction. In *Proceedings of CoNLL*.

Hakan Ringbom. 2001. Lexical transfer in L3 production. volume 31, pages 59–68. Multilingual Matters.

Heath Rose and Lorna Carson. 2014. Introduction. *Language Learning in Higher Education*, 4(2):257–269.

Keisuke Sakaguchi, Yuki Arase, and Mamoru Komachi. 2013. Discriminative Approach to Fill-in-the-Blank Quiz Generation for Language Learners. In *Proceedings of the 51st Annual Meeting of the Association for Computational Linguistics*, pages 238–242.

Ben Swanson and Eugene Charniak. 2014. Data Driven Language Transfer Hypotheses. *EACL 2014*, page 169.

Joel Tetreault, Daniel Blanchard, and Aoife Cahill. 2013. A Report on the First Native Language Identification Shared Task. In *Proceedings of the Eighth Workshop on Innovative Use of NLP for Building Educational Applications*, pages 48–57, Atlanta, Georgia, June. Association for Computational Linguistics.

Linda Tsung and Ken Cruickshank. 2011. *Teaching and Learning Chinese in Global Contexts: CFL Worldwide*. Bloomsbury Publishing.

Kam-Fai Wong, Wenjie Li, Ruifeng Xu, and Zheng-sheng Zhang. 2009. Introduction to Chinese Natural Language Processing. *Synthesis Lectures on Human Language Technologies*, 2(1):1–148.

Martin Wynne, editor. 2005. *Developing Linguistic Corpora: A Guide to Good Practice*. Oxbow Books Oxford.

Helen Yannakoudakis, Ted Briscoe, and Ben Medlock. 2011. A new dataset and method for automatically grading ESOL texts. In *Proceedings of the 49th Annual Meeting of the Association for Computational Linguistics: Human Language Technologies-Volume 1*, pages 180–189. Association for Computational Linguistics.

Liang-Chih Yu, Lung-Hao Lee, and Li-Ping Chang. 2014. Overview of Grammatical Error Diagnosis for Learning Chinese as a Foreign Language. In *Proceedings of the 22nd International Conference on Computers in Education*, Nara, Japan.

Hongqin Zhao and Jianbin Huang. 2010. Chinas policy of Chinese as a foreign language and the use of overseas Confucius Institutes. *Educational Research for Policy and Practice*, 9(2):127–142.

Reducing Annotation Efforts in Supervised Short Answer Scoring

Torsten Zesch
Language Technology Lab
University of Duisburg-Essen

Michael Heilman* **Aoife Cahill**
Educational Testing Service
660 Rosedale Rd
Princeton, NJ 08541, USA

Abstract

Automated short answer scoring is increasingly used to give students timely feedback about their learning progress. Building scoring models comes with high costs, as state-of-the-art methods using supervised learning require large amounts of hand-annotated data. We analyze the potential of recently proposed methods for semi-supervised learning based on clustering. We find that all examined methods (centroids, all clusters, selected pure clusters) are mainly effective for very short answers and do not generalize well to several-sentence responses.

1 Introduction

Automated short answer scoring is getting more and more important, e.g. in the context of large-scale assessment in MOOCs or PISA (OECD, 2010). The state of the art is currently to use supervised systems that are trained for a certain assessment item using manually annotated student responses. For high-stakes assessments like PISA, the effort that goes into manually scoring a large number of responses in order to train a good model might be justified, but it becomes a large obstacle in settings where new items need to be generated more frequently, like in MOOCs. Thus, in this paper we explore ways to reduce the number of annotated training instances required to train a model for a new item.

In the traditional setting, human annotators score responses until a certain total or score distribution is reached that is deemed sufficient to train the model. As long as responses are randomly chosen for manual scoring, it is inevitable that annotators will see a lot of similar answers that will not add much new knowledge to the trained model. Another drawback is that the class distribution in the data is often highly skewed (e.g. because there are only very few excellent answers). Thus, the number of responses that need to be manually scored is much higher than it perhaps needs to be. It should be possible to replace the random selection of responses to be annotated with a more informed approach. In this paper, we explore two approaches: (i) annotating single selected instances, and (ii) annotating whole answer clusters. The difference between the two approaches is visualized in Figure 1.

In the first approach, we try to maximize lexical diversity based on the assumption that the classifier is best informed by responses that are as different as possible (i.e. in the words used). In the second approach, we simulate letting annotators score whole clusters with a label that is used for all instances in this cluster. The main advantage of this method is that it yields multiple training instances with just one decision from the annotator. At the same time, judging whole clusters – especially if they are large – is more difficult than judging a single response, so we need to take this into consideration when comparing the results.

2 Related Work

Basu et al. (2013) describe a related study on *Powergrading*, an approach for computer-assisted scoring of short-answer questions. They carry out experiments using crowd-sourced responses to questions from the US citizenship test. The end goal of that

*Michael Heilman is now a Data Scientist at Civis Analytics.

Proceedings of the Tenth Workshop on Innovative Use of NLP for Building Educational Applications, 2015, pages 124–132,
Denver, Colorado, June 4, 2015.

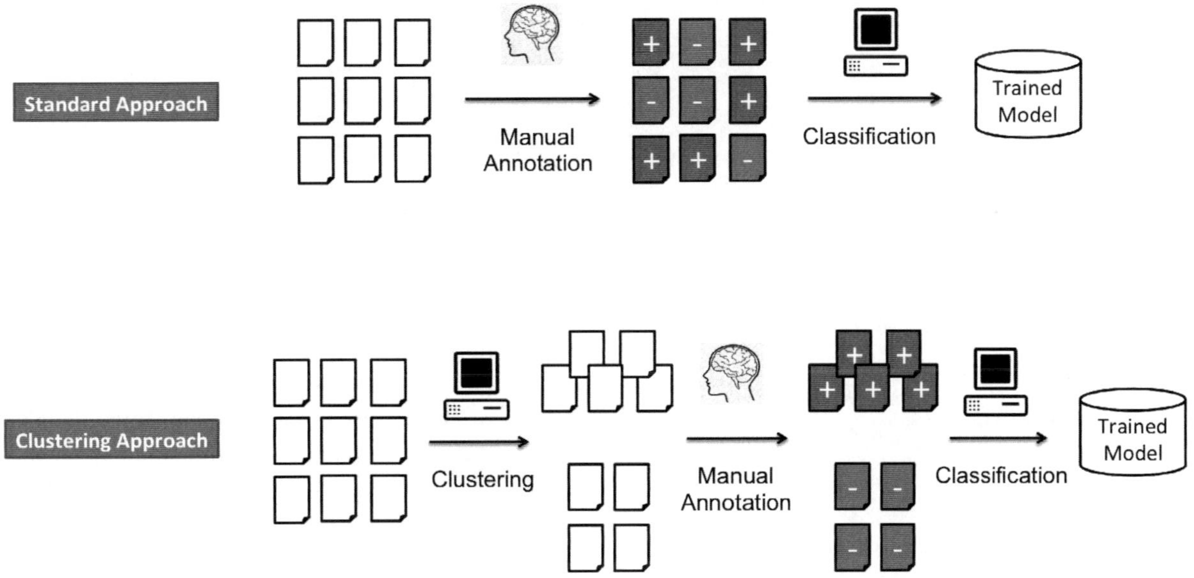

Figure 1: Comparison of the classical supervised approach with clustering approach where a subset of instances is selected for manual annotation.

work is the clustering itself, which they argue is useful for the teacher to understand the misconceptions of the students, while for us it is only an intermediate step towards a trained model for complete automatic scoring of responses. Another major difference between our work and theirs is that we cluster the same feature space that is also used for supervised classification (in order to ensure direct comparability), while Basu et al. (2013) use a pairwise similarity-based space.

The work closest to ours is Horbach et al. (2014) who investigate approaches for selecting the optimum response from within a cluster of responses for a human to score in order to train automated scoring models. They propagate the human score for this optimum response to the rest of the cluster and use this to train an automated scoring system. In experiments on 1,668 very short German responses, they show that a scoring accuracy of over 85% can be achieved by only annotating 40% of the training data. It is unclear what the distribution of scores is in this dataset, and since they only report accuracy and do not report agreement measures such as quadratic weighted kappa, we cannot easily interpret the changes in performance between models.

Basu et al. (2013) and Horbach et al. (2014) both use datasets with very short responses. As we will show later, shorter responses are easier to cluster and it is unclear whether these techniques generalize to several-sentence responses.

While we only focus on the side of the training data, it is also possible to change the learning process itself. Lewis and Gale (1994) introduce *uncertainty sampling*, a form of active learning where a classifier is trained on a small annotated sample and the classifier then finds examples where it is uncertain, which are then also labeled by the teacher. Ienco et al. (2013) combine active learning and clustering to avoid sampling bias which is especially important for streaming data, i.e. when not all answers are available at the beginning. Those first answer might have a strong bias towards a certain outcome class, e.g. better grades because the unmotivated students wait until the last minute to submit. However, this is less of a problem in standardized testing when all students take the test at the same time.

A completely different approach that fully eliminates the need for training data is to use peer-grading (Kulkarni et al., 2014), where the grading process is farmed out to students. The approach relies on the assumption that (at least) some of the students know the correct answer. However, if a misconception is shared by a majority of students, peer-grading will give fatally flawed results.

	# items	# classes	∅ # responses		∅ # tokens		type/token ratio	
ASAP	10	3-4	1,704	(±157)	48	(±12)	.040	(±.016)
PG	10	2	486	(±157)	4	(±2)	.100	(±.005)

Table 1: Overview of datasets

3 Experimental Setup

In this section, we describe the datasets used for evaluation as well as the principal setup of our supervised scoring system.

3.1 Evaluation Datasets

We use two publicly available datasets. Table 1 gives an overview of their properties.

Automated Student Assessment Prize (ASAP) This dataset was used to run the 2012 short answer scoring competition. See Higgins et al. (2014) for a good overview of the challenge and the results. The dataset contains 10 items with approximately 20,000 graded student answers. All responses were written by students primarily in grade 10 and mostly consist of multiple sentences. The responses were graded on a 0-2 or 0-3 scale (i.e. 3–4 classes).

Powergrading (PG) The dataset was created by Basu et al. (2013) and contains about 5,000 crowdsourced responses to 10 questions from the US citizenship test.[1] As can be quickly seen from Table 1, the responses in this dataset are rather short with on average 4 tokens. Looking into the data, it quickly becomes clear that there is relatively little variance in the answers. We thus expect clustering to work rather well on this dataset.

We are not aware of any supervised systems using the PG dataset before. In order to have a point of reference for the performance of the automatic scoring, we computed an average pairwise inter-annotator-agreement of .86 (quadratic weighted kappa) for the three human annotators.

3.2 Scoring System

In order to allow for a fair comparison of all approaches, we implement a basic short answer scoring system using the DKPro TC (Daxenberger et al., 2014) framework. We preprocess the answers using the ClearNLP tools[2] (segmenter, POS-tagger, lemmatizer, and dependency parser). As we are not interested in tuning every last bit of performance, we use a standard feature set (length, ngrams, dependencies) described in more detail in Table 2. We use the DKPro TC wrapper for Weka and apply the SMO learning algorithm in standard configuration.

3.3 Evaluation Metric

We use the evaluation metric that was also used in the ASAP challenge: quadratic weighted kappa κ. We follow the ASAP challenge procedure by applying Fisher-Z transformation when averaging kappas. According to Bridgeman (2013), quadratic weighted kappa is very similar to Pearson correlation r in such a setting.

4 Baseline Results

Applying our basic scoring system and using all available training data, we get a kappa of .67 for the ASAP dataset and .96 for the PG dataset. The extraordinarly high result on the PG dataset (even much higher than the inter-annotator agreement) immediately stands out. As we have already discussed above, the answers in the PG dataset are very short and show very limited lexical variance making it quite easy to learn a good model.

Our results on the ASAP dataset are about 10 percentage points lower than the best results from the literature (Higgins et al., 2014). This is due to our feature set and classifier not being tuned directly on this dataset. The results are in line with what similar systems achieved in the original competition. Results closer to the best results in the literature can be reached by using more specialized features (Tandalla, 2012) or by ensembling multiple scoring models (Zbontar, 2012).

With our system, we get quite consistent results on all ASAP items, while attempts to tune the sys-

[1] In all our experiments, we excluded item #13 as it has multiple correct answers and is thus an anomaly amongst all the other items.

[2] http://clearnlp.wikispaces.com

Name	Configuration	Description
length	Number of words in the response	Longer responses are often better.
ngrams	1-3 grams of words	Which word sequences appear in good or bad responses.
skipNgrams	2-3 skip grams of words, 2 tokens maximum skip	This accounts for non adjacent token combinations.
charNgrams	3-5 grams of characters	This mainly accounts for spelling errors as also partially correct word fragments can influence the score.
dependencies	All dependencies, no threshold	Like skipNgrams this measures whether a certain combination of tokens appears in the document, but also makes sure they are in the same dependency relation.

Table 2: List of features

tem on a certain item led to decreased performance on the others. For our experiments consistency is more important than especially good baseline results, and so we choose to run the same system on all ten items rather than developing ten separate systems that require individual tuning.

Impact of Training Data Size The main question that we are exploring in this paper is whether some answers are more valuable for training than others (Lewis and Gale, 1994; Horbach et al., 2014). By carefully selecting the training instances, we should be able to train a model with performance comparable to the full model that uses less training data and thus is cheaper to create. In order to assess the potential of this approach, it will be useful to compare against the upper and lower bound in performance. For this purpose, we need to find the best and worst subset of graded answers. As the number of possible combinations of k instances from n answers is much too high to search in its entirety, we test 1,000 random samples while making sure that all outcome classes are found in the sample. In Figure 2, we show the performance of the best and worst subset, as well as the mean over all subsets. In order to avoid clutter, we show averaged curves over all items in a dataset.

Looking at the ASAP dataset first, we see that in the average case doubling the amount of training data yields a steady performance increase, but with diminishing returns. Using about 100 (2^7) answers means sacrificing more than 10 percentage points of performance compared with using about 1,000 (2^10) answers. However, it should be noted that in an average practical setting annotating 1,000 answers is next to impossible and 100 still means a considerable effort even if one is willing to live with the suboptimal performance.

For the PG dataset, the pattern is similar in the average case, but we need more training examples in the worst case to get up and running, while the ASAP worst case has a much steeper climb.

We see that the selection of instances actually has an enormous effect for both datasets. Especially for small numbers of training instances, depending on how lucky or unlucky we are in picking instances to score, we might end up with performance near zero, or performance very close to what we can expect when training on all instances. When inspecting the selected subsets it becomes clear that one crucial factor is the lexical variance that we see in instances. We explore this in more detail in the next section.

5 Selecting Answers for Annotation

The idea behind this approach is that given a limited amount of training instances, we should only annotate answers that inform the machine learner in an optimal way. Our hypothesis is that the learning algorithm should gain more from a lexically diverse sample than from a sample of very similar answers. For example, if we have already scored an answer like *Edison invented the light bulb*, rating another very similar one like *The light bulb was invented by Edison* adds little additional information to the model.

Setup We cluster all answers and then select the centroid of each cluster for manual annotation. We use Weka k-means clustering and set the k to the

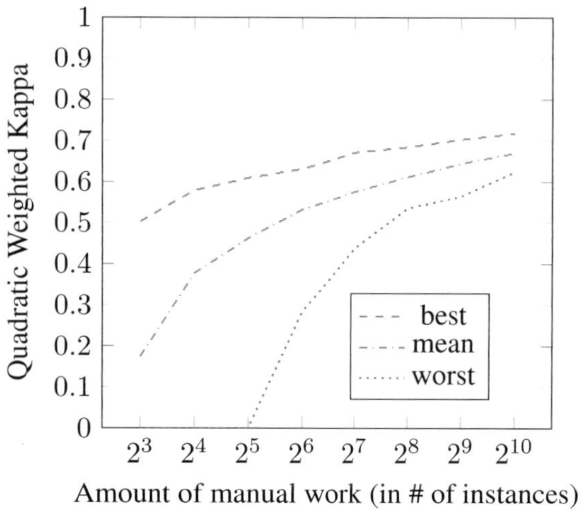

(a) ASAP dataset

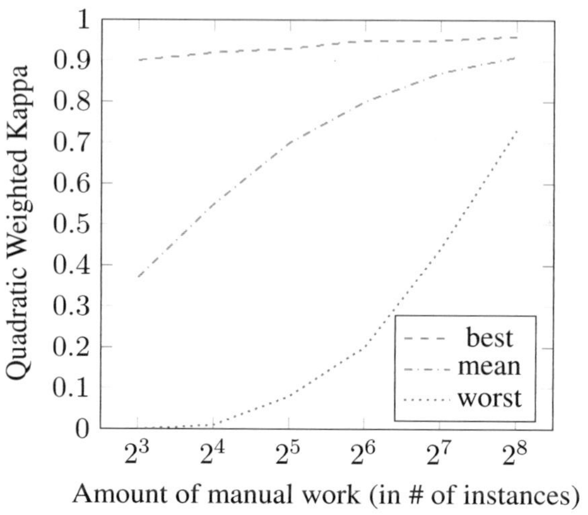

(b) PG dataset

Figure 2: Learning curves for the supervised approach. Best and worst lines indicate the range of potential for selecting good/bad subsamples for training.

desired number of instances we want to annotate. As k-means might result in 'virtual' centroids that do not correspond to any real instance, we determine the instance that is closest to the centroid. In a practical setting, this selected instance would now be presented to a teacher to be scored. In our setting, we simulate this step by using data that was already scored before. (Note that we do not use the score during clustering so that a cluster might contain answers with different scores.) The classifier is then trained using the selected instances.

Results Figure 3 shows the resulting performance when using only the centroids for training. We also show the corresponding learning curves from Figure 2 for comparison.

For the ASAP dataset, results are very close to the average performance, but most of the time slightly worse. For the PG dataset, results are slightly above average with the highest gains for the smallest amount of training data. In both cases, the centroids are obviously not the instances that maximize the performance, as there is quite some room for improvement to reach the best performance.

However, we believe that the result is more important than it might seem, as the average case against which we are comparing here is only a statistical observation. When selecting a subset of instances for manual annotation, we might be lucky and get even better performance than compared with all instances, or we might be very unlucky and get a model that does not generalize at all. Using centroids, we can at least be sure of getting a reasonable minimum performance even if it does not reach the model's full potential.

A disadvantage of maximizing lexical diversity is that similar but contradicting answers like *The solution is A* and *The solution is not A* will be in the same cluster and the difference cannot be learned. This implies a need for better features so that the clustering can get better at distinguishing those cases.

In the next section, we explore whether using the whole clusters might get us closer to the optimal performance as was proposed in previous work.

6 Annotating Whole Clusters

In this section, we explore whether we can take the clustering idea one step further. We explore how we can make use of the whole clusters, not just the centroids.

6.1 Using all clusters

If the teacher has already scored the centroid of a cluster, we could use the same score for all other instances in that cluster. This results in more instances for training without incurring additional annotation

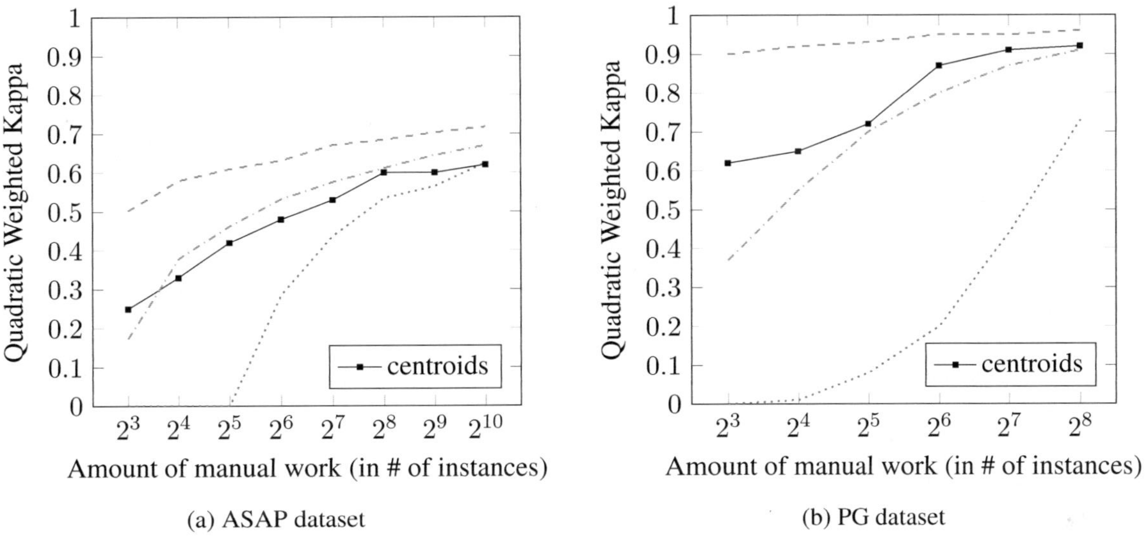

Figure 3: Results for training only on answers selected using **cluster centroids**. Learning curves from Figure 2 are shown for comparison.

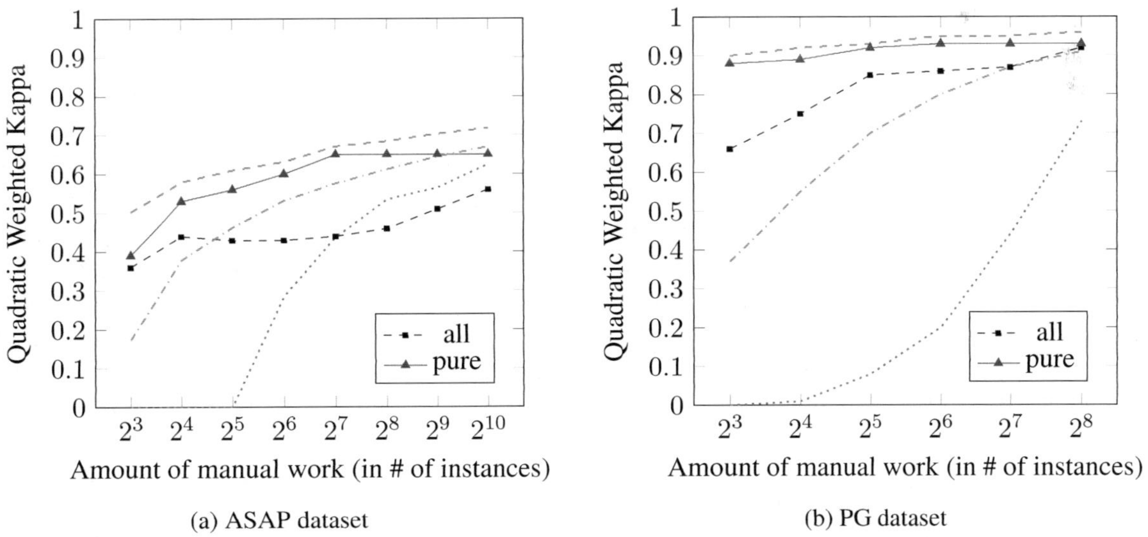

Figure 4: Results for projecting centroid score to **whole clusters** (all) and when selecting **pure clusters** (pure). Learning curves from Figure 2 are shown for comparison.

costs. However, this might obviously also result in a large training error if the clusters are not pure, as we would assign incorrect labels to some instances in that case.

Following Horbach et al. (2014), we use the score assigned to the centroid for the whole cluster and obtain the results shown in Figure 4. For the ASAP dataset, the curve is almost flat, i.e. no matter how many cluster centroids the teacher annotates, prediction results do not improve. The results even dip below the 'worst' line which can be explained by the fact that we are using a lot of noisy training data in this case instead of fewer correct instances. For the PG dataset, results are better due to the much easier clustering. In this case, we can get a significant performance increase compared to just using centroids especially for smaller amounts of annotated instances.

As we are always clustering the whole set of answers, selecting a small number of clusters and at the same time asking for noise-free clusters is equivalent to finding a perfect solution for the scoring problem. For example, if we have 4 scores (0,1,2,3) and 4 clusters, than the clusters can only be pure if all the answers for each score are in their own cluster. This is unlikely to happen. If the number of clusters grows, we expect to have some smaller, purer clusters where similar answers are grouped together, and some larger clusters with a lot of noise.[3] We thus need to find a way to minimize the impact of noise in our training data.

6.2 Using only pure clusters

One possible approach to reduce noise in the clustered data would be to have the teacher look at the whole clusters instead of individual answers only. The teacher would then select only those clusters that are relatively pure, i.e. only contain answers corresponding to the same score. We simulate this step by computing the purity of each cluster using the already known scores for each answer. The solid line in Figure 4 shows the result for this scenario. We see that for both datasets, the results are significantly above average, getting close to the optimal performance. We believe that this is due to the pure clusters representing frequent correct answers or frequent misconceptions shared between students, while impure clusters represent noisy answers that lead to overfitting in the learned model.

[3]Note that, if we ask for as many clusters as there are answers in the set, each answer gets its own cluster and we get the baseline results.

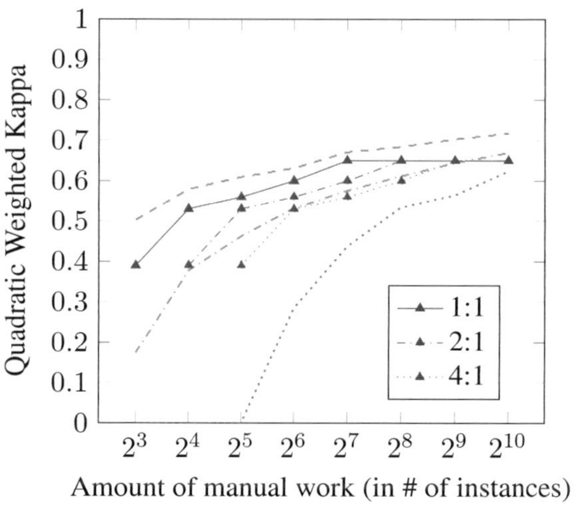

Figure 5: Results annotating pure clusters for different 'exchange rates', where 1:1 means that annotating a cluster and a single answer takes the same time, 2:1 a cluster takes twice as long as a single answer, etc.

Annotation Difficulty One obvious criticism of this approach is that scoring a large cluster takes much longer than scoring a single answer. As a consequence, the 'exchange rate' between scoring an individual answer and a cluster is not 1:1. For example, a 4:1 rate would mean that it takes 4 longer to annotate a cluster compared to a single answer, or in other terms, while annotating a single cluster a teacher could annotate 4 single answers in the same time. In Figure 5, we plot the results on the ASAP dataset for the pure clusters using exchange rates of 1:1, 2:1, and 4:1. With a 2:1 ratio, the pure ASAP clusters are still somewhat ahead of the average performance, with a 4:1 ratio slightly below. While estimating the exact exchange ratio is left to future annotation studies with real teachers annotating clusters, it seems safe to argue that it will be closer to 4:1 than to 1:1, thus resulting in no benefit to the method on the ASAP dataset in terms of manual work to be saved. For the PG dataset, the results are obviously above average and very close to the optimal performance no matter what exchange rate is used. We can thus conclude that the effectiveness of this method strongly depends on how well the answers can be clustered. This in turn depends on both the nature of the answers and the quality of the feature space (or similarity function for graph clustering). As we are using the same feature set for both datasets, the good results on PG can only be explained with the rather short answers and the low lexical variance. However, a better baseline model of answer similarity might also push results on the ASAP dataset more towards the optimal result.

7 Conclusions

In this paper, we explored approaches for minimizing the required amount of annotated instances when training supervised short answer scoring systems. Instead of letting a teacher annotate all instances in advance, we argue that by carefully selecting the instances we might be able to train a comparable model at much lower costs. We do this by clustering the answers and having the teacher only annotate the cluster centroids. We find that – especially for small amounts of instances to be annotated – using centroids yields results comparable to the average random selection of the same number of instances. This means that centroids provide a convenient way to select suitable instances for annotation instead of random selection, but only if one is comfortable with significantly sacrificing scoring quality.

In a second experiment, we follow Horbach et al. (2014) projecting the score assigned to the centroid to the whole cluster. Especially for longer answers that doesn't work well due to the noise introduced by imperfect clustering. Having the teacher select and annotate only pure clusters counters the noise problem, but introduces quite high annotation costs that probably negate any gains.

To summarize: the results indicate that clustering has limited potential for reducing the annotation effort if the answers are short enough to be partitioned well, but is not well suited for longer answers. It remains an open question whether better clustering based on a deeper understanding of multiple sentence answers could change that picture. We make the full source code publicly available so that our experiments can be easily replicated.[4]

[4]https://github.com/zesch/exp-grading-bea2015

Acknowledgements

We thank Nitin Madnani for helpful discussions. We also thank Keelan Evanini, Matthew Mulholland and the anonymous reviewers for thoughtful comments and suggestions.

References

Sumit Basu, Chuck Jacobs, and Lucy Vanderwende. 2013. Powergrading: a Clustering Approach to Amplify Human Effort for Short Answer Grading. *Transactions of the Association for Computational Linguistics (TACL)*, 1:391–402.

Brent Bridgeman. 2013. Human Ratings and Automated Essay Evaluation. In Mark D Shermis and Jill Burstein, editors, *Handbook of Automated Essay Evaluation: Current Applications and New Directions*, chapter 13, pages 221–232. Routledge, New York.

Johannes Daxenberger, Oliver Ferschke, Iryna Gurevych, and Torsten Zesch. 2014. DKPro TC: A Java-based Framework for Supervised Learning Experiments on Textual Data. In *Proceedings of the 52nd Annual Meeting of the Association for Computational Linguistics. System Demonstrations*, pages 61–66, Baltimore, MD, USA, June.

Derrick Higgins, Chris Brew, Michael Heilman, Ramon Ziai, Lei Chen, Aoife Cahill, Michael Flor, Nitin Madnani, Joel R Tetreault, Daniel Blanchard, Diane Napolitano, Chong Min Lee, and John Blackmore. 2014. Is getting the right answer just about choosing the right words? The role of syntactically-informed features in short answer scoring. *Computation and Language*.

Andrea Horbach, Alexis Palmer, and Magdalena Wolska. 2014. Finding a Tradeoff between Accuracy and Rater's Workload in Grading Clustered Short Answers. In *Proceedings of the Ninth International Conference on Language Resources and Evaluation (LREC'14)*, pages 588–595, Reykjavik.

Dino Ienco, Albert Bifet, Indre Zliobaite, and Bernhard Pfahringer. 2013. Clustering based active learning for evolving data streams. In *Proceedings of Discovery Science - 16th International Conference*, pages 79–93.

Chinmay E. Kulkarni, Richard Socher, Michael S. Bernstein, and Scott R. Klemmer. 2014. Scaling short-answer grading by combining peer assessment with algorithmic scoring. In *Proceedings of the first ACM conference on Learning @ scale conference - L@S '14*, pages 99–108. ACM Press.

David D. Lewis and William A. Gale. 1994. A sequential algorithm for training text classifiers. In *Proceedings of the 17th Annual International ACM SIGIR Conference on Research and Development in Information Retrieval*, SIGIR '94, pages 3–12.

OECD. 2010. *PISA 2009 Assessment Framework: Key Competencies in Reading, Mathematics and Science*. PISA, OECD Publishing.

Luis Tandalla. 2012. Scoring short answer essays. Technical report, ASAP Short Answer Scoring Competition System Description. Downloaded from http://kaggle.com/asap-sas/.

Jure Zbontar. 2012. Short answer scoring by stacking. Technical report, ASAP Short Answer Scoring Competition System Description. Downloaded from http://kaggle.com/asap-sas/.

Annotation and Classification of Argumentative Writing Revisions

Fan Zhang
University of Pittsburgh
Pittsburgh, PA, 15260
zhangfan@cs.pitt.edu

Diane Litman
University of Pittsburgh
Pittsburgh, PA, 15260
litman@cs.pitt.edu

Abstract

This paper explores the annotation and classification of students' revision behaviors in argumentative writing. A sentence-level revision schema is proposed to capture why and how students make revisions. Based on the proposed schema, a small corpus of student essays and revisions was annotated. Studies show that manual annotation is reliable with the schema and the annotated information helpful for revision analysis. Furthermore, features and methods are explored for the automatic classification of revisions. Intrinsic evaluations demonstrate promising performance in high-level revision classification (surface vs. text-based). Extrinsic evaluations demonstrate that our method for automatic revision classification can be used to predict a writer's improvement.

1 Introduction

Rewriting is considered as an important factor of successful writing. Research shows that expert writers revise in ways different from inexperienced writers (Faigley and Witte, 1981). Recognizing the importance of rewriting, more and more efforts are being made to understand and utilize revisions. There are rewriting suggestions made by instructors (Wells et al., 2013), studies modeling revisions for error correction (Xue and Hwa, 2010; Mizumoto et al., 2011) and tools aiming to help students with rewriting (Elireview, 2014; Lightside, 2014).

While there is increasing interest in the improvement of writers' rewriting skills, there is still a lack of study on the details of revisions. First, to find out what has been changed (defined as **revision extraction** in this paper), a typical approach is to extract and analyze revisions at the word/phrase level based on edits extracted with character-level text comparison (Bronner and Monz, 2012; Daxenberger and Gurevych, 2012). The semantic information of sentences is not considered in the character-level text comparison, which can lead to errors and loss of information in revision extraction. Second, the differentiation of different types of revisions (defined as **revision categorization**) is typically not fine-grained. A common categorization is a binary classification of revisions according to whether the information of the essay is changed or not (e.g. text-based vs. surface as defined by Faigley and Witte (1981)). This categorization ignores potentially important differences between revisions under the same high-level category. For example, changing the evidence of a claim and changing the reasoning of a claim are both considered as text-based changes. Usually changing the evidence makes a paper more grounded, while changing the reasoning helps with the paper's readability. This could indicate different levels of improvement to the original paper. Finally, for the automatic differentiation of revisions (defined as **revision classification**), while there are works on the classification of Wikipedia revisions (Adler et al., 2011; Bronner and Monz, 2012; Daxenberger and Gurevych, 2013), there is a lack of work on revision classification in other datasets such as student writings. It is not clear whether current features and methods can still be adapted or new features and methods are required.

To address the issues above, this paper makes

Proceedings of the Tenth Workshop on Innovative Use of NLP for Building Educational Applications, 2015, pages 133–143,
Denver, Colorado, June 4, 2015.

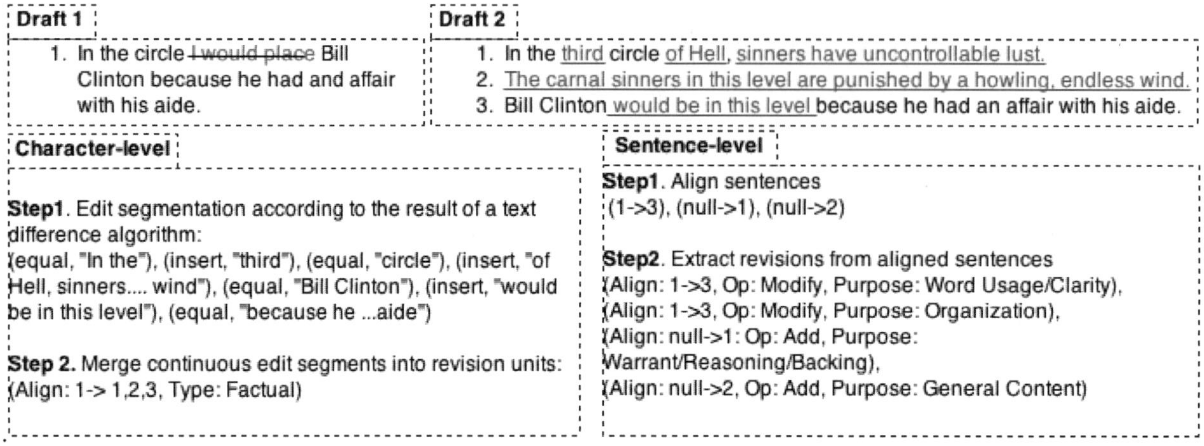

Figure 1: In the example, words in sentence 1 of Draft 1 are rephrased and reordered to sentence 3 of Draft 2. Sentences 1 and 2 in Draft 2 are newly added. Our method first marks 1 and 3 as aligned and the other two sentences of Draft 2 as newly added based on semantic similarity of sentences. The purposes and operations are then marked on the aligned pairs. In contrast, previous work extracts differences between drafts at the character level to get edit segments. The revision is extracted as a set of sentences covering the contiguous edit segments. Sentence 1 in Draft 1 is wrongly marked as being modified to 1, 2, 3 in Draft 2 because character-level text comparison could not identify the semantic similarity between sentences.

the following efforts. First, we propose that it is better to extract revisions at a level higher than the character level, and in particular, explore the sentence-level. This avoids the misalignment errors of character-level text comparisons. Finer-grained studies can still be done on the sentence-level revisions extracted, such as fluency prediction (Chae and Nenkova, 2009), error correction (Cahill et al., 2013; Xue and Hwa, 2014), statement strength identification (Tan and Lee, 2014), etc. Second, we propose a sentence-level revision schema for argumentative writing, a common form of writing in education. In the schema, categories are defined for describing an author's revision operations and revision purposes. The revision operations can be directly decided according to the results of sentence alignment, while revision purposes can be reliably manually annotated. We also do a corpus study to demonstrate the utility of sentence-level revisions for revision analysis. Finally, we adapt features from Wikipedia revision classification work and explore new features for our classification task, which differs from prior work with respect to both the revision classes to be predicted and the sentence-level revision extraction method. Our models are able to distinguish whether the revisions are changing the content or not. For fine-grained classification, our models also demonstrate good performance for some categories. Beyond the classification task, we also investigate the pipelining of revision extraction and classification. Results of an extrinsic evaluation show that the automatically extracted and classified revisions can be used for writing improvement prediction.

2 Related work

Revision extraction To extract the revisions for revision analysis, a widely chosen strategy uses character-based text comparison algorithms first and then builds revision units on the differences extracted (Bronner and Monz, 2012; Daxenberger and Gurevych, 2013). While theoretically revisions extracted with this method can be more precise than sentence-level extractions, it could suffer from the misalignments of revised content due to character-level text comparison algorithms. For example, when a sentence is rephrased, a character-level text comparison algorithm is likely to make alignment errors as it could not recognize semantic similarity. As educational research has suggested that revision analysis can be done at the sentence level (Faigley and Witte, 1981), we propose to extract revisions at the sentence level based on semantic sentence alignment instead. Figure 1 provides an example comparing revisions annotated in our work to revisions extracted in prior work (Bronner and Monz, 2012). Our work identifies the fact that the student added new information to the essay and modified the organization of old sentences. The previous work, however, extracts all the modifications as one unit and cannot distinguish the different kinds of revisions inside the unit. Our method is similar to Lee and Webster's method (Lee and Webster, 2012), where a sentence-level revision corpus is built from college students' ESL writings. However, their corpus only includes the comments of the teachers and does not have every revision annotated.

Revision categorization In an early educational work from Faigley and Witte (1981), revisions are categorized to *text-based change* and *surface change* based on whether they changed the information of the essay or not. A similar categorization (factual vs. fluency) was chosen by Bronner and Monz (2012) for classifying Wikipedia edits. However, many differences could not be captured with such coarse grained categorizations. In other works on Wikipedia revisions, finer categorizations of revisions were thus proposed: vandalism, paraphrase, markup, spelling/grammar, reference, information, template, file etc. (Pfeil et al., 2006; Jones, 2008; Liu and Ram, 2009; Daxenberger and Gurevych, 2012). Corpus studies were conducted to analyze the relationship between revisions and the quality of Wikipedia papers based on the categorizations. Unfortunately, their categories are customized for Wikipedia revisions and could not easily be applied to educational revisions such as ours. In our work, we provide a fine-grained revision categorization designed for argumentative writing, a common form of writing in education, and conduct a corpus study to analyze the relationship between our revision categories and paper improvement.

Revision classification Features and methods are widely explored for Wikipedia revision classifications (Adler et al., 2011; Mola-Velasco, 2011; Bronner and Monz, 2012; Daxenberger and Gurevych, 2013; Ferschke et al., 2013). Classification tasks include binary classification for coarse categories (e.g. factual vs. fluency) and multi-class classification for fine-grained categories (e.g. 21 categories defined by Daxenberger and Gurevych (2013)). Results show that the binary classifications on Wikipedia data achieve a promising result. Classification of finer-grained categories is more difficult and the difficulty varies across different categories. In this paper we explore whether the features used in Wikipedia revision classification can be adapted to the classification of different categories of revisions in our work. We also utilize features from research on argument mining and discourse parsing (Burstein et al., 2003; Burstein and Marcu, 2003; Sporleder and Lascarides, 2008; Falakmasir et al., 2014; Braud and Denis, 2014) and evaluate revision classification both intrinsically and extrinsically. Finally, we explore end-to-end revision processing by combining automatic revision extraction and categorization via automatic classification in a pipelined manner.

3 Sentence-level revision extraction and categorization

This section describes our work for sentence-level revision extraction and revision categorization. A corpus study demonstrates the use of the sentence-level revision annotations for revision analysis.

3.1 Revision extraction

As stated in the previous section, our method takes semantic information into consideration when extracting revisions and uses the sentence as the basic semantic unit; besides the utility of sentence revisions for educational analysis (Faigley and Witte, 1981; Lee and Webster, 2012), automatic sentence segmentation is quite accurate. Essays are split into sentences first, then sentences across the essays are aligned based on semantic similarity.[1] An added sentence or a deleted sentence is treated as aligned to *null* as in Figure 1. The aligned pairs where the sentences in the pair are not identical are extracted as revisions. For the automatic alignment of sentences,

[1]We plan to also explore revision extraction at the clause level in the future. Our approach can be adapted to the clause level by segmenting the clauses first and aligning the segmented clauses after. A potential benefit is that clauses are often the basic units of discourse structures, so extracting clause revisions will allow the direct use of discourse parser outputs (Feng and Hirst, 2014; Lin et al., 2014). However, potential problems are that clauses contain less information for alignment decisions and clause segmentation is noisier.

we used the algorithm in our prior work (Zhang and Litman, 2014) which considers both sentence similarity (calculated using TF*IDF score) and the global context of sentences.

3.2 Revision schema definition

As shown in Figure 2, two dimensions are considered in the definition of the revision schema: the author's behavior (**revision operation**) and the reason for the author's behavior (**revision purpose**).

Revision operations include three categories: *Add*, *Delete*, *Modify*. The operations are decided automatically after sentences get aligned. For example, in Figure 1 where Sentence 3 in Draft 2 is aligned to sentence 1 in Draft 1, the revision operation is decided as *Modify*. The other two sentences are aligned to null, so the revision operations of these alignments are both decided as *Add*.

The definitions of revision purposes come from several works in argumentative writing and discourse analysis. *Claims/Ideas*, *Warrant/Reasoning/Backing*, *Rebuttal/Reservation*, *Evidence* come from *Claim*, *Rebuttal*, *Warrant*, *Backing*, *Grounds* in Toulmin's model (Kneupper, 1978). *General Content* comes from *Introductory material* in the essay-based discourse categorization of Burstein et al. (2003). The rest come from the categories within the surface changes of Faigley and Witte (1981). Examples of all categories are shown in Table 1. These categories can further be mapped to surface and text-based changes defined by Faigley and Witte (1981), as shown in Figure 2.

Note that while our categorization comes from the categorization of argumentative writing elements, a key difference is that our categorization focuses on revisions. For example, while an evidence revision must be related to the evidence element of the essay, the reverse is not necessarily true. The modifications on an evidence sentence could be just a correction of spelling errors rather than an evidence revision.

3.3 Data annotation

Our data consists of the first draft (Draft 1) and second draft (Draft 2) of papers written by high school students taking English writing courses; papers were revised after receiving and generating peer feedback. Two assignments (from different teachers) have been annotated so far. Corpus C1 comes from an AP-level course, contains papers about Dante's Inferno and contains drafts from 47 students, with 1262 sentence revisions. A Draft 1 paper contains 38 sentences on average and a Draft 2 paper contains 53. Examples from this corpus are shown in Table 1. After data was collected, a score from 0 to 5 was assigned to each draft by experts (for research prior to our study). The score was based on the student's performance including whether the student stated the ideas clearly, had a clear paper organization, provided good evidence, chose the correct wording and followed writing conventions. The class's average score improved from 3.17 to 3.74 after revision. Corpus C2 (not AP) contains papers about the poverty issues of the modern reservation and contains drafts from 38 students with 495 revisions; expert ratings are not available. Papers in C2 are shorter than C1; a Draft 1 paper contains 19 sentences on average and a Draft 2 paper contains 26.

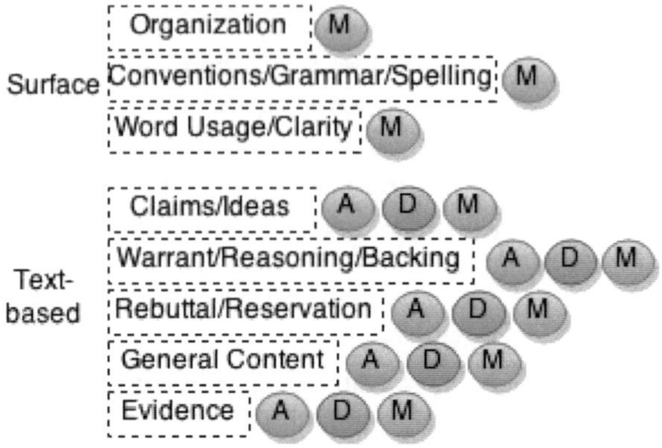

Figure 2: For the revision purpose, 8 categories are defined. These categories can be mapped to surface and text-based changes. Revision operations include *Add*, *Delete*, *Modify* (A, D, M in the figure). Only text-based changes have *Add* and *Delete* operations.

Two steps were involved in the revision scheme annotation of these corpora. In the first step, sentences between the two drafts were aligned based on semantic similarity. The kappa was 0.794 for the sentence alignment on C1. Two annotators discussed about the disagreements and one annotator's work was decided to be better and chosen as the gold standard after discussion. The sentence alignment on C2 is done by one annotator after his annotation and discussion of the sentence alignment on C1. In

Codes	*Claims/Ideas*: change of the position or claim being argued for *Conventions/Grammar/Spelling*: changes to fix spelling or grammar errors, misusage of punctuation or to follow the organizational conventions of academic writing
Example	Draft 1: (1, "**Saddam Hussein and Osama Bin Laden come** to mind when mentioning wrathful people") Draft 2: (1, "**Fidel Castro comes** to mind when mentioning wrathful people")
Revisions	(1->1, Modify, "claims/ideas"), (1->1, Modify, "conventions/grammar/spelling")

Codes	*Evidence*: change of facts, theorems or citations for supporting claims/ideas *Rebuttal/Reservation*: change of development of content that rebut current claim/ideas
Example	Draft 1: (1, "In this circle I would place Fidel.") Draft 2: (1, "In the circle I would place Fidel"), (2, "**He was annoyed with the existence of the United States and used his army to force them out of his country**"), (3, "**Although Fidel claimed that this is for his peoples' interest, it could not change the fact that he is a wrathful person.**")
Revisions	(null->2, "Add", "Evidence"), (null->3, "Add", "Rebuttal/Reservation")

Codes	*Word-usage/Clarity*: change of words or phrases for better representation of ideas *Organization*: changes to help the author get a better flow of the paper *Warrant/Reasoning/Backing*: change of principle or reasoning of the claim *General Content*: change of content that do not directly support or rebut claims/ideas
Example	As in Figure 1

Table 1: Examples of different revision purposes. Note that in the second example the alignment is not extracted as a revision when the sentences are identical.

the second step, revision purposes were annotated on the aligned sentence pairs. Each aligned sentence pair could have multiple revision purposes (although rare in the annotation of our current corpus). The full papers were also provided to the annotators for context information. The kappa score for the revision purpose annotation is shown in Table 2, which demonstrates that our revision purposes could be annotated reliably by humans. Again one annotator's annotation is chosen as the gold standard after discussion. Distribution of different revision purposes is shown in Tables 3 and 4.

3.4 Corpus study

To demonstrate the utility of our sentence-level revision annotations for revision analysis, we conducted a corpus study analyzing relations between the number of each revision type in our schema and student writing improvement based on the expert paper scores available for C1. In particular, the number of revisions of different categories are counted for each student. Pearson correlation between the number of revisions and the students' Draft 2 scores is calculated. Given that the student's Draft 1 and Draft 2 scores are significantly correlated ($p < 0.001$, $R = 0.632$), we controlled for the effect of Draft 1 score by regressing it out of the correlation.[2] We expect surface changes to have smaller impact than text-based changes as Faigley and Witte (1981) found that advanced writers make more text-based changes comparing to inexperienced writers.

As shown by the first row in Table 5, the overall number of revisions is significantly correlated with students' writing improvement. However, when we compare revisions using Faigley and Witte's binary categorization, only the number of text-based revisions is significantly correlated. Within the text-based revisions, only *Claims/Ideas*, *Warrant/Reasoning/Backing* and *Evidence* are significantly correlated. These findings demonstrate that revisions at different levels of granularity have different relationships to students' writing success,

[2]Such partial correlations are one common way to measure learning *gain* in the tutoring literature, e.g. (Baker et al., 2004).

Revision Purpose	Kappa (C1)	Kappa (C2)
Surface		
Organization	1	1
Conventions	0.74	0.87
Word-usage	1	1
Text-based		
Claim	0.76	0.89
Warrant	0.78	0.85
Rebuttal	1	1
General Content	0.76	0.80
Evidence	1	1

Table 2: Agreement of annotation on each category.

Rev Purpose	# Add	# Delete	#Modify
Total	800	96	366
Surface	0	0	297
Organization	0	0	35
Conventions	0	0	84
Word-usage	0	0	178
Text-based	800	96	69
Claim	80	23	8
Warrant	335	40	14
Rebuttal	1	0	0
General	289	23	42
Evidence	95	10	5

Table 3: Distribution of revisions of corpus C1.

Rev Purpose	# Add	# Delete	#Modify
Total	280	53	162
Surface	0	0	141
Organization	0	0	1
Conventions	0	0	29
Word-usage	0	0	111
Text-based	280	53	21
Claim	42	12	4
Warrant	153	23	10
Rebuttal	0	0	0
General	60	13	6
Evidence	25	5	1

Table 4: Distribution of revisions of corpus C2.

Revision Purpose	R	p
# All revisions (N = 1262)	0.516	**<0.001**
# Surface revisions	0.137	0.363
# Organization	0.201	0.180
# Conventions	-0.041	0.778
# Word-usage/Clarity	0.135	0.371
# Text-based revisions	0.546	**<0.001**
# Claim/Ideas	0.472	**0.001**
# Warrant	0.462	**0.001**
# General	0.259	0.083
# Evidence	0.415	**0.004**

Table 5: Partial correlation between number of revisions and Draft 2 score on corpus C1 (partial correlation regresses out Draft 1 score); rebuttal is not evaluated as there is only 1 occurrence.

which suggests that our schema is capturing salient characteristics of writing improvement.

While correlational, these results also suggest the potential utility of educational technologies based on fine-grained revision analysis. For teachers, summaries of the revision purposes in a particular paper (e.g. "The author added more reasoning sentences to his old claim, and changed the evidence used to support the claim.") or across the papers of multiple students (e.g. "90% of the class made only surface revisions") might provide useful information for prioritizing feedback. Fine-grained revision analysis might also be used to provide student feedback directly in an intelligent tutoring system.

4 Revision classification

In the previous section we described our revision schema and demonstrated the utility of it. This section investigates the feasibility of automatic revision analysis. We first explore classification assuming we have revisions extracted with perfect sentence alignment. After that we combine revision extraction and revision classification in a pipelined manner.

4.1 Features

As shown in Figure 3, besides using unigram features as a baseline, our features are organized into *Location*, *Textual*, and *Language* groups following prior work (Adler et al., 2011; Bronner and Monz, 2012; Daxenberger and Gurevych, 2013).

Baseline: unigram features. Similarly to Daxenberger and Gurevych (2012), we choose the count of unigram features as a baseline. Two types of uni-

Draft 1 5 paragraphs, the third paragraph contains 5 sentences	Draft 2 7 paragraphs, the third paragraph contains 9 sentences
In Paragraph 3: 1. The third circle is for Wrathful people. 2. **Saddam Hussein and Osama Bin Laden come to mind when mentioning wrathful people.** ...	In Paragraph 3: 1. The third circle contains wrathful people. 2. **Fidel Castro comes to mind when mentioning wrathful people.** ...

Unigram	Location	Textual	Language
Unigrams of all: ["Saddam", "Hussein", "and", "Osama", "Bin", "Laden", "come", "to", "mind", "when", "mentioning", "wrathful", "people", "Fidel", "Castro", "comes"] ***Unigrams of diff:*** ["Saddam", "Hussein", "and", "Osama", "Bin", "Laden", "Fidel", "Castro", "come", "comes"]	First sentence of paragraph? **Old Draft:** No **New Draft:** No Last sentence of paragraph? **Old Draft:** No **New Draft:** No First paragraph of the essay? **Old Draft:** No **New Draft:** No Last paragraph of the essay? **Old Draft:** No **New Draft:** No Sentence in the paragraph(Ratio): **Old Draft:** (2-1)/(5-1) = 0.25 **New Draft:** 0.125 **Diff:** -0.125 Sentence in the paragraph (Num): **Old Draft:** 2 **New Draft:** 2 **Diff:** 0 paragraph in the essay (Ratio) ...	***Named entity:*** # of PERSON? **Old Draft:** 2 **New Draft:** 1 **Diff:** -1 # of LOCATION? **Old Draft:** 0 **New Draft:** 0 ***Discourse markers:*** Contains "because", "due to"? **Old Draft:** No **New Draft:** No ... ***Sentence difference:*** Diff in commas:0 Diff in digits: 0 ... Edit distance: 31 ... ***Revision Operation:*** *Modify*	***POS tags:*** # of adjectives: **Old Draft:** 1 **New Draft:**1 **Diff:** 0 # of nouns: ... Ratio of adjectives: **Old Draft:** 0.077 **New Draft:** 0.111 **Diff:** 0.034 Ratio of nouns: ... ***Spelling mistakes:*** Old Draft: 0 New Draft: 0 Diff: 0 ***Grammar mistakes:*** Old Draft: 0 New Draft: 0 Diff: 0

Figure 3: An example of features extracted for the aligned sentence pair (2->2).

grams are explored. The first includes unigrams extracted from all the sentences in an aligned pair. The second includes unigrams extracted from the differences of sentences in a pair.

Location group. As Falakmasir et al. (2014) have shown, the positional features are helpful for identifying thesis and conclusion statements. Features used include the location of the sentence and the location of paragraph .[3]

Textual group. A sentence containing a specific person's name is more likely to be an example for a claim; sentences containing "because" are more likely to be a sentence of reasoning; a sentence generated by text-based revisions is possibly more different from the original sentence compared to a sentence generated by surface revisions. These intuitions are operationalized using several feature groups: *Named entity features*[4] (also used in Bronner and Monz (2012)'s Wikipedia revision classification task), *Discourse marker features* (used by Burstein et al. (2003) for discourse structure identification), *Sentence difference features* and *Revision operation* (similar features are used by Daxenberger and Gurevych (2013)).

Language group. Different types of sentences can have different distributions in POS tags (Daxenberger and Gurevych, 2013). The difference in the number of spelling/grammar mistakes[5] is a possible indicator as Conventions/Grammar/Spelling revisions probably decrease the number of mistakes.

4.2 Experiments

Experiment 1: Surface vs. text-based As the corpus study in Section 3 shows that only text-based revisions predict writing improvement, our first experiment is to check whether we can distinguish between the surface and text-based categories. The classification is done on all the non-identical aligned sentence pairs with *Modify* operations[6]. We choose 10-fold (student) cross-validation for our experi-

[3]Since Add and Delete operations have only one sentence in the aligned pair, the value of the empty sentence is set to 0.

[4]Stanford parser (Klein and Manning, 2003) is used in named entity recognition.

[5]The spelling/grammar mistakes are detected using the languagetool toolkit (https://www.languagetool.org/).

[6]*Add* and *Delete* pairs are removed from this task as only text-based changes have *Add* and *Delete* operations.

N = 366	**Precision**	**Recall**	**F-score**
Majority	32.68	50.00	37.12
Unigram	45.53	49.90	46.69
All features	**62.89**∗	**58.19**∗	**55.30**∗

Table 6: Experiment 1 on corpus C1 (Surface vs. Text-based): average unweighted precision, recall, F-score from 10-fold cross-validation; ∗ indicates significantly better than majority and unigram.

N = 162	**Precision**	**Recall**	**F-score**
Majority	31.57	40.00	33.89
Unigram	50.91	50.40	51.79
All features	**56.11**∗	**55.03**∗	**54.49**∗

Table 7: Experiment 1 on corpus C2.

ment. Random Forest of the Weka toolkit (Hall et al., 2009) is chosen as the classifier. Considering the data imbalance problem, the training data is sampled with a cost matrix decided according to the distribution of categories in training data in each round. All features are used except *Revision operation* (since only *Modify* revisions are in this experiment).

Experiment 2: Binary classification for each revision purpose category In this experiment, we test whether the system could identify if revisions of each specific category exist in the aligned sentence pair or not. The same experimental setting for surface vs. text-based classification is applied.

Experiment 3: Pipelined revision extraction and classification In this experiment, revision extraction and Experiment 1 are combined together as a pipelined approach[7]. The output of sentence alignment is used as the input of the classification task. The accuracy of sentence alignment is 0.9177 on C1 and 0.9112 on C2. The predicted *Add* and *Delete* revisions are directly classified as text-based changes. Features are used as in Experiment 1.

4.3 Evaluation

In the intrinsic evaluation, we compare different feature groups' importance. Paired t-tests are utilized to compare whether there are significant differences in performance. Performance is measured using unweighted F-score. In the extrinsic evaluation, we repeat the corpus study from Section 3 using the predicted counts of revision. If the results in the intrinsic evaluation are solid, we expect that a similar conclusion could be drawn with the results from either predicted or manually annotated revisions.

Intrinsic evaluation Tables 6 and 7 present the results of the classification between surface and text-based changes on corpora C1 and C2. Results show that for both corpora, our learned models significantly beat majority and unigram baselines for all of unweighted precision, recall and F-score; the F-score for both corpora is approximately 55.

Tables 8 and 9 show the classification results for the fine-grained categories. Our results are not significantly better than the unigram baseline on *Evidence* of C1, C2 and *Claim* of C2. While the poor performance on *Evidence* might be due to the skewed class distribution, our model also performs better on *Conventions* where there are not many instances. For the categories where our model performs significantly better than the baselines, we see that the location features are the best features to add to unigrams for the text-based changes (significantly better than baselines except *Evidence*), while the language and textual features are better for surface changes. We also see that using all features does not always lead to better results, probably due to over fitting. Replicating experiments in two corpora also demonstrates that our schema and features can be applied across essays with different topics (Dante vs. poverty) written in different types of courses (advanced placement or not) with similar results.

For the intrinsic evaluation of our pipelined approach (**Experiment 3**), as the revisions extracted are not exactly the same as the revisions annotated by humans, we only report the unweighted precision and unweighted recall here; C1 (p: 40.25, r: 45.05) and C2 (p: 48.08, r: 54.30). Paired t-test shows that the results significantly drop compared to Tables 6 and 7 because of the errors made in revision extraction, although still outperform the majority baseline.

Extrinsic evaluation According to Table 10 , the conclusions drawn from the predicted revisions and annotated revisions are similar (Table 5). Text-based changes are significantly correlated with writing improvement, while surface changes are not. We can also see that the coefficient of the predicted text-

[7] We leave pipelined fine-grained classification to the future.

N = 1261	Text-based				Surface		
Experiments	**Claim**	**Warrant**	**General**	**Evidence**	**Org.**	**Word**	**Conventions**
Majority	39.24	32.25	29.38	27.47	25.49	27.75	31.23
Unigram	65.64	63.24	69.21	60.40	49.23	62.07	56.05
All features	66.20	**70.76**∗	72.65∗	60.57	**54.01**∗	73.79∗	70.95∗
Textual+unigram	**71.54**∗	68.13∗	70.76	59.73	52.62∗	**75.92**∗	**71.98**∗
Language+unigram	67.76∗	66.27∗	69.23	59.81	49.21	65.01∗	69.62∗
Location+unigram	69.90∗	67.78∗	**72.94**∗	59.14	49.25	62.40	66.85∗

Table 8: Experiment 2 on corpus C1: average unweighted F-score from 10-fold cross-validation; ∗ indicates significantly better than majority and unigram baselines. *Rebuttal* is removed as it only occurred once.

N = 494	Text-based				Surface	
Experiments	**Claim**	**Warrant**	**General**	**Evidence**	**Word**	**Conventions**
Majority	24.89	32.05	28.21	27.02	13.00	32.67
Unigram	54.34	64.06	55.00	56.99	49.56	60.09
All features	50.22	67.50∗	56.50	53.90	56.07∗	77.78∗
Textual+unigram	52.19	65.79	55.74	56.08	54.19∗	76.08∗
Language+unigram	50.54	**68.24**∗	56.42	56.15	**58.83**∗	**78.92**∗
Location+unigram	53.20	66.45∗	**58.08**∗	52.57	51.55	75.39∗

Table 9: Experiment 2 on corpus C2; *Organization* is removed as it only occurred once.

Predicted purposes	**R**	**p**
#All revisions (N = 1262)	0.516	**<0.001**
#Surface revisions	0.175	0.245
#Text-based revisions	0.553	**<0.001**
Pipeline predicted purposes	**R**	**p**
#All (predicted N = 1356)	0.509	**<0.001**
#Surface revisions	0.230	0.124
#Text-based revisions	0.542	**<0.001**

Table 10: Partial correlation between number of predicted revisions and Draft 2 score on corpus C1. (Upper: Experiment 1, Lower: Experiment 3)

based change correlation is close to the coefficient of the manually annotated results.

5 Conclusion and current directions

This paper contributes to the study of revisions for argumentative writing. A revision schema is defined for revision categorization. Two corpora are annotated based on the schema. The agreement study demonstrates that the categories defined can be reliably annotated by humans. Study of the annotated corpus demonstrates the utility of the annotation for revision analysis. For automatic revision classification, our system can beat the unigram baseline in the classification of higher level categories (surface vs. text-based). However, the difficulty increases for fine-grained category classification. Results show that different feature groups are required for different purpose classifications. Results of extrinsic evaluations show that the automatically analyzed revisions can be used for writer improvement prediction.

In the future, we plan to annotate revisions from different student levels (college-level, graduate level, etc.) as our current annotations lack full coverage of all revision purposes (e.g., "Rebuttal/Reservation" rarely occurs in our high school corpora). We also plan to annotate data from other educational genres (e.g. technical reports, science papers, etc.) to see if the schema generalizes, and to explore more category-specific features to improve the fine-grained classification results. In the longer-term, we plan to apply our revision predictions in a summarization or learning analytics systems for teachers or a tutoring system for students.

Acknowledgments

We would like to thank Wencan Luo, Christian Schunn, Amanda Godley, Kevin Ashley and other members of the SWoRD group for their helpful feedback and all the anonymous reviewers for their suggestions.

This research is funded by IES Award R305A120370 and NSF Award #1416980.

References

B. Thomas Adler, Luca De Alfaro, Santiago M. Mola-Velasco, Paolo Rosso, and Andrew G. West. 2011. Wikipedia vandalism detection: Combining natural language, metadata, and reputation features. In *Proceedings of the 12th International Conference on Computational Linguistics and Intelligent Text Processing - Volume Part II*, CICLing'11, pages 277–288, Berlin, Heidelberg. Springer-Verlag.

Ryan Shaun Baker, Albert T Corbett, Kenneth R Koedinger, and Angela Z Wagner. 2004. Off-task behavior in the cognitive tutor classroom: when students game the system. In *Proceedings of the SIGCHI conference on Human factors in computing systems*, pages 383–390.

Chloé Braud and Pascal Denis. 2014. Combining natural and artificial examples to improve implicit discourse relation identification. In *Proceedings of COLING 2014, the 25th International Conference on Computational Linguistics: Technical Papers*, pages 1694–1705, Dublin, Ireland, August. Dublin City University and Association for Computational Linguistics.

Amit Bronner and Christof Monz. 2012. User edits classification using document revision histories. In *Proceedings of the 13th Conference of the European Chapter of the Association for Computational Linguistics*, EACL '12, pages 356–366, Stroudsburg, PA, USA. Association for Computational Linguistics.

Jill Burstein and Daniel Marcu. 2003. A machine learning approach for identification of thesis and conclusion statements in student essays. *Computers and the Humanities*, 37(4):pp. 455–467.

Jill Burstein, Daniel Marcu, and Kevin Knight. 2003. Finding the write stuff: Automatic identification of discourse structure in student essays. *Intelligent Systems, IEEE*, 18(1):32–39.

Aoife Cahill, Nitin Madnani, Joel Tetreault, and Diane Napolitano. 2013. Robust systems for preposition error correction using wikipedia revisions. In *Proceedings of the 2013 Conference of the North American Chapter of the Association for Computational Linguistics: Human Language Technologies*, pages 507–517, Atlanta, Georgia, June. Association for Computational Linguistics.

Jieun Chae and Ani Nenkova. 2009. Predicting the fluency of text with shallow structural features: case studies of machine translation and human-written text. In *Proceedings of the 12th Conference of the European Chapter of the Association for Computational Linguistics*, pages 139–147. Association for Computational Linguistics.

Johannes Daxenberger and Iryna Gurevych. 2012. A corpus-based study of edit categories in featured and non-featured Wikipedia articles. In *Proceedings of COLING 2012*, pages 711–726, Mumbai, India, December. The COLING 2012 Organizing Committee.

Johannes Daxenberger and Iryna Gurevych. 2013. Automatically classifying edit categories in Wikipedia revisions. In *Proceedings of the 2013 Conference on Empirical Methods in Natural Language Processing*, pages 578–589, Seattle, Washington, USA, October. Association for Computational Linguistics.

Elireview. 2014. Eli review. `http://elireview.com/support/`. [Online; accessed 11-17-2014].

Lester Faigley and Stephen Witte. 1981. Analyzing revision. *College composition and communication*, pages 400–414.

Mohammad Hassan Falakmasir, Kevin D Ashley, Christian D Schunn, and Diane J Litman. 2014. Identifying thesis and conclusion statements in student essays to scaffold peer review. In *Intelligent Tutoring Systems*, pages 254–259. Springer.

Vanessa Wei Feng and Graeme Hirst. 2014. A linear-time bottom-up discourse parser with constraints and post-editing. In *Proceedings of The 52nd Annual Meeting of the Association for Computational Linguistics (ACL 2014), Baltimore, USA, June*.

Oliver Ferschke, Johannes Daxenberger, and Iryna Gurevych. 2013. A survey of nlp methods and resources for analyzing the collaborative writing process in wikipedia. In *The Peoples Web Meets NLP*, pages 121–160. Springer.

Mark Hall, Eibe Frank, Geoffrey Holmes, Bernhard Pfahringer, Peter Reutemann, and Ian H Witten. 2009. The weka data mining software: an update. *ACM SIGKDD explorations newsletter*, 11(1):10–18.

John Jones. 2008. Patterns of revision in online writing a study of wikipedia's featured articles. *Written Communication*, 25(2):262–289.

Dan Klein and Christopher D Manning. 2003. Accurate unlexicalized parsing. In *Proceedings of the 41st Annual Meeting on Association for Computational Linguistics-Volume 1*, pages 423–430. Association for Computational Linguistics.

Charles W Kneupper. 1978. Teaching argument: An introduction to the toulmin model. *College Composition and Communication*, pages 237–241.

John Lee and Jonathan Webster. 2012. A corpus of textual revisions in second language writing. In *Proceedings of the 50th Annual Meeting of the Association for Computational Linguistics: Short Papers-Volume 2*, pages 248–252. Association for Computational Linguistics.

Lightside. 2014. lightside revision assistant. `http://lightsidelabs.com/ra/`. [Online; accessed 11-17-2014].

Ziheng Lin, Hwee Tou Ng, and Min-Yen Kan. 2014. A pdtb-styled end-to-end discourse parser. *Natural Language Engineering*, pages 1–34.

Jun Liu and Sudha Ram. 2009. Who does what: Collaboration patterns in the wikipedia and their impact on data quality. In *19th Workshop on Information Technologies and Systems*, pages 175–180.

Tomoya Mizumoto, Mamoru Komachi, Masaaki Nagata, and Yuji Matsumoto. 2011. Mining revision log of language learning sns for automated japanese error correction of second language learners. In *Proceedings of 5th International Joint Conference on Natural Language Processing*, pages 147–155. Asian Federation of Natural Language Processing.

Santiago M Mola-Velasco. 2011. Wikipedia vandalism detection. In *Proceedings of the 20th international conference companion on World wide web*, pages 391–396. ACM.

Ulrike Pfeil, Panayiotis Zaphiris, and Chee Siang Ang. 2006. Cultural differences in collaborative authoring of wikipedia. *Journal of Computer-Mediated Communication*, 12(1):88–113.

Caroline Sporleder and Alex Lascarides. 2008. Using automatically labelled examples to classify rhetorical relations: An assessment. *Nat. Lang. Eng.*, 14(3):369–416, July.

Chenhao Tan and Lillian Lee. 2014. A corpus of sentence-level revisions in academic writing: A step towards understanding statement strength in communication. In *Proceedings of the 52nd Annual Meeting of the Association for Computational Linguistics (Volume 2: Short Papers)*, pages 403–408, Baltimore, Maryland, June. Association for Computational Linguistics.

Jaclyn M. Wells, Morgan Sousa, Mia Martini, and Allen Brizee. 2013. Steps for revising your paper. `http://owl.english.purdue.edu/owl/resource/561/05`.

Huichao Xue and Rebecca Hwa. 2010. Syntax-driven machine translation as a model of esl revision. In *Proceedings of the 23rd International Conference on Computational Linguistics: Posters*, pages 1373–1381. Association for Computational Linguistics.

Huichao Xue and Rebecca Hwa. 2014. Improved correction detection in revised esl sentences. In *Proceedings of the 52nd Annual Meeting of the Association for Computational Linguistics (Volume 2: Short Papers)*, pages 599–604, Baltimore, Maryland, June. Association for Computational Linguistics.

Fan Zhang and Diane Litman. 2014. Sentence-level rewriting detection. In *Proceedings of the Ninth Workshop on Innovative Use of NLP for Building Educational Applications*, pages 149–154, Baltimore, Maryland, June. Association for Computational Linguistics.

Embarrassed or Awkward?
Ranking Emotion Synonyms for ESL Learners' Appropriate Wording

Wei-Fan Chen
Academia Sinica
viericwf@iis.sinica.edu.tw

Mei-Hua Chen
Department of Foreign Language and Literature,
Tunghai University
chen.meihua@gmail.com

Lun-Wei Ku
Academia Sinica
lwku@iis.sinica.edu.tw

Abstract

We introduce a novel framework based on the probabilistic model for emotion wording assistance. The example sentences from the on-line dictionary, *Vocabulary.com* are utilized as the training data; and the writings in a designed ESL's writing task are the testing corpus. The emotion events are captured by extracting patterns of the example sentences. Our approach learns the joint probability of contextual emotion events and the emotion words from the training corpus. After extracting patterns in the testing corpus, we then aggregate their probabilities to suggest the emotion word that describes the ESL's context most appropriately. We evaluate the proposed approach by the NDCG@5 of the suggested words for the writings in the testing corpus. The experiment result shows our approach can more appropriately suggest the emotion words compared to SVM, PMI and two representative on-line reference tools, PIGAI and *Thesaurus.com.*

1 Introduction

Most English-as-a-second-language (ESL) learners have been found to have difficulties in emotion vocabulary (Pavlenko, 2008). With limited lexical knowledge, learners tend to use common emotion words such as angry and happy to describe their feelings. Moreover, the learner's first language seems to lead to inappropriate word choices (Altarriba and Basnight-Brown, 2012). Many learners consult the thesaurus for synonyms of emotion words; typically, the synonyms suggested come with little or no definition or usage information. Moreover, the suggested synonyms seldom take into account contextual information. As a result, the thesaurus does not always help language learners select appropriately nuanced emotion words, and can even mislead learners into choosing improper words that sometimes convey the wrong message (Chen *et al.*, 2013). Take *embarrassed* and *awkward* for example: although they both describe situations where people feel uneasy or uncomfortable, in practice they are used in different scenarios. According to *Vocabulary.com*, *embarrassed* is more self-conscious and can result from shame or wounded pride: for instance, *He was too embarrassed to say hello to his drunken father on the street*. On the other hand, *awkward* would be "socially uncomfortable" or "unsure and constrained in manner": *He felt awkward and reserved at parties.* These examples illustrate not only the nuances between synonymous emotion words, but also the difficulty for language learners in determining proper words. There is a pressing need for a reference resource providing a sufficient number of emotion words and their corresponding usage information to help language learners expand their knowledge of emotion words and learn proper emotional expressions.

To address this issue, we propose a novel approach to help differentiate synonyms of emotion words based on contextual clues—Ranking Emotional SynOnyms for language Learners' Vocabulary Expansion (RESOLVE). This involves first the learning of emotion event scores between an event and an emotion word from a corpus: these

Proceedings of the Tenth Workshop on Innovative Use of NLP for Building Educational Applications, 2015, pages 144–153,
Denver, Colorado, June 4, 2015. ©2015 Association for Computational Linguistics

scores quantify how appropriate an emotion word is to describe a given event. Subsequently, based on the emotion event in the learner's text, RESOLVE suggests a list of ranked emotion words.

2 Related Work

Previous studies related to RESOLVE can be divided into four groups: **paraphrasing**, **emotion classification**, **word suggestion** and **writing assessment**. The aim of paraphrasing research is how to express the same information in various ways. Such alternative expressions of the same information rely on paraphrase pairs which map an expression to a previously learned counterpart, or inference rules that re-structure the original sentences. Most work uses machine translation techniques such as statistical machine translation or multiple-sequence alignment to extract paraphrase pairs from monolingual corpora (Barzilay and McKeown, 2001; Keshtkar and Inkpen, 2010), or bilingual corpora (Bannard and Callison-Burch, 2005; Callison-Burch, 2008; Chen *et al.*, 2012). Approaches based on inference rules, on the other hand, derive these rules by analyzing the dependency relations of paraphrase sentences (Lin and Pantel, 2001; Dinu and Lapata, 2010). Alternative expressions can be achieved by applying inference rules to rephrase the original sentence. In general, the focus of paraphrasing is sentence variation, which involves sentence re-structuring, phrase alternation and word substitution. Generating an alternative sentence without changing the sentence's original meaning is the main concern. For RESOLVE, in contrast, rather than attempting preservation, the focus is on appropriate in-context word substitution. There are several online paraphrasing tools. PREFER[1] (Chen *et al.*, 2012) is an online paraphrase reference interface that generates phrase-level paraphrases using a combination of graph and PageRank techniques. Chen shows a significant improvement in learner paraphrase writing performance. For RESOLVE, instead of pursuing participant improvements in semantically equivalent rephrasing, the aim is to suggest contextually appropriate wording. Microsoft Contextual Thesaurus[2] (MCT) is similar to PREFER: it is an online reference tool that smartly rephrases an input sentence into various alternative expressions, using both word-level and phrase-level substitution. However, we know of no study that evaluates learning effectiveness when using MCT. Finally, SPIDER (Barreiro, 2011) targets document-level editing; it relies on derivations from dictionaries and grammars to paraphrase sentences, aiming at reducing wordiness and clarifying vague or imprecise terms. In short, rather than offering better suggestions, paraphrasing tools provide equivalent expressions.

Emotion classification concerns approaches to detect the underlying emotion of a text. Related work typically attempts this using classifiers. These classifiers are trained with features such as n-grams (Tokuhisa *et al.*, 2008), word-level pointwise mutual information (PMI) values (Agrawal *et al.*, 2012; Bullinaria *et al.*, 2007; and Church *et al.*, 1990) or a combination of word POS and sentence dependency relations (Ghazi *et al.*, 2012). The remained works of emotion classification in above mentioned research to deal with emotions aroused by events inspires us to relate events to emotion words in RESOLVE. In addition, in terms of emotion classification, RESOLVE classifies texts into fine-grained classes where each emotion word can be viewed as a single class; in contrast, most emotion classification work focuses only on coarse-grained (6 to 10 classes) emotion labeling. It is a challenging work.

Word suggestion involves guessing a possible replacement for a given word in a sentence, or finding word collocations. A representative research task for word suggestion is the SemEval 2007 English Lexical Substitution task: the problem is to find a word substitute for the designated word given a sentence. Zhao *et al.* (2007) first uses rules to find possible candidates from WordNet and verifies the sentence after substitution using Web search results; Dahl *et al.* (2007) utilizes a more traditional n-gram model but uses statistics from web 5-grams. Although closely related to our work, this task is different in several ways. First, the word for which a substitute is required is already an appropriate word, as it appears in a sentence from a well-written English corpus, the Internet Corpus of English[3]. However, the goal of our work is to determine whether a word selected by ESL learners is appropriate, and if necessary to

[1] http://service.nlpweb.org/PREFER

[2] http://labs.microsofttranslator.com/thesaurus/

[3] http://corpus.leeds.ac.uk/internet.html

suggest appropriate alternatives. Observation of our corpus has shown that typically, the word selected by ESL learners is not the most appropriate one. This is in contrast to the cited related works in which the original in-context wording is usually the most appropriate one. However, in our research the context often does not support the way the ESL learner's word(s) are used. Second, the context of the given word in SemEval is a sentence, while in this work it is a document. Third, annotators for SemEval were limited to at most three possible substitutions, all of which were to be equally appropriate, while in our work annotators are asked to assign ranks to all candidates (synonyms of the given word). Fourth, in SemEval the words to be substituted come from various syntactic or semantic categories, while we only suggest appropriate emotion words to the learners.

For writing assessment, existing works are known as automatic essay assessment (AEA) systems, which analyze user compositions in terms of wording, grammar and organization. PIGAI[4], targeted at generating suggested revisions, suggests unranked synonyms for words. However, unranked synonyms easily confuse Chinese learners (Ma, 2013). E-rater (Leading *et al.* 2005), a writing evaluation system developed by the Educational Testing Service (ETS), offers a prompt-specific vocabulary usage score, a scoring feature which evaluates the word choice and compares words in the writing with samples in low- to high-quality writings. Ma shows that students' scores on PIGAI increase after using PIGAI, and that these results are in proportion to the frequency they use PIGAI. As for E-rater, to our best knowledge, its focus is on helping judges to score writing rather than on assisting learners. In contrast, the purpose of RESOLVE is to directly assist language learners in finding appropriate wording, especially for emotion words.

As context and events are crucial to appropriate emotion wording, both have been taken into account in the development of RESOLVE. For context, learner writings describing emotions have been utilized to extract contextual clues. For events, Jeong and Myaeng (2012) find that in the well-annotated TimeBank corpus, 65% of the event conveyance was accomplished using verbs; thus we detect events from verb phrases. In contrast to paraphrasing and emotion analysis, the goal of RESOLVE is to distinguish the nuances among emotion synonyms in order to aid in language learning: this makes it a novel research problem.

[4] http://www.pigai.org

3 Method

We postulate that patterns can describe emotion events, and that event conveyance is accomplished primarily using verbs (Jeong and Myaeng, 2012). In RESOLVE, verb-phrase patterns are selected for use in differentiating emotion word synonyms, that is, candidate emotion words, using their relationships with these patterns. Figure 1 shows the two-stage RESOLVE framework. First we learn corpus patterns (patterns extracted from the corpus) and their emotion event scores, *EES*, for all emotion words, and then, given the target emotion word, we rank the candidate emotion words to suggest appropriate wording using the writing patterns (patterns extracted from learner writing) and associated emotion event scores learned in the first stage. To determine the similarity between corpus patterns and writing patterns, we also propose a pattern matching algorithm which takes into account the cost of wildcard matching. Finally, to verify the effectiveness of RESOLVE in aiding precise wording, a learning experiment is designed. In an example RESOLVE scenario, the learner writes the following: "I love guava but one day I ate a rotten guava with a maggot inside, which made me **disgust**." She is not sure about the wording so she turns to RESOLVE for help. She is given a ranked word suggestion list: *repugnance*, *disgust*, *repulsion*, *loathing* and *revulsion*; which are more appropriate than the list *Theasurus.com* provides: *antipathy*, *dislike*, *distaste*, *hatred* and *loathing*.

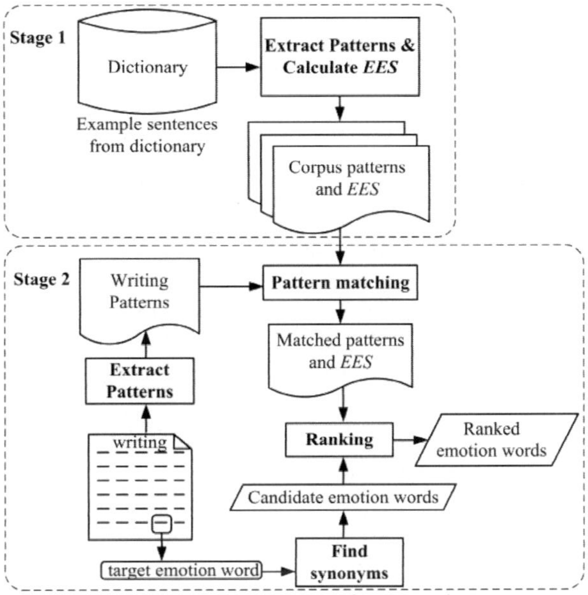

Figure 1: RESOLVE framework.

3.1 Stage One: Learning Corpus Patterns for All Emotion Words

In this stage, we learn patterns and their relations to emotion words from the corpus. Sentences are first pre-processed, after which patterns are extracted from the corpus and their emotion event scores calculated.

Pre-processing. As compound sentences can be associated with more than one emotion event, they must be pre-processed before we extract patterns. Compound sentences are first broken into clauses according to the Stanford phrase structure tree output (Klein and Manning, 2003). In the experiments, these clauses are treated as sentences.

Pattern Extraction. Emotion events are characterized by verb-phrase patterns, derived from the output of the Stanford dependency parser (De Marneffe *et al.*, 2006). This parser generates the grammatical relations of word pairs and determines the ROOT, which is often the verb, after parsing each sentence. We describe the extraction steps given the sentence "*We gave the poor girl a new book*.". A total of 746,919 patterns were extracted in this process.

Step1: Identify the ROOT (*gave*) and all its dependents based on the parsing result.

Step2: Replace the words having no dependency relation to the *ROOT* with wildcards; consecutive wildcards were combined into one. (*we gave * girl * book*)

Step3: Filter out less informative dependents (i.e., those nodes that are not the children of the ROOT in the dependency parse tree) by replacing with wildcards the dependents in the following relations to the ROOT: *subj, partmod, comp, parataxis, advcl, aux, poss, det, cc, advmod* and *dep*. (** gave * girl * book*)

Step4: Generalize the grammatical objects by replacing them with their top-level semantic class in *WordNet*. (** gave * <person> * <artifact>*)

Step5: Lemmatize the verbs using *WordNet*. (** give * <person> * <artifact>*)

Step6: Removing the starting and ending wildcards. (*give * <person> * <artifact>*)

Emotion Event Score Calculation. Once the patterns are extracted, RESOLVE learns their emotion event scores (EES) to quantize their relations to each emotion word. Here we discover an interesting issue: the extracted pattern may summarize an emotion event, but it may also tell the emotion it bears directly with emotion words. To determine whether patterns containing emotion words have different characteristics and effects on performance, we term them self-containing patterns. Hence two pattern sets are used in experiments: one that includes all extracted patterns (P_{all}), and the other that excludes all self-containing patterns ($P_{-scPattern}$).

As shown in equation (1), we define the emotion event score ($EES_{p,e}$) of a pattern p for an emotion word e by the conditional probability of e given p.

$$EES_{p,e} = P(e \mid p) \qquad (1)$$

3.2 Stage Two: Ranking Synonyms of the Emotion Word to Suggest Appropriate Wording

In previous stage we built a pattern set for each emotion word. In this stage, there are four tasks: enumerate candidate emotion words for the target emotion word, extract writing patterns, match the writing patterns to the corpus patterns of the candidates, and rank the candidates. To enumerate the candidate emotion words, RESOLVE first looks up synonyms of the target emotion word in *WordNetSynsets* and in *Merriam Webster's Dictionary*.

Pattern Matching. For each candidate e_i, RESOLVE compares writing patterns $P_{writing}=(pw_1,pw_2,...pw_N)$ with corpus patterns P_{corpus}, and returns the matching corpus patterns $P_{match}=(p_1,p_2,...p_N)$ and their corresponding emotion event scores; where N is number of clauses in the writing. Edit distance is utilized to calculate the similarity between a writing pattern and a corpus pattern, where the matching corpus pattern is defined as that with the maximum pattern similarity to the writing pattern (in a one-to-one matching). The emotion scores of this matched corpus pattern for different emotion words will be used as the writing pattern scores.

We propose a variation of edit distance which accepts wildcards (that is, edit-distance with wildcards, *EDW*) that allows for partial matching, including similar patterns, and hence increases hit rates. Therefore, we add a *wildcard replacement cost* (WRC) to the edit cost (*general edit cost*, GEC) in the traditional definition of the edit distance. For this purpose, a two-dimensional vector (GEC, WRC) which considers two edit costs separately is used to measure the *EDW* between patterns S_1 and S_2. *EDW* is defined as

$$EDW(S_1 \rightarrow S_2) = D_{I,J} = (GEC,\ WRC) \quad (2)$$

where $S_1=\{s_1(1), s_1(2), s_1(3),...,s_1(I)\}$ and $S_2=\{s_2(1), s_2(2), s_2(3),..., s_2(J)\}$ are tokens of the corpus pattern S1 and the writing pattern S_2; I and J are the lengths of S_1 and S_2; i and j are the indices of S_1 and S_2; and $D_{I,J}$ is recursively calculated from 1 to I and 1 to J using the edit distance formula. Note that $D_{0,0}$ is (0,0). A wildcard may be replaced with one or more tokens, or vice versa. When calculating *EDW*, if there is a wildcard replacement, the replacement cost is added to the WRC; for other cases, the edit cost is added to the GEC.

We here define the value of the WRC. The traditional edit-distance algorithm takes into account only single-token costs, whereas wildcards in our patterns may replace more than one token. Wildcard insertion and deletion costs hence depend on the number of tokens a wildcard may replace. After some experiments, we empirically choose e (Euler's number) as the cost of wildcard insertion and deletion. Note that e is also very close to the mean of the number of words replaced by one wildcard (positively skewed distribution). Table 1 shows the costs of all EDW operations.

Operation	Cost
Wildcard Insertion (ø → *)	e
Wildcard Deletion (* →ø)	e
Wildcard Replacement (* →token)	1
Wildcard Replacement (token → *)	e

Table 1: Edit distance costs for EDW operations.

Empirically, if no exact pattern is found, to represent the pattern we seek a more general pattern rather than a specific one. A general pattern's meaning includes the meaning of the original pattern, but a specific pattern's meaning is part of the original. For example, consider the pattern "*eat * tomorrow morning quickly.*" If unable to find an exactly matching pattern, it would be better to use "*eat * tomorrow * quickly*" rather than "*eat breakfast tomorrow morning quickly*" to represent it. Hence "*→token" wildcard replacements ("* →morning" in the example) should be assigned a lower cost than "token→*" wildcard replacements ("breakfast→*" in the example), as a wildcard token may represent several general tokens: "token→*" wildcard replacement (token →*) is equivalent to inserting more than zero tokens and "*→token" wildcard replacements are equivalent to deleting more than zero tokens. Therefore, we define the cost of "*→token" wildcard replacement as 1 and "token→*" wildcard replacement as e.

$$\begin{aligned} p_{match} &= \underset{p_{corpus} \in P_{corpus}}{\arg\max}\ similarity\left(p_{corpus} \rightarrow p_{wiriting}\right) \\ &= \underset{p_{corpus} \in P_{corpus}}{\arg\max}\ -\sqrt{GEC^2 + WRC^2} \end{aligned} \quad (3)$$

The Euler equation, equation (3), takes into account both GEC and WRC to calculate the similarity of two patterns. The matching corpus pattern is that with the maximum similarity.

Candidate Emotion Word Ranking. The scoring function for ranking candidates $S=\{e_1,e_2,...,e_I\}$ depends on the conditional probability of candidate e_i given writing patterns and candidates as defined in equation (4), which equals equation (5), assuming the patterns in $P_{writing}$ are mutually independent.

$$P(e_i \mid P_{writing}, S) = P(e_i \mid pw_1, pw_2, ..., pw_N, S) \quad (4)$$

$$P(e_i \mid pw_1, pw_2, ..., pw_N, S) \propto \left(\prod_n P(e_i \mid pw_n, S) \right) \cdot P(e_i \mid S)^{1-N} \quad (5)$$

The second term in equation (5), $P(e_i|S)^{1-N}$, denotes the learner's preference with respect to writing topics. As we have no learner corpus, we assume that there are no such preferences and thus that $P(e_i|S)$ is uniformly distributed among e_i in S. As a result, when ranking e_i, $P(e_i|S)^{1-N}$ can be omitted. In addition, for the scores of the writing patterns we must use the scores of the matching corpus pattern found by the EDW algorithm for the corpus. Therefore, we rewrite the first term of equation (5) as follows.

$$\prod_n P(e_i \mid pw_n, S) = \prod_n \frac{P(pw_n, e_i, S)}{P(p_n, e_i, S)} \cdot \frac{P(p_n, S)}{P(pw_n, S)} \cdot P(e_i \mid p_n, S) \propto \prod_n \frac{P(pw_n, e_i, S)}{P(p_n, e_i, S)} \cdot P(e_i \mid p_n, S) \quad (6)$$

$P(e_i|p_n,S)$ in equation (6) can be calculated by *EES*, and the similarity value from equation (3) is utilized in equation (7) to estimate the first term. Equation (8), its logarithmic form, is the final scoring function for ranking.

$$scr(e_i, P_{writing}, S) = \prod_n e^{similarity(p_n \rightarrow pw_n)} \cdot P(e_i \mid p_n, S) \quad (7)$$

$$\ln\left(scr(e_i, P_{writing}, S)\right) = \sum_n \left(\ln\left(\frac{EES_{p_n,e_i}}{\sum_{e_i \in S} EES_{p_n,e_i}} \right) - \sqrt{GEC_n^{\,2} + WRC_n^{\,2}} \right) \quad (8)$$

Modified EES. After observing the corpus characteristics, we further modified *EES* by adding the weighting factors ICZ_e (the Inverse Corpus-siZe-ratio for emotion word e, where the corpus size denotes the number of patterns) and CTP^l_p (the emotion Category Transition Penalty for pattern p, where l denotes the level of the emotion word hierarchy, as explained later) in equation (9). *ICZ* in equation (10) normalizes the effect of the emotion word corpus size. When an emotion word appears more frequently, more example sentences are collected, resulting in a larger corpus. This can lead to a suggestion bias toward commonly seen emotion words.

$$EES'_{p,e} = EES_{p,e} \cdot ICZ_e \cdot \prod_{l=1}^{3} \left(1 - CTP^l_p\right) \quad (9)$$

$$ICZ_e = \log\left(P(e)^{-1}\right) \quad (10)$$

The other weighting factor, *CTP*, takes into account emotion word similarity. As mentioned, emotion words are derived from *WordNet-Affect* and then extended via *WordNetSynset* and *Webster Synonyms*; as shown in Figure 2, we build a three-layered hierarchy of emotion words. Level 1 is the six major emotion categories in *WordNet-Affect* (*anger, disgust, fear, joy, sadness,* and *surprise*), level 2 is the 1,000 emotion words from *WordNet-Affect*, and level 3 is the synonyms of the level-2 emotion words.

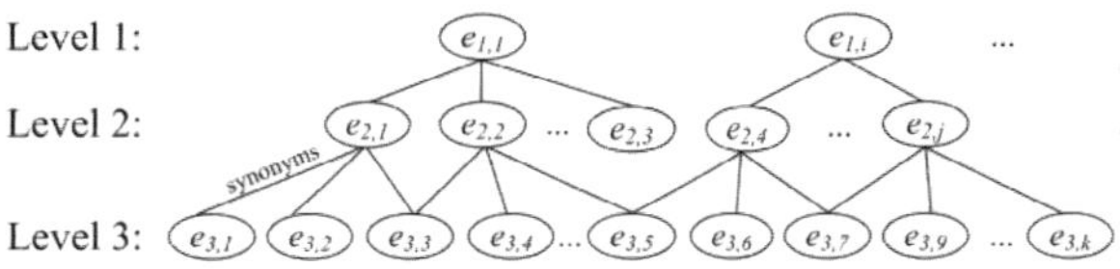

Figure 2: The emotion word hierarchy.

$$CTP^l_p = \frac{\frac{(P(p))^2}{\sum_c (P(c,p))^2} - 1}{m_{level}}, 0 \le CTP^l_p \le 1 \quad (11)$$

Intuitively, patterns that co-occur with many different emotion words are less informative. To assign less importance to these patterns, *CTP* estimates how often a pattern transits among emotion categories and adjusts its score accordingly in equation (11), where m is the number of categories in each level; c is the emotion category. High-*CTP* patterns appear in more emotion categories or are evenly distributed among emotion categories and are hence less representative. Note that categories in lower levels (for instance level 1) are less similar, and transitions among these make patterns less powerful.

4 Experiment

4.1 Emotion Words and Corpus

The corpora used in this study include *WordNet-Affect* (Strapparava and Valitutti, 2004), *WordNetSynset* (Fellbaum, 1999), *Merriam Webster Dictionary*, and *Vocabulary.com*. The WordNet-

Affect emotion list contains 1,113 emotion terms categorized into six major emotion categories: *anger*, *disgust*, *fear*, *joy*, *sadness*, and *surprise* (Ekman, 1993). 113 of the 1,113 terms were excluded because they were emotion phrases as opposed to words; thus a total of 1,000 emotion words were collected. Then, to increase coverage, synonyms of these 1,000 emotion words from *WordNetSynset* and *Merriam Webster Dictionary* were included. Thus we compiled a corpus with 3,785 emotion words. For each of these 3,785 emotion words there was an average of 13.1 suggested synonyms, with a maximum of 57 and a minimum of 1. Moreover, we extracted from *Vocabulary.com* a total of 2,786,528 example sentences, each containing emotion words. The maximum number of example sentences for a given emotion word was 1,255; the minimum was 3.

4.2 Testing Data and Gold Standard

A writing task was designed for the evaluation. To create the testing data, 240 emotion writings written by ESL learners were collected. The participants were non-native English speakers (native Chinese speakers), all undergraduates or higher. Each writing was a short story about one of the six emotions defined by Ekman, and each had three requirements: (1) a length of at least 120 words; (2) a consistent emotion throughout the story; and (3) a sentence at the end that contains an emotion word (hereafter referred to as the *target emotion word*) summarizing the feeling of the writing. The target emotion word and its synonyms were taken as candidates of the most appropriate word (hereafter termed *candidate emotion words*). From these, RESOLVE proposes for each writing the five most appropriate words.

To create the gold standard, two native-speaker judges ranked the appropriateness of the emotion word candidates for each target emotion word given the writing. The judges scored the candidates ranging from 0 (worst) to 6 (best) based on contextual clues. When two or more words were considered equally appropriate, equal ranks were allowed, i.e., skips were allowed in the ranking. For example, given the synonym list *angry, furious, enraged, mad* and *annoyed*, if the judge considered enraged and furious to be equally appropriate, followed by angry, mad and annoyed, then the ranking scores from highest to lowest would be *enraged*-6, *furious*-6, *angry*-4, *mad*-3 and *annoyed*-2, respectively. In addition, words not in the top five but that fit the context were assigned 1 whereas those that did not fit the context were assigned 0.

In order to gauge the quality of judges' ranks, Cohen's KAPPA value was utilized to measure the inter-judge agreement. KAPPA (k) is calculated by considering the ranking score to be either zero (0) or non-zero (1-6). In addition, a weighted KAPPA value for ranked evaluation (k_w) was adopted (Sim and Wright, 2005) to quantify the agreement between the native scores. On average, k=0.51, and k_w=0.68; both values indicate substantial inter-judge agreement.

5 Performance of RESOLVE

In this section, we first evaluate the performance of RESOLVE from several aspects: (1) the performance of EDW and modified EES, (2) a comparison of RESOLVE with commonly-adopted mutual information and machine learning algorithms for classification, and (3) a comparison of RESOLVE with tools for ESL learners. Then we utilize and compare the pattern sets P_{all} and $P_{-scPattern}$ (no self-containing patterns) introduced in Section 4.1. We adopt NDCG@5 as the evaluation metric, which evaluates the performance when viewing this work as a word suggestion problem.

5.1 EDW and Modified EES

We evaluate the effect of the pattern-matching algorithm EDW, EES modified by three layers of CTP weighting, and ICZ weighting. First we compare EDW matching with wildcard matching. For the baseline, we use conventional wildcard matching with neither ICZ nor CTP. The results in Table 2 show that EDW outperforms the baseline wildcard matching algorithm. In addition, using ICZ to account for the influence of the corpus size improves performance. Level-1 CTP performs best. Thus for the remaining experiments we use EDW and EES modified by ICZ weighting and level-1 CTP.

RESOLVE Components	NDCG@5
Baseline	0.5107
EDW	0.5138
EDW + level-1 CTP	0.5150
EDW + level-1 CTP + ICZ	**0.5529**
EDW + level-1, 2 CTP + ICZ	0.5104
EDW + level-1, 2, 3 CTP + ICZ	0.5098

Table 2: Performance with various components.

5.2 Comparison to MI/ML Methods

After demonstrating that the proposed EDW and modified EES for RESOLVE yield the best performance, we compare RESOLVE to representative methods in related work to demonstrate its superiority. As mentioned in Section 2, related works view similar research problems as emotion classification problems or word suggestion problems. Commonly-adopted approaches for the former are based on mutual information (MI) and the latter on machine learning (ML). To represent these two types of approaches, we selected PMI and SVM, respectively, to which we compare the performance of RESOLVE.

PMI, SVM and RESOLVE all used the same corpus. Note that NAVA words (noun, adjective, verb and adverb) are the major sentiment-bearing terms (Agrawal and An, 2012). Hence for comparison with the feature set of extracted patterns we selected NAVA words as the additional feature set. For the PMI approach we calculated PMI values (1) between NAVA words and emotion words, (2) between patterns and emotion words. The PMI values between features from the writing and one emotion word candidate are then summed as the ranking score of the candidate. For the SVM approach, we used libsvm (Chang *et al.*, 2011). We used a linear kernel to train for a classifier for each emotion by selecting all positive samples and an equal number of randomly-selected negative samples. We ran tests using various SVM parameter settings and found the performance differences to be within 1%. PMI, SVM and RESOLVE were all trained on the prepared three feature sets. SVM simply classifies each emotion word candidate as fitting the context or not. The confidence value of each answer is used for ranking.

From Table 3, we found the best features for the PMI and SVM approaches are NAVA words. NDCG@5 (BD) shows the binary decision performance when giving a score of 1 to all candidates with ranking scores from 1 to 6, and 0 otherwise. Note that it is possible that SVM when using NAVA words is too sparse to ensure satisfactory performance, as the number of corpus-extracted patterns exceeds one million; thus the result is not shown here, as this leads to excessive feature counts for SVM. Experimental results show that RESOLVE achieves the best performance; the significance test shows that RESOLVE (pattern) significantly outperforms PMI (NAVA) and SVM (NAVA) at tail p-values of less than 0.001.

Feature		PMI	SVM	RESOLVE
NAVA word	NDCG@5	**0.4275**	0.5122	0.5048
	NDCG@5(BD)	0.4778	**0.5229**	0.5236
Pattern	NDCG@5	0.4126	N/A	**0.5529**
	NDCG@5(BD)	0.4530	N/A	0.5627

Table 3: NDCG@5 for various feature sets.

As to RESOLVE, recall that there are two configurations for testing the effectiveness of self-containing patterns: RESOLVE including self-containing patterns (RESOLVE-P_{all}), and RESOLVE excluding self-containing patterns (RESOLVE-$P_{-scPattern}$). Six different emotion categories are analyzed individually to reveal their different characteristics (De Choudhury *et al.*, 2012). Table 4 shows the NDCG@5 averaged by the number of writings in six emotion categories for PMI (NAVA), SVM (NAVA), and RESOLVE-P_{all} and RESOLVE-$P_{-scPattern}$. A further analysis of the writings shows that when expressing *disgust* or *sadness*, extensive uses of emotion words are found. Therefore, RESOLVE-P_{all} yields better performance. The remaining four emotions are expressed through descriptions of events rather than using emotion words. These results conform to the conclusion from (De Choudhury, Counts and Gamon, 2012): negative moods tend to be described in limited context. Based on the finding in Table 4, RESOLVE-P_{all} is used for emotion writings about *disgust* and *sadness*, and RESOLVE-$P_{-scPattern}$ is used for writings about *anger, fear, joy* and *surprise* when building the final conditional RESOLVE system.

Emotion	PMI (NAVA)	SVM (NAVA)	RESOLVE $-P_{all}$	RESOLVE $-P_{-scPattern}$
Anger	0.3295	0.4706	0.4886	**0.5071**
Disgust	0.3103	0.3738	**0.3773**	0.2584
Fear	0.4064	0.5381	0.5168	**0.6152**
Joy	0.4849	**0.5764**	0.4456	0.5708
Sadness	0.2863	0.3495	**0.3999**	0.3194
Surprise	0.7346	0.7651	0.8037	**0.8400**

Table 4 NDCG@5 for six emotion categories.

5.3 Comparison to Tools for ESL Learners

In the final part of the system evaluation, we show the effectiveness of RESOLVE by evaluating the performance of the most commonly-used tools by ESL learners. One traditional and handy tool is the thesaurus. For this evaluation we selected Roget's Thesaurus[5]. Another tool is online language learning systems, of which PIGAI is the most well-known online rating system for writing for Chinese ESL learners. This system can also suggest to learners several easily-confused words as substitutes for several system-selected words. For evaluation, we posted the experimental writing to PIGAI to check whether there were any suggested substitutes for the target emotion word. Replacement suggestions were found for the target emotion word in 71 out of 240 writings. Therefore, we compared the performance of PIGAI and RESOLVE on these 71 writings. Note that what the thesaurus and PIGAI suggested are both appropriate word sets, where words are listed in alphabetic order. Learners must select by themselves (or most conveniently, simply select the first one). Table 5 shows that RESOLVE provides a better set of top-5 suggestions than both the thesaurus and PIGAI.

Tool	NDCG@5	NDCG@5 (BD)	Precision@5 (BD)
PIGAI (71/240)	0.3300	0.3095	0.8732
RESOLVE (71/240)	**0.4755**	**0.4728**	**0.9789**
Thesaurus	0.3708	0.4237	0.9146
RESOLVE	**0.5529**	**0.5627**	**0.9479**

Table 5: Performance using ESL learner tools.

[5] http://Thesaurus.com

6 Conclusion

We presented a probabilistic model that can suggest emotion word based on the context. The modified *EES* that considered the distribution of emotion word help our algorithm rank the candidate emotion words better. Besides, the matching algorithm, EDW, can find the most similar emotional event from the writings. Furthermore, the example sentences can be used as our training corpus without any handcraft annotations. The evaluation shows that the proposed approach can more appropriately suggest emotion words than other models and reference tools like PIGAI and Thesaurus.

Acknowledgements

Research of this paper was partially supported by National Science Council, Taiwan, under the contract MOST 101-2628-E-001-005-MY3.

References

Agrawal, A., and An, A. 2012. Unsupervised Emotion Detection from Text using Semantic and Syntactic Relations. In *Web Intelligence and Intelligent Agent Technology (WI-IAT), 2012 IEEE/WIC/ACM International Conferences on* (Vol. 1, pp. 346-353). IEEE.

Altarriba, J., and Basnight-Brown, D. M. 2012. The acquisition of concrete, abstract, and emotion words in a second language. *International Journal of Bilingualism*, *16*(4), 446-452.

Bannard, C., and Callison-Burch, C. 2005. Paraphrasing with bilingual parallel corpora. In *Proceedings of the 43rd Annual Meeting on Association for Computational Linguistics* (pp. 597-604). Association for Computational Linguistics.

Barreiro, A. 2011. SPIDER: A System for Paraphrasing in Document Editing and Revision—Applicability in Machine Translation Pre-editing. In *Computational Linguistics and Intelligent Text Processing* (pp. 365-376). Springer Berlin Heidelberg.

Barzilay, R., and Lee, L. 2003. Learning to paraphrase: an unsupervised approach using multiple-sequence alignment. In *Proceedings of the 2003 Conference of the North American Chapter of the Association for Computational Linguistics on Human Language Technology-Volume 1* (pp. 16-23). Association for Computational Linguistics.

Barzilay, R., and McKeown, K. R. 2001. Extracting paraphrases from a parallel corpus. In *Proceedings of the 39th Annual Meeting on Association for Computational Linguistics* (pp. 50-57). Association for Computational Linguistics.

Bullinaria, J. A., and Levy, J. P. 2007. Extracting semantic representations from word co-occurrence statistics: A computational study. *Behavior research methods*, *39*(3), 510-526.

Callison-Burch, C. 2008. Syntactic constraints on paraphrases extracted from parallel corpora. In *Proceedings of the Conference on Empirical Methods in Natural Language Processing* (pp. 196-205). Association for Computational Linguistics.

Chang, C. C., and Lin, C. J. 2011. LIBSVM: a library for support vector machines. *ACM Transactions on Intelligent Systems and Technology (TIST)*, *2* (3), 27.

Chen, M. H., Huang, S. T., Chang, J. S., and Liou, H. C. 2013. Developing a corpus-based paraphrase tool to improve EFL learners' writing skills. *Computer Assisted Language Learning*, (ahead-of-print), 1-19.

Chen, M. H., Huang, S. T., Huang, C. C., Liou, H. C., and Chang, J. S. 2012. PREFER: using a graph-based approach to generate paraphrases for language learning. In *Proceedings of the Seventh Workshop on Building Educational Applications Using NLP* (pp. 80-85). Association for Computational Linguistics.

Church, K. W., and Hanks, P. 1990. Word association norms, mutual information, and lexicography. *Computational linguistics*, *16*(1),

Dahl, G., Frassica, A. M., and Wicentowski, R. (2007, June). SW-AG: Local context matching for English lexical substitution. In *Proceedings of the 4th International Workshop on Semantic Evaluations* (pp. 304-307). Association for Computational Linguistics. 22-29.

De Choudhury, M., Counts, S., and Gamon, M. 2012. Not all moods are created equal! exploring human emotional states in social media. In *Sixth International AAAI Conference on Weblogs and Social Media.*

De Marneffe, M. C., MacCartney, B., and Manning, C. D. 2006. Generating typed dependency parses from phrase structure parses. In *Proceedings of LREC* (Vol. 6, pp. 449-454).

Dinu, G., and Lapata, M. 2010. Topic models for meaning similarity in context. In *Proceedings of the 23rd International Conference on Computational Linguistics: Posters* (pp. 250-258). Association for Computational Linguistics.

Ekman, P. 1993. Facial expression and emotion. *American Psychologist*, *48* (4), 384.

Fellbaum, C. 1999. *WordNet*. Blackwell Publishing Ltd.

Ghazi, D., Inkpen, D., and Szpakowicz, S. 2012. Prior versus Contextual Emotion of a Word in a Sentence. In *Proceedings of the 3rd Workshop in Computational Approaches to Subjectivity and Sentiment Analysis* (pp. 70-78). Association for Computational Linguistic

Jeong, Y., and Myaeng, S. H. 2012. Using Syntactic Dependencies and WordNet Classes for Noun Event Recognition. In *The 2nd Workhop on Detection, Representation, and Exploitation of Events in the Semantic Web in Conjunction with the 11th International Semantic Web Conference* (pp. 41-50).

Keshtkar, F., and Inkpen, D. 2010. A corpus-based method for extracting paraphrases of emotion terms. In *Proceedings of the NAACL HLT 2010 Workshop on Computational approaches to Analysis and Generation of emotion in Text* (pp. 35-44). Association for Computational Linguistics.

Klein, D., and Manning, C. D. 2003. Accurate unlexicalized parsing. In *Proceedings of the 41st Annual Meeting on Association for Computational Linguistics-Volume 1* (pp. 423-430). Association for Computational Linguistics.

Leading, L. L., Monaghan, W., and Bridgeman, B. 2005. E-rater as a Quality Control on Human Scores.

Lin, D. 1998. An information-theoretic definition of similarity. In *ICML* (Vol. 98, pp. 296-304).

Lin, D., and Pantel, P. 2001. DIRT—discovery of inference rules from text. In *Proceedings of the seventh ACM SIGKDD international conference on Knowledge discovery and data mining* (pp. 323-328). ACM.

Ma, K. (2013). Improving EFL Graduate Students' Proficiency in Writing through an Online Automated Essay Assessing System. *English Language Teaching*, *6*(7).

Pavlenko, A. 2008. Emotion and emotion-laden words in the bilingual lexicon. *BILINGUALISM LANGUAGE AND COGNITION*, *11*(2), 147.

Sim, J., and Wright, C. C. 2005. The kappa statistic in reliability studies: use, interpretation, and sample size requirements. *Physical therapy*, *85*(3), 257-268.

Strapparava, C., and Valitutti, A. 2004. WordNet Affect: an Affective Extension of WordNet. In *LREC* (Vol. 4, pp. 1083-1086).

Tokuhisa, R., Inui, K., and Matsumoto, Y. 2008. Emotion classification using massive examples extracted from the web. In *Proceedings of the 22nd International Conference on Computational Linguistics-Volume 1* (pp. 881-888). Association for Computational Linguistics.

Zhao, S., Zhao, L., Zhang, Y., Liu, T., and Li, S. (2007, June). Hit: Web based scoring method for english lexical substitution. In *Proceedings of the 4th International Workshop on Semantic Evaluations* (pp. 173-176). Association for Computational Linguistics.

RevUP: Automatic Gap-Fill Question Generation from Educational Texts

Girish Kumar
NUS High School of Math and Science
Singapore 129957
girishvill@gmail.com

Rafael E. Banchs, Luis F. D'Haro
Institute for Infocomm Research
Singapore 138632
{rembanchs,luisdhe}@i2r.a-star.edu.sg

Abstract

This paper describes RevUP which deals with automatically generating gap-fill questions. RevUP consists of 3 parts: Sentence Selection, Gap Selection & Multiple Choice Distractor Selection. To select topically-important sentences from texts, we propose a novel sentence ranking method based on topic distributions obtained from topic models. To select gap-phrases from each selected sentence, we collected human annotations, using the Amazon Mechanical Turk, on the relative relevance of candidate gaps. This data is used to train a discriminative classifier to predict the relevance of gaps, achieving an accuracy of 81.0%. Finally, we propose a novel method to choose distractors that are semantically similar to the gap-phrase and have contextual fit to the gap-fill question. By crowd-sourcing the evaluation of our method through the Amazon Mechanical Turk, we found that 94% of the distractors selected were good. RevUP fills the semantic gap left open by previous work in this area, and represents a significant step towards automatically generating quality tests for teachers and self-motivated learners.

1 Introduction

In today's educational systems, a student needs to recall and apply major concepts from study material to perform competently in assessments. Crucial to this is practice and self-assessment through questions. King [1992] found that questioning is an effective method of helping students learn better. However, the continued crafting of varied questions is extremely time consuming for teachers as mentioned in Mitkov et al. [2006]. Furthermore, learners are increasingly moving from the traditional classroom setting to an independent learning setting online. Here, there is a need for leveraging upon online educational texts to provide practice material for students. Automatic Question Generation (AQG) shows promise for both these use-cases.

1.1 Related Work

Work in Automatic Question Generation(AQG) has mostly involved transforming sentences into questions and can be divided into two categories: Wh-Question Generation (WQG) and Gap-Fill Question Generation (GFQG). Most work in WQG has involved transforming sentences into grammatically correct Wh-questions (Why, What, How, etc.) with little attention given to the semantics and educational relevance of the questions (Heilman and Smith [2009], Mitkov et al. [2006], Mostow and Chen [2009], Wolfe et al. [1975], Wyse and Piwek [2009]). On the other hand, previous works in GFQG have generally worked with vocabulary-testing and language learning (Smith et al. [2010], Sumita et al. [2005]). Smith et al. presented TedClogg which took gap-phrases as input and found multiple choice distractors from a distributional thesaurus. 53.3% of the questions generated were acceptable. Our work aligns more closely to that of Aggarwal et al. where a weighted sum of lexical, syntactic features were utilised to select sentences, gaps and distractors from informative texts (Agar-

Proceedings of the Tenth Workshop on Innovative Use of NLP for Building Educational Applications, 2015, pages 154–161,
Denver, Colorado, June 4, 2015. ©2015 Association for Computational Linguistics

wal and Mannem [2011]). Becker et al. [2012] built upon the former's work by collecting human ratings of questions generated from a Wikipedia-based corpus. A machine-learning model was trained to effectively replicate these judgments, achieving a true positive rate of 83% and false positive rate of 19%.

RevUP focuses on GFQG which overcomes WQG's need for grammaticality by blanking out meaningful words (gaps) in known good sentences.

1.2 Key Contributions

Our key contribution is the employment of data-driven but domain independent methods to construct RevUP: an automated system for GFQG from educational texts. RevUP consists of 3 components: Sentence Selection, Gap Selection & Distractor Selection.

Sentence Selection
: Current systems use extractive summarization methods which may not suitable as they aim to choose sentences that cover the most content, which could result in complexity or incoherence. As such, we propose selecting *topically important* sentences by ranking them based on topic distributions obtained from a topic model.

Gap Selection
: Here, we train a machine learning classifier to replicate human judgements on the relevance of gaps. We propose collecting human rankings of the educational relevance of gaps. This is because ratings of gaps on a points scale resulted in inter-rater agreement issues in past work as each annotator had different thresholds for each point. We then propose semantic and domain-independent features for classifier training on these rankings and the trained classifier predicts the educational relevance of gap candidates with an accuracy of 81.0%.

Distractor Selection
: Contrary to previous work which use thesauruses or syntactic features, we propose using vector representation of words (word2vec), language model probabilities and dice coefficients to find semantically similar distractors with contextual fit to the question. 94% of the distractors selected by RevUP were found to be good.

A Biology text book titled *Campbell Biology, 9th Edition* has been used for work throughout this paper. The textbook consists of 35621 sentences, with each sentence consisting of an average of 20 words.

2 Sentence Selection

Previous work in AQG used extractive summarisation for selecting sentences Becker et al. [2012]. Since these methods aim to select sentences that maximise content coverage, they might not be suitable as such sentences can be complex and incoherent. As such, we aim to choose topically-important sentences that have a peaked topic distribution and $w = [0.5, 0.3, 0.2]$. Sentences with the top-n scores are selected. This is because sentence with peaked distributions have the following two properties.

1. The sentence belongs only to a few topics
2. These topics are expressed to a high degree

The first property implies that the sentence is coherent in terms of the ideas and content it expresses.The second property implies that the sentence contains important and interesting information. Each sentence is assigned a score as follows.

$$\text{score} = \sum_{i=1}^{k} w_i \cdot \max(\mathbf{t}, i) \quad (1)$$

where $\max(\mathbf{t}, i)$ is the ith largest probability in topic distribution $\mathbf{t}$ obtained from a topic model and w_i is its associated weight. For RevUP, we set $k = 3$. Table 1 shows a list of good and bad sentences with their scores.
It is to be noted that the assumption that topically important and coherent sentences make good questions does not always hold. We leave it to future work to account for more factors.

3 Gap Selection

We over-generated a list of candidate gap-phrases from every sentence and trained a binary classifier on human judgements of the relative relevance of the gap-words. Though similar to Becker et al., we

Good Sentences	Score	Bad Sentences	Score
Within the cortex, sensory areas receive and process sensory information, association areas integrate the information, and motor areas transmit instructions to other parts of the body.	0.48	As the water warms or cools, so does the body of the bass.	0.14
Roots were another key trait, anchoring the plant to the ground and providing additional structural support for plants that grew tall.	0.41	The scientific community reflects the cultural standards and behaviors of society at large.	0.14
Each nucleotide added to a growing DNA strand comes from a nucleoside triphosphate, which is a nucleoside with three phosphate groups.	0.29	In one study, researchers spread low concentrations of dissolved iron over 72 km 2 of ocean and * C uptake by cultures measures primary production.	0.16

Table 1: Good and bad sentences according to proposed sentence ranking metric

propose ranking gap-phrases instead of rating them to improve inter-rater agreement. Furthermore, we propose semantic features for classifier training. We used sentences from the Campbell Biology Textbook.

3.1 Methodology

3.1.1 Candidate Extraction

We extracted candidate gap-phrases that span up to three words. To prevent a skew towards irrelevant gap-phrases, we employed domain-independent syntactic rules. We first ran the Stanford Part-of-Speech (POS) Tagger to obtain the POS tags for each word in the sentence and the Stanford Parser to obtain a syntactic parse tree (Toutanova et al. [2003a,b]). We extracted all the nouns, adjectives, cardinals and noun-phrases with a Wikipedia page.

3.1.2 Crowd-Sourcing Annotations

Pinpointing a relevant gap is a complex task which relies on human judgement. Amazon Mechanical Turk, MTurk, was used to collect such human annotations in a cost and time efficient manner. In MTurk, requesters can pay human workers (Turkers) a nominal fee to complete Human Intelligence Tasks (HITs). To gather quality annotations, a HIT must be easy to complete and must take into account limitations with human judgement. We first piloted a HIT where a turker was tasked to rate gap-phrases from a source sentence on a scale from 1 to 5. However, we found very poor inter-annotator agreement as the task was tedious (up to 10 candidate gap-phrases per task) and each annotator had different thresholds for each point on the scale. However, the ratings preserved the relative educational relevance of the gaps. As such, we decided to redesign the HIT as a ranking task. Also, for shortening purposes, each HIT involved the ranking of 3 gap-phrases from one source-sentence. As such, for every source sentence,we created multiple sets of gap-phrase triplets as in Figure 1.

Gap A		Trp 1: A,B,C
Gap B	→	Trp 2: B,C,D
Gap C		Trp 3: C,D,A
Gap D		Trp 4: D,A,B

Figure 1: Triplet Generation. Trp refers to Triplet.

Each gap-phrase is part of three ranking HITs and each triplet shares two gap phrase pairs with two other triplets. In Figure 1,Trp 1 shares A,B with Trp 4 and B,C with Trp 2. Since conventional inter-annotator agreement metrics, e.g. Cohen's Kappa, cannot be used for a ranking task, we proposed an inter-ranker agreement measure as in Equation 2.

$$\text{Agreement} = \frac{\sum_{X,Y \in Gap-Pairs} \begin{cases} 1, & \text{if } \operatorname{sgn}(r_1(X) - r_1(Y)) = \operatorname{sgn}(r_2(X) - r_2(Y)) \\ 0, & \text{otherwise} \end{cases}}{\text{Num. of HITs}} \quad (2)$$

Sentence	Selected Gap
Sister chromatids are attached along their lengths by protein complexes called ________.	cohesins
Using an ATP-driven pump, the ________ expel hydrogen ions into the lumen	parietal cells
Unlike ________, leukocytes are also found outside the circulatory system, patrolling both interstitial fluid and the lymphatic system.	erythrocytes
A shoot apical meristem is a ________ mass of dividing cells at the shoot tip.	dome-shaped

Table 2: Gaps selected by RevUP. Red indicates bad gaps.

where $\text{sgn}(\cdot)$ is the sign function and $r_n(Z)$ is the rank assigned by ranker n to gap Z.

To collect sentences for HIT deployment, we first ranked all the sentences from the Campbell's Biology textbook as in Section 2.2. From the top sentences, we hand-picked sentences to ensure a good mix of topics, sentence-lengths and gap-phrase lengths so as not to introduce a bias. 200 sentences were deployed with rankings collected for 1306 gaps in total. The inter-ranker agreement was high at 0.783.

3.1.3 Automatic Gap Classification

Since every gap was ranked thrice, we assigned each gap a score by summing up the three ranks. Ranks ranged from 1 to 3: 1 for best and 3 for worst. Scores ranged from 3 to 9. For binary classification, gap-phrases with scores less than 6 were considered good and the rest bad. Data filtering was done by removing gap-phrases that had been ranked first, second and third due to the uncertainty associated with the relevance of the gap. Gap-phrases that were part of triplets that showed no agreement with both the triplets that they shared gap-phrase pairs with, were removed. 285 gaps were removed. Our final dataset had a slight skew towards bad gaps with 554 bad gaps and 468 good gaps.

A good set of features are vital for training a good classifier. Table 4 lists all the features used for classification. Note that all the features are domain-independent. Using the scikit-learn python package, we trained a Support Vector Machine (SVM) with a Radial Basis Function (RBF) kernel (Pedregosa et al. [2011]).

3.2 Results

Table 3 details the average accuracy, precision, recall and F1 score achieved for a 10-fold cross validation test. Given an accuracy of 81%, we can conclude that RevUP performs fairly well for gap selection, on par with Becker et al. [2012].

	Filtered Gaps	All Gaps
Accuracy	0.81 ± 0.024	0.77 ± 0.026
Precision	0.81 ± 0.061	0.74 ± 0.045
Recall	0.77 ± 0.066	0.71 ± 0.082
F1-Score	0.79 ± 0.032	0.72 ± 0.043

Table 3: SVM Cross-Validation Results.

Besides, the results prove the huge impact preprocessing had on classifier performance. To understand impact of each feature on classifier performance, we obtained the classifier accuracy without each feature over 10-folds (Figure 2).

We can observe that most features have an equal effect on classifier performance with the exception of WordVec (Feature 10). Without WordVec, classifier performance drops to 76.6%. The large impact of WordVec is mainly because it strongly encodes the semantics of candidate gap-phrases. Word2Vec employs a Skip-gram model to learn and obtain distributed representations of words, from input texts, in a vector space which spatially encodes the semantic information and meaning of words. We believe that interesting and important words are separated from unimportant words in this vector space. This could have also helped in improving classifier accuracy.
Examples of gaps selected by RevUP are in Table 2.

4 Distractor Selection

The final component of RevUP pipeline involves the selection of relevant multiple-choice distractors to ensure that the learner has a good grasp of the relevant concepts put to test. Past work has involved the usage of thesauruses, LSA and rule-based approaches. Contrary to this, we propose a domain-

No.	Name	Description
0	Char Length	Number of characters in gap-phrase
1	Char Overlap	Character length of gap divided by character length of sentence
2	Height	Height of the gap-phrase in the syntactic parse tree
3	TF	Number of times gap-phrase occurs in the source sentence
4*	Corpus TF	Number of times gap-phrase occurs in the biology textbook
5*	Corpus IDF	Inverse document frequency of the gap-phrase in the biology textbook. Sentences are treated as documents.
6*	Sent. Words	Number of words in the source sentence
7*	Word Overlap	No. of Words in the gap-phrase divided by Sent. Words
8	Index	Position of the gap-phrase in the source sentence
9*	WN Synsets	Number of WordNet synsets of the gap-phrase
10*	WordVec	Vector of the gap-phrase as computed with the Word2Vec Tool. Refer to Section 4.1 for more details on word2vec.
11	Prev. POS Tag	Part-of-Speech Tags of the two words before the gap-phrase
12	Post. POS Tag	Part-of-Speech Tags of the two words after the gap-phrase
13	NER Tag	Name-Entity Tag of the gap-phrase
14	SRL	Semantic Role Label of the gap-phrase
15*	Topic Distribution	Topic Distribution of the gap phrase as computed by the proposed deep learning model
16*	Topic Distribution Change	Jensen Shannon Divergence between topic distribution of the gap phrase and the source sentence
17*	Transition Prob.	Transition probability from Kneser Ney Back-off Language Model trained on the biology textbook corpus

Table 4: Features Used to Train Binary Classifier. * represents features proposed by the authors. The rest correspond to that by Becker et al. [2012]

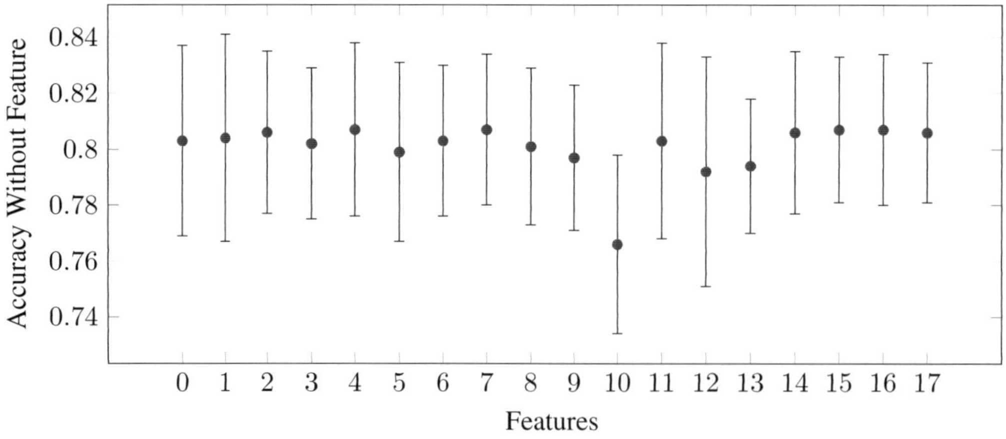

Figure 2: The effect of features on classifier performance. Note that Feature Number Correspond to Table 4

independent, data-driven approach to select distractors with semantic similarity and contextual fit. We leave it to future work to reject distractors that are correct answers to their respective questions.

Sentence	Selected Gap	Distractor
Sister chromatids are attached along their lengths by protein complexes called ________.	cohesins	1) spindle microtubules 2) myosin filaments 3) thick filaments 4) kinetochores
________ worsen pain by increasing nociceptor sensitivity to noxious stimuli.	Prostaglandins	1) nitric oxides 2) steroid hormones 3) signaling molecules 4) lipid-soluble hormones
Instead, a hypha grows into a tube formed by ________ of the root cells membrane.	invagination	1) vegetal pole 2) undifferentiated cell 3) neural plate 4) frog embryo
________ bodies are reinforced by ossicles, hard plates composed of magnesium carbonate and calcium carbonate crystals.	Echinoderms	1) sense organs 2) salamanders 3) birds 4) turtles

Table 5: Examples of distractors generated by RevUP. Red indicates bad distractors.

4.1 Methodology

To choose distractors semantically similar to the gap-phrase, we used the word2vec tool (Mikolov et al. [2013]). However, word2vec requires input texts with millions of words to learn quality vector representations. To rapidly expand our biology training dataset, we downloaded and processed the latest dumps of Wikipedia. Thereafter, to ensure that we only obtained texts relevant to the textbook used, we implemented a TF-IDF search engine through the gensim python package (Řehůřek and Sojka [2010]). The Campbell's Biology textbook was split into 548 batches of 50 sentences each and texts from the top 50 Wikipedia pages for each batch were used. The final data-set consisted of 900,000 sentences and 21 million words. This data-augmentation method keeps our proposed solution domain-independent as only the relevant textbook is needed. For word2vec training, the dimension of the vector space was set to be 70. A n-best list of candidate distractors can be chosen by ranking words in the vocabulary according to the cosine similarity of their vectors with respect to that of the gap-phrase. Thereafter, we removed candidates that already appear in the question sentence and that are of different parts-of-speech. Finally, we validated the semantic similarity of each candidate with the gap-phrase with WordNet (Miller [1995]). WordNet is a lexical graph database where words are grouped into sets of synonyms (synsets). Synsets are linked through a number of relations. We measured the semantic similarity of two terms, x, y, using path similarity.

$$\text{pathsim}(x, y) = \frac{1}{1 + \text{len(shortest\_path(x,y))}} \quad (3)$$

where $len(shortest\_path(x, y))$ is the shortest path between words x and y in WordNet. We eliminated candidates with path_sim < 0.1. We then proceeded to re-rank the candidates to obtain the 4 best distractors. Often, syntactic similarities between distractors and their respective gap-phrases help confuse students. For example, *s-phase* is a good distractor for *g-phase*. We captured such syntactic similarities by computing the Dice Coefficient, DC, for the gap-phrase and each candidate (Equation 4).

$$DC(X, Y) = \frac{2 \cdot |X \cap Y|}{|X| + |Y|} \quad (4)$$

To take into account the context of the question, we calculated the language model probability of the candidate given the words that appear before the gap-phrase in the question-sentence. We trained a 5-gram Kneser Ney Back-off Language Model with the data used for word2vec training. Finally, we re-weighted and ranked the candidates according to their word2vec similarity, dice coefficient and language model probabilities and we picked the top 4 candidates as the final distractors.

4.2 Results

Amazon Mechanical Turk was used to evaluate our distractor selection method. Turkers were presented with a Gap-Fill Question, gap-phrase and were tasked to evaluate whether each of the top 4 distractors were good or bad. 75 sentences with 300 distractors from the Campbell's Biology Textbook were deployed. Since every distractor was rated by 5 turkers, we assigned each distractor a score by summing up the five ratings (1 for Good and 0 for Bad). Scores ranged from 0 to 5. Results are summarized in Table 7.

	Very Good	**Fair**	**Bad**
Percentage of Distractors	43%	51%	6%

Table 6: Distractor Selection Results

Mean	**Variance**
3.19	1.51

Table 7: Distractor Rating Statistics

Distractors with a score > 3 were considered very good, score < 2 were considered bad and the rest fair. We found that 51% of the distractors had a score of 2 or 3 which meant that there was low inter-annotator agreement. This reflects the complexity of the task as well as a lack of biological . As such, a more precise evaluation of our system can be performed with students/teachers as our annotators instead. Nonetheless, with 94% of the distractors being at least fair, RevUP's distractor selection component works fairly well.

Examples of distractors selected by RevUP are in Table 5.

5 Conclusion & Future Work

In summary, we have leveraged upon data-driven machine learning methods to propose RevUP: an automated, domain-independent pipeline for GFQG. Leveraging on topic models, a new topic-distribution based ranking method was proposed for sentence selection. For gap-selection, a discriminative binary classifier was trained on human annotations. With the classifier, RevUP could predict the relevance of a gap-phrase with an accuracy of 81.0%. We finally proposed a novel method for generating semantically-similar distractors with contextual fit and demonstrated that a 94% of the generated distractors were fair.

For future work, we hope to utilise more parameters to more accurately pinpoint better sentences. As for gap selection, we could explore the usage of more features and the usage of learning-to-rank methods e.g. SVMRank. We intend to cast the distractor selection problem as a machine learning problem to be trained from human judgments. Another possibility is the integration of RevUP into e-learning platforms such as Moodle to allow public usage of the tool. This could pave the way for usability tests to be conducted to understand the impact RevUP has on the learning process and educational performance of students. Furthermore, RevUP could be used to generate questions from transcribed lectures on MOOC platforms such as Coursera and Udacity.

References

Manish Agarwal and Prashanth Mannem. Automatic gap-fill question generation from text books. In *Proceedings of the 6th Workshop on Innovative Use of NLP for Building Educational Applications*, pages 56–64. Association for Computational Linguistics, 2011.

Lee Becker, Sumit Basu, and Lucy Vanderwende. Mind the gap: Learning to choose gaps for question generation. In *HLT-NAACL*, pages 742–751. The Association for Computational Linguistics, 2012. ISBN 978-1-937284-20-6.

Michael Heilman and Noah A Smith. Question generation via overgenerating transformations and ranking. Technical report, DTIC Document, 2009.

Alison King. Comparison of self-questioning, summarizing, and notetaking-review as strategies for learning from lectures. *American Educational Research Journal*, 29(2):303–323, 1992.

Tomas Mikolov, Ilya Sutskever, Kai Chen, Greg S Corrado, and Jeff Dean. Distributed representations of words and phrases and their compositionality. In *Advances in Neural Information Processing Systems*, pages 3111–3119, 2013.

George A. Miller. Wordnet: A lexical database for english. *COMMUNICATIONS OF THE ACM*, 38: 39–41, 1995.

Ruslan Mitkov, Le An Ha, and Nikiforos Karamanis. A computer-aided environment for generating multiple-choice test items. *Nat. Lang. Eng.*, 12(2):177–194, June 2006. ISSN 1351-3249. doi: 10.1017/S1351324906004177.

Jack Mostow and Wei Chen. Generating instruction automatically for the reading strategy of self-questioning. In *Proceedings of the 2009 Conference on Artificial Intelligence in Education: Building Learning Systems That Care: From Knowledge Representation to Affective Modelling*, pages 465–472, Amsterdam, The Netherlands, The Netherlands, 2009. IOS Press. ISBN 978-1-60750-028-5.

F. Pedregosa, G. Varoquaux, A. Gramfort, V. Michel, B. Thirion, O. Grisel, M. Blondel, P. Prettenhofer, R. Weiss, V. Dubourg, J. Vanderplas, A. Passos, D. Cournapeau, M. Brucher, M. Perrot, and E. Duchesnay. Scikit-learn: Machine learning in Python. *Journal of Machine Learning Research*, 12:2825–2830, 2011.

Radim Řehůřek and Petr Sojka. Software Framework for Topic Modelling with Large Corpora. In *Proceedings of the LREC 2010 Workshop on New Challenges for NLP Frameworks*, pages 45–50, Valletta, Malta, May 2010. ELRA.

Adam Kilgarriff Simon Smith, PVS Avinesh, and Adam Kilgarriff. Gap-fill tests for language learners: Corpus-driven item generation. In *Proceedings of ICON-2010: 8th International Conference on Natural Language Processing*, 2010.

Eiichiro Sumita, Fumiaki Sugaya, and Seiichi Yamamoto. Measuring non-native speakers' proficiency of english by using a test with automatically-generated fill-in-the-blank questions. In *Proceedings of the second workshop on Building Educational Applications Using NLP*, pages 61–68. Association for Computational Linguistics, 2005.

Kristina Toutanova, Dan Klein, Christopher D Manning, and Yoram Singer. Feature-rich part-of-speech tagging with a cyclic dependency network. In *Proceedings of the 2003 Conference of the North American Chapter of the Association for Computational Linguistics on Human Language Technology-Volume 1*, pages 173–180. Association for Computational Linguistics, 2003a.

Kristina Toutanova, Dan Klein, Christopher D Manning, and Yoram Singer. Feature-rich part-of-speech tagging with a cyclic dependency network. In *Proceedings of the 2003 Conference of the North American Chapter of the Association for Computational Linguistics on Human Language Technology-Volume 1*, pages 173–180. Association for Computational Linguistics, 2003b.

John H. Wolfe, Navy Personnel Research, and CA. Development Center, San Diego. *An Aid to Independent Study through Automatic Question Generation (AUTOQUEST) [microform] / John H. Wolfe*. Distributed by ERIC Clearinghouse [Washington, D.C.], 1975.

Brendan Wyse and Paul Piwek. Generating questions from openlearn study units. 2009.

Preliminary Experiments on Crowdsourced Evaluation of Feedback Granularity

Nitin Madnani[1], Martin Chodorow[2], Aoife Cahill[1], Melissa Lopez[1], Yoko Futagi[1] and Yigal Attali[1]

[1]*Educational Testing Service, Princeton, NJ*
[2]*Hunter College and the Graduate Center, City University of New York, NY*

Abstract

Providing writing feedback to English language learners (ELLs) helps them learn to write better, but it is not clear what type or how much information should be provided. There have been few experiments directly comparing the effects of different types of automatically generated feedback on ELL writing. Such studies are difficult to conduct because they require participation and commitment from actual students and their teachers, over extended periods of time, and in real classroom settings. In order to avoid such difficulties, we instead conduct a crowdsourced study on Amazon Mechanical Turk to answer questions concerning the effects of type and amount of writing feedback. We find that our experiment has several serious limitations but still yields some interesting results.

1 Introduction

A core feature of learning to write is receiving feedback and making revisions based on the information provided (Li and Hegelheimer, 2013; Biber et al., 2011; Lipnevich and Smith, 2008; Truscott, 2007; Rock, 2007). However, an important question to answer before building automated feedback systems is what type of feedback (and degree of interactivity) can best support learning and retention. Is it better to restrict the system to providing feedback which indicates that an error has been made but does not suggest a possible correction? Or is it better for the learner to receive feedback, which provides a clear indication of the error location as well as the correction itself, or even an explanation of the underlying grammatical rule? In this study, we refer to the first type of feedback as *implicit* feedback and to the second type as *explicit* feedback.

To the best of our knowledge, there is no empirical study that directly compares several different amounts of detail (granularities) in automatically generated feedback in terms of their impact on learning outcomes for language learners. This is not surprising since the ideal study would involve conducting controlled experiments in a classroom setting, requiring participation from actual language learners and teachers.

In this paper, we examine whether a large-scale crowdsourcing study conducted on Amazon Mechanical Turk, instead of in classrooms, can provide any answers about the effect of feedback granularity on learning. Our experiments are preliminary in nature but nevertheless yield results that — despite not being directly applicable to ELLs — are interesting. We also report on lessons we have learned about the deficiencies in our study and suggest possible ways to overcome them in future work.

For the purpose of this study, we define an "improvement in learning outcome" as an improvement in the performance of the Turkers on a specific task: detecting and correcting preposition selection errors in written text. Obviously, learning to use the correct preposition in a given context is only one, albeit an important, aspect of better writing. However, we concentrate on this single error type since: (a) doing so will allow us to remove any unintended effects of interactions among multiple errors, ensuring that the feedback message is the only variable in our experiment, and (b) automated systems for correcting

Proceedings of the Tenth Workshop on Innovative Use of NLP for Building Educational Applications, 2015, pages 162–171,
Denver, Colorado, June 4, 2015.

preposition selection errors have been studied and developed for many years. Reason (b) is important since we can use the output of these automated systems as part of the feedback.

Briefly, a high-level description of the study is as follows:

1. Over multiple sessions, Turkers detect and correct preposition errors in sentences.
2. We provide sub-groups of Turkers with different types of feedback as they proceed through the sessions.
3. We measure the differences in Turker performance and see if the differences vary across feedback types.

Section 2 describes related work. Section 3 describes the experimental design of our study in more detail. Section 4 presents our analysis of the results from the study and, finally, Section 5 concludes with a summary of the study along with the lessons we learned from conducting it.

2 Related Work

One automated writing evaluation tool that helps students plan, write and revise their essays guided by instant diagnostic feedback and a score is Criterion. Attali (2004) and Shermis et al. (2004) examine the effect of feedback in general in the Criterion system and find that students presented with feedback are able to improve the overall quality of their writing. Those studies do not investigate different feedback types; they look at the issue of whether feedback in general is a useful tool. We propose to look at varying levels of detail in feedback messages to see what effect this has on student learning.

We have found no large-scale empirical studies comparing the types of feedback on grammatical errors in the field of second language acquisition, and no work at all on using computer-generated corrections. In the field of second language acquisition, the main focus has been on explicit vs. implicit feedback in a general sense.

The major focus of studies on Corrective Feedback, or "CF", for grammatical errors has been on whether CF is effective or not following the controversial claim by Truscott (1996) that it may actually be harmful to a learner's writing ability.

Russell and Spada (2006) used 56 studies in their meta-analysis of CF research, and of those, 22 focused on written errors and one looked at both oral and written errors. Meihami and Meihami (2013) list a few more studies, almost all of which are from 2006 or later. Some of the studies were conducted in classroom settings, while others were in "laboratory" settings. In all of the studies, corrective feedback was given by humans (teachers, researchers, peers, other native speakers), so the sample sizes are most likely limited (unfortunately, that information is missing from the Russell and Spada meta-analysis).

Doughty and Williams (1998) summarize the findings of the Lyster and Ranta (1997) classroom study of the effectiveness of various feedback techniques. Lyster and Ranta (1997) found that one of the effective types of feedback for stimulating learner-generated repairs was a repaired response from the teacher. There were also several other feedback types that were found to be effective including meta-linguistic cues, clarification requests and repetition of the learner error. Carroll and Swain (1993) found that in general some kind of feedback is better than no feedback.

There are very few studies that have compared the effectiveness of different types of written corrective feedback. Bitchener et al. (2005) and Bitchener (2008) seem to show that direct feedback (oral or written) is more effective than indirect, while in (Bitchener and Knoch, 2008; Bitchener and Knoch, 2009), which have larger sample sizes, the difference disappeared. Bitchener and Knoch (2010) investigated different types of corrective feedback over a 10-month period and also show that there are no differences among different types of feedback. However, Sheen (2007) found that the group receiving meta-linguistic explanations performed better than the one who received direct error corrections in the delayed post-test 2 months later. All of these studies focused only on English articles.

Biber et al. (2011) present a synthesis of existing work on the influences of feedback for writing development. One point from this report that is very relevant to our current work is that "Truscott (2007) focuses on the quite restricted question of the extent to which error correction influences writing accuracy for L2-English students. This study concluded that overt error correction actually has a small negative influence on learners' abilities to write accurately. However, the meta-analysis was based on only six research studies, making it somewhat difficult to be confident about the generalizability of the findings." Biber et al. (2011) also mention that "In actual practice, direct feedback is rarely used as a treatment in empirical research."

The work most directly relevant to our study is that of Nagata and Nakatani (2010), who attempt to measure actual impact of feedback on learning outcomes for English language learners whose native language is Japanese. At the beginning of the study, students wrote English essays on 10 different topics. Errors involving articles and noun number were then flagged either by a human or by two different automatic error detection systems: one with high precision and another with high recall. A control group received no error feedback. Learning was measured in terms of reduction of error rate for the noun phrases in the students' essays. Results showed that learning was quite similar for the human-supplied feedback and the high-precision automated feedback conditions, and that both were better than the no-feedback condition. In contrast, the high-recall automated feedback condition actually yielded results worse than the no-feedback condition. This latter finding supports the commonly held assumption that it is better to provide less feedback than to provide incorrect feedback. Note, however, that their study only compares providing implicit feedback to providing no feedback.

3 Experimental Setup

We designed a crowdsourcing experiment to examine the differences in learning effects resulting from different types of feedback. The overall design of the experiment consists of three phases:

1. **Phase 1**. Recruit Turkers and measure their pre-intervention preposition error detection and correction skills. All Turkers are provided with the same minimal feedback during the pre-intervention session, i.e., they are on equal footing when it comes to writing feedback.
2. **Phase 2**. Divide the recruited Turkers into different, mutually exclusive groups. Each group participates in a series of intervention sessions where the Turkers in that group receive one specific type of feedback.
3. **Phase 3**. Measure the post-intervention performance for all Turkers. Similar to the pre-intervention session, the same minimal feedback is provided during the post-intervention session.

We chose to use five different feedback granularities in our study, which are outlined below. The first one represents implicit feedback and the last four represent explicit feedback.

1. **Minimal Feedback**. Messages are of the form: *There may be an error in this sentence.*
2. **Moderate Feedback**. The incorrect preposition is highlighted and the feedback message is of the form: *The highlighted preposition P_1 may be incorrect.*
3. **Detailed Feedback 1**. The incorrect preposition is highlighted and the feedback message is of the form: *The highlighted preposition P_1 may be incorrect; the preposition P_2 may be more appropriate*, where P_2 is a human expert's suggested correction for the error.
4. **Detailed Feedback 2**. The incorrect preposition is highlighted and the feedback message is of the form: *The highlighted preposition P_1 may be incorrect; the preposition P_2 may be more appropriate*, where P_2 is the correction assigned the highest probability by an automated preposition error correction system (Cahill et al., 2013).
5. **Detailed Feedback 3**. The incorrect preposition is highlighted and the feedback message is of the form: *The highlighted preposition P_1 may be incorrect; the following is a list of prepositions that may be more appropriate*, where the list contains the top 5 suggested corrections from the automated error correction system.

For all three detailed feedback types, Turkers were told that the corrections were generated by an automated system. Table 1 shows the design of our experimental study wherein all recruited Turkers were divided into five mutually exclusive groups, each corresponding to one of the feedback types described above.

For our pre-intervention/recruitment session (Session 1), we collected judgments from 450 Turkers

	Session 1	Session 2	Session 3	Session 4	Session 5
Group 1	Minimal		Minimal		Minimal
Group 2	Minimal		Moderate		Minimal
Group 3	Minimal		Detailed 1		Minimal
Group 4	Minimal		Detailed 2		Minimal
Group 5	Minimal		Detailed 3		Minimal

Table 1: The experimental design of the study. Turkers were divided into five mutually exclusive groups and always shown the same type of feedback during the intervention (sessions 2–4). All Turkers were shown the same minimal feedback during the pre- and the post-intervention (sessions 1 and 5, respectively).

	Session 1	Session 2	Session 3	Session 4	Session 5
Group 1	82	78	76	74	72
Group 2	82	72	70	68	66
Group 3	82	72	70	70	65
Group 4	83	74	72	70	70
Group 5	83	75	74	73	72
Total	412	371	362	355	345

Table 2: The number of Turkers that participated in each group for each session.

without regard for qualification requirements. One Turker's work was rejected for carelessness, and the remaining 449 received approved payments of $1. After scoring the responses, removing questionable work, and reviewing the distribution of scores, we reduced this number to 412 (approximately 82 Turkers per group). We then randomly assigned Turkers to one of the five feedback groups.[1] We administered Session 2 approximately two weeks after Session 1. We created a unique task for each feedback group, and Turkers were only permitted to access the task for their assigned group. Upon review, their work was approved for payment, and a new qualification score was assigned for entrance into the next session. The remaining sessions were posted every other day up to Session 5, and each task remained available for two weeks after posting. The payment amount increased by 50 cents for each new session, adding up to a total of $10 per Turker if they completed all five sessions. Table 2 shows the number of Turkers assigned to each group who participated in each of the five sessions.

We used the CLC-FCE corpus (Yannakoudakis et al., 2011), which has been manually annotated for preposition errors by professional English language instructors. We randomly selected 90 sentences with preposition errors and 45 sentences without errors and manually reviewed them to ensure their suitability. Unsuitable sentences were replaced from the pool of automatically extracted sentences until we had a total of 135 suitable sentences. We annotated each sentence containing an error with a correct preposition. The 135 sentences were then randomly divided into 5 HITs (Human Intelligence Tasks, the basic unit of work on MTurk), one for each of the five sessions. Each HIT was generated automatically, with manual human review. Given a sentence containing an error and a correction, we automatically extracted the following additional data:

- A version of the sentence where the only error is the preposition error (specifically errors where an incorrect preposition is used).

[1] An MTurk feature that was essential to this study was the ability to designate "qualifications" to recruit and target specific Turkers. MTurk requesters can use these qualifications to assign Turkers to conditions and keep a record of their status. After Turkers completed Session 1, we were able to use our own qualifications and a range of qualification scores to assign Turkers to groups and control the order in which they completed the sessions. Although the Turkers were assigned randomly to groups, we manually ensured that the distributions of Session 1 scores were similar across groups.

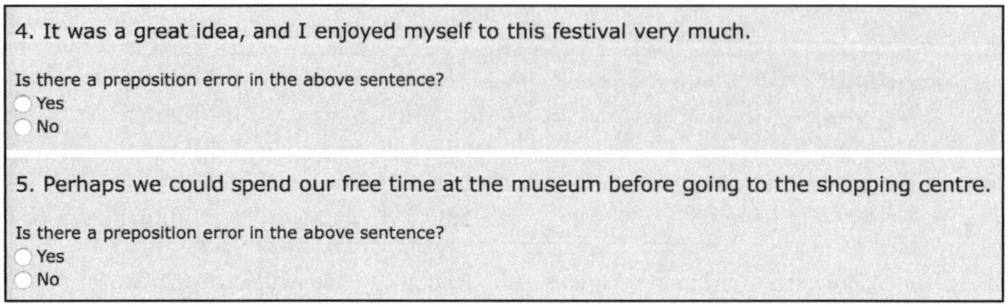

Figure 1: A partial screenshot of the HIT shown to the Turkers. The first sentence contains a preposition error and the second does not.

- The incorrect preposition, its position in the sentence, and the human correction.
- A version of the sentence that has the preposition error corrected.

The pre- and post-intervention HITs consisted of 30 sentences and the intervention sessions consisted of 25 sentences each. About a third of the sentences in each HIT contained no errors (to measure detection ability) and the remaining contained a single preposition error (to measure correction ability). Turkers were first asked to indicate whether or not there was a preposition error in each sentence, in order to test their error detection skills. Once the Turker answered, they received a feedback message of the appropriate granularity directing them to correct the error in the sentence, if there was one. If there were no errors annotated in the sentence, Turkers received a message saying that the sentence contained no errors. Figure 1 shows a partial screenshot of a HIT.

In order to understand more about our participants, we geo-located Turkers using their IP addresses. A significant majority of the Turkers — 319 out of the 345 who participated in all five sessions — were from the United States with the remaining located in India (21), Mexico (3), Ireland (1), and Sweden (1).

4 Analysis

To prepare data for analysis, we automatically scored the Turker responses and manually adjusted these scores to account for sentences where more than one correction was appropriate. Scoring for each sentence depended on the presence of an error. For sentences with errors, Turkers could score a maximum of two independent points: 1 point for detection and 1 point for correction. Because Turkers were not asked to correct sentences without errors, these were only worth 1 point for detection.

4.1 Prepositions Used

Before examining the Turker responses, we analyzed the actual prepositions that were involved in each erroneous sentence in each session. Figure 2 shows this distribution. We observe that not all prepositions are represented across all sessions and that the distributions of prepositions are quite different. In fact, only three prepositions errors ("of", "in" and "to") appear in all five sessions.

4.2 Turker Motivation

One of the most common problems with using crowdsourcing solutions like MTurk is that of quality control. In our study, we excluded 37 Turkers at the pre-intervention stage for quality control. However, after that session, no Turkers were excluded since we wanted all recruited Turkers to finish all five sessions. Therefore, it is important to examine the recruited Turkers' responses provided for all three intervention sessions for any strange patterns indicating that a Turker was trying to game the task by not providing good-faith answers. For example, a Turker who was only motivated to earn the HIT payment and not to make a useful contribution to the task could:

- answer 'yes' or 'no' to *all* error detection questions or at random
- *always* accept the suggested preposition
- *always* use a random preposition as their answer

- *always* pick the first preposition from a given list of prepositions

We analyze the Turkers' error detection responses all together and their error correction responses by feedback type.

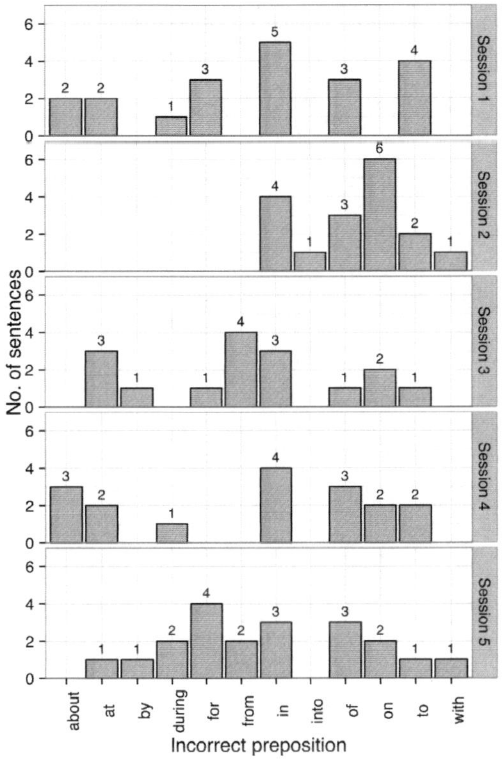

Figure 2: The distribution of prepositions involved in the erroneous sentences for each session.

4.2.1 Analyzing Detection Responses

First, we examine the possibility that Turkers may have answered 'yes' or 'no' at the error detection stage for all questions or may have selected one of those answers at random for each question. To do this, we simply compute the proportion of sentences for which each Turker accurately detected the error, if one was present. The faceted plot in Figure 3 shows that almost all of the Turkers seem to have answered the error detection questions accurately, and without trying to game the system. Each facet shows a histogram of the average accuracy (across all sentences) of the Turkers from one of the five feedback groups and for each of the five sessions. The dotted line in each plot indicates the accuracy that would

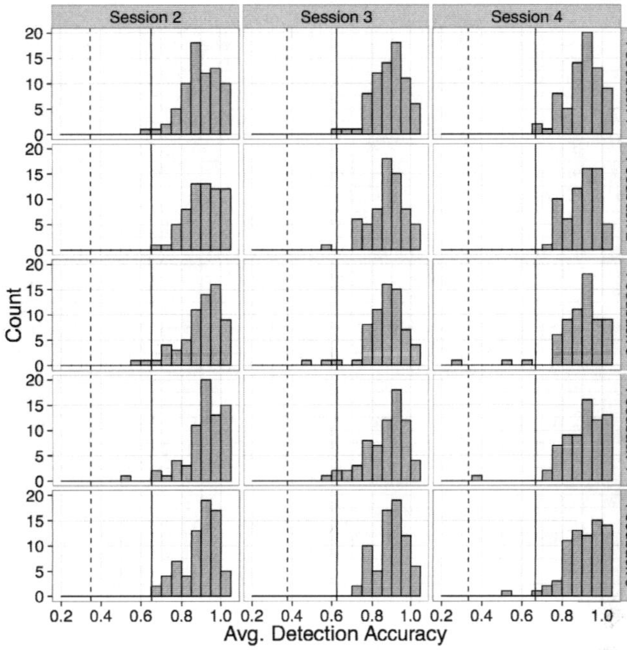

Figure 3: A histogram of the Turkers' average error detection accuracy for the three intervention sessions. The dotted and solid lines indicate accuracies that a Turker would have obtained had they answered every question in a session with 'No' or 'Yes', respectively.

have been obtained by a Turker had they simply said 'no' to all the error detection questions and the solid line indicates the accuracy that would have been obtained by answering 'yes' to all of them. Note that these lines are the same across feedback groups because the sentences are the same for a session, irrespective of the feedback group.

4.2.2 Analyzing Correction Responses

In this section, we analyze the Turker error correction responses by feedback type. First, we examine the responses from the Turkers in Group 3, i.e., those who received messages of the **Detailed Feedback 1** type. Figure 4 shows that most of the Turkers accepted the suggested correction. Note that since Turkers were not informed that the suggestion came from an expert, this is still an indicator of good Turker performance. Furthermore, the figure shows that even a majority of the Turkers who decided not to accept the suggestion actually answered with an alternative correct preposition of their own. The "*Not Accepted - Incorrect (Other)*" category in the

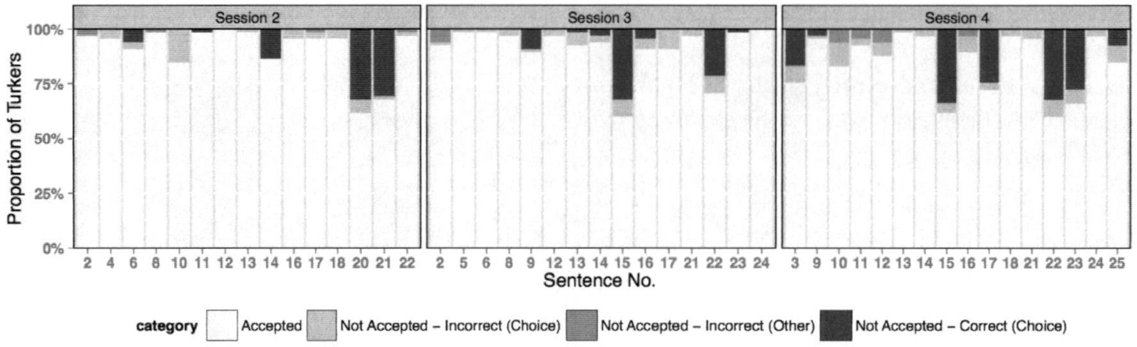

Figure 4: By session and sentence, the proportion of Turkers in Group 3 accepting the (always correct) suggested preposition, and, if not accepting it, the correctness of their repairs.

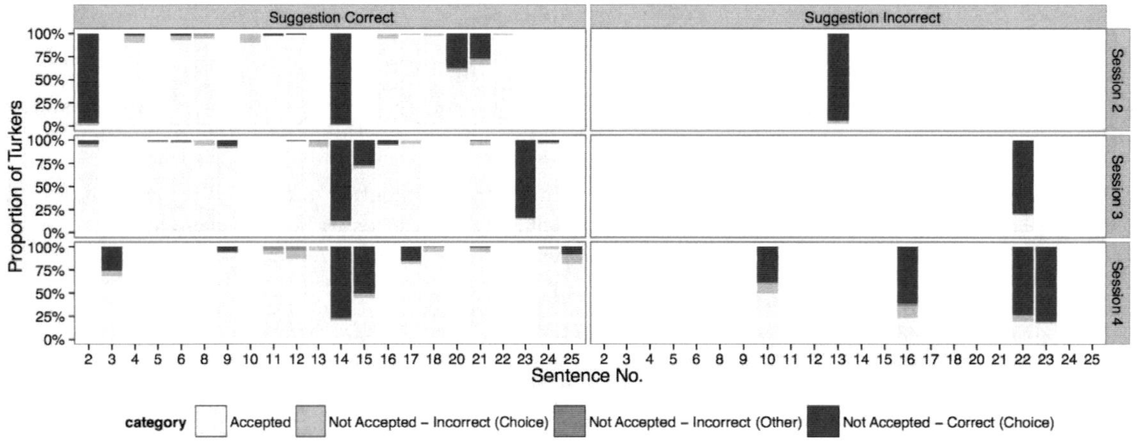

Figure 5: By session and sentence, the proportion of Turkers in Group 4 accepting the (possibly incorrect) suggested preposition, and, if not accepting it, the correctness of their repairs.

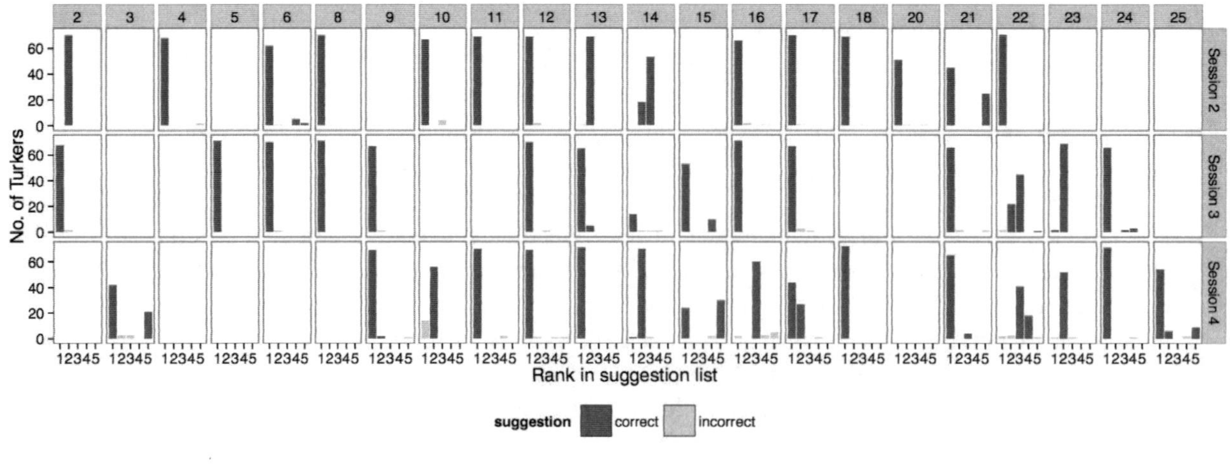

Figure 6: By session and sentence, the number of Turkers in Group 5 selecting a preposition at each rank position in the suggestion list and the correctness of their selection.

figure refers to rare cases where the Turkers deleted the erroneous preposition or made other changes in the sentence instead of fixing the preposition error.

Next, we examine responses from Turkers in Group 4. Figure 5 shows – similar to Figure 4 – the proportion of Turkers that simply accepted the suggestion provided as compared to those who did not. However, in this case, we have the additional possibility of the suggested preposition being incorrect, since it is generated by an automated system. Again, we see that most Turkers accept the suggested preposition when it's correct, but when it's incorrect, they answer with a different correct preposition of their own.

Our analysis for Group 5 shows similar trends, i.e., most Turkers take the time to find a contextually accurate answer even if it's not on the list of suggested prepositions. Therefore, we do not include a corresponding plot for Group 5 in the paper.

Instead, we thought it would be interesting to examine the Turkers' responses from another angle. Since a correct suggestion may not always be the top-ranked preposition in the suggestion list, it would be interesting to include suggestion ranks into the analysis. Figure 6 shows, for each sentence in each session, the number of Turkers that accepted each ranked suggestion. The color of the bar indicates whether that particular suggestion was correct or incorrect. Note that there may be multiple correct suggestions in a list. Again, we observe that, although there are some Turkers who accepted the top ranked answer even if it was incorrect, the great majority took the time to select a correct preposition no matter what its rank was. Note that the blank facets in the figure represent sentences for a session that did not contain any errors.

4.3 Learning Effects

In this section, we attempt to answer the primary question for the study, i.e., assuming that sessions 2-4 constitute the intervention, is there a significant difference in the pre-intervention and post-intervention Turker performance across the various feedback conditions?

To answer this question, we first compute the log-odds of Turkers accurately detecting (and correcting) errors for the pre-intervention and post-intervention sessions — sessions 1 and 5 respectively — and plot them in Figure 7. We observe that for detection, the changes in performance between pre- and post-intervention are similar across feedback groups and no group seems to have performed better than Group 1, post-intervention. As far as correction is concerned, there is improvement across all feedback conditions, but the change in Group 3's performance seems much more dramatic than that for the other groups.

However, we need to determine whether these improvements are statistically significant or instead can simply be explained away by sampling error due to random variation among the Turkers or among the sentences. To do so, we use a linear mixed-effects model.[2] The advantages of using such a model are that, in addition to modeling the fixed effects of the intervention and the type of feedback, it can also model the random effects represented by the Turker ID (Turkers have different English proficiencies) and the sentence (a sentence may be easier or more difficult than another). In addition, it can also help us account for further random effects, e.g., the effect of Turkers in different groups learning at different rates and the sentences being affected differently by the different feedback conditions. Specifically, we fit the following mixed-effects logistic regression model using the `lme4` package in R:

$$\begin{aligned}\texttt{accurate} \sim \texttt{group} * \texttt{session} & \\ + (1 + \texttt{session} \mid \texttt{mturkid}) & \\ + (1 + \texttt{group} \mid \texttt{sentnum}) &\end{aligned}$$

where `accurate` (0 or 1) represents whether a Turker accurately detected or corrected the error in the sentence, `group` represents the feedback type, and `session` is either the pre- or the post-intervention session (1 or 5). The $*$ in the model indicates the inclusion of the interaction between `group` and `session`, which is necessary since our model is focused on a second order measure (the differences between changes in performance). We fit two models of this form, one for detection and one for correction. Examination of the results indicates:

1. In the detection model, there was a significant effect of `session` ($p < 0.05$). However, neither the effect of `group` nor any of the interactions of

[2]cf. Chapter 7, Baayen (2008).

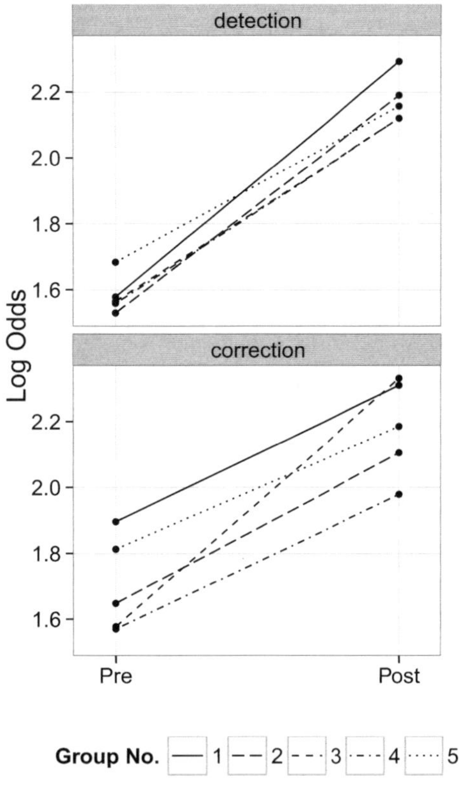

Figure 7: Log-odds of Turkers accurately detecting or correcting preposition errors, pre- and post-intervention.

group by session were significant.

2. In the correction model, the effect of group was significant only for Group 3. In addition, the interaction of group by session was also significant only for Group 3.

From the above results, we can conclude that:

- Irrespective of the feedback type they were shown, Turkers exhibited significant improvements in their detection performance between the pre- and post-intervention sessions, probably due to practice. This was *not* the case for correction.
- Only Turkers from Group 3 (i.e., those shown expert suggestions as feedback - **Detailed Feedback 1**) exhibited a significantly larger improvement in correction performance due to the intervention, as compared to the Turkers that were shown minimal feedback (no explicit feedback).

5 Summary

In this paper, we presented a study that uses crowdsourcing to evaluate whether the granularity of writing feedback can have a measurable impact on learning outcomes. The study yields some interesting results. In particular, it provides some evidence to support the finding from Nagata and Nakatani (2010) that only high precision feedback can help learners improve their writing. However, the study is quite preliminary in nature and focuses on the outcomes for a *single* writing skill. In addition, there were several other deficiencies:

- The distributions of preposition errors across sessions varied considerably which might have made it harder for Turkers to generalize what they learned from one session to another. Another possible confounding factor may have been the fact that the Turker population we recruited was largely located in the U.S. whereas the sentences were chosen from a corpus of British English.
- It is clear from the high levels of pre-intervention error detection and correction performance that the recruited Turkers are not English language learners. We had hoped to recruit Turkers with varied English proficiencies by not restricting participation to any specific countries. However, a more explicit strategy is likely necessary.
- Even though we were fortunate that the Turkers were well-motivated throughout our task, enforcing quality control in a study of this type is challenging.
- Note that in our experimental set up, Turkers receive, as part of the feedback message, an explicit indication of whether or not their detection answers were correct, but no such indication is provided for their correction answers. This could be why session had a significant effect for detection but not for correction.

We believe that our study, along with all its deficiencies, represents a useful contribution to the field of assessing the impact of writing feedback, and that it can help the community design better studies in the future, whether they be conducted using crowdsourcing or with actual students in a classroom.

Acknowledgments

We would like to thank the three anonymous reviewers. We would also like to thank Keelan Evanini, Beata Beigman Klebanov and Lin Gu for their comments.

References

Yigal Attali. 2004. Exploring the Feedback and Revision Features of *Criterion*. Paper presented at the National Council on Measurement in Education (NCME), Educational Testing Service, Princeton, NJ.

R. H. Baayen. 2008. *Analyzing Linguistic Data: A Practical Introduction to Statistics using R*. Cambridge University Press.

Douglas Biber, Tatiana Nekrasova, and Brad Horn. 2011. The Effectiveness of Feedback for L1-English and L2-Writing Development: A Meta-Analysis. Research Report RR-11-05, Educational Testing Service, Princeton, NJ.

J. Bitchener and U. Knoch. 2008. The Value of Written Corrective Feedback for Migrant and International Students. *Language Teaching Research Journal*, 12(3):409–431.

J. Bitchener and U. Knoch. 2009. The Relative Effectiveness of Different Types of Direct Written Corrective Feedback. *System*, 37(2):322–329.

J. Bitchener and U. Knoch. 2010. *The Contribution of Written Corrective Feedback to Language Development: A Ten Month Investigation*.

J. Bitchener, S. Young, and D. Cameron. 2005. The Effect of Different Types of Corrective Feedback on ESL Student Writing. *Journal of Second language Writing*.

J. Bitchener. 2008. Evidence in Support of Written Corrective Feedback. *Journal of Second Language Writing*, 17:69–124.

Aoife Cahill, Nitin Madnani, Joel Tetreault, and Diane Napolitano. 2013. Robust Systems for Preposition Error Correction Using Wikipedia Revisions. In *Proceedings of NAACL*, pages 507–517, Atlanta, GA, USA.

S. Carroll and M. Swain. 1993. Explicit and Implicit Negative Feedback. *Studies in Second Language Acquisition*, 15:357–386.

C. Doughty and J Williams. 1998. *Pedagogical Choices in Focus on Form*.

Z. Li and V. Hegelheimer. 2013. Mobile-assisted Grammar Exercises: Effects on Self-editing in L2 Writing. *Language Learning & Technology*, 17(3):135–156.

Anastasiya A. Lipnevich and Jeffrey K. Smith. 2008. Response to Assessment Feedback: The Effects of Grades, Praise, and Source of Information. Research Report RR-08-30, Educational Testing Service, Princeton, NJ.

R. Lyster and L. Ranta. 1997. Corrective Feedback and Learner Uptake. *Studies in Second Language Acquisition*, 19:37–66.

B. Meihami and H. Meihami. 2013. Correct I or I Dont Correct Myself: Corrective Feedback on EFL Students Writing. In *International Letters of Social and Humanistic Sciences*, page 8695.

Ryo Nagata and Kazuhide Nakatani. 2010. Evaluating Performance of Grammatical Error Detection to Maximize Learning Effect. In *Proceedings of COLING (Posters)*, pages 894–900, Beijing, China.

JoAnn Leah Rock. 2007. The Impact of Short-Term Use of Criterion on Writing Skills in Ninth Grade. Research Report RR-07-07, Educational Testing Service, Princeton, NJ.

J. Russell and N. Spada. 2006. The Effectiveness of Corrective Feedback for the Acquisition of L2 Grammar: A Meta-analysis of the Research. In J. D. Norris and L. Ortega, editors, *Synthesizing Research on Language Learning and Teaching*, pages 133–164. John Benjamins, Philadelphia.

Y. Sheen. 2007. The Effect of Focused Written Corrective Feedback and Language Aptitude on ESL Learners Acquisition of Articles. *TESOL Quarterly*, 41:255–283.

Mark D. Shermis, Jill C. Burstein, and Leonard Bliss. 2004. The Impact of Automated Essay Scoring on High Stakes Writing Assessments. In *Annual Meeting of the National Council on Measurement in Education*.

J. Truscott. 1996. The Case against Grammar Correction in L2 Writing Classes. *Language Learning*, 46:327–369.

John Truscott. 2007. The Effect of Error Correction on Learners' Ability to Write Accurately. *Journal of Second Language Writing*, 16(4):255–272.

Helen Yannakoudakis, Ted Briscoe, and Ben Medlock. 2011. A New Dataset and Method for Automatically Grading ESOL Texts. In *Proceedings of the ACL: HLT*, pages 180–189, Portland, OR, USA.

Oracle and Human Baselines for Native Language Identification

Shervin Malmasi[1]**, Joel Tetreault**[2] **and Mark Dras**[1]

[1]Centre for Language Technology, Macquarie University, Sydney, NSW, Australia
[2] Yahoo Labs, New York, NY, USA

shervin.malmasi@mq.edu.au, tetreaul@yahoo-inc.com
mark.dras@mq.edu.au

Abstract

We examine different ensemble methods, including an oracle, to estimate the upper-limit of classification accuracy for Native Language Identification (NLI). The oracle outperforms state-of-the-art systems by over 10% and results indicate that for many misclassified texts the correct class label receives a significant portion of the ensemble votes, often being the runner-up. We also present a pilot study of human performance for NLI, the first such experiment. While some participants achieve modest results on our simplified setup with 5 L1s, they did not outperform our NLI system, and this performance gap is likely to widen on the standard NLI setup.

1 Introduction

Native Language Identification (NLI) is the task of inferring the native language (L1) of an author based on texts written in a second language (L2). Machine Learning methods are usually used to identify language use patterns common to speakers of the same L1 (Tetreault et al., 2012). The motivations for NLI are manifold. The use of such techniques can help SLA and ESL researchers identify important L1-specific learning and teaching issues, enabling them to develop pedagogical material that takes into consideration a learner's L1. It has also been used to study language transfer hypotheses and extract common L1-related learner errors (Malmasi and Dras, 2014).

NLI has drawn the attention of many researchers in recent years. With the influx of new researchers, the most substantive work in this field has come in the last few years, leading to the organization of the inaugural NLI Shared Task in 2013which was attended by 29 teams from the NLP and SLA areas (Tetreault et al., 2013).

An interesting question about NLI research concerns an upper-bound on the accuracy achievable for a dataset. More specifically, given a dataset, a selection of features and classifiers, what is the maximal performance that could be achieved by an NLI system that always picks the best candidate? This question, not previously addressed in the context of NLI to date, is the primary focus of the present work. Such a measure is an interesting and useful upper-limit baseline for researchers to consider when evaluating their work, since obtaining 100% classification accuracy may not be a reasonable or even feasible goal. In this study we investigate this issue with the aim of deriving such an upper-limit for NLI accuracy.

A second goal of this work is to measure human performance for NLI, something not attempted to date. To this end we design and run a crowdsourced experiment where human evaluators predict the L1 of texts from the NLI shared task.

2 Oracle Classifiers

One possible approach to estimating an upper-bound for classification accuracy, and one that we employ here, is the use of an "Oracle" classifier. This method has previously been used to analyze the limits of majority vote classifier combination (Kuncheva et al., 2001). An oracle is a type of multiple classifier fusion method that can be used to combine the results of an ensemble of classifiers which are all used to classify a dataset.

The oracle will assign the correct class label for an instance if at least one of the constituent classifiers in the system produces the correct label for that data point. Some example oracle results for an ensemble of three classifiers are shown in Table 1. The probability of correct classification of a data point by the oracle is:

$$P_{\text{Oracle}} = 1 - P(\text{All Classifiers Incorrect})$$

Proceedings of the Tenth Workshop on Innovative Use of NLP for Building Educational Applications, 2015, pages 172–178,
Denver, Colorado, June 4, 2015. ©2015 Association for Computational Linguistics

Instance	True Label	Classifier Output C_1	C_2	C_3	Oracle
18354.txt	ARA	TUR	ARA	ARA	Correct
15398.txt	CHI	JPN	JPN	KOR	Incorrect
22754.txt	HIN	GER	TEL	HIN	Correct
10459.txt	SPA	SPA	SPA	SPA	Correct
11567.txt	ITA	FRE	GER	SPA	Incorrect

Table 1: Example oracle results for an ensemble of three classifiers.

Oracles are usually used in comparative experiments and to gauge the performance and diversity of the classifiers chosen for an ensemble (Kuncheva, 2002; Kuncheva et al., 2003). They can help us quantify the *potential* upper limit of an ensemble's performance on the given data and how this performance varies with different ensemble configurations and combinations.

One scenario is the use of an oracle to evaluate the utility of a set of feature types. Here each classifier in the ensemble is trained on a single feature type. This is the focus of our first experiment (§5).

Another scenario involves the combination of different learning algorithms trained on similar features, to form an ensemble in order to evaluate the potential benefits and limits of combining different classification approaches. This is the focus of our second experiment (§6), using all of the entries from the 2013 shared task as systems.

3 Data

Released as part of the 2013 NLI Shared task, the TOEFL11 corpus (Blanchard et al., 2013) [1] is the first dataset designed specifically for the task of NLI and developed with the aim of addressing the deficiencies of other previously used corpora. By providing a common set of L1s and evaluation standards, the shared task set out to facilitate the direct comparison of approaches and methodologies. TOEFL11 includes 12,100 learner essays sampled evenly from 11 different L1 backgrounds: Arabic, Chinese, French, German, Hindi, Italian, Japanese, Korean, Spanish, Telugu and Turkish.

4 Ensemble Combination Methods

We experiment with several ensemble combination methods to draw meaningful comparisons.

Oracle The correct label is selected if predicted by any ensemble member, as described in §2.

Plurality Voting This is a standard combination strategy that selects the label with the highest number of votes,[2] regardless of the percentage of votes it received (Polikar, 2006).

Accuracy@N To account for the possibility that a classifier may predict the correct label by chance (with a probability determined by the random baseline), we propose an Accuracy@N combiner. This method is inspired by the "Precision at k" metric from Information Retrieval (Manning et al., 2008) which measures precision at fixed low levels of results (*e.g.* the top 10 results). Here, it is an extension of the Plurality vote combiner where instead of selecting the label with the highest votes, the labels are ranked by their vote counts and an instance is correctly classified if the true label is in the top N ranked candidates.[3] In other words, it is a more restricted version of the Oracle combiner that is limited to the top N ranked candidates in order to minimize the influence of a single classifier having chosen the correct label by chance. In this study we experiment with $N = 2$ and 3. We also note that setting $N = 1$ is equivalent to the Plurality voting method.

Mean Probability All classifiers provide probability estimates for each possible class. Each class' estimates are summed and the one with the highest mean wins (Polikar, 2006, §4.2).

Simple Combination combines all features into a single feature space.

5 Feature Set Evaluation

Our first experiment attempts to derive the potential accuracy upper-limit of our feature set. We train a single linear Support Vector Machine (SVM) classifier for each feature type to create our classifier ensemble. Linear SVMs have been shown to be effective for such text classification problems and was the classifier of choice in the 2013 NLI Shared Task. We do not experiment with combining different machine learning algorithms here, instead we focus on gauging the potential of the feature set. We employ a standard set of previously used feature types: character/word n-grams, Part-of-Speech (POS) n-grams, function words, Context-free grammar production rules, Tree Substitution Grammar fragments and Stanford Dependencies. Descriptions of these features can be

[1] http://catalog.ldc.upenn.edu/LDC2014T06

[2] This differs with a *majority* vote combiner where a label must obtain over 50% of the votes.

[3] In case of ties we choose randomly from the labels with the same number of votes.

	Accuracy (%)	
	10-fold CV	**Test Set**
Random Baseline	9.1	9.1
Shared Task Best	84.3 (84.5)	83.6 (85.3)
Oracle	95.6	95.4
Accuracy@3	92.5	92.2
Accuracy@2	88.6	88.0
Plurality Vote	78.2	77.6
Simple Combination	78.2	77.5
Mean Probability	79.4	78.7

Table 2: Oracle results using our feature set.

	Accuracy (%)	
	Best Run	**All Runs**
Random Baseline	9.1	9.1
Shared Task Best	84.3 (84.5)	83.6 (85.3)
Oracle	97.9	99.5
Accuracy@3	95.5	95.6
Accuracy@2	92.2	92.5
Plurality Vote	84.5	84.4

Table 3: Oracle results on the shared task systems.

found in §4.1 of Tetreault et al. (2012).[4]

We report classification accuracy under 10-fold cross-validation using the TOEFL11 training data and also on the test set from the 2013 shared task, shown in Table 2. For both Tables 2 and 3 we report a random baseline and the best performances on the Shared Task: the first number is the top performer from the shared task (Jarvis et al., 2013), and the number in parentheses is the best published performance after the shared task (Ionescu et al., 2014) . The cross-validation and test results are very similar, with the oracle accuracy at 95%, suggesting that for each document there is in most cases at least one feature type that correctly predicts it. This drops to 88% with the Accuracy@2 combiner, still much higher than the plurality vote and the best results from the shared task. This suggests that there is a noticeable tail of feature types dragging the plurality vote down.

6 2013 Shared Task Evaluation

In the second experiment we apply our methods to the submissions in the 2013 NLI Shared Task, aiming to quantify the potential upper limit for combining a range of different systems.

The data comes from the closed-training sub-task.[5] Each team was allowed to submit up to 5 different runs for each task, allowing them to experiment with different feature and parameter variations of their system. Each team's systems produce predictions using their own set of features and learning algorithms, with several of these systems using ensembles themselves.

In total, 115 runs were submitted by 29 teams, with the winning entry achieving the highest accuracy of 83.6% on the test set. We experiment under two conditions: using only each team's best run and using all 115 runs. Results are compared against the random baseline and winning entry.

Table 3 shows the results for this experiment. The oracle results are higher than the previous experiment, which is not unexpected given the much larger number of predictions per document. Results for the other combiners are also higher here.

The Accuracy@2 results are 92% in both conditions, much higher than the winning entry's 83%. Results from the Accuracy@2 combiner, both here and in the previous experiment, show that a great majority of the texts are close to being correctly classified: this value is significantly higher than the plurality combiner[6] and not much lower than the oracle. This shows that the correct label receives a significant portion of the votes and when not the winning label, it is often the runner-up.[7]

One implication of this concerns practical applications of NLI, *e.g.* in a manual analysis, where it may be worthwhile for researchers to also consider the runner-up label in their evaluation.

This knowledge could also be used to increase NLI accuracy by aiming to develop more sophisticated classifiers that can take into account the top N labels in their decision making, similar to discriminative reranking methods applied in statistical parsing (Charniak and Johnson, 2005).

Using the Accuracy@2 combiner, we isolate the cases where the actual label was the runner up and extract the most frequent pairs of top 2 labels, presented in Table 4. We see that a quarter of the errors are confusion between Hindi and Telugu. The Korean and Turkish confusion could be due to both being Altaic languages.

We also examine the confusion matrices for the plurality, Accuracy@2 and oracle combiners,[8] shown

[4]For features comparisons see Malmasi and Cahill (2015)

[5]The shared task consisted of three sub-tasks. For each task, the test set was TOEFL11-TEST; only the type of training data varied by task where the other two sub-tasks allowed the use of external training data.

[6]Which is itself equivalent to an Accuracy@1 combiner.

[7]In approx. 8% of the cases here, to be more precise.

[8]Where the Accuracy@2 and oracle combiners could not predict the correct label the plurality vote was used.

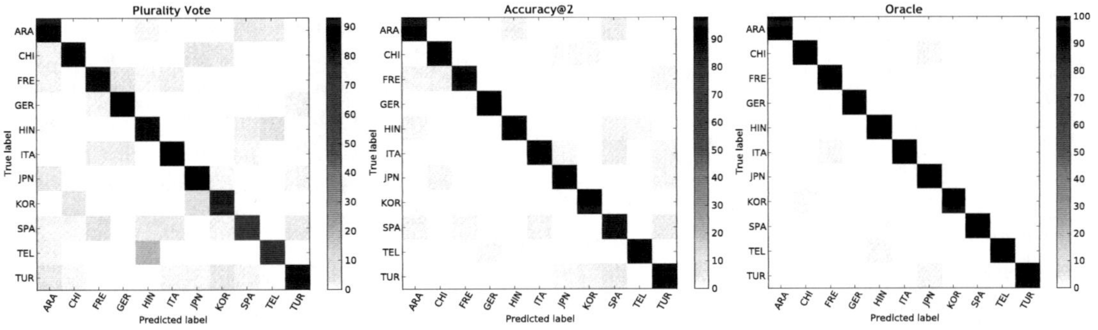

Figure 1: Confusion matrices for the plurality (L), Accuracy@2 (M) and oracle (R) combiners..

Confused Pair	Percent	Cumulative Percent
HIN–TEL	15.9	15.9
TEL–HIN	10.2	26.1
CHI–KOR	6.8	33.0
JPN–KOR	6.8	39.8
KOR–TUR	4.5	44.3

Table 4: Most commonly predicted top 2 label pairs where the runner-up is the true label.

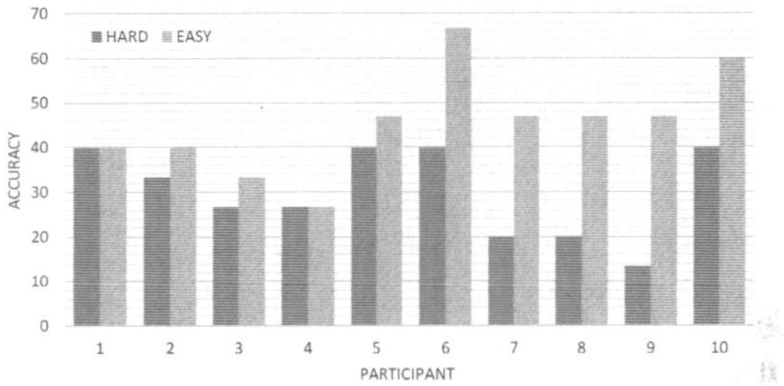

Figure 2: Prediction accuracy for each of our 10 participants under both easy and hard conditions.

in Figure 1. They show that Hindi–Telugu is the most commonly confused pair and confirm the directionality of the confusion: more Telugu texts are misclassified as Hindi than vice versa.

7 Human NLI Performance

While most NLI work has focused on improving system performance, to our knowledge there has not been any corresponding study which looks at human performance for this task. To give our preceding results more context, as well as the results of the field, we ran an exploratory study to determine how accurate humans are for this task.

7.1 Experiment Design

Our initial hypothesis was to use the Amazon Mechanical Turk to collect crowdsourced judgments. However, unlike simpler NLP tasks, e.g. sentiment analysis and word sense disambiguation, which can be effectively annotated by untrained Turkers (Snow et al., 2008), NLI requires raters with knowledge and exposure to writers with different L1s. Optimally, one would use a set of ESL teachers and researchers who have experience in working with ESL writers from all of the 11 L1s, though such people are rarity. As a reasonable compromise, we chose 10 professors and researchers who have varied linguistic backgrounds, speak multiple languages, and have had exposure with the particular L1s, either as a speaker or through working with ESL students. We also constrained the task from 11 L1s to 5 (Arabic, Chinese, German, Hindi, and Spanish) as we believed that 11 L1s would be too much of an overload on the judges. The 5 L1s were selected since they all belong to separate language families.

The experiment consisted of rating 30 essays from TOEFL11-TEST, 15 of which most Shared Task systems could predict correctly (easy), and the remaining 15 were essays in which the Shared Task systems had difficulty (hard). The L1s were distributed evenly over the essays and easy/hard conditions (3 "easy" and 3 "hard" essays per L1).

7.2 Results

Figure 2 shows the accuracy for each rater in this pilot study. The top rater accurately identified 16 out of 30 L1s (53.3%), with the lowest raters at 30.0% overall and an average of 37.3%. All raters did better on the "easy" cases than on the "hard." A paired-samples t-test was conducted to compare human accuracy in the easy and hard conditions. A significant difference was found for easy (M=45.33, SD=11.67) and hard (M=30, SD=10.06), t(9)=−3.851, p = .004.

Next, we compared human accuracy with our NLI system, which we re-trained using only the five selected L1s. Results are shown in Table 5. All ensembles outperform human raters and a plurality vote composed of the human raters. Interestingly, the human plurality vote was only 3% higher than the top human score, suggesting that the raters tended to get the same essays correct.

	Accuracy (%)		
	Easy	**Hard**	**All**
Random Baseline	20.0	20.0	20.0
NLI Plurality Vote	100.0	33.3	66.7
NLI Mean Probability	**100.0**	**46.7**	**73.3**
Top Human	66.7	40.0	53.3
Human Plurality Vote	73.3	40.0	56.7

Table 5: Comparing human participant performance against an NLI system on 30 selected texts.

We also note that some L1s received more correct predictions than others,[9] but the difference is not statistically significant.[10] Some participants noted that while they had familiarity with L1 Spanish/Chinese non-native writing, they did not have much exposure to the other L1s, possibly due to international student cohorts.

Our belief, based on these pilot results, is that as the number of classes increases, the system will outpace the human raters by a widening margin. It should also be noted that we purposefully selected disparate L1s to make easier for the human raters. As there are several other L1s in the TOEFL11 that are in the Romance family class, and others where it is less likely for raters to have seen student essays (such as Telugu), including those will also likely affect human performance.

8 Related Work

Prior work has shown that ensemble classification can improve NLI performance. Tetreault et al. (2012) established that ensembles composed of classifiers trained on different feature types were useful for NLI and we also take this approach. Several shared task systems also found improvements using different ensemble classifications. Goutte et al. (2013) used plurality voting in their shared task submission which placed seventh. Cimino et al. (2013) found that a meta-classifier approaches outperformed plurality voting, while both outperformed their basic system. Malmasi et al. (2013) experimented with 7 different methods of ensemble classification and found that the mean probability method performed best, though they note that all ensemble methods were within about 1% of each other. This method, performed after the final submission phase, performed at 83.6%, the same as the top performing system (Jarvis et al., 2013).

More recently, Bykh and Meurers (2014) extended their shared task submission (Bykh et al., 2013) by investigating the use of model selection and tuning for ensemble classification. Their method outperformed plurality voting, and when combined with improvements to syntactic and n-gram features, produced a performance of 84.82%. Finally, Ionescu et al. (2014) used string kernels to achieve the highest reported result on the TOEFL11-TEST: 85.3% and 10-fold CV: 84.5%.

In contrast to the prior work, our work in combining the outputs of each system could not make use of the development set since that would require the actual code from all 29 systems. If that were available, then a meta-classifer could be used to further improve performance.

9 Discussion

We presented a novel analysis for predicting the "potential" upper limit of NLI accuracy on a dataset. This upper limit can vary depending on which components – feature types and algorithms – are used in the system. Alongside other baselines, oracle performance can assist in interpreting the relative performance of an NLI system.[11]

A useful application of this method is to isolate the subset of wholly misclassified texts for further investigation and error analysis. This segregated data can then be independently studied to better understand the aspects that make it hard to classify them correctly. This can also be used to guide feature engineering practices in order to develop features that can distinguish these challenging texts. In practice, this type of oracle measure can be used to guide the process of choosing the pool of classifiers that form an ensemble.

We also note that these oracle figures would be produced by an optimal system that always makes the correct decision using this pool of classifiers. While these oracle results could be interpreted as potentially attainable, this may not be feasible and practical limits could be substantially lower.

A potentially fruitful direction for future work is the investigation of meta-classification methods that can overcome the limitations of the plurality voting methods to achieve higher results. It should be noted that the human study described in this paper is a pilot. We plan on conducting a larger rating where we sample randomly across essays and include more experts for each L1.

[9] CHI: 50%, SPA: 46.7%, HIN: 33.3%, GER: 31.7%, ARA: 26.7%

[10] Our sample size is too small, but this is still suggestive.

[11] *e.g.* an NLI system with 70% accuracy against an Oracle baseline of 80% is relatively better compared to one with 74% accuracy against an Oracle baseline of 93%.

Acknowledgments

We would like to thank the three anonymous reviewers as well as our raters: Martin Chodorow, Carla Parra Escartin, Marte Kvamme, Aasish Pappu, Dragomir Radev, Patti Spinner, Robert Stine, Kapil Thadani, Alissa Vik and Gloria Zen.

References

Daniel Blanchard, Joel Tetreault, Derrick Higgins, Aoife Cahill, and Martin Chodorow. 2013. TOEFL11: A Corpus of Non-Native English. Technical report, Educational Testing Service.

Serhiy Bykh and Detmar Meurers. 2014. Exploring Syntactic Features for Native Language Identification: A Variationist Perspective on Feature Encoding and Ensemble Optimization. In *Proceedings of COLING 2014, the 25th International Conference on Computational Linguistics: Technical Papers*, pages 1962–1973, Dublin, Ireland, August. Dublin City University and Association for Computational Linguistics.

Serhiy Bykh, Sowmya Vajjala, Julia Krivanek, and Detmar Meurers. 2013. Combining Shallow and Linguistically Motivated Features in Native Language Identification. In *Proceedings of the Eighth Workshop on Innovative Use of NLP for Building Educational Applications*, pages 197–206, Atlanta, Georgia, June. Association for Computational Linguistics.

Eugene Charniak and Mark Johnson. 2005. Coarse-to-fine n-best parsing and MaxEnt discriminative reranking. In *Proceedings of the 43rd Annual Meeting on Association for Computational Linguistics*, pages 173–180. Association for Computational Linguistics.

Andrea Cimino, Felice Dell'Orletta, Giulia Venturi, and Simonetta Montemagni. 2013. Linguistic Profiling based on General–purpose Features and Native Language Identification. In *Proceedings of the Eighth Workshop on Innovative Use of NLP for Building Educational Applications*, pages 207–215, Atlanta, Georgia, June. Association for Computational Linguistics.

Cyril Goutte, Serge Léger, and Marine Carpuat. 2013. Feature Space Selection and Combination for Native Language Identification. In *Proceedings of the Eighth Workshop on Innovative Use of NLP for Building Educational Applications*, pages 96–100, Atlanta, Georgia, June. Association for Computational Linguistics.

Radu Tudor Ionescu, Marius Popescu, and Aoife Cahill. 2014. Can characters reveal your native language? a language-independent approach to native language identification. In *Proceedings of the 2014 Conference on Empirical Methods in Natural Language Processing (EMNLP)*, pages 1363–1373, Doha, Qatar, October. Association for Computational Linguistics.

Scott Jarvis, Yves Bestgen, and Steve Pepper. 2013. Maximizing Classification Accuracy in Native Language Identification. In *Proceedings of the Eighth Workshop on Innovative Use of NLP for Building Educational Applications*, pages 111–118, Atlanta, Georgia, June. Association for Computational Linguistics.

Ludmila I Kuncheva, James C Bezdek, and Robert PW Duin. 2001. Decision templates for multiple classifier fusion: an experimental comparison. *Pattern Recognition*, 34(2):299–314.

Ludmila I Kuncheva, Christopher J Whitaker, Catherine A Shipp, and Robert PW Duin. 2003. Limits on the majority vote accuracy in classifier fusion. *Pattern Analysis & Applications*, 6(1):22–31.

Ludmila I Kuncheva. 2002. A theoretical study on six classifier fusion strategies. *IEEE Transactions on pattern analysis and machine intelligence*, 24(2):281–286.

Shervin Malmasi and Aoife Cahill. 2015. Measuring Feature Diversity in Native Language Identification. In *Proceedings of the Tenth Workshop on Innovative Use of NLP for Building Educational Applications*, Denver, Colorado, June. Association for Computational Linguistics.

Shervin Malmasi and Mark Dras. 2014. Language Transfer Hypotheses with Linear SVM Weights. In *Proceedings of the 2014 Conference on Empirical Methods in Natural Language Processing (EMNLP)*, Doha, Qatar, October. Association for Computational Linguistics.

Shervin Malmasi, Sze-Meng Jojo Wong, and Mark Dras. 2013. NLI Shared Task 2013: MQ Submission. In *Proceedings of the Eighth Workshop on Innovative Use of NLP for Building Educational Applications*, pages 124–133, Atlanta, Georgia, June. Association for Computational Linguistics.

Christopher D Manning, Prabhakar Raghavan, and Hinrich Schütze. 2008. Evaluation in information retrieval. In *Introduction to Information Retrieval*, pages 151–175. Cambridge university press Cambridge.

Robi Polikar. 2006. Ensemble based systems in decision making. *Circuits and systems magazine, IEEE*, 6(3):21–45.

Rion Snow, Brendan O'Connor, Daniel Jurafsky, and Andrew Ng. 2008. Cheap and Fast – But is it Good? Evaluating Non-Expert Annotations for Natural Language Tasks. In *Proceedings of the 2008 Conference on Empirical Methods in Natural Language Processing*, pages 254–263, Honolulu, Hawaii, October. Association for Computational Linguistics.

Joel Tetreault, Daniel Blanchard, Aoife Cahill, and Martin Chodorow. 2012. Native Tongues, Lost and Found: Resources and Empirical Evaluations in Native Language Identification. In *Proceedings of COLING 2012*, pages 2585–2602, Mumbai, India, December. The COLING 2012 Organizing Committee.

Joel Tetreault, Daniel Blanchard, and Aoife Cahill. 2013. A Report on the First Native Language Identification Shared Task. In *Proceedings of the Eighth Workshop on Innovative Use of NLP for Building Educational Applications*, pages 48–57, Atlanta, Georgia, June. Association for Computational Linguistics.

Using PEGWriting® to Support the Writing Motivation and Writing Quality of Eighth-Grade Students: A Quasi-Experimental Study

Joshua Wilson
University of Delaware
213E Willard Hall
Newark, DE 19716
joshwils@udel.edu

Trish Martin
Measurement Incorporated
423 Morris Street
Durham, NC 27701
tmartin@measinc.com

Abstract

A quasi-experimental study compared the effects of feedback condition on eighth-grade students' writing motivation and writing achievement. Four classes of eighth-graders were assigned to a combined feedback condition in which they received feedback on their writing from their teacher and from an automated essay evaluation (AEE) system called PEGWriting®. Four other eighth-grade classes were assigned to a teacher feedback condition, in which they solely received feedback from their teacher via GoogleDocs. Results indicated that students in the combined PEGWriting+Teacher Feedback condition received feedback more quickly and indicated that they were more likely to solve problems in their writing. Equal writing quality was achieved between feedback groups even though teachers in the PEGWriting condition spent less time providing feedback to students than in the GoogleDocs condition. Results suggest that PEGWriting enabled teachers to offload certain aspects of the feedback process and promoted greater independence and persistence for students.

1. Introduction

In the 21st century, possessing strong writing skills is essential for success in K-12 education, college acceptance and completion, and stable gainful employment (National Commission on Writing, 2004, 2005). Yet, more than two-thirds of students in grades four, eight, and twelve fail to achieve grade-level proficiency in writing, as indicated by recent performance on the National Assessment of Educational Progress (NCES, 2012; Salahu-Din, Persky, & Miller, 2008). Without sufficient writing skills, students are at-risk of performing worse in school, suffering lower grades, and experiencing school dropout (Graham & Perin, 2007).

One effective method for improving students' writing skills is providing instructional feedback (Graham, McKeown, Kiuhara, & Harris, 2012; Graham & Perin, 2007). Struggling writers, in particular, need targeted instructional feedback because they tend to produce shorter, less-developed, and more error-filled texts than their peers (Troia, 2006). However, instructional feedback is often difficult and time-consuming for teachers to provide. Indeed, educators in the primary and secondary grades report that the time-costs of evaluating writing are so prohibitive that they rarely assign more than one or two paragraphs of writing (Cutler & Graham, 2008; Kiuhara, Graham, & Hawken, 2009). Consequently, educators are increasingly relying on automated essay evaluation (AEE) systems (Warschauer & Grimes, 2008) to provide students with immediate feedback in the form of essay ratings and individualized suggestions for improving an essay—i.e., automated feedback.

Previous research on AEE indicates that, in isolation of teacher feedback, automated feedback appears to support modest improvements in students' writing quality. Findings from studies of ETS's Criterion® (Kellogg, Whiteford, & Quinlan; Shermis, Wilson Garvan, & Diao, 2008), Pearson's Summary Street (Franzke, Kintsch, Caccamise, Johnson, & Dooley, 2005; Wade-Stein & Kintsch, 2004), and Measurement Incorporated's PEGWriting® system (Wilson & Andrada, in press; Wilson, Olinghouse, & Andrada, 2014), indicate that automated feedback assists students in improving the overall quality of their essays while concomitantly reducing the frequency of their mechanical errors.

Less research has explored the effects of AEE on writing motivation. However, in two studies, Warschauer and Grimes (2008; 2010), found that

Proceedings of the Tenth Workshop on Innovative Use of NLP for Building Educational Applications, 2015, pages 179–189,
Denver, Colorado, June 4, 2015.

teachers and students who had used ETS' Criterion or Pearson's My Access programs, agreed that AEE had positive effects on student motivation. Teachers also reported that the AEE systems saved them time on grading, and to be more selective about the feedback they gave.

1.1 Study purpose

The purpose of the present study was to extend previous research in the following ways. First, previous studies of AEE have focused on the use of automated feedback in isolation of teacher feedback, despite the intended use of such systems for complementing, not replacing, teacher feedback (Kellogg et al., 2010). To date, no research has evaluated the effects of a combined AEE-and-teacher-feedback condition against a teacher-feedback-only condition. Furthermore, studies have employed a weak control condition, typically a no-feedback condition, to test the effects of AEE on writing quality.

Furthermore, additional research is needed regarding the possible effects of AEE on writing motivation. Theoretical models of writing (e.g., Hayes, 2006; 2012), and empirical research (e.g., Graham, Berninger, & Fan, 2007) underscore the importance of a student's motivation and dispositions towards writing for promoting writing achievement. As AEE systems become more widely-used, it is important for stakeholders to know the degree, and limitations, of their effect on these affective dimensions of writing ability.

Therefore, the present study compared a combined teacher-plus-AEE feedback condition to a teacher-feedback-only condition with regards to their effect on eighth-grade students' writing motivation and writing quality. The combined feedback condition utilized an AEE system called PEGWriting. The teacher-feedback-only condition utilized the comments function of GoogleDocs to provide students with feedback. We hypothesized that students in the combined feedback condition would report greater motivation due to PEGWriting's capacity to provide immediate feedback in the form of essay ratings and individualized suggestions for feedback. With respect to writing quality, it was difficult to generate a priori hypotheses given the aforementioned limitations of previous research. Exploratory analyses considered whether students in the combined feedback condition outperformed their peers on measures of writing quality, or whether quality was commensurate across groups.

2. Methods

2.1 Setting and Participants

This study was conducted in a middle school in an urban school district in the mid-Atlantic region of the United States. The district serves approx. 10,000 students in 10 elementary schools, three middle schools, and one high school. In this district, 43% of students are African-American, 20% are Hispanic/Latino, and 33% White. Approximately 9% of students are English Language Learners, and 50% of students come from low income families.

Two eighth-grade English Language Arts (ELA) teachers agreed to participate in this study. The teachers were experienced, having taught for a total of 12 and 19 years, respectively. One teacher had earned a Master's degree and the other was in the process of earning it (Bachelor's +21 credits). Each teacher taught a total of four class periods of ELA per day.

Given that the school did not use academic tracking and each class exhibited a range of reading and writing ability, teachers were asked to randomly select two classes from each of their schedules to assign to the combined automated-and-teacher-feedback condition (hereafter referred to as PEG+Teacher), and two classes to assign to a teacher-feedback-only condition (hereafter referred to as GoogleDocs). Thus, teachers instructed classes assigned to both feedback condition.

A total of 74 students were assigned to the PEG+Teacher condition and 77 students to the GoogleDocs condition. Though classes were randomly assigned to feedback conditions, the study sampled intact classes, resulting in a quasi-experimental design. Table 1 reports demographics for each sample. Chi-Square and *t*-tests confirmed that the groups were equal with respect to all variables. In addition, all students received free-lunch. No students received special education services.

	PEG + Teacher	GoogleDocs
Gender (*n*)		
Male	41	38
Female	33	39
Race (*n*)		
Hispanic/Latino	20	20
African American	31	24
White	22	30
Asian	1	1
Unreported	0	2
ELL (*n*)	2	0
Age (months)		
M	169.03	169.51
SD	5.90	4.90

Table 1: Demographics of Study Participants

2.2 Description of PEGWriting

PEGWriting is a web-based formative writing assessment program developed by Measurement Incorporated (MI). It is designed to provide students and teachers with an efficient and reliable method of scoring student writing in order to promote students' writing skills.

PEGWriting is built around an automated essay scoring engine called PEG, or Project Essay Grade. PEG was developed by Ellis Batten Page (Page, 1966; 1994; 2003) and acquired by MI in 2002. PEG uses a combination of techniques such as natural language processing, syntactic analysis, and semantic analysis to measure more than 500 variables that are combined in a regression-based algorithm that predicts human holistic and analytic essay ratings. A number of empirical studies have established the reliability and criterion validity of PEG's essay ratings (Kieth, 2003; Shermis, 2014; Shermis, Koch, Page, Keith, & Harrington, 2002).

Students and teachers access PEGWriting by visiting www.pegwriting.com and inputting their individual username and passwords. Teachers can assign system-created prompts in narrative, argumentative, or informative genres. They can also create and embed their own prompts, which can use words, documents, images, videos, or even music as stimuli.

Once a prompt is assigned, students can select from several embedded graphic organizers to support their brainstorming and prewriting activities. After prewriting, students have up to 60 minutes to complete and submit their drafts for evaluation by PEG. Once submitted, students immediately receive essay ratings for six traits of writing ability: idea development, organization, style, sentence structure, word choice, and conventions. Each of these traits is scored on a 1-5 scale and combined to form an Overall Score ranging from 6-30. In addition, students receive feedback on grammar and spelling, as well as trait-specific feedback that encourages students to review and evaluate their text with regard to the features of that specific trait. Students also receive customized links to PEGWriting's skill-building mini-lessons. These lessons are multimedia interactive lessons on specific writing skills such as elaboration, organization, or sentence variety.

Once students receive their feedback, they may revise and resubmit their essays up to a total of 99 times—the default limit is 30—and receive new essay ratings, error corrections, and trait-specific feedback. Teachers are also able to provide students with feedback by embedding comments within the students' essays or through summary comments located in a text box following the PEG-generated trait-specific feedback. Students may also leave comments for their teacher using a similar function.

2.3 Study Procedures

After classes were assigned to feedback conditions, all students completed a pretest writing motivation survey (Piazza & Siebert, 2008; see Section 2.4). Then, teachers began instruction in their district-assigned curriculum module on memoir writing. Teachers introduced the key features of memoir writing to all their classes. During this initial instructional phase, students in the PEG+Teacher condition were given an opportunity to learn how to use PEGWriting. Earlier in the school year, the first author trained the two teachers on the use PEGWriting during three 30 minute training sessions. Then, teachers subsequently trained their students how to use the program in one 45 minute class period following completion of the pretest writing motivation survey.

Teachers then assigned their district-created writing prompt for the memoir unit, which read:

> We have all had interesting life experiences. Some are good, funny, or exciting, while

> others are bad, sad, or devastating. Choose one experience from your life and tell the story. Once you have chosen your topic, you may choose to turn it into a scary story, drama, elaborate fiction, science fiction, comedy, or just tell it how it is. Be sure to organize your story and elaborate on your details. Your audience wasn't there so you need to tell them every little detail.

Students then proceeded to brainstorm, organize their ideas, and draft their memoirs using the technology available to them. Students in the PEG+Teacher condition used the built-in graphic organizers to plan out their memoirs. Students in the GoogleDocs condition used teacher-provided graphic organizers. Subsequent class periods were devoted to drafting, revising, and editing the memoirs. During this time, teachers delivered mini-lessons on features of memoir writing such as "Show, not tell," "Using dialogue in memoirs," and "Using transitions." Both teachers kept a log of their instructional activities, documenting that they delivered the same instruction as each other and to each of the classes they taught.

Teachers were instructed to review and provide feedback on their students' writing a minimum of one, and a maximum of two times, across both conditions. Teachers were allowed to provide feedback as they normally would, commenting on those aspects of students' text which they deemed necessary. They gave feedback to students in the GoogleDocs condition by (a) directly editing students' texts, and (b) providing comments similar to the comment feature in Microsoft Word. Since students in the PEG+Teacher feedback condition were already receiving feedback from PEG, teachers could supplement the feedback with additional comments as they deemed necessary. Feedback was delivered in the form of embedded comments (similar to the GoogleDocs condition) and in the form of summary comments. Students in this condition were allowed to receive as much feedback from PEG as they wished by revising and resubmitting their memoir to PEG for evaluation. But, the amount of teacher feedback was held constant across conditions.

At the conclusion of the instructional period (approx. three weeks), students submitted the final drafts of their memoir. Then, students were administered a post-test writing motivation survey that mirrored the initial survey with additional items that specifically asked about their perceptions of the feedback they received. Teachers also completed a brief survey regarding their experiences providing feedback via PEGWriting and GoogleDocs.

2.4 Study Measures

Writing Motivation was assessed using the Writing Disposition Scale (WDS; Piazza & Siebert, 2008), which consisted of 11 Likert-scale items that are combined to form three subscales measuring the constructs of confidence, persistence, and passion. Cronbach's Alpha was reported as .89 for the entire instrument, and .81, .75, and .91, respectively for the three subscales (Piazza & Siebert, 2008). The WDS was administered at pretest and at posttest. The posttest administration of the WDS also include additional researcher-developed items asking students to share their perceptions of the feedback they received. These items included Likert-scale ratings followed by an open-ended response option.

Writing quality was assessed using the PEG Overall Score, PEG trait scores, and teacher grades. Details on the PEG Overall Score and the PEG trait scores are found in Section 2.2. Teacher grades were generated by using a primary trait narrative rubric developed by the local school district. The rubric evaluated ten traits of personal narrative writing, each on a 0-10 scale. Final grades were assigned by totaling students' scores on each of the ten traits (range: 0-100). Traits assessed included: the presence of a compelling introduction; logical organization; establishment of a setting, narrator, and point of view; effective conclusion which reflects on the life event; sufficient details and description; effective use of figurative language and dialogue; presence of accurate sentence structure; strong and vivid word choice; and absence of errors of spelling, punctuation, and usage.

2.5 Data Analysis

Non-parametric analyses were used to estimate differences between feedback conditions on individual items of the Writing Dispositions Scale (WDS). A series of one-way analysis of variance (ANOVA) were used to estimate differences between groups on the Confidence, Persistence, and

	PEG+Teacher					GoogleDocs				
Item	SA	A	N	D	SD	SA	A	N	D	SD
1. My written work is among the best in the class.	8	17	34	13	2	9	13	39	10	5
2. Writing is fun for me.	4	25	29	8	8	10	23	15	18	10
3. I take time to try different possibilities in my writing.	3	33	23	13	2	7	35	20	10	4
4. I would like to write more in school.	2	11	25	22	14	5	18	18	17	18
5. I am NOT a good writer.	3	12	23	20	16	6	8	28	25	9
6. Writing is my favorite subject in school.	3	6	24	31	10	3	11	22	22	18
7. I am will to spend time on long papers.	3	21	21	14	15	8	23	13	19	13
8. If I have choices during free time, I usually select writing.	0	4	13	27	30	1	8	8	27	32
9. I always look forward to writing class.	3	10	27	21	13	1	10	24	18	23
10. I take time to solve problems in my writing.	11	34	17	8	4	5	34	20	13	4
11. Writing is easy for me.	10	24	31	2	7	17	22	27	5	5

Table 2: Frequencies of Student Responses to the Pretest Writing Disposition Scale (WDS) by Feedback Condition SA = Strongly Agree; A = Agree; N = Neutral; D = Disagree; SD = Strongly Disagree

Passion subscales. Confidence was formed as the average of items 1, 5 (reverse coded), and 11. Reverse coding was achieved by translating self-reports of strongly agree to strongly disagree, agree to disagree, and vice versa. Neutral responses remained the same. Persistence was formed as the average of items 3, 4, 7, and 10. Passion was formed as the average of items 2, 6, 8, and 9. Finally, a series of one-way ANOVAs was used to compare conditions with respect to the writing quality measures. Full data was available for all students on the PEG Overall and Trait scores. Data on teacher grades was only available for 62 students in each group at the time of this reporting. Data coded from open-ended response items from teachers and students was used to contextualize the results. Missing data for posttest measures of motivation and writing quality resulted in listwise deletion of cases from analyses

3. Results

3.1 Pretest Analyses of Writing Motivation

Data from the pretest administration of the WDS is presented in Table 2 (above). Non-parametric analyses performed on the individual survey items revealed that the null hypothesis of equal distributions across feedback conditions was retained in all cases. Thus, it is possible to assume that students' writing motivation did not differ as a function of their feedback condition. Means and standard deviations for the subscales of Confidence, Persistence, and Passion are presented in Table 3. *T*-tests indicated no-statistically significant differences in subscale scores by feedback condition. Hence, at pretest, groups were equivalent with respect to their writing motivation and writing dispositions.

	PEG+Teacher		GoogleDocs	
Subscale	*M*	*SD*	*M*	*SD*
Confidence	2.75	.91	2.58	.78
Persistence	3.05	.85	2.86	.69
Passion	3.64	.88	3.42	.76

Table 3: Descriptives for WDS Subscales at Pretest

3.2 Posttest Analyses of Writing Motivation

Non-parametric analyses were performed on the individual posttest survey items, examining statistically significant differences in the distribution of responses across conditions. All contrasts were non-statistically significant, except for item 10—"I take time to solve problems in my writing." The mean ranks of the PEG+Teacher and GoogleDocs conditions were 62.52 and 75.53, respectively: U = 1921.50, Z = -2.03, p = .04. Examination of the individual frequency data for this item (see Table 4) shows that 66% of students in the PEG+Teacher feedback condition agreed or strongly agreed with this statement, as compared to 50% of students in the GoogleDocs condition.

	SA	A	N	D	SD
PEG+Teacher	11	31	17	4	1
GoogleDocs	7	30	27	7	3

Table 4: Posttest Frequencies to WDS Item 10

When comparing pre-/posttest responses to item 10 (see Figure 1), the percentage of students in the PEG+Teacher condition who agreed or strongly agreed that they take time to solve problems in their writing increased by 5%, whereas those in the GoogleDocs condition stayed the same. One-way ANOVAs comparing subscale scores across condition were not statistically significant.

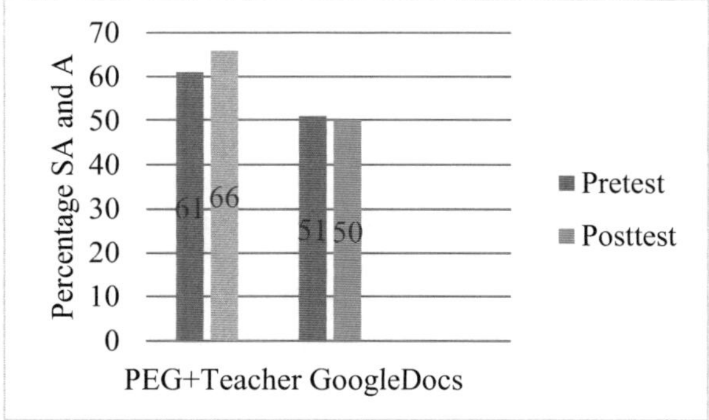

Figure 1: Pretest/Posttest Comparison of SA/A Responses to WDS Item 10

To further investigate this finding we compared the average number of essay drafts completed by students in each condition using a one-way ANOVA. Results indicated that students in the PEG+Teacher condition completed a higher average number of essay drafts (M = 11.28, SD = 6.81) than students in the GoogleDocs condition (M = 7.18, SD = 2.29): F (1, 138) = 22.287, p < .001. Thus, students' self-report information and behavior appears to be consistent in this regard.

In addition to the 11 items on the WDS scale, seven other Likert-scale items were administered at posttest assessing students' perceptions of the feedback they received. Non-parametric analyses indicated a statistically significant difference between feedback conditions on item 18—"I received feedback quickly"—favoring the PEG+Teacher feedback condition (Mean rank = 56.34) as compared to the GoogleDocs condition (Mean rank = 79.31): U = 1526.00, Z = -3.57, p < .001. A total of 78% of students in the PEG+Teacher condition agreed or strongly agreed that they received feedback quickly, as compared to 63% of students in the GoogleDocs condition. Examination of the frequency data for the other feedback-specific items (see Table 5 following page) suggests that students in both conditions perceived feedback to be useful for helping them improve their writing. Students exhibited greater variation with regard to their desire to receive more feedback (Item 15). Open-ended response data suggests that feedback can serve to both encourage and discourage student writers. For some, feedback is a supportive and motivating factor.

> I wish that because it'll help me make my writing pieces better. Than that way I know what to do and what mistakes not to do next time. (ID #2324)

Yet for others, feedback serves to highlight a student's deficits and cause discomfort.

> I got tired of so much feedback. (ID #2403)
> Not really because I wouldn't like people to know what I'm writing. (ID #2301)

Still, for some students it is the absence of feedback, not the presence of it, which tells them that they are doing a good job.

> I chose three because yes I would like to receive feedback but if I don't I think I'm doing fine. (ID #2321)

Item	PEG+Teacher					GoogleDocs				
	SA	A	N	D	SD	SA	A	N	D	SD
12. The Feedback I received helped me improve my writing.	27	31	4	2	0	26	42	4	0	1
13. I received the right amount of feedback.	24	27	12	1	0	23	36	11	2	1
14. The feedback I received made sense to me.	23	29	7	4	0	25	39	8	1	0
15. I wish I had more opportunities to receive feedback.	14	15	16	14	4	17	19	20	11	6
16. I received feedback about a variety of writing skills.	15	32	9	8	0	14	27	20	9	3
17. Receiving feedback on my essay score helped me improve my writing.	33	25	8	4	2	34	27	7	3	2
18. I received feedback quickly.	30	20	12	2	0	12	33	17	10	0

Table 5: Frequencies by Condition of Student Responses to the Posttest Survey Items Regarding Feedback

3.3 Posttest Analyses of Writing Quality

A series of one-way ANOVAs examined the effects of feedback condition on the PEG Overall Score and PEG trait scores. The null hypothesis of equal means was retained in all cases. However, the one-way ANOVA comparing groups on the "Conventions" trait approached statistical significance, showing a small effect size favoring the PEGWriting group: $F(1, 138) = 3.33, p = .07, D = .31$. There was also a small effect size favoring the PEGWriting condition on the Sentence Structure trait: $D = .18$. The one-way ANOVA of Teacher Grades was not statistically significant, but a small effect size favored the PEGWriting group: $D = .19$.

Writing Skills	GoogleDocs	PEG+Writing
Capitalization	✓	
Grammar	✓	
Idea Development & Elaboration		✓
Organization		✓
Punctuation	✓	
Spelling	✓	
Word Choice		✓

Figure 2. Writing Skill Feedback by Condition

3.4 Teacher Survey Data

Results of surveys administered to teachers at the conclusion of the study indicated that teachers varied their feedback across conditions. Teachers were asked to rank the following skills in order of the frequency with which they were commented on in students' writing: spelling, punctuation, capitalization, organization, idea development and elaboration, and word choice. For the GoogleDocs condition, teachers agreed that they most frequently provided feedback on low-level writing skills, such as spelling, punctuation, capitalization, and grammar. For the PEG+Teacher condition, teachers agreed that they most frequently provided feedback on high-level writing skills: idea development and elaboration, organization, and word choice. Indeed, one teacher said she did not need to give any feedback on capitalization or grammar. When asked to decide which of the two systems—PEGWriting or GoogleDocs—enabled them to devote more energy to commenting on content, both teachers selected PEGWriting.

Teachers further agreed that they needed to give less feedback to students who had been using PEGWriting. Consequently, when asked to estimate the amount of time spent providing feedback to students in each condition, teachers agreed that providing feedback in the GoogleDocs condition took twice as long as doing so in the PEG+Teacher condition. For this reason, both teachers agreed that PEGWriting was more efficient for providing feedback than GoogleDocs.

When asked to select which system was easier for teachers and students to use, teachers agreed that GoogleDocs was easier for teachers, but PEGWriting and GoogleDocs were equally easy for students to use. However, both teachers agreed that PEGWriting was more motivating for students and that it promoted greater student independence.

4. Discussion

This study was the first of its kind to compare the effects of a combined automated feedback and teacher feedback condition and a teacher-feedback-only condition (GoogleDocs) on writing motivation and writing quality. Students in the combined feedback condition composed memoirs with the aid of feedback from an AEE system called PEGWriting® and their teacher (provided within the environment of PEGWriting). Students in the teacher-feedback-only condition composed their texts using GoogleDocs which enabled their teacher to edit their text and embed comments.

Based on prior research (Grimes & Warschauer, 2010; Warschauer & Grimes, 2008), we hypothesized that students would report greater writing motivation in the PEG+Teacher feedback condition. However, we were unable to generate an a priori hypothesis regarding the effects of feedback condition on writing quality since prior research has not contrasted feedback conditions in the manner investigated in the current study.

With respect to writing motivation, our hypothesis was partially confirmed. Students in the PEG+Teacher feedback condition reported stronger agreement with Item 10 of the WDS—"I take time to solve problems in my writing"—than did students in the GoogleDocs condition. This self-report data was confirmed with a statistically significant difference, favoring the PEG+Teacher feedback condition, in the number of drafts students completed. However, effects on broader constructs of writing motivation—confidence, persistence, and passion—were not found. This may have been due, in part, to the duration of the study. The study spanned just over three weeks; hence, it is likely that additional exposure and engagement with PEGWriting is needed to register effects on these broader constructs.

Nevertheless, it is encouraging that students reported greater agreement with Item 10. Revision is a challenging and cognitively-demanding task (Flower & Hayes, 1980; Hayes, 2012), requiring students to re-read, evaluate, diagnose, and select the appropriate action to repair the problem. Many struggling writers lack the motivation to engage in this process, and consequently make few revisions to their text (MacArthur, Graham, & Schwartz, 1991; Troia, 2006). Perhaps, the use of an AEE system, such as PEGWriting, provides sufficient motivation for students to persist in the face of the substantial cognitive demands of revision. Future research should explore the use of AEE systems over extended timeframes. It may be possible that these initial gains in persistence are leveraged to increase writing motivation more broadly.

With respect to writing quality, results showed no statistically significant differences between conditions for the PEG Overall Score or PEG trait scores. While on this surface this may appear to indicate that the feedback provided by PEGWriting yielded no value-added over simply receiving teacher feedback in the form of edits and comments via GoogleDocs, we do not believe this to be the case.

First, though AEE systems are designed and marketed as supporting and complementing teacher feedback, previous research has solely examined the use of automated feedback in isolation from teacher feedback. Furthermore, prior studies have typically employed weak control conditions, such as a no-feedback condition (Kellogg et al., 2010) or a spelling-and-text-length condition (Franzke et al., 2005; Wade-Stein & Kintsch, 2004). While these studies provide important initial evidence of the effects of automated feedback and AEE, their design lacks ecological validity as they do not reflect the intended use of such systems. Lack of statistically significant effects on our measures of writing quality may simply be due to the presence of a stronger counterfactual. Thus, the presence of a stronger control condition in our study should not be confused with absence of value-added.

Second, results from the additional posttest survey items administered to students (see Table 5) and from the survey administered to teachers may point to where the value added by AEE. The provision of immediate feedback in the form of essay ratings, error correction, and trait-specific feedback appears to have enabled students to increase their persistence and independence in solving problems in their writing. Consequently, teachers spent half the amount of time providing feedback to students as they did to students in the GoogleDocs condition. Moreover, the use of PEGWriting enabled teachers to devote attention to higher-level skills such as idea development and elaboration, organization, and word choice, while offloading feedback on lower-level skills to the AEE system.

Thus, the value-added of PEGWriting appears to be its ability to promote an equivalent level of writing quality as is achieved using a more time consuming and effortful method of providing feedback (i.e., teacher-feedback-only). In other words, by enabling teachers to be more selective and focused in their comments, PEGWriting saved teachers time and effort without sacrificing the quality of students' writing. Forthcoming analyses will determine whether this hypothesis holds true across other measures of writing quality.

4.1 Limitations and Future Research

Study findings and implications must be interpreted in light of the following limitations. First, though teachers randomly assigned classes to feedback conditions, in absence of a pretest measure of writing ability it is not possible to test whether groups were truly equivalent in terms of prior writing ability. Nevertheless, the pretest measure of writing motivation indicated equivalence across conditions with regards to specific writing dispositions and subscales of confidence, persistence, and passion. It is likely, that if one condition exhibited significantly greater writing achievement this would also have been reflected in the disposition ratings (see Graham et al., 2007).

Second, the study examined the effects of feedback on just a single writing assignment: memoir writing. Furthermore, the prompt allowed for substantial student choice, both in terms of the content of their memoir and the form. Students had the freedom to turn their memoir into a comedy, a drama, a science fiction story, or simply recount the events as they happened. It is unclear whether similar results would have been found had a prompt been assigned that was more restrictive in terms of student choice and that placed greater demands on students in terms of background knowledge. Given the literature on prompt and task effects in writing (Baker, Abedi, Linn, & Niemi, 1995; Chen, Niemi, Wang, Wang, & Mirocha, 2007), it is important that future research attempt to replicate results across different writing tasks.

Finally, the sample was drawn from classes taught by two teachers in a single middle school in a school district in the mid-Atlantic region of the United States. Therefore, it is unclear the degree to which study results reflect generalizable or local trends. Nonetheless, study findings on the utility of AEE are consistent with prior research which has used much larger samples (Warschauer & Grimes, 2008). Further, since the study utilized a novel design—comparing a combined AEE and teacher feedback condition to teacher-feedback-only condition—it is logical to initially test the design using smaller samples. Future research should seek to utilize similar feedback conditions in larger samples.

5. Conclusion

The increasing application of AEE in classroom settings necessitates careful understanding of its effects on students' writing motivation and writing quality. Research should continue to illustrate methods of how AEE can complement, not replace, teacher instruction and teacher feedback. The current study provides initial evidence that when such a combination occurs, teachers save time and effort and they provide greater amounts of feedback relating to students' content and ideas. In addition, students receive feedback more quickly, report increases in their persistence to solve problems in their writing. In sum, AEE may afford the opportunity to shift the balance of energy from teachers to students without sacrificing the final quality of students' writing.

Acknowledgements

This research was supported in part by a Delegated Authority contract from Measurement Incorporated® to University of Delaware (EDUC432914).

References

Baker, E. L., Abedi, J., Linn, R. L., & Niemi, D. (1995). Dimensionality and generalizability of domain independent performance assessments. *Journal of Educational Research, 89*(4), 197-205.

Chen, E., Niemie, D., Wang, J., Wang, H., & Mirocha, J. (2007). *Examining the generalizability of direct writing assessment tasks. CSE Technical Report 718*. Los Angeles, CA: National Center for Research on Evaluation, Standards, and Student Testing (CRESST).

Cutler, L., & Graham, S. (2008). Primary grade writing instruction: A national survey. *Journal of Educational Psychology, 100*, 907-919.

Flower, L. S., & Hayes, J. R. (1980). The dynamics of composing: making plans and juggling constraints. In L.W. Gregg, & E.R. Sternberg (Eds.), *Cognitive processes in writing* (pp. 3- 29). Hillsdale, NJ: Lawrence Erlbaum Associates.

Franzke, M., Kintsch, E., Caccamise, D., Johnson, N., and Dooley, S. (2005). Summary Street®: Computer support for comprehension and writing. *Journal of Educational Computing Research, 33*, 53–80

Graham, S., Berninger, V., & Fan, W. (2007). The structural relationship between writing attitude and writing achievement in first and third grade students. *Contemporary Educational Psychology, 32*(3), 516-536.

Graham, S., McKeown, D., Kiuhara, S., & Harris, K. R. (2012). A meta-analysis of writing instruction for students in the elementary grades. *Journal of Educational Psychology, 104*, 879-896.

Graham, S., & Perin, D. (2007). *Writing next: Effective strategies to improve writing of adolescents in middle and high schools – A report to Carnegie Corporation of New York.* Washington, DC: Alliance for Excellent Education.

Grimes, D. & Warschauer, M. (2010). Utility in a fallible tool: A multi-site case study of automated writing evaluation. *Journal of Technology, Learning, and Assessment, 8*(6), 1-44. Retrieved December 12, 2014 from http://www.jtla.org.

Hayes, J. R. (2006). New directions in writing theory. In C. MacArthur, S. Graham, J. Fitzgerald (Eds.), *Handbook of writing research* (pp. 28-40). New York: Guilford Press.

Hayes, J. R. (2012). Modeling and remodeling writing. *Written Communication, 29*(3), 369-388.

Keith, T. Z. (2003). Validity and automated essay scoring systems. In M. D. Shermis, & J. C. Burstein (Eds.), *Automated essay scoring: A cross-disciplinary perspective* (pp.147-167). Mahwah, NJ: Lawrence Erlbaum Associates, Inc.

Kellogg, R. T., Whiteford, A. P., & Quinlan, T. (2010). Does automated feedback help students learn to write? *Journal of Educational Computing Research, 42*(2), 173-196.

Kiuhara, S. A., Graham, S., & Hawken, L. S. (2009). Teaching writing to high school students: A national survey. *Journal of Educational Psychology, 101*, 136-160.

MacArthur, C. A., Graham, S., & Schwartz, S. (1991). Knowledge of revision and revising behavior among students with learning disabilities. *Learning Disability Quarterly, 14*, 61-73.

McNamara, D.S., Louwerse, M.M., Cai, Z., & Graesser, A. (2013). *Coh-Metrix version 3.0.* Retrieved from http://cohmetrix.com.

National Center for Education Statistics (2012).*The Nation's Report Card: Writing 2011*(NCES 2012–470). Institute of Education Sciences, U.S. Department of Education, Washington, D.C.

National Commission on Writing for America's Families, Schools, and Colleges. (2004). *Writing: A ticket to work...or a ticket out. A survey of business leaders.* Iowa City, IA: The College Board.

National Commission on Writing for America's Families, Schools, and Colleges. (2005). *Writing: A powerful message from state government.* Iowa City, IA: The College Board.

Page, E. B. (1994). Computer grading of student prose, using modern concepts and software. *The Journal of Experimental Education, 62*(2), 127-142.

Page, E. B. (1966). The imminence of grading essays by computer. *Phi Delta Kappan, 48*, 238-243.

Page, E. B. (2003). Project Essay Grade: PEG. In M. D. Shermis, & J. C. Burstein (Eds.), *Automated essay scoring: A cross-disciplinary perspective* (pp.43-54). Mahwah, NJ: Lawrence Erlbaum Associates, Inc.

Piazza, C. L., & Siebert, C. F. (2008). Development and validation of a writing dispositions scale for elementary and middle school students. *The Journal of Educational Research, 101*(5), 275-286.

Salahu-Din, D., Persky, H., and Miller, J. (2008). *The Nation's Report Card: Writing 2007* (NCES 2008–468). National Center for Education Statistics, Institute of Education Sciences, U.S. Department of Education, Washington, D.C.

Shermis, M. D. (2014). State-of-the-art automated essay scoring: Competition, results, and future directions from a United States demonstration. *Assessing Writing, 20*, 53-76.

Shermis, M. D., Koch, C. M., Page, E. B., Keith, T. Z., & Harrington, S. (2002). Trait ratings for automated essay grading. *Educational and Psychological Measurement, 62*, 5-18.

Shermis, M. D., Wilson Garvan, C., & Diao, Y. (2008, March). *The impact of automated essay scoring on writing outcomes.* Paper presented at the annual meeting of the National Council on Measurement in Education, New York, NY.

Troia, G. A. (2006). Writing instruction for students with learning disabilities. In C. A. MacArthur, S. Graham, & J. Fitzgerald (Eds.), Handbook of Writing Research (pp. 324-336. New York, NY: Guilford.

Wade-Stein, D., & Kintsch, E. (2004). Summary Street: Interactive computer support for writing. *Cognition and Instruction, 22*, 333-362.

Warschauer, M., & Grimes, D. (2008). Automated writing assessment in the classroom. *Pedagogies: An International Journal, 3*, 22-36.

Wilson, J., & Andrada, G. N. (in press). Using automated feedback to improve writing quality: Opportunities and challenges. In In Y. Rosen, S. Ferrara, & M. Mosharraf (Eds.), *Handbook of Research on Computational Tools for Real-World Skill Development.* IGI Global.

Wilson, J., Olinghouse N. G., & Andrada, G. N. (2014). Does automated feedback improve writing quality? *Learning Disabilities: A Contemporary Journal, 12*, 93-118.

Towards Creating Pedagogic Views from Encyclopedic Resources

Ditty Mathew, Dhivya Eswaran, Sutanu Chakraborti

Department of Computer Science and Engineering
Indian Institute of Technology Madras
Chennai 600 036, India
{ditty, dhivyae, sutanuc }@cse.iitm.ac.in

Abstract

This paper identifies computational challenges in restructuring encyclopedic resources (like Wikipedia or thesauri) to reorder concepts with the goal of helping learners navigate through a concept network without getting trapped in circular dependencies between concepts. We present approaches that can help content authors identify regions in the concept network, that after editing, would have maximal impact in terms of enhancing the utility of the resource to learners.

1 Introduction

The digital age opens up the possibility of using a mix of online resources for self-study. Not all of these resources have rich pedagogical content, tailored to suit the user's learning goals. Therefore, while greedily looking out for pages of interest, a learner often finds a stop gap solution using a resource like Wikipedia, but may need to put in substantial effort to stitch together a set of content pages to address her learning needs. In this paper, we distinguish between two kinds of resources: encyclopedic and pedagogic. Encyclopedic resources like Wikipedia or thesauri have good reference value and broad coverage, but are not necessarily structured with the goal of assisting learning of concepts. An online textbook, in contrast, is a pedagogic resource in that it has its content organized to realize specific tutoring goals. However, textbooks in their current form have definite limitations. Firstly, the content is often not dynamic, and does not adapt to learner requirements. Second, unlike Wikipedia, textbooks are often not collaboratively authored, some are expensive, and many subjects have no structured learning resources at all. This paper is motivated by the central question - "How can we effectively create a pedagogic view of content from encyclopedic resources?"

At the current state of the art, it would be ambitious to conceive of fully automated solutions to this question. The more pragmatic goal would be to examine the extent to which tools can be devised that can effectively aid humans in (a) constructing such views (b) facilitating the learner in navigating through such views. For the purpose of analysis, we present an abstraction of an encyclopedic resource in the form of a concept network, and show how graph theoretic approaches can be used to restructure such a network with the goal of making it pedagogically useful. While the formal development of this idea is detailed in Section 2, the central idea is as follows. Consider a concept network constructed using Wikipedia articles as concept nodes and hyperlinks as directed edges. Since Wikipedia articles are authored independently, it is not unusual that the author of an article A assumes that a concept B is known when the reader is on the Wikipedia page of A, while the author of concept B assumes exactly the opposite. This results in a circular definition of concepts, thus making the learner flip back and forth between these articles. A pedagogical resource overcomes this bottleneck by ensuring that the corresponding concept network is a directed acyclic graph. A textbook, for example, structures concepts in a way that ensures that no concept is used before being defined (Agrawal et al., 2012) (an exception

Proceedings of the Tenth Workshop on Innovative Use of NLP for Building Educational Applications, 2015, pages 190–195,
Denver, Colorado, June 4, 2015. ©2015 Association for Computational Linguistics

is the set of concepts that the textbook assumes the learner is already familiar with). Thus, a well written textbook, together with a set of such prerequisites, ensures that the concept network is cycle-free. If experts were to analyse Wikipedia content to create pedagogic views on specific subjects, they would benefit from tools that can potentially make best use of their time and effort, by identifying regions in the network that need expert attention.

In the context of this paper, we use a dictionary of words as an example of an encyclopedic resource, where a word is treated as a concept, and an edge exists from a concept to the concept whose definition mentions it. Using a dictionary as opposed to Wikipedia simplifies the discussion and allows us to read into our empirical findings more readily. Though not much is sacrificed in terms of generality, we identify issues in scaling the idea to Wikipedia. We also note that the emphasis of the current paper is largely on the problem of creating views, and not on presenting the views to the end user (learner). Thus we envisage that the current paper is a first in a line of research aimed at creating tools that complement both content creators and learners in creating and using pedagogical resources crafted from diverse starting points.

2 Our Approach

The central assumption in our work is that circular definitions in the concept network are detrimental for learning since the learner is led to flip back and forth between concepts involved in a cycle. The goal is to identify and help content editors eliminate such cycles, so that we can eventually create a pedagogically sound partial order of concepts.

2.1 Mathematical model

We model the concept network as a directed graph $\mathbb{G} = (\mathbb{V}, \mathbb{E})$. The nodes ($\mathbb{V}$) represent concepts, and the edges ($\mathbb{E}$) signify the dependency between these concepts. More specifically, for any two nodes u and v in the graph, a directed edge $u \rightarrow v$ exists if and only if u is useful or necessary in understanding v. So, while modeling a dictionary, the edges are from the words (which we assume to have been sense-disambiguated) in the definition of $v \in \mathbb{V}$ to v.

At each concept node v, we can assume a composition operator Π that composes its in-neighbors by ordering them and augmenting them appropriately with stop words like *the*, *of*, *on*, etc to constructively create a definition for v. The operation Π is assumed to be grounded, in the sense that the terms used for augmentation do not need definitions themselves. We distinguish between two specific compositions, AND and OR. In the former, all in-neighbors of a concept node are needed to understand it, and in the latter any one suffices. Later in this section, we note that in practice, a combination of (soft)AND and (soft)OR accounts for most concept definitions.

In the general case, for a given node v, all its in-neighbors are not required to understand v, as there can be alternate definitions for a word. More precisely, if the two definitions of a word according to the dictionary involve concept sets $\{a_1, a_2, \dots a_n\}$ and $\{b_1, b_2, \dots, b_m\}$, then the user has to know either all a_is or all b_js to understand the word, which shows the presence of AND-OR composition. In practice, the learner does not need to know all a_is as one can guess the word meaning using a_is that are known. Thus by imposing relaxation on AND, we have a soft AND-OR composition in the network.

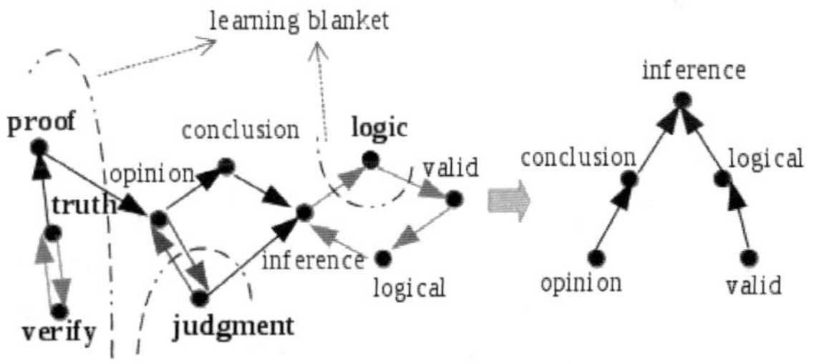

Figure 1: An example of a sub-graph of a concept graph based on a dictionary is shown on the left side and the corresponding reordering of the concepts needed to understand the word *inference* given on the right side.

The left part of Figure 1 depicts an example of a sub-graph of the concept graph constructed using a dictionary. Here, we note that the word *truth* is used in the definition of *verify* and vice versa. There are two other cycles present in this example which result in circular definitions. However, if the learner knows the meaning of *verify*, the circularity involving *truth* and *verify* will not exist any more. We can capture this idea by defining a *learning blanket* for each learner, which encompasses the set of concepts in the concept graph that he/she is familiar with. In Figure 1, all words in bold are assumed to be below the learning blanket with respect to a learner. We observe that the circularities situated below the learning blanket do not challenge the learner. Thus, content editors don't need to spend effort in resolving such cycles. For example, *hat-trick* is defined as *"three goals scored by one player in one game"*. For a learner who knows the meaning of *goal*, and is interested in the definition of *hat-trick*, we do not resolve cycles that involve concepts that are used to define *goal*. So our focus is to find the regions of interest which are situated above the learning blanket and then help experts resolve those circularities.

2.2 Methods to resolve circular dependencies

We identify three methods which can be used by content editors to resolve circular dependencies. The algorithms discussed later on feed into these.

1. Perceptual grounding: Miller et al. (1990) distinguish between constructive and discriminatory definitions. While the former applies to words that can be easily defined using other words, the latter is appropriate for words like *red*, which can be better defined by contrasting against other colors. Attempts to constructively define such words is a common cause of circularities (*red* defined using color, and vice versa). This grounding involves use of images, videos, etc. to avoid such circularities.

2. Collapsing : This method provides single definition simultaneously to a set of concepts. For example, we can define the concepts *polite* and *courteous* using a single definition *showing good manners.*

3. Linguistic grounding : Linguistic grounding involves redefining a concept. For example, in Figure 1 the circular definition of *opinion* can be broken by redefining it as *a personal view* instead of the current definition *a judgment of a person.*

Algorithms to discover concepts to be grounded and concepts to be collapsed are described in Sections 2.3 and 2.4 respectively

2.3 Greedy discovery of concepts for grounding

In order to discover concepts that need expert attention, we present a greedy algorithm that ranks the concepts in the graph based on the extent to which they adversely affect learning by contributing to cycles. We exploit the idea of Relative Coverage proposed by Smyth and McKenna (1999) and PageRank proposed by Page et al. (1998) to score concepts.

Relative coverage is used to order concepts according to their individual contributions for learning. In our context we define the terminologies for finding this measure as follows,

Def 2.1. A concept a helps in understanding another concept b, abbreviated $helpsUnderstand(a, b)$, if and only if a occurs in the definition of b.

Def 2.2. The Coverage Set of a concept a is, $\text{Coverage}(a) = \{b \mid \textit{helpsUnderstand}(a, b)\}$

Def 2.3. The Reachability Set of a concept b is, $\text{Reachability}(b) = \{a \mid \textit{helpsUnderstand}(a, b)\}$

Def 2.4. The Relative Coverage of a concept a is, $\text{RelativeCoverage}(a) = \sum_{b \in \text{Coverage}(a)} \frac{1}{|\text{Reachability}(b)|}$

The intuition behind Def 2.4 is as follows: a concept has high relative coverage if it helps in understanding concepts that cannot be alternatively explained using other concepts.

We make two observations regarding the notion of Relative Coverage. Firstly, it ignores transitive dependencies. Thus, if a concept A helps in understanding B, and B in turns helps in understanding C, the role of A in understanding C is ignored while estimating the Relative Coverage of A. The second observation is that Relative Coverage implicitly assumes an OR composition, or else the presence of a directed edge from a concept A to a concept B would suggest that A is imperative for understanding B, irrespective of all other concepts that help understand B. To overcome the first limitation, we need a recursive formulation, and we use PageRank to this end. On the network of web pages, PageRank estimates the importance of a web page by making a circular hypothesis that a page is important if it is pointed to by several important pages. We can extend the PageRank algorithm to recursively estimate importance of concepts in the concept network. However, one observation is that the score of a concept increases (decreases) with increase (decrease) in the score of any of its in-neighbors. While this monotonicity is desirable, it ignores the fact that a learner unfamiliar with a concept needed to understand the target concept T can often make up for the lapse if he knows other in-neighbors of T. We noted

Algorithm 1: Discover concepts for grounding

Input: Graph $\mathbb{G} = (\mathbb{V}, \mathbb{E})$, **Output**: GroundConcepts
Initialize $\mathbb{C} \leftarrow$ Set of cycles in $\mathbb{G}$
ConceptsToGround = ϕ
while $\mathbb{C} \neq \phi$ **do**
    $\mathbb{N} \leftarrow \{n \mid n \in c,\ c \in \mathbb{C}\}$ # nodes involved in cycles
    Compute Importance(n), $\forall\, n \in \mathbb{N}$
    $v \leftarrow \text{argmax}_{n \in \mathbb{N}}$ Importance(n)
    $\mathbb{C} \leftarrow \mathbb{C} - \{c \in \mathbb{C} | v \in c\}$
    $\mathbb{V} \leftarrow \mathbb{V} - \{v\}$
    $\mathbb{E} \leftarrow \mathbb{E} - \{(n_1, n_2) \in \mathbb{E} | n_1 = v \text{ or } n_2 = v\}$
    ConceptsToGround $\leftarrow$ ConceptsToGround $\cup\ v$
end

that Relative Coverage captures this aspect, except that it does not support recursion in its definition. This leads us to conceptualize a weighted version of the PageRank that exploits the Relative Coverage of the concept nodes.

The importance scores can be used to identify concepts that do not take part in any cycle, and rank the remaining concepts in a partial order that they need to be presented to the content editor. Algorithm 1 greedily identifies and ranks concepts till there are no more cycles in the graph.

2.4 Identifying regions for collapsing

We use the term collapsing to refer to the process of simultaneously defining multiple concepts. This method is inspired by the way in which a dictionary groups together different forms of a word (such as noun, verb, etc). For example, words like *humility, humble* can be grouped together. This idea can be extended to words which do not share a root as well.

In order to perform collapsing, we first identify the strongly connected components (SCCs) of the graph. Only the nodes which are present inside the same SCC are related well enough to be defined simultaneously. Also, the lesser the number of nodes in an SCC, the stronger the dependency between its nodes. So, we propose that all the SCCs whose number of nodes is less than some threshold ϵ can be collapsed, where ϵ is very small (We set it to 5). However, this may be infeasible if the content in the resource under consideration is too large. In such cases, we may need to rank these SCCs based on the effect in which their collapsing has on the entire learning graph. We do this by topologically sorting these SCCs (Haeupler et al., 2012). This process is

Algorithm 2: Identify the regions for collapsing

Input: Graph $\mathbb{G}$, **Output**: CollapsedSet
CollapsedSet $\leftarrow\ \phi$
SCC $\leftarrow$ StronglyConnectedComponents(G)
SortedSCC $\leftarrow$ TopologicalOrder(SCC)
for *each component c in SortedSCC* **do**
    if *No of nodes in c* $< \epsilon$ **then**
        CollapsedSet $\leftarrow$ CollapsedSet $\cup$ c
    end
end

depicted in Algorithm 2. It may be noted that the constraint that nodes belong to a small SCC is generally a weak compared to the one that requires them to participate in a cycle.

3 Experiments

In our experiments, we have used standard corpora Brown and Gutenberg as learning resources and Wordnet (Miller et al., 1990) to obtain the definition of words. The words present in Indian English textbooks published by NCERT[1] are used to come up with an approximation to the set of words an average user is expected to know (acts as the average learning blanket). We tested our experiment across the different levels of average learning blanket. First level includes all the words present in English textbooks upto first grade and likewise for higher levels.

We lemmatized the words in the corpus and then removed the stop words from the standard list in the Python NLTK package. The remaining words constitute the nodes in our concept graph $\mathbb{G}$. In the next step, we obtain the dependencies that exist amongst this set of words by using the definition of the first sense of these words from WordNet. At the end of this step, we have the complete concept graph $\mathbb{G}$.

The concept graph contains 18,361 nodes for Gutenberg corpus and 23,238 nodes for Brown corpus. Then, we labeled each node as blanket or non-blanket nodes using the data obtained for the average learning blanket. Then, we implemented Algorithms 1 and 2 after removing blanket nodes from the concept graph. As a crude baseline, we picked concepts randomly until there are no more cycles in the graph. This baseline method was then compared against Algorithm 1 using different estimates for concept

[1] http://www.ncert.nic.in/ncerts/textbook/textbook.htm

Avg. level of learning blanket	Relative Coverage		Pagerank		Pagerank (Rel. Cov.)		Random	
	Brown	Gut.	Brown	Gut.	Brown	Gut.	Brown	Gut.
1	13.9	14.7	14.7	14.8	**13.6**	**13.9**	28.5	29.5
2	13.0	12.9	12.7	12.5	**11.4**	**11.3**	24.1	25.9
3	12.5	12.3	12.5	10.9	**10.6**	**10.7**	25.7	23.8
4	11.2	9.9	10.4	9.2	**9.0**	**8.8**	19.3	20.3
5	13.4	**10.8**	9.3	12.2	**8.5**	12.9	18.1	20.2

Table 1: Comparison of methods in terms of percentage of concepts flagged to experts (%)

sleeve armhole	enfold enclose	pasture herbage
displeasure displease	magnificent grandeur	tumult commotion
deceit, deceive defraud dishonest	stubborn obstinate tenaciously	existence extant exist

Table 2: Sample sets of concepts suggested for collapsing

scoring, such as Relative Coverage, PageRank and weighted PageRank with Relative Coverage. Table 1 shows the comparison of percentage of discovered concepts for grounding across various levels of average learning blanket, in Brown and Gutenberg corpora. It is desirable that only a small fraction of the total concepts are flagged to experts for editing. The figures in bold correspond to the best reductions. Table 1 shows that PageRank with Relative Coverage outperforms other approaches in most settings, and all the three scoring methods presented in this paper beat the baseline approach comprehensively.

The experiment for finding regions for collapsing is conducted with ϵ=5. A few sets of concepts identified for collapsing are shown in Table 2. Each set looks meaningful as it has closely related words.

4 Discussion and Related Work

This paper is concerned with automating the discovery of concepts that need expert attention. This helps humans invest their creative resources in the right direction. Bottom up knowledge of how the concepts are actually used and accessed by learners, and closing the loop by receiving learner feedback are also useful components in the big picture, that are not addressed in the current work. While we have demonstrated the effectiveness of computational approaches in creating pedagogic views, there are specific issues that we have not adequately addressed. It is not unusual that an attempt to eliminate one cycle by redefining a concept can lead to creation of fresh cycles. Thus, the user interface used by content editors should not only flag concepts (or cycles) identified by the approaches we presented in this paper, but also advise them on choosing a grounding strategy that minimizes side effects. We also have to account for a situation where multiple content authors simultaneously edit the concept network.

It would be interesting to extend this work to propose approaches that help the learner explore the pedagogic space of concepts effectively. As observed earlier, each learner has a different learning blanket, and we need to devise interfaces that establish conversation with the learner to discover her learning blanket in order to specifically address her learning needs. In the context of Wikipedia, we can treat each article name as a concept, which also defines a learning goal. After progressively working backwards from this goal through the concept network, we generate sub-goals eventually hitting the learning blanket. We can also aggregate information from trails followed by learners and such usage patterns can guide content editing by revealing regions where most learners face difficulties.

While the problem of restructuring the concept graph to eliminate circularities in concept definitions is novel, the following papers are related in parts. In (Agrawal et al., 2013), the goals and underlying hypotheses are substantially different, but the authors formulate a reader model as a random walk over a concept graph. Levary et al. (2012) analyse loops and self-reference in dictionaries, though not from a pedagogic standpoint. Roy (2005) shows the connections between language and perceptual grounding in infant vocabulary acquisition.

5 Conclusion

The paper presented approaches to help experts construct pedagogical views from encyclopedic resources. The work is based on the assumption that circularities in concept definitions are an impediment to learning. Empirical studies are promising in that the algorithms proposed significantly reduce the number of concepts that need to be examined by content editors.

References

David Levary, Jean-Pierre Eckmann, Elisha Moses and Tsvi Tlusty. 2012. *Loops and Self-Reference in the Construction of Dictionaries* Physical Review X 2, 031018

Barry Smyth and Elizabeth McKenna. 1999. *Footprint-Based Retrieval* Proceedings of the Third International Conference on Case-Based Reasoning and Development, Pages 343 - 357

Deb Roy. 2005. *Grounding words in perception and action: computational insights* Trends in Cognitive Sciences, Vol.9 No.8, Pages 389 - 396

Rakesh Agrawal, Sunandan Chakraborty, Sreenivas Gollapudi, Anitha Kannan, Krishnaram Kenthapadi. 2012. *Quality of textbooks: an empirical study* ACM Symposium on Computing for Development (ACM DEV), ACM.

Larry Page, Sergey Brin, R. Motwani, T. Winograd . 2012. *The PageRank Citation Ranking: Bringing Order to the Web* In Stanford InfoLab.

Rakesh Agrawal, Sreenivas Gollapudi, Anitha Kannan, Krishnaram Kenthapadi. 2013. *Studying from Electronic Textbooks* 22nd ACM International Conference on Information and Knowledge Management, CIKM'13, Pages 1715 - 1720

George A. Miller, Richard Beckwith, Christiane Fellbaum, Derek Gross, and Katherine Miller. 1990. *Introduction to WordNet: An On-line Lexical Database* International Journal of Lexicography, Vol.3 No.4, Pages 235 - 244.

Taher H. Haveliwala. 2002. *Topic-sensitive PageRank* Proceedings of the 11th international conference on World Wide Web, Pages 517 - 526.

Bernhard Haeupler, Telikepalli Kavitha, Rogers Mathew, Siddhartha Sen, and Robert E Tarjan. 2012. *Incremental Cycle Detection, Topological Ordering, and Strong Component Maintenance* ACM Trans. Algorithms, Vol.8 No.1, Article 3.

Judging the Quality of Automatically Generated Gap-fill Question using Active Learning

Nobal B. Niraula and Vasile Rus
Department of Computer Science and Institute for Intelligent Systems
The University of Memphis
Memphis, TN, 38152, USA
{nbnraula,vrus}@memphis.edu

Abstract

In this paper, we propose to use active learning for training classifiers to judge the quality of gap-fill questions. Gap-fill questions are widely used for assessments in education contexts because they can be graded automatically while offering reliable assessment of learners' knowledge level if appropriately calibrated. Active learning is a machine learning framework which is typically used when unlabeled data is abundant but manual annotation is slow and expensive. This is the case in many Natural Language Processing tasks, including automated question generation, which is our focus. A key task in automated question generation is judging the quality of the generated questions. Classifiers can be built to address this task which typically are trained on human labeled data. Our evaluation results suggest that the use of active learning leads to accurate classifiers for judging the quality of gap-fill questions while keeping the annotation costs in check. We are not aware of any previous effort that uses active learning for question evaluation.

1 Introduction

Recent explosion of massive open online courses (MOOCs) such as Coursera[1] and Udacity[2] and the success of Intelligent Tutoring Systems (ITSs), e.g. AutoTutor (Graesser et al., 2004) and DeepTutor (Rus et al., 2013), at inducing learning gains comparable to human tutors indicate great opportunities for online education platforms. These systems typically deliver knowledge to learners via video streaming or direct interaction with the system, e.g. dialogue based interaction. If adaptive to individual learners, such online platforms for learning must assess learners' knowledge before, during, and after students' interaction with the platform. For instance, in order to identify knowledge deficits before and/or after a session a pre- and/or post-test can be used. The knowledge deficits discovered based on the pre-test can guide the online platform to select appropriate instructional tasks for the learner. Furthermore, the pre- and post-test can be used to measure the learning gains with the online platform, e.g. by subtractic the pre-test score from the post-test score. The bottom line is that assessment is critical for adaptive instruction. Various kinds of questions are used to assess students' knowledge levels varying from True/False questions to multiple choice questions to open answer questions.

Indeed, a main challenge in online learning platforms such as MOOCs and ITSs is test construction (assessment question generation). Automated test construction is a demanding task requiring significant resources. Any level of automation in question generation would therefore be very useful for this expensive and time-consuming process. In fact, it has been proven that computer-assisted test construction can dramatically reduce costs associated with test construction activities (Pollock et al., 2000). Besides test construction, automatic question generation are very useful in several other applications such as reading comprehension (Eason et al., 2012), vocabulary assessment (Brown et

[1]http://www.coursera.org
[2]http://www.udacity.com

Proceedings of the Tenth Workshop on Innovative Use of NLP for Building Educational Applications, 2015, pages 196–206,
Denver, Colorado, June 4, 2015.

al., 2005), and academic writing(Liu et al., 2012). Consequently, particular attention has been paid by Natural Language Processing (NLP) and educational researchers to automatically generating several types of questions. Some examples include *multiple choice questions* (Mitkov et al., 2006; Niraula et al., 2014), *gap-fill* questions (Becker et al., 2012) and *free-response* questions (Mazidi and Nielsen, 2014a; Heilman and Smith, 2009). The more general problem of question generation has been systematically addressed via shared tasks (Rus et al., 2010).

Mitkov et al. (2006) reported that automatic question construction followed by manual correction is more time-efficient than manual construction of the questions alone. Automated method for judging the question quality would therefore make the question generation process much more efficient. To this end, we present in this paper an efficient method to rank *gap-fill* questions, a key step in generating the questions. We formulate the problem next.

1.1 Gap-fill Question Generation

Gap-fill questions are *fill-in-the-blank* questions consisting of a sentence/paragraph with one or more gaps (blanks). A typical gap-fill question is presented below:

Newton's _____ law is relevant after the mover doubles his force as we just established that there is a non-zero net force acting on the desk then.

The gap-fill question presented above has a word missing (i.e. a gap). A gap-fill question can have one more than one gaps too. Students (test takers) are supposed to predict the missing word(s) in their answer(s). Gap-fill questions can be of two types: with alternative options (*key and distractors*) and without choices. The former are called *cloze* questions and the latter are called *open-cloze* questions. In this paper, we use the term gap-fill question as an alternative to open-cloze question.

The attractiveness of gap-fill questions is that they are well-suited for automatic grading because the correct answer is simply the original word/phrase corresponding to the gap in the original sentence. As a result they are frequently used in educational contexts such as ITSs and MOOCs.

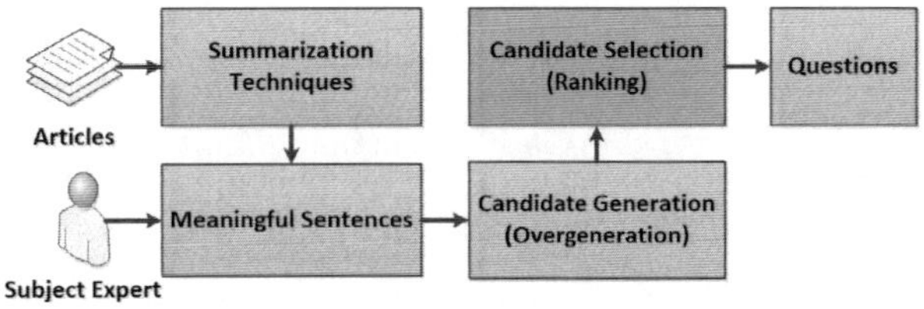

Figure 1: A pipeline for gap-fill question generation

A typical pipeline to automatically generate gap-fill questions is shown in Figure 1. It follows the three steps paradigm for question generation (Rus and Graesser, 2009) : *Sentence Selection*, *Candidate Generation* (overgeneration) and *Candidate Selection* (ranking).

Step 1 - Sentence Selection: To generate gap-fill questions, a set of meaningful sentences are needed first. The sentences can be selected from a larger source, e.g. a chapter in a textbook, using particular instructional criteria such as being difficult to comprehend or more general informationl criteria such as being a good summary of the source (Mihalcea, 2004) or directly from subject matter experts.

Step 2 - Candidate Generation: This step generates a list of candidate questions (*overgeneration*) from the target sentences selected in Step 1. The simplest method might be a brute force approach which generates candidate questions by considering each word (or a phrase) as a gap. A more advanced technique may target the content words as gaps or exploit the arguments of semantic roles for the gaps (Becker et al., 2012). An example of overgeneration of questions is shown in Table 1.

Step 3 - Candidate selection: Not all of the questions generated in the candidate generation step are of the same quality. The classes can be *Good*, *Okay* and *Bad* as in Becker *et al.* (2012) or simply the binary classes *Good* and *Bad*. *Good* questions are the questions that ask about key concepts from the sentence and are reasonable to answer, *Okay* questions are questions that target the key concepts but are difficult to answer (e.g. too long, ambiguous), and *Bad* questions are questions which ask about unimportant aspect of the sentence or their answers are easy to guess from the context. The candidate selection step is about rating the question candidates. Supervised machine learning models are typically em-

Bad	.... net force is equal to the mass times its acceleration.
Good	The .... force is equal to the mass times its acceleration.
Good	The net .... is equal to the mass times its acceleration.
Good	.... is equal to the mass times its acceleration.
Bad	The net force .... equal to the mass times its acceleration.
Okay	The net force is .... to the mass times its acceleration.
Bad	The net force is equal .... the mass times its acceleration.
Good	The net force is equal to the .... times its acceleration.
Okay	The net force is equal to the mass .... its acceleration.
Bad	The net force is equal to the mass times .... acceleration.

Table 1: *Typical overgenerated questions from a sentence with their ratings* ***Good, Okay*** *and* ***Bad.***

ployed in the form of classifiers to label the candidate questions as Good, Okay, or Bad.

1.2 Question Quality

Question quality can be judged linguistically or pedagogically. In linguistic evaluation, questions are evaluated with respect to whether they are grammatically and semantically correct. In pedagogical evaluation, questions are evaluated to see whether they are helpful for understanding and learning the target concepts. Our focus here is on the pedagogical evaluation of automatically generated gap-fill questions since they are always linguistically correct.

The third step i.e. candidate selection is expensive when supervised approaches are used because model building in supervised learning requires large amount of human annotated examples. The advantage of supervised methods, however, is that their performances are in general better than, for instance, that of unsupervised methods. As such, ideally, we would like to keep the advantages of supervised methods while reducing the costs of annotating data. Such a method that offers a good compromise between annotation costs and performance is *active learning*, which we adopt in this work. Such models are always attractive choices especially when there is a limited budget e.g. fixed annotation time / cost, a highly probable case.

Active learning and *interactive learning* are two well-known approaches that maximize performance of machine learning methods for a given budget. They are successfully applied for rapidly scaling dialog systems (Williams et al., 2015), parts-of-speech tagging (Ringger et al., 2007), sequence labeling (Settles and Craven, 2008), word sense disambiguation (Chen et al., 2006), named entity tagging (Shen et al., 2004), etc. Instead of selecting and presenting to an annotator a random sample of unlabeled instances to annotate, these approaches intelligently rank the set of unlabeled instances using certain criteria (see Section 3) and present to the annotator the best candidate(s). This characteristic of active learning and interactive labeling hopefully demands fewer instances than random sampling to obtain the same level of performance.

In this paper, we propose an active learning based approach to judge the quality of gap-fill questions with the goal of reducing the annotation costs. We are not aware of any previous effort that uses active learning for question generation. We chose active learning particularly because it is well-suited when unlabeled data is abundant but manual annotation is tedious and expensive. As mentioned, this is the case in gap-fill question question generation in overgeneration approaches when plenty of questions are available but their quality needs to be specified. The remaining challenge is to judge the quality of these questions. Our plan is to build a probabilistic classifier at reduced costs that would automatically label each candidate questions as *good* or *bad* using an active learnign approach.

The rest of the paper is organized as follows. In Section 2, we present the relevant works. In Section 3, we present the active learning techniques that we are going to employ. In Section 4 and Section 5, we describe our experiments and results respectively. We present the conclusions in Section 6.

2 Related Works

Currently, statistical and machine learning based approaches are the most popular approaches that are used to rank the automatically generated questions of various kinds e.g. free-response (e.g. What, When etc.) and gap-fill questions. For example, Heilman et al. (2010) used logistic regression, a supervised method, to predict the acceptability of each free-response question candidate. The candidate questions were automatically generated by using a set of rules. They used fifteen native English-speaking university students for the construction of training examples required for building the logistic regression model.

Hoshino and Nakagawa (2005) proposed a machine learning approach to generate multiple-choice questions for language testing. They formed a question sentence by deciding the position of the gap i.e. missing word(s). To decide whether a given word can be left blank (i.e. serve as a gap) in the declarative stem, they trained classifiers using the training instances which were generated by collecting fill-in-the-blank questions from a TOEIC preparation book. The positive examples were the exact blank positions in the question from the book whereas the negative examples were generated by shifting the blank position.

Similarly, Becker *et al.* (2012) proposed *Mind the Gap* system that applied logistic regression to rank automatically generated gap-fill questions. They used text summarization technique to select useful sentences from text articles for which gap-fill questions are to be generated. From each of the selected sentence, it generated potential gap-fill candidates using semantic constraints. Each candidate question was then labeled by four Amazon's Mechanical Turkers to one of *Good*, *Bad* and *Okay* classes. In total, 85 unique Turkers were involved in the annotation. The data set was used to build a logistic regression classifier and ranked the candidate questions. They reported that the classifier largely agreed with the human judgment on question quality.

In recent works Mazidi and Nielsen (2014a; 2014b) generated free-response questions from sentences by using the patterns which were manually authored by exploiting the semantic role labels. They evaluated the questions linguistically and pedagogically using human annotators and reported that their systems produced higher quality questions than comparable systems. The main limitation of their approaches is that they do not exploit the examples obtained from the annotation process to evaluate unseen (or not yet evaluated) questions. Moreover, their approaches do not provide any ranking for the questions they generated using those patterns.

3 Active Learning for Judging Question Quality

As mentioned before, active learning fits well when abundant data can be available but manual labeling costs are high. As a result, the technique has been applied to many NLP tasks such as text classification, Word Sense Disambiguation, sequence labeling, and parsing. We use active learning for guiding our annotation process for judging the quality of automatically generated gap-fill questions.

3.1 Active Learning Algorithms

An active learning system mainly consists of a classification model and querying algorithm. Typically the classification models are the probabilistic classifiers such as Naïve Bayes and Logistic Regression which provide a class probability distribution for a given instance. Querying algorithms/functions actively choose unlabeled instance samples by exploiting these probabilities.

We follow the standard pool-based active learning algorithm as shown in Algorithm 1. It starts with a set of initially labeled instances (seed examples) and a set of unlabeled instances (U). A new model is built using the labeled examples in L. Next, a batch of instances are extracted from the unlabeled set U using a query function $f(.)$ and then the selected instances are labeled by human judges. The new labeled instances are added to the labeled list L. The process repeats until a stopping criterion is met. The criteria could be the number of examples labeled, expected accuracy of the model, or something else.

3.1.1 Querying Algorithms

Many query functions exist. They differ on how they utilize the class probability distributions. We use two variants of query functions: uncertainty sampling and query by committee sampling.

Input: Labeled instances L, unlabeled instances U, query batch size B, query function $f(.)$;
while *some stopping criterion* **do**
  θ = Train the model using *L*;
  for i = *1 to* B **do**
    $b_i^* = \arg\max_{u \in U} f(u)$;
    $L = L \cup < b_i^*, label(b_i^*) >$;
    $U = U - b_i^*$;
  end
end

Algorithm 1: Pool-based active learning algorithm

A. Query By Uncertainty or Uncertainty Sampling

Uncertainty sampling chooses the samples for which the model's predictions are least certain. These examples reside very near to the decision boundary. We use three functions that predict the samples in the decision boundary.

(a) Least Confidence: This function chooses the sample x that has the highest $f_{LC}(.)$ score and is defined as : $f_{LC}(x) = 1 - P(y^*|x;\theta)$ where y^* is the most likely class predicted by the model (Settles and Craven, 2008).

(b) Minimum Margin: This function chooses the sample x that has the least $f_{MM}(.)$ score and is defined as: $f_{MM}(x) = |P(y_1^*|x;\theta) - P(y_2^*|x;\theta)|$ where y_1^* and y_2^* are the first and the second most likely classes predicted by the model (Chen et al., 2006).

(c) Entropy: This function chooses the sample x that has the highest entropy i.e. $f_{EN}(.)$ score and is defined as: $f_{EN}(x) = -\sum_{c=1}^{C} P(y_c|x;\theta) * \log(P(y_c|x;\theta))$ where C is the total number of classes (Chen et al., 2006).

B. Query By Committee

Our query by committee sampling algorithm consists of a committee of models. These models are trained on the same labeled examples but learn different hypotheses. We compute for a given instance the class distribution mean over all committee members and assume that the mean scores represent the votes received from the committee. Next we apply $f_{LC}(.)$, $f_{MM}(.)$ and $f_{EN}(.)$ over the mean class distribution and view them as selection scores.

4 Experiments

In this section we describe our experiments in detail.

4.1 Data set

Although an active learning system doesn't require all the unannotated instances to be labeled initially, having such an annotated data set is very useful for simulations since it allows us to conduct experiments to inverstigate active learning, in our case, for judging the quality of automatically generated questions. To this end, we used the existing data set called *Mind the Gap data set* which was created and made publicly available by Becker *et al.* (2012) [3]. The data set consists of 2,252 questions generated using sentences extracted from 105 Wikipedia's articles across historical, social, and scientific topics. Each question was rated by four Amazon Mechanical Turkers as *Good*, *Okay*, or *Bad* (see definitions in Section 1.1).

For our experiments, we binarized the questions into *positive* and *negative* examples. We considered a question *positive* when all of its ratings were *Good* or at most one rating was *Okay* or *Bad*. The rest of the questions were considered as *negative* examples. This way we obtained 747 positive and 1,505 were negative examples. The chosen requirement for being a positive example was needed in order to focus on high quality questions.

4.2 Features

In order to build models to judge the quality of questions, we implemented five types of features as in Becker et al. (2012) including *Token Count, Lexical, Syntatic, Semantic* and *Named Entity*. In total we had 174 features which are summarized in Table 2. The numbers inside parentheses are the indices of the features used.

Questions with many gaps (with many missing words) are harder to answer. Similarly, gaps with many overlapped words with the remaining words in the question are not suitable since they can be easily inferred from the context. We used 5 different *Token Count* features to capture such properties. We also used 9 *Lexical* features to capture different

[3] http://research.microsoft.com/s̃umitb/questiongeneration

Type	Features
Token Count - 5	no. of tokens in answer(1) and in sentence(2), % of tokens in answer (3), no.(4) and %(5) of tokens in answer matching with non-answer tokens
Lexical - 9	% of tokens in answer that are capitalized words(6), pronouns(7), stopwords(8), and quantifiers(9), % of capitalized words(10) and pronouns(11) in sentence that are in answer, does sentence start with discourse connectives ?(12), does answer start with quantifier ?(13), does answer end with quantifier ?(14)
Syntatic - 116	is answer before head verb ? (15), depth of answer span in constituent parse tree (16), presence/absence of POS tags right before the answer span(17-54), presence/absence of POS tags right after the answer span(55-92), no. of tokens with each POS tag in answers(93-130)
Semantic - 34	Answer covered by (131-147), answer contains(148-164) the semantic roles: {A0, A1, A2, A3, A4, AM-ADV, AM-CAU, AM-DIR, AM-DIS, AM-LOC, AM-MNR, AM-PNC, AM-REC, AM-TMP, CA0, CA1, Predicate}
Named Entities - 11	does answer contain a LOC(165), PERS(166), and ORG(167) named entities ? does non-answer span contain a LOC(168), PERS(169), and ORG(164) named entities ? no. (170) and % (171) of tokens in answer that are named entities, no. (172) and % (173) of tokens in sentence that are named entities, % of named entities in sentence present in answer (174)

Table 2: List of features used

statistics of pronouns, stop words, quantifiers, capitalized words, and discourse connectives. Similarly, we used 116 *Syntatic* features that include mostly binary features indicating presence/absence of a particular POS tag just before the gap and just after the gap, and number of occurrences of each POS tag inside the gap. Our semantic features includes 34 binary features indicating whether the answer contained a list of semantic roles and whether semantic roles cover the answer. In addition, we used 11 *Named Entities* features to capture presence/absence of LOC, PERS and ORG entities inside the answer and outside the answer. We also computed the entity density i.e. number of named entities present in the answer. We used Senna tool for getting semantic roles (Collobert et al., 2011) and Stanford CoreNLP package (Manning et al., 2014) for getting POS tags and named entities.

5 Results and Discussions

We conducted a number of experiments to see how active learning performs at judging the quality of questions at different settings: type of classifiers (simple and committee), evaluation metrics (accuracy and F-Measure), seed data size, batch size, and sampling algorithms. An experiment consists of a number of runs. In each run, we divided the data set into three folds using stratified sampling. We considered one of the folds as the *test data set* and

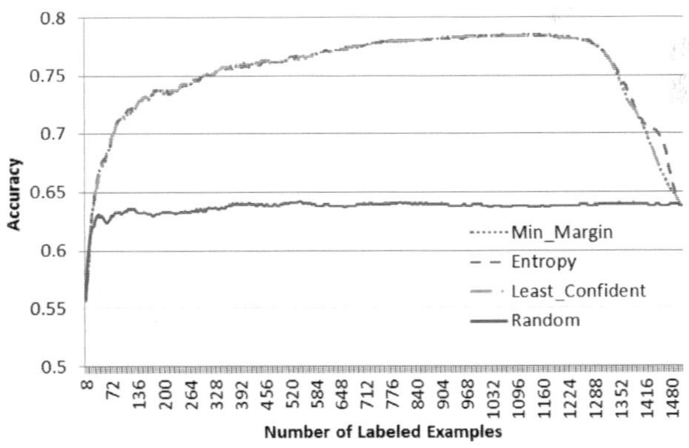

Figure 2: Full Simulation for Naïve Bayes Accuracy

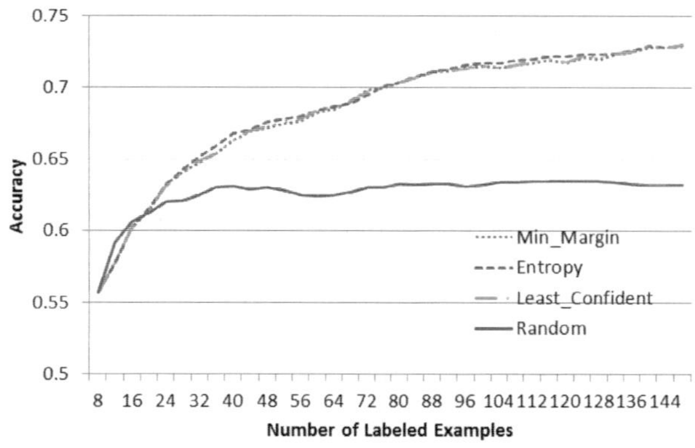

Figure 3: Close-up view of Naïve Bayes Accuracy

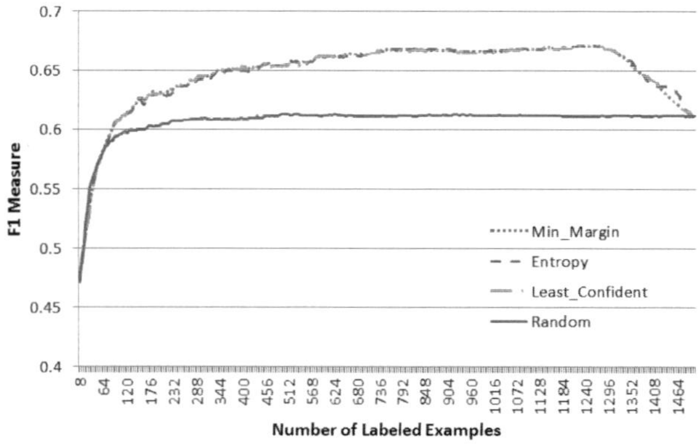

Figure 4: Full Simulation for Naïve Bayes F1

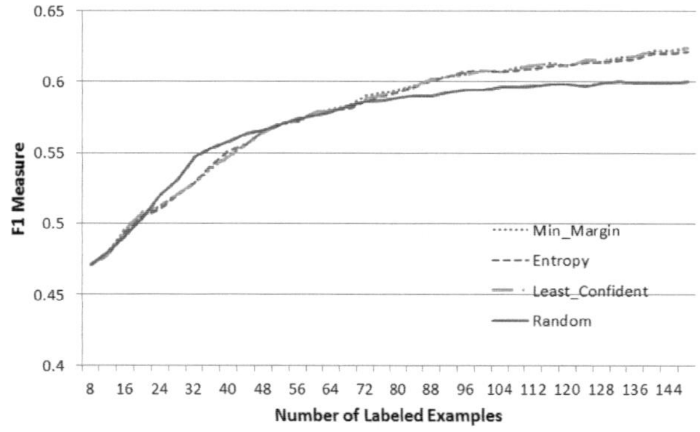

Figure 5: Close-up view of Naïve Bayes F1

merged the other two to construct the *unlabeled data set* (U). Remember that our data set is already labeled but we pretended that it is unlabeled U. Typically, the selected instances from U have to be labeled by a human. Since we already know all the labels in the data set, we mimic the human labeling by simply using the existing labels. This allows us to conduct several experiments very efficiently.

In the first experiment, we compared the various sampling techniques in terms of their impact of the overall performance of question quality classifier. To this end, we randomly selected 8 examples (four positive and 4 negative) from U for the seed data set, removed them from U and put them into the labeled data set (L). We then built a Naïve Bayes model for judging the quality of questions using L. All the machine learning algorithms we used are available in Weka (Hall et al., 2009). Next, we applied a given sampling strategy to select 4 best examples (i.e. a batch of size 4) to be labeled. These new labeled examples were added to L and the question quality classifier was retrained with this extended data set. We used the test data subset to evaluate the question quality classifier at each iteration and report accuracy and F-measure. The process was iterated until the unlabeled data set U was empty.

We used the four sampling algorithms (i.e. least confidence, minimum margin, entropy and random) and report results in terms of average across 100 different runs; in each such run we ran the active learning approach entirely on all the data we had available. Figure 2 and Figure 4 present the accuracy and F1 scores of Naïve Bayes for each of the sampling algorithms with respect to the number of labeled instances used. Figure 3 and Figure 5 are close-ups of leftmost part of the curves in Figure 2 and Figure 4, respectively. As we can see, all uncertainty sampling methods (Min-margin, Entropy and Least confident) outperformed random sampling for both accuracy and F1 measures after few annotations were made. For instance, with 200 examples selected by active learning, the model provided 10% more in accuracy and 4% more in F1 measure compared to the case when the same number of instances were used by sample randomly. It is a promising observation that can save annotation budgets significantly. Moreover, close-up graphs show that all three uncertainty sampling approaches rival each other. Note that all the sampling methods converged (i.e. have same accuracy and F1 measure) at the end of the simulation. It is normal because they would have the same set of labeled instances by then.

In the second experiment, we formed a committee of three probabilistic classifiers provided by Weka:

Naïve Bayes, Logistic Regression, and SMO. These classifiers learnt different hypotheses from the same set of training examples. As discussed in Section 3.1.1, we generated three models from the same labeled set of examples and computed mean probability distributions. For this experiment, we set seed size of 8, batch size of 4, and 100 runs as in experiment 1 and measured the performances of the sampling algorithms. Figure 6 and Figure 8 show the accuracy and F-measure for several sampling strategies as a function of the number of annotated examples. Figure 7 and Figure 9 are the close-up views for Figure 6 and Figure 8 respectively. Again, the uncertainty based sampling algorithms are very competitive to each other and they outperform random sampling significantly in both accuracy and F-measure. This suggests that committee based active learning is also useful for checking question quality.

To get an idea of the level of annotation savings when using active learning, consider we have a budget for annotating about 160 instances. With this budget (in Figure 6), uncertainty sampling algorithms provide 70% accuracy whereas random sampling provides only 65% accuracy. To attain 70% accuracy, random sampling needs at least 360 samples (i.e. 200 examples more) to be labeled. With 360 samples, uncertainty sampling algorithms provide 74% accuracy. Similar observations can be made when focusing on the F-measure. These observations clearly show the effectiveness of using active learning for judging the quality of automatically generated questions.

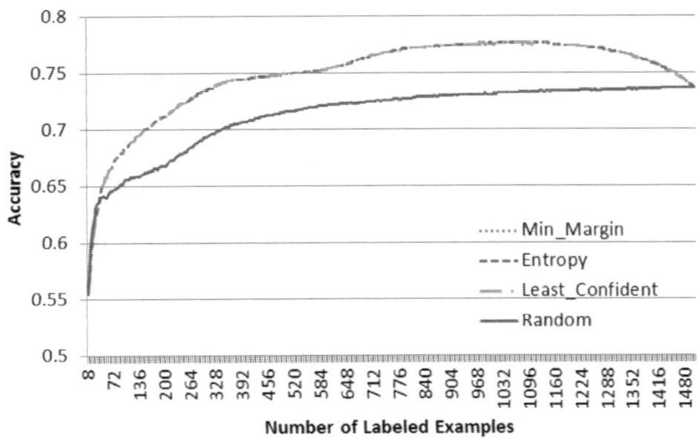

Figure 6: Full Simulation for Committee Accuracy

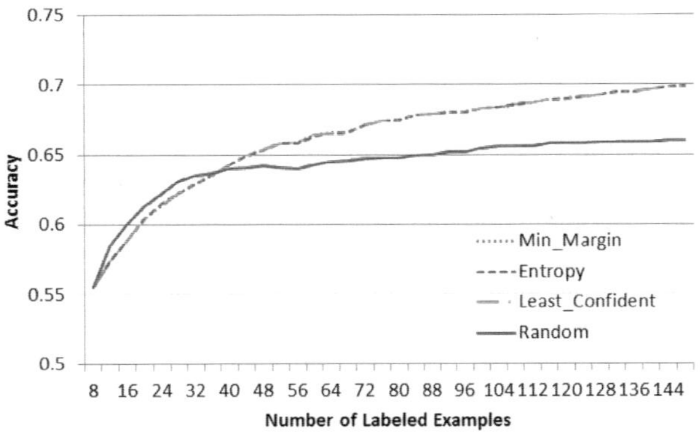

Figure 7: Close-up view of Committee Accuracy

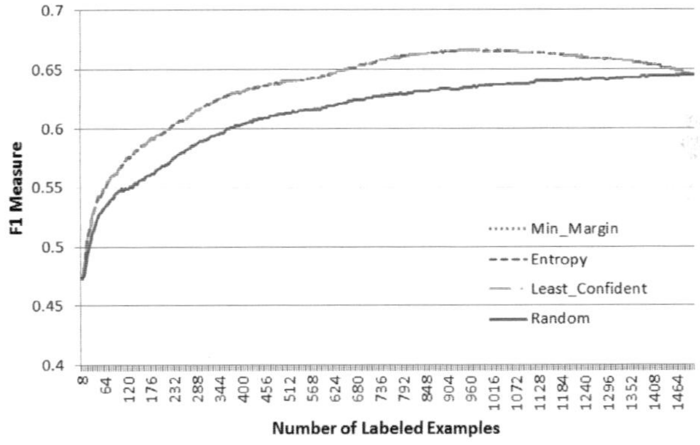

Figure 8: Full Simulation for Committee F1

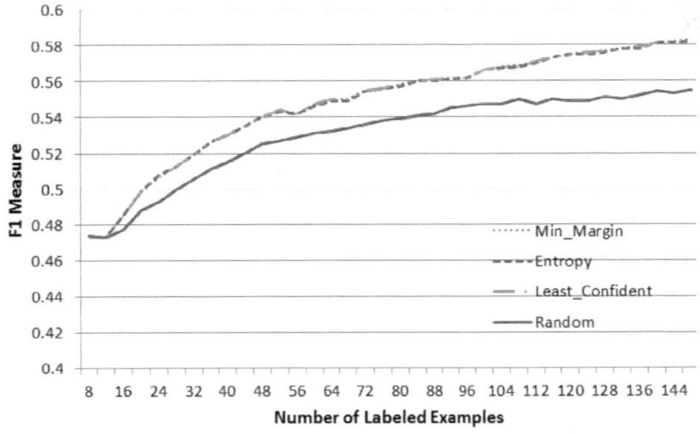

Figure 9: Close-up view of Committee F1

In a third experiment, we focused on the effect of the batch size on the behavior of the active learning approach. Note that we generate a new model as soon as a new batch of labeled instances is ready. For instance, a batch size of 2 means as soon as the annotators provide two annotated instances, we add them to the labeled set and generate a new model from all the available labeled instances. The new model is generally a better one as it is trained on a larger training set than the previous one. However, the smaller the batch size the larger the computational cost because we need to generate a model frequently. So, a balance between the computation cost and the better model should be determined.

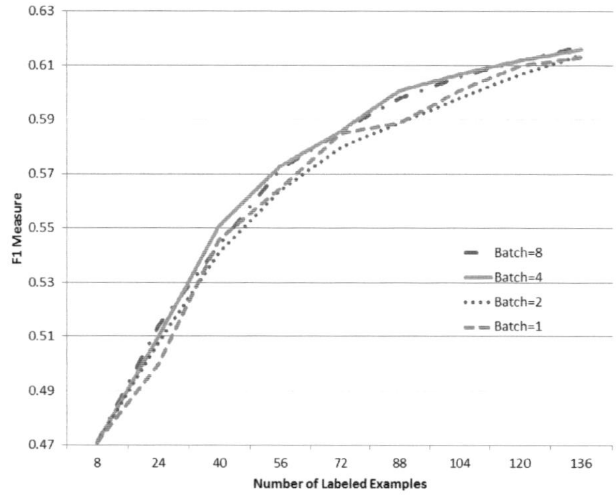

Figure 10: Effect of Batch Size

To this end, we chose Naïve based active learning with entropy based sampling. We varied the batch size from 1, 2, 4 and 8 and ran the experiment for 50 runs. The plot can be seen in Figure 10. As the plot suggests, the performances are less sensitive to batch sizes. A reasonable choice could be a batch size of 4. But again, it depends on the amount of computation cost available for model construction.

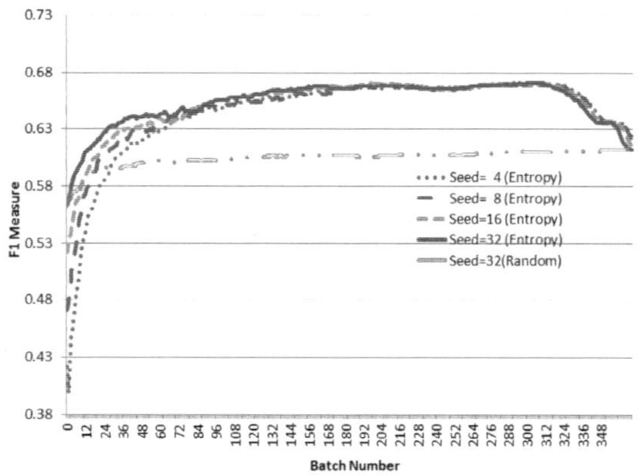

Figure 11: Effect of seed data

In the last experiment, we varied initial seed size to see its effect of the initial seed size on our active learning approach. We experimented with seed sizes of 4, 8, 16 and 32. We applied Naïve based active learning with the batch size of 4 and 100 runs. The plot in Figure 11 shows F1 measures of Entropy based sampling at different seed set sizes. It can be seen that the smaller the seed size, the smaller the F1 score initially. Having a larger seed data initially is beneficial which is obvious because in general the larger the training set the better. We also included a plot of the F1 measure corresponding to random sampling with 32 seeds in Figure 11. It is interesting to note that although random sampling with 32 seeds has larger F1 score initially, it eventually performs poorly when more data is added.

6 Conclusion

In this paper, we proposed to use active learning for training classifiers for judging the quality of automatically generated gap-fill questions, which is the first attempt of its kind to the best of our knowledge. Our experiments showed that active learning is very useful for creating cost-efficient methods for training question quality classifiers. For instance, it is observed that a reasonably good classifier can be built with 300-500 labeled examples using active learning (a potential stopping criteria) that can provide about 5-10% more in accuracy and about 3-5% more in F1-measure than with random sampling. Indeed, the proposed approach can accelerate the question generation process, saving annotation time and budget.

Although the proposed method is investigated in the context of judging the quality of gap-fill questions, the method is general and can be applied to other types of questions e.g., stem generation for multiple choice questions and ranking of free-response questions. We plan implement the remaining steps (i.e. sentence selection and candidate generation) of the question generation pipeline and make it a complete system.

Acknowledgments

This research was partially sponsored by The University of Memphis and the Institute for Education Sciences (IES) under award R305A100875 to Dr. Vasile Rus.

References

Lee Becker, Sumit Basu, and Lucy Vanderwende. 2012. Mind the gap: learning to choose gaps for question generation. In *Proceedings of the 2012 Conference of the North American Chapter of the Association for Computational Linguistics: Human Language Technologies*, pages 742–751. Association for Computational Linguistics.

Jonathan C Brown, Gwen A Frishkoff, and Maxine Eskenazi. 2005. Automatic question generation for vocabulary assessment. In *Proceedings of the conference on Human Language Technology and Empirical Methods in Natural Language Processing*, pages 819–826. Association for Computational Linguistics.

Jinying Chen, Andrew Schein, Lyle Ungar, and Martha Palmer. 2006. An empirical study of the behavior of active learning for word sense disambiguation. In *Proceedings of the main conference on Human Language Technology Conference of the North American Chapter of the Association of Computational Linguistics*, pages 120–127. Association for Computational Linguistics.

Ronan Collobert, Jason Weston, Léon Bottou, Michael Karlen, Koray Kavukcuoglu, and Pavel Kuksa. 2011. Natural language processing (almost) from scratch. *The Journal of Machine Learning Research*, 12:2493–2537.

Sarah H Eason, Lindsay F Goldberg, Katherine M Young, Megan C Geist, and Laurie E Cutting. 2012. Reader–text interactions: How differential text and question types influence cognitive skills needed for reading comprehension. *Journal of educational psychology*, 104(3):515.

Arthur C Graesser, Shulan Lu, George Tanner Jackson, Heather Hite Mitchell, Mathew Ventura, Andrew Olney, and Max M Louwerse. 2004. Autotutor: A tutor with dialogue in natural language. *Behavior Research Methods, Instruments, & Computers*, 36(2):180–192.

Mark Hall, Eibe Frank, Geoffrey Holmes, Bernhard Pfahringer, Peter Reutemann, and Ian H Witten. 2009. The weka data mining software: an update. *ACM SIGKDD explorations newsletter*, 11(1):10–18.

Michael Heilman and Noah A Smith. 2009. Question generation via overgenerating transformations and ranking. Technical report, DTIC Document.

Michael Heilman and Noah A Smith. 2010. Good question! statistical ranking for question generation. In *Human Language Technologies: The 2010 Annual Conference of the North American Chapter of the Association for Computational Linguistics*, pages 609–617. Association for Computational Linguistics.

Ayako Hoshino and Hiroshi Nakagawa. 2005. A real-time multiple-choice question generation for language testing: a preliminary study. In *Proceedings of the second workshop on Building Educational Applications Using NLP*, pages 17–20. Association for Computational Linguistics.

Ming Liu, Rafael A Calvo, and Vasile Rus. 2012. G-asks: An intelligent automatic question generation system for academic writing support. *Dialogue & Discourse*, 3(2):101–124.

Christopher D Manning, Mihai Surdeanu, John Bauer, Jenny Finkel, Steven J Bethard, and David McClosky. 2014. The stanford corenlp natural language processing toolkit. In *Proceedings of 52nd Annual Meeting of the Association for Computational Linguistics: System Demonstrations*, pages 55–60.

Karen Mazidi and Rodney D Nielsen. 2014a. Linguistic considerations in automatic question generation. In *Proceedings of Association for Computational Linguistics*, pages 321–326.

Karen Mazidi and Rodney D Nielsen. 2014b. Pedagogical evaluation of automatically generated questions. In *Intelligent Tutoring Systems*, pages 294–299. Springer.

Rada Mihalcea. 2004. Graph-based ranking algorithms for sentence extraction, applied to text summarization. In *Proceedings of the ACL 2004 on Interactive poster and demonstration sessions*, page 20. Association for Computational Linguistics.

Ruslan Mitkov, Le An Ha, and Nikiforos Karamanis. 2006. A computer-aided environment for generating multiple-choice test items. *Natural Language Engineering*, 12(2):177–194.

Nobal B Niraula, Vasile Rus, Dan Stefanescu, and Arthur C Graesser. 2014. Mining gap-fill questions from tutorial dialogues. pages 265–268.

MJ Pollock, CD Whittington, and GF Doughty. 2000. Evaluating the costs and benefits of changing to caa. In *Proceedings of the 4th CAA Conference*.

Eric Ringger, Peter McClanahan, Robbie Haertel, George Busby, Marc Carmen, James Carroll, Kevin Seppi, and Deryle Lonsdale. 2007. Active learning for part-of-speech tagging: Accelerating corpus annotation. In *Proceedings of the Linguistic Annotation Workshop*, pages 101–108. Association for Computational Linguistics.

Vasile Rus and Arthur C Graesser. 2009. The question generation shared task and evaluation challenge. In *The University of Memphis. National Science Foundation*.

Vasile Rus, Brendan Wyse, Paul Piwek, Mihai Lintean, Svetlana Stoyanchev, and Cristian Moldovan. 2010. The first question generation shared task evaluation challenge. In *Proceedings of the 6th International Natural Language Generation Conference*, pages 251–257. Association for Computational Linguistics.

Vasile Rus, Nobal Niraula, Mihai Lintean, Rajendra Banjade, Dan Stefanescu, and William Baggett. 2013. Recommendations for the generalized intelligent framework for tutoring based on the development of the deeptutor tutoring service. In *AIED 2013 Workshops Proceedings*, volume 7, page 116.

Burr Settles and Mark Craven. 2008. An analysis of active learning strategies for sequence labeling tasks. In *Proceedings of the Conference on Empirical Methods in Natural Language Processing*, pages 1070–1079. Association for Computational Linguistics.

Dan Shen, Jie Zhang, Jian Su, Guodong Zhou, and Chew-Lim Tan. 2004. Multi-criteria-based active learning for named entity recognition. In *Proceedings of the 42nd Annual Meeting on Association for Computational Linguistics*, page 589. Association for Computational Linguistics.

Jason D Williams, Nobal B Niraula, Pradeep Dasigi, Aparna Lakshmiratan, Carlos Garcia Jurado Suarez, Mouni Reddy, and Geoff Zweig. 2015. Rapidly scaling dialog systems with interactive learning.

Generating Reference Texts for Short Answer Scoring Using Graph-based Summarization

Lakshmi Ramachandran[1] and **Peter Foltz**[1,2]
[1]Pearson, [2]University of Colorado
{lakshmi.ramachandran,peter.foltz}@pearson.com

Abstract

Automated scoring of short answers often involves matching a students response against one or more sample reference texts. Each reference text provided contains very specific instances of correct responses and may not cover the variety of possibly correct responses. Finding or hand-creating additional references can be very time consuming and expensive. In order to overcome this problem we propose a technique to generate alternative reference texts by summarizing the content of top-scoring student responses. We use a graph-based cohesion technique that extracts the most representative answers from among the top-scorers. We also use a state-of-the-art extractive summarization tool called MEAD. The extracted set of responses may be used as alternative reference texts to score student responses. We evaluate this approach on short answer data from Semeval 2013's Joint Student Response Analysis task.

1 Introduction

Short answer scoring is a critical task in the field of automated student assessment. Short answers contain brief responses restricted to specific terms or concepts. There is a great demand for new techniques to handle large-scale development of short-answer scoring engines. For example an individual state assessment may involve building scoring algorithms for over two hundred prompts (or questions). The past few years have seen a growth in the amount of research involved in developing better features and scoring models that would help improve short answer scoring (Higgins et al., 2014; Leacock and Chodorow, 2003). The Automated Student Assessment Prize (ASAP-SAS (2012)) competition had a short answer scoring component.

Table 1: Question text, sample reference and some top-scoring answers from a prompt in the ASAP-SAS (2012) competition.

Prompt question: "Explain how pandas in China are similar to koalas in Australia and how they both are different from pythons. Support your response with information from the article."
Sample reference answer: "Specialists are limited geographically to the area of their exclusive food source. Pythons are different in both diet or eating habits and habitat from koalas. Generalists are favored over specialists. Adaptability to change. Koalas and pandas are herbivores and pythons are carnivores."
Some top-scoring student responses: "A panda and a koala are both vegetarians. Pandas eat bamboo, and koalas eat eucalyptus leaves. Pythons are not vegetarians they eat meat, and they kill there pray by strangling them or putting venom into them." "Pandas and koalas are both endangered animals. They can only be found in certain places where their food supply is. They are different from pythons because they move to a new environment and adapt as well. They be at a loss of food and climate change."

Short answer datasets are typically provided with one or more sample human references, which are representative of ideal responses. Student responses that have a high text overlap with these human references are likely to get a higher score than those that have a poor overlap. However often these sample human references are not representative of all possible correct responses. For instance consider the question, sample reference and a set of top-scoring student responses for a prompt from the ASAP-SAS (2012) competition in Table 1. The human reference provided does not encompass all possible alternative ways of expressing the correct response.

A number of approaches have been used to extract regular expressions and score student responses. Pulman and Sukkarieh (2005) use hand-crafted patterns to capture different ways of expressing the correct answer. Bachman et al. (2002) extract tags from a model answer, which are matched with stu-

Proceedings of the Tenth Workshop on Innovative Use of NLP for Building Educational Applications, 2015, pages 207–212,
Denver, Colorado, June 4, 2015.

dent responses to determine their scores. Mitchell et al. (2003) use a mark scheme consisting of a set of acceptable or unacceptable answers. This marking scheme is similar to a sample reference. Each student response is matched with these marking schemes and scored accordingly. The winner of the ASAP competition spent a lot of time and effort hand-coding regular expressions from the human samples provided, in order to obtain better matches between student responses and references (Tandalla, 2012). Although hand-crafting features might seem feasible for a few prompts, it is not an efficient technique when scoring large datasets consisting of thousands of prompts. Hence there is a need to develop automated ways of generating alternate references that are more representative of top-scoring student responses.

We use two summarization techniques to identify alternative references from top-scoring student responses for a prompt. Klebanov et al. (2014) use summarization to generate content importance models from student essays. We propose a graph-based cohesion technique, which uses text structure and semantics to extract representative responses. We also use a state-of-the-art summarization technique called MEAD (Radev et al., 2004), which extracts a summary from a collection of top-scoring responses. The novelty of our work lies in the utilization of summarization to the task of identifying suitable references to improve short-answer scoring.

2 Approach

Top-scoring responses from each prompt or question are summarized to identify alternate reference texts with which student responses could be compared to improve scoring models.

2.1 Graph-based Cohesion Technique

We use an agglomerative clustering technique to group lexico-semantically close responses into clusters or topics. The most representative responses are extracted from each of the clusters to form the set of alternate references. Just as in a cohesion-based method only the most well-connected vertices are taken to form the summary (Barzilay and Elhadad, 1997), likewise in our approach responses with the highest similarities within each cluster are selected as representatives.

Steps involved in generating summaries are:

Generating Word-Order Graphs: Each top-scoring response is first represented as a word-order graph. We use a word-order graph representation because it captures structural information in texts. Graph matching makes use of the ordering of words and context information to help identify lexical changes. According to Makatchev and VanLehn (2007) responses classified by human experts into a particular semantic class may be syntactically different. Thus word-order graphs are useful to identify representatives from a set of responses that are similar in meaning but may be structurally different.

During graph generation, each response is tagged with parts-of-speech (POS) using the Stanford POS tagger (Toutanova et al., 2003). Contiguous subject components such as nouns, prepositions are grouped to form a subject vertex, while contiguous verbs or modals are grouped into a verb vertex and so on for the other POS types. Ordering is maintained with the edges capturing subject—verb, verb—object, subject—adjective or verb—adverb type of information. Graph generation has been explained in detail in Ramachandran and Gehringer (2012).

Calculating Similarity: In this step similarities between all pairs of top-scoring responses are calculated. Similarities between pairs of responses are used to cluster them and then identify representative responses from each cluster. *Similarity* is the average of the best vertex and edge matches.

$$\begin{aligned} \mathit{Similarity}(A,B) = \; & \tfrac{1}{2}\Big(\tfrac{1}{|V_A|+|V_B|}\Big(\sum_{\forall V_A} \operatorname{argmax}_{\forall V_B}\{\mathit{sem}(V_A,V_B)\} \\ & + \sum_{\forall V_B} \operatorname{argmax}_{\forall V_A}\{\mathit{sem}(V_B,V_A)\}\Big) + \\ & \tfrac{1}{|E_A|+|E_B|}\Big(\sum_{\forall E_A} \operatorname{argmax}_{\forall E_B}\{\mathit{sem}_e(E_A,E_B)\} \\ & + \sum_{\forall E_B} \operatorname{argmax}_{\forall E_A}\{\mathit{sem}_e(E_B,E_A)\}\Big)\Big) \end{aligned} \quad (1)$$

In equation 1 V_A and V_B are the vertices and E_A and E_B are the edges of responses A and B respectively. We identify the best semantic match for every vertex or edge in response A with a vertex or edge in response B respectively (and vice-versa). *sem* is identified using WordNet (Fellbaum, 1998).

Clustering Responses: We use an agglomerative clustering technique to group responses into clusters. The clustering algorithm starts with assigning every response in the text to its own cluster. Initially every cluster's similarity is set to 0. A cluster's similarity is the average of the similarity between all pairs of responses it contains.

We rank response pairs based on their similarity (highest to lowest) using merge sort, and assign one response in a pair to the other's cluster provided it satisfies the condition in Equation 2. The condition ensures that a response (S) that is added to a cluster (C) has high similarity, i.e., is close in meaning and context to that cluster's responses (S_C).

$$\left(C.\mathit{clusterSimilarity} - \sum_{\forall S_C \in C} \frac{\mathit{Similarity}(S, S_C)}{|C|} \right) \leq \alpha \quad (2)$$

The choice of cluster to which a response is added depends on the cluster's similarity, i.e., a response is added to the cluster with higher similarity. If both responses (in the pair) have same cluster similarities, then the larger cluster is chosen as the target. If cluster similarity and the number of responses are the same, then the target is selected randomly.

Identifying Representatives: In this step the most representative responses from each cluster are identified. The aim is to identify the smallest set of representatives that *cover* every other response in the cluster. We use a list heuristic to handle this problem (Avis and Imamura, 2007). We order responses in every cluster based on (a) decreasing order of their average similarity values, and (b) decreasing order of the number of responses they are adjacent to.

Our approach ensures that responses with the highest semantic similarity that cover previously uncovered responses are selected. Representatives from all clusters are grouped together to generate the representative responses for a prompt.

2.2 MEAD

We use MEAD as an alternative summarization approach. Radev et al. (2004) proposed the use an automated multi-document summarization technique called MEAD. MEAD was developed at the University of Michigan as a centroid-based summarization approach. MEAD is an extractive summarization approach that relies on three features: position, centroid and the length of sentences to identify the summary. MEAD's classifier computes a score for each sentence in the document using a linear combination of these three features. Sentences are then ranked based on their scores and the top ranking sentences are extracted to generate summaries. The extraction can be restricted to the top N words to generate a summary of specified length.

In our study each document contains a list of top-scoring responses from the dataset, i.e., each top-scoring response would constitute a sentence. For our study we use MEAD[1] to extract summaries of length that match the lengths of the summaries generated by the graph-based cohesion technique.

3 Experiment

3.1 Data

Semeval's Student Response Analysis (SRA) corpus contains short answers from two different sources: Beetle and SciEntsBank (Dzikovska et al., 2013)[2]. Beetle contains responses extracted from transcripts of interactions between students and the Beetle II tutoring system (Dzikovska et al., 2010). The SciEntsBank dataset contains short responses to questions collected by Nielsen et al. (2008).

Beetle contains 47 questions and 4380 student responses, and SciEntsBank contains 135 questions and 5509 student responses (Dzikovska et al., 2013). Each dataset is classified as: (1) 5-way, (2) 3-way and (3) 2-way. The data in the SRA corpus was annotated as follows for the 5-way classification: *correct:* student response that is correct, *partially_correct_incomplete:* response that is correct but does not contain all the information in the reference text, *contradictory:* response that contradicts the reference answer, *irrelevant:* response that is relevant to the domain but does not contain information in the reference, *non_domain:* response is not relevant to the domain. The 3-way classification contains the contradictory, correct and incorrect classes, while the 2-way classification contains correct and incorrect classes.

Dzikovska et al. (2013) provide a summary of the results achieved by teams that participated in this task. Apart from the dataset, the organizing committee also released code for a baseline, which included lexical overlap measures. These measures

[1]We use the code for MEAD (version 3.10) available at `http://www.summarization.com/mead/`.

[2]The data is available at `http://www.cs.york.ac.uk/semeval-2013/task7/index.php?id=data`

Table 2: Comparing performance of system-generated summaries of top-scoring short answers with the performance of sample reference texts provided for the Semeval dataset.

		5-way		3-way		2-way	
Data Type	**System**	**F1-overall**	**Weighted-F1**	**F1-overall**	**Weighted-F1**	**F1-overall**	**Weighted-F1**
Beetle	Baseline features (Dzikovska et al., 2013)	0.424	0.483	0.552	0.578	0.788	
	Graph (~62 words)	0.436	0.533	**0.564**	**0.587**	**0.794**	**0.803**
	MEAD (~63 words)	**0.446**	**0.535**	0.537	0.558	0.744	0.757
SciEntsBank	Baseline features (Dzikovska et al., 2013)	0.375	0.435	0.405	0.523	0.617	
	Graph (~39 words)	0.372	0.458	**0.438**	**0.567**	**0.644**	**0.658**
	MEAD (~40 words)	**0.379**	**0.461**	0.429	0.554	0.631	0.645

Table 3: Comparing f-measures (f) and mean cosines (cos) of every class for features generated by graph and MEAD summaries.

		5-way					3-way			2-way	
Classes	**Feature**	**correct**	**partially _correct _incomplete**	**contra-dictory**	**non _domain**	**irrel-evant**	**correct**	**contra-dictory**	**inco-rrect**	**correct**	**inco-rrect**
					Beetle						
MEAD	f	0.702	**0.443**	**0.416**	**0.667**	0.000	0.687	0.400	0.523	0.679	0.809
Graph	f	**0.736**	0.400	0.404	0.640	0.000	**0.732**	**0.422**	**0.539**	0.747	**0.840**
MEAD	cos	0.690	0.464	**0.438**	0.058	**0.319**	0.690	**0.438**	0.387	0.690	**0.408**
Graph	cos	**0.720**	**0.470**	0.425	**0.065**	0.286	**0.720**	0.425	**0.388**	**0.720**	0.404
					SciEntsBank						
MEAD	f	0.601	**0.332**	0.082	NA	**0.500**	0.563	**0.062**	**0.661**	0.528	0.733
Graph	f	**0.617**	0.302	0.087	NA	0.482	**0.605**	0.059	0.649	**0.548**	**0.741**
MEAD	cos	0.441	0.337	0.337	0.138	0.268	0.441	0.337	0.298	0.441	0.305
Graph	cos	**0.498**	**0.372**	**0.350**	**0.229**	**0.271**	**0.498**	**0.350**	**0.316**	**0.498**	**0.323**

compute the degree of overlap between student responses and sample reference texts and the prompt or question texts. Both human references as well as question texts were provided with the dataset. The lexical overlap measures include: (1) Raw count of the overlaps between student responses and the sample reference and question texts, (2) Cosine similarity between the compared texts, (3) Lesk similarity, which is the sum of square of the length of phrasal overlaps between pairs of texts, normalized by their lengths (Pedersen et al., 2002) and (4) f-measure of the overlaps between the compared texts[3]. These four features are computed for the sample reference text and the question text, resulting in a total of eight features. We compute these eight features for every system and compare their raw and weighted (by their class distributions) f-measure values.

3.2 Results and Discussion

The graph-based cohesion technique produced summaries containing an average of 62 words for Beetle and an average of 39 words for SciEntsBank. Therefore, we chose to extract summaries containing nearly the same number of words using the MEAD summarization tool.

From the results in Table 2[4] we see that, compared to the baseline approach, the summarization approaches are better at scoring short answers. We also tested the use of all top-scoring student responses as alternate references (i.e. with no summarization). These models perform worse than the baseline, producing an average *decrease* in overall f-measure of 14.7% for Beetle and 14.3% for SciEntsBank. This suggests the need for a summarization technique. Our results indicate that the summarizers produce representative sentences that are more useful for scoring than just the sample reference text. MEAD performs better on the 5-way task while the graph-based cohesion approach performs well on 3-way and 2-way classification tasks.

In the case of both the datasets, the performance of the graph-based approach on the "correct" class is higher. We looked at the average cosine similarity for data from each class with their corre-

[3] f-measure is the harmonic mean of the precision and recall of the degree of overlaps between two texts. Precision is computed as the number of overlaps divided by the length of student response, while recall of overlap is computed as the degree of overlap divided by the number of tokens in the human reference text.

[4] We report results only on the unseen answers test set from Semeval because the train and test sets contain data from different prompts for the unseen domains and unseen questions sets. Summaries generated from the top-scoring responses from one set of prompts or questions in the train set may not be relevant to different prompts in the other test sets.

Table 4: Comparing references generated by the summarizers with a sample reference for a prompt from the Beetle dataset.

Sample Reference: "Terminal 1 and the positive terminal are separated by the gap OR Terminal 1 and the positive terminal are not connected. OR Terminal 1 is connected to the negative battery terminal. OR Terminal 1 is not separated from the negative battery terminal. OR Terminal 1 and the positive battery terminal are in different electrical states"	**Graph-based Cohesion:** "The terminal is not connected to the positive battery terminal. OR The terminals are not connected. OR The positive battery terminal and terminal 1 are not connected. OR Because there was not direct connection between the positive terminal and bulb terminal 1. OR Terminal one is connected to the negative terminal and terminal 1 is separated from the positive terminal by a gap. OR The positive battery terminal is separated by a gap from terminal 1."	**MEAD:** "Positive battery terminal is separated by a gap from terminal 1. OR Terminal 1 is not connected to the positive terminal. OR Because there was not direct connection between the positive terminal and bulb terminal 1. OR The terminals are not connected. OR Because they are not connected. OR Terminal 1 is connected to the negative battery terminal. OR The two earnt connected."

sponding reference texts (Table 3). Magnitude of the average cosine between student responses and the reference texts for classes such as non_domain and partially_correct_incomplete in Beetle and for non_domain, partially_correct_incomplete, contradictory and irrelevant in SciEntsBank are higher in case of the graph-based approach than MEAD. As a result, the graph's features tend to classify more data points as correct, leaving fewer data points to be classified into the other classes, thus producing lower f-measures in both datasets.

In the case of 3-way and 2-way classifications, performance on the correct class was higher for the graph-based approach (Table 3). The cosine similarity between the correct data and the summaries from the graph-based approach are higher than the cosines between the correct data and MEAD's summaries. The graph-based approach tends to predict more of the correct data points accurately, resulting in an improvement in the graph-based approach's performance. A similar trend was observed in the case of the 2-way classification.

Sample reference and representatives from the graph-based approach and MEAD for question BULB_C_VOLTAGE_EXPLAIN_WHY1 from Beetle are listed in Table 4. The samples follow the structure X and Y are <relation> OR X <relation> Y. A correct response such as "The terminals are not connected." would get a low match with these samples. Both the graph-based approach and MEAD extract references that may be structurally different but have the same meaning.

The team that performed best on the Semeval competition on both the Beetle and SciEntsBank datasets for the unseen answers task (Heilman and Madnani, 2013), used the baseline features (listed above) as part of their models. CoMeT was another team that performed well on Beetle on the unseen answers dataset (Ott et al., 2013). They did not use the baseline features directly but did use the sample reference text to generate several text overlap measures. Since the best performing models used sample references to generate useful features, the use of representative sentences generated by a summarization approach is likely to help boost the performance of these models. We have not been able to show the improvement to the best models from Semeval since the code for the best models have not been made available. These alternate references also generate improved baselines, thus encouraging teams participating in competitions to produce better models.

4 Conclusion

In this paper we demonstrated that an automated approach to generating alternate references can improve the performance of short answer scoring models. Models would benefit a great deal from the use of alternate references that are likely to cover more types of correct responses than the sample. We evaluated two summarization techniques on two short answer datasets: Beetle and SciEntsBank made available through the Semeval competition on student response analysis. We showed that references generated from the top-scoring responses by the graph-based cohesion approach and by MEAD performed better than the baseline containing the sample reference.

The results indicate that the approach can be successfully applied for improving scoring of short answers responses. These results have direct applications to automated tutoring systems, where students are in a dialogue with a computer-based agent and the system must match the student dialogue against a set of reference responses. In each of these cases, the technique provides a richer set of legal reference texts and it can be easily incorporated as a preprocessing step before comparisons are made to the student responses.

References

ASAP-SAS. 2012. Scoring short answer essays. ASAP short answer scoring competition system description. `http://www.kaggle.com/c/asap-sas/`.

David Avis and Tomokazu Imamura. 2007. A list heuristic for vertex cover. volume 35, pages 201–204. Elsevier.

Lyle F Bachman, Nathan Carr, Greg Kamei, Mikyung Kim, Michael J Pan, Chris Salvador, and Yasuyo Sawaki. 2002. A reliable approach to automatic assessment of short answer free responses. In *Proceedings of the 19th international conference on Computational linguistics-Volume 2*, pages 1–4. Association for Computational Linguistics.

Regina Barzilay and Michael Elhadad. 1997. Using lexical chains for text summarization. In *In Proceedings of the ACL Workshop on Intelligent Scalable Text Summarization*, pages 10–17.

Myroslava O Dzikovska, Johanna D Moore, Natalie Steinhauser, Gwendolyn Campbell, Elaine Farrow, and Charles B Callaway. 2010. Beetle ii: a system for tutoring and computational linguistics experimentation. In *Proceedings of the ACL 2010 System Demonstrations*, pages 13–18. Association for Computational Linguistics.

Myroslava O Dzikovska, Rodney D Nielsen, Chris Brew, Claudia Leacock, Danilo Giampiccolo, Luisa Bentivogli, Peter Clark, Ido Dagan, and Hoa T Dang. 2013. Semeval-2013 task 7: The joint student response analysis and 8th recognizing textual entailment challenge. Technical report, DTIC Document.

Christiane Fellbaum. 1998. Wordnet: An electronic lexical database. *MIT Press*.

Michael Heilman and Nitin Madnani. 2013. ETS: Domain adaptation and stacking for short answer scoring. In *Proceedings of the 2nd joint conference on lexical and computational semantics*, volume 2.

Derrick Higgins, Chris Brew, Michael Heilman, Ramon Ziai, Lei Chen, Aoife Cahill, Michael Flor, Nitin Madnani, Joel Tetreault, Dan Blanchard, Diane Napolitano, Chong Min Lee, and John Blackmore. 2014. Is getting the right answer just about choosing the right words? The role of syntactically-informed features in short answer scoring. *arXiv*.

Beata Beigman Klebanov, Nitin Madnani, Swapna Somasundaran, and Jill Burstein. 2014. Content importance models for scoring writing from sources. In *Proceedings of the 52nd Annual Meeting of the Association for Computational Linguistics (Volume 2: Short Papers)*, pages 247–252. Association for Computational Linguistics.

Claudia Leacock and Martin Chodorow. 2003. C-rater: Automated scoring of short-answer questions. In *Computers and the Humanities*, volume 37, pages 389–405. Springer.

Maxim Makatchev and Kurt VanLehn. 2007. Combining bayesian networks and formal reasoning for semantic classification of student utterances. In *Proceedings of the 2007 Conference on Artificial Intelligence in Education: Building Technology Rich Learning Contexts That Work*, pages 307–314, Amsterdam, The Netherlands.

Tom Mitchell, Nicola Aldridge, and Peter Broomhead. 2003. Computerised marking of short-answer free-text responses. In *Manchester IAEA conference*.

Rodney D Nielsen, Wayne Ward, James H Martin, and Martha Palmer. 2008. Annotating students' understanding of science concepts. In *LREC*.

Niels Ott, Ramon Ziai, Michael Hahn, and Detmar Meurers. 2013. Comet: integrating different levels of linguistic modeling for meaning assessment.

Ted Pedersen, Satanjeev Banerjee, and Siddharth Patwardhan. 2002. Lesk similarity. `http://search.cpan.org/dist/Text-Similarity/lib/Text/Similarity/Overlaps.pm`.

Stephen G Pulman and Jana Z Sukkarieh. 2005. Automatic short answer marking. In *Proceedings of the second workshop on Building Educational Applications Using NLP*, pages 9–16.

Dragomir R Radev, Hongyan Jing, Małgorzata Styś, and Daniel Tam. 2004. Centroid-based summarization of multiple documents. *Information Processing & Management*, 40(6):919–938.

Lakshmi Ramachandran and Edward F. Gehringer. 2012. A word-order based graph representation for relevance identification (poster). *Proceedings of the 21st ACM Conference on Information and Knowledge Management*, pages 2327–2330, October.

Luis Tandalla. 2012. Scoring short answer essays. ASAP short answer scoring competition–Luis Tandalla's approach. `https://kaggle2.blob.core.windows.net/competitions/kaggle/2959/media/TechnicalMethodsPaper.pdf`.

Kristina Toutanova, Dan Klein, Christopher D. Manning, and Yoram Singer. 2003. Feature-rich part-of-speech tagging with a cyclic dependency network. In *In Proceedings of HLT-NAACL*, pages 252–259.

Evaluating the performance of Automated Text Scoring systems

Helen Yannakoudakis
The ALTA Institute
Computer Laboratory
University of Cambridge
helen.yannakoudakis@cl.cam.ac.uk

Ronan Cummins
The ALTA Institute
Computer Laboratory
University of Cambridge
ronan.cummins@cl.cam.ac.uk

Abstract

Various measures have been used to evaluate the effectiveness of automated text scoring (ATS) systems with respect to a human gold standard. However, there is no systematic study comparing the efficacy of these metrics under different experimental conditions. In this paper we first argue that *measures of agreement* are more appropriate than *measures of association* (i.e., correlation) for measuring the effectiveness of ATS systems. We then present a thorough review and analysis of frequently used *measures of agreement*. We outline desirable properties for measuring the effectiveness of an ATS system, and experimentally demonstrate using both synthetic and real ATS data, that some commonly used measures (e.g., Cohen's kappa) lack these properties. Finally, we identify the most appropriate *measures of agreement* and present general recommendations for best evaluation practices.

1 Introduction

Automated assessment of text was introduced in the early 1960s in an attempt to address several issues with manual assessment (e.g., expense, speed, and consistency). Further advantages become more pronounced when it comes to scoring extended texts such as essays, a task prone to an element of subjectivity. Automated systems enable rigid application of scoring criteria, thus reducing the inconsistencies which may arise, in particular, when many human examiners are employed for large-scale assessment.

There is a substantial literature describing and evaluating ATS systems (Page, 1968; Powers et al., 2002; Rudner and Liang, 2002; Burstein et al., 2003; Landauer et al., 2003; Higgins et al., 2004; Attali and Burstein, 2006; Attali et al., 2008; Williamson, 2009; Briscoe et al., 2010; Chen and He, 2013). Such systems are increasingly used but remain controversial. Although a comprehensive comparison of the capabilities of eight existing commercial essay scoring systems (Shermis and Hamner, 2012) across five different performance metrics in the recent ATS competition organised by Kaggle[1] claimed that ATS systems grade similarly to humans, critics (Wang and Brown, 2007; Wang and Brown, 2008; Perelman, 2013) have continued to dispute this.

For the evaluation of ATS systems (Williamson, 2009; Williamson et al., 2012), emphasis has been given to the "agreement" of machine-predicted scores (ordinal grades) with that of a human gold standard; that is, scores assigned by human examiners to the same texts that the machine is evaluated on. Various metrics have been used, the most prominent being Pearson's correlation, percentage of agreement, and variations of Cohen's kappa statistic. Inconsistencies in the reporting of, and misconceptions in the interpretation of, these metrics in published work makes cross-system comparisons on publicly-available datasets more difficult. The lack of careful motivation of any metric fuels opposition to the deployment of ATS. To date, several ATS systems are being used operationally for high-stakes assessment in addition to them being part of self-assessment and self-tutoring sys-

[1] https://www.kaggle.com/c/asap-aes

Proceedings of the Tenth Workshop on Innovative Use of NLP for Building Educational Applications, 2015, pages 213–223,
Denver, Colorado, June 4, 2015.

tems, underscoring the need for common and well-motivated metrics that establish true system performance.

In this paper, we define the task of ATS as the accurate prediction of gold-standard scores (predefined ordinal grades), and we experimentally examine the robustness and efficacy of *measures of agreement* for a number of different conditions under two different experimental setups. First, we use synthetic data to simulate various experimental conditions, and second, we use real ATS data to assess the effectiveness of the metrics under realistic scenarios. For the latter, we run a series of experiments on the output of state-of-the-art ATS systems. We outline some deficiencies in commonly used metrics that have been previously overlooked, and consequently we propose more appropriate metrics for evaluating ATS systems focusing primarily on optimising system effectiveness and facilitating cross-system comparison.

The focus on measures of agreement is motivated by their use as the primary metric for evaluating system effectiveness in the recent Kaggle essay scoring competition. To the best of our knowledge, there is no systematic study comparing the efficacy of different measures of agreement under different experimental conditions. Although we focus on the task of ATS, the recommendations regarding the metrics covered in this paper extend naturally to many similar NLP tasks, i.e., those where the task is to accurately predict a gold-standard score.

The remainder of the paper is structured as follows: Section 2 defines our task and objectives. Section 3 reviews a number of performance metrics relevant to the ATS task. Section 4 describes a set of desired metric properties and presents an analysis of some prominently used metrics for the ATS task that uses the output of both simulated and real systems. Section 5 concludes with a discussion, general recommendations for evaluation practices and an outline of future work.

2 Task Definition

In the standard ATS evaluation, there exists a set of n texts where each text is indexed t_1 to t_n. Each text t_i is assigned a gold standard score $gs(t_i)$ by a human assessor (or group of human assessors). This score is one of g ordinal scores, which for convenience we index 1 to g. It is worth noting that, in general, it is not a requirement that the differences in scores are uniform. Furthermore, there exists some number of ATS systems ats_j indexed $j = 1$ to $j = m$ that predict scores $ats_j(t_i)$ for each of the n texts.

Given two ATS systems ats_1 and ats_2, we would like to determine a metric $\mathcal{M}$ that returns a measure of performance for ats_1 and ats_2 for which $\mathcal{M}(ats_1, gs, t) > \mathcal{M}(ats_2, gs, t)$ when ats_1 is a *better* system than ats_2. Note that we have not defined what "better" means at this stage. We will return to describing some desirable properties of $\mathcal{M}$ in Section 4.

From an educational point of view, our task is to ascertain whether the writing abilities required to warrant a particular score/grade have been attained. From this perspective, measures of agreement seem the appropriate type of measurement to apply to the output of ATS systems to address the accuracy of the (numerical) solution compared to the gold standard.

3 Measuring Performance of ATS systems

In this section, we review and critique metrics that have been frequently used in the literature to ascertain the performance of ATS systems. These performance metrics can be broadly categorised into *measures of association* and *measures of agreement* (e.g., see Williamson et al. (2012)).

3.1 Measures of Association

Measures of association (i.e., correlation coefficients) have been widely used in ATS (e.g., Yannakoudakis et al. (2011)), with Pearson's product-moment correlation coefficient being the most common. Pearson's correlation is a parametric measure of association that quantifies the degree of linear dependence between two variables and, more specifically, describes the extent to which the variables co-vary relative to the degree to which they vary independently. The greater the association, the more accurately one can use the value of one variable to predict the other. As the data depart from the coefficient's assumptions (e.g., unequal marginals), its maximum values may not be attainable (Carroll, 1961). For ordinal data, unequal marginals will always involve ties.[2] As the number of ties increases relative to the number of observations, its appropriateness largely diminishes.[3]

Spearman's rank correlation coefficient is a non-parametric measure of association that has the same range as Pearson, and it is calculated by ranking the variables and computing Pearson on the ranks rather than the raw values. In contrast to Pearson, it assesses the strength of a monotonic rather than linear relation between two variables, and has the advantage of independence from various assumptions. Unlike Pearson, it exhibits robustness to outliers; however, its reliability also decreases as the number of ties increases. It is worth noting at this point Kendall's τ_b, which is a more effective tie-adjusted non-parametric bivariate coefficient that quantifies the degree of agreement between rankings, and it is defined in terms of concordant and discordant pairs, although ties also affect its reliability.

3.1.1 Discussion

In essence, non-parametric measures are measures of *rank* correlation. In the context of the evaluation of ATS, they measure agreement with respect to the ranks, that is, whether an ATS system ranks texts similarly to the gold standard. However, this is not an appropriate type of measurement given the task definition in Section 2, where we would like to ascertain actual agreement with respect to the scores. Furthermore, correlation coefficients do not account for any systematic biases in the data; for example, a high correlation can be observed even if the predicted scores are consistently n points higher than the gold standard.

In the presence of outliers, the coefficient can be misleading and pulled in either direction. For example, for Pearson's correlation an outlier can influence the value of the correlation to the extent that a high correlation is observed even though the data may not be linearly dependent. Furthermore, it is well known that the value of the correlation will be greater if there is more variability in the data than if there is less. This is caused by the mathematical constraints in their formulation, and does not necessarily reflect the true relationship of predicted to gold standard scores. Finally, their reliability decreases as the number of ties increases. We come back to the appropriateness and recommended use of correlation metrics in Section 5.

In summary, (non-parametric) correlation measures are more apt at measuring the ability of the ATS system to correctly *rank* texts (i.e., placing a well written text above a poorly written text), rather than the ability of the ATS system to correctly assign a score/grade. In other words, correlation measures do not reward ATS systems for their ability to correctly identify the thresholds that separate score/grade boundaries ($1 : 2$ to $g - 1 : g$).

3.2 Measures of Agreement

A simple way of gauging the agreement between gold and predicted scores is to use percentage agreement, calculated as the number of times the gold and predicted scores are the same, divided by the total number of texts assessed. A closely-related variant is percentage of adjacent agreement, in which agreement is based on the number of times the gold and predicted scores are no more than n points apart.

Despite its simplicity, it has been argued (Cohen, 1960) that this measure can be misleading as it does not exclude the percentage of agreement that is expected on the basis of pure chance. That is, a certain amount of agreement can occur even if there is no systematic tendency for the gold and predicted scores to agree. The kappa coefficient (C_κ) was introduced by Cohen (1960) as a measure of agreement adjusted for chance. Let P_a denote the percentage of observed agreement and P_e the percentage of agreement expected by chance, Cohen's kappa coefficient is calculated as the ratio between the "true" observed agreement and its maximum value:

$$C_\kappa = \frac{P_a - P_e(\kappa)}{1 - P_e(\kappa)} \qquad (1)$$

where $P_e(\kappa)$ is the estimated agreement due to chance, and is calculated as the inner-product of the marginal distribution of each assessor (a worked example of this follows in Section 3.2.1). The values of the coefficient range between -1 and 1, where 1 represents perfect agreement and 0 represents no agreement beyond that occurring by chance. Most

[2] Of course, ties exist even when the marginals are identical if the number of observations is larger than the number of scores.

[3] For more details see (Maimon et al., 1986; Goodwin and Leech, 2006; Hauke and Kossowski, 2011) among others.

measures of agreement that are corrected for chance agreement, of which there are many, follow the general formula above where P_e varies depending on the specific measure. The disadvantage of this basic measure applied to ordinal data (scores in our case) is that it does not allow for weighting of different degrees of disagreement.

Weighted kappa (Cohen, 1968) was developed to address this problem. Note that this was the main metric used for evaluation and cross-system comparison of essay scoring systems in the recent Kaggle shared-task competition on ATS. It is commonly employed with ordinal data and can be defined either in terms of agreement or disagreement weights. The most common weights used are the (absolute) linear error weights and the quadratic error weights (Fleiss, 1981). The linear error weights are proportional to the actual difference between the predicted scores and the gold standard, while the quadratic error weights are proportional to the squared actual difference between these scores. The choice of weights is important as they can have a large effect on the results (Graham and Jackson, 1993).

In what follows, we discuss two of the main problems regarding the kappa coefficient: its dependency on trait prevalence and on marginal homogeneity. We note that the properties kappa exhibits (as shown below) are *independent* of the type of data on which it is used, that is, whether there is a categorical or an ordinal (gold standard) scale.

3.2.1 Trait Prevalence

Trait prevalence occurs when the underlying characteristic being measured is not distributed uniformly across items. It is usually the case that gold standard scores are normally distributed in the ATS task (i.e., the scores/grades are biased towards the mean).

Table 1 shows an example of the effect of trait prevalence on the C_κ statistic using a contingency table. In this simple example there are two scores/grades (i.e., pass P or fail F) for two different sets of 100 essays with different gold-score distributions, gs_1 and gs_2. The rows of the matrix indicate the frequency of the scores predicted by the ATS, while the columns are the gold-standard scores. Although percentage agreement (along the main diagonal) in both cases is quite high, $P_a = 0.8$, the C_κ statistic varies quite considerably. As the observed marginals (i.e., the totals either vertically or horizontally, or otherwise, the distribution of the scores / grades) in ats\gs$_1$ are uniformly distributed, the correction for chance agreement is much lower (i.e., $P_e(\kappa) = 0.5 \times 0.5 + 0.5 \times 0.5 = 0.5$) than for ats\gs$_2$ (i.e., $P_e(\kappa) = 0.68 \times 0.8 + 0.32 \times 0.2 = 0.61$) with unequal marginals, which leads to a lower absolute C_κ value for ats\gs$_2$. In this example, it is not clear why one would want a measure of agreement with this behaviour, where P_e is essentially artificially increased when the marginals are unequal.

ats \gs$_1$	P	F	
P	40	10	50
F	10	40	50
	50	50	100

ats \gs$_2$	P	F	
P	64	4	68
F	16	16	32
	80	20	100

Table 1: Cohen's κ for an ats system on two sets of essays. Although percentage agreement is 0.8 for both sets of essays, $C_\kappa = 0.6$ (left) and $C_\kappa = 0.49$ (right).

Fundamentally, this implies that the comparison of systems across datasets (or indeed the comparison of datasets given the same system) is very difficult because the value of C_κ not only depends on actual agreement, but crucially also on the distribution of the gold standard scores.

3.2.2 Marginal Homogeneity

A second problem with C_κ is that the difference in the marginal probabilities affects the coefficient considerably. Consider Table 2, which shows two different ATS system ratings (ats_1 and ats_2) along the same gold standard scores. The value of C_κ for ats_2 is much smaller (and actually it is 0) compared to that for ats_1 (0.12), even though ats_2 has higher percentage and marginal agreement; that is, ats_2 predicts scores with frequencies that are more similar to those in the gold standard.[4] The root cause of this paradox is similar to the one described earlier, and arises from the way P_e is calculated, and more specifically the assumption that marginal probabilities are classification propensities that are fixed, that is, they are known to the assessor before classifying the instances/texts into categories/scores. This

[4]Of course higher marginal agreement does not translate to overall higher agreement if percent agreement is low.

ats_1 \gs	P	F	
P	20	0	20
F	60	20	80
	80	20	100

ats_2 \gs	P	F	
P	60	15	75
F	20	5	25
	80	20	100

Table 2: C_κ for two systems ats_1 and ats_2 for the same set of gold scores. Although percentage agreement for ats_1 and ats_2 is 0.4 and 0.65 respectively, C_κ for ats_1 and ats_2 is $C_\kappa = 0.12$ (left) and $C_\kappa = 0$ (right).

is clearly not the case for ATS systems, and therefore the dependence of chance agreement on the level of marginal agreement is questionable when the marginals are free to vary (Brennan and Prediger, 1981).[5]

Essentially, the end result when a system predicts scores with a marginal distribution that is more similar to the gold standard (i.e., ats_2), is that any misclassification is penalised more severely even though percent agreement may be high. This is not the behaviour we want in a performance metric for ATS systems. Using kappa as an objective function in any machine learning algorithm could easily lead to learning functions that favour assigning distributions that are *different* to that of the gold standard (e.g., Chen and He (2013)).

3.2.3 Discussion

Previous work has also demonstrated that there exist cases where high values of (quadratic) kappa can be achieved even when there is low agreement (Graham and Jackson, 1993). Additionally, Brenner and Kliebsch (1996) investigated the effect of the score range on the magnitude of weighted kappa and found that the quadratic weighted kappa coefficient tends to have high variation and increases as the score range increases, particularly in ranges between two and five distinct scores. In contrast, linearly weighted kappa appeared to be less affected, although a slight increase in value was observed as the range increased.

The correction for chance agreement in Cohen's kappa has been the subject of much controversy (Brennan and Prediger, 1981; Feinstein and Cicchetti, 1990; Uebersax, 1987; Byrt et al., 1993; Gwet, 2002; Di Eugenio and Glass, 2004; Sim and Wright, 2005; Craggs and Wood, 2005; Artstein and Poesio, 2008; Powers, 2012). Firstly, it assumes that when assessors are unsure of a score, they *guess* at random according to a fixed prior distribution of scores. Secondly, it includes chance correction for every single prediction instance (i.e., not only when an assessor is in doubt). Many have argued (Brennan and Prediger, 1981; Uebersax, 1987) that this is a highly improbable model of assessor error and vastly over-estimates agreement due to chance, especially in the case when prior distributions are free to vary. Although it is likely that there is some agreement due to chance when an assessor is unsure of a score (Gwet, 2002), it is unlikely that human assessors simply guess at random, and it is unlikely that this happens for *all* predictions. For the task of ATS, the distribution of scores to assign are not *fixed* a priori. Although trained assessors may have a certain expectation of the final distribution, it is certainly not fixed.[6]

Consequently, there are a number of different agreement metrics – for example, Scott's π (Scott, 1955), which is sensitive to trait prevalence but not the marginals, and Krippendorff's α (Krippendorff, 1970) which is nearly equivalent to π (Artstein and Poesio, 2008) – all of which vary in the manner in which chance agreement (i.e., P_e) is calculated, but have similar problems (Zhao, 2011; Gwet, 2014). It is also worth noting that weighted versions of kappa do not solve the issues of trait prevalence and marginal homogeneity.

The two most noteworthy variants are the *agreement coefficient* AC (Gwet, 2002) and the Brennan-Prediger (BP) coefficient (Brennan and Prediger, 1981), which both estimate P_e more conservatively using more plausible assumptions. In particular, the BP coefficient estimates P_e using $1/g$, with the assumption that the probability that an assessor would guess the score of an item by chance is inversely related to the number of scores g in the rating scale.[7] Substituting P_e in equation (1) gives $(P_a - 1/g)/(1 - 1/g)$, which is better suited when one or both of the marginals are free to vary. When

[5] However, we would like to penalise trivial systems that e.g., always assign the most prevalent gold score, in which case the marginals are indeed fixed.

[6] See Brennan and Prediger (1981) for a more detailed discussion.

[7] We note that this is equivalent to the S coefficient (Bennett et al., 1954) discussed in (Artstein and Poesio, 2008).

the grades are not uniformly distributed, P_e may be higher than $1/g$; nevertheless, it can be a useful lower limit for P_e (Lawlis and Lu, 1972). Note that in the example in Table 1, BP would be the same for both ats\gs$_1$ and ats\gs$_2$, $(0.8 - 0.5)/(1 - 0.5) = 0.6$, and thus effectively remains unaltered under the effects of trait prevalence.[8]

The AC coefficient calculates P_e as follows:

$$P_e = \frac{1}{(g-1)} \sum_{k=1}^{g} \pi_k (1 - \pi_k) \quad (2)$$

$$\pi_k = (p_{a,k} + p_{b,k})/2 \quad (3)$$

where π_k represents the probability of assigning grade/score k to a randomly selected item by a randomly selected assessor, calculated based on $p_{a,k}$ and $p_{b,k}$, which are the marginal probabilities of each assessor a and b respectively for grade/score k. More specifically, $p_{a,k} = n_{a,k}/n$ and $p_{b,k} = n_{b,k}/n$, where $n_{a,k}$ refers to the number of instances assigned to grade k by assessor a, $n_{b,k}$ refers to the number of instances assigned to grade k by assessor b, and n refers to the total number of instances. Gwet (2002;2014) defines chance agreement as the product of the probability that two assessors agree given a non-deterministic instance,[9] defined as $1/g$, by the propensity for an assessor to assign a non-deterministic grade/score, estimated as $\sum_{k=1}^{g} \pi_k (1 - \pi_k)/(1 - 1/g)$.[10]

In the example in Table 1, $P_e = (0.5 \times (1-0.5) + 0.5 \times (1 - 0.5))/(2 - 1) = 0.5$ for ats\gs$_1$ (for which $\pi_{pass} = \pi_{fail} = 0.5$), and $P_e = (0.74 \times (1 - 0.74) + 0.26 \times (1-0.26))/(2-1) = 0.38$ for ats\gs$_2$, which is in contrast to C_κ that overestimated P_e for ats\gs$_2$ with unequal marginals. More specifically, the AC coefficient would be higher for ats\gs$_2$ than for ats\gs$_1$: 0.67 versus 0.60 respectively.[11]

4 Metric Properties

On the basis of the discussion so far, we propose the following list of desirable properties of an evaluation measure for an ATS system:

- Robustness to trait prevalence
- Robustness to marginal homogeneity
- Sensitivity to magnitude of misclassification
- Robustness to score range

In this section, we analyse the aforementioned metrics of agreement (with different weights) with respect to these properties using both synthetic and real ATS-system scores (where applicable).

4.1 Robustness to Trait Prevalence

In order to test metrics for robustness to trait prevalence, we simulated 5,000 gold standard scores on a 5-point scale using a Gaussian (normal) distribution with a mean score at the mid-point. By controlling the variance of this Gaussian, we can create gold standard scores that are more *peaked* at the center (high trait prevalence) or more uniform across all grades (low trait prevalence). We simulated systems by randomly introducing errors in these scores. The system output in Figure 1 (left) was created by randomly sampling 25% of the gold standard scores and perturbing them by 2 points in a random direction.[12] This led to a simulated system with 75% percentage agreement, which also translates to a constant mean absolute error (MAE) of 0.5 (i.e., on average, each predicted score is 0.5 scores away from its gold counterpart).

Figure 1 (left) shows that nearly all evaluation measures are very sensitive to the distribution of the gold standard scores, and the magnitude of the metrics does change as the distribution becomes more peaked. The AC measure is less sensitive than C_κ (and actually rewards systems), but the only measure of agreement that is invariant under changes in trait prevalence is the BP coefficient, which actually is in line with percentage agreement and assigns 75% agreement using quadratic weights.

To study the effect of trait prevalence on real systems, we replicated an existing state-of-the-art ATS system (Yannakoudakis et al., 2011). The model

[8] However, it can be artificially increased as the scoring scale increases.

[9] That is, it is a hard-to-score instance, which is the case where random ratings occur.

[10] See (Gwet, 2014) for more details regarding the differences between AC and Aickin's alpha (Aickin, 1990).

[11] The reader is referred to (Gwet, 2014; Brennan and Prediger, 1981) for more details on AC and BP and their extensions to at least ordinal data and to more than two assessors.

[12] If this could not be done (i.e., a score of 4 cannot be changed by +2 on a 5-point scale), a different score was randomly sampled.

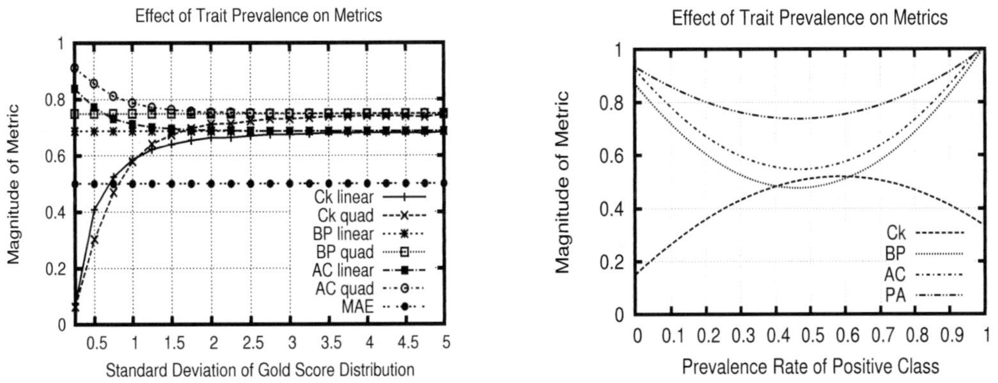

Figure 1: Effect of trait prevalence on metrics of agreement for synthetic (left) and real (right) ATS scores.

evaluates writing competence on the basis of lexical and grammatical features, as well as errors, and achieves a correlation of around 0.75 on the publicly available First Certificate in English (FCE) examination scripts, that have been manually annotated with a score in the range 1 to 40 (with 40 being the highest). In this setting, robustness to trait prevalence was evaluated by plotting the magnitude of the metrics as a function of the prevalence rate, calculated as the proportion of passing scores in the data, as judged by both the ATS system and the examiner, as we varied the passing threshold from 1 to 40.

In Figure 1 (right) we can see that all metrics are sensitive to trait prevalence.[13] In order to get a clearer picture on the effect of trait prevalence on real systems, it is important we plot percent agreement (PA) along with the metrics. The reason is that chance-corrected agreement measures should remain reasonably close to the quantity that they adjust for chance, as this quantity varies (Gwet, 2014). AC and BP remain reasonably close to PA as the prevalence rate increases. On the other hand, C_κ is further away, and at times considerably lower. The behaviour of kappa is difficult to explain, and in fact, even when the prevalence rate approaches 1, C_κ still produces very low results. Note that in the binary pass/fail case, linear and quadratic weights do not affect the value of kappa and produce the same results.

[13]Curve fitting is performed to be able to observe the tendency of the metrics.

4.2 Robustness to Marginal Homogeneity

In order to test the metrics for robustness to marginal homogeneity, we simulated 5,000 gold standard scores on a 10-point scale using a Gaussian distribution with a mean score at the mid-point and a standard deviation of one score. We simulated different systems by randomly introducing errors in these scores. In particular, we simulated outputs that had distributions different to that of the gold standard by drawing a number of incorrect scores from a different Gaussian centred around a different mean (0–9 in Figure 2). We kept percentage agreement with linear weights constant, which again also translates to a constant MAE (1.0). We are looking for metrics that are less sensitive to varying marginals, and ideally which promote systems that distribute scores similarly to the gold standard when agreement is otherwise identical.

For the measures of agreement, as expected, Cohen's kappa (both linear and quadratic) penalises systems that distribute scores similarly to those of the gold standard. However, AC (with linear and quadratic weights) and quadratic BP promote systems that distribute scores similarly to the gold scores. On the other hand, BP linear remains unchanged.

To study the sensitivity of the metrics to the variations in the marginal distributions in real ATS systems, we plot their variation as a function of the similarity of the passing-score distributions, where the similarity is calculated as $sim_{pass} = 1 - |p_{gold,pass} - p_{ats,pass}|$, which is based on the absolute difference

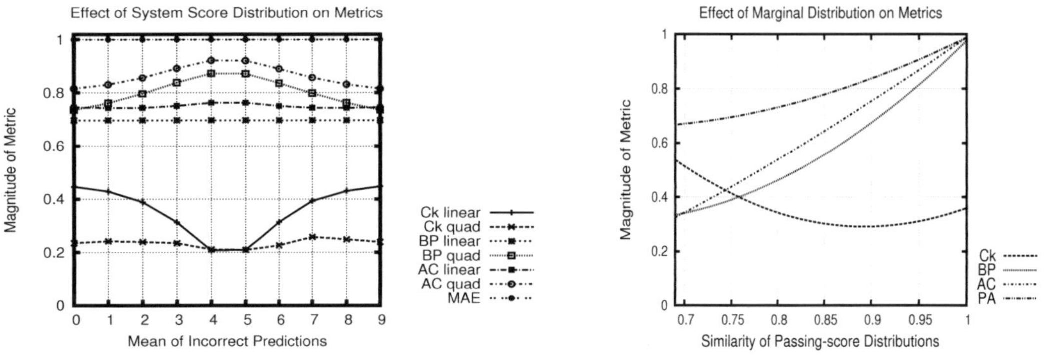

Figure 2: Sensitivity of metrics on the marginal distribution of synthetic (left) and real (right) ATS scores.

between the marginal probabilities of the gold and predicted passing scores. The higher the value of sim, the more similar the distributions are. Again, we employ Yannakoudakis et al. (2011)'s ATS system.

Similarly to the simulated experiments, we observe increases in the magnitude of AC and BP as the similarity increases, whereas C_κ is considerably lower and has a decreasing tendency which does not stay close to PA. In fact, marginal homogeneity does not guarantee the validity of the results for Cohen's kappa. This can be seen more clearly in Figure 3, where we plot the magnitude of the metrics as a function of the overall probability of assigning a passing score, as judged by both the human assessor and the ATS system. That is, $(p_{gold,pass} + p_{ats,pass})/2$. As the overall probability of a passing score becomes very large or very small, C_κ yields considerable lower results, regardless of whether the marginal probabilities are equal or not.

4.3 Sensitivity to Magnitude of Misclassification

It is common that human assessors disagree by small margins given the subjectivity of the ATS task. However, larger disagreements are usually treated more seriously. Therefore, given two ATS systems, we would prefer a system that makes more small misclassifications over a system that makes a few large misclassifications when all else is equal. A metric with quadratic-weighting is likely to adhere to this property.

To test the sensitivity of the metrics to the magnitude of misclassification, we simulated 5,000 gold standard scores on a 10-point scale using a Gaussian (normal) distribution with a mean score at the midpoint. Again, we simulated systems by randomly introducing errors to the scores. For each system, we varied the magnitude of the misclassification while the total misclassification distance (i.e., MAE or PA) was kept constant. Figure 4 confirms that measures of agreement that use quadratic weights decrease as the magnitude of each error increases. The metrics of agreement that use linear weights actually increase slightly.[14]

4.4 Robustness to score scales

Robustness of the metrics to the score range or scale was tested by binning the gold and predicted scores at fixed cutpoints and re-evaluating the results. In the FCE dataset, the scale was varied between 40 and 3 points by successively binning scores. Metrics that are less sensitive to scoring scales facilitate cross-dataset comparisons.

All metrics were affected by the scale, although those with quadratic weights appeared to be more sensitive compared to those with linear ones. Quadratic C_κ was the most sensitive metric and showed larger decreases compared to the others as the scoring scale was reduced, while AC quadratic exhibited higher stability compared to BP quadratic.[15]

[14]Note that such an experiment cannot be controlled and reliably executed for real systems.

[15]Detailed results omitted due to space restrictions.

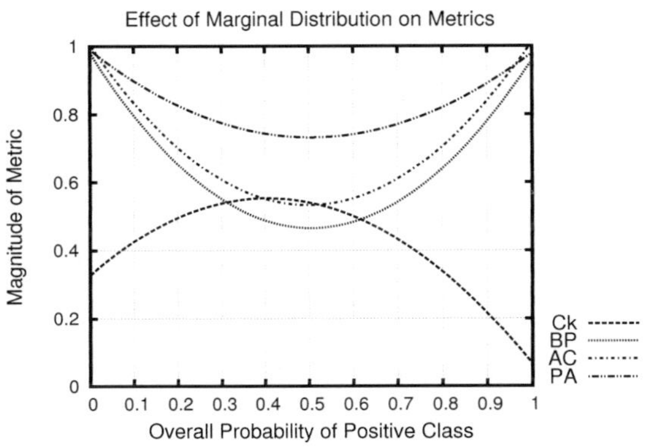

Figure 3: Sensitivity of metrics on the marginal distribution of real ATS-model scores.

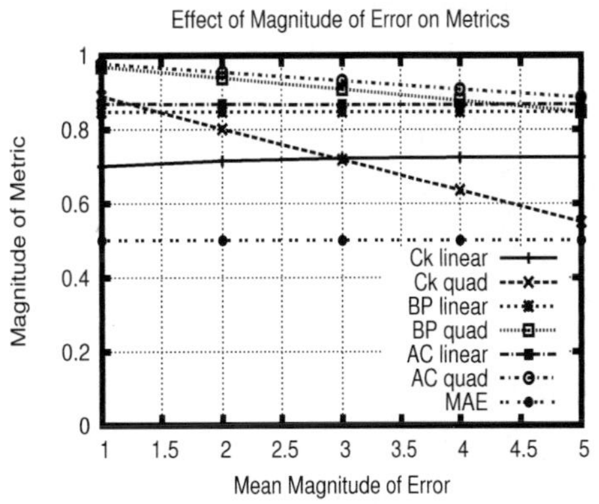

Figure 4: Change in the magnitude of performance metrics as only the size of each misclassification increases.

5 Recommendations and Conclusion

Our results suggest that AC and BP (with quadratic weights) overall are the most robust agreement coefficients. On the basis of this analysis, we make the following recommendations:

- We recommend against using Cohen's kappa. Interpretation of the magnitude of kappa within / across system and dataset comparisons is problematic, as it depends on trait prevalence, the marginal distributions and the scoring scale. It is worth noting at this point that the inefficacy of kappa is *independent* on the type of data that it is being used on, that is, whether there is a categorical or ordinal (gold standard) scale.

- We recommend using the AC coefficient with quadratic weights. Although BP is a good alternative as it adjusts percent agreement simply based on the inverse of the scoring scale, it is more sensitive to, and directly affected by the scoring scale.

- We recommend *reporting* a rank correlation coefficient (Spearman's or Kendall's τ_b rank correlation coefficient), rather than using it for system evaluation and comparison, as it can facilitate error analysis and system interpretation; for example, low agreement and high rank correlation would indicate a large misclassification magnitude, but high agreement with respect to the ranking (i.e., the system ranks texts similarly to the gold standard); high agreement and low rank correlation would indicate high accuracy in predicting the gold scores, but small ranking errors.[16] Kendall's τ_b may be preferred, as it is a more effective tie-adjusted coefficient that is defined in terms of concordant and discordant pairs; however, further experiments beyond the scope of this paper would be needed to confirm this.

It is worth noting that given the generality of the ATS task setting as presented in this paper (i.e., aiming to predict gold standard scores on an ordinal scale) and the metric-evaluation setup (using synthetic data in addition to real output), the properties discussed and resulting recommendations may be more widely relevant within NLP and may serve as a useful benchmark for the wider community (Siddharthan and Katsos, 2010; Bloodgood and Grothendieck, 2013; Chen and He, 2013; Liu et al., 2013, among others) as well as for shared task organisers.

An interesting direction for future work would be to explore the use of evaluation measures that lie outside of those commonly used by the ATS community, such as macro-averaged root mean squared error that has been argued as being suitable for ordinal regression tasks (Baccianella et al., 2009).

[16] A low correlation could also point to effects of the underlying properties of the data as the metric is sensitive to trait prevalence (see Section 3.1.1).

Acknowledgments

We would like to thank Ted Briscoe for his valuable comments and suggestions, Cambridge English Language Assessment for supporting this research, and the anonymous reviewers for their useful feedback.

References

Mikel Aickin. 1990. Maximum likelihood estimation of agreement in the constant predictive probability model, and its relation to Cohen's kappa. *Biometrics*, 46(2):293–302.

Ron Artstein and Massimo Poesio. 2008. Inter-coder agreement for computational linguistics. *Computational Linguistics*, 34(4):555–596.

Yigal Attali and Jill Burstein. 2006. Automated essay scoring with e-Rater v.2.0. *Journal of Technology, Learning, and Assessment*, 4(3):1–30.

Yigal Attali, Don Powers, Marshall Freedman, Marissa Harrison, and Susan Obetz. 2008. Automated Scoring of short-answer open-ended GRE subject test items. Technical Report 04, ETS.

Stefano Baccianella, Andrea Esuli, and Fabrizio Sebastiani. 2009. Evaluation measures for ordinal regression. In *9th IEEE International Conference on Intelligent Systems Design and Applications*, pages 283–287. IEEE Comput. Soc.

E M Bennett, R Alpert, and A C Goldstein. 1954. Communications through limited-response questioning. *Public Opinion Quarterly*, 18(3):303–308.

Michael Bloodgood and John Grothendieck. 2013. Analysis of Stopping Active Learning based on Stabilizing Predictions. In *Proceedings of the Seventeenth Conference on Computational Natural Language Learning*, pages 10–19.

Robert L Brennan and Dale J Prediger. 1981. Coefficient kappa: Some uses, misuses, and alternatives. *Educational and psychological measurement*, 41(3):687–699.

Hermann Brenner and Ulrike Kliebsch. 1996. Dependence of weighted kappa coefficients on the number of categories. *Epidemiology*, 7(2):199–202.

Ted Briscoe, Ben Medlock, and Øistein E. Andersen. 2010. Automated assessment of ESOL free text examinations. Technical Report UCAM-CL-TR-790, University of Cambridge, Computer Laboratory, nov.

Jill Burstein, Martin Chodorow, and Claudia Leacock. 2003. Criterion: Online essay evaluation: An application for automated evaluation of student essays. In *Proceedings of the fifteenth annual conference on innovative applications of artificial intelligence*, pages 3–10.

Ted Byrt, Janet Bishop, and John B Carlin. 1993. Bias, prevalence and kappa. *Journal of clinical epidemiology*, 46(5):423–429.

John B. Carroll. 1961. The nature of the data, or how to choose a correlation coefficient. *Psychometrika*, 26(4):347–372, December.

Hongbo Chen and Ben He. 2013. Automated Essay Scoring by Maximizing Human-machine Agreement. In *Empirical Methods in Natural Language Processing*, pages 1741–1752.

Jacob Cohen. 1960. A Coefficient of Agreement for Nominal Scales. *Educational and Psychological Measurement*, 20(1):37–46, April.

Jacob Cohen. 1968. Weighted kappa: nominal scale agreement with provision for scaled disagreement or partial credit. *Psychological bulletin*, 4(70):213–220.

Richard Craggs and Mary McGee Wood. 2005. Evaluating discourse and dialogue coding schemes. *Computational Linguistics*, 31(3):289–295.

Barbara Di Eugenio and Michael Glass. 2004. The kappa statistic: A second look. *Computational linguistics*, 30(1):95–101.

Alvan R Feinstein and Domenic V Cicchetti. 1990. High agreement but low kappa: I. the problems of two paradoxes. *Journal of clinical epidemiology*, 43(6):543–549.

Joseph L. Fleiss. 1981. *Statistical methods for rates and proportions*. Wiley series in probability and mathematical statistics. Applied probability and statistics. Wiley.

Laura D. Goodwin and Nancy L. Leech. 2006. Understanding Correlation: Factors That Affect the Size of r. *The Journal of Experimental Education*, 74(3):249–266, April.

Patrick Graham and Rodney Jackson. 1993. The analysis of ordinal agreement data: beyond weighted kappa. *Journal of clinical epidemiology*, 46(9):1055–1062, September.

Kilem Gwet. 2002. Inter-rater reliability: dependency on trait prevalence and marginal homogeneity. *Statistical Methods for Inter-Rater Reliability Assessment Series*, 2:1–9.

Kilem L. Gwet. 2014. *Handbook of Inter-Rater Reliability, 4th Edition: The Definitive Guide to Measuring The Extent of Agreement Among Raters*. Advanced Analytics, LLC.

Jan Hauke and Tomasz Kossowski. 2011. Comparison of Values of Pearson's and Spearman's Correlation Coefficients on the Same Sets of Data. *Quaestiones Geographicae*, 30(2):87–93, January.

Derrick Higgins, Jill Burstein, Daniel Marcu, and Claudia Gentile. 2004. Evaluating multiple aspects of coherence in student essays. In *Proceedings of the Human Language Technology Conference of the North American Chapter of the Association for Computational Linguistics*.

Klaus Krippendorff. 1970. Estimating the reliability, systematic error and random er- ror of interval data. *Educational and Psychological Measurement*, 30(1):61–70.

Thomas K. Landauer, Darrell Laham, and Peter W. Foltz. 2003. Automated scoring and annotation of essays with the Intelligent Essay Assessor. In M.D. Shermis and J. C. Burstein, editors, *Automated essay scoring: A cross-disciplinary perspective*, pages 87–112.

G Frank Lawlis and Elba Lu. 1972. Judgment of counseling process: reliability, agreement, and error. *Psychological bulletin*, 78(1):17–20, July.

Tsun-Jui Liu, Shu-Kai Hsieh, and Laurent PREVOT. 2013. Observing Features of PTT Neologisms: A Corpus-driven Study with N-gram Model. In *Twenty-Fifth Conference on Computational Linguistics and Speech Processing (ROCLING 2013)*, pages 250–259.

Zvi Maimon, Adi Raveh, and Gur Mosheiov. 1986. Additional cautionary notes about the Pearson's correlation coefficient. *Quality and Quantity*, 20(4).

Ellis B. Page. 1968. The use of the computer in analyzing student essays. *International Review of Education*, 14(2):210–225, June.

L Perelman. 2013. Critique (ver. 3.4) of mark d. shermis and ben hammer,contrasting state-of-the-art automated scoring of essays: Analysis. *New York Times*.

Donald E. Powers, Jill C. Burstein, Martin Chodorow, Mary E. Fowles, and Karen Kukich. 2002. Stumping e-rater: challenging the validity of automated essay scoring. *Computers in Human Behavior*, 18(2):103–134.

David M W Powers. 2012. The problem with kappa. In *13th Conference of the European Chapter of the Association for Computational Linguistics*, pages 345–355.

Lawrence M. Rudner and Tahung Liang. 2002. Automated essay scoring using Bayes' theorem. *The Journal of Technology, Learning and Assessment*, 1(2):3–21.

William A Scott. 1955. Reliability of content analysis: The case of nominal scale coding. *Public opinion quarterly*, 19(3):321–325.

Mark D Shermis and Ben Hamner. 2012. Contrasting state-of-the-art automated scoring of essays: Analysis. In *Annual National Council on Measurement in Education Meeting*, pages 14–16.

Advaith Siddharthan and Napoleon Katsos. 2010. Reformulating Discourse Connectives for Non-Expert Readers. In *North American Chapter of the ACL*, pages 1002–1010.

Julius Sim and Chris C Wright. 2005. The Kappa Statistic in Reliability Studies: Use, Interpretation, and Sample Size Requirements. *Physical Therapy*, 85(3):257–268, March.

John S Uebersax. 1987. Diversity of decision-making models and the measurement of interrater agreement. *Psychological Bulletin*, 101(1):140.

Jinhao Wang and Michelle Stallone Brown. 2007. Automated Essay Scoring Versus Human Scoring: A Comparative Study. *The Journal of Technology, Learning and Assessment*, 6(2).

Jinhao Wang and Michelle Stallone Brown. 2008. Automated Essay Scoring Versus Human Scoring: A Correlational Study. *Contemporary Issues in Technology and Teacher Education*, 8(4):310–325.

David M. Williamson, Xiaoming Xi, and Jay F. Breyer. 2012. A framework for evaluation and use of automated scoring. *Educational Measurement: Issues and Practice*, 31(1):2–13.

David M. Williamson. 2009. A Framework for Implementing Automated Scoring. In *Proceedings of the Annual Meeting of the American Educational Research Association and the National Council on Measurement in Education*, San Diego, CA.

Helen Yannakoudakis, Ted Briscoe, and Ben Medlock. 2011. A New Dataset and Method for Automatically Grading ESOL Texts. In *Proceedings of the 49th Annual Meeting of the Association for Computational Linguistics: Human Language Technologies*.

Xinshu Zhao. 2011. When to use scott's π or krippendorff's α, if ever? In *The annual Conference of the Association for Education in Journalism and Mass Communication*.

Task-Independent Features for Automated Essay Grading

Torsten Zesch **Michael Wojatzki**
Language Technology Lab
University of Duisburg-Essen

Dirk Scholten-Akoun
Center of Teacher Education
University of Duisburg-Essen

Abstract

Automated scoring of student essays is increasingly used to reduce manual grading effort. State-of-the-art approaches use supervised machine learning which makes it complicated to transfer a system trained on one task to another. We investigate which currently used features are task-independent and evaluate their transferability on English and German datasets. We find that, by using our task-independent feature set, models transfer better between tasks. We also find that the transfer works even better between tasks of the same type.

1 Introduction

Having students write an essay is a widely used method for assessment, e.g. universities use essay writing skills as a proxy for the prospects of applicants. As manually grading essays is costly, automated essay grading systems are increasingly used becasue they – once developed – do not introduce additional costs for grading new essays.

Automated essay grading systems usually follow a supervised approach and yield a quality of holistic grading comparable to human performance (Valenti et al., 2003; Dikli, 2006). These systems make use of certain properties of essays (called features) in order to estimate the essay quality. In the grading process, these features are extracted and ratings are assigned according to the manifestations of the features (Attali and Burstein, 2006). In order to automatically learn the association between feature values and ratings a high amount of manually rated essays is required for training. Hence, it seems desirable to develop systems that work without this initial input, which means – expressed in terms of machine learning – that features should not be defined by the present task but by general essay grading. A task is defined here as prompting a group of humans to solve a particular writing task. Tasks differ in attributes such as the grade-level of underlying subjects or characteristics of the prompt.

Many kinds of features have been proposed for essay grading (Valenti et al., 2003; Dikli, 2006). They differ in the degree of dependency to the task at hand. There are features that are strongly dependent on a task, e.g. when they detect important words or topics (Chen and He, 2013). Other features are less dependent, e.g. when they capture general characteristics of essays like the number of words in the essay (Östling, 2013; Lei et al., 2014), usage of connectors (Burstein and Chodorow, 1999; Lei et al., 2014), etc.

We assume that a system which considers only task-independent features should perform well no matter what task it is trained on. However, it is unclear how much explanatory power the model might lose in this step. In this paper, we test this hypothesis by performing experiments with a state-of-the-art essay grading system on English and German datasets. We categorize features into task-dependent and task-independent ones and evaluate the difference in grading accuracy between the corresponding models. We find that the task-independent models show a better performance for both languages tested, but the resulting losses are relatively high in general. Moreover, we examine the tasks more closely and group them according to whether they offer a textual source as a reference point. We show that the transfer works better if the model is derived from the same task type.

Proceedings of the Tenth Workshop on Innovative Use of NLP for Building Educational Applications, 2015, pages 224–232,
Denver, Colorado, June 4, 2015.

2 Features

In this section, we describe state-of-the-art features and how they relate to the quality of an essay. For each feature, we discuss whether it belongs to the strongly task-dependent or weakly task-dependent group.

2.1 Length Features

This very simple but quite valuable feature deals with the **essay length** (Mahana et al., 2012; Chen and He, 2013; Östling, 2013; Lei et al., 2014). The core idea is that essays are usually written under a time limit. So the amount of produced text can be a useful predictor of the productivity of the writer and thus the quality of the essay (Shermis and Burstein, 2002). Therefore, we measure the text length by counting all tokens and sentences in an essay. The degree of task-dependence of this feature is directly connected to the time limit.

The average **sentence length** in words and **word length** in characters can be an indicator for the degree of complexity a writer can master (Attali and Burstein, 2006; Mahana et al., 2012; Chen and He, 2013; Östling, 2013). As this is not particularly tied to a specific task, these features are weakly task-dependent.

2.2 Occurrence Features

According to Mahana et al. (2012) the occurrences of linguistic phenomena such as **commas, quotations**, or **exclamation marks** can serve as valuable features in a grade prediction. These features focus more on the structuring of an essay and are thus weakly task-dependent.

For tasks that are source-based (i.e. a source text is provided on which the task is based), we augment this approach by also counting **formal references** like citations and line references. Source-based features are obviously strongly task-dependent.

Using third party sources to support an argument can be a valuable hint for evidence (Bergler, 2006). Therefore, we use the approach of Krestel et al. (2008) to detect **direct, indirect**, and **reported speech** in essays. The approach relies on set of reporting verbs and rules to identify and distinguish these forms.

If a task is based on a certain text source, the occurrence of **core concepts** in the essay should be an indicator for high quality (Foltz et al., 1999). We determine core concepts from the source using words or phrases with a high tf.idf weight. Again these features are just meaningful if the related task offers a textual source.

2.3 Syntax Features

Variation in the syntactic structures used in an essay may indicate proficiency in writing (Burstein et al., 1998). Following Chen and He (2013), we operationalize this by measuring the ratio of distinct parse trees to all the trees and the average depths of the trees to compute **syntactic variation** features.

Further, the parsing trees are used to measure the proportion of **subordinate, causal** and **temporal clauses**. Causal and temporal clauses are detected by causal or temporal conjunctions that could be found in subordinate-clauses. For example, a subordinate clause beginning with *when* is considered as temporal. The detection of causal- and temporal clauses is used to enrich the syntactic variability by a discourse element (Burstein et al., 1998; Chen and He, 2013; Lei et al., 2014). As syntactic features are relatively independent of the task, we categorize them as weakly task-dependent.

2.4 Style Features

Another important aspect of essay quality is an appropriate style. Following Östling (2013), we use the relative ratio of POS-tags to detect style preferences of writers. We complemented this by a feature that measures the formality F of an essay (Heylighen and Dewaele, 2002) defined as:

$$F = \frac{\sum_{i \in A} \frac{c(i)}{n} - \sum_{j \in B} \frac{c(j)}{n} + 100}{2}$$

where A = {N, ADJ, PP, DET}, B = {PR, V, ADV, UH}, and n is the number of tokens in the text. The **formality**-feature should be strongly task-dependent, as the correct style depends on the task and the target audience.

The words used in the essay tell us something about the vocabulary the writer actively uses. In accordance with Chen and He (2013), we measure the

type-token-ratio to estimate whether an essay has a relatively rich or rather poor vocabulary.

As noted by Breland et al. (1994), word knowledge of a writer is highly tied to the corpus frequency of the words used. The lower the frequency the higher the writer's language proficiency. We model this idea by calculating the average **word frequency** in the Web1T-corpus (Brants and Franz, 2006). We expect this average frequency to be relatively stable and thus categorize the feature as weakly task-dependent.

2.5 Cohesion Features

The structure of an essay reflects the writer's ability to organize her ideas and compose a cohesive response to the task. Following Lei et al. (2014) the use of **connectives** (like *therefore* or *accordingly*) can be a hint for a cohesive essay. We count occurrences of connectives (from a fixed list) and normalize by the total number of tokens. As cohesion is relatively independent from the topic of an essay, we categorize this feature as weakly task-dependent.

2.6 Coherence Features

In order to make an essay understandable, writers need to ensure that the whole text is coherent and the reader can follow the argumentation (Chen and He, 2013; Lei et al., 2014). Features based on Rhetorical Structure Theory (William and Thompson, 1988) could be used (Burstein et al., 2001), but there are no reliable parsers available for German and performance is also not yet robust enough for English. Instead, we operationalize coherence measuring the **topical overlap** between adjacent sentences. We use similarity measures based on n-gram overlap and redundancy (e.g. of nouns). This operationalization of coherence is weakly task-dependent, as the degree of topical overlap is independent of the actual topic.

2.7 Error Features

Grammatical or spelling errors are one of the most obvious indicators of bad essays, but have been found to have only little impact on scoring quality (Chen and He, 2013; Östling, 2013). We add a simple rule-based **grammar error** feature in our system based on LanguageTool.[1] We do not expect grammar errors to be bound to specific topics and categorize the feature as weakly task-dependent.

[1] https://www.languagetool.org

2.8 Readability Features

We use a set of established **readability** features (Flesch, Coleman-Liau, ARI, Kincaid, FOG, Lix, and SMOG), that rely on normalized counts of words, letters, syllables or other phenomena (like abbreviations) which affect the readability (McLaughlin, 1969; McCallum and Peterson, 1982; Smith and Taffler, 1992). Depending on which writing style is considered as appropriate, high scoring essays might be associated with different levels of readability. However, a certain level of formal writing is required for most essays and very simple or very complex writing are both indicators for bad essays. Thus, we categorize the features as weakly task-dependent.

2.9 Task-Similarity Features

For source-based essays, we can determine the **task similarity** of an essay by computing the similarity between essay and the task specific source (Östling, 2013). There should be a certain degree of similarity between the source and the essay, but if the similarity is too high the essay might be plagiarized. We use Kullback–Leibler divergence between source and essay.

A variant of this feature computes the **corpus similarity** to a neutral background corpus (Brown corpus (Marcus et al., 1993) in our case) in order to determine whether the essay was written specific enough.

While the corpus similarity should be weakly task-dependent, the task similarity is of course strongly dependent on the task.

2.10 Set-Dependent Features

So far, all features have only used the characteristics of a single essay, but it is also useful to take the whole set of essays into account. Instead of detecting characteristics of an individual essay the differences between essays in the set is examined. Set-based features can be based on topics (Burstein et al., 1998) or n-grams (Chen and He, 2013). We use **word n-gram** features for the 1,000 most frequent uni-, bi- and tri-grams in the essay set. Following

Chen and He (2013), we further use the same number of **POS n-grams** as features.

As a consequence of writing conventions, wording in an essay usually differs between regions in a text. For example, words that indicate a summary or a conclusion are indicators for a good essay only if they occur at the end, not at the beginning. Thus, we partition the essay in n equally sized parts based on word counts (we found five parts to work well) and compute **partition word n-grams** using the same settings as described above.

As all features described in this section deal with frequent wording or essay topics, they are strongly task-dependent.

3 Experimental Setup

We now describe the experimental setup used to examine our research question regarding task-independent models.

3.1 Datasets

As we want to compare models across tasks, we need datasets that contain different tasks.

English A suitable English dataset is the ASAP essay grading challenge.[2] The dataset contains eight independent tasks of essay-writing with each about 1,800 graded essays (except the last one with only 723). The essays were written by students in grade levels between 7 and 10 of a US high-school. The tasks cover a wide range of different settings and can be grouped on whether they were source-based or not:

The **source-based tasks** have in common that the participants first received a text as input and then had to write an essay that refers to this source. The following task belong to this group:

- Task 3: Given a source of someone who is traveling by bicycle, students should describe how the environment influences the narrator.
- Task 4: On the basis of the text 'winter hibiscus' participants should explain why the text ends in a particular way.
- Task 5: Students were requested to describe the mood of a given memoir.
- Task 6: Based on an excerpt on the construction of the Empire State Building, participants had to describe the obstacles the builders faced.

The **opinion tasks** ask for an opinion about a certain topic, but without referring to a specific source text.

- Task 1: Students should convince readers of a local newspaper of their opinion on the effects computers have on people.
- Task 2: Participants were asked to write about their opinion on whether certain media should be banned from libraries. They were prompted to include own experiences.
- Task 7: Participants should freely write on 'patience'. They could either write entirely free or about a situation in which they or another person proved patience.
- Task 8: Participants were told to tell a true story in which laughter was a part.

As the different tasks use different scoring schemes, we use holistic scores and normalize to a scale from 0 to 9 in order to make the trained model exchangeable.

German The German dataset contains two independent tasks each with 197 and 196 annotated essays. The essays were written by first-year university students of degree programs for future teachers. Both writing tasks had in common that the participants first received a text as an input. After reading the given text they were supposed to write an essay by summarizing the argumentative structure of the text. However, students were also asked to include their own pro and contra arguments.

- T1: Students were requested to summarize and to discuss a newspaper article of a national German newspaper which deals with an educational topic.
- T2: Participants were asked to summarize and to discuss a newspaper article of a national German newspaper which focusses on the quality of contributions in the participatory media.

Again, we use the holistic scores. No normalization was necessary as both tasks use the same 6-point scoring scale.

[2] https://www.kaggle.com/c/asap-aes

Group	Feature
strongly task-dependent	essay length partition word n-gram POS n-gram word n-gram
	**core concepts* **formal references* **task similarity*
weakly task-dependent	connectives commas/quotations/exclamation corpus similarity direct, indirect and reported speech formality grammar error readability subordinate, causal & temporal clauses syntactic variation topical overlap type-token-ratio word frequency word/sentence length

Table 1: List of features grouped into strongly and weakly task-dependent. Source-based features (marked with a *) are not used in our experiments.

3.2 Strongly vs. Weakly Dependent Features

Our theoretic considerations on the commonly used features show that they differ in their degree of dependence on a specific essay writing task. As not all tasks refer to a source, we exclude – for the sake of comparability – features that rely heavily on the source text, i.e. features like core concepts. We argue that set-dependent features are strongly task-dependent and most others are weakly dependent. Table 1 gives an overview of the two feature groups used in our experiments. The **full** feature set uses both strongly and weakly task-dependent features, while the **reduced** set only uses the weakly task-dependent ones.

3.3 Essay Grading System

In order to ensure a fair comparison, we re-implemented a state-of-the-art essay grading system based on DKPro TC (Daxenberger et al., 2014)[3] which ensures easy reproducibility and replicability.

Our system takes a set of graded essays and performs preprocessing using tokenization, POS-tagging, stemming, and syntactic parsing.[4] The feature extraction takes a list of features (either the **full** or **reduced** set of features) and extracts the corresponding feature values from the instances. The machine learning algorithm[5] then learns a model of essay quality from the extracted features.

In a second and independent step, the learned model is applied in order to grade essays. In the usual in-task setting (our baseline), we train on a part of the available data for a specific essay writing task and then evaluate on the held-out rest (10-fold cross validation). In our task-adaptation setting, we train the model on all the data for one task, but evaluate on another task.

For the German essays, we need to adapt some components of the system. For example, the lists of **connectives**, **causal** and **temporal** clause detection were replaced by German equivalents. The detection of **direct, indirect, and reported speech** was done following Brunner (2013). Further, **corpus similarity** was computed based on the Tiger corpus (Brants et al., 2004) instead of the Brown corpus, and the **word frequency** was calculated using the German part of Web1T. In all other aspects, the English and German setups are equal.

3.4 Evaluation Metric

Following the recommendation of the ASAP challenge, we use as evaluation metric **quadratic weighted kappa** computed as:

$$\kappa = 1 - \frac{\sum_{i,j} w_{i,j} O_{i,j}}{\sum_{i,j} w_{i,j} E_{i,j}}$$

with $O_{i,j}$ as the number of times one annotator graded j and the other i, with $E_{i,j}$ as the expected grades given a random distribution and with

$$w_{i,j} = \frac{(i-j)^2}{(N-1)^2}$$

as the weight of the grades. The metric produces a value for the agreement between the human gold standard and the machine grading.

[3]version: 0.7

[4]The preprocessing was realized with the DKPro Core 1.7.0 components used within DKPro TC: BreakIterator, TreeTagger, SnowballStemmer and StanfordParser.

[5]Support Vector Machine provided by DKPro TC

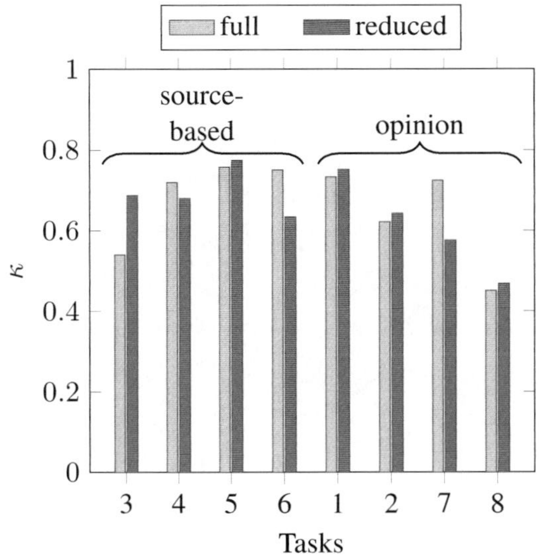

Figure 1: ASAP dataset: Comparison of the full and reduced model.

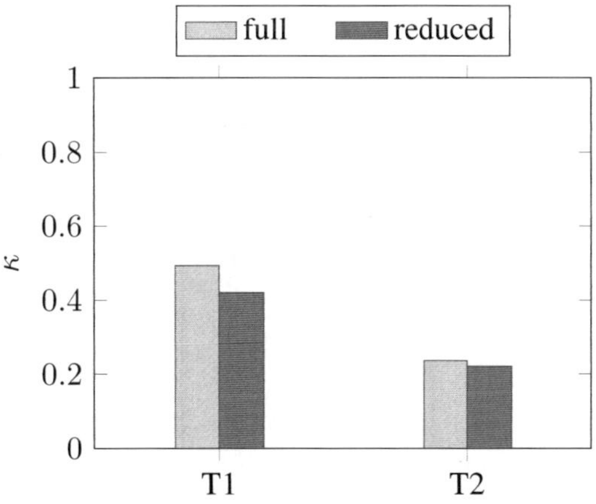

Figure 2: German dataset: Comparison of the full and reduced model

4 Results

We now report and discuss the results of our task adaptation experiments. The difference in performance will be an indicator of how well the models can be transferred from one essay set to another. We first establish the within-task results as a baseline and then compare them with the cross-task results.

4.1 Baseline: Within-Task Models

Figure 1 gives an overview of the results obtained when training a dedicated model for each task, either with the strongly task-dependent full model or the weakly task-dependent reduced model. Task8 shows very low performance due to the much smaller amount of available training data. We expected that the full model would always perform better than the reduced model, but we get a mixed picture instead. It seems that even within a task, the full feature set overfits on specific words used in the training data while they do not need to be necessarily mentioned in order to write a good essay.

Figure 2 shows the results for the German essays. The kappa values are much lower than for the English essays. This can be explained by the fact that the German tasks focus more on content issues than on language proficiency aspects, as the German essays are targeted towards university students compared to school students for the English essays. As content issues are hardly covered by our features, the results could probably be improved by adding content features like the occurrence of core concepts (see 2.2). However, for both German tasks we see the expected drop in performance when going from the full to the reduced model although it is rather small.

After having calculated the baselines, we can now transfer the models and determine the loss associated with the transfer.

4.2 Experiment: Cross-Task Models

We now examine the task-adaptivity of models by training on one task and testing on another, and then compare the result to the baseline established above.

Table 2 shows the resulting loss in performance for the full model. The table rows represent the tasks on which the model has been trained and the columns the tasks on which the trained model was tested. The average loss over all model transfers is .42, which shows that the full models do not work very well when transferred to another task.[6] For most cases, the observed behavior is symmetric, i.e. we see a similar drop when training on task 5 and testing on 4 or training on 4 and testing on 5. Though there are some remarkable exceptions. The model

[6]Note that the average loss in terms of quadratic weighted kappa is not equal the mean, as Fishers-Z transformation (Fisher, 1915) has to be performed before averaging variance ratios like quadratic weighted kappa.

		Opinion				Source-based			
		3	4	5	6	1	2	7	8
Opinion	3	-	-0.41	-0.24	-0.44	-0.42	-0.56	-0.34	-0.43
	4	-0.35	-	-0.48	-0.48	-0.35	-0.55	-0.38	-0.41
	5	-0.41	-0.47	-	-0.55	-0.13	-0.46	-0.25	-0.35
	6	-0.46	-0.59	-0.61	-	-0.43	-0.36	-0.45	-0.13
Source-based	1	-0.45	-0.60	-0.55	-0.65	-	+0.01	-0.37	-0.12
	2	-0.46	-0.60	-0.60	-0.63	-0.40	-	-0.61	-0.10
	7	-0.39	-0.49	-0.42	-0.53	-0.28	-0.19	-	-0.19
	8	-0.41	-0.53	-0.50	-0.60	-0.52	-0.24	-0.33	-

Table 2: Loss of the **full** models compared with using the tasks own model (loss >-0.3 highlighted)

		Opinion				Source-based			
		3	4	5	6	1	2	7	8
Opinion	3	-	-0.11	-0.29	-0.25	-0.66	-0.61	-0.31	-0.46
	4	-0.04	-	-0.24	-0.24	-0.67	-0.60	-0.29	-0.46
	5	-0.23	-0.18	-	+0.03	-0.54	-0.60	-0.16	-0.44
	6	-0.41	-0.34	-0.24	-	-0.39	-0.57	-0.06	-0.40
Source-based	1	-0.54	-0.43	-0.45	-0.37	-	-0.12	-0.07	-0.20
	2	-0.48	-0.40	-0.48	-0.43	-0.35	-	-0.36	-0.05
	7	-0.54	-0.39	-0.39	-0.38	-0.09	-0.28	-	-0.25
	8	-0.56	-0.49	-0.57	-0.50	-0.49	-0.25	-0.31	-

Table 3: Loss of the **reduced** models compared with using the tasks own model (loss >-0.3 highlighted)

trained on set 1 performs even better on set 2 than its own model, while training on set 2 and testing on set 1 results in a .4 drop. In addition, all source-based models (1, 2, and 7) work quite well as models for set 8 – the drop is only about .1 in all those cases. However, set 8 has relatively little training data so that this might be rather an effect of the other models being generally of higher quality than a task transfer effect.

The same procedure was carried out for the model with the reduced feature set that excludes task-dependent features. The results are shown in table 3. We see that the average loss is reduced (.36 compared to .42 for the full model) which is in line with our hypothesis that the reduced feature set should transfer better between tasks. However, the effect is not very strong when averaged over all tasks.

We also observe noticeable difference in the transferability between the groups (source-based vs. opinion tasks). Looking only within the source-based tasks the loss falls between +.03 and -.41, while for training on the opinion tasks and yields much higher losses (from -.37 to -.57). The same

	Opinion	Source-based
Opinion	-0.22	-0.46
Source-based	-0.47	-0.23

Table 4: Average loss of reduced model by task type

effect can be found for the opinion tasks (with the exceptions of set 7). In order to better see the difference, we show the average loss for each group in table 4. It is obvious that a transfer within source-based or opinion tasks works much better than across the groups. Within a group, the loss is only half as big as between groups.

We perform the same set of experiments on the German data set. The results of the full model are shown in table 5a and the results of the reduced model are shown in figure 5b. Again the losses of the reduced model are much smaller than of the full model confirming our results on the English dataset.

5 Conclusion

In this work, we investigated the research question to what extend supervised models for automatic essay

	T1	T2
T1	-	-0.15
T2	-0.47	-

(a) Full

	T1	T2
T1	-	-0.07
T2	-0.28	-

(b) Reduced

Table 5: Loss on the German dataset

grading can be transferred from one task to another. We discussed a wide range of features commonly used for essay grading regarding their task dependence and found that they can be categorized into strongly and weakly task-dependent. Our hypothesis was that the latter model should transfer better between tasks. In order to test that, we implemented a state-of-the-art essay grading system for English and German and examined the task transferability by comparing the baseline performance (training on the actual task) with the models trained on the other tasks. We found, consistent with our hypothesis, that the reduced models performed better on average. The transfer worked even better if the underlying tasks are similar in terms of being source-based or opinionated. The fact that the losses on average are still quite high raises the question of whether a more fine-grained discrimination of features is necessary or whether models for essay grading can be transferred at all.

In future work we plan to further investigate the connection of task attributes to their task-transferability (e.g. the language proficiency level of participants or differences in the task description). In addition, we think that there are facets of quality that are independent of tasks, like the complexity of essays. Grading essays not only holistically, but according to facets is likely to transfer better between tasks and at the same time provides teachers with reliable sub-scores that may support their decisions without the demand of training data.

References

Yigal Attali and Jill Burstein. 2006. Automated essay scoring with e-rater® v. 2. *The Journal of Technology, Learning and Assessment*, 4(3).

Sabine Bergler. 2006. Conveying attitude with reported speech. In *Computing attitude and affect in text: Theory and applications*, pages 11–22. Springer.

Thorsten Brants and Alex Franz. 2006. Web 1t 5-gram corpus version 1.1. *Google Inc.*

Sabine Brants, Stefanie Dipper, Peter Eisenberg, Silvia Hansen-Schirra, Esther König, Wolfgang Lezius, Christian Rohrer, George Smith, and Hans Uszkoreit. 2004. Tiger: Linguistic interpretation of a german corpus. *Research on Language and Computation*, 2(4):597–620.

Hunter M Breland, Robert J Jones, Laura Jenkins, Marion Paynter, Judith Pollack, and Y Fai Fong. 1994. The college board vocabulary study. *ETS Research Report Series*, 1994(1):i–51.

Annelen Brunner. 2013. Automatic recognition of speech, thought, and writing representation in german narrative texts. *Literary and linguistic computing*, 28(4):563–575.

Jill Burstein and Martin Chodorow. 1999. Automated essay scoring for nonnative english speakers. In *Proceedings of a Symposium on Computer Mediated Language Assessment and Evaluation in Natural Language Processing*, pages 68–75. Association for Computational Linguistics.

Jill Burstein, Karen Kukich, Susanne Wolff, Chi Lu, Martin Chodorow, Lisa Braden-Harder, and Mary Dee Harris. 1998. Automated scoring using a hybrid feature identification technique. In *Proceedings of the 17th international conference on Computational linguistics-Volume 1*, pages 206–210. Association for Computational Linguistics.

Jill Burstein, Claudia Leacock, and Richard Swartz. 2001. *Automated evaluation of essays and short answers*. Loughborough University Press.

Hongbo Chen and Ben He. 2013. Automated essay scoring by maximizing human-machine agreement. In *EMNLP*, pages 1741–1752.

Johannes Daxenberger, Oliver Ferschke, Iryna Gurevych, and Torsten Zesch. 2014. Dkpro tc: A java-based framework for supervised learning experiments on textual data. In *Proceedings of 52nd Annual Meeting of the Association for Computational Linguistics: System Demonstrations*, pages 61–66, Baltimore, Maryland, June. Association for Computational Linguistics.

Semire Dikli. 2006. An overview of automated scoring of essays. *The Journal of Technology, Learning and Assessment*, 5(1).

Ronald A Fisher. 1915. Frequency distribution of the values of the correlation coefficient in samples from an indefinitely large population. *Biometrika*, pages 507–521.

Peter W Foltz, Darrell Laham, and Thomas K Landauer. 1999. Automated essay scoring: Applications to educational technology. In *World Conference on Educational Multimedia, Hypermedia and Telecommunications*, volume 1999, pages 939–944.

Francis Heylighen and Jean-Marc Dewaele. 2002. Variation in the contextuality of language: An empirical measure. *Foundations of Science*, 7(3):293–340.

Ralf Krestel, Sabine Bergler, René Witte, et al. 2008. Minding the source: Automatic tagging of reported speech in newspaper articles. *Reporter*, 1(5):4.

Chi-Un Lei, Ka Lok Man, and TO Ting. 2014. Using learning analytics to analyze writing skills of students: A case study in a technological common core curriculum course. *IAENG International Journal of Computer Science*, 41(3).

Manvi Mahana, Mishel Johns, and Ashwin Apte. 2012. Automated essay grading using machine learning. *Mach. Learn. Session, Stanford University*.

Mitchell P Marcus, Mary Ann Marcinkiewicz, and Beatrice Santorini. 1993. Building a large annotated corpus of english: The penn treebank. *Computational linguistics*, 19(2):313–330.

Douglas R McCallum and James L Peterson. 1982. Computer-based readability indexes. In *Proceedings of the ACM'82 Conference*, pages 44–48. ACM.

G Harry McLaughlin. 1969. Smog grading: A new readability formula. *Journal of reading*, 12(8):639–646.

Robert Östling. 2013. Automated essay scoring for swedish. In *Proceedings of the Eighth Workshop on Innovative Use of NLP for Building Educational Applications*, pages 42–47.

Mark D Shermis and Jill C Burstein. 2002. *Automated essay scoring: A cross-disciplinary perspective*. Routledge.

Malcolm Smith and Richard Taffler. 1992. Readability and understandability: Different measures of the textual complexity of accounting narrative. *Accounting, Auditing & Accountability Journal*, 5(4):0–0.

Salvatore Valenti, Francesca Neri, and Alessandro Cucchiarelli. 2003. An overview of current research on automated essay grading. *Journal of Information Technology Education: Research*, 2(1):319–330.

Mann William and Sandra Thompson. 1988. Rhetorical structure theory: Towards a functional theory of text organization. *Text*, 8(3):243–281.

Using Learner Data to Improve Error Correction in Adjective–Noun Combinations

Ekaterina Kochmar
Alta Institute
Computer Laboratory
University of Cambridge
ek358@cl.cam.ac.uk

Ted Briscoe
Alta Institute
Computer Laboratory
University of Cambridge
ejb@cl.cam.ac.uk

Abstract

This paper presents a novel approach to error correction in content words in learner writing focussing on adjective–noun (AN) combinations. We show how error patterns can be used to improve the performance of the error correction system, and demonstrate that our approach is capable of suggesting an appropriate correction within the top two alternatives in half of the cases and within top 10 alternatives in 71% of the cases, performing with an MRR of 0.5061. We then integrate our error correction system with a state-of-the-art content word error detection system and discuss the results.

1 Introduction

The task of error detection and correction (EDC) on non-native texts, as well as research on learner language in general, has attracted much attention recently (Leacock et al., 2014; Ng et al., 2014; Ng et al., 2013; Dale et al., 2012). The field has been dominated by EDC for grammatical errors and errors in the use of articles and prepositions (Ng et al., 2013; Rozovskaya and Roth, 2011; Chodorow et al., 2010; Gamon et al., 2008; Brockett et al., 2006; Han et al., 2006).

More recently, however, the need to address other error types has been recognised (Kochmar and Briscoe, 2014; Ng et al., 2014; Rozovskaya et al., 2014; Sawai et al., 2013; Dahlmeier and Ng, 2011). Among these, errors in content words are the third most frequent error type after errors in articles and prepositions (Leacock et al., 2014; Ng et al., 2014).

The correct use of content words is notoriously hard for language learners to master, while importance of the correct word choice for successful writing has long been recognised (Leacock and Chodorow, 2003; Johnson, 2000; Santos, 1988).

The major difficulty is that correct word choice is not governed by any strictly defined rules: native speakers know that *powerful computer* is preferred over *strong computer*, while *strong tea* is preferred over *powerful tea* (Leacock et al., 2014), but language learners often find themselves unsure of how to choose an appropriate word. As a result, they often confuse words that are similar in meaning or spelling, overuse words with general meaning, or select words based on their L1s (Kochmar and Briscoe, 2014; Dahlmeier and Ng, 2011).

Previous work on EDC for content words has also demonstrated that since these error types are substantially different from errors with function words, they require different approaches. The most widely adopted approach to EDC for function words relies on availability of finite confusion sets. The task can then be cast as multi-class classification with the number of classes equal to the number of possible alternatives. Detection and correction can be done simultaneously: if the alternative chosen by the classifier is different from the original word, this is flagged as an error. However, content word errors cannot be defined in terms of a general and finite set of confusion pairs, and the set of alternatives in each case depends on the choice of original word. Moreover, it has been argued that error detection for content words should be performed independently from error correction (Kochmar and Briscoe, 2014).

Proceedings of the Tenth Workshop on Innovative Use of NLP for Building Educational Applications, 2015, pages 233–242,
Denver, Colorado, June 4, 2015.

In this work, we focus on error correction in content words and, in particular, investigate error correction in adjective–noun (AN) combinations using several publicly-available learner error datasets for this type of construction. At the same time, we believe that a similar approach can be applied to other types of content word combinations. Specifically, we make the following contributions:

1. We explore different ways to construct the correction sets and to rank the alternatives with respect to their appropriateness. We report the coverage of different resources and assess the ranked lists of suggestions.

2. We show that learner text is a useful source of possible corrections for content words. In addition, we demonstrate how error patterns extracted from learner text can be used to improve the ranking of the alternatives.

3. We present an EDC system for AN combinations which compares favourably to the previous published approaches of which we are aware.

4. We explore the usefulness of self-propagating for an error correction system.

2 Related work

Leacock *et al.* (2014) note that the usual approach to EDC in content words relies on the idea of comparing the writer's choice to possible alternatives, so that if any of the alternatives score higher than the original combination then the original combination is flagged as a possible error and one or more alternatives are suggested as possible corrections. The performance of an EDC algorithm that uses this approach depends on:

- the choice of the source of alternatives;

- the choice of the metric for ranking the alternatives.

The source of alternatives defines the *coverage* of the error correction algorithm, while the *quality* of the system suggestions depends on the choice of an appropriate metric for ranking the alternatives.

Early work on EDC for content words (Wible et al., 2003; Shei and Pain, 2000) relied on the use of reference databases of known learner errors and their corrections. While such approaches can achieve good quality, they cannot provide good coverage.

Previous research considered semantically related confusions between content words as the most frequent type of confusion in learner writing and used WordNet (Miller, 1995), dictionaries and thesauri to search for alternatives (Östling and Knutsson, 2009; Futagi et al., 2008; Shei and Pain, 2000). Since these resources cannot cover alternatives that are not semantically related to the original words, other resources have been considered as well: for example, Dahlmeier and Ng (2011) consider spelling alternatives and homophones as possible corrections.

L1-specific confusions have been reported to cover a substantial portion of errors in content words for some groups of language learners (Chang et al., 2008; Liu, 2002), and some previous EDC approaches have considered using parallel corpora and bilingual dictionaries to generate and rank alternatives (Dahlmeier and Ng, 2011; Chang et al., 2008). L1-specific approaches have shown the best results in EDC for content words so far, but it should be noted that their success relies on availability of high-quality L1-specific resources which is hard to guarantee for the full variety of learner L1s.

At the same time, good performance demonstrated by L1-specific approaches shows the importance of taking learner background into consideration. In contrast to the other resources like WordNet and thesauri, which can only cover confusions between words in the L2, use of parallel corpora and bilingual dictionaries gives access to the types of confusions which cannot be captured by any L2 resources. Learner corpora and databases of text revisions can be used to similar effect.

For example, Rozovskaya and Roth (2011) show that performance of an EDC algorithm applied to articles and prepositions can be improved if the classifier uses L1-specific priors, with the priors being set using the distribution of confusion pairs in learner texts. Sawai *et al.* (2013) show that an EDC system that uses a large learner corpus to extract confusion sets outperforms systems that use WordNet and roundtrip translations. Madnani and Cahill (2014) use a corpus of Wikipedia revisions containing annotated errors in the use of prepositions and their corrections to improve the ranking of the suggestions.

Finally, we note that a number of previous approaches to errors in content words have combined error detection and correction, flagging an original choice as an error if an EDC algorithm is able to find a more frequent or fluent combination (Östling and Knutsson, 2009; Chang et al., 2008; Futagi et al., 2008; Shei and Pain, 2000), while some focussed on error correction only (Dahlmeier and Ng, 2011; Liu et al., 2009). Kochmar and Briscoe (2014) argue that error detection and correction should be performed separately. They show that an EDC algorithm is prone to overcorrection, flagging originally correct combinations as errors, if error detection is dependent on the set of alternatives and if some of these alternatives are judged to be more fluent than the original combination.

We follow Kochmar and Briscoe (2014) and treat error detection and error correction in content words as separate steps. We focus on the correction step, and first implement a simple error correction algorithm that replicates previous approaches to EDC for content words. We believe that performance of this algorithm on our data reflects the state-of-the-art in content error correction. Next, we show how learner data and distribution of confusion pairs can be used to improve the performance of this algorithm.

3 Data

In our experiments, we use three publicly-available datasets of learner errors in AN combinations: the AN dataset extracted from the *Cambridge Learner Corpus* (*CLC*)[1] and annotated with respect to the learner errors in the choice of adjectives and nouns;[2] the AN dataset extracted from the CLC-FCE dataset;[3] and the set of errors in ANs that we have extracted for the purposes of this work from the training and development sets used in the CoNLL-2014 Shared Task on Grammatical Error Correction.[4] We discuss these datasets below.

3.1 Annotated dataset

We use the dataset of AN combinations released by Kochmar and Briscoe (2014). This dataset presents typical learner errors in the use of 61 adjectives that are most problematic for language learners. The examples are annotated with respect to the types of errors committed in the use of adjectives and nouns, and corrections are provided.

Kochmar and Briscoe note that learners often confuse semantically related words (e.g., synonyms, near-synonyms, hypo-/hypernyms). Examples (1) and (2) from Kochmar and Briscoe (2014) illustrate the confusion between the adjective *big* and semantically similar adjectives *large* and *great*:

(1) *big*/large* quantity

(2) *big*/great* importance

In addition, in Kochmar and Briscoe (2014) we note that the adjectives with quite general meaning like *big*, *large* and *great* are often overused by language learners instead of more specific ones, as is illustrated by examples (3) to (6):

(3) *big*/long* history

(4) *bigger*/wider* variety

(5) *greatest*/highest* revenue

(6) *large*/broad* knowledge

Words that seem to be similar in form (either related morphologically or through similar pronunciation) are also often confused by learners. Examples (7) and (8) illustrate this type of confusions:

(7) *classic*/classical* dance

(8) *economical*/economic* crisis

The dataset contains 798 annotated AN combinations, with 340 unique errors.

Table 1 presents the statistics on the error types detected in this dataset. The majority of the errors

[1] http://www.cup.cam.ac.uk/gb/elt/catalogue/subject/custom/item3646603/Cambridge-International-Corpus-Cambridge-Learner-Corpus/

[2] http://ilexir.co.uk/media/an-dataset.xml

[3] http://ilexir.co.uk/applications/adjective-noun-dataset/

[4] http://www.comp.nus.edu.sg/~nlp/conll14st.html

Error type	Distribution
S	56.18%
F	25.88%
N	17.94%

Table 1: Distribution of error types in the annotated dataset.

Word	**Ann. data**	**CLC-FCE**	**NUCLE**
A	63.24%	43.20%	34.15%
N	30.29%	52.63%	60.16%
Both	6.47%	4.17%	5.69%

Table 2: Distribution of errors in the choice of adjectives (A), nouns (N) or both words in the datasets.

involve semantically related words (type S). Form-related confusions occur in 25.88% of the cases (type F); while 17.94% are annotated as errors committed due to other reasons (type N), possibly related to learners' L1s.

3.2 CLC-FCE dataset

The CLC-FCE AN dataset is extracted from the publicly-available CLC-FCE subset of the CLC released by Yannakoudakis *et al.* (2011). The CLC error coding (Nicholls, 2003) has been used to extract the correctly used ANs and those that are annotated as errors due to inappropriate choice of an adjective or/and noun, but the error subtypes for the AN errors are not further specified. We have extracted 456 combinations that have adjective–noun combinations as corrections.

3.3 NUCLE dataset

We have also used the training and development sets from the CoNLL-2014 Shared Task on Grammatical Error Correction (Ng et al., 2014) to extract the incorrect AN combinations. The data for the shared task has been extracted from the *NUCLE* corpus, the *NUS Corpus of Learner English* (Dahlmeier et al., 2013). Unlike the other two datasets it represents a smaller range of L1s, and similarly to the CLC-FCE dataset the errors are not further annotated with respect to their subtypes.

We have preprocessed the data using the RASP parser (Briscoe et al., 2006), and used the error annotation provided to extract the AN combinations that contain errors in the choice of either one or both words. Additionally, we have also checked that the suggested corrections are represented by AN combinations. The extracted dataset contains 369 ANs.

Table 2 reports the distribution of the errors with respect to the incorrect choice of an adjective, noun or both words within AN combinations in all three datasets.

4 Error Correction Algorithm

First, we implement a basic error correction algorithm that replicates the previous approaches to error correction overviewed in §2, and investigate the following aspects of the algorithm:

1. We explore different resources to retrieve alternatives for the adjectives and nouns within incorrect ANs and report the coverage of these resources;
2. The alternative ANs are generated by crossing the sets of alternatives for the individual words, and ranked using a metric assessing AN frequency or fluency in native English. We assess the quality of the ranking using *mean reciprocal rank* (*MRR*) by comparing the system suggestions to the gold standard corrections;
3. Finally, we also show how the confusion sets extracted from the learner data can help improve the ranking and the quality of the suggested corrections.

When reporting the results, we specifically focus on two aspects of the error correction algorithm: the *coverage* estimated as the proportion of gold standard corrections that can be found in any of the resources considered, and the ability of the algorithm to rank the more appropriate corrections higher than the less appropriate ones measured by *MRR* of the gold standard corrections in the system output.

4.1 Word alternatives

We extract word alternatives using three resources:

1. We use the notion of Levenshtein distance (henceforth, Lv) (Levenshtein, 1966) to find the words that learners might have accidentally confused or misspelled. These alternatives can cover errors annotated as form related. To avoid introducing too much change

to the original words, we only consider alternatives that differ from the original words by no more than $1/3$ of the characters in the original word and that start with the same letter as the original word. The generated alternatives are checked against the *British National Corpus (BNC)*[5] and the *ukWaC* corpus[6] to avoid generating non-words. This allows the algorithm to find alternatives like *customer* for *costumer* (in **important costumer*), *metropolis* for *metropole* (in **whole metropole*), or *electronic* for *electric* (in **electric society*).

2. We look for further alternatives in WordNet (henceforth, `WN`) (Miller, 1995), which has previously been widely used to find semantically related words. For each original noun, we extract a set of synonyms and hypo-/hypernyms. For each original adjective, we extract synonyms and the adjectives related via the `WN` relation *similar-to*. This allows us to cover semantically related confusions, and find alternatives such as *luck* for *fate* (in **good fate*) and *steep* for *heavy* (in **heavy decline*).

3. Both `Lv` and `WN` cover confusions that occur in L2, but none of them can cover confusions that occur due to L1-transfer. Therefore, we extract the corrections provided by the annotators in the *Cambridge Learner Corpus* (henceforth, `CLC`). This approach is similar to that of Madnani and Cahill (2014), but it uses learner data as the database. We believe that the confusion pairs extracted this way cover a substantial portion of errors committed due to L1-transfer, while, computationally, it is much less expensive than the use of bilingual dictionaries or parallel corpora as in Dahlmeier and Ng (2011) or Chang *et al.* (2008). This approach allows us to extract confusion pairs that are covered by the `CLC` only, for example, *novel* for *roman* (in **historical roman*), *narrow*, *short* and *brief* for *small* (in **small interruption*) or *big*, *high* and *loud* for *strong* (in **strong noise*).

[5]http://www.natcorp.ox.ac.uk

[6]http://wacky.sslmit.unibo.it/doku.php?id=corpora

Setting	Ann. data	CLC-FCE	NUCLE
Lv	0.1588	0.0833	0.0897
WN	0.4353	0.3904	0.2880
CLC	0.7912	0.8684	0.5625
CLC+Lv	0.7971	0.8706	0.5951
CLC+WN	0.8558	0.8904	0.6141
All	**0.8618**	**0.8925**	**0.6467**

Table 3: Coverage of different sets of alternatives.

We assess how many of the gold standard corrections can be found in each of these confusion sets as well as in different combinations of these sets. Coverage of the different resources is reported in Table 3. We note that the `CLC` as a single source of corrections provides the highest coverage: for example, 79% of erroneous ANs from the annotated dataset and 87% of erroneous ANs in the CLC-FCE can potentially be corrected using only the previous corrections for the content words from the CLC. We note that although the ANs in the annotated dataset have been extracted from the CLC, they have been error-annotated independently. The lower figure of 56% on the NUCLE dataset can be explained by the difference between the CLC and NUCLE corpora since the distribution of errors in these corpora is also different (see Table 2). Nevertheless, we note that the corrections extracted from the CLC still cover a substantial amount of the errors in the NUCLE dataset. A combination of the corrections from the CLC and semantically related words from WordNet covers an additional 6% of ANs in the annotated dataset, 5% in the NUCLE dataset, and 2% in the CLC-FCE dataset, which demonstrates that the majority of the semantically related confusions are already covered by the corrections extracted from the CLC, so WordNet improves the coverage of this resource only marginally. Addition of the form related words (`Lv`) does not improve coverage significantly.

4.2 Alternative ANs ranking

Once the alternatives for the words within the combinations are collected, the alternative AN combinations are generated by the Cartesian product of the sets of alternatives for the adjectives and the nouns. The alternatives then need to be ranked with respect to their appropriateness.

We apply two simple methods to rank the alternatives: we use the frequency of the generated ANs in a combined BNC and ukWaC corpus, and we also measure collocational strength of the alternative combinations using *normalised pointwise mutual information* (*NPMI*) since PMI-based metrics have been widely used before (see §2):

$$NPMI(AN) = \frac{PMI(AN)}{-log_2(P(AN))} \quad (1)$$

where

$$PMI(AN) = log_2 \frac{P(AN)}{P(A)P(N)} \quad (2)$$

We have noticed that when the full sets of alternatives for the adjectives and nouns are used to generate the AN alternatives, the resulting sets of ANs contain many combinations, with both original words changed to alternative suggestions, that are dissimilar in meaning to the original ANs while often being quite frequent or fluent. As a result, such alternatives are ranked higher than the appropriate corrections. To avoid this, we only consider the alternative ANs where one of the original words is kept unchanged, i.e.:

$\{alternative\ ANs\} = (\{alternative\ adjs\} \times noun) \cup (adj \times \{alternative\ nouns\})$

We evaluate the ranking using the *mean reciprocal rank* (*MRR*):

$$MRR = \frac{1}{|N|} \sum_{i=1}^{|N|} \frac{1}{rank_i} \quad (3)$$

where N is the total number of erroneous ANs considered by our algorithm. *MRR* shows how high the gold standard alternative is ranked in the whole set of alternatives provided.

The results are reported in the upper half of the Table 4. We note that often the wider sets of alternatives for the individual words yield lower ranks for the gold standard corrections since some other frequent AN alternatives are ranked higher by the algorithm.

4.3 Exploitation of confusion probabilities

Next, we consider a novel approach to ranking the alternative ANs. Since we are using the CLC corrections for the adjectives and nouns within the ANs, in addition to the possible corrections themselves we can also use the confusion probabilities – probabilities associated with the words used as corrections given the incorrect word choice – for the pairs of words that we extract from the CLC.

Setting	Ann. set	CLC-FCE	NUCLE
$\texttt{CLC}_{freq}$	**0.3806**	0.3121	0.2275
$\texttt{CLC}_{NPMI}$	0.3752	0.2904	0.1961
$(\texttt{CLC+Lv})_{freq}$	0.3686	**0.3146**	**0.2510**
$(\texttt{CLC+Lv})_{NPMI}$	0.3409	0.2695	0.1977
$(\texttt{CLC+WN})_{freq}$	0.3500	0.2873	0.2267
$(\texttt{CLC+WN})_{NPMI}$	0.3286	0.2552	0.1908
$\texttt{All}_{freq}$	0.3441	0.2881	0.2468
$\texttt{All}_{NPMI}$	0.3032	0.2407	0.1943
$\texttt{All}_{\mathbf{freq'}}$	**0.5061**	**0.4509**	**0.2913**
$\texttt{All}_{\mathbf{NPMI'}}$	0.4843	0.4316	0.2118

Table 4: *MRR* for the alternatives ranking.

We use a refined formula to rank the possible corrections:

$$\begin{aligned} M' = M & \times CP(a_{orig} \to a_{alt}) \\ & \times CP(n_{orig} \to n_{alt}) \end{aligned} \quad (4)$$

where M is the measure for ranking the alternatives (frequency or *NPMI*, as before), and CP is the confusion probability of using the alternative word (possible correction) instead of the original one (error) estimated from the examples in the CLC. We set $CP(a/n_{orig} \to a/n_{orig})$ to 1.0.

For instance, consider an incorrect AN **big enjoyment* and its gold standard correction *great pleasure*. Table 5 shows some alternatives for the words *big* and *enjoyment* with the corresponding corrections and their probabilities extracted from the CLC. If we use these sets of confusion pairs to generate the alternative ANs and rank them with raw frequency, the algorithm will choose *great fun* (7759 in the native corpus) over the gold standard correction *great pleasure* (2829 in the native corpus). However, if we use the confusion probabilities with the new measure (4) the gold standard correction *great pleasure* ($Freq' = 3.8212$) will be ranked higher than *great fun* ($Freq' = 1.1620$). The new measure helps take into account not only the fluency of the correction in the native data but also the appropriateness of a

Original	Alternatives	CP(orig → alt)
big	*great*	0.0144
	large	0.0141
	wide	0.0043
	...	...
	significant	$5.1122 * 10^{-5}$
enjoyment	*pleasure*	0.0938
	entertainment	0.0313
	fun	0.0104
	happiness	0.0052

Table 5: CLC confusion pairs

particular correction given a learner error.

In addition, this algorithm allows us to consider both words as possibly incorrectly chosen: equation (4) ensures that the alternative combinations where both original words are changed are only ranked higher if they are both very frequent in the native corpus and very likely as a confusion pair since $CP(a/n_{orig} \rightarrow a/n_{orig})$ is set to 1.0.

Finally, if no confusion pairs are found for either an adjective or a noun in the CLC, the algorithm considers the alternatives from other resources and uses standard measures to rank them.

The lower half of Table 4 presents the results of this novel algorithm and compares them to the previous results from §4.2. The new metric consistently improves performance across all three datasets, with the difference in the results being significant at the 0.05 level.

5 Discussion

5.1 Analysis of the results

An *MRR* of 0.4509 and 0.5061 reported in §4.3 implies that for a high number of the ANs from the CLC-FCE and annotated dataset the gold standard correction is ranked first or second in the list of all possible corrections considered by the system. Table 6 presents the breakdown of the results and reports the proportion of ANs for which the gold standard correction is covered by the top N alternatives.

We note the small difference between the number of cases covered by the top 10 system alternatives for the annotated dataset (71.18%) and the upper bound – the total number of corrections that can potentially be found by the system (74.71%)

Top N	Ann. data	CLC-FCE	NUCLE
1	41.18	34.21	21.20
2	49.12	45.18	27.99
3	56.77	50.88	33.70
4	61.77	55.04	38.04
5	65.29	58.55	40.49
6	66.18	61.40	42.39
7	67.35	62.28	43.21
8	68.53	63.60	44.29
9	69.71	65.35	45.38
10	71.18	66.45	46.20
Not found	25.29	19.96	48.64

Table 6: Results breakdown: % of errors covered.

Type	S	F	N
MRR_{found}	0.6007	0.8486	0.6507
Not found	0.1990	0.1705	0.5410

Table 7: Subtype error analysis for the annotated dataset.

– which shows that the system reaches its potential around the top 10 suggestions. These results also compare favourably to those reported in previous research (Chang et al., 2008; Dahlmeier and Ng, 2011), although direct comparison is not possible due to the differences in the data used.

We also further investigate the performance of the error correction algorithm on the different error subtypes in the annotated dataset (see Table 1). Table 7 presents the proportion of the gold standard corrections for each subtype that are not found by the algorithm, as well as the *MRR* for those corrections that are identified. We see that the highest proportion of gold standard corrections that are not found by the algorithm are the corrections that are not related to the originally used words (type N). This result is not surprising: if the original words and their corrections are not related semantically or in form, it is hard to find the appropriate suggestions. The results also suggest that the system performs best on the errors of type F: a possible reason for this is that errors of this type are more systematic and have smaller confusion sets. For example, the average *MRR* on the set of ANs involving errors in the use of the adjective *elder* in the annotated dataset is 0.875 since most often such ANs require changing

Corpus	MRR_{adj}	MRR_{noun}
Ann	0.5188	0.4312
CLC	0.3986	0.4665
NUCLE	0.3191	0.2608

Table 8: Average *MRR* on the sets of ANs with the errors in the choice of adjectives and nouns.

Setting	Ann. set	CLC-FCE	NUCLE
`CLC`	0.3806	0.3121	0.2275
`CLC+Lv`	0.3686	0.3146	0.2510
`Augm`	**0.4420**	**0.3533**	**0.2614**

Table 9: Augmented sets of alternatives.

the adjective for form related alternatives *elderly* or *older*.

At the same time, we note that the results on the NUCLE dataset are lower than on the two other datasets. In Table 3 we report that about 35% of the gold standard corrections from this dataset are not covered by any of the available sets of alternatives for adjectives and nouns, while the confusion sets extracted from the CLC can only cover about 56% of the cases. We conclude that there might be a substantial difference between the two learner corpora in terms of topics, vocabulary used, learner levels and the distribution of the L1s. We assume that a high number of errors in NUCLE dataset can be caused by reasons other than semantic or form similarity of the words in L2. For example, our system does not suggest the gold standard correction *bill* for **debt* in **medical debt*, or *infrastructural* for **architectural* in **architectural development* because these suggestions are not originally covered by any of the sets of alternatives, including the set of confusion pairs extracted from the CLC.

Table 8 reports the average *MRR* on the sets of ANs involving errors in the choice of adjectives and nouns separately. The NUCLE dataset contains ANs with 105 adjectives and 185 nouns, with 76 adjectives and 145 nouns occurring in the NUCLE ANs only. The low overlap between the sets of individual words explains the differences in performance. Since the annotated dataset contains ANs within a set of frequent adjectives, the algorithm achieves highest performance in correcting adjective-specific errors in this dataset.

5.2 Augmenting sets of alternatives

We investigate whether self-propagation of the system can mitigate the problem of gold standard suggestions not covered by the original sets of alternatives. Some previous research (Shei and Pain, 2000; Chang et al., 2008) has suggested that if an error correction system is implemented in an interactive way, learners can be asked to accept the suggested corrections so that the error–correction pairs can be added to the error database for future reference. We add the gold standard suggestions for the adjectives and nouns from all three datasets to the sets of alternatives and run our error correction system using the augmented sets. For example, we add *bill* to the set of alternatives for *debt* and *infrastructural* to the set of alternatives for *architectural* and check whether the results of the error correction system improve.

Table 9 reports the results. Since we focus on the effect of the sets of alternatives, we run the experiments using one setting of the system only. We note that, since the datasets contain only a few examples for each adjective and noun, we cannot expect to see a significant change in the results if we updated the confusion probabilities and used the refined measure from §4.3. Therefore, we rank the AN alternatives using frequency of occurrence in the corpus of native English. For ease of comparison, we copy the relevant results from Table 4.

The best results obtained in experiments in §4.2 with the original sets of alternatives are underlined, while the results obtained with the augmented sets of alternatives are marked in bold. We note that the results improve, although the difference is not statistically significant across the three datasets.

5.3 Error Detection and Correction System

Finally, we combine the error correction algorithm from §4.3 with the error detection algorithm from Kochmar and Briscoe (2014): the error correction algorithm is applied to the set of erroneous ANs correctly detected by the error detection algorithm.

In Kochmar and Briscoe (2014) we report precision of 0.6850 and recall of 0.5849 on the incorrect examples in the annotated dataset. Some of the errors identified cannot be further corrected by our algorithm since the corrections are longer than two words. MRR of the error correction system applied to the set of detected errors is 0.2532, while for 24.28% of the cases the system does not find a gold standard correction. If these cases are not considered, $MRR_{found} = 0.6831$. We believe that these results reflect state-of-the-art performance for the combined EDC system for AN combinations.

6 Conclusion

In this paper, we have addressed error correction in adjective–noun combinations in learner writing using three publicly available datasets. In particular, we have explored different ways to construct the correction sets and to rank the suggested corrections, and showed that the confusion patterns extracted directly from the learner data not only provide the highest coverage for the system, but can also be used to derive confusion probabilities and improve the overall ranking of the suggestions. We have shown that an error correction system can reach an *MRR* of 0.5061 which compares favourably to the results reported previously.

Further analysis shows that the majority of errors not covered by the algorithm involve confusion between words that are not related semantically or in form and, therefore, cannot be found in L2 resources like WordNet. Our experiments with the augmented sets of alternatives, where we use known learner confusion pairs to further extend the sets of correction candidates, show improvement in the results and suggest that extension of the learner corpus can help system find appropriate corrections. At the same time, the difference in the results obtained on the datasets extracted from the CLC and the NUCLE corpora can be explained by the difference in the topics, learner levels and L1s represented by the two learner corpora. Future research should explore further ways to extend the learner data.

We also note that in the current work we do not consider the wider context for error detection and correction in ANs. In future work we plan to investigate the use of surrounding context for EDC for ANs.

Finally, we have integrated our error correction system with a state-of-the-art content word error detection system. To the best of our knowledge, this is the first attempt to combine two such systems, and we believe that the results obtained – an *MRR* of 0.2532 on the set of errors identified by the error detection algorithm – reflect state-of-the-art performance on the EDC task for AN combinations. Our future work will also extend this approach to other types of content word combinations.

Acknowledgments

We are grateful to Cambridge English Language Assessment and Cambridge University Press for supporting this research and for granting us access to the CLC for research purposes. We also thank the anonymous reviewers for their valuable comments.

References

Ted Briscoe, John Carroll, and Rebecca Watson. 2006. *The second release of the RASP system.* In ACL-Coling06 Interactive Presentation Session, pp. 77–80.

Chris Brockett, William B. Dolan, and Michael Gamon. 2006. *Correcting ESL errors using phrasal SMT techniques.* In Proceedings of the 21st International Conference on Computational Linguistics and the 44th annual meeting of the Association for Computational Linguistics, pp. 249–256.

Yu-Chia Chang, Jason S. Chang, Hao-Jan Chen, and Hsien-Chin Liou. 2008. *An automatic collocation writing assistant for Taiwanese EFL learners: A case of corpus-based NLP technology.* Computer Assisted Language Learning, 21(3), pp. 283–299.

Martin Chodorow, Michael Gamon, and Joel Tetreault. 2010. *The utility of grammatical error detection systems for English language learners: Feedback and Assessment.* Language Testing, 27(3):335–353.

Daniel Dahlmeier, Hwee Tou Ng, and Siew Mei Wu. 2012. *Building a large annotated corpus of learner English: The NUS Corpus of Learner English.* In Proceedings of the Eighth Workshop on Innovative Use of NLP for Building Educational Applications, pp. 22–31.

Daniel Dahlmeier and Hwee Tou Ng. 2011. *Correcting Semantic Collocation Errors with L1-induced Paraphrases.* In Proceedings of the EMNLP-2011, pp. 107–117.

Robert Dale, Ilya Anisimoff, and George Narroway. 2012. *HOO 2012: A Report on the Preposition and Determiner Error Correction Shared Task.* In Proceedings of the 7th Workshop on the Innovative Use of NLP for Building Educational Applications, pp. 54–62.

Yoko Futagi, Paul Deane, Martin Chodorow and Joel Tetreault. 2009. *A computational approach to detecting collocation errors in the writing of non-native speakers of English.* Computer Assisted Language Learning, 21(4), pp. 353–367.

Michael Gamon, Jianfeng Gao, Chris Brockett, Alexander Klementiev, William Dolan, Dmitriy Be- lenko, and Lucy Vanderwende. 2008. *Using contextual speller techniques and language modeling for ESL error correction.* In Proceedings of IJCNLP, pp. 491–511.

Na-Rae Han, Martin Chodorow, and Claudia Leacock. 2006. *Detecting errors in English article usage by non-native speakers.* Journal of Natural Language Engineering, 12(2):115–129.

Dale D. Johnson. 2000. *Just the Right Word: Vocabulary and Writing.* In R. Indrisano & J. Squire (Eds.), *Perspectives on Writing: Research, Theory, and Practice*, pp. 162–186.

Ekaterina Kochmar and Ted Briscoe. 2014. *Detecting Learner Errors in the Choice of Content Words Using Compositional Distributional Semantics.* In Proceedings of COLING 2014, the 25th International Conference on Computational Linguistics: Technical Papers, pp. 1740–1751.

Claudia Leacock and Martin Chodorow. 2003. *Automated Grammatical Error Detection.* In M. D. Shermis and J. C. Burstein (eds.), *Automated Essay Scoring: A Cross-Disciplinary Perspective*, pp. 195–207.

Claudia Leacock, Martin Chodorow, Michael Gamon and Joel Tetreault. 2014. *Automated Grammatical Error Detection for Language Learners*, Second Edition. Synthesis Lectures on Human Language Technologies, Morgan & Claypool Publishers.

Vladimir I. Levenshtein. 1966. *Binary codes capable of correcting deletions, insertions, and reversals.* Soviet Physics Doklady, 10(8):707–710.

Anne Li-E Liu. 2002. *A corpus-based lexical semantic investigation of verb-noun miscollocations in Taiwan learners English.* Masters thesis, Tamkang University, Taipei.

Anne Li-E Liu, David Wible and Nai-Lung Tsao. 2009. *Automated suggestions for miscollocations.* In Proceedings of the 4th Workshop on Innovative Use of NLP for Building Educational Applications, pp. 47–50.

Nitin Madnani and Aoife Cahill. 2014. *An Explicit Feedback System for Preposition Errors based on Wikipedia Revisions.* In Proceedings of the Ninth Workshop on Innovative Use of NLP for Building Educational Applications, pp. 79–88.

George A. Miller. 1995. *WordNet: A Lexical Database for English.* Communications of the ACM, 38(11):39–41.

Hwee Tou Ng, Siew Mei Wu, Yuanbin Wu, Christian Hadiwinoto, and Joel Tetreault. 2013. *The CoNLL- 2013 Shared Task on Grammatical Error Correction.* In Proceedings of the Seventeenth Conference on Computational Natural Language Learning: Shared Task (CoNLL-2013 Shared Task), pp. 1–12.

Hwee Tou Ng, Siew Mei Wu, Ted Briscoe, Christian Hadiwinoto, Raymond Hendy Susanto, and Christopher Bryant. 2014. *The CoNLL-2014 Shared Task on Grammatical Error Correction.* In Proceedings of the Eighteenth Conference on Computational Natural Language Learning: Shared Task, pp. 1–14.

Diane Nicholls. 2003. *The Cambridge Learner Corpus: Error coding and analysis for lexicography and ELT.* In Proceedings of the Corpus Linguistics 2003 conference, pp. 572–581.

Robert Östling and Ola Knutsson. 2009. *A corpus-based tool for helping writers with Swedish collocations.* In Proceedings of the Workshop on Extracting and Using Constructions in NLP, pp. 28–33.

Alla Rozovskaya and Dan Roth. 2011. *Algorithm Selection and Model Adaptation for ESL Correction Tasks.* In Proceedings of the 49th Annual Meeting of the Association for Computational Linguistics: Human Language Technologies - Volume 1, pp. 924–933.

Alla Rozovskaya, Kai-Wei Chang, Mark Sammons, Dan Roth, and Nizar Habash. 2014. *Correcting Grammatical Verb Errors.* In Proceedings of the 14th Conference of the European Chapter of the Association for Computational Linguistics, pp. 358–367.

Terry Santos. 1988. *Professors' reaction to the academic writing of nonnative speaking students.* TESOL Quarterly, 22(1):69–90.

Yu Sawai, Mamoru Komachi, and Yuji Matsumoto. 2013. *A Learner Corpus-based Approach to Verb Suggestion for ESL.* In Proceedings of the 51st Annual Meeting of the Association for Computational Linguistics, pp. 708–713.

Chi-Chiang Shei and Helen Pain. 2000. *An ESL Writer's Collocation Aid.* Computer Assisted Language Learning, 13(2), pp. 167–182.

David Wible, Chin-Hwa Kuo, Nai-Lung Tsao, Anne Liu and H.-L. Lin. 2003. *Bootstrapping in a language-learning environment.* Journal of Computer Assisted Learning, 19(4), pp. 90–102.

Helen Yannakoudakis, Ted Briscoe, and Ben Medlock. 2011. *A New Dataset and Method for Automatically Grading ESOL Texts.* In Proceedings of the 49th Annual Meeting of the Association for Computational Linguistics: Human Language Technologies, pp. 180–189.

Using NLP to Support Scalable Assessment of Short Free Text Responses

Alistair Willis
Department of Computing and Communications
The Open University
Milton Keynes, UK
alistair.willis@open.ac.uk

Abstract

Marking student responses to short answer questions raises particular issues for human markers, as well as for automatic marking systems. In this paper we present the Amati system, which aims to help human markers improve the speed and accuracy of their marking. Amati supports an educator in incrementally developing a set of automatic marking rules, which can then be applied to larger question sets or used for automatic marking. We show that using this system allows markers to develop mark schemes which closely match the judgements of a human expert, with the benefits of consistency, scalability and traceability afforded by an automated marking system. We also consider some difficult cases for automatic marking, and look at some of the computational and linguistic properties of these cases.

1 Introduction

In developing systems for automatic marking, Mitchell et al. (2002) observed that assessment based on short answer, free text input from students demands very different skills from assessment based upon multiple-choice questions. Free text questions require a student to present the appropriate information in their own words, and without the cues sometimes provided by multiple choice questions (described respectively as improved verbalisation and recall (Gay, 1980)). Work by Jordan and Mitchell (2009) has demonstrated that automatic, online marking of student responses is both feasible (in that marking rules can be developed which mark at least as accurately as a human marker), and helpful to students, who find the online questions a valuable and enjoyable part of the assessment process. Such automatic marking is also an increasingly important part of assessment in Massive Open Online Courses (MOOCs) (Balfour, 2013; Kay et al., 2013).

However, the process of creating marking rules is known to be difficult and time consuming (Sukkarieh and Pulman, 2005; Pérez-Marín et al., 2009). The rules should usually be hand-crafted by a tutor who is a domain expert, as small differences in the way an answer is expressed can be significant in determining whether responses are correct or incorrect. Curating sets of answers to build mark schemes can prove to be a highly labour-intensive process. Given this requirement, and the current lack of availability of training data, a valuable progression from existing work in automatic assessment may be to investigate whether NLP techniques can be used to support the manual creation of such marking rules.

In this paper, we present the Amati system, which supports educators in creating mark schemes for automatic assessment of short answer questions. Amati uses information extraction-style templates to enable a human marker to rapidly develop automatic marking rules, and inductive logic programming to propose new rules to the marker. Having been developed, the rules can be used either for marking further unseen student responses, or for online assessment.

Automatic marking also brings with it further advantages. Because rules are applied automatically, it improves the *consistency* of marking; Williamson et al. (2012) have noted the potential of automated

Proceedings of the Tenth Workshop on Innovative Use of NLP for Building Educational Applications, 2015, pages 243–253,
Denver, Colorado, June 4, 2015.

marking to improve the reliability of test scores. In addition, because Amati uses symbolic/logical rules rather than stochastic rules, it improves the *traceability* of the marks (that is, the marker can give an explanation of *why* a mark was awarded, or not), and increases the *maintainability* of the mark scheme, because the educator can modify the rules in the context of better understanding of student responses. The explanatory nature of symbolic mark schemes also support issues of auditing marks awarded in assessment. Bodies such as the UK's Quality Assurance Agency[1] require that assessment be fully open for the purposes of external examination. Techniques which can show exactly why a particular mark was awarded (or not) for a given response fit well with existing quality assurance requirements.

All experiments in this paper were carried out using student responses collected from a first year introductory science module.

2 Mark Scheme Authoring

Burrows et al. (2015) have identified several different eras of automatic marking of free text responses. One era they have identified has treated automatic marking as essentially a form of information extraction. The many different ways that a student can correctly answer a question can make it difficult to award correct marks[2]. For example:

> *A snowflake falls vertically with a constant speed. What can you say about the forces acting on the snowflake?*

Three student responses to this question were:

(1) *there is no net force*

(2) *gravitational force is in equilibrium with air resistance*

(3) *no force balanced with gravity*

The question author considered both responses (1) and (2) correct. However, they share no common words (except *force* which already appears in the question, and *is*). And while *balance* and *equilibrium* have closely related meanings, response (3) was not considered a correct answer to the question[3]. These examples suggest that bag of words techniques are unlikely to be adequate for the task of short answer assessment. Without considering word order, it would be very hard to write a mark scheme that gave the correct mark to responses (1)-(3), particularly when these occur in the context of several hundred other responses, all using similar terms.

In fact, techniques such as Latent Semantic Analysis (LSA) have been shown to be accurate in grading longer essays (Landauer et al., 2003), but this success does not appear to transfer to short answer questions. Haley's (2008) work suggests that LSA performs poorly when applied to short answers, with Thomas et al. (2004) demonstrating that LSA-based marking systems for short answers did not give an acceptable correlation with an equivalent human marker, although they do highlight the small size of their available dataset.

Sukkarieh and Pulman (Sukkarieh and Pulman, 2005) and Mitchell et al. (2002) have demonstrated that hand-crafted rules containing more syntactic structure can be valuable for automatic assessment, but both papers note the manual effort required to develop the set of rules in the first place. To address this, we have started to investigate techniques to develop systems which can support a subject specialist (rather than a computing specialist) in developing a set of marking rules for a given collection of student responses. In addition, because it has been demonstrated (Butcher and Jordan, 2010) that marking rules based on regular expressions can mark accurately, we have also investigated the use of a symbolic learning algorithm to propose further marking rules to the author.

Enabling such markers to develop computational marking rules should yield the subsequent benefits of speed and consistency noted by Williamson et al., and the potential for embedding in an online systems to provide immediate marks for student submissions (Jordan and Mitchell, 2009). This proposal fits with the observation of Burrows et al. (2015), who suggest that rule based systems are desirable for "re-

[1] `http://www.qaa.ac.uk`

[2] Compared with multiple choice questions, which are easy to mark, although constructing suitable questions in the first place is far from straightforward (Mitkov et al., 2006).

[3] As with all examples in this paper, the "correctness" of answers was judged with reference to the students' level of study and provided teaching materials.

term(R, Term, I)	The Ith term in R is *Term*
template(R, Template, I)	The Ith term in R matches *Template*
precedes(I_i, I_j)	The I_i^{th} term in a response precedes the I_j^{th} term
closely_precedes(I_i, I_j)	The I_i^{th} term in a response precedes the I_j^{th} within a specified window

Figure 1: Mark scheme language

peated assessment" (i.e. where the assessment will be used multiple times), which is more likely to repay the investment in developing the mark scheme. We believe that the framework that we present here shows that rule-based marking can be more tractable than suggested by Burrows.

2.1 The Mark Scheme Language

In this paper, I will describe a set of such marking rules as a "mark scheme", so Amati aims to support a human marker in hand crafting a mark scheme, which is made up of a set of marking rules. In Amati, the mark schemes are constructed from sets of prolog rules, which attempt to classify the responses as either correct or incorrect. The rule syntax closely follows that of Junker et al. (1999), using the set of predicates shown in figure 1.

The main predicate for recognising keywords is *term(R, Term, I)*, which is true when *Term* is the Ith term in the response R. Here, we use "term" to mean a word or token in the response, subject to simple spelling correction. This correction is based upon a Damerau-Levenshtein (Damerau, 1964) edit distance of 1, which represents the replacement, addition or deletion of a single character, or a transposition of two adjacent characters. So for example, if R represented the student response:

(4) *no force ballanced with gravity*

then *term(R, balanced, 3)* would be true, as the 3rd token in R is *ballanced*, and at most 1 edit is needed to transform *ballanced* to *balanced*.

The predicate *template* allows a simple form of stemming (Porter, 1980). The statement *template(R, Template, I)* is true if *Template* matches at the beginning of the Ith token in R, subject to the same spelling correction as *term*. So for example, the statement:

template(R, balanc, 3)

would match example (4), because *balanc* is a single edit from *ballanc*, which itself matches the beginning of the 3rd token in R. (Note that it would not match as a *term*, because *ballance* is two edits from *balanc*.) Such templates allow rules to be written which match, for example, *balance*, *balanced*, *balancing* and so on.

The predicates *precedes* and *closely_precedes*, and the index terms, which appear as the variables I and J in figure 1, capture a level of linear precedence, which allow the rules to recognise a degree of linguistic structure. As discussed in section 2, techniques which do not capture some level of word order are insufficiently expressive for the task of representing mark schemes. However, a full grammatical analysis also appears to be unnecessary, and in fact can lead to ambiguity. Correct responses to the *Rocks* question (see table 1) required the students to identify that the necessary conditions to form the rock are *high temperature* and *high pressure*. Both *temperature* and *pressure* needed to be modified to earn the mark. Responses such as (5) should be marked correct, with an assumption that the modifier should distribute over the conjunction.

(5) *high temperature and pressure*

While the *precedence* predicate is adequate to capture this behaviour, using a full parser creates an ambiguity between the analyses (6) and (7).

(6) *(high (pressure)) and temperature* ×

(7) *(high (pressure and temperature))* √

The example suggest that high accuracy can be difficult to achieve by systems which commit to an early, single interpretation of the ambiguous text.

So a full example of a matching rule might be:

$$
\begin{aligned}
&term(R,\ oil,\ I) \wedge \\
&term(R,\ less,\ J) \wedge \\
&template(R,\ dens,\ K) \\
&precedes(I,\ J) \rightarrow correct(R)
\end{aligned}
$$

which would award the correct marks to responses (8) and (9):

(8) *oil is less dense than water* √

(9) *water is less dense than oil* ×

The use of a template also ensures the correct mark is awarded to the common response (10), which should also be marked as correct:

(10) *oil has less density than water*

2.2 Incremental rule authoring

The Amati system is based on a bootstrapping scheme, which allows an author to construct a rule-set by marking student responses in increments of 50 responses at a time, while constructing marking rules which reflect the marker's own judgements. As the marker develops the mark scheme, he or she can correct the marks awarded by the existing mark scheme, and then edit the mark scheme to more accurately reflect the intended marks.

The support for these operations are illustrated in figures 2 and 3. To make the system more usable by non-specialists (that is, non-specialists in computing, rather than non-specialists in the subject being taught), the authors are not expected to work directly with prolog. Rather, rules are presented to the user via online forms, as shown in figure 2. As each rule is developed, the system displays to the user the responses which the rule marks as correct.

As increasingly large subsets of the student responses are marked, the system displays the set of imported responses, the mark that the current mark scheme awards, and which rule(s) match agains each response (figure 3). This allows the mark scheme author to add or amend rules as necessary.

2.3 Rule Induction

As the marker constructs an increasingly large collection of marked responses, it can be useful to use the marked responses to induce further rules automatically. Methods for learning relational rules to

Figure 2: Form for entering marking rules

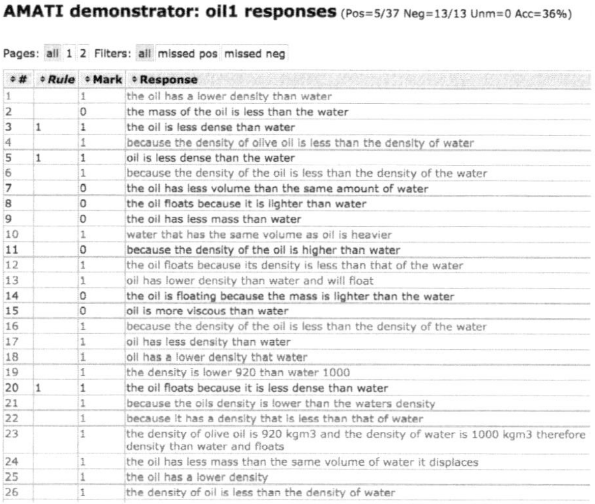
AMATI demonstrator: oil1 responses (Pos=5/37 Neg=13/13 Unm=0 Acc=36%)

Pages: all 1 2 Filters: all missed pos missed neg

#	Rule	Mark	Response
1		1	the oil has a lower density than water
2		0	the mass of the oil is less than the water
3	1	1	the oil is less dense than water
4		1	because the density of olive oil is less than the density of water
5	1	1	oil is less dense than the water
6		1	because the density of the oil is less than the density of the water
7		0	the oil has less volume than the same amount of water
8		0	the oil floats because it is lighter than water
9		0	the oil has less mass than water
10		1	water that has the same volume as oil is heavier
11		0	because the density of the oil is higher than water
12		1	the oil floats because its density is less than that of the water
13		1	oil has lower density than water and will float
14		0	the oil is floating because the mass is lighter than the water
15		0	oil is more viscous than water
16		1	because the density of the oil is less than the density of the water
17		1	oil has less density than water
18		1	oil has a lower density that water
19		1	the density is lower 920 than water 1000
20	1	1	the oil floats because it is less dense than water
21		1	because the oils density is lower than the waters density
22		1	because it has a density that is less than that of water
23		1	the density of olive oil is 920 kgm3 and the density of water is 1000 kgm3 therefore density than water and floats
24		1	the oil has less mass than the same volume of water it displaces
25		1	the oil has a lower density
26		1	the density of oil is less than the density of water

Figure 3: Application of rule to the *Oil* response set

perform information extraction are now well established (Califf and Mooney, 1997; Soderland, 1999), with Inductive Logic Programming (ILP) (Quinlan, 1990; Lavrač and Džeroski, 1994) often proving a suitable learning learning technique (Aitken, 2002; Ramakrishnan et al., 2008). ILP is a supervised learning algorithm which attempts to generate a logical description of a set of facts in the style of a prolog program. Amati embeds the ILP system Aleph (Srinivasan, 2004) as the rule learner, which itself implements the Progol learning algorithm (Muggleton, 1995), a bottom up, greedy coverage algorithm. This allows an author to mark the current set of questions (typically the first or second block of 50 responses), before using the ILP engine to generate a rule set which he or she can then modify. We return to the question of editing rule sets in section 4.1.

Our use of ILP to support markers in developing rules has several parallels with the Powergrading project (Basu et al., 2013). Both our work and that of Basu et al. focus on using NLP techniques primarily to support the work of a human marker, and reduce marker effort. Basu et al. take an approach whereby student responses are clustered using statistical topic detection, with the marker then able to allocate marks and feedback at the cluster level, rather than at the individual response level. Similarly, the aim of Amati is that markers should be able to award marks by identifying, via generated rules, commonly occurring phrases. The use of such phrases can then be analysed at the cohort level (or at least, incrementally at the cohort level), rather than at the individual response level.

In practice, we found that markers were likely to use the predicted rules as a "first cut" solution, to gain an idea of the overall structure of the final mark scheme. The marker could then concentrate on developing more fine-grained rules to improve the mark scheme accuracy. This usage appears to reflect that found by Basu et al., of using the machine learning techniques to automatically identify groups of similar groups of responses. This allows the marker to highlight common themes and frequent misunderstandings.

Short name	Question text
Sandstone	A sandstone observed in the field contains well-sorted, well rounded, finely pitted and reddened grains. What does this tell you about the origins of this rock?
Snowflake	A snowflake falls vertically with a constant speed. What can you say about the forces acting on the snowflake?
Charge	If the distance between two electrically charged particles is doubled, what happens to the electric force between them?
Rocks	Metamorphic rocks are existing rocks that have "changed form" (metamorphosed) in a solid state. What conditions are necessary in order for this change to take place?
Sentence	What is wrong with the following sentence? *A good idea.*
Oil	The photograph *(not shown here)* shows a layer of oil floating on top of a glass of water. Why does the oil float?

Table 1: The questions used

3 Evaluation

The aim of the evaluation was to determine whether a ruleset built using Amati could achieve performance comparable with human markers. As such, there were two main aims. First, to determine whether the proposed language was sufficiently expressive to build successful mark schemes, and second, to determine how well a mark scheme developed using the Amati system would compare against a human marker.

3.1 Training and test set construction

A training set and a test set of student responses were built from eight questions taken from an entry-level science module, shown in table 1. Each student response was to be marked as either correct or incorrect. Two sets of responses were used, which were built from two subsequent presentations of the same module. Amati was used to build a mark scheme using a training set of responses from the 2008 student cohort, and then that scheme was applied to an unseen test set constructed from the responses to the same questions from the 2009 student cohort.

The difficulties in attempting to build any corpus in which the annotations are reliable are well documented (Marcus et al.'s (1993) discussion of the Penn Treebank gives a good overview). In this case, we exploited the presence of the original question setter and module chair to provide as close to a "ground truth" as is realistic. Our gold-standard marks were obtained with a multiple-pass annotation process, in which the collections of responses were initially marked by two or more subject-specialist tutors, who mainly worked independently, but who were able to confer when they disagreed on a particular response. The marks were then validated by the module chair, who was also called upon to resolve any disputes which arose as a result of disagreements in the mark scheme. The cost of constructing a corpus in this way would usually be prohibitive, relying as it does on subject experts both to provide the preliminary marks, and to provide a final judgement in the reconciliation phase. In this case, the initial marks (including the ability to discuss in the case of a dispute) were generated as part of the standard marking process for student assessment in the University[4].

3.2 Effectiveness of authored mark schemes

To investigate the expressive power of the representation language, a set of mark schemes for the eight questions shown in table 1 were developed using the Amati system. The training data was used to build the rule set, with regular comparisons against the gold standard marks. The mark scheme was then applied to the test set, and the marks awarded compared against the test set gold standard marks.

The results are shown in table 2. The table shows the total number of responses per question, and the accuracy of the Amati rule set applied to the unseen data set. So for example, the Amati rule set correctly marked 98.42% of the 1711 responses to the *Sandstone* question. Note that the choice of accuracy as the appropriate measure of success is determined by the particular application. In this case, the important measure is how many responses are marked correctly. That is, it is as important that incorrect answers are marked as incorrect, as it is that correct answers are marked as correct.

To compare the performance of the Amati ruleset against the human expert, we have used Krippendorf's α measure, implemented in the python Natural Language Toolkit library (Bird et al., 2009) following Artstein and Poesio's (2008) presentation. The rightmost column of table 2 shows the α measure between the Amati ruleset and the post-reconciliation marks awarded by the human expert. This column shows a higher level of agreement than was obtained with human markers alone. The

[4]We have not presented inter-annotator agreement measures here, as these are generally only meaningful when annotators have worked independently. This model of joint annotation with a reconciliation phase is little discussed in the literature, although this is a process used by Farwell et al. (2009). Our annotation process differed in that the reconciliation phase was carried out face to face following each round of annotation, in contrast to Farwell et al.'s, which allowed a second anonymous vote after the first instance.

Question	# responses	accuracy/%	α/%
Sandstone	1711	98.42	97.5
Snowflake	2057	91.0	81.7
Charge	1127	98.89	97.6
Rocks	1429	99.00	89.6
Sentence	1173	98.19	97.5
Oil	817	96.12	91.5

Table 2: Accuracy of the Amati mark schemes on unseen data, and the Krippendorf α rating between the marks awarded by Amati and the gold standard

agreement achieved by independent human markers ranged from a maximum of $\alpha = 88.2\%$ to a minimum of $\alpha = 71.2\%$, which was the agreement on marks awarded for the *snowflake* question. It is notable that the human marker agreement was worst on the same question that the Amati-authored ruleset performed worst on; we discuss some issues that this question raises in section 4.3.

The marks awarded by the marker supported with Amati therefore aligned more closely with those of the human expert than was achieved between independent markers. This suggests that further development of computer support for markers is likely to improve overall marking consistency, both across the student cohort, and by correspondence with the official marking guidance.

4 Observations on authoring rulesets

It is clear from the performance of the different rule sets that some questions are easier to generate mark schemes for than others. In particular, the mark scheme authored on the responses to the *snowflake* question performed with much lower accuracy than the other questions. This section gives a qualitative overview of some of the issues which were observed while authoring the mark schemes.

4.1 Modification of generated rules

A frequently cited advantage of ILP is that, as a logic program, the output rules are generated in a human-readable form (Lavrač and Džeroski, 1994; Mitchell, 1997). In fact, the inclusion of templates means that several of the rules can be hard to interpret at first glance. For example, a rule proposed to mark the *Rocks* question was:

$$template(R, bur, I) \wedge$$
$$template(R, hea, J) \rightarrow correct(R)$$

As the official marking guidance suggests that *High temperature and pressure* is an acceptable response, *hea* can easily be interpreted as *heat*. However, it is not immediately clear what *bur* represents. In fact, a domain expert would probably recognise this as a shortened form of *buried* (as the high pressure, the second required part of the solution, can result from burial in rock). As the training set does not contain terms with the same first characters as *burial*, such as *burnished*, *Burghundy* or *burlesque*, then this term matches. However, a mark scheme author might prefer to edit the rule slightly into something more readable and so maintainable:

$$template(R, buri, I) \wedge$$
$$term(R, heat, J) \rightarrow correct(R)$$

so that either *buried* or *burial* would be matched, and to make the recognition of *heat* more explicit.

A more complex instance of the same phenomenon is illustrated by the generated rule:

$$term(R, high, I) \wedge$$
$$term(R, temperature, J) \rightarrow correct(R)$$

Although the requirement for the terms *high* and *temperature* is clear enough, there is no part of this rule that requires that the student also mention *high pressure*. This has come about because all the student responses that mention *high temperature* also explicitly mention *pressure*. Because Progol and Aleph use a greedy coverage algorithm, in this case Amati did not need to add an additional rule to capture . Again, the mark scheme author would probably wish to edit this rule to give:

$$term(R, high, I) \wedge$$
$$term(R, temperature, J) \wedge$$
$$term(R, pressure, K) \wedge$$
$$precedes(I, J) \rightarrow correct(R)$$

which covers the need for *high* to precede *temperature*, and also contain a reference to *pressure*. A similar case, raised by the same question, is the following proposed rule:

$$term(R, high, I) \wedge$$
$$term(R, pressure, J) \wedge$$
$$term(R, and, K) \wedge$$
$$precedes(I, K) \rightarrow correct(R)$$

which requires a conjunction, but makes no mention of *temperature* (or *heat* or some other equivalent). In this case, the responses (11) and (12):

(11) *(high (pressure and temperature))* √

(12) *(high (pressure and heat))* √

are both correct, and both appeared amongst the student responses. However, there were no incorrect responses following a similar syntactic pattern, such as, for example, (13) or (14):

(13) *high pressure and altitude* ×

(14) *high pressure and bananas* ×

Students who recognised that *high pressure* and *something else* were required, always got the *something else* right. Therefore, the single rule above had greater coverage than rules that looked individually for *high pressure and temperature* or *high pressure and heat.*

This example again illustrates the Amati philosophy that the technology is best used to support human markers. By hand-editing the proposed solutions, the marker ensures that the rules are more intuitive, and so can be more robust, and more maintainable in the longer term. In this case, an author might reasonably rewrite the single rule into two:

$$term(R, high, I) \wedge$$
$$term(R, pressure, J) \wedge$$
$$term(R, temperature, K) \wedge$$
$$precedes(I, K) \rightarrow correct(R)$$

$$term(R, high, I) \wedge$$
$$term(R, pressure, J) \wedge$$
$$term(R, heat, K) \wedge$$
$$precedes(I, K) \rightarrow correct(R)$$

removing the unnecessary conjunction, and providing explicit rules for *heat* and *temperature*.

4.2 Spelling correction

It is questionable whether spelling correction is always appropriate. A question used to assess knowledge of organic chemistry might require the term *butane* to appear in the solution. It would not be appropriate to mark a response containing the token *butene* (a different compound) as correct, even though *butene* would be an allowable misspelling of *butane* according to the given rules. On the other hand, a human marker would probably be inclined to mark responses containing *buttane* or *butan* as correct. These are also legitimate misspellings according the table, but are less likely to be misspellings of *butene*.

The particular templates generated reflect the linguistic variation in the specific datasets. A template such as *temp*, intended to cover responses containing *temperature* (for example), would also potentially cover *temporary*, *tempestuous*, *temperamental* and so on. In fact, when applied to large sets of homogenous response-types (such as multiple responses to a single question), the vocabulary used across the complete set of responses turns out to be sufficiently restricted for meaningful templates to be generated. It does not follow that this hypothesis language would continue to be appropriate for datasets with a wider variation in vocabulary.

4.3 Diversity of correct responses

As illustrated in table 2, the *Snowflake* question was very tricky to handle, with lower accuracy than the other questions, and lower agreement with the gold standard. The following are some of the student responses:

(15) *they are balanced*

(16) *the force of gravity is in balance with air resistance*

(17) *friction is balancing the force of gravity*

(18) *only the force of gravity is acting on the hailstone and all forces are balanced*

The module chair considered responses (15), (16) and (17) to be correct, and response (18) to be incorrect.

The most straightforward form of the answer is along the lines of response (15). In this case, there are no particular forces mentioned; only a general comment about the forces in question. Similar cases were *there are no net forces, all forces balance, the forces are in equilibrium* and so on.

However, responses (16) and (17) illustrate that in many cases, the student will present particular examples to attempt to answer the question. In these cases, both responses identify gravity as one of the acting forces, but describe the counteracting force differently (as *air resistance* and *friction* respectively). A major difficulty in marking this type of question is predicting the (correct) examples that students will use in their responses, as each correct pair needs to be incorporated in the mark schemes. A response suggesting that *air resistance* counteracts *drag* would be marked incorrect. As stated previously, developing robust mark schemes requires that mark scheme authors use large sets of previous student responses, which can provide guidance on the range of possible responses.

Finally, response (18) illustrates a difficult response to mark (for both pattern matchers and linguistic solutions). The response consists of two conjoined clauses, the second of which, *all forces are balanced*, is in itself a correct answer. It is only in the context of the first clause that the response is marked incorrect, containing the error that it is **only** *the force of gravity* which acts.

This question highlights that the ease with which a question can be marked automatically can depend as much on the question being asked as the answers received. Of course, this also applies to questions intended to be marked by a human; some questions lead to easier responses to grade. So a good evaluation of a marking system needs to consider the questions (and the range of responses provided by real students) being asked; the performance of the system is meaningful only in the context of the nature of the questions being assessed, and an understanding of the diversity of correct responses. In this case, it appears that questions which can be correctly answered by using a variety of different examples should be avoided. We anticipate that with increasing maturity of the use of automatic marking systems, examiners would develop skills in setting appropriate questions for the marking system, just as experienced authors develop skills in setting questions which are appropriate for human markers.

4.4 Anaphora Ambiguity

The examples raise some interesting questions about how anaphora resolution should be dealt with. Two responses to the *oil* question are:

(19) *The oil floats on the water because it is lighter*

(20) *The oil floats on the water because it is heavier*

These two responses appear to have contradictory meanings, but in fact are both marked as correct. This initially surprising result arises from the ambiguity in the possible resolutions of the pronoun *it*:

(21) *[The oil]$_i$ floats on the water because it$_i$ is lighter.*

(22) *The oil floats on [the water]$_j$ because it$_j$ is heavier.*

When marking these responses, the human markers followed a general policy of giving the benefit of the doubt, and, within reasonable limits, will mark a response as correct if any of the *possible* interpretations would be correct relative to the mark scheme.

As with the ambiguous modifier attachment seen in responses (6) and (7), this example illustrates that using a different (possibly better) parser is unlikely to improve the overall system performance. Responses such (21) and (22) are hard for many parsers to handle, because an early commitment to a single interpretation can assume that *it* must refer to *the oil* or *the water*. Again, this example demonstrates that a more sophisticated approach to syntactic ambiguity is necessary if a parsing-based system is to be used. (One possible approach might be to use underspecification techniques (König and Reyle, 1999; van Deemter and Peters, 1996) and attempt to reason with the ambiguous forms.)

5 Discussion and Conclusions

We have presented a system which uses information extraction techniques and machine learning to support human markers in the task of marking free text responses to short answer questions. The results suggest that a system such as Amati can help markers create accurate, reusable mark schemes.

The user interface to Amati was developed in collaboration with experienced markers from the Open University's Computing department and Science department, who both gave input into the requirements for an effective marking system. We intend to carry out more systematic analyses of the value of using such systems for marking, but informally, we have found that a set of around 500-600 responses was enough for an experienced marker to feel satisfied with the performance of her own authored mark scheme, and to be prepared to use it on further unseen cases. (This number was for the *Snowflake* question, which contained approximately half correct responses. For the other questions, the marker typically required fewer responses.)

The work described in this paper contrasts with the approach commonly taken in automatic marking, of developing mechanisms which assign marks by comparing student responses to one or more target responses created by the subject specialist (Ziai et al., 2012). Such systems have proven effective where suitable linguistic information is compared, such as the predicate argument structure used by c-rater (Leacock and Chodorow, 2003), or similarity between dependency relationships, as used by AutoMark (now FreeText (Mitchell et al., 2002)) and Mohler et al. (2011). Our own experiments with FreeText found that incorrect marks were often a result of an inappropriate parse by the embedded Stanford parser (Klein and Manning, 2003)), as illustrated by the parses (6) and (7). In practice, we have found that for the short answers we have been considering, pattern based rules tend to be more robust in the face of such ambiguity than a full parser.

A question over this work is how to extend the technique to more linguistically complex responses. The questions used here are all for a single mark, all or nothing. A current direction of our research is looking at how to provide support for more complicated questions which would require the student to mention two or more separate pieces of information, or to reason about causal relationships. A further area of interest is how the symbolic analysis of the students' responses can be used to generate meaningful feedback to support them as part of their learning process.

Acknowledgments

The author would like to thank Sally Jordan for her help in collecting the students' data, for answering questions about marking as they arose and for making the data available for use in this work. Also, David King who developed the Amati system, and Rita Tingle who provided feedback on the usability of the system from a marker's perspective. We would also like to thank the anonymous reviewers for their valuable suggestions on an earlier draft of the paper.

References

James Stuart Aitken. 2002. Learning information extraction rules: An inductive logic programming approach. In *ECAI*, pages 355–359.

Ron Artstein and Massimo Poesio. 2008. Inter-coder agreement for computational linguistics. *Computational Linguistics*, 34(4):555–596.

Stephen P Balfour. 2013. Assessing writing in MOOCs: Automated essay scoring and calibrated peer review. *Research & Practice in Assessment*, 8(1):40–48.

Sumit Basu, Chuck Jacobs, and Lucy Vanderwende. 2013. Powergrading: A clustering approach to amplify human effort for short answer grading. *Transactions of the Association for Computational Linguistics*, 1:391–402.

Steven Bird, Ewan Klein, and Edward Loper. 2009. *Natural Language Processing with Python*. O'Reilly Media.

Steven Burrows, Iryana Gurevych, and Benno Stein. 2015. The eras and trends of automatic short answer grading. *International Journal of Artificial Intelligence in Education*, 25(1):60–117.

Philip G. Butcher and Sally E. Jordan. 2010. A comparison of human and computer marking of short free-text student responses. *Computers and Education*.

Mary Elaine Califf and Raymond J. Mooney. 1997. Relational learning of pattern-match rules for information extraction. In T.M. Ellison, editor, *Computational Natural Language Learning*, pages 9–15. Association for Computational Linguistics.

F. J. Damerau. 1964. Technique for computer detection and correction of spelling errors. *Communications of the Association of Computing Machinery*, 7(3):171–176.

David Farwell, Bonnie Dorr, Rebecca Green, Nizar Habash, Stephen Helmreich, Eduard Hovy, Lori Levin, Keith Miller, Teruko Mitamura, Owen Rambow, Florence Reeder, and Advaith Siddharthan. 2009. Interlingual annotation of multilingual text corpora and framenet. In Hans C. Boas, editor, *Multilingual FrameNets in Computational Lexicography : Methods and Applications*. Mouton de Gruyter, Berlin.

Lorraine R Gay. 1980. The comparative effects of multiple-choice versus short-answer tests on retention. *Journal of Educational Measurement*, 17(1):45–50.

Debra T. Haley. 2008. *Applying Latent Semantic Analysis to Computer Assisted Assessment in the Computer Science Domain: A Framework, a Tool, and an Evaluation*. Ph.D. thesis, The Open University.

Sally Jordan and Tom Mitchell. 2009. E-assessment for learning? The potential of short free-text questions with tailored feedback. *British Journal of Educational Technology*, 40(2):371–385.

Markus Junker, Michael Sintek, and Matthias Rinck. 1999. Learning for text categorization and information extraction with ILP. In J. Cussens, editor, *Proceedings of the First Workshop Learning Language in Logic*, pages 84–93.

Judy Kay, Peter Reimann, Elliot Diebold, and Bob Kummerfeld. 2013. MOOCs: So Many Learners, So Much Potential.... *IEEE Intelligent Systems*, 3:70–77.

Dan Klein and Christopher D. Manning. 2003. Accurate unlexicalized parsing. In *Proceedings of the 41st Meeting of the Association for Computational Linguistics*, pages 423–430. Association for Computational Linguistics.

Esther König and Uwe Reyle. 1999. A general reasoning scheme for underspecified representations. In Hans Jürgen Ohlbach and U. Reyle, editors, *Logic, Language and Reasoning. Essays in Honour of Dov Gabbay*, volume 5 of *Trends in Logic*. Kluwer.

T. K. Landauer, D. Laham, and P. W. Foltz. 2003. Automated scoring and annotation of essays with the intelligent essay assessor. In M. Shermis and J. Burstein, editors, *Automated essay scoring: a cross-disciplinary approach*, pages 87–112. Lawrence Erlbaum Associates, Inc.

Nada Lavrač and Sašo Džeroski. 1994. *Inductive Logic Programming*. Ellis Horwood, New York.

Claudia Leacock and Martin Chodorow. 2003. C-rater: Automated scoring of short-answer questions. *Computers and the Humanities*, 37(4):389–405.

Mitchell P Marcus, Mary Ann Marcinkiewicz, and Beatrice Santorini. 1993. Building a large annotated corpus of English: The Penn Treebank. *Computational linguistics*, 19(2):313–330.

Tom Mitchell, Terry Russell, Peter Broomhead, and Nicola Aldridge. 2002. Towards robust computerised marking of free-text responses. In *6th International Computer Aided Assessment Conference*, Loughbrough.

Tom M. Mitchell. 1997. *Machine Learning*. Computer Science Series. McGraw Hill International Editions.

Ruslan Mitkov, Le An Ha, and Nikiforos Karamanis. 2006. A computer-aided environment for generating multiple-choice test items. *Natural Language Engineering*, 12(2):177–194.

Michael Mohler, Razvan Bunescu, and Rada Mihalcea. 2011. Learning to grade short answer questions using semantic similarity measures and dependency graph alignments. In *Proceedings of the 49th Annual Meeting of the Association for Computational Linguistics: Human Language Technologies-Volume 1*, pages 752–762. Association for Computational Linguistics.

Stephen Muggleton. 1995. Inverse entailment and Progol. *New Generation Computing*.

Diana Pérez-Marín, Ismael Pascual-Nieto, and Pilar Rodríguez. 2009. Computer-assisted assessment of free-text answers. *Knowledge Engineering Review*.

M. F. Porter. 1980. An algorithm for suffix stripping. *Program*, 14(3):130–137, July.

J. R. Quinlan. 1990. Learning logical definitions from relations. *Machine learning*, 5(3):239–266.

Ganesh Ramakrishnan, Sachindra Joshi, Sreeram Balakrishnan, and Ashwin Srinivasan. 2008. Using ILP to construct features for information extraction from semi-structured text. In *Inductive Logic Programming*, volume 4894 of *Lecture Notes in Computer Science*, pages 211–224. Springer.

Stephen Soderland. 1999. Learning information extraction rules for semi-structured and free text. *Machine Learning*, 34(1-3):233–272, February.

Ashwin Srinivasan. 2004. The Aleph manual. http://www.comlab.ox.ac.uk/activities/machinelearning/Aleph/.

Jana Sukkarieh and Stephen Pulman. 2005. Information extraction and machine learning: Auto-marking short free text responses to science questions. In *Proceeding of the 2005 conference on Artificial Intelligence in Education*, pages 629–637.

Pete Thomas, Debra Haley, Anne De Roeck, and Marian Petre. 2004. E-assessment using latent semantic analysis in the computer science domain: A pilot study. In *Proceedings of the Workshop on eLearning for Computational Linguistics and Computational Linguistics for eLearning table of contents*, pages 38–44. Association for Computational Linguistics.

Kees van Deemter and Stanley Peters. 1996. *Semantic Ambiguity and Underspecification*. CSLI.

David M Williamson, Xiaoming Xi, and F Jay Breyer. 2012. A framework for evaluation and use of automated scoring. *Educational Measurement: Issues and Practice*, 31(1):2–13.

Ramon Ziai, Niels Ott, and Detmar Meurers. 2012. Short answer assessment: Establishing links between research strands. In *Proceedings of the Seventh Workshop on Building Educational Applications Using NLP*, pages 190–200. Association for Computational Linguistics.

Automatically Scoring Freshman Writing: A Preliminary Investigation

Courtney Napoles[1] and **Chris Callison-Burch**[2]
[1]Center for Language and Speech Processing
Johns Hopkins University, Baltimore, MD
[2]Computer and Information Science Department
University of Pennsylvania, Philadelphia, PA

Abstract

In this work, we explore applications of automatic essay scoring (AES) to a corpus of essays written by college freshmen and discuss the challenges we faced. While most AES systems evaluate highly constrained writing, we developed a system that handles open-ended, long-form writing. We present a novel corpus for this task, containing more than 3,000 essays and drafts written for a freshman writing course. We describe statistical analysis of the corpus and identify problems with automatically scoring this type of data. Finally, we demonstrate how to overcome grader bias by using a multi-task setup, and predict scores as well as human graders on a different dataset. Finally, we discuss how AES can help teachers assign more uniform grades.

1 Introduction

Automatic essay scoring (AES) is the task of automatically predicting the scores of written essays. AES has primarily focused on high-stakes standardized tests and statewide evaluation exams. In this paper, we consider a classroom application of AES to evaluate a novel corpus of more than 3,000 essays written for a first-year writing program.

Many colleges have first-year writing programs, which are typically large courses divided into multiple sections taught by different teachers. These essays are more representative of college writing than assessment-based datasets used for AES, and we wish to examine how AES can help students and teachers in the classroom. These preliminary experiments could help teachers evaluate students and colleges gain insight into variance across instructors.

This corpus may be more difficult to model compared to previous datasets because it lacks multiple grades to establish validity and the essays are not constrained by a prompt. Foltz et al. (2013) reported that prompt-independent scoring generally had 10% lower reliability than prompt-specific scoring.

We address several issues surrounding automatically scoring essays of this nature:

1. Is it possible to model essays graded by several different teachers with no overlapping grades?
2. ...even when scores given by each teacher have different distributions?
3. Can a single model predict the scores of long essays that are (a) not constrained by an essay prompt and (b) written in different styles?
4. How can AES provide constructive feedback to teachers and administrators?

In this work, we describe how multi-task learning can accommodate the differences in teacher scoring patterns by jointly modeling the scores of individual teachers, while sharing information across all teachers. Our multi-task model correlates strongly with actual grades. We also provide an example of how to provide feedback to help teachers grade more uniformly, using the weights learned by a linear model.

Our corpus is described in Section 3. In Section 4 we describe our experimental setup and the features used. Section 5 presents results from our system that achieve human-like levels of correlation. Section 6 discusses our results and proposes a new way to provide feedback to teachers about their grading.

Proceedings of the Tenth Workshop on Innovative Use of NLP for Building Educational Applications, 2015, pages 254–263,
Denver, Colorado, June 4, 2015.

Project	Target word count	Description
1	600-770	A personal narrative that describes an experience and uses that experience to tell readers something important about the writer.
2	600	A bibliographic essay that asks you to understand the conversation surrounding your chosen topic by examining four relevant sources. Two of these sources must be at least ten years apart so that you can see how interpretations of an event, concept, or person evolve over time and that textual scholarship is an ongoing conversation.
3	600–800	A reflection that asks you to think carefully about how audience and purpose, as well as medium and genre, affect your choices as composers and reflect carefully on a new dimension of your topic.
4	1000–1200	A polished essay that asserts an arguable thesis that is supported by research and sound reasoning.

Table 1: Brief description of the assignments in the FWC, as provided by the syllabus.

2 Related Work

While AES has traditionally been used for grading tests, there are some previous applications of AES in a non-testing environment. For example, Elliot et al. (2012) used AES to assist with placement and Chali and Hasan (2012) automatically graded essays written for an occupational therapy course by comparing them to the course material.

Corpora for AES include English-language learner writing, specifically the First Certification Exam corpus (FCE), a portion of the Cambridge Learner Corpus consisting of 1,244 essays written for an English-language certification exam (Yannakoudakis et al., 2011), and the International Corpus of Learner English (ICLE), 6,085 essays written by university students across the world (Granger, 2003). The Kaggle ASAP–AES dataset has primarily native-English writing, with 22,000 short essays written by middle- and high-school students the United States (Shermis and Hamner, 2013). The FCE and Kaggle data were collected during examinations while the ICLE data was written during an exam or as part of a class assignment.

Student writing collections not suitable for AES include the Michigan Corpus of Upper-level Student Papers, with 829 academic papers that received an A grade, written by college seniors and graduate students across several disciplines (Mic, 2009). A separate corpus of freshman writing was collected at University of Michigan containing 3,500 ungraded pre-entrance essays (Gere and Aull, 2010).

Methods previously used for AES include linear regression (Attali and Burstein, 2006), rank algorithms (Yannakoudakis et al., 2011; Chen and He, 2013), LSA (Pearson, 2010; Chali and Hasan, 2012), and Bayesian models (Rudner and Liang, 2002). Recent approaches focus on predicting specific aspect of the score by using targeted features such as coherence (McNamara et al., 2010; Yannakoudakis and Briscoe, 2012).

Draft	Tokens	Sentences	Paragraphs
Intermed.	840.3	35.6	5.2
Final	938.5	39.6	5.7

Table 2: Average length of essays from the Fall 2011 semester.

Multi-task learning jointly models separate tasks in a single model using a shared representation. It has been used in NLP for tasks such as domain adaptation (Finkel and Manning, 2009), relation extraction (Jiang, 2009), and modeling annotator bias (Cohn and Specia, 2013).

3 Data

The Freshman Writing Corpus (FWC) is a new corpus for AES that contains essays written by college students in a first-year writing program. The unique features of this corpus are multiple essay drafts, teacher grades on a detailed rubric, and teacher feedback. The FWC contains approximately 23,000 essays collected over 6 semesters. To our knowledge, this is the first collection of take-home writing assignments that can be used for AES.

In this work, we consider one semester of es-

Category	Weight	Level	Possible Points	Brief Description
Focus	25%	Basics	0–4	Meeting assignment requirements
		Critical thinking	0–4	Strength of thesis and analysis
Evidence	25%	Critical thinking	0–4	Quality of sources and how they are presented
Organization	25%	Basics	0–4	Introduction, supporting sentences, transitions, and conclusion
		Critical thinking	0–4	Progression and cohesion of argument
Style	20%	Basics	0–4	Grammar, punctuation, and consistent point of view
		Critical thinking	0–4	Syntax, word choice, and vocabulary
Format	5%	Basics	0–4	Paper formatting and conformance with style guide

Table 3: The rubric for grading essays. The teachers used a more detailed rubric that provided guidelines at each possible score.

says from the FWC, for a total of 3,362 essays written by 639 students during the Fall 2011 semester.[1] Students were enrolled in the same Composition I course, which was divided into 55 sections taught by 21 teachers. All sections had the same curriculum and grading rubric.

The course had four writing projects, and for each project students could hand in up to three drafts: Early, Intermediate, and Final. Each project focused on a different type of essay, specifically a personal narrative, a bibliographic essay, a remediation, and a thesis-driven essay, but the topic was open-ended. A description of the requirements for each essay is found in Table 1.

Submission and grading was done on My Reviewers.[2] Students uploaded PDF versions of their essays to the site, where teachers graded them. Teachers could also comment on the PDFs to provide feedback to the students.

We downloaded the essays in PDF format from MyReviewers, extracted text from PDFs using the PDFMiner library[3], and automatically labeled text by document section based on its (x, y) position on the page. Document sections include header, title, paragraph, page number, and teacher annotation.

To anonymize the data, we replaced student and teacher names with numeric IDs. We ran sentence segmentation on the paragraphs using Splitta (Read et al., 2012) and added several layers of annotation to the sentences: constituent and dependency parses, named entities, and coreference chains using Stanford Core NLP (Manning et al., 2014); 101 discourse markers with the Explicit Discourse Connectives Tagger[4]; and 6,791 opinion words defined by Hu and Liu (2004).

In this work, we only consider the Intermediate and Final drafts. We leave out Early drafts because less than half of Final essays have an Early draft (80% have an Intermediate draft) and Early drafts are typically short outlines or project proposals, while Intermediate drafts generally have a similar form to the Final draft. The average essay has 899 words, 38 sentences, and 5.5 paragraphs (Table 2 has lengths by draft).

3.1 Scores

All essays were graded on the same rubric, which has five categories broken into eight sub-categories, with bulleted requirements for each. The overall score is a weighted combination of the individual category scores that ranges from 0–4, which corresponds to a letter grade. (A condensed version of the rubric is shown in Table 3, and the correspondence between score and grade is shown in Figure 1.) This grading scheme has two immediate advantages, the first that students have a clear sense of how different aspects of their paper contributes to the grade,

[1] There were 3,745 graded essays in total, but we were unable to automatically extract text from 383 of the PDFs.

[2] www.myreviewers.com/

[3] http://www.unixuser.org/~euske/python/pdfminer/index.html

[4] http://www.cis.upenn.edu/~epitler/discourse.html

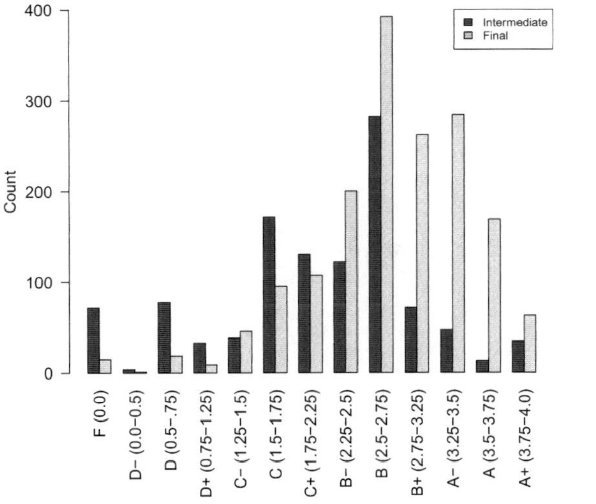

Figure 1: Number of essays by grade. Each letter grade corresponds to a range of numeric scores, in parentheses.

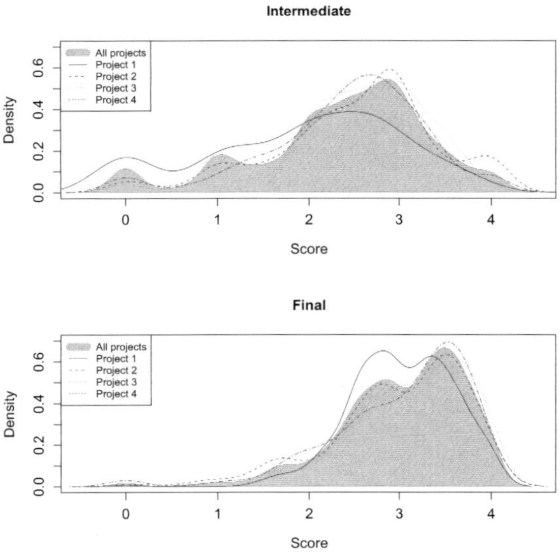

Figure 2: Distribution of scores by project and draft.

Project	Intermediate	Final	Change
1	1.94	3.02	+1.08
2	2.51	2.98	+0.70
3	2.31	3.09	+0.87
4	2.35	3.02	+0.69
All	2.35	3.03	+0.86

Table 4: Average score for each draft by project, including the average change in score between the Intermediate and Final drafts. The standard deviation of the Intermediate and Final draft scores are 0.92 and 0.68, respectively.

and the second to promote consistent grading across teachers (Graham et al., 2012).

The grade "curve" is different for Intermediate and Final drafts (Kolmogorov-Smirnov test, $D = 0.332$, $p < 10^{-10}$) and the scores of neither draft are normally distributed by the Shapiro-Wilk test (Intermediate: $W = 0.948$, $p < 10^{-10}$, Final: $W = 0.932$, $p < 10^{-10}$). Figure 2 illustrates the distribution of grades across projects and drafts. Intermediate scores have higher variance and tend to be below 2.5 (corresponding to a B grade), while Final scores are more tightly distributed, the majority of them at least a B grade (Figure 5 and Table 4).

3.2 Teachers

Since each essay is graded by one teacher, we cannot guarantee that teachers grade consistently. To illustrate the differences between teacher grades, we randomly selected nine teachers who graded at least 150 Intermediate and Final drafts and graphically represented the score distribution assigned by each one (Figure 3).

A one-way ANOVA on the Intermediate draft scores revealed a significant difference between at least one pair of teachers' scores (17 teachers, $F(16, 1079) = 51.9$, $p < 10^{-10}$), and Tukey's post-hoc analysis revealed significant differences between 66 pairs of teachers ($p < 0.001$). Similar results were found for the Final drafts (20 teachers, $F(19, 1642) = 15.57$, $p < 10^{-10}$; 44 pairs significantly different $p < 0.001$). Even with a detailed rubric, teachers appear to grade differently.

In Figure 4, we compare the correlation of four features to the scores assigned by different teachers. This figure provides an example of how teachers exhibit a considerable amount of variance in how they unconsciously weight different criteria.

3.3 Students

We do not have access to specific demographic information about the students, but we can make es-

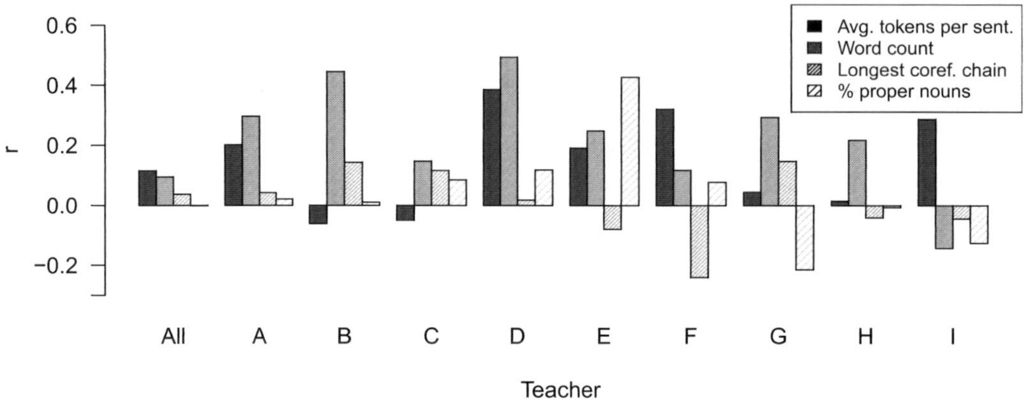

Figure 4: The correlation of four different features with Final draft scores, compared across nine teachers.

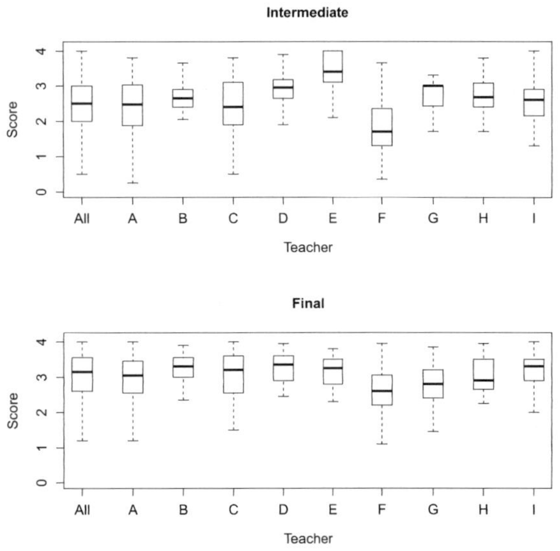

Figure 3: Distribution of scores given by nine teachers.

timates of their writing ability and native language. The writing course is a university requirement that students can place out of if they have completed a comparable course or received a sufficient grade in any number of pre-college standardized tests.[5] Therefore, we assume that the students in this course require additional support to develop college-level writing skills.

We also assume that the majority of students in this course are native English speakers. Because native English speakers and English language learners generally have different difficulties with writing, we wished to estimate how many of the students in the course were native English speakers. 96% the student body as a whole are American citizens, whom we assume are native English speakers. If the demographics of the writing course are the same as the university as a whole, then at most 4% of the students are non-native English speakers, which is our lower-bound estimate.

We arrive at an upper bound if we assume that every international student in the freshman class (168 out of 4,200 total students) is in the writing class, or at most 26% of the writing class are non-native speakers. In reality, the number is probably somewhere between 4–26%.

4 Experiments

We separated 3,362 essays by draft, Intermediate and Final (1,400 and 1,962 essays, respectively, skipping 31 Intermediate drafts that had no grade assigned). We randomly selected 100 essays for development and 100 for testing from each draft type and

[5]For example, students need a 4 in an English Language/Literature AP course, or a 5 in an IB English course to place out.

represented all essays with feature vectors.[6]

4.1 Model

In this work, we establish a single-task model and explain how it can be extended for multi-task learning. The single-task model represents essays graded by every teacher in the same feature space.

We have n essays graded by T teachers and m features. In the single-task setup, we represent each essay by a vector containing the values of these m features calculated over that essay. An essay $\boldsymbol{x}$ is represented as an m-dimensional vector:

$$\boldsymbol{x} = (x_1, x_2, \ldots, x_m)$$

For multi-task learning, we make a copy of the entire feature set for each of the T teachers. Each of the original features has a global feature and one feature specific to each teacher, for a total of $(1 + T) \times m$ features. For example, an essay graded by teacher A has a set of global features that are equal to the teacher-A-specific feature values. The features specific to other teachers are assigned zero value.

Specifically, we have an n-dimensional teacher vector $\boldsymbol{t}$, such that t_i is the teacher that graded essay i. In the multi-task framework, each essay is represented by a $(1 + T) \times m$-dimensional vector, $\boldsymbol{x}^*$. The new vector $\boldsymbol{x}^*$ contains twice as many non-zero features as the original vector $\boldsymbol{x}$,

$$\boldsymbol{x}^* = (x_1, x_2, \ldots, x_m, x_{t_i1}, x_{t_i2}, \ldots, x_{t_im}, \ldots) \quad \text{s.t. } x_j = x_{t_ij} \tag{1}$$

We favor linear models in this work because the contribution of each feature is transparent, which allows us to provide teachers with feedback based on the weights learned by the model. In the multi-task setup, we used principal component analysis to transform the features into a lower dimension to reduce computational burden. scikit-learn was used for dimensionality reduction and model learning.

Since there is a mapping between scores and letter grades, we experimented with closed-class classification as well as ranking classification, but linear regression yielded the best results on the development set. We predicted scores using linear regression over a number of features, described in Section 4.2 below.

[6] Analysis in Section 3 was done over the training set only.

For evaluation, we report the correlation between predicted and actual scores as Pearson's r and Kendall's τ, as well as the mean squared error. We round all predictions to the nearest 0.05, to conform with the actual scores. We also report the exact agreement and quasi-adjacent agreement, which we define as a predicted score within 0.25 points of the actual score (approximately the difference between a grade G and a G+ or G-).

Using the same experimental setup, we learn different models to predict

- the overall score of Intermediate and Final drafts,
- the score of individual rubric components, and
- the score improvement from an Intermediate to Final draft.

4.2 Features

We broadly categorize features as surface, structural, lexical, syntactic, and grammatical.

Surface features include average word, sentence, and paragraph lengths; lengths of the longest and shortest sentences; and number of tokens, sentences, and paragraphs. Another feature indicates the ratio of unique first three words of all sentences to the total number of sentences, to loosely capture sentence variety. (9 features)

Structural features include the frequency of discourse markers and the number of sentences containing discourse markers, as well as measures of cohesion, specifically the average and longest coreference chain lengths and the number of coreference chains (representing the number of entities discussed in the essay). Finally, we calculate the following statistics over the first, last, and body paragraphs: number of polarity words, number of "complex" words (with more than 3 syllables), and Flesch–Kincaide grade level. (25 features)

Lexical features are token trigrams skipping singletons and bag of words without stop words. We also include ratios of each of the following to the number of tokens: stop words, out-of-vocabulary words, proper nouns, and unique token types. (5 + # tokens - # stopwords + # token trigrams features)

Syntactic features include the average and longest lengths between the governor and dependent in all dependency relations; the number of clauses in an essay, specifying subordinating clauses, direct

Model	Intermediate Drafts r	τ	MSE	Exact	Adj.	Final Drafts r	τ	MSE	Exact	Adj.
Baseline	0.045	-0.008	1.995	0.094	0.323	0.101	0.098	0.876	0.180	0.450
Single-task	0.399	0.274	0.980	0.198	0.469	0.252	0.157	0.997	0.130	0.440
Multi-task	*0.755*	*0.558*	*0.474*	*0.323*	*0.708*	*0.558*	*0.408*	*0.397*	*0.250*	*0.760*

Table 5: Correlation between predictions and teacher scores, measured by Pearson's r and Kendall's τ, as well as the mean squared error (MSE) and exact and adjacent agreements. The baseline is a random balanced sample.

questions, and inverted declarative sentences and questions; the number of passive and active nominal subjects; the tallest and average parse-tree heights; and the ratios of adjective, prepositional, and verb phrases to noun phrases. (14 features)

Grammatical features are trigram counts of part-of-speech (POS) tags and the number of POS 5-grams unseen in a 24-million-token portion of the English Gigaword corpus. We also include the perplexity assigned to the text by three language models: a 500k-token Gigaword LM, and LMs estimated over the correct and incorrect learner text from the NUCLE 3.2 corpus. (4 + # POS trigrams features)

5 Results

5.1 Predicting the overall score by draft

We learned two single-task models using the features described above, one for Intermediate drafts and one for Final drafts, and the correlation between the predicted and actual scores was well below human levels. By introducing a multi-task approach (Section 4), the model made significant gains, with the correlation increasing from $r = 0.422$ to $r = 0.755$ and from $r = 0.252$ to $r = 0.558$ for the Intermediate and Final drafts, respectively. The Intermediate model predicts scores that very strongly correlate with the human score, and does as well as a human grader. Results are summarized in Table 5.

Using the same setup, we trained separate models for each of the projects, and found that the individual models did not do as well as a composite model (Table 6).

5.2 Predicting specific rubric scores

Next, we predicted individual rubric scores with multi-task learning. The rubric scores that correlate most with overall score are Organization, Evidence, and Focus ($r >= 0.84$), and we were curious whether our model would do better predicting those rubric categories than the others. Focus and Evidence predictions correlated very strongly, but the Organization predictions had weaker correlation with the actual scores (Table 7).

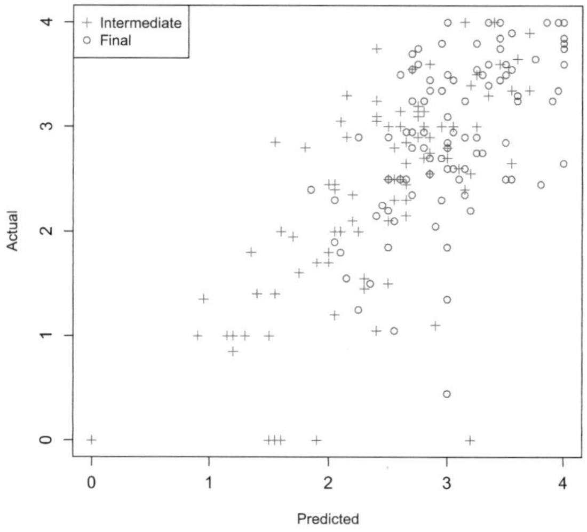

Figure 5: Predicted versus actual essay scores.

5.3 Predicting score change

In a preliminarily experiment to predict the improvement between draft pairs, we represent each draft pair by a vector that was the difference between the feature vector of the Intermediate and the Final drafts. Less than 10% of Final drafts show a decrease in score and on average the score increases 0.86 between the Intermediate and Final draft, so a binary classification of whether the score improved would be trivial. Instead we aim to predict the *amount* of the score change.

Training single-task and multi-task models over 794 draft pairs from the same training set above, we tested 50 pairs of essays. The single-task model pre-

Project	Intermediate	Final
P1	0.859	0.511
P2	0.706	0.483
P3	0.571	0.463
P4	0.591	0.382
P1–4	0.704	0.454

Table 6: The correlation (Pearson's r) of actual scores to predictions made by individual models for each project/draft pair. P1–4 represents predictions of all project models.

Model	r	MSE
Baseline	0.067	0.815
Single-task	0.346	4.304
Single-task, no content	0.087	0.399
Multi-task	-0.027	5.841
Multi-task, no content	*0.356*	*1.702*

Table 8: Correlation between the predicted and actual change between Intermediate and Final draft scores.

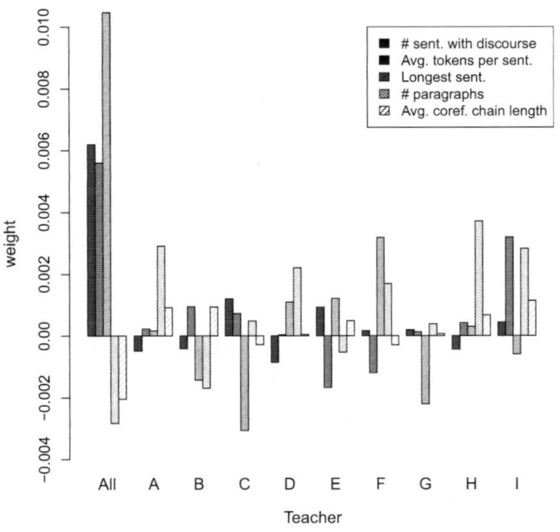

Figure 6: A comparison of feature weights learned in individual, teacher-specific models.

dicted the change much better than the multi-task, ($r = 0.346$ versus $r = -0.027$, which is worse than a random balanced baseline). When we removed content features (unigrams and trigrams), the multi-task model outperformed the single-task model with content, both by correlation and MSE. Removing content features significantly degraded the performance of the single-task model (Table 8).

5.4 Potential for providing feedback

We trained individual models for each of 17 teachers over Intermediate drafts, without dimensionality reduction. The predicted scores correlated strongly with the instructor scores ($r = 0.650$). We isolated the features with the heaviest average weights across all 17 models to examine whether teachers weighted these features differently in the individual models, and found that these weights varied by magnitude and polarity (Figure 6).

A graphical representation of this type could provide useful feedback to teachers. For example, the longest sentence feature has a high negative weight for teachers C and G, but is positively weighted for the other teachers. Given this information, teachers C and G could slightly alter their grading practices to better match the other teachers. However, before such a technology is deployed, we would need to develop more reliable models, examine the essays to check that the features is not a proxy for some other aspect of the text, and perform pilot testing.

6 Discussion and Future Work

One of the primary challenges of our dataset is the lack of multiple annotations. We only have one score for each essay, and the scores are provided by 21 different teachers whose grades are from different distributions. Modeling scores from different distributions in a single task yields predictions that only weakly correlate with the actual scores.

A joint model across all teachers and all projects does better than individual models for predicting essay scores. The multi-task setup enables us to jointly model characteristics of individual teachers while taking advantage of shared information across all teachers, and the models' predictions strongly correlate with human scores. On the Intermediate drafts, the correlation is very strong and within the range of human–human correlation (inter-human correlations ranged from 0.61 to 0.85 on the Kaggle ASAP–AES data (Shermis and Hamner, 2013)).

Unlike the Kaggle data, these essays are open ended, and open-ended topics are thought to be more difficult to score (Foltz et al., 2013). Furthermore,

Draft	Overall	Focus	Evidence	Organization	Style	Format
Intermediate	0.755	0.720	0.789	0.666	0.594	0.787
Final	0.558	0.340	0.324	0.329	0.350	0.432

Table 7: Correlation (Pearson's r) of predicted to actual scores for individual rubric categories.

the form of each project is different (personal narrative, bibliographic essay, remediation, thesis-driven essay), and we are able to score these different types of open-ended essays using a single model.

Our model predicts Intermediate scores better than Final scores, possibly because Intermediate drafts have higher variance than Final drafts, which are more tightly clustered, with more than 50% of the scores between 2.5 and 3.5. The adjacent agreement and MSE are better for Final drafts than Intermediate, suggesting that even though the correlation of Final drafts is weaker, the predictions are within a close range of the true scores.

We have shown that multi-task learning makes better predictions, and in the future we will apply multi-task learning to grading new teachers.

In addition to predicting the overall essay scores, we applied the same setup to two other tasks facilitated by this dataset: predicting individual rubric scores and predicting the score change from Intermediate to Final drafts. We found room for improvement in both tasks. To predict isolated rubric scores, future work will include investigating different features tailored to specific aspects of the rubric.

Our experiments in predicting improvement from Intermediate to Final draft revealed that content features confound a multi-task model but a single-task model does better with content features. This suggests that the single-task, no-content model underfits the data while the multi-task, with-content model overfits, illustrating the potential benefit of a multi-task setup to low-dimensional space.

There are inconsistencies in the paired-essay data, which may confound the model. 23 essays did not change between the Intermediate and Final drafts. Of these essays, the score decreased for 9, remained unchanged for 5, and increased for 9 essays–in two instances, the score increase was 2 points or more. Further analysis is warranted to determine whether there was a rationale for how the scores of unchanged essays were assigned.

Future work includes having the essays re-scored by another grader to establish validity. Until then, we cannot claim to have developed a reliable system, only to have robustly modeled the grading tendencies of this particular set of teachers for this class.

7 Conclusion

Consistent grading across teachers is difficult to achieve, even with training and detailed rubrics (Graham et al., 2012). Automatic tools to provide constant feedback may help promote consistency across teachers. This work is the first step aiming to identify when and how teachers grade differently. In the future, we hope to drill down to separate rubric scores so that we can provide specific feedback when teachers use different internal criteria.

In this work we introduced a new set of essays for evaluating student writing that is more representative of college writing than previous AES datasets. We developed a single, robust system for automatically scoring open-ended essays of four different forms (personal narrative, bibliographic, reflective and thesis driven), graded by 21 different teachers. Our predictions correlate strongly with the actual scores, and predicts the scores of Intermediate drafts as well as human raters on a different set of essays. We present a method for handling a dataset labeled by multiple, non-overlapping annotators.

This is an exciting new dataset for educational NLP, and this paper presents just a sample project facilitated by its unique characteristics. At this time we cannot release the corpus due to privacy concerns, but we hope it will be available to the community at some point in the future.

Acknowledgments

We thank Joseph Moxley for his assistance in obtaining the corpus, Burr Settles for his ideas in developing a multi-task approach, and Benjamin Van Durme and the reviewers for their feedback.

References

Yigal Attali and Jill Burstein. 2006. Automated essay scoring with e-rater® v. 2. *The Journal of Technology, Learning and Assessment*, 4(3).

Yllias Chali and Sadid A. Hasan. 2012. Automatically assessing free texts. In *Proceedings of the Workshop on Speech and Language Processing Tools in Education*, pages 9–16, Mumbai, India, December. The COLING 2012 Organizing Committee.

Hongbo Chen and Ben He. 2013. Automated essay scoring by maximizing human-machine agreement. In *Proceedings of the 2013 Conference on Empirical Methods in Natural Language Processing*, pages 1741–1752, Seattle, Washington, USA, October. Association for Computational Linguistics.

Trevor Cohn and Lucia Specia. 2013. Modelling annotator bias with multi-task gaussian processes: An application to machine translation quality estimation. In *Proceedings of the 51st Annual Meeting of the Association for Computational Linguistics (Volume 1: Long Papers)*, pages 32–42, Sofia, Bulgaria, August. Association for Computational Linguistics.

Norbert Elliot, Perry Deess, Alex Rudniy, and Kamal Joshi. 2012. Placement of students into first-year writing courses. *Research in the Teaching of English*, 46(3):285–313.

Jenny Rose Finkel and Christopher D. Manning. 2009. Hierarchical bayesian domain adaptation. In *Proceedings of Human Language Technologies: The 2009 Annual Conference of the North American Chapter of the Association for Computational Linguistics*, pages 602–610, Boulder, Colorado, June. Association for Computational Linguistics.

Peter W. Foltz, Lynn A. Streeter, Karen E. Lochbaum, and Thomas K. Landauer. 2013. Implementation and applications of the intelligent essay assessor. *Handbook of Automated Essay Evaluation*, pages 68–88.

Anne Ruggles Gere and Laura Aull. 2010. Questions worth asking: Intersections between writing research and computational linguistics. In *Proceedings of the NAACL HLT 2010 Workshop on Computational Linguistics and Writing: Writing Processes and Authoring Aids*, pages 51–55, Los Angeles, CA, USA, June. Association for Computational Linguistics.

Matthew Graham, Anthony Milanowski, and Jackson Miller. 2012. Measuring and promoting inter-rater agreement of teacher and principal performance ratings. *Online Submission*.

Sylviane Granger. 2003. The international corpus of learner english: a new resource for foreign language learning and teaching and second language acquisition research. *Tesol Quarterly*, 37(3):538–546.

Minqing Hu and Bing Liu. 2004. Mining and summarizing customer reviews. In *Proceedings of the tenth ACM SIGKDD international conference on Knowledge discovery and data mining*, pages 168–177. ACM.

Jing Jiang. 2009. Multi-task transfer learning for weakly-supervised relation extraction. In *Proceedings of the Joint Conference of the 47th Annual Meeting of the ACL and the 4th International Joint Conference on Natural Language Processing of the AFNLP*, pages 1012–1020, Suntec, Singapore, August. Association for Computational Linguistics.

Christopher D. Manning, Mihai Surdeanu, John Bauer, Jenny Finkel, Steven J. Bethard, and David McClosky. 2014. The Stanford CoreNLP natural language processing toolkit. In *Proceedings of 52nd Annual Meeting of the Association for Computational Linguistics: System Demonstrations*, pages 55–60.

Danielle S. McNamara, Scott A. Crossley, and Philip M. McCarthy. 2010. Linguistic features of writing quality. *Written Communication*, 27(1):57–86.

2009. Michigan corpus of upper-level student papers. The Regents of the University of Michigan.

Pearson. 2010. Intelligent Essay Assessor fact sheet. Technical report, Pearson.

Jonathon Read, Rebecca Dridan, Stephan Oepen, and Lars Jrgen Solberg. 2012. Sentence boundary detection: A long solved problem? In *Proceedings of COLING 2012: Posters*, pages 985–994, Mumbai, India, December. The COLING 2012 Organizing Committee.

Lawrence M. Rudner and Tahung Liang. 2002. Automated essay scoring using Bayes' theorem. *The Journal of Technology, Learning and Assessment*, 1(2).

Mark D. Shermis and Ben Hamner. 2013. 19 contrasting state-of-the-art automated scoring of essays. *Handbook of automated essay evaluation: Current applications and new directions*, page 313.

Helen Yannakoudakis and Ted Briscoe. 2012. Modeling coherence in ESOL learner texts. In *Proceedings of the Seventh Workshop on Building Educational Applications Using NLP*, pages 33–43, Montréal, Canada, June. Association for Computational Linguistics.

Helen Yannakoudakis, Ted Briscoe, and Ben Medlock. 2011. A new dataset and method for automatically grading esol texts. In *Proceedings of the 49th Annual Meeting of the Association for Computational Linguistics: Human Language Technologies*, pages 180–189, Portland, Oregon, USA, June. Association for Computational Linguistics.

Author Index